THE

PACIFIC

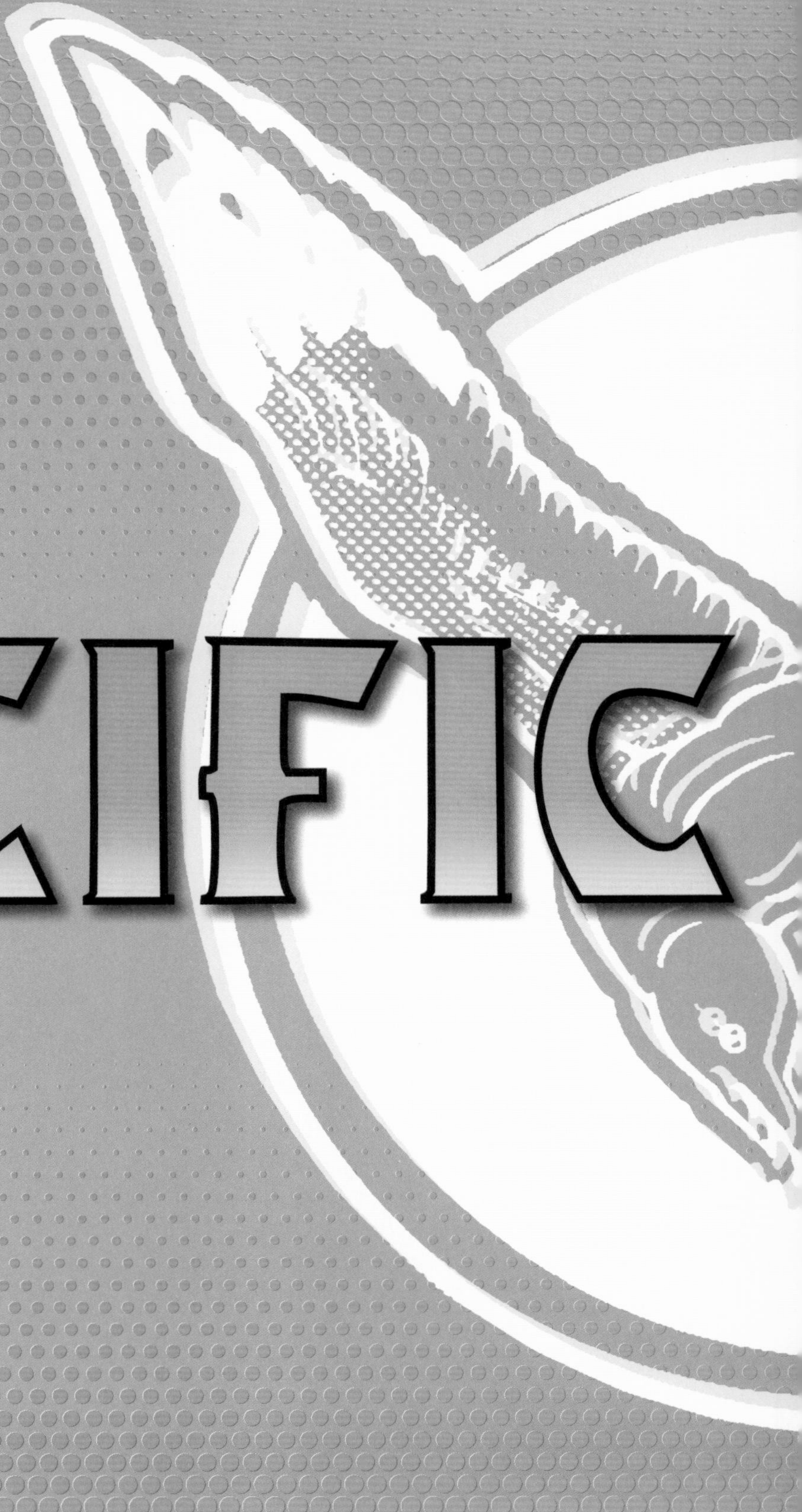

TwoMorrows Publishing
Raleigh, North Carolina USA

COMICS
COMPANION

by Stephan Friedt
with Jon B. Cooke

The Pacific Comics Companion
by Stephan Friedt
with Jon B. Cooke

Published by John Morrow
Edited, Designed, and Co-written by Jon B. Cooke
Proofread by John Morrow & Kevin Sharp
Cover art by Dave Stevens, with color by Homer Reyes
Cover art courtesy of The Rocketeer Trust & Jennifer Stevens Bawcum

Please note that some low-resolution photos in this book were enhanced by image software.

Copyrights

Next page: Left to right, Steve Schanes, David Scroggy, and Bill Schanes, Pacific warehouse in 1983. Photo by Jackie Estrada.

First Printing, July 2023 • Printed in China • ISBN 978-1-60549-121-9

Published by
TwoMorrows Publishing
Raleigh, North Carolina USA • www.twomorrows.com

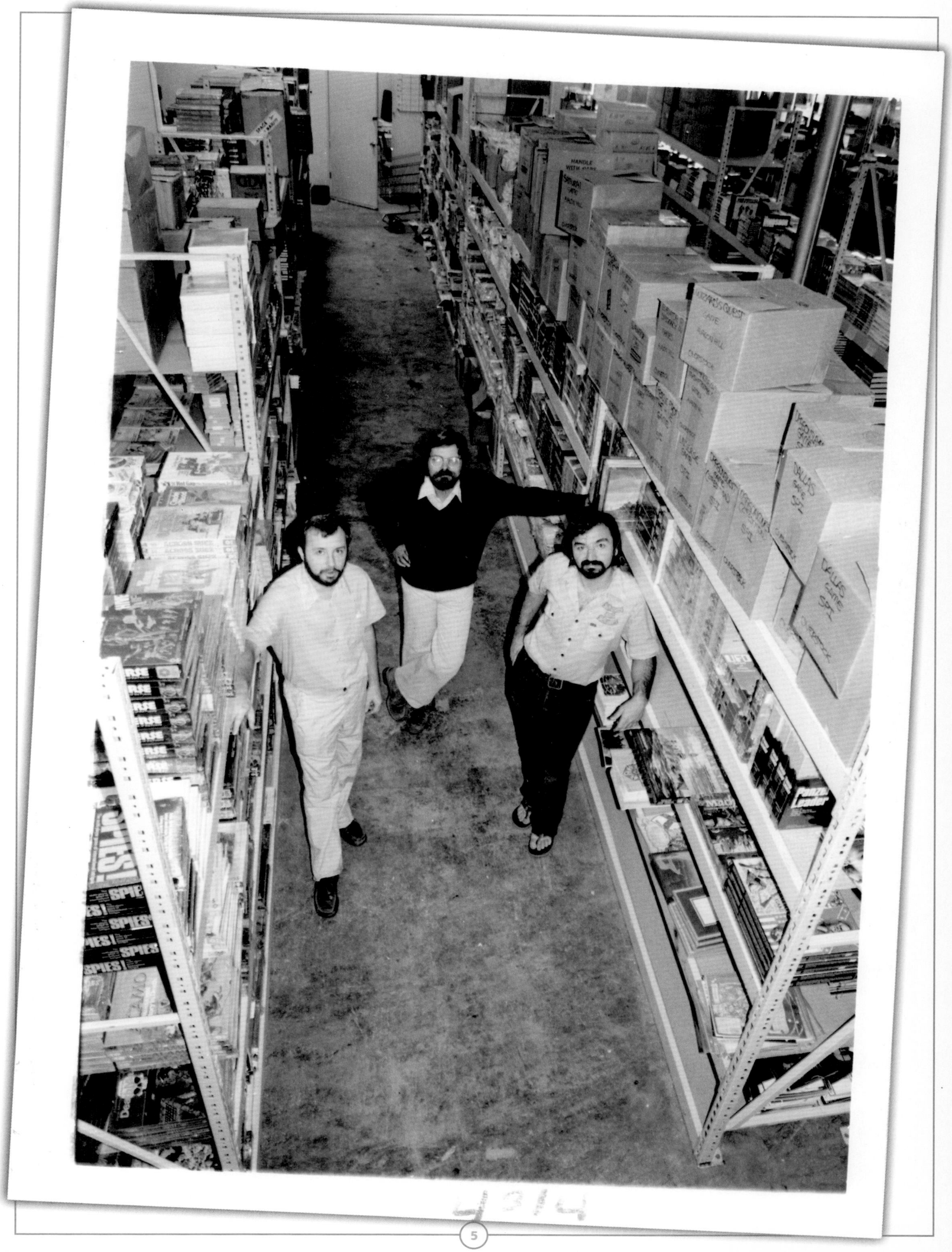
SPIES!
Panzer Leader
DALLAS GAME SPI

Dedications

To my parents:

My dad, **Jacob Friedt** [1926–2013]. My earliest memories are of sitting on my dad's lap while he read to me the Sunday funnies each week — *Alley Oop, Tarzan,* and *Steve Canyon* among his favorites — and his flood of comic book recollections when I brought my first copy of *Action Comics #*1 home.

My mom, **Delores Friedt** [1932–2018]. When I was four, she would take me to the library once a week to feed my voracious appetite for books, allowing me to bring home the weekly maximum allowed. The stacks began with Dr. Seuss and evolved into Walter Farley, Edgar Rice Burroughs, Arthur Conan Doyle, and others, as my reading abilities increased. Thanks to her, I was able to read and write when I entered first grade. Both parents always added comic books to the package when they came home from shopping trips. Comics held no stigma in their eyes… reading was reading.

To my siblings:

My brother, **Donald**, who joined me in my comic book adventures from our first and only San Diego Comic-Con in 1978, to my first foray into owning a comic book shop, Fantasy World, and all the trials and tribulations that come with self-ownership.

To my sister, **Pam**, who is always there to support and encourage my efforts.

To my brother, **Jason**, who always lent a hand when it was needed.

To my own family:

My wife, **Carla**, who has always supported my efforts, even when it meant not having the use of the kitchen table or spare bedrooms when projects or collections were involved.

To my daughters, **Stephanie** and **Katie**, who always tolerated and, on occasion, shared my love of collecting.

Our Thanks

ACKNOWLEDGMENT must be extended to **Jay Allen Sanford** for his comprehensive feature article on Pacific Comics, which he wrote for the Aug. 19, 2004, issue of the *San Diego Reader*. "The Rise and Fall of Pacific Comics: The Inside Story of a Pioneering Publisher," available online at *www. sandiegoreader.com/news/2004/aug/19/two-men-and-their-comic-books*, was the first in-depth examination of the Schanes brothers' company, and the author is indebted to Mr. Sanford for his fine retrospective.

Also a nod of grateful appreciation to the magazines, *The Comics Journal, Amazing Heroes,* and *Comics Interview*, for their contemporaneous reporting and interviews which helped to shed vital information regarding the history of Pacific Comics.

SPECIAL THANKS to **STEVE SCHANES, BILL SCHANES**, and, most of all, **DAVID SCROGGY**, all of whom consulted and contributed mightily to this history. We are also grateful to the many people whose assistance and contributions — whether given wittingly or not! — were essential for this retrospective: **Neal Adams, Brent Anderson, Sergio Aragonés, Richard Arndt, Darren Auck, Mike Baron, Jennifer Stevens Bawcum, Rick Burchett, Tim Burgard, Lee Caplin, Shaun Clancy,** Columbia University's Rare Book and Manuscript Library, **JoAnn Conrad, Tim Conrad, Richard Corben, Glynn Crain, Ray Cuthbert, Craig Deeley, Scott Dunbier, Jackie Estrada, Mark Evanier, Mike Friedrich, Rick Geary, Michael T. Gilbert, Karen Green, Scott Hampton, Ron Harris, Jon Hartz, Richard Howell, Rob Imes, Bruce Jones, Mat Klickstein, Alan Light, Russ Maheras, Kelvin Mao, Emanuel Maris, Will Meugniot, John Morrow, Michael Netzer, Paul S. Power, Greg Preston, Trina Robbins, Steve Rude, Arlen Schumer, Scott Shaw!, Ken Steacy, William Stout, Walter Stuart, Roy Thomas, Mark Wheatley, John Wooley,** and **Thomas Yeates.**

Next page: From left, the Schanes brothers, Bill and Steve, and David Scroggy, at the Pacific Comics warehouse in 1983. Photo by Jackie Estrada.

Pgs. 10–11: Bill, David, and Steve posing alongside a painter, outside the Pacific Comics facilities. Photo by Jackie Estrada.

Contents

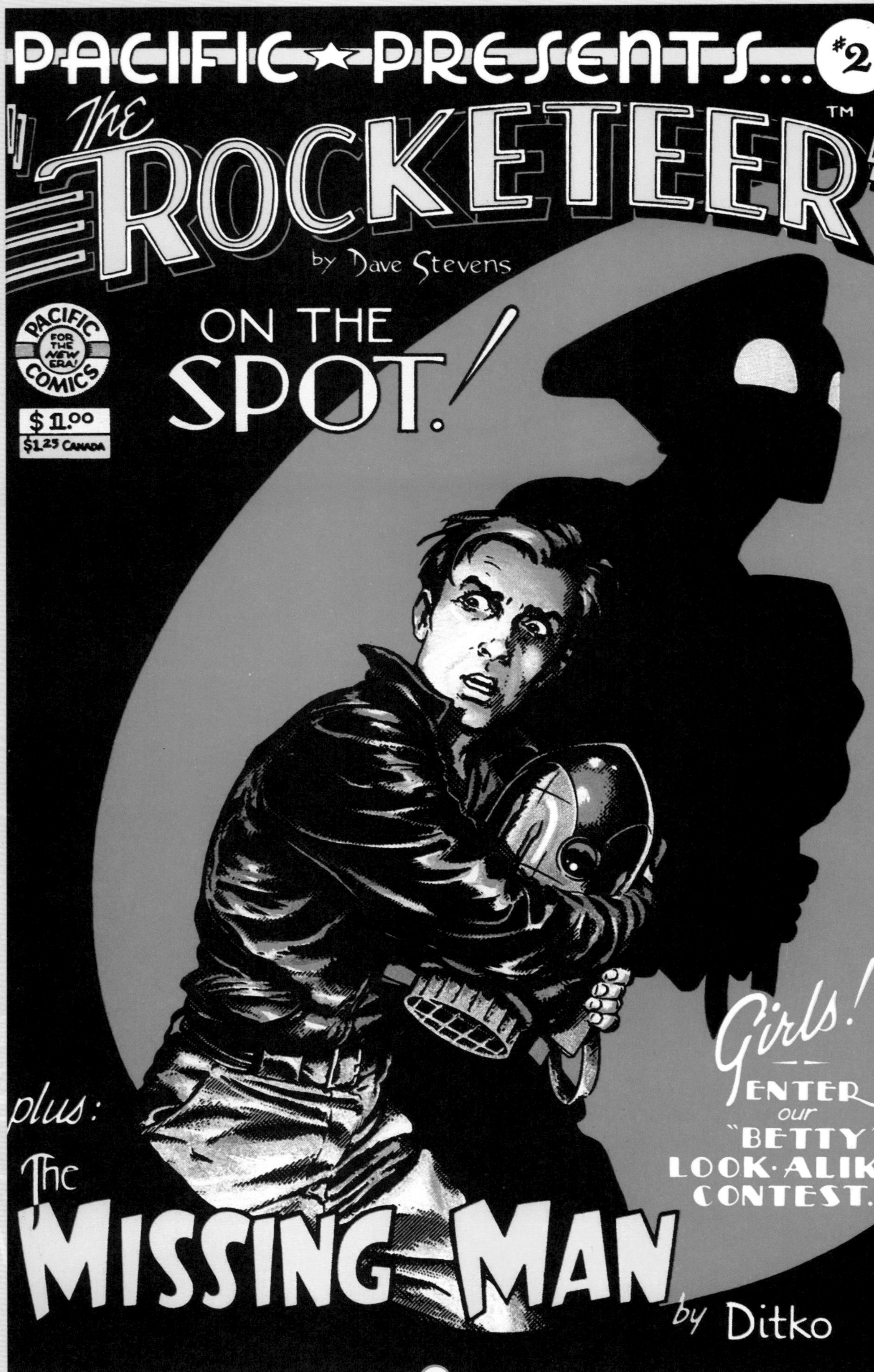
PACIFIC ★ PRESENTS... #2
"The ROCKETEER" ™
by Dave Stevens
PACIFIC FOR THE NEW ERA! COMICS
$1.00
$1.25 CANADA
ON THE SPOT!
Girls! ENTER our "BETTY" LOOK-ALIKE CONTEST!
plus: The MISSING MAN by Ditko

The Promise of Pacific Comics

A Preface of Sorts

Pacific Comics was a bright spot in the new comics scene when they surfaced in shops in the beginning of the 1980s. When they hit, I was in my second attempt at owning a comic shop, Curiosity Shoppe, in central Washington state. They offered a higher cover price, better paper stock, some of the very best work of the mainstream professionals, and a surprising crop of talented newcomers. While it wasn't always everybody's finest work, it was consistently done with a love for the art. This was material the creators wanted to do, not what they were *told* to do or *had* to do to get a paycheck.

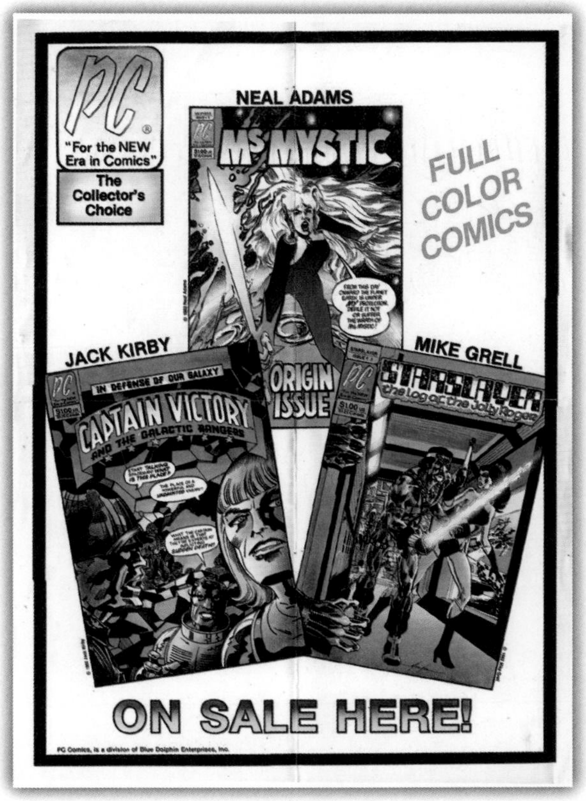
PC
"For the NEW Era in Comics"
The Collector's Choice
NEAL ADAMS
Ms MYSTIC
FULL COLOR COMICS
JACK KIRBY
IN DEFENSE OF OUR GALAXY
CAPTAIN VICTORY AND THE GALACTIC RANGERS
ORIGIN ISSUE
MIKE GRELL
STARSLAYER
The log of the Jolly Roger
ON SALE HERE!
PC Comics, is a division of Blue Dolphin Enterprises, Inc.

Changes were taking place in the way comic books were provided for the multitude of outlets that were springing up across the country, mine included. New approaches in the way professionals were paid, and how rights to their creations would be assigned, were tried for the first time. That was the legacy of Bill and Steve Schanes' Pacific Comics.

This book is an effort to relive fond memories — both mine and some of the professionals involved — and to document the titles, their individual issues, and the professionals who contributed. It is also an attempt to provide a checklist of sorts, along with some insight into their various contents for those who wish to collect the entire library or track down particular issues with specific contributors.

Bill and Steve have related the history in several interviews over the years (including those conducted by others) and I've personally had the opportunity to speak with Bill and David Scroggy, both in person and through correspondence; and I also interviewed a number of the creators who participated in the groundbreaking experiment, as did my editor.

I've also had the opportunity to read every online history and reference I could find — some of which is quoted by a grateful author in this book — as well as refer to my own near-complete collection of their output (all of the comics, 90% of the books, and about a third of the portfolios). The effort that follows is a factual history interspersed with personal remembrances of the people involved, often after many, many years.

While Pacific Comics was a business entity existing for over a decade, only four of those years were as a publisher, and yet this book has taken almost four decades to come to completion.

While I had the pleasure of meeting many of the creators who worked with Pacific Comics, several of the intended interviews as originally planned never came to be. Real life, complicated schedules, and the unfortunate passing of a number of the creators over the years became speed bumps. May you get some enjoyment or usefulness from the contents.

— **Stephan Friedt**

Previous page: Dave Stevens' moody cover featuring his trademark character, Cliff Secord, the Rocketeer. *Pacific Presents* #2 [Apr. 1983]. **Inset top:** Promotional poster sent to comics retailers. **Inset left:** Pacific Comics logo.

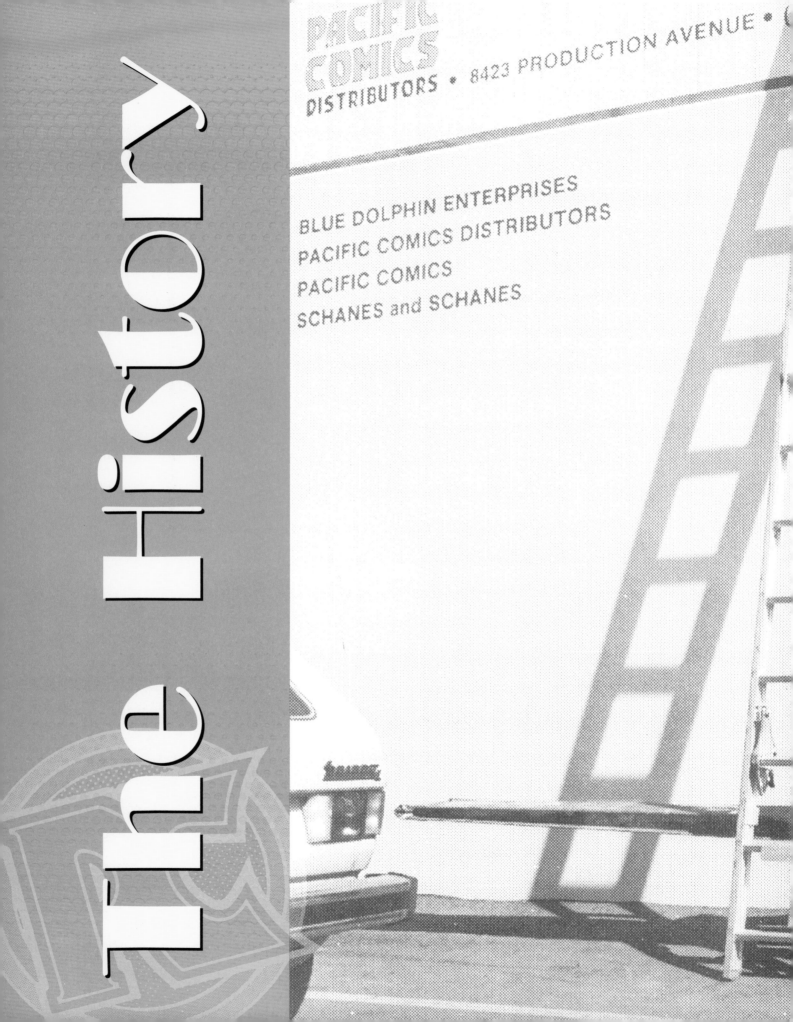

The History

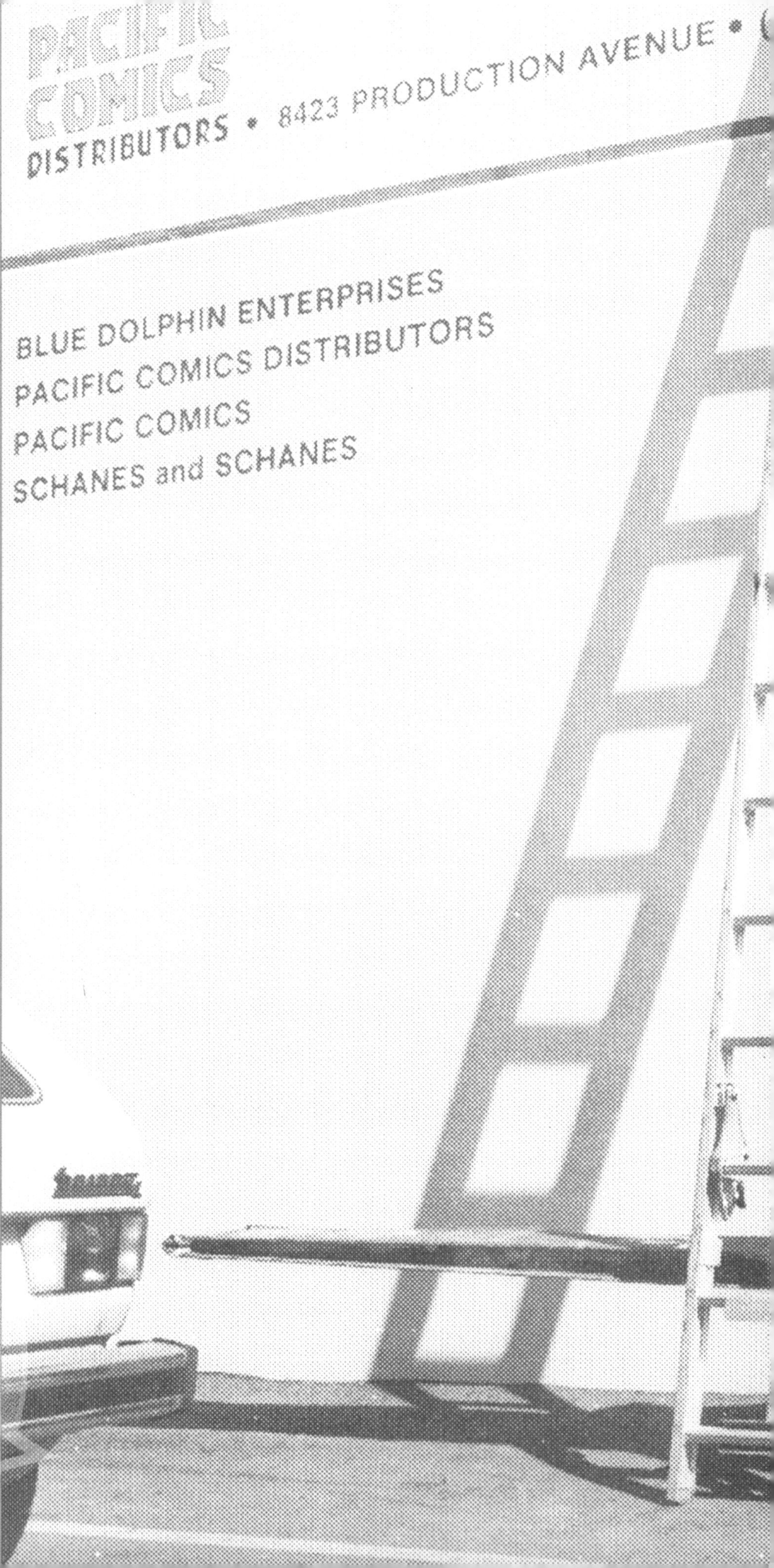
PACIFIC COMICS DISTRIBUTORS • 8423 PRODUCTION AVENUE •
BLUE DOLPHIN ENTERPRISES
PACIFIC COMICS DISTRIBUTORS
PACIFIC COMICS
SCHANES and SCHANES

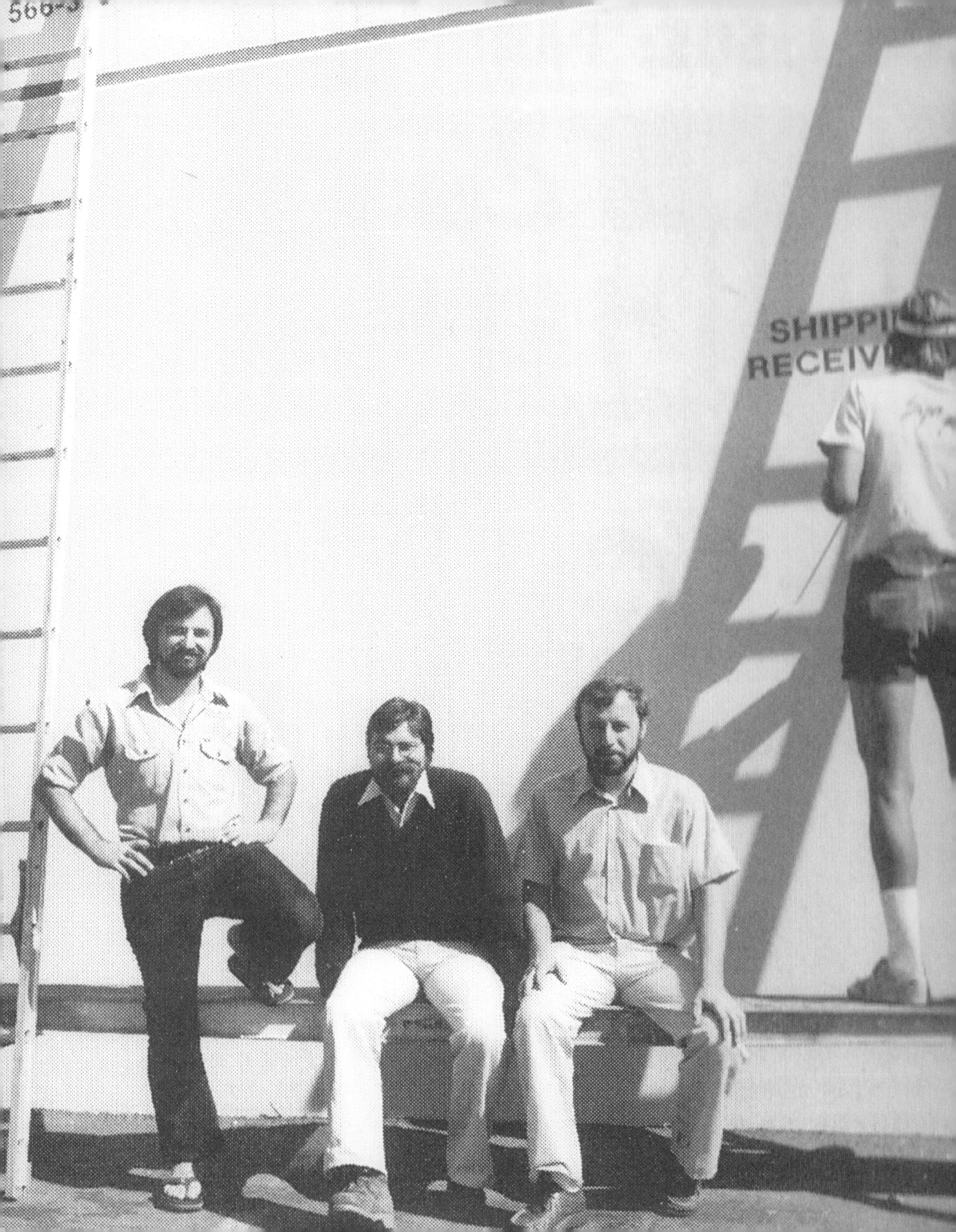
SHIPPI
RECEIV

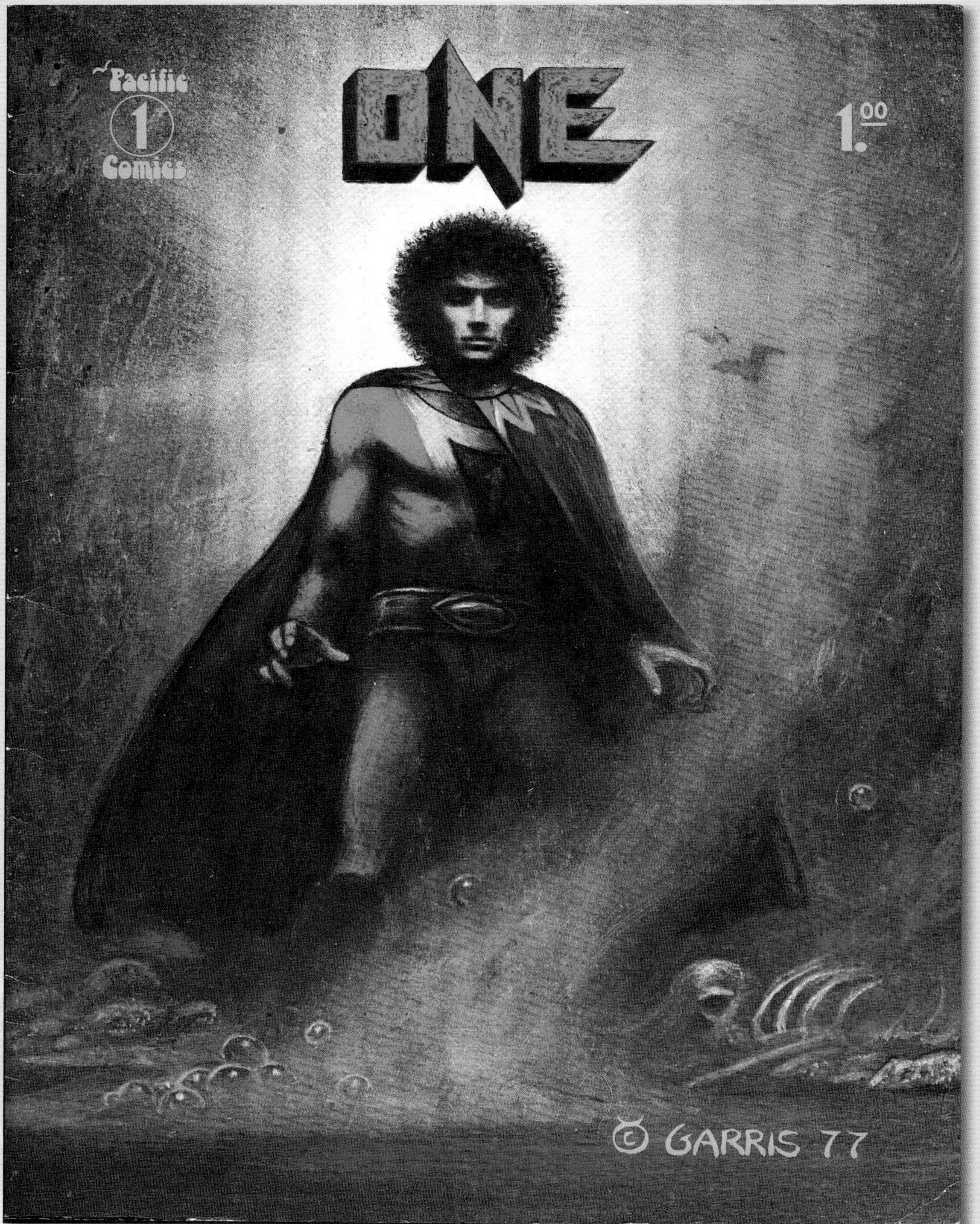
Pacific 1 Comics
ONE
1.00
© GARRIS 77

Beginnings

It all started at a swap meet…

Steve and Bill Schanes, they weren't the first. The New Jersey-born siblings didn't create the inaugural direct sales distribution company in the comic book industry. Nor were they first to publish independent comics for sale exclusively to the nation's ever-growing network of shops dedicated to comic books. Certainly, there were others who came before them, but, as Jay Allen Sanford observed, these two had the drive to succeed in the world of funnybooks. "[T]he brothers were industrious," Sanford wrote, "not to mention ballsy."[1]

THE BIG SCORE

Launching their endeavors in 1971, when Steven J. was 17 and William D. 14, the first commercial realm in which the San Diego-based brothers invested their energies was to sell back issues of comic books out of their parents' home, a form of reading material to which the older brother felt indebted. "My high school days were really challenging," Steve told Mat Klickstein, "because I was getting C's, D's in every class, except for athletics. I did keep comic books in my backpack and teachers were actually very supportive of me reading them during our break time. Specific teachers would take an interest in me because they thought I was intelligent and was just having trouble reading — which is why they were encouraged by my reading comics."[2]

Bill, too, suffered the same reading ailment as his older sibling, recalling to Klickstein, "In 1971, my brother and I were riding bicycles to a swap meet. And when we got there, we were walking up and down the rows of just junk and stuff that people had all laid on the asphalt. This lady had an old wagon just chockful of comic books. I have dyslexia, but I had actually never seen a comic book before. So, I sat down and did my best to read a couple of them in front of her stand. I really enjoyed them. I read all of them completely through and said to my brother, 'Let's buy these.' We asked how much she wanted for all the books she had. And she said she had about 900 comics, mostly Marvels and DCs from the '60s and early '70s, a few from the '50s and from the '40s. Fifty dollars for the whole 900 comics. Well, as two teenagers, we didn't have $50. So, we asked her to hold onto them for about an hour. 'Would you give us enough time to ride our bicycles back to our parents' house?' We asked our parents for $50 — and, of course, a ride down with the car to pick all these comics up. Luckily, my mother saw my enthusiasm for reading, which was not one of my top priorities back then, due in large part to my dyslexia. 'Gee, if he's going to be excited about reading something, at least let him read some comic books.' She drove us down, gave us the 50 bucks, and we bought the comics, loaded them all up in her station wagon, and brought them back to our house."[3]

In an essay for *The Jack Kirby Collector,* Steve recalled the exact same number of comics purchased as well as the identical price, though some other details differed. "I was age 17, walking through a flea market looking

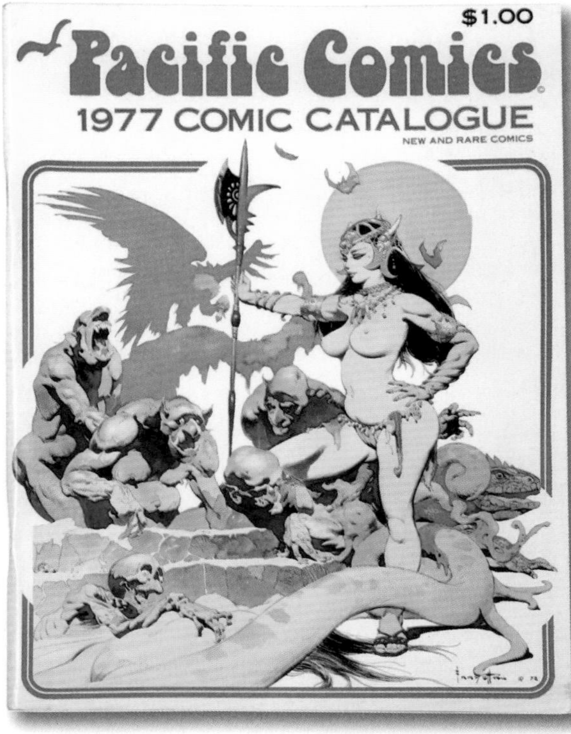
$1.00
Pacific Comics
1977 COMIC CATALOGUE
NEW AND RARE COMICS

Left: Frank Frazetta's provocative illo graces the cover of the Schanes bros' mail order catalogue.

Pacific Profiles

Steven J. Schanes

Born: *Apr. 1954*
It goes without saying that Steve and his brother Bill were the founders of Pacific Comics, an outfit whose origin dates back to 1971, when Steve was 17. After Pacific closed, he immediately began Blackthorne Comics, an imprint lasting until 1990. Today he runs Schanes Products and Services, a pop culture consulting firm.

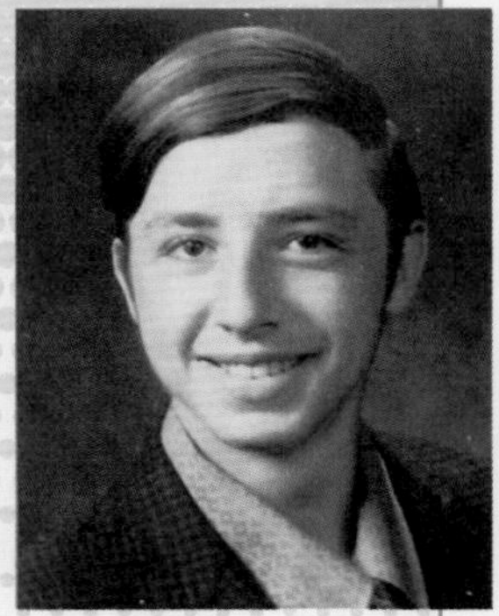

Above: Steve Schanes in his 1972 University City High School yearbook senior portrait.
Previous page: Cover of the first Pacific title, *One*.

William D. Schanes

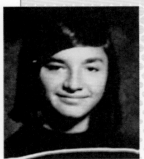

Born: *Sept. 1958*
With brother Steve, Bill is the principal partner in Pacific, and he went on to work for many years with Diamond Comic Distributors, said to be essentially second-in-command behind owner Steve Geppi. Bill retired from Diamond in 2013 and is today Oni Press' publishing consultant.

Above: Bill Schanes in his 1972 University of San Diego High School yearbook sophmore portrait.

THE BUYER'S GUIDE FOR COMIC FANDOM-39
SPECIAL BONUS ISSUE!
Presenting:
INSIDE COMIX
Who Runs The Comic Industry?
...inside!

for unique items," he explained. "I came upon a man who had several boxes of comic books for sale. I always liked comic books and learned to read with the help of comics. (I was born with a severe case of dyslexia and could not read well because the words would be configured in my mind differently than they were actually printed. Comic books enabled me to see pictures along with words; the words now made sense.) I bought the collection of 900 comics for $50. I was a big fan of DC Comics and could not relate to Marvels. I gave the Marvels to my brother Bill, age 14. Immediately we decided to become comic book dealers."[4]

Bill remembered their transition into becoming entrepreneurs as happening literally while the comics were being hauled out of the family station wagon. "As we were unloading them," he said to Klickstein, "my next door neighbor came over and was really excited. He saw we had a bunch of comics, and he was our age, and he said, 'Hey! Here's *Fantastic Four* #2! I'll give you $38 for it.' Well, we didn't know comic books had issue numbers or creators or anything. All we wanted to do was read the 900 comics. And we were thinking, 'This guy wants to pay $38 for one comic after we spent only $50 on 900 of them?!' We said to him, 'Sure! You can take *Fantastic Four* #2 for $38.' And that was our little introductory lesson to comics. We ended up with about 30 people over at our house — our parents' house — rummaging through these boxes, buying stuff. We made hundreds of dollars on that very first weekend selling comics. The only rule, of course, was my brother and I had to read them before we could sell them. That was the only rule of engagement. We had no idea there's a business involved. We were just enjoying the idea of having friends over, all kindred spirits, who loved comics, too. That little bit of interest there that weekend really initiated our creating 'Pacific Comics.'"[5]

Steve described how they kept the fledgling business growing: by going on the prowl to refresh their inventory. "Every day after school," he wrote in the *Kirby Collector*, "I would ride my bike around the small town of Pacific Beach looking for old comics at used book stores. The collection grew rapidly. The next year we issued our first mail order catalogue, placed our first ad in *The Buyer's Guide For Comic Fandom* [#39, July 1, 1973], and attended our first San Diego Comic Convention. (I met Jack Kirby at the 1972 con.) The response to that first catalogue was overwhelming. People we didn't know were sending us thousands of dollars. The collection grew too big for our parents' home; both bedrooms were full, floor to ceiling."[6]

The siblings decided to christen the new enterprise after their own California neighborhood (to where, in the '60s, they had moved from New Jersey), as Bill explained the name to Klickstein. It was, he said, "A combination of 'Pacific Beach' in San Diego and 'comic books.'"[7]

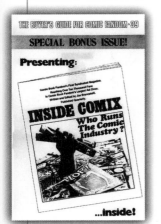

Right: The two ads in *The Buyer's Guide for Comic Fandom* that would launch the Schanes brothers' Pacific Comics. Immediate right is their first ad, *TBG* #39 [July 1, 1973] — cover above — and, far right, their follow-up, in *TBG* #44 [Sept. 15, 1973].

①
Pacific Comics
NO.1
4884 SAN JOAQUIN DR, SAN DIEGO, CALIF. 92109
Pacific Comics is a brand new comic warehouse. We have over 15,000 comics.
• We have a no rip off policy...
To get catalogue No1.mail us a 8¢ stamp to cover postage.
Included in our vast stock are rare comics, little big books, and hard cover.
We also feature side lines ... plastic protector bags, catalogue sheets, and much more.
Below are just a few great buys.
#1 Conan (fine) $2.00
#1 Defenders (mint) $1.00
#1 Doc Savage (mint) $1.00
#1 Frankenstein (mint) $ .50
#1 Dare Devil (fine) $5.00
#1 Hero for Hire (mint) $1.25
#1 Kull (mint) $2.00
#1 Marvel Spectacular $ .35
#1 Shield New Mint $ .75
#1 Tomb of Dracula (mint$ .75
#1 Warlock $1.25
#1 World's Unknown (mint)$.75
#1 Aquaman $2.50
#1 Bomba $ .75
#1 Creeper $ .75
#1 Demon (mint) $1.50
#1 Forever People (mint $2.50
#1 Hawkman Mint $3.50
#1 Kamand (mint) $ .75
#1 Mister Miracle (mint)$2.50
#1 New Gods (mint) $2.50
#1 Secret Origin (mint) $ .35
#1 Shazam (mint) $1.00
#1 Spectrum (mint) $1.25
#1 Supergirl (mint $ .75
* the above prices are at sale price this ad only.
Golden Age
#1 Star Spangled (fine) $75.00
#1 Hulk old (fine) $21.00
#2 Wonder Woman (fine) $30.00
#124 Action $7.00
#40 Action (NFO
#40 Action (nf) $23.00
#18 All-Flash (good) $9.00
#19 Batman (good) $17.00
#21 Batman (Mint) $23.00
#22 Batman (mint) $23.00
#40 Batman (mint) $17.00
#47 Batman (v.fine) $20.00
Origin retold
#76 Batman (good $5.00
#86 Detective (n.mint)$15.00
#15 Mad (good) $10.00
#32 Superman (mint) $20.00
#31 Superman (good) $11.00
#17 World,s Finest $15.00
#29 World,s Finest $ 8.00
#4 Kid Eternity $4.50
#58 Flash (good) $12.00
There is no minimum order but on orders less than 10.00 there will be a .65 postage and handling charge. Foreign orders 1.25 cents.
SEND FOR YOUR BIG CATALOGUE TODAY — just a 8¢ stamp

①
TIRED OF HIGH PRICES?
TRY
Pacific Comics
P.O. Box 99217, San Diego, Ca. 92109
CATALOGUE NO. 1 DISCOUNT OFFER
BECAUSE OF THE FINE RESPONSE TO OUR FIRST AD, WE HAVE BEEN ABLE TO ENLARGE OUR STOCK AND TO PASS ON MORE SAVINGS TO YOU..
TO RECEIVE A 10% DISCOUNT:
JUST SEND IN THE DISCOUNT COUPON WITH YOUR CAT.NO. 1 ORDER. IF YOU DON'T HAVE CATALOGUE NO. 1, SEND FOR IT TODAY, WITH AN 8¢ STAMP TO COVER POSTAGE.
WE HAVE A NO-RIP-OFF POLICY, WITH A MONEY-BACK GUARANTEE. IF THE CONDITION OF COMIC IS NOT AS STATED, WE WILL PROMPTLY REFUND YOUR MONEY UPON RETURN OF COMIC.
clip here
Pacific Comics Discount Coupon
10% off
on all items listed except Golden Age. Good only for Cat. #1
P.O. Box 99217
San Diego, Ca. 92109
we buy collections

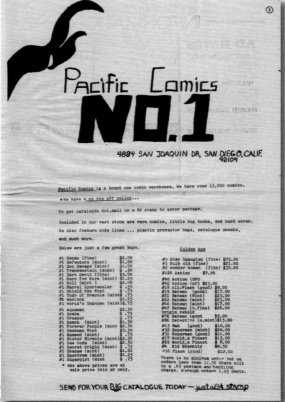

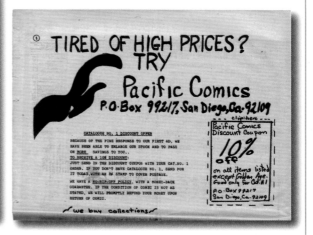

COMIC BOOK
STORE
1972

1972

Left: Snapshots of the Schanes boys in 1972 at their first retail comic shop location, on Cass Street. Note Bill reading a copy of *The Buyer's Guide for Comic Fandom* behind the counter.

Pacific Comics

NEW & RARE COMICS ©

PACIFIC COMICS A'BORNING!

The first *TBG* Pacific Comics ad, which featured a suburban San Diego address of San Joaquin Drive, was a full-pager that boasted the company had a brand-new warehouse and over 15,000 comics, and it also declared, "We have a no rip-off policy."[8] Listed items for sale included *Conan the Barbarian* #1, in fine condition, for $2, and the Golden Age *Star Spangled Comics* #1 for $75, in fine condition.

Indeed, the initial advertisement proved a success for the new enterprise as, five issues later, in *TBG* #44 [Sept. 15, 1973], the boys purchased a half-page (now listing a post office box as address), which had a discount coupon for 10% off "on all items except Golden Age."[9] The first incarnation of Pacific Comics was off to a profitable start.

However effective they were in generating sales, those early ads put together by the Schanes brothers were pretty crude efforts, with hand-drawn headlines and a curious logo design, with an illustration that vaguely looked either like a seagull or duck's head, depending on one's perspective. That same branding image was used on signage when the Schaneses established their first shop.

About their brick-&-mortar endeavor, Steve told *Comics Interview* #55, "We opened a small retail store in Pacific Beach, on Cass Street, basically to give my mother some space in her house, which had been lost to the comic books, which, by that time, had monopolized most of the house. For the sake of getting them out of the house, we started the store, and we started [*it*] on a $400 budget… Myself, Bill, and my mother worked at the store."[10]

Their retail and mail order enterprises were making copious amounts of money, a bounty which had its own unique, if temporary, drawback for the young partners. Bill wrote in a Facebook post, "We needed to open our first business bank account at Crocker National Bank, which was located in San Diego, California. I was told I was too young, and I must come with a parent to co-sign, to open up a bank account. I went back home and told my parents, who didn't understand and were a little upset. The next day, my mother came to the bank with me and the teller explained about the co-sign to my mother.

"My mother said that I wanted my own account under the 'Pacific Comics' name and I plunked down several

Left: Fuzzy photos originally printed in a San Diego newspaper that show their warehouse set-up in the 1980s and, in pic at immediate left, a rare shot of the entire Schanes clan, including older brother Paul at far left (known as Pablo, who would eventually work with his younger siblings), and on the right, Mom and Dad — a.k.a. Christine and Steven Schanes.

Pacific Profiles

David Scroggy

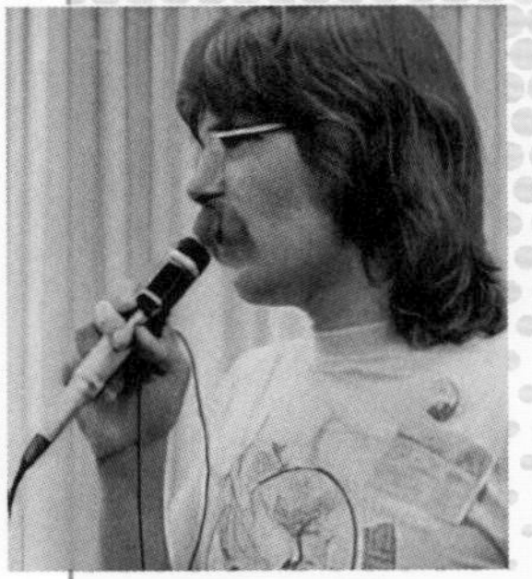

Above: David at a San Diego Comic-Con auction event in the 1970s or '80s. Photo by Jackie Estrada.

Born: *Dec. 1951* David would have a long career in comics after his Pacific stint as editorial director, prominently as head of new product development at Dark Horse until retiring in 2017. Today he lives with wife Rosemary in Scotland. He went to high school with rock star Chrissie Hynde, Craig Yoe, and Paul Mavrides.

thousand dollars in currency and coins, from all the Pacific Comics mail-order catalogue orders (we hadn't gotten any orders for actual products yet, as mail wasn't very fast at that time). The teller had the bank manager come over and, after I explained why I wanted my own account, he allowed me to have one, without having my mother as a co-signer."[11]

Bill added, "As a side note, when you opened a new account at Crocker National Bank, you got a teddy bear as a welcome gift. I told the manager that, if I owned the bank and I was giving a gift to new customers opening an account, I would give them a 'Crocker Spaniel,' a play off of the name of the bank versus a bear — which was cute, but once you brought it home, you wouldn't remember where you got it from. A few months later, the bank started handing out 'Crocker Spaniel' plush dogs to new accounts."[12]

About his memory of launching their first retail operation, Bill said to Klickstein, "Within a couple of years, we were doing a couple hundred thousand dollars out of my parents' house, and were having almost like mini-conventions on weekends — tons and tons of fans coming over to buy, sell, and trade. This encouraged us to get out of the house, make it an official business, and find a location. Which is what we did: a small retail store in San Diego, of course in Pacific Beach."[13]

He continued, "It was about a two-mile bike ride — our mode of transportation in those days — from our parents' house. The store was about 1,000 square feet and our hours were basically after we got out of school. Noon-to-six on weekdays and nine-to-five or nine-to-six on weekends. I had gotten permission from my high school to attend early classes so I could do all of this. I'd go to school on my bicycle, be there at 7:00 in the morning, then bike 30 minutes to the store to open at noon. And I did that for several years.

"So, Pacific Comics started off as a house business, thanks to a swap meet, transitioned to a mail order business, and then our first store in Pacific Beach. Pretty crazy. Through the store, we met Shel Dorf. As a young teenager, he seemed like such an older guy. It was like, 'Why is he involved in reading comic books?' But then I quickly realized that comic books bridge all gaps. They bridge age groups. Really, if you just enjoy entertainment, enjoy escapism, enjoy the idea of reading books, it could be anybody out there. And Shel was just one of those guys. He treated me really well as a kid."[14]

Below: Though they missed the very first San Diego Comic-Con, the Schanes brothers became perennial exhibitors during the lifespan of Pacific Comics and they were also active participants in various capacities at the annual event. *The Buyer's Guide* publisher Alan Light took this snapshot of Steve [left] talking with a con attendee at the 1982 show.

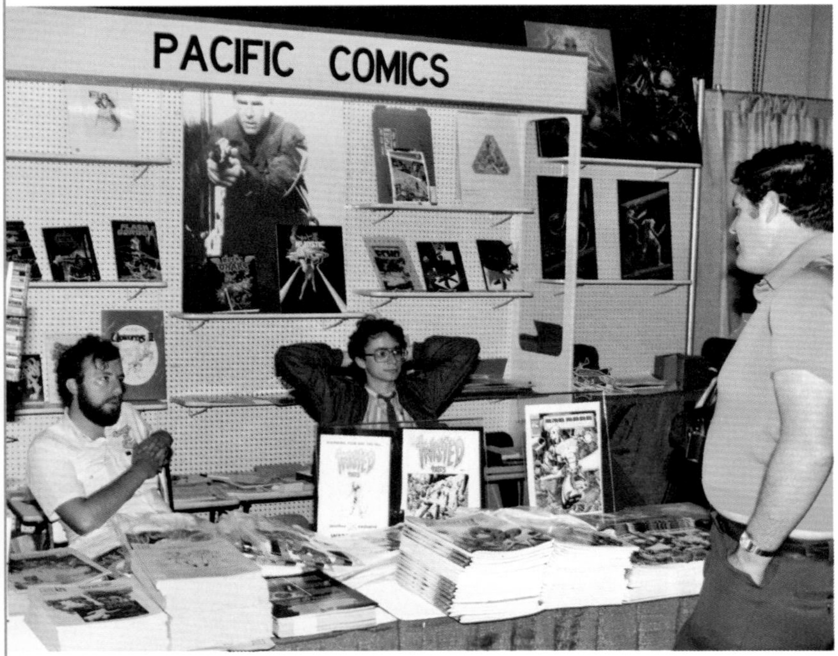
PACIFIC COMICS

SCROGGY MAKES THE SCENE

In 1975, newly arrived to San Diego from his native Ohio, 23-year-old David Scroggy was helped by San Diego Comic-Con co-founder Shel Dorf, resulting in David volunteering for the con and Shel arranging with *TBG* publisher Alan Light for David to write a regular column for the bi-weekly. In a tribute to Dorf (who died in 2009), David said, "Comic-Con and the column got me a job at Pacific Comics."[15]

David explained to the author, "Initially, I managed the Cass Street location of Pacific Comics. I opened and closed the store, scheduled our staff of part-time help, worked the counter, sorted the back-issue stock, and things like that. Bill and Steve handled the accounting, purchasing, dealings with vendors and the landlord, and the 'big picture' financial planning."[16]

Included in that "big picture" was a significant move for Pacific, as David told the author. "Not long after I joined the company, the Schanes brothers, who had been challenged in obtaining a reliable supply of new comics, became an early account of direct-sales comic market pioneer Phil Seuling. Prior to that, their main

Pacific Comics
1979 Oceanside

Pacific Comics

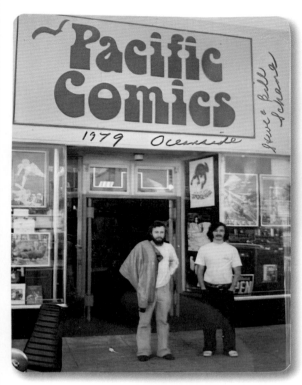

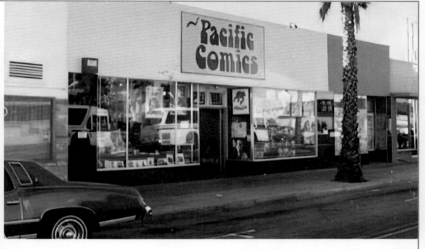

source of supply was local magazine distributor San Diego Periodicals. They were an example of what was called the 'I.D.' [*independent distributor*] distribution system, which was an unfriendly, wasteful, and corrupt network of magazine distributors. They were unfriendly to comic books in general, and, as Pacific's needs grew, increasingly, to the Schanes brothers."[17]

David continued, "It wasn't long before the Schanes brothers realized that the non-returnable discount offered by Seuling's Sea Gate firm, while a big improvement over the local I.D. distributor, was also unfair. Seuling had been granted national exclusivity as distributor to the fledgling comics specialty retailer market. 'Why,' the Schaneses asked, 'should one person be granted our entire market?' Pretty much simultaneously, Pacific Comics and a company called New Media Irjax challenged the legality of the unwillingness of Marvel and DC to set terms and open their wholesale sales to other qualified entities. This caused the corporate higher-ups at Marvel and DC to look more closely at the comics specialty channel, which, up until then, had escaped their notice. They quickly saw that Seuling's sweetheart deal was rife with potential liabilities for their comics imprints. Non-returnable wholesale terms were set, and Pacific, along with a number of other companies, were able to purchase in bulk directly from the publishers and become distributors themselves."[18] Pacific seized this opportunity.

Pacific Comics

Above: Top left and right are pix of the Oceanside store and, above, is the Clairemont branch of Pacific Comics.

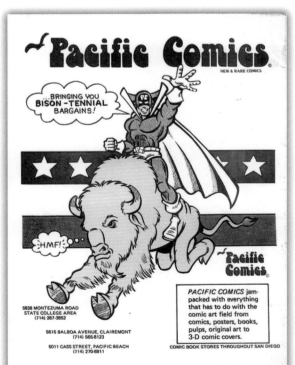

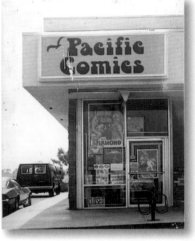

During all this, Steve and Bill recruited local San Diego cartoonist Scott Shaw! to render a mascot for the company, resulting in "Captain Terrific Pacific," a cloaked super-hero who appeared in Pacific Comics ads and, according to the *San Diego Reader,* "on bus benches all over San Diego in the mid-1970s."[18]

By decade's end, the Schanes brothers had expanded their retail empire and opened three other shops. The second was located in San Diego's Clairemont neighborhood, and the third was established near the San Diego State University campus. The fourth was located in Oceanside, about 35 miles north of San Diego.

Pacific Comics
NEW & RARE COMICS
...BRINGING YOU BISON-TENNIAL BARGAINS!
HMF!
Pacific Comics
PACIFIC COMICS jam-packed with everything that has to do with the comic art field from comics, posters, books, pulps, original art to 3-D comic covers.
5838 MONTEZUMA ROAD STATE COLLEGE AREA (714) 287-3852
5615 BALBOA AVENUE, CLAIREMONT (714) 565-8123
5011 CASS STREET, PACIFIC BEACH (714) 270-6911
COMIC BOOK STORES THROUGHOUT SAN DIEGO

Inset left: Scott Shaw!, San Diego cartoonist, produced many illustrations for Pacific Comics, including amusing spot illos in their catalogue, and he designed and rendered the character Captain Terrific Pacific, the company's mascot super-hero.

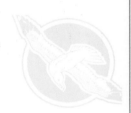

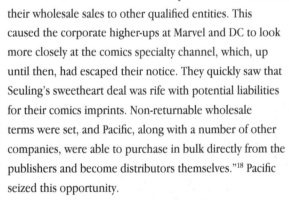

This page: Just a few of the Pacific Comics mascot Captain Terrific Pacific cartoons rendered by Scott Shaw!, whose association with the Schanes brothers ultimately resulted in the funny animals anthology, *Wild Animals*. Below is an ad targeting area college students and, at bottom, the ad seen by a zillion Marvel Comics readers, this repro'd from *Star Wars* #3 [Sept. 1977].

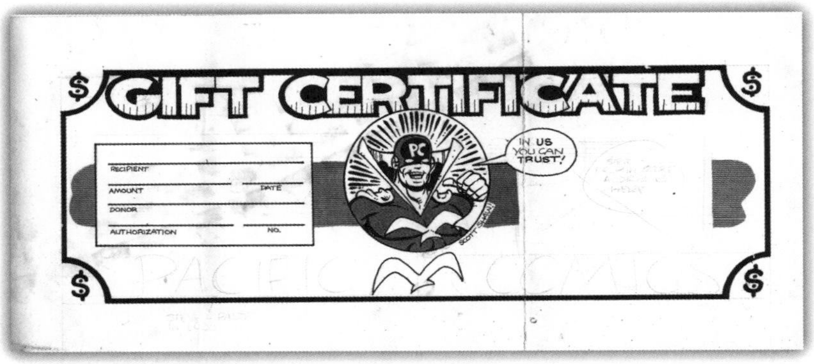
$ GIFT CERTIFICATE $
RECIPIENT
AMOUNT
DATE
DONOR
AUTHORIZATION
NO.
IN US YOU CAN TRUST!
PACIFIC COMICS

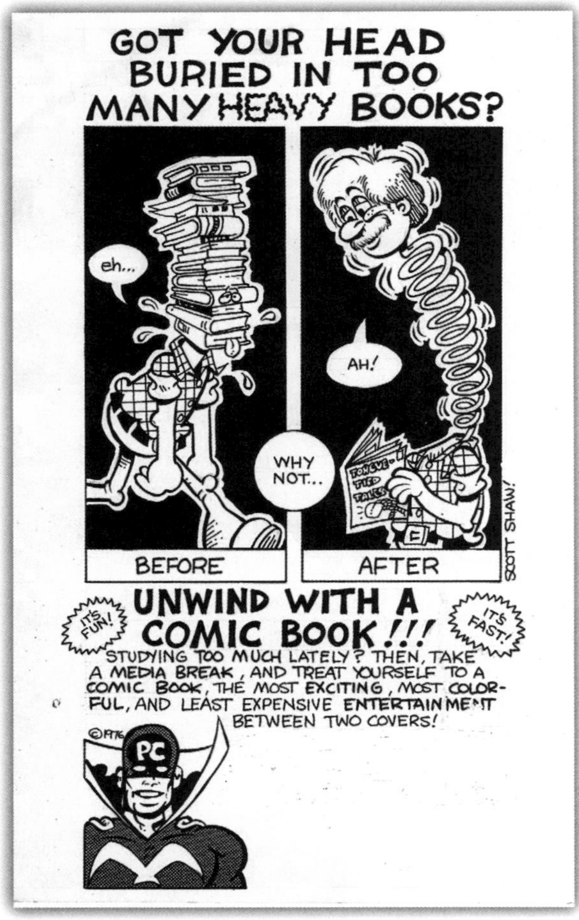
GOT YOUR HEAD BURIED IN TOO MANY HEAVY BOOKS?
eh...
AH!
WHY NOT...
BEFORE
AFTER
SCOTT SHAW!
IT'S FUN!
UNWIND WITH A COMIC BOOK!!!
IT'S FAST!
STUDYING TOO MUCH LATELY? THEN, TAKE A MEDIA BREAK, AND TREAT YOURSELF TO A COMIC BOOK, THE MOST EXCITING, MOST COLORFUL, AND LEAST EXPENSIVE ENTERTAINMENT BETWEEN TWO COVERS!
©1976
PC

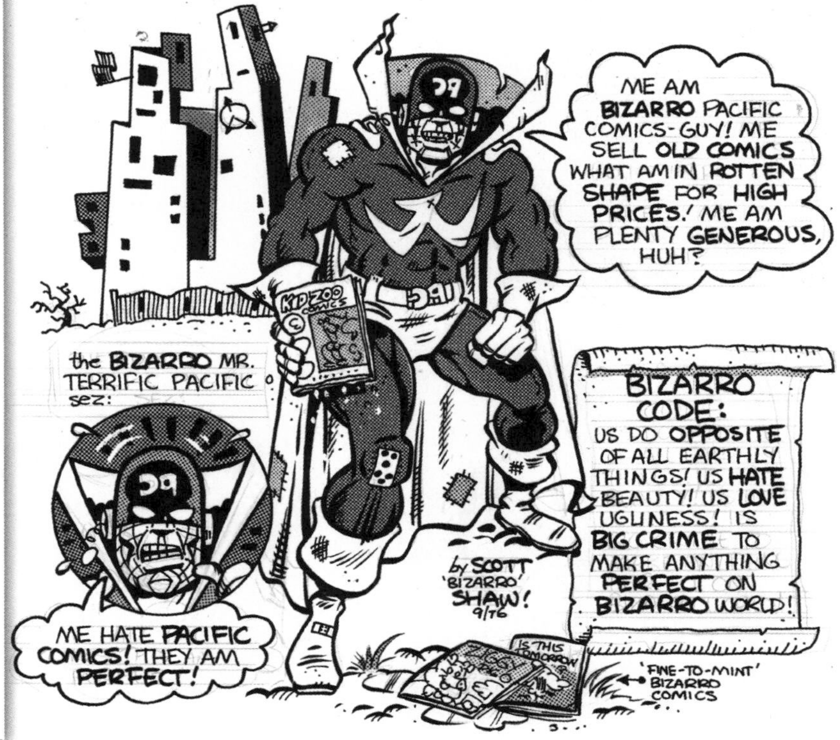
ME AM BIZARRO PACIFIC COMICS-GUY! ME SELL OLD COMICS WHAT AM IN ROTTEN SHAPE FOR HIGH PRICES! ME AM PLENTY GENEROUS, HUH?
the BIZARRO MR. TERRIFIC PACIFIC sez:
KID ZOO COMICS
BIZARRO CODE: US DO OPPOSITE OF ALL EARTHLY THINGS! US HATE BEAUTY! US LOVE UGLINESS! IS BIG CRIME TO MAKE ANYTHING PERFECT ON BIZARRO WORLD!
by SCOTT 'BIZARRO' SHAW! 9/76
ME HATE PACIFIC COMICS! THEY AM PERFECT!
IS THIS TOMORROW
'FINE-TO-MINT' BIZARRO COMICS

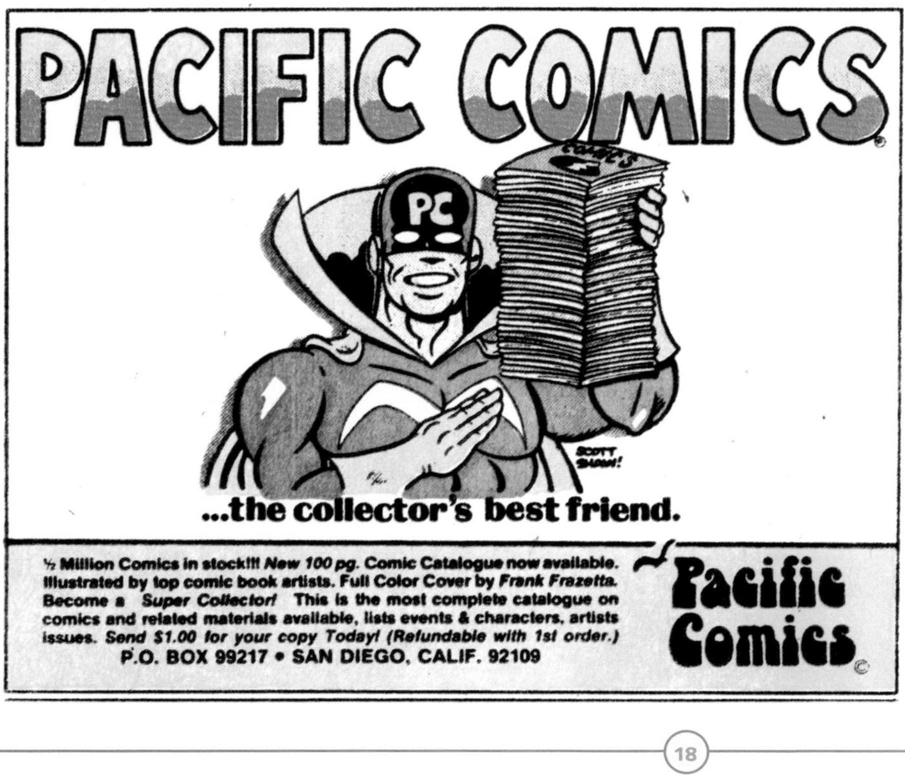
PACIFIC COMICS
PC
SCOTT SHAW!
...the collector's best friend.
½ Million Comics in stock!!! New 100 pg. Comic Catalogue now available. Illustrated by top comic book artists. Full Color Cover by Frank Frazetta. Become a Super Collector! This is the most complete catalogue on comics and related materials available, lists events & characters, artists issues. Send $1.00 for your copy Today! (Refundable with 1st order.)
P.O. BOX 99217 • SAN DIEGO, CALIF. 92109
Pacific Comics

Pacific Profiles

Scott Shaw!

Born: *Sept. 1958*

Scott has worked on underground comix, funny animal comics, Saturday morning animated shows, licensing art, and toiled for advertising agencies. A mainstay at the San Diego Comic-Con, you can always find the talented cartoonist exhibiting next to longtime friend Sergio Aragonés in Artists Alley!

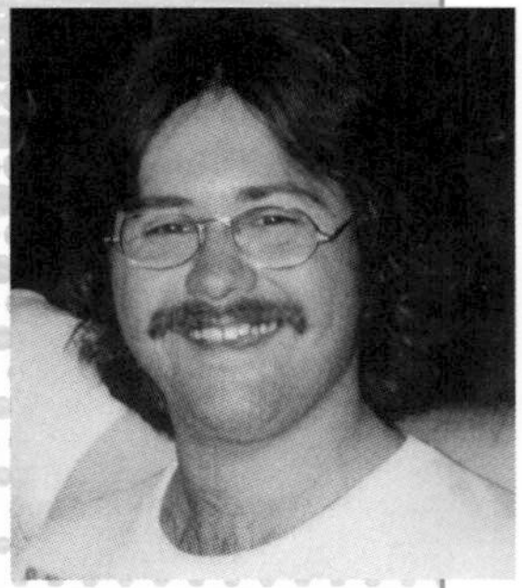

Above: Scott Shaw! grins for the camera in a pic taken at the 1976 San Diego Comic-Con.

Next page: Scott Shaw! drew this Pacific Comics flyer.

...MAKE WAY FOR
PACIFIC COMICS!
...HE HAS THE STRENGTH OF TEN, FOR HIS PRICES ARE LOW!
BY SCOTT SHAW!
Pacific Comics
5011 Cass St., San Diego, CA 92109
(714) 270-6911
Comic Catalogue
250,000 COMICS IN STOCK • 64 PAGES
COMICS • PULPS • BOOKS WE BUY & SELL!
SEND 50¢ FOR OUR HUGE CATALOGUE
Pacific Comics

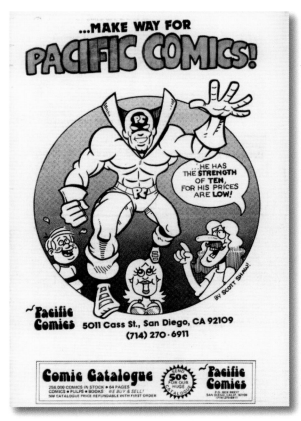

THE DISTRIBUTION GAME

Steve Schanes explained a whole new Pacific Comics endeavor to Rod Underhill. "By '76, we had five retail stores and we decided that was not the direction we wanted to go. What had happened was that we had experienced a lot of robberies and we got very demoralized, so we liquidated the stores, and got solely into wholesale. So, we contracted. Pacific Comics went through a series of contractions and expansions. That was our first major contraction. We then became a distributor, because we thought that we'd have more control, less labor, and we could more easily manage it. With one of the stores, if an employee didn't show up, my brother or myself would have to go to that physical store and work it.

"We began running the wholesale out of the small Pacific Beach store. We picked up a lot of accounts; the weak link at that time in retailing was getting product to the stores — there was no direct distribution. The local distributors were not tuned to the specialty market. They were more interested in the mass market, like 7-Elevens and that sort of thing. So we opened a warehouse in San Diego, then one in Los Angeles, and then one in Illinois."[19]

David talked about his perspective in *Back Issue* magazine: "Although it seems hard to imagine today, one of the big problems comic-book stores had in those days was getting a reliable supply of new comic books.

Bill Schanes Goes to DC

After buying from Sea Gate for about two years, our monthly orders were really growing, as we opened more stores, plus other comic book specialty retailers started to buy their new comics from Pacific Comics.

I had called Sol Harrison, then DC Vice President (I think) about buying new DC comics directly from DC versus Sea Gate. After a few phone calls, Sol asked me to come to New York City to meet with him and, to show DC Comics our level of commitment, I was to bring a check in the amount of no less than $10,000, which would act as an advance payment on our first order. I viewed this as a huge development, as I thought, if Sol was asking for this advance payment, it was a sign he was going to allow Pacific Comics to buy direct from DC Comics (our discount from Sea Gate was 50% off, and switching to going direct with DC would mean we'd now be buying at 60% off the cover price) — a real game changer from our overall profitability standpoint.

This tremendous opportunity presented several challenges at that time. First, and most importantly, we had to raise $10,000, while still continuing to run our ongoing businesses, plus buy a round-trip plane ticket and pay for a hotel room.

This would be my very first solo plane trip other than flights with my family when I was younger. I was a teenager and felt it was important I "dressed up" to meet Sol, to make sure I presented a good impression of not only me, but my company, so I wore a polo shirt, jeans, and sneakers (I normally wore an old T-shirts, shorts, and flip-flops, although back then everyone called them thongs, but, boy, has the meaning of *that* word changed over the years). I didn't own a dress jacket of any kind and, coming from San Diego, I only had a light wind-breaker, which didn't really go with what else I had packed, but I wasn't going for a fashion show, so...

A few weeks later, I left San Diego for New York City, with a check in the amount of $10,000 already made out to DC Comics. I had been to N.Y.C. as a child, as our family grew up in Montclair, New Jersey, not very far from Manhattan. My father would drive us into the big city on special occasions in the early '60s, not that I remembered much from that time period, except I remember our family home address — 106 Buckingham Road — and can recall what the inside and exterior of the house looked like. (I don't know why, but I still know every address I've ever lived at, including homes and apartments.)

I stayed in a Manhattan hotel on the evening I arrived, as I had scheduled an appointment with Sol at 10:00 A.M. the next morning. I was very nervous, as this was my first meeting with any of the major publisher business representatives. (I had met many of the creators and editors since I attended the early San Diego Comic-Con, and I also served as the "dealers room coordinator" for the convention, as well.)

The next morning, I didn't want to be late, so I arrived in front of the DC Comics building about 30 minutes early, and I just paced back and forth in front of the building for a few minutes. I had to ask businessmen dressed in suits what time it was, as I didn't wear a wristwatch. At 9:50 A.M., I entered the building, I asked the building receptionist what floor DC Comics was located on, and up I went.

I was just a couple of minutes early, which is what I wanted. I walked into the DC reception area, and told the receptionist that I had a 10:00 A.M. meeting scheduled with Mr. Harrison. She asked me to sit in the reception waiting area, while she pushed a button on her phone, which was kinda like an intercom system. I could hear it buzz, then a man answered (Sol, I assumed), and the receptionist told him, "Mr. Schanes is here for his 10:00 A.M. appointment." Sol indicated he'd be out in a few minutes, and the receptionist told me the same thing, even though I could hear both of them through the loud intercom system. I was sweating, my hands were wet, and I was continually rubbing them on my Levi's.

Sol Harrison, DC President

I'm guessing about 20 minutes had passed and I thought Sol may have forgotten I was here for my scheduled appointment, so I walked back up to the receptionist, and asked if she could call Sol to remind him I'm here, which she did.

A few minutes later, a door opened, and a much older man walked into the reception area, looked around, and then left through the same door he had entered. A few minutes after that, I was actually starting to get a little frustrated, and again walked up to the receptionist, again asking her to call Sol, which she did. I could hear from the tone in his voice, he was a bit grumpy, as he kinda barked out that he just walked out to the reception area and I wasn't there. The receptionist said I was and asked him to come out to meet me.

This time Sol came right out and walked right up to the receptionist asking where I was. The receptionist started to point in my direction as I stood up and said, "Mr. Harrison, my name is Bill Schanes, and we have spoken on the phone a few times, and I am here for our 10:00 A.M. scheduled appointment" (even though it was now closer to 10:45 A.M.). It's important to know that I've always had a very low voice, even when I was a teenager, it was normal to me, but I often got confused for someone much older when I was making a telephone call.

I wiped my hands on my Levi's one last time, then reached out my hand to shake Sol's hand. I'm 100% certain Sol thought I would be someone in my late 20s or early 30s. Still in the lobby, we shook hands, but neither of us said anything for a short time afterwards. (I know I was very nervous, and I think Sol was thinking, "Why am I wasting time meeting with a kid?") I finally blurted out that I had brought the $10,000 check he had requested I bring with me, and that was the icebreaker that was needed, as Sol then invited me into his office to finalize our new business arrangement between DC Comics and Pacific Comics. The actual meeting was very orderly, as Sol explained how the ordering process worked, timing, order increments, payment terms, and other important business points. I was taking notes the whole time, hoping Sol would slow down, so I could make sure I noted the key points.

The meeting went well, and in the taxi ride back to my hotel afterwards, I was shaking with excitement, as I knew this was a huge step for our company.[22]

Distribution of comics, as with other dated periodicals, was controlled by the newsstand wholesaler network. Sometimes the principals were pretty shady characters. To these companies, comics were a nuisance business. The distributors seldom kept track of the titles, let alone the issue number, and did not care much about the condition of the books. The price point of comics, deemed to have an audience solely of children, had been kept low for decades. Cover prices had not kept pace with those of other magazines, so comics were hardly worth carrying for either distributor or retailer. Often, new titles were not even put out for sale, but pulped or sold out the back door without ever leaving the warehouse.

"Phil Seuling, an energetic dealer and entrepreneur from Brooklyn, had approached the New York publishers with an offer: he would buy and sell comic books on a non-returnable basis and serve these collector shops. The publishers had nothing to lose, and Seuling could be described as persuasive; the direct sales market was born. Shops had a steady supply source, and fans knew that these stores would have all the new comics on a weekly basis. The entire market's output was paltry by today's standards, but then, as now, the comic-book readers were loyal and enthusiastic. A number of related items also became viable by utilizing this emerging distribution channel: fanzines, limited-edition prints,

and fantasy-art portfolios all found a wider audience among true fans. Pacific, who had by then shed their retail stores and back-issue mail-order businesses in favor of distributing, got active in this area."[20]

In his 2004 epic *San Diego Reader* history of Pacific Comics, Jay Allen Sanford reported, "Greg Pharis ran a shop in Kensington called Golden State Comics. Currently the owner of San Diego Comics, near [*San Diego State University*], Pharis recalls, 'Steve was really worried about rumors that guys from the local ARA [*periodical distributors*], which was said to be Mafia-controlled, were out to get him and Bill. He told me once that someone had knocked out his windows and he'd been personally threatened a few times… he was obviously anxious and scared, rightfully so, but you could tell he was also a little pleased and proud that he'd gotten the big guys' attention in such a big way.'"[21]

In his book *Comic Shop*, Dan Gearino described the Schanes brothers as "unshaven and often dressed in flip-flops and shorts, [*and they*] were part of a laid-back California scene." He continued, "Much less laid-back were the news distributors in the region, some of whom were rumored to have ties to organized crime. 'My car had a series of unfortunate incidences where I was getting four flat tires a day, and you knew where that was coming from,' [*Bill*] Schanes said. But vandalism turned out to be the extent of the push-back. Evidently, comics were too small a business to warrant actual violence."[23]

"Skywise"

COPYRIGHT ©1980   WENDY PINI   Plate 1
Schanes & Schanes • Box 99217 • San Diego, California 92109 • All Rights Reserved

EXPANDING THEIR PORTFOLIOS

David Scroggy recalled that shortly after he came on board, Pacific entered yet another new realm: publishing, though it was not funnybooks but high-end art portfolios to start. "And during that time," he told Klickstein, "we morphed from retailer with three or four stores in San Diego to an early direct sales distributor, to an early publisher of things like fantasy art and comic art portfolios."[24]

David described this new product line in his *Back Issue* essay: "Generally consisting of six to ten individual illustration plates in an illustrated folder, signed and numbered by the artist, these joined the comic books as part of the product mix."[25] And, for whatever reason, this profuse number of portfolios, which included work of innumerable top artists, from Howard Chaykin to Wendy Pini, were published under the "Schanes and Schanes" imprint. And, amid this foray into publishing, the brothers produced *One*, their first comic book. [*See page 24.*]

Above: In 1980, the Pacific Comics Catalogue boasted the following: "Schanes & Schanes published the first *Elfquest* portfolio. It was the fastest-selling portfolio in their history and was completely sold out in six weeks." Wendy Pini's *Elfquest: A Gallery of Portraits* was published by S&S in 1981. **Previous page:** Steve Schanes in 1975 with others at his Cass Street store. **Inset left:** Lovely fantasy illustration by Frank Cirocco.

This page: Clockwise from right is Rick Geary's one-pager from *Vanguard Illustrated* #4 [Apr. 1984]; two Geary booklets published by Pacific Comics in 1978; and his design of the Comic-Con International: San Diego close-up eye logo and the Comic-Con toucan mascot, both for which Geary is probably most recognized. **Next page:** Geary contributed his cartooning to Pacific's catalogue and marketing needs early on. These items, courtesy of Scott Shaw!, include some paste-ups that indicate the illos had subsequent uses after the Pacific years.

WHENEVER MY GRANDKIDS CLIMB UP FOR A STORY, I TELL THEM OF MY DAYS AS A . . .
STUDENT FILMMAKER
RICK GEARY © 1982
THAT'S ME WITH THE OLD BELL & HOWELL.
HERE I FALL OVER BACKWARD.
TOO COLD TO SHOOT TODAY —
NOW TOO WINDY!
ONE CAST MEMBER CHANGES HIS MIND.
NOW THE LIGHTS FALL OVER.
TRIPOD COLLAPSES.
HERE SOMEONE STANDS IN FRONT OF THE CAMERA.
TOO DARK TO SHOOT.
EDITING
OH NO! EDITING ROOM'S LOCKED.
I FALL OVER BACKWARD AGAIN!
THIS IS ALL THAT REMAINS.

Mister San Diego

Among the very first publications Pacific produced were two booklets by Rick Geary, a cartoonist whose name would become synonymous with the San Diego Comic-Con. "I moved to Pacific Beach in 1976 and lived very close to the Schaneses' comic store on Cass Street," he said. "They hired me to do two little cartoon books, *Television* and *Hello from San Diego*. As I recall, the *San Diego* subject was assigned to me and *Television* was my own choice, and they're both 5½" vertical x 8½" horizontal, a popular format at the time, à lá the Kliban cartoon books. I assume that they were ganged for printing, but I can't be certain.

"Later on, I contributed one- and two-page comic stories to their anthology titles, like *Vanguard Illustrated* and *Wild Animals*. But these were through my agent at the time, Dave Scroggy, who fortunately was also an editor at Pacific. I had very little direct contact with the brothers, only to say hi to at the Comic-Con and when I dropped into their store. I remember attending a big party when they opened a warehouse in San Diego."[27] As seen on the next page, Geary also drew art for Pacific's distribution side.

While at first distributing only to the Southern California region, the new Pacific incarnation was coveting wider territory. Jay Allen Sanford wrote, "To service the growing network of comic-book stores, Pacific expanded its distribution nationwide, after raising $200,000 by closing its four San Diego retail locations and selling off inventory. The Schaneses' rise in the industry put them atop a brand-new distribution network that would be called the 'direct market,' i.e., comic publishers bypassing the traditional distributors and making direct sales to comic shops through independent distributors like Pacific."[26]

Poised to conquer, Pacific pondered making their own items to distribute and thus took note when another upstart distributor new to the scene, Capital City, decided to create their own product. Capital took a bold step and launched their line of comics, a move that was watched carefully by a certain ambitious competitor based in sunny San Diego.

Hello from SAN DIEGO
$2.50
DRAWN BY RICK GEARY

$2.50
TELEVISION
DRAWN BY RICK GEARY

COMIC-CON INTERNATIONAL

Pacific Profiles
Rick Geary

Above: Rick Geary.

Born: *Feb. 1946*
Outside of his adopted San Diego, the cartoonist first made a mark as contributor to *National Lampoon* and *Heavy Metal*. Besides adapting famous literature for *Classics Illustrated,* Geary is well-regarded for his entertaining non-fiction graphic albums on famous historical murders. He won a 2007 Eisner Award.

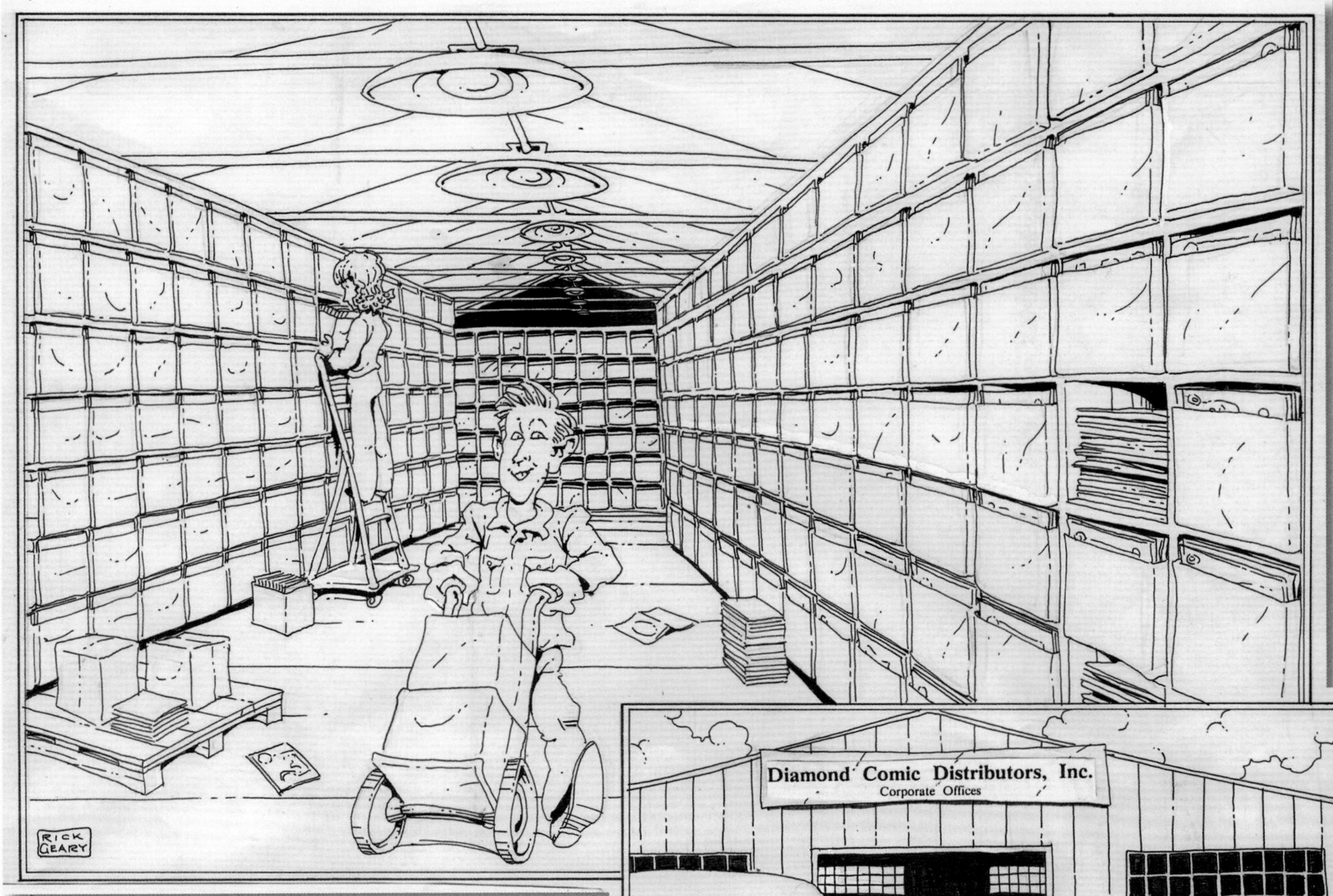
RICK GEARY

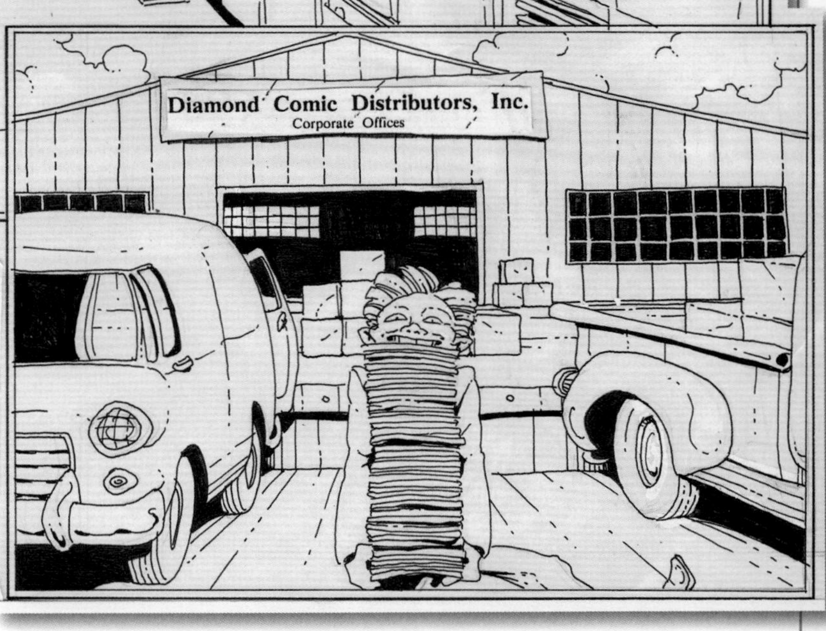
Diamond Comic Distributors, Inc.
Corporate Offices

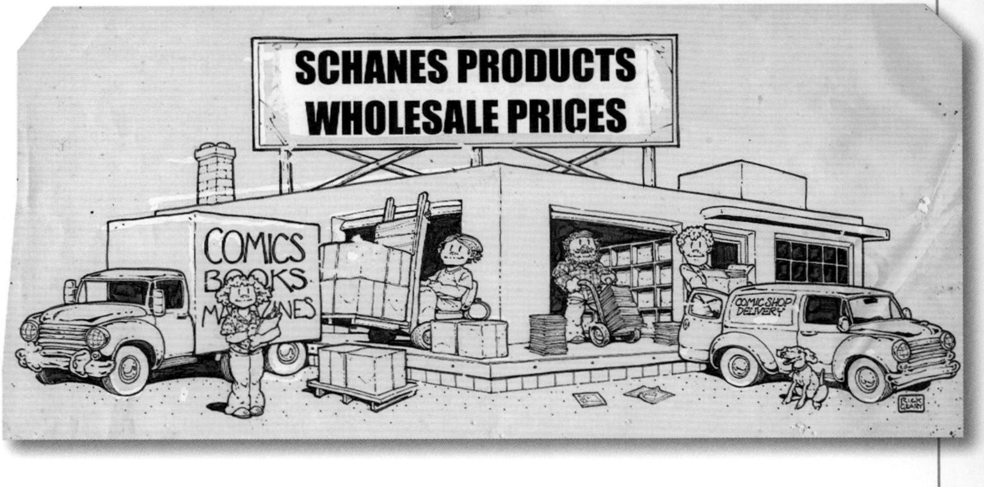
SCHANES PRODUCTS
WHOLESALE PRICES
COMICS
BOOKS
COMIC SHOP DELIVERY

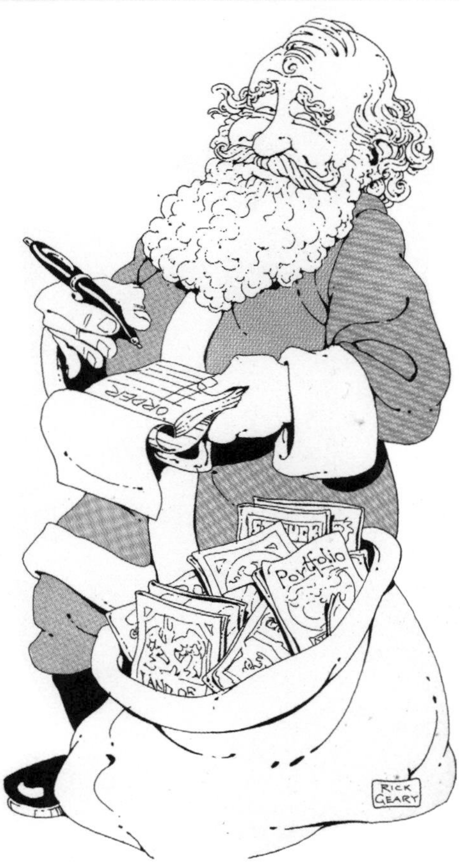
ORDER
Portfolio
RICK GEARY

The Story of the *One* and Only

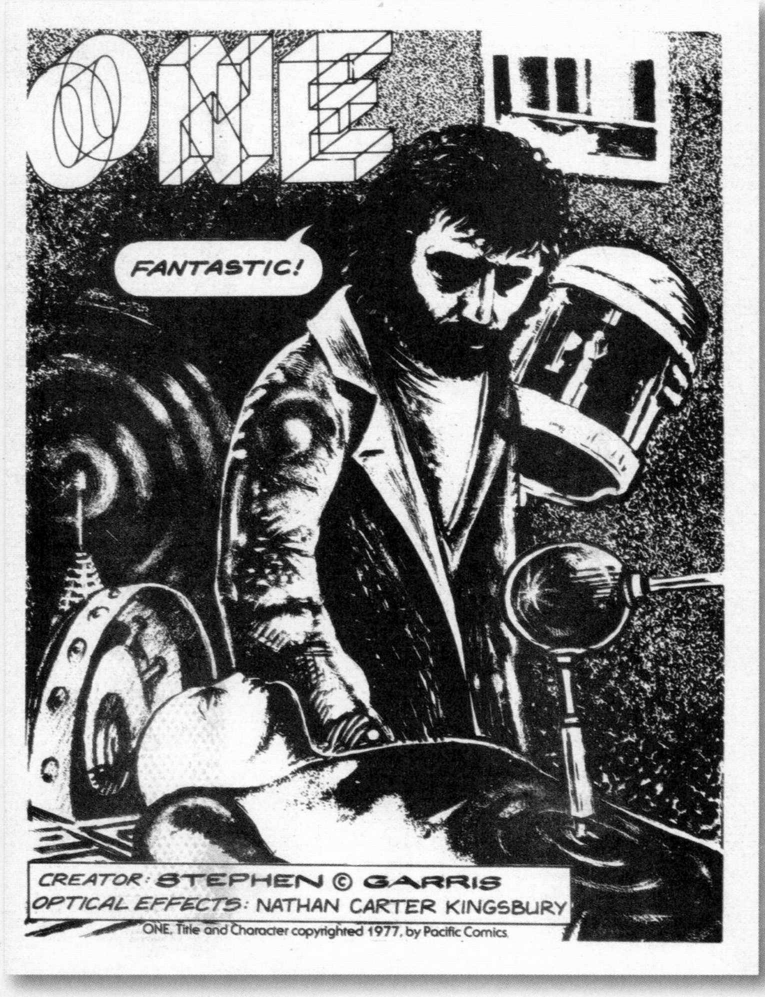
ONE
FANTASTIC!
CREATOR: STEPHEN © GARRIS
OPTICAL EFFECTS: NATHAN CARTER KINGSBURY
ONE, Title and Character copyrighted 1977, by Pacific Comics

Above: Opening splash page of *One* [July 1977]. Note the copyright notice attributed to "Pacific Comics."

Well before the company dove headfirst into comic book publishing, Pacific Comics made an initial attempt with *One*, a magazine-sized effort sporting black-&-white interiors and dated July 1977, intended to be a quarterly, but lasting only (ahem) one issue.

In 2015, Steve Schanes told Ed Catto, "We first published a black-&-white comic book called *One*, which was part photo-illustration, and part traditional comic book style of artwork. We did this to make sure we fully understood how the whole editorial production cycle worked, plus we felt *One* had enough potential on its own to reach a wide range of consumers."[28]

Judging it by the cover, *One* is impressive with its painting of the titular character by Phil Garris, an artist renowned for his Grateful Dead album cover, *Blues for Allah.* (Phil's *One* is an image so nice, they repro'd it twice, again on the back cover with a notice that posters of the illustration were available for three bucks.) But the main story inside written by Phil's brother Stephen and Nathan Carter Kingsbury was less than stellar, called "underwhelming, with much of it basically just poorly Xeroxed photos and word balloons."[29]

The back-up stories were an improvement, but the most important aspect of *One* was the inclusion of copyright notices crediting the magazine's contributors as owners of their own material (though the title character was curiously copyrighted to "Pacific Comics"), a harbinger of the central appeal for comics creators to contribute to the imprint in the future. Such copyright notices had been generally only found in underground comix and the "ground-level" publications of Mike Friedrich's Star*Reach.

The inside back cover's statements, "Pacific Comics, the wave of the future," and "*One* is just beginning; alternative views, attitudes, and concepts — that is what Pacific Comics is all about,"[30] might have been a bit hyperbolic and overwrought, but the little-known comic magazine was an opening volley by the Schanes brothers, one that would culminate in a full-on barrage that altered the course of the American comic book. But that fusillade was still a few years off so, in the meantime, the siblings' publishing efforts would focus on their S&S art portfolios.

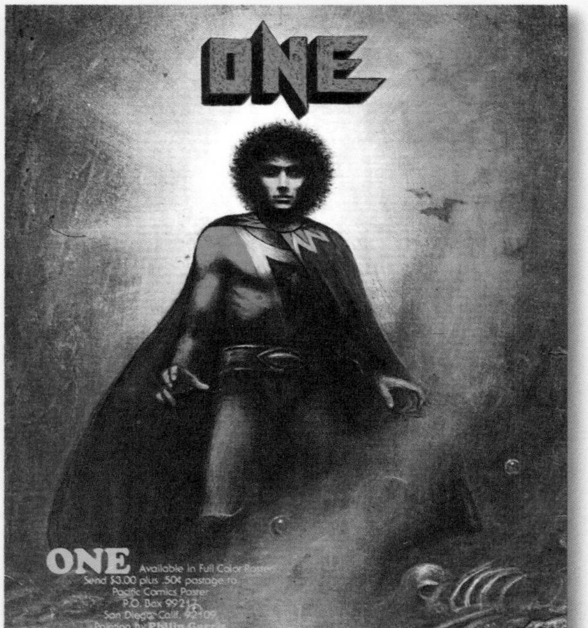
ONE
ONE Available in Full Color Poster
© GARRIS 77

Inset right: À lá the Gold Key Comics of the 1960s, Pacific repeated Phil Garris' cover painting sans logo on the back cover, which did include a promotional blurb, "*One*: Available in Full Color Poster" for $3.00.

Chapter Notes

1 Jay Allen Sanford, "The Rise & Fall of Pacific Comics: The Inside Story of a Pioneering Publisher," *San Diego Reader* website [Aug. 19, 2004], *https://www.sandiegoreader.com/news/2004/aug/19/two-men-and-their-comic-books/*.

2 Steve Schanes, testimonial, *See You in San Diego: An Oral History of Comic-Con, Fandom, and the Triumph of Geek Culture* [Fantagraphics, 2022], pg. 22.

3 Bill Schanes, testimonial, *See You in San Diego*, pg. 86.

4 Steve Schanes, "Captain Victory & Pacific Comics," *The Jack Kirby Collector* #15 [TwoMorrows, Apr. 1997], pg. 47.

5 Bill Schanes, testimonial, *See You in San Diego*, pg. 86.

6 Steve Schanes, *TJKC* #15.

7 Bill Schanes, testimonial, *See You in San Diego*, pg. 86.

8 Pacific Comics display ad, *The Comic Buyer's Guide for Comic Fandom* #39 [July 1, 1973], pg. 3.

9 Pacific Comics display ad, *The Comic Buyer's Guide for Comic Fandom* #44 [Sept. 15, 1973], pg. 6.

10 Steve Schanes, "Steve Schanes," interviewed by Rod Underhill, *Comics Interview* #55 [1988], pg.52.

11 Bill Schanes, Facebook posting [Apr. 27, 2020].

12 Ibid.

13 Bill Schanes, testimonial, *See You in San Diego*, pg. 87.

14 Ibid.

15 David Scroggy, "Hal Scroggy's Watercolor Portrait of Shel," Shel Dorf tribute website [Nov. 29, 2009], *https://www.sheldorftribute.com/2009/11/29/hal-scroggys-watercolor-portrait-of-shel/*.

16 David Scroggy, e-mail interview with author.

17 Ibid.

18 Sanford.

19 Steve Schanes, "Steve Schanes," interviewed by Rod Underhill, *Comics Interview* #55 [Summer 1988], pg. 52.

20 David Scroggy, "Pacific Comics Memories," guest editorial, *Back Issue* #75 [Sept. 2014], pg. 45.

21 Sanford.

22 Bill Schanes, Facebook post [Sept. 24, 2022].

23 Dan Gearino, *Comic Shop: The Retail Mavericks Who Gave Us a New Geek Culture,* expanded edition [Swallow Press, 2019], pg. 83.

24 David Scroggy, testimonial, *See You in San Diego*, pg. 87–88.

25 Scroggy, *Back Issue #75*, pg. 45.

26 Sanford.

27 Rick Geary, e-mail to Jon B. Cooke [May 6, 2023].

28 Bill Schanes, "Ed Catto: The (Not Quite) Secret Origin of Pacific Comics," interviewed by Ed Catto, Comicmix website [Aug. 31, 2015], *https://www.comicmix.com/2015/08/31/ed-catto-the-not-quite-secret-origin-of-pacific-comics/*.

29 "One by Stephen Garris & c.," Totally Pacific website [May 29, 2019], *https://totally-pacific.kwakk.info/2019/05/1977-one/*.

30 Editorial matter, *One #1* [July 1977], inside back cover.

31 Bill Schanes, Facebook post [Oct. 7, 2018], *https://www.facebook.com/william.schanes/posts/10157447681423273*.

32 David Scroggy, e-mail to Jon B. Cooke [Apr. 7, 2023].

Schanes & Schanes Art Portfolios

Between 1978–83, the Schanes and Schanes art portfolios were being published at a rapid clip, featuring the work of an astounding array of artists, including the names listed below, a thorough — if not definitive — list. Bill Schanes wrote on Facebook, "One of the companies my brother Steve and I owed in the '70s and '80s was a publishing company called Schanes & Schanes. S&S was really focused on prints, posters, and portfolios. Over the years, we released over 40 different portfolios, each was hand-signed and numbered, in limited editions."

He continued, "David Scroggy, who worked with us for many years, was really instrumental in reaching out to many of those we wanted to work with. My personal favorite portfolio we published

was *The Portfolio of Underground Art.* The final release of *TPOUA* included 13 brand-new illustrated pieces, featuring artwork by [*the underground comix artists listed below*]. (Others we couldn't track down, some didn't want to participate, and some we just never asked.)"[31]*

Other notable Schanes and Schanes releases included Howard Chaykin' *Starbuck* and *Robin Hood* sets; William Stout's *Dragon Slayers*; Wendy Pini's *Elfquest* trio of sets; P. Craig Russell's *The Curse of the Ring*; Marshall Rogers' *Strange*; sets by Filipino masters Alex Niño, Alfredo Alcala, and Nestor Redondo; and, of particular note in regards to the company's comic book line, a Mike Grell set of six black-&-white plates depicting *Starslayer*.

Alfred Alcala	Guy Colwell	Richard Hescox	Chris Miller	Marshall	Frank Thorne
Alicia Austin	Tim A. Conrad	Greg Hildebrandt	Alex Niño	Rogers	Larry Todd
Jean Braley	R. Crumb	Rand Holmes	Dan O'Neil	Rowena Morrill	Boris Vallejo
Frank Brunner	Lela Dowling	Greg Irons	Wendy Pini	P. Craig Russell	John A.
Rick Bryant	Mike Grell	Jack "Jaxon"	John Pound	Dave Sim	Williams
Tim Burgard	Rick Griffin	Jackson	Nestor	William Stout	Robert Williams
Howard Chaykin	Gary Hallgren	Josh Kirby	Redondo	Arthur Suydam	S. Clay Wilson
Frank Cirocco	Rory Hayes	Val Mayerik	Spain Rodriguez	Steve Swenston	Corey Wolfe

* David Scroggy noted, "In fact, the portfolio was only supposed to have 10 plates at first. As it was getting underway, Rick Griffin complained to me that 'There weren't enough of the *ZAP* artists,' and also lobbied strongly to include neo-primitive artist Rory Hayes. I carried that message to the Schanes brothers, asking to increase the budget to include the additional plates. They agreed. It is true that there were several worthy candidates that we didn't solicit, but we were able to reach everybody we had picked. There was no underground comix artist who was left out because they couldn't be reached."[32]

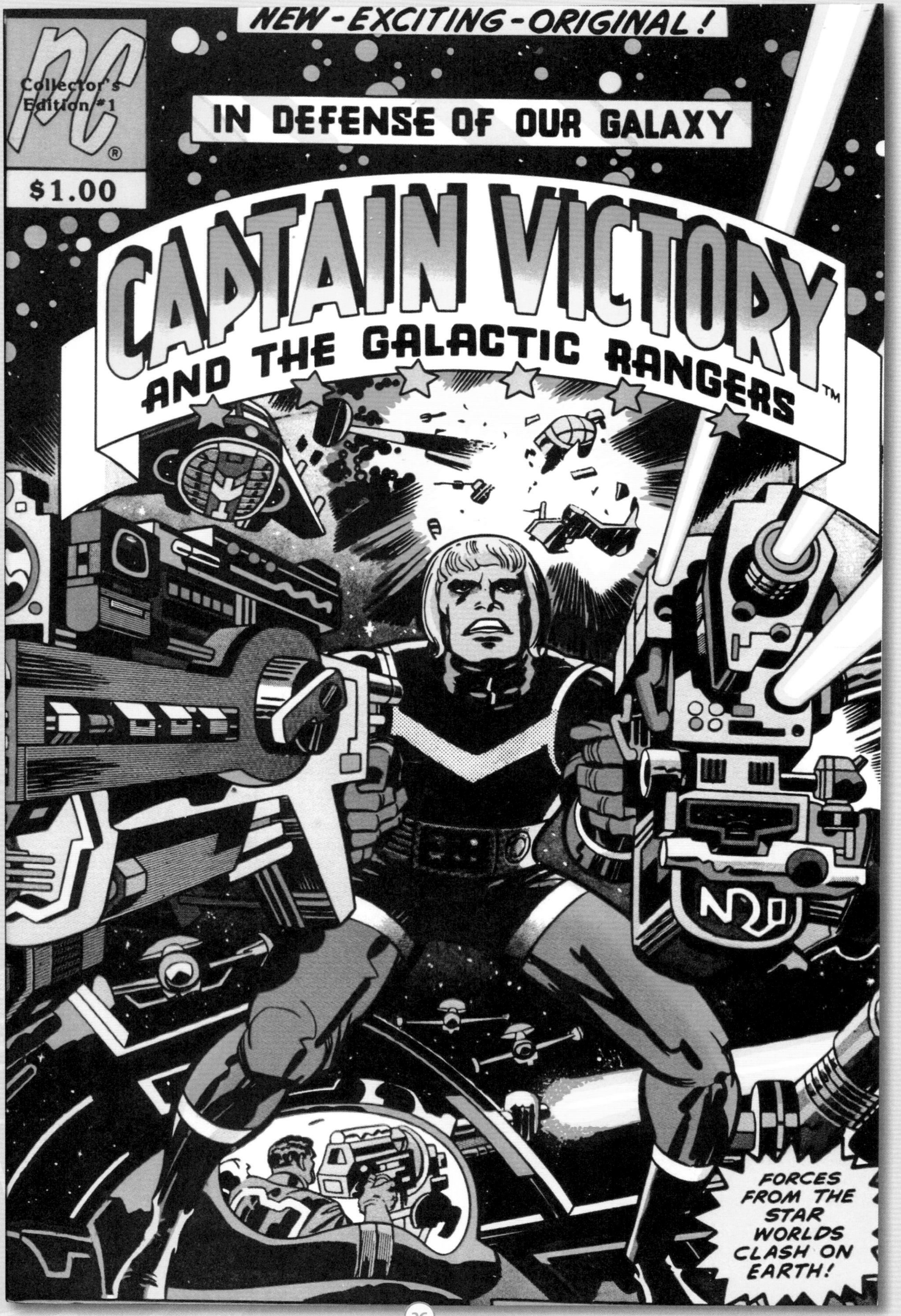

NEW-EXCITING-ORIGINAL!
PC
Collector's Edition #1
$1.00
IN DEFENSE OF OUR GALAXY
CAPTAIN VICTORY
AND THE GALACTIC RANGERS
FORCES FROM THE STAR WORLDS CLASH ON EARTH!

"Pacific's glorious experiment"

Who better than the King?

Steve Schanes told Jay Allen Sanford he knew who he wanted to launch a comics line. The Pacific co-owner hoped for comic book royalty. "I figured," he said, "if you want to get people's attention with a new comic book, who better to do it with than the King of Comics, Jack Kirby! We were already friends with Jack. We used to send him free copies of comics he'd drawn for other publishers because they never sent him any! So I just went ahead and called him on the phone, and he turned out to be a nice guy, completely accessible… we negotiated a whole detailed publishing deal between the two of us. No middlemen."[1]

MAKING AN IMPRINT

In an essay for *The Jack Kirby Collector,* Steve recalled starting their new business. "Bill and I decided we would become a comic book publisher. There were no books on this subject, and the major companies weren't about to give us any free advice. We needed an approach that was unique and fair. After discussions with comic book artists and writers, we became aware that these creative people did not own or control the concepts they created. Opportunity knocked: we would offer creator rights and a progressive royalty program… The talent was very thrilled by this radical new approach, but… hesitant because they could be blacklisted if they bucked the established system."[2]

It was 1981, Bill remembered, when they started to formulate a plan. "As we began to figure out how to approach this," he told the author, "we looked at what DC Comics and Marvel Comics were publishing at the time, plus we also learned what both companies were paying the creators/talent on both a per-page rate, as well as who owned what (company-owned intellectual properties versus creator-owned properties)." To that end, he added, "We engaged Mike Friedrich early on into this process as a consultant to help us craft a creator-friendly agreement."[3]

Back in the '70s, Mike Friedrich (who started off as a comics writer for the "Big Two") was publisher of *Star∗Reach* and its sister magazines, comics that were dubbed as neither underground nor mainstream, but instead called "ground-level." Of his company, Gerard Jones and Will Jacobs explained, "Star∗Reach Productions, with its creator-owned, Comics Code-free, personal artistic efforts, was for him what Wally Wood had once called 'the real stuff.' 'I think that if people are actually involved from the top to the bottom in a common endeavor, really involved,' Friedrich said, 'everybody is going to be more productive… If the writers and artists have a piece of it, they're going to be more involved and going to do a little bit more than if they don't.'"[4] (By 1979, Friedrich had shut down Star∗Reach as a publishing company, but as he remained acutely aware, comics creators needed to take charge of their own creations and keep rapacious

Previous page: *Captain Victory and the Galactic Rangers* #1 [Nov. 1981]. **Below:** Jack Kirby at the Pacific Comics booth during the 1982 San Diego Comic-Con. Note the *CV* comics in the spinner rack. Photo by Jackie Estrada.

S5871 ★ 75¢ ★ A BANTAM BOOK
BLACKMARK
THE NEW FULL-LENGTH ACTION ADVENTURE IN WORDS AND PICTURES
FIRST IN A SERIES OF DARING ADVENTURES
BLACKMARK™ IN THE PRIMITIVE WORLD OF
BY GIL KANE

publishers at bay as best as possible. To that end, he established a comic creator agency in 1981, under the same Star*Reach name.)

David Scroggy told Mat Klickstein, "My bosses Bill and Steve Schanes had come to an epiphany early on, realizing that, 'Hey, we could publish better comics than the ones we're distributing and selling!' In those days, it was a very unfair deal (and, in many ways, still is today) for creators. Very few of them got ownership of their own material. Nothing in the way of royalties; they just simply got a flat fee: whether their books sold a hundred thousand or a million copies, they were paid the same. Creators had no ownership of the intellectual property of their comics."

Top: Gil Kane's *Blackmark* paperback [1971]. **Above:** Captain Glory was originally named Captain Victory. **Below:** CV character designs.

David continued, "So, the Schanes brothers had a very simple but brilliant idea, which was to make a better deal for creators. They offered them ownership of their intellectual property and they offered to pay on a royalty basis. And this, in turn, attracted some of the biggest names ever in the industry. Our first comics were by Jack Kirby. *Captain Victory*."[5]

THE MARK OF KANE

But the King of Comics was actually *not* the first creator approached to kick off Pacific Comics. Bill told Ed Catto, "Most people don't know this next tidbit, but we intended on our first major release to be a project Gil Kane was working on at the time – *Blackmark*."[6] Bill expanded on that fact in a Facebook post: "We had originally reached out to Gil Kane to launch our Pacific Comics line of full-color comic books. Gil had a very interesting project called *Blackmark*, which had originally been published as a paperback book in 1971, by Bantam Books. We sold these in our chain of retail comic book stores back in the day.

"Gil very much liked our creator-friendly contract, but Gil was really old school, and he wanted to have *Blackmark* [*as a comic book*] on newsstands nationwide. Gil was quite stubborn and was challenging to have a conversation with. We didn't believe in the newsstand channel as a viable distribution model, as the sell through percentages often were as low as 20%, and we felt the whole old school fully-returnable system was so out of date and fundamentally flawed. Also, when we were going to launch our line of full-color comic books, we wouldn't have any advertising revenue, just sales from the actual comic books." Bill added, "We couldn't come to terms with Gil, but instead lead with the king, Jack Kirby! Can't get any better than that. (Side note: I seem to recall Gil wanted *Blackmark* published as a black-&-white comic book versus full-color.)"[7]

THE ROAD TO *VICTORY*

The latter '70s was a period in flux for Jack Kirby. He had bounced between DC Comics and Marvel earlier in the decade, when he encountered disrespect and his comic books were disparaged by some in editorial positions. By 1979, he had left mainstream comics behind and found work in animation, drew a syndicated newspaper strip, and worked on visual concepts for a science-fiction movie (later used in a daring — and successful — scheme to covertly rescue diplomats from Iran, as depicted in the film, *Argo*).

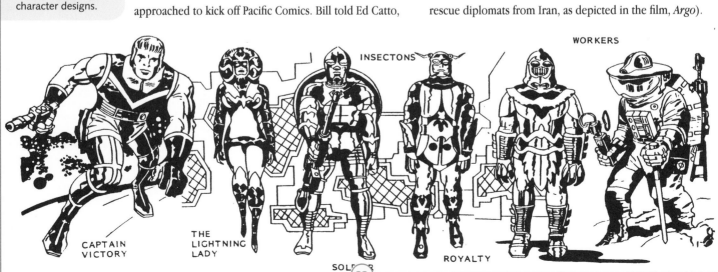

WORKERS
INSECTONS
CAPTAIN VICTORY
THE LIGHTNING LADY
ROYALTY

KEEP AN EYE ON CAPTAIN VICTORY'S "BACK UP" CREW--- THEY ARE STAR CREATURES WHO WILL SURPRISE AND EXCITE YOU!!!
ORCA
FROM EPSILON ERIDANI, IS EXACTLY WHAT HE APPEARS TO BE!
MAJOR KLAVUS
FROM FAR ANTARES--- IS NOT WHAT HE APPEARS TO BE!
TARIN
OF ALPHA CENTAURI. LIKES HIS JOB-- HATES HIS SHIP---
MISTER MIND
ORIGIN UNKNOWN--- A SWASHBUCKLER AT HEART. BUT NEVER IN DEED!!
LOVALEEN
FROM URSA MINOR IS SIMPLE, HUMBLE, -- THE MOST BEAUTIFUL SPORE IN ALL OF CREATION!!

As lucrative and satisfying as Kirby found storyboard, concept, and presentation work at Hanna-Barbera and Ruby-Spears, he was willing to take on another assignment, and he responded positively when the Schanes brothers came to call. Not long thereafter, the comics creator told *Comics Scene*, "I cooperate with Pacific Comics and Pacific cooperates with me. It's a good relationship, without conflict. It's living proof that, if you give the next guy a fair break, or cooperate with him, he's going to help you. And it's certainly not going to hurt the world."[8]

For the Schaneses' consideration, Kirby retrieved an unused project lingering on his shelf: *Captain Victory and the Galactic Rangers,* the first portion of a saga starring "an intergalactic policeman," with his "bizarre team of humans and aliens," determined to "combat the efforts of an alien 'beehive society' to take over the Earth."[9]

The theme behind the concept is cautionary. "Kirby says that he chose to do *Captain Victory* as a kind of warning," Howard Zimmerman reported in *Comics Scene*. "'I think there's a complacency now among the young' [*Kirby said*]. 'Sometimes we go overboard on trust.' As an example, Kirby cites Steven Spielberg's *Close Encounters of the Third Kind.* 'I thought his *Raiders of the Lost Ark* was terrific, but I felt he was too much of an idealist in *Close Encounters*.' Kirby feels that Spielberg's vision of benevolent aliens was as far off-base as the peaceful greeting they received from the American military and governmental advisors."[10]

(What Kirby didn't mention was the influence of *Star Wars* and his simmering resentment toward that movie, as director George Lucas was obviously inspired by Kirby's "Fourth World" series at DC, given the parallel Vader/Skywalker and Darkseid/Orion father-son plot devices.)

As mentioned, the Schanes brothers previously were in touch with Kirby. When starting up Pacific Comics, "We would send him copies of his printed work; Jack did not get complimentary samples from Marvel, especially of the foreign reprints. Jack appreciated this gesture," Steve Schanes mentioned in the *Kirby Collector.*[11]

"Jack Kirby had no fear," Steve continued. "He sent us a 48-page comic book he called *Captain Victory,* a graphic novel. This work was complete. What a man Jack was to take such a risk on two young men with a dream. We couldn't believe a top talent like Jack Kirby would work with us. We jumped at the opportunity.

"That first story was broken into the first two 32-page

Inset left: Likely presentation art done in the latter '70s, which was inked by Mike Thibodeaux and colored by Steve Oliff for use as the back cover of *Captain Victory* #2 [Jan. 1982]. **Below:** *Comics Scene* #2 [Mar. 1982] cover-credited Ruby-Spears co-workers Alan Huck and Ric Gonzalez for "executing the cel" that included Kirby's art and the photo by Sam Emerson. The issue contained an interview conducted by Howard Zimmerman, where Kirby was critical of his treatment by Marvel Comics in the '70s.

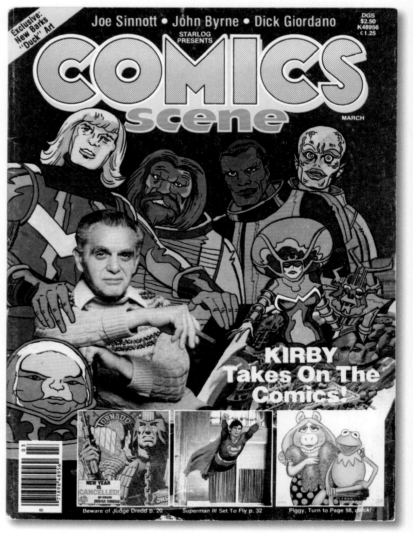

Exclusive: New Barks "Duck" Art
Joe Sinnott • John Byrne • Dick Giordano
STARLOG PRESENTS
COMICS Scene
MARCH
KIRBY Takes On The Comics!
NEW YEAR IS CANCELLED!
Beware of Judge Dredd p. 20
Superman III Set To Fly p. 32
Piggy, Turn to Page 58, quick!

Pacific Profiles

Jack Kirby

Above: Jack Kirby, 1982 San Diego Comic-Con, at the Pacific Comics booth. Photo by Alan Light.

Born: *Aug. 1917*
Perhaps the greatest comic book creator in the realm of adventure and the quintessential super-hero storyteller, the man born Jacob Kurtzberg in the slums of New York City continues to be revered by devotees, and his concepts have so far generated billions in the realm of movies.

issues of *Captain Victory*. It's always hard to start with the top talent because you get comfortable with the professional level. Jack was the ultimate professional. Here was a man who had done it all, but still had the patience and maturity to work with new people."[12]

What the Schanes boys maybe didn't know was the fact the package they were handed was actually produced a few years prior, when some Kirby-fan entrepreneurs stepped briefly into the King's life.

THE LEGEND THAT CAME TO LIFE
THUNDER FOOT
TM
LAST OF THE HALF-HUMANS

SATAN'S SIX
TM
THE DEVIL'S REJECTS

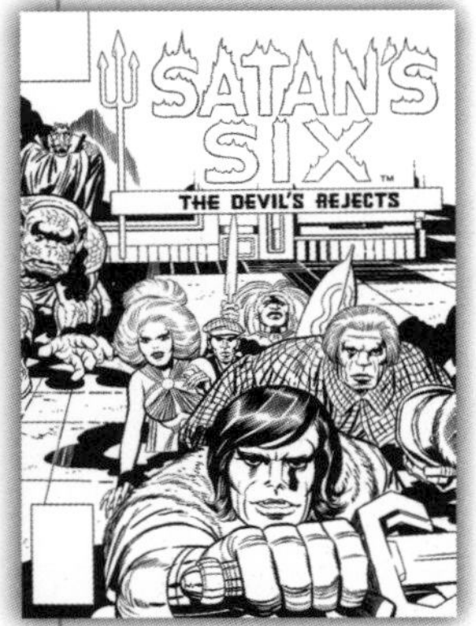

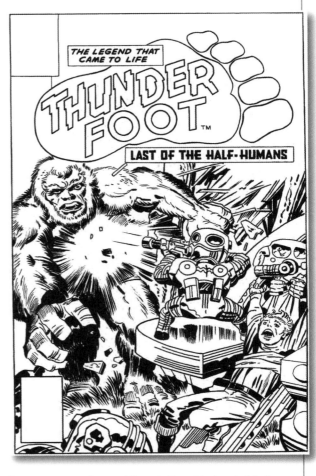

Above & below: *Satan's Six* cover and presentation art by Jack Kirby. **Inset right:** Kirby Comics *Thunderfoot* cover.

KIRBY COMICS

The particulars surrounding the short-lived proposal look to be lost to the ages, but some tantalizing evidence remains about a 1977 or '78 project called "Kirby Comics," as then-Kirby inker Mike Royer related in an interview with *Jack Kirby Quarterly*, a British 'zine. Referring to when Kirby left Marvel in that latter year, Royer said, "I remember, at some point during that period, there were a couple of guys who were apparently going to fund a new line of comic books. And I think they were going to be called — this is quite original — 'Kirby Comics.'

"Jack created three new books… *Satan's Six, Captain Victory,* and *Thunderfoot*. And the first thing I did was design the magazines logos. So that *Captain Victory* logo was my work — and *Satan's Six,* with the pitchfork. And *Thunderfoot*, which you've never seen, was a huge footprint with the lettering on it.

"We did a whole, double-length *Captain Victory,* and a number of pages for *Satan's Six,* as I recall. We never did any *Thunderfoot*, to my knowledge. And then, what happened is that the guys with the money, as so often happens, really didn't *have* the money.

"So then, subsequently, I guess *Captain Victory* was sold to Pacific Comics by that time I was at Disney. I think, the way they published the pages, they added some stuff that Mike Thibodeaux inked."[13]

Satan's Six lay dormant until 1993, when Topps Comics published the eight finished pages penciled by Kirby and a double-page spread featuring his character designs, which Topps extrapolated — for their "Kirbyverse" imprint — to a four-issue mini-series. And, actually, Royer seemed to have forgotten there were a few items produced regarding Thunderfoot, a Sasquatch-like character friendly to kids, including a cover. (*TJKC* editor John Morrow did some sleuthing: "No one can remember who the entrepreneurs were who convinced Jack to draw complete stories 'on spec,' but Mike at least was paid for his work.")[14]

JACK KIRBY'S
SATAN'S SIX
TM
SIX LOVABLE DOPES FROM LIMBO. IN ORDER TO GET RID OF THEM, SATAN SENDS THEM BACK TO EARTH TO EARN THEIR PITCHFORKS!
THIS IS WHAT CHARACTERS LOOK LIKE WHEN NOT IN COSTUME...
BRIAN BLUEDRAGON
THIS ERRING KNIGHT HAS THE WORST OF INTENTIONS... BUT HIS BAD DEEDS ALWAYS TURN OUT TO BE GOOD...
HARD LUCK HARRIGAN
PETTY GAMBLER AND BOOKIE WHO DROVE THE MOBSTERS --OUT OF THEIR BIRD!
DOCTOR MORDIUS
NO SELF-RESPECTING MASS-MURDERER WOULD ASSOCIATE WITH HIM...
KUGA THE LION-KILLER
THE TRUTH IS--HE'LL FIGHT ONE--BUT HE WON'T KILL ONE... KUGA SECRETLY LOVES ANIMALS...
DEZIRA OF BABYLON. SHE'S TOO CUTE AND DIZZY TO BE A BONAFIDE TEMPTRESS. SHE'S LIKE GOLDIE HAWN...
FRIGHTFUL-- HE'S A REAL, BONA-FIDE FIEND FROM HELL. HIS POWERS ARE AWESOME... HE'S SENT ALONG TO KEEP THE OTHERS IN LINE, BUT HE WINDS UP HELPING THEM...

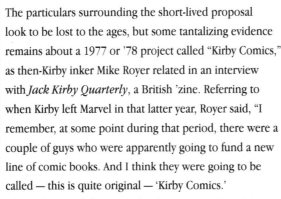

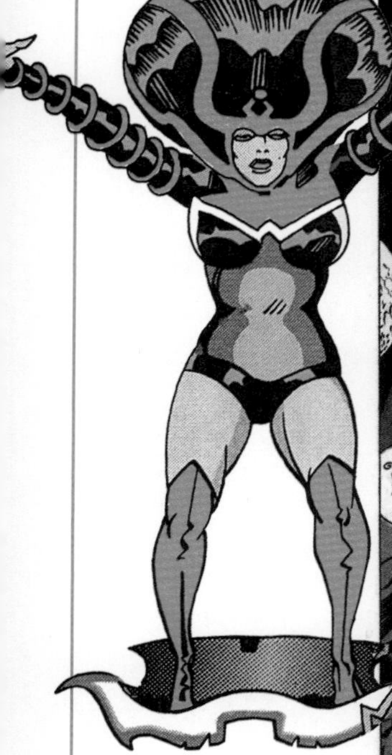

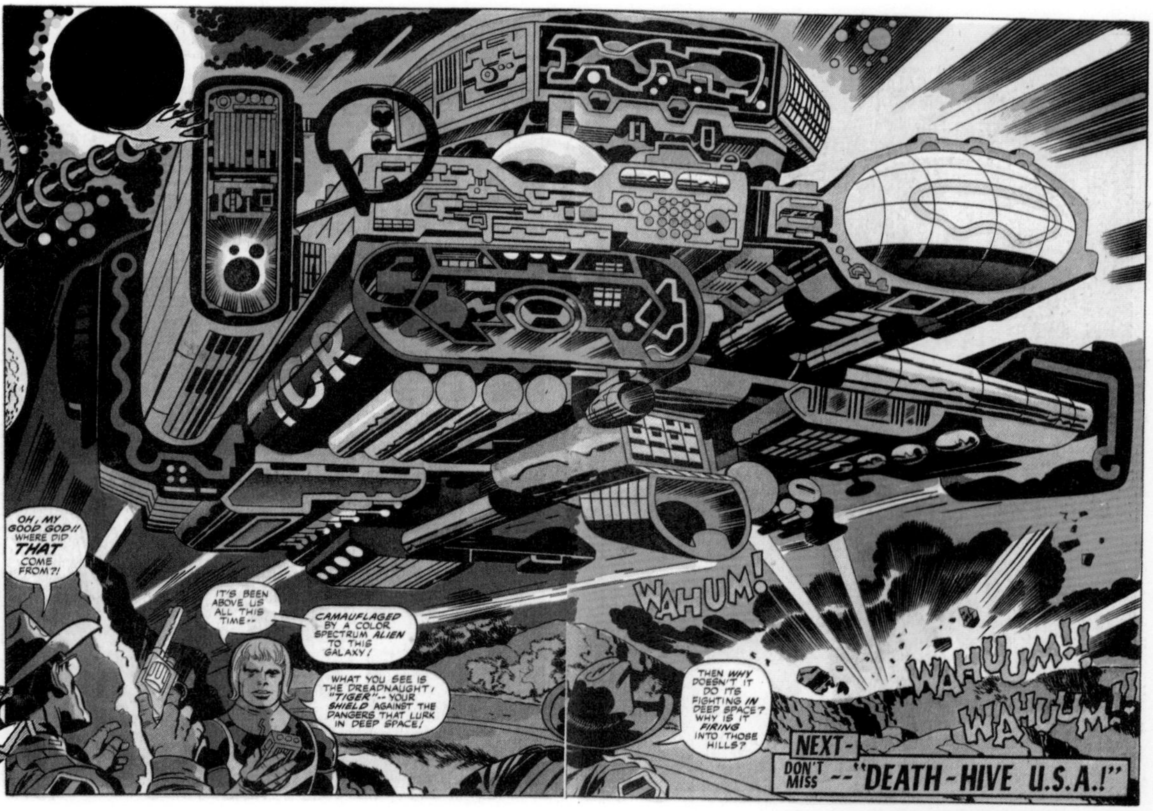

OH, MY GOOD GOD!! WHERE DID THAT COME FROM?!
IT'S BEEN ABOVE US ALL THIS TIME--
CAMAUFLAGED BY A COLOR SPECTRUM ALIEN TO THIS GALAXY!
WHAT YOU SEE IS THE DREADNAUGHT, "TIGER"-- YOUR SHIELD AGAINST THE DANGERS THAT LURK IN DEEP SPACE!
WAHUM!
THEN WHY DOESN'T IT DO ITS FIGHTING IN DEEP SPACE? WHY IS IT FIRING INTO THOSE HILLS?
WAHUUM!!
WAHUUM!!
NEXT- DON'T MISS --"DEATH-HIVE U.S.A.!"

THE ORIGINAL FORM

In *Captain Victory: Graphite Edition* [June 2003], John Morrow explained the slightly complicated reconfiguring *Captain Victory* endured on its way to become Pacific Comics' first regular title. "[*Kirby*] penciled a 17-page *Captain Victory* story meant for a new start-up comics imprint called Kirby Comics… Jack then expanded it into a 50-page graphic novel with inks by Mike Royer, the first of a planned three-part saga, but there were no takers, so the pages languished in his files. With the help of assistant Steve Sherman, he prepared a *Captain Victory* movie screenplay in 1977… but nothing came of it, so the character remained grounded until Pacific Comics came calling in 1981. Kirby split-up his 50-page novel to make Pacific's *Captain Victory* #1 and #2, adding new filler art, and jettisoning one page that made it into issue #3."[15]

Jeremy Lewis, in a series assessment published in *Jack Kirby Quarterly*, shared, "Certainly, *Captain Victory* was the only occasion since the Fourth World on which Kirby enjoyed that creative freedom for which he had fought so hard. There are no redrawn faces. No superfluous characters imposed from without. No editorial interference. *Captain Victory* was Kirby's baby from start to finish and it runs along at an absolutely cracking pace."[16] And, while Lewis notes Kirby was having "a ball" with the title, the writer tellingly noted a degree of rage therein.

RESPECT

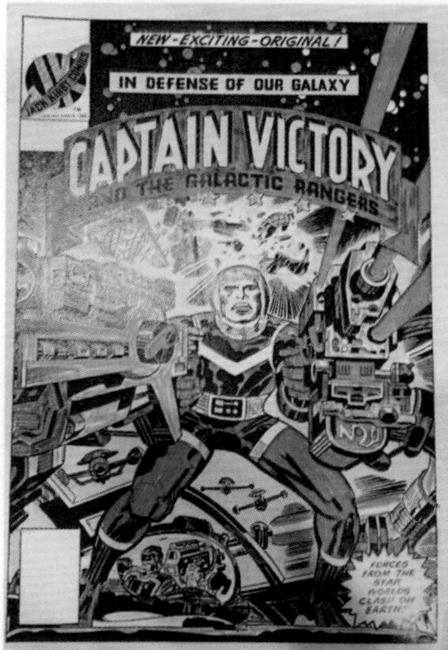

NEW-EXCITING-ORIGINAL!
IN DEFENSE OF OUR GALAXY
CAPTAIN VICTORY
AND THE GALACTIC RANGERS

"Perhaps, through this work," Lewis then surmised about Kirby and *Captain Victory*, "he was expressing some of the anger and frustration he felt as a consequence of having been cut-off, trammeled, and limited in the '70s."[17]

In truth, resentment over his being exploited had stretched to prior decades, starting in 1941 when Kirby and then-partner Joe Simon were being cheated out of a promised cut of profits from the wildly popular *Captain America Comics*, not to mention coming to the realization that all of his work as the major creator at Marvel Comics in the '60s earned him nothing more than a page rate.

Since its inception, the comic book industry had treated its creative talent with contempt, Jay Allen Sanford explained, with artists and writers, "forced to sign contracts that granted them no proprietary rights to their own creations. To cash their paychecks, they had to waive all rights to their work, even to characters, storylines, and entire series they had thought up and developed. The publisher owned it all, right down to the original, hand-drawn artwork, and the notion of royalties was unheard of."[18] The Schanes men dramatically changed that equation.

This page: At top left is the spectacular double-page spread concluding *Captain Victory* #1 [Nov. 1982] by Jack Kirby. Top left is detail from *CV* #1's back cover, Victory's nemesis, Lightning Lady. Above is the Jack Kirby Comics circa 1977 cover mock-up for *CV* #1. Inks by Royer and Thibodeaux.

Pacific Plots to Take Over the World

STEELEVILLE
PC
8423 PRODUCTION AVE.
SAN DIEGO, CA 92121
COMICS

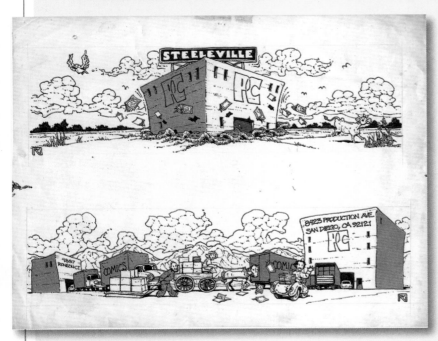

Above: Rick Geary created this cartoon of Pacific's facilities in San Diego and Steeleville, Illinois.

Inset right: *Southern Illinoisan* newspaper article, from Mar. 9, 1983 mentioning the Steeleville warehouse.

Below: Typical Pacific Comics product catalogue, this from 1982.

PACIFIC COMICS
1982 FANTASY CATALOGUE
PC
• COMICS
• BOOKS
• MAGAZINES
• DELUXE PRODUCTS
• PORTFOLIOS
• PRINTS
• SCIENCE FICTION
• FANTASY
• DISNEY
• FANZINES

While Pacific Comics did launch a brand-new comic book publishing house, it retained the distribution branch of the outfit — the parent company being dubbed Blue Dolphin Enterprises — which had grown into a powerhouse by the early 1980s. "When Marvel opened itself up to working with new distributors, Pacific signed up," wrote Dan Gearino, "and became the regional player in Southern California."[19]

The Schaneses began eying the national scene and made a move to expand beyond their 17,000-square-foot office/warehouse, where the company was based by July 1982. "That same year, the Schaneses purchased a firehouse in Steeleville, Illinois, for $50,100, near World Color Press in Sparta, where the majority of U.S. comic books were printed," Sanford reported. "Pacific converted the firehouse into a distribution hub. It was also operating warehouses in Los Angeles and Phoenix at the time."[20]

Sanford himself got a job at the Pacific home warehouse around 1983. "I was in nerd nirvana, shuffling around wide-eyed and speechless as I checked out the seemingly endless, depth-less shelves overflowing with new comics, graphic novels, magazines, toys, Japanese models, and hundreds of other items, including years' worth of back issues of *Cerebus, ZAP Comix,* and *The Fabulous Furry Freak Brothers*. Pacific-published comics in sealed boxes[*that*] were stacked up by the pallet-load and being shuffled around by guys on forklifts. About a half-dozen employees packed customer orders in various departments spread out over two floor levels in the warehouse."

Pacific Comics comes to town

By Arlene Hill
Southern Illinoisan Correspondent

It's a long way from Brooklyn to Steeleville if you go by way of Los Angeles, Calif. That's the route Ken Krueger took. The layover in Los Angeles lasted 15 years. Mr. Krueger is manager/buyer for Steeleville's newest industry, Pacific Comic Distributors.

He says that Steeleville's close proximity to World Color Press was a primary factor in his company's decision to purchase the old fire station and set up their business here, but the real deciding factor was the co-operation from local community and business leaders.

Pacific Comics intended for people on the site to handle their own product, to sort and distribute their comic books and comic oriented books. That was August 1982. In September they shipped 5,000 pieces. They are now shipping a total of 120,000. There are four full-time employees and two part-time besides Krueger and his wife, Patty.

Sanford soon met with the younger Schanes brother. "Bill hired me as a shipping and receiving clerk. My job involved filling orders from back-stock and breaking up shipments of new comics from dozens of publishers once a week. This last endeavor, 'new-comic day,' was everyone's favorite part of the workweek. The center aisle of the warehouse would be filled with rows and rows of brand-new issues, sometimes even overseas and underground comics, all fresh from the presses and smelling of damp ink and newsprint. First we had to fill invoices for San Diego customers, who'd be pounding at the door in a few hours to get their goodies in order to open their shops, but then there was time to read the comics, to catch up on the numerous titles and types of creative offerings coming out from publishers and producers all over the planet.

"On a typical workday, I might be putting together sets of *Elfquest* magazines for an account in Germany or designing a start-up rack with Mobile Suit Gundam blueprints, *Battle of the Planets* toys, and *Speed Racer* Viewmaster reels for a local retail store about to go into Japanimation. Or I could be standing in an assembly line, going through hand-drawn animation cels from the movie, *Heavy Metal,* and throwing away damaged or chipped cels, stuffing the rest into portfolio packets printed by the Schaneses. (They'd bought a huge stash of production cels from the film company.) Of course, we put aside the best cels for ourselves, using our 25% employee discount to pay only $56.25 (retail $75) for ten complete cels — today, *Heavy Metal* animation cels go for $500 to $2,000 each."[21]

Sanford was surprised that the company ran as well as it did. "I had to admit that it *did* seem to work, marveling at the inventive low-tech verve it took to just jump in and do something, learning how to do so as you go along. That was the vibe in the front office at Pacific — a bunch of overgrown kids whose clubhouse had suddenly, overnight, become a corporation — a corporation that published upward of a dozen comic books each month.

"It didn't feel like a corporation, however — running the company had become a family affair, with the duo's father, Steven E. Schanes, hired in 1982 as financial vice president, and mother Christine Marra serving as office manager. Bill and Steve's older brother Paul (everyone called him Pablo) quit his job as a welder to work in the financial records department, and sister Chris, an L.A.-based attorney, provided counsel on legal affairs."[22]

In the March 15, 1984 edition of *Amazing Heroes,* Pacific Comics Distributors took out a double-page ad mapping out their territory, which had expanded by then to 12 countries, including the US. Gearino wrote, "Pacific Comics grew as a regional distributor and then as a national publisher. The two sides of the business seemed complementary, especially when *Captain Victory* caused a big sensation among longtime fans of Kirby. But soon one side of Pacific would run into trouble, and both sides would feel the pain."[23]

Pacific's dual businesses were heading for an inevitable clash. Steve Schanes would later confess to Rod Underhill, "Being a publisher caused damage to the distribution end of the business, because the people we were distributing were also in competition with us as a publisher."[24]

PC
PACIFIC COMICS DISTRIBUTORS
FANTASY CATALOG — WINTER 1982 —

Above: Rick Geary drew St. Nick on the cover of Pacific's Winter 1982 catalogue. **Below:** Spread from *Amazing Heroes* #43 [Mar. 15, 1984], showing the breadth of Pacific's distribution division.

Pacific Comics Distributors
OFFERS
FAST DISTRIBUTION
ALASKA
Sparta
Steeleville
LOS ANGELES
SAN DIEGO
HAWAII
BY UPS
2 days to Chicago
2 days to Detroit
3 days to Baltimore
3 days to Dallas
3 days to Houston
3 days to Miami
3 days to New York
3 days to Phoenix
3 days to San Fran.
4 days to Seattle
BY AIR
1 day to Ala
1 day to Hawaii
From our Steeleville, IL warehouse, we offer:
One to four day service by UPS (depending on where you are located).
Next day service by air to most cities.
Next day service by air to Hawaii and Alaska.
WE SHIP THE NEW COMICS EVERY THURSDAY MORNING
Along with our fast and efficient service we now offer store owners new discounts and terms that make Pacific Comics one of the most effective distributors in the country.
PACIFIC COMICS DISTRIBUTORS
206 North Sparta
Steeleville, IL 62288
Phone: (618) 965-3464 Telex: 282500
Pacific Comics Distributors
OFFERS
WORLDWIDE DISTRIBUTION
CURRENTLY SERVING: Canada, Brazil, England, France, Switzerland, West Germany, Italy, Japan, China, Australia, New Zealand—and ever expanding!
SWITZERLAND
FRANCE
W. GERMANY
ENGLAND
ITALY
JAPAN
CANADA
CHINA
BRAZIL
AUSTRALIA
NEW ZEALAND
We offer the following products:
Comics: DC, First, Marvel, Pacific, Capital, Americomics, Vortex, Eagle, Comico, Texas, Aardvark, Spectrum, Continuity, Eclipse.
Magazines: Amazing Heroes, Analog, Asimov, American Cinematographer, Comics Journal, Fangoria, Starlog, Cinefex, Heavy Metal, Imago, National Lampoon, Cinefantastique, Drago, Wargamer, and more.
Also: Calendars, t-shirts, posters, hardcovers, trade papers, paperbacks, games, miniatures, portfolios, toys, masks, albums, plus much, much, more.
We offer the following services:
Accurate records. Fast and efficient service. Orders shipped in specially made double wall boxes. Orders can be shipped by: mail bag, parcel post, air mail, ocean freight, or air freight. We can get you your books in a week and a half after they are printed, by air freight. We have some of the best prices available on ocean freight and air freight.
Plus: we are one of the few distributors that has a separate department designed especially for the processing and shipping of foreign accounts.
PACIFIC COMICS
8423 PRODUCTION AVENUE
SAN DIEGO, CA 92121-2278
Phone: (619) 566-3290 Telex: 695206

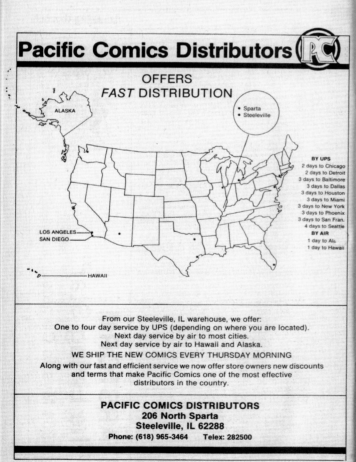

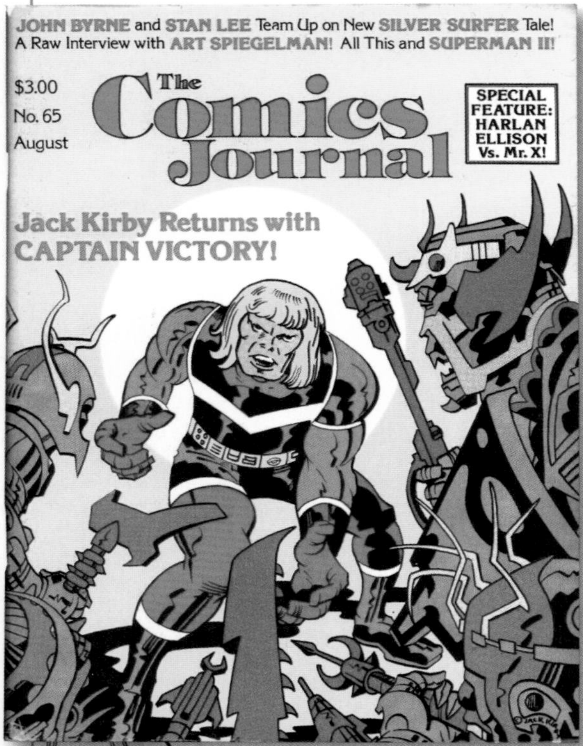
JOHN BYRNE and STAN LEE Team Up on New SILVER SURFER Tale!
A Raw Interview with ART SPIEGELMAN! All This and SUPERMAN III!
$3.00
No. 65
August
The Comics Journal
SPECIAL FEATURE: HARLAN ELLISON Vs. Mr. X!
Jack Kirby Returns with CAPTAIN VICTORY!

Steve and Bill offered a contract more aligned with actual book publishing, "The Schaneses told Kirby that they wanted only publishing rights to new works; he could keep ownership of anything new and copyrightable he created," Sanford explained. "They'd even help him license characters for use overseas or in television, film or other media. Pacific was also the first company to offer Kirby royalty payments according to a comic's sales figures: eight cents on the dollar and 10¢ for comics selling over 100,000 copies. If Marvel Comics, selling around 150,000 on average, had offered royalties akin to Pacific's, this would have worked out to $13,000 in payments to the artist."[25]

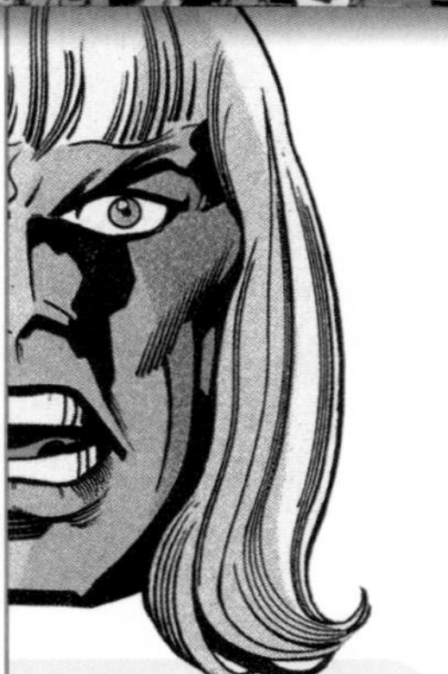

This page: Clockwise, top left, *TCJ* #65 [Aug. 1981] cover by Kirby; *CV* #1 original art; *Dazzler* #1 [Mar. 1981], the first mainstream comic book published just for the direct market; and detail from *CV* #4 [May 1982] splash.

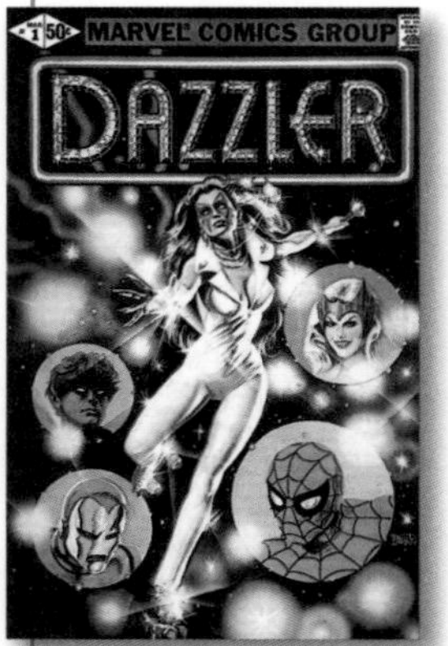
MARVEL COMICS GROUP
DAZZLER

A BOOK OF OUR OWN

A lot had happened in the tumultuous comic book market before the Summer 1981 publication of *Captain Victory and the Galactic Rangers* #1. David Scroggy put that landmark event in context. "The single biggest development in Pacific Comics' evolution, of course, was the decision to publish their own comic books. As the comics specialty market had grown, there was an increasing clamor for a title that would be distributed solely by the direct sales market. It was hard to get reliable information from Marvel or DC, but the consensus at the time was that the direct market was nearing 10% of Marvel's sales."[26]

David continued, "In 1979, Marvel President James Galton came to San Diego Comic-Con, and a meeting with the comics specialty distributors and key retailers was arranged. The most vocal request, put forward by Steve Schanes, was 'give us a book.' Marvel decided to accept, and *Dazzler* #1, published in December 1980, became the first 'direct-sales only' comic book. The retailers all took big positions on *Dazzler*, wanting to send a strong message to Marvel. It worked. This, once and for all, proved the viability of the direct-sales comics specialty market to support its own tiles."

Dazzler #1 sold an eye-popping — and non-returnable! — 428,000 copies,* and David told Jeff Gelb, "This was a great awakening to everyone that the comics specialty shops had become a market of their own, fully capable of supporting a book's entire print run, often distributed through Pacific. We felt we were more in touch with the needs of these shops than anyone, including Marvel, and that we could probably do just as well or better at producing comics for that marketplace."[27]

In an interview with Stanley Wiater and Steve Bissette, one-time Image Comics executive director Larry Marder declared that, after the emergence of *The First Kingdom, Cerebus,* and *Elfquest* (all black-&-white comic magazines created for the direct market), and the publication of *Sabre* (the first graphic novel produced exclusively for the d-m), the signing of Jack Kirby was the next landmark event in the growth of the direct sales marketplace. He described *Captain Victory*: "It was a color comic book that was indistinguishable from a mainstream DC or Marvel comic — though it was available only through the direct sales market. So, in a very short period of time, within five years or so, this new market went from an idea by Phil Seuling to having material produced for it that was indistinguishable from mainstream product. It's really quite extraordinary that it happened that quickly."[28]

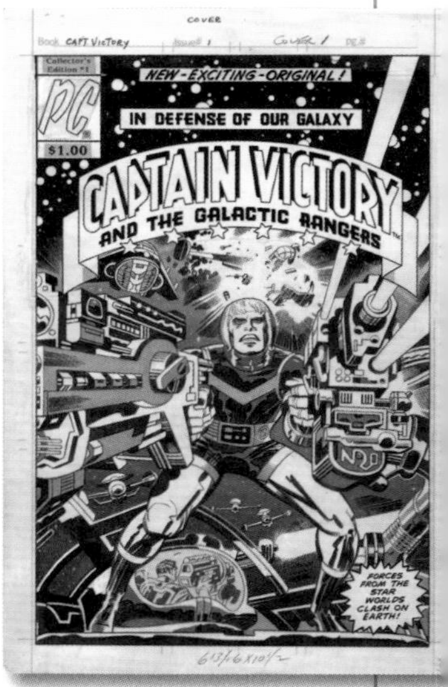
NEW-EXCITING-ORIGINAL!
IN DEFENSE OF OUR GALAXY
$1.00
CAPTAIN VICTORY
AND THE GALACTIC RANGERS
FORCES FROM THE STAR WORLDS CLASH ON EARTH!

VINDICATION

In the years since, most critics of Pacific's 13-issue and one *Special* run of *Captain Victory* by Jack Kirby have been less than kind, though more than a few others are willing to argue it is a worthy addition to Kirby's pantheon of heroes. Speaking for the majority, Gerard Jones and Will Jacobs opined, "It wasn't great Kirby material. His eyes and energy were beginning to fail him, and being a producer-consultant at Ruby-Spears was still his principal

* That number relayed by Jim Shooter, in his "Comic Book Distribution — Part 3" blogpost, Nov. 22, 2011, at jimshooter.com.

job. Fans who'd been saying, 'He can draw, but he can't write,' were now smirking, 'He can't draw anymore either.' Premiering in late 1981, *Captain Victory* was out of step with its moment, looking like some strange reprint from another era next to *Daredevil, X-Men,* and *Teen Titans.* But the fans *noticed* it, and a fair number of them bought it, so refreshing was it to have something other than Marvel and DC to satisfy their super-hero cravings."[29]

Of course, the Pacific Comics equation was based on creating their own product exclusively for the direct sales market, thus avoiding newsstand distribution entirely, and *Captain Victory #1* became not only Pacific's' inaugural release, but also the first non-mainstream full-color comic title sold only in comic shops. And while the Big Two cover price was typically 50¢ or 60¢ an issue, Pacific audaciously slapped a $1.00 price tag on their debut effort and, undeterred by a cover price double that of competitors, retailers purchased 130,000 copies* of #1. "Those were incredible numbers, right up there with Marvel and DC," Steve told Jay Allen Sanford, who explained, "Within six months, circulation was up to 85,000 per issue, and the comic had been licensed in seven foreign countries. The third issue of *Captain Victory* netted Kirby a $6,000 royalty check, and Pacific's publishing and distribution ventures together that year grossed about $1.2 million."[30]

* Bill Schanes reports that staggering number in sidebar below!

SO BEGINS THE REVOLUTION

The repercussions of *Captain Victory #1*'s success cannot be overstated. Every comic book creator of that era, many disheartened by the industry's lack of respect for their contributions, and some who had even quit the business in

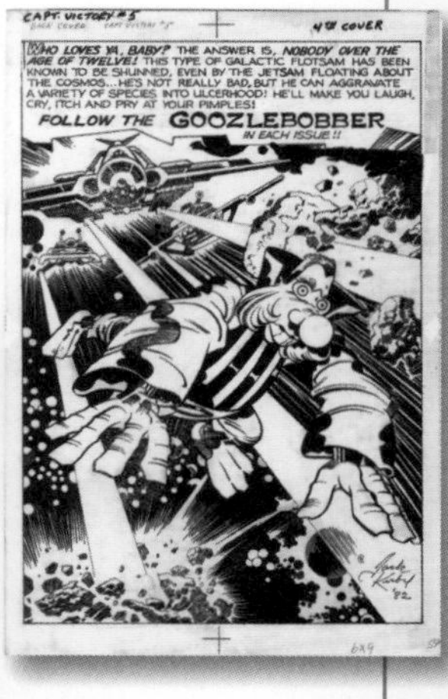

CAPT. VICTORY #5
4TH COVER
WHO LOVES YA, BABY? THE ANSWER IS, NOBODY OVER THE AGE OF TWELVE! THIS TYPE OF GALACTIC FLOTSAM HAS BEEN KNOWN TO BE SHUNNED, EVEN BY THE JETSAM FLOATING ABOUT THE COSMOS... HE'S NOT REALLY BAD, BUT HE CAN AGGRAVATE A VARIETY OF SPECIES INTO ULCERHOOD! HE'LL MAKE YOU LAUGH, CRY, ITCH AND PRY AT YOUR PIMPLES!
FOLLOW THE GOOZLEBOBBER
IN EACH ISSUE!!

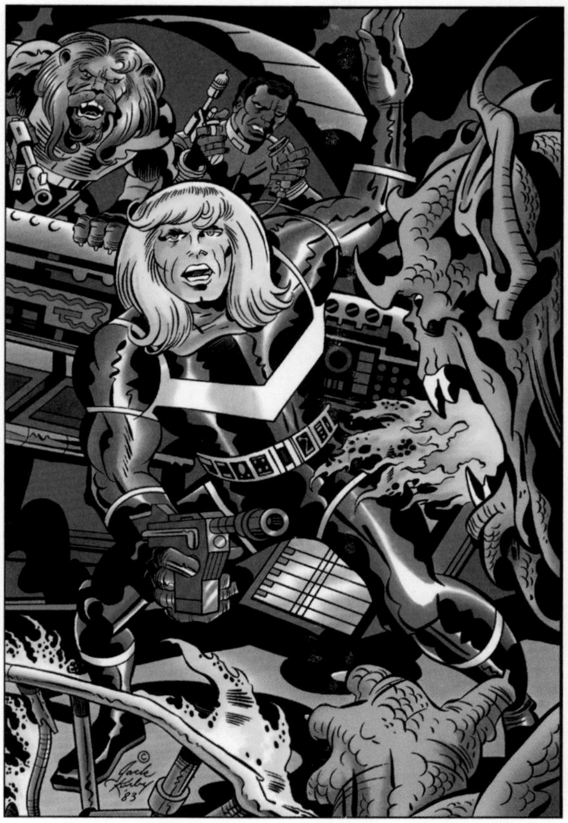

Above: Original art for Kirby's *Captain Victory* #5 [July 1982], featuring his absurd back-up character, Goozlebobber. **Left:** This piece originally appeared as the back cover of *The Jack Kirby Collector* #12 [Oct, 1996]. The caption accompanying the art stated, "Jack drew this Captain Victory art for a 1980s French portfolio. Inks by Michael Thibodeaux. Color by Tom Ziuko."

Bill Schanes on Competing with the Big Two

In the late '70s, both DC and Marvel Comics were offering 60% off of the retail cover price to those distributors who purchased directly from them on a non-returnable basis. At that time, both companies published standard 32-page, full-color comic books, with a cover price of 50¢ on each new issue.

My older brother, Steve, and I already had four comic-book specialty retail stores — CBSR — a large mail order company, and a couple of small publishing companies: Schanes & Schanes and Pacific Comics.

We felt there was an opportunity to create a new business model within the comic-book publishing industry, but with DC and Marvel both having characters which were well-established for decades, and had loyal consumers who were buying their entire lines (i.e., many Marvel Comics collectors were often referred to as "Marvel Zombies," as they bought every book Marvel put out, regardless of what the title, theme, and/or creative team were). The relative low cover price and small number of new monthly releases made it possible for fans and collectors to buy the whole line if they enjoyed the books and wanted to be completists.

We needed a creator who was a juggernaut, one which every collector and every CBSR would recognize, even if the character(s) involved would be entirely new. And we found one in Jack Kirby. So Pacific Comics was created when we published the King's new creator-owned title called *Captain Victory.*

Since we were going to launch our 32-page, full-color comic books with a $1 cover price, twice as much as DC or Marvel were currently pricing their new 32-page full-color comic books, we knew we would need to incentivize the same distributors of DC and Marvel.

We felt we'd have one chance to get enough copies into the marketplace, that we'd have to make the deal points irresistible, so we announced a unique set of discounts and terms, as we offered a sliding scale discount, based on the total quantity purchased on a per disgust, now saw in the sales numbers of Kirby's creator-owned title and in Pacific's courage to take on the big guns, a viable formula to achieve independence and maybe financially thrive in the process. By fall, the Schanes brothers were fielding inquiries by comics pros expressing interest in the San Diego-based publisher's creator-friendly contracts, with artists and writers rifling through their filing cabinets for unrealized projects to pitch.* Competitors, such as Eclipse, were looking to start their own full-color lines. Ushered in by Kirby and the Schanes brothers, the age of creator-owned comics had arrived!

* This is not to deny that the siblings didn't actively pursue creators. In fact, they sent out a brochure composed by Mike Friedrich that detailed the better deal Pacific offered to artists and writers over Marvel and DC.

CAPTAIN VICTORY
AND HIS GALACTIC RANGERS
YOU'LL BEG TO DIE!! WHEN YOU DISCOVER THE PENALTY FOR LOSING THIS BATTLE!
Jack Kirby
A MAN RISKED MORE THAN HIS LIFE IN THE SPACE ARENAS OF

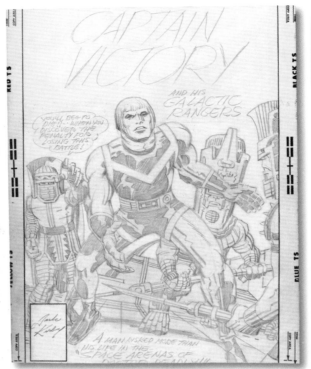

Left: Unpublished *Captain Victory and the Galactic Rangers* cover, perhaps — given the good captain's hairdo — drawn during the "Jack Kirby Comics" pitch of 1977–78.

TO EDIT A KING

Steve spoke with Jeff Gelb about editing *Captain Victory.* "You don't really edit a Jack Kirby," he said. "You give him an idea: do an origin story, create a super-hero for us, but he's pretty well set in his ways so far as his book's direction is concerned. We do pass along all the letters received from readers to each book's creator(s), which may help to determine editorial policy over a period of time."[31]

issue basis. Our discount schedule was:

1,000 copies or more 60% off the cover price.

5,000 copies or more 65% off the cover price.

10,000 copies or more 70% off the cover price.

We originally had thought a couple of the distributors would stretch to get to the 10,000 per issue level, at least for a few issues — or at least on first issues — and then their discount would drop to 65% or 60% respectively, which was still 5% more at retail than DC or Marvel was offering at the 5,000 copy per issue purchase commitment.

At that time, the distributors also were offering a sliding scale discount to the CBSR based on the total purchases made on a pre-order monthly basis. Small accounts would get books at 40% off the cover price, while the largest accounts might get up to 55% off the cover price. The average discount was probably closer to 50% off the cover price, so that's what I'm going use below to illustrate the Pacific Comics versus DC/Marvel discount comparisons. Here's what the numbered ended up looking like:

	Retail cover	Gross cover (60% off)	Cost to retailers	Profit
DC	50¢	20¢	25¢	5¢
Marvel	50¢	20¢	25¢	5¢
	Retail cover	**Gross cover (70% off)**	**Cost to retailers**	**Profit**
Pacific	$1	30¢	50¢	20¢

From a distributor perspective, the logistics and operations costs of soliciting, receiving, fulling, and invoicing DC, Marvel, and Pacific were identical, as the comic books were the same size, same page count, same paper stock, and price points, plus they were printed and delivered from the same printer. The fundamental difference was the distributor had the opportunity to earn four times more each time they sold a Pacific comic versus a DC comic book or a Marvel comic book. We also thought both distributors and CBSR would rally for the non-New York publishing company, who was creator-friendly, but also had a background as an active CBSR and distributor (one who understood the business from the ground floor-up).

We also offered a 2% net discount for payment made within 10 days of shipment, while DC and Marvel didn't offer this option.

So, with the most important part being Jack Kirby's return to the comic book industry, and choosing Pacific Comics creator-owned friendly agreement, plus an incredibly favorable pricing model, we felt we had the right ingredients to launch our new line of full-color comic books. What we didn't anticipate was that instead of one or two of distributors ordering at the 10,000 per issue level, I seem to remember eight or nine distributors each ordered 10,000 copies or more of *Captain Victory* #1. I had conservatively forecast sales on *Captain Victory* #1 at 35,000 copies, and when our total orders came in at over 130,000 copies, we were shocked in the best of ways. I called each distributor to reconfirm their purchase order quantities, as at first I thought many of the mid-sized and small distributors had put the wrong quantity down on their purchase orders. The quantities didn't change.

Mike Grell's *Starslayer* #1: initial orders over 140,000 units.

Neal Adams' *Ms. Mystic* #1: initial orders just shy of 225,000 units.[32]

Open Bar Partying with the Big Bird

BILL SCHANES ON PACIFIC'S *VICTORY* PARTY

In 1981, my brother, David Scroggy, and I wanted to throw a huge party to celebrate our just released, first new full-color comic book, *Captain Victory*, by none other than Jack Kirby. We decided to hold the party at the Pacific Comics offices on one of the nights during the San Diego Comic-Con. Our offices were located about a 20-minute drive north from downtown San Diego.

It was a logistical challenge, as we really wanted a big bash, one which would include us hiring a fleet of buses to shuttle business people, artists, retailers, media, printers, family, and friends from downtown to our offices and back (we wanted the buses to run non-stop from 5:00 P.M. to midnight), as we thought it would start slow and pick up speed as the hours passed, and our invited guests finished up their day's activities at the show. We invited the Who's Who within our industry, from all aspects of the business, including select loyal fans from our four retail stores, all by invitation only. It was a hot ticket at the time.

We had food catered but, for some reason I can't recall, we decided to run the bar by ourselves. At that time, the owners of Hi De Ho Comics in Santa Monica, California, were good friends of ours, and had told us they all had been bartenders in the past and that they would volunteer to tend our open bar for the evening. They had supplied us with a very detailed list of name brand types of alcohol, related drink-making requirements, and other details that would be best to use. The bar set-up was positioned in the back, near the loading docks.

Our staff had spent several days spritzing up the offices and kinda cleaning up the two-level warehouse in the back, as the idea was to allow everyone to roam everywhere, including the long rows of inventory, except for the offices, which we purposely kept locked.

The day of the party, our staff was doing split duty, as we still had a huge booth to man during the show hours, plus we had to staff the party (I seem to recall we recruited spouses, best friends, and others we knew).

On the night of the party, everything was set up, and we waited for the first busload of guests to arrive around 5:20 P.M., which is pretty much exactly when the bus pulled up. As in all parties, the first thing guests head for is the bar, but unfortunately for us, the three guys from Hi De Ho hadn't shown up yet and, being somewhat short-staffed, I started to take drink orders. Sounds great, except for one huge problem: I don't drink alcohol, never had, still don't, and I really didn't know what was in each drink or what proportions to pour.

So, my first time tending a bar, 60-plus people got off the bus and made their way to our bar, with me behind the makeshift counter. People started to shout out drink requests, rum and Coke — seemed easy, as I had heard of both, and we had both — so I poured 50/50 of each, almost to the top of the cup (seemed right to me), sometimes with ice and sometimes without. The drink orders were being shouted out at a frenzied pace; many of the drinks requests had specific names, which didn't include the type of alcohol included, so I guessed. I pulled a bottle that I felt sounded like a dark alcohol and poured

Vol. 1, No. 3
June, 1983
PACIFIC PREMIERES
CAPTAIN VICTORY SPECIAL #1
THIS ISSUE ON "BAXTER" STOCK
NEW COMICS SHIPPING in AUGUST

Above: In addition to 13 regular issues, Pacific published a *Captain Victory Special* in 1983. Here's their house organ promoting it.

Above: Not Bill's actual "Big Boy," but an African Macaw, the breed of his bird.

50/50 and either a soda or water. I liked it when someone just ordered a soft drink or an orange juice, as I knew I got those right!

The looks on the faces of the people sipping their first drink served up by me, was either, "Wow, this is really, really strong!" or "Wow, this is really, really strong! What is this? It's not what I asked for."

The three Hi De Ho guys showed up around 7:00 P.M., and immediately took over (I've never been so relieved). One of the Hi De Ho gentlemen asked where was the rest of the boozes, as they had previously told us how much to buy, but over half was used in just the 90 minutes, 100% because I was a more than a bit heavy-handed on the alcohol portions. We had to send folks out for an alcohol restock right away.

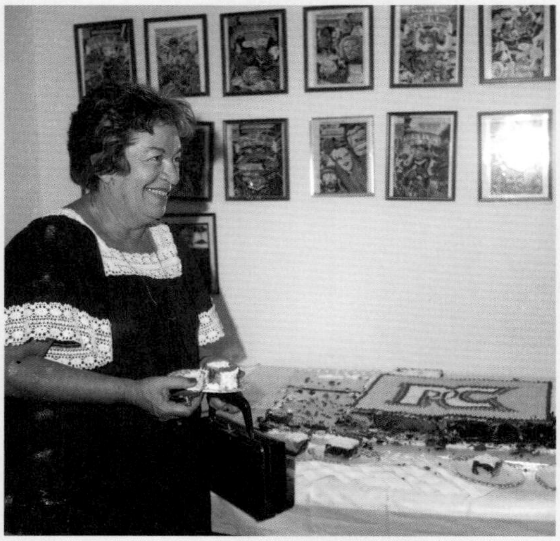

Needless to say, a large number of our guests were feeling no pain early into the evening. I was so glad we had hired buses to pick up and drop off our guests from the SDCC convention area.

It was a night to remember!

A side note: my beautiful wife had agreed to make a huge flat cake to serve 500 guests. The Pacific Comics main corporate color was a rich blue, so my wife hand-mixed the icing to reflect the exact color of blue. Unfortunately, she used a wee bit too much food dye, and a number of our guests had blue teeth for the evening. Many folks couldn't stop from laughing while talking with someone else, as the teeth discoloration was very obvious, and you couldn't help be stare.

In addition, I had decided to bring my African blue and gold macaw from my house to the party (whose name was Big Bird), to add as a conversation piece. I had raised Big Bird from when he was young, so he didn't bite, would sit on your arm, eat from your mouth, and could say ten or so words.[27]

DAVID SCROGGY ALSO REMEMBERS THE BIG NIGHT

This was one of my most memorable nights ever. I was co-bartender with Mike Smith of Hi De Ho. The reason you had to start alone, Bill, is that Rosemary and I took Mike out for dinner, which was his "pay" for bartending. He thought he could handle it alone. There weren't many restaurants around the warehouse, so our dining spot was further away than was convenient. So, we were late. As you discovered the hard way, the bartending chore was not a one-person job! Hence, I was pressed into service just like you were. We kicked ass (I think) and although we knew how much alcohol went into a drink (sort of), the furious pace made our mixology kind of imprecise. I am guessing that, like you, we erred on the side of "more" rather than "less." It was indeed a Who's Who of comics. I recall you looking over at Jack Kirby, Will Eisner, and Joe Shuster chatting, and said, "I wish we had thought to bring a camera!" D'oh. There were certainly many great photo ops. I remember B. Kliban ordering some kind of really oddball drink — bourbon and orange juice, perhaps. We had a giant bowl of cheese dip with tortilla chips around, so, of course, Sergio drew a big cartoon of Groo over it. Et cetera. The next day, several guests told me they were getting worried on the bus ride up, since it was aways from downtown in the Mira Mesa industrial park area, but, by the time they poured themselves into the buses for the ride back, they were all singing loudly all the way to the El Cortez Hotel. The first real industry party of Comic-Con — another Pacific Comics innovation![33]

Above: Steve and Bill's mom, Christine, smiles before she eats the frosting that turned her (and everyone's who ate the cake) teeth blue!

Victory by Moonlight

Ronin Ro shared about the creator's nocturnal work habits on *Captain Victory and the Galactic Rangers* in his 2004 book, *Tales To Astonish: Jack Kirby, Stan Lee, and the American Comic Book Revolution*:

"Every night, Jack worked on the series until three or four in the morning. His grandson, Jeremy, remembered waking up in the middle of the night: 'You could see him with his back facing the window, just drawing on the board.' He filled *Captain Victory* with insect villains that resembled armored warriors in *New Gods*, animal sidekicks Orca and Tarin that evoked the Inhumans and Kamandi, and a hero with direct ties to the Fourth World. 'Captain Victory was supposed to be the grandson of Darkseid,' explained Mike Thibodeaux, who inked the books. 'That was his plan.' And about Victory's biggest opponent, Blackmass, Jack told the inker, 'That's really Darkseid.'"[34]

In 2000, Jeremy would briefly revive *Captain Victory and the Galactic Rangers* for a two-issue run that repurposed his late grandfather's art to accommodate the grandson's new scripts. These were published by the short-lived Jack Kirby Comics imprint.

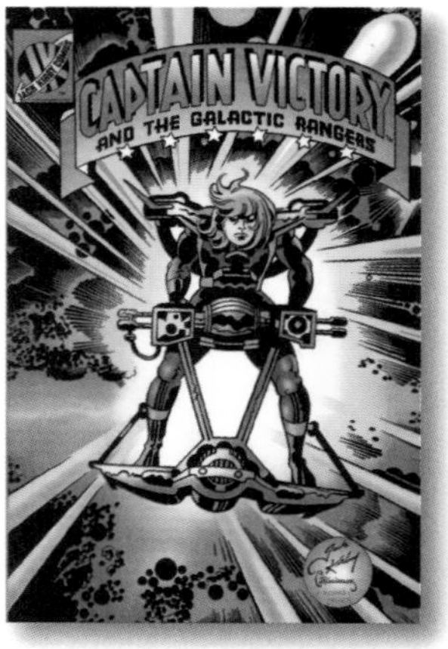
CAPTAIN VICTORY
AND THE GALACTIC RANGERS

Left: Cover of the first ish of Jack Kirby Comics' revival of *Captain Victory and the Galactic Rangers* [2000].

Chapter Notes

[1] Jay Allen Sanford, "The Rise & Fall of Pacific Comics: The Inside Story of a Pioneering Publisher," *San Diego Reader* website [Aug. 19, 2004], *https://www.sandiegoreader.com/news/2004/aug/19/two-men-and-their-comic-books/*.
[2] Steve Schanes, testimonial, *See You in San Diego: An Oral History of Comic-Con, Fandom, and the Triumph of Geek Culture* [Fantagraphics, 2022], pg. 22.
[3] Bill Schanes, Facebook post.
[4] Will Jacobs and Gerard Jones, *The Comic Book Heroes* [Prima, 1997], pg. 210.
[5] David Scroggy, testimonial, *See You in San Diego: An Oral History of Comic-Con, Fandom, and the Triumph of Geek Culture* [Fantagraphics, 2022], pg. 88.
[6] Bill Schanes, "Ed Catto: The (Not Quite) Secret Origin of Pacific Comics," interviewed by Ed Catto, Comicmix website [Aug. 31, 2015], *https://www.comicmix.com/2015/08/31/ed-catto-the-not-quite-secret-origin-of-pacific-comics/*.
[7] Bill Schanes, Facebook post [Dec. 29, 2018].
[8] Jack Kirby, "Kirby Takes on the Comics," interviewed by Howard Zimmerman, *Comics Scene* #2 [Mar. 1982], pg. 26.
[9] Pacific Comics press release, quoted, *The Comics Journal* #65 [Aug. 1981], pg. 23.
[10] Howard Zimmerman, "Kirby Takes on the Comics," *Comics Scene* #2 [Mar. 1982], pg. 27.
[11] Steve Schanes, "Captain Victory & Pacific Comics," *The Jack Kirby Collector* #15 [TwoMorrows, Apr. 1997], pg. 47.
[12] Ibid.
[13] Mike Royer, "Mrs. Royer's Boy — Mike," interviewed by Chris Harper, *Jack Kirby Quarterly* #8 [Spr. 1997], pg. 9.
[14] John Morrow, "Collector Comments," editor's reply, *The Jack Kirby Collector* #44 [Fall 2005], pg. 78.
[15] John Morrow, untitled introduction, *Captain Victory: Graphite Edition* [June 2003], inside front cover.
[16] Jeremy Lewis, "In Defense of Our Galaxy," *Jack Kirby Quarterly* #8 [Spr. 1997], pg. 15.
[17] Ibid.
[18] Sanford.
[19] Dan Gearino, *Comic Shop: The Retail Mavericks Who Gave Us a New Geek Culture,* expanded edition [Swallow Press, 2019], pg. 83.
[20] Sanford.
[21] Ibid.
[22] Ibid.
[23] Gearino.
[24] Steve Schanes, "Steve Schanes," interviewed by Rod Underhill, *Comics Interview* #55 [Summer 1988], pg. 53.
[25] Sanford.
[26] David Scroggy, correspondence with author.
[27] David Scroggy, "Pacific Comics," interviewed by Jeff Gelb, *Comics Scene* #9, May 1983], pg. 21.
[28] Larry Marder, interviewed by Stanley Wiater and Stephen Bissette, *Comic Book Rebels: Conversations with the Creators of the New Comics* [Primus, 1993] pg. 20.
[29] Jacobs and Jones, pgs. 251–252.
[30] Steve Schanes, "The Rise & Fall of Pacific Comics: The Inside Story of a Pioneering Publisher," interviewed by Jay Allen Sanford, *San Diego Reader* website [Aug. 19, 2004], *https://www.sandiegoreader.com/news/2004/aug/19/two-men-and-their-comic-books/*.
[31] Steve Schanes, "Pacific Comics," interviewed by Jeff Gelb, *Comics Scene* #9, May 1983], pg. 21.
[32] Bill Schanes, Facebook post [Jan. 9, 2019].
[33] Bill Schanes, Facebook post [Oct. 18, 2018].
[34] David Scroggy, Facebook post [Oct. 18, 2018].
[35] Ronin Ro, *Tales To Astonish: Jack Kirby, Stan Lee, and the American Comic Book Revolution* [Bloomsbury, 2004], pg. 212.

Captain Victory Foreign Editions

French and German editions of *Captain Victory and the Galactic Rangers.*

Nr. 1 DM 4,80 Schweiz Fr. 4.80 Österreich S. 38.—
Jetzt NEU!
Das neue Superhelden-COMIC-Album
CAPTAIN VICTORY
UND DIE GALACTIC RANGERS

Dans les solitudes glacées et infinies des galaxies
La lutte d'un homme pour la sauvegarde de la vie
CAPTAIN VICTORY
ET SES CHASSEURS GALACTIQUES

Nr. 2 DM 4,80 Schweiz Fr. 4.80 Österreich S. 38.—
Jetzt NEU!
Das neue Superhelden-COMIC-Album
CAPTAIN VICTORY
UND DIE GALACTIC RANGERS
JACK KIRBYS neues SUPERHELDEN-COMIC! Jetzt erstmals in DEUTSCHER SPRACHE!

Nr. 3 DM 4,80 Schweiz Fr. 4.80 Österreich S. 38.—
Jetzt NEU!
Das neue Superhelden-COMIC-Album
CAPTAIN VICTORY
UND DIE GALACTIC RANGERS
JACK KIRBYS neues SUPERHELDEN-COMIC! Jetzt erstmals in DEUTSCHER SPRACHE!

Nr. 4 DM 4,80
Jetzt NEU!
Das neue Superhelden-COMIC-Album
CAPTAIN VICTORY
UND DIE GALACTIC RANGERS
JACK KIRBYS neues SUPERHELDEN-COMIC! Jetzt erstmals in DEUTSCHER SPRACHE!

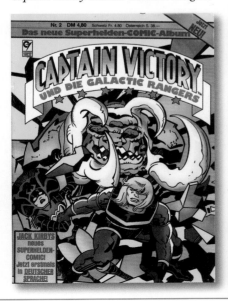

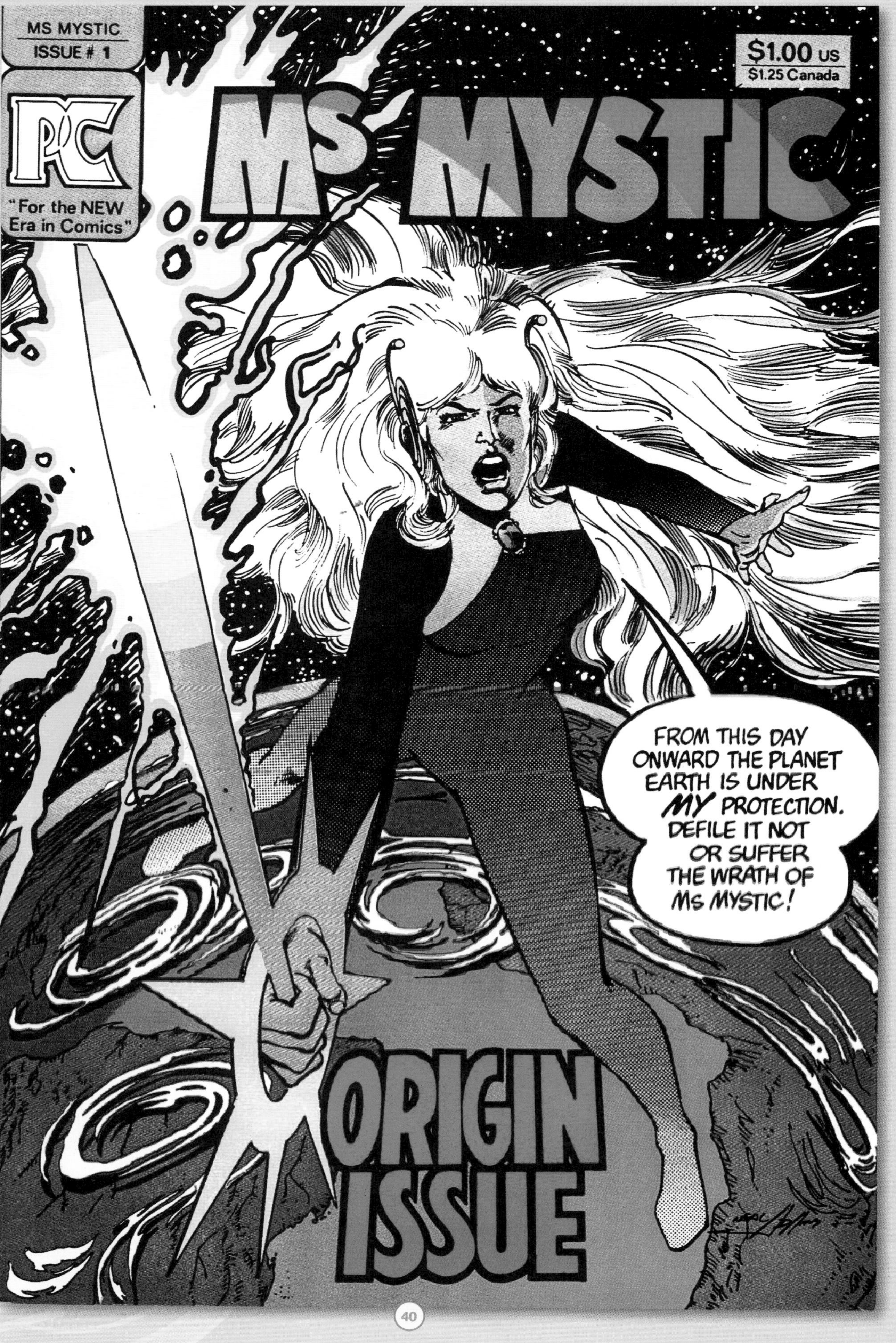
MS MYSTIC
ISSUE # 1
$1.00 US
$1.25 Canada
PC
"For the NEW Era in Comics"
Ms MYSTIC
FROM THIS DAY ONWARD THE PLANET EARTH IS UNDER MY PROTECTION. DEFILE IT NOT OR SUFFER THE WRATH OF Ms MYSTIC!
ORIGIN ISSUE

Riding the Pacific Wave

Starslayer is the anti-Warlord.

That's basically how Mike Grell described the star of Pacific Comics' second regular title. The artist-writer told Dewey Cassell, "*Starslayer* originated as a concept that I pitched to DC Comics. It was intended as a direct counterpart to *Warlord*. With the Warlord, I had a modern man in a very primitive society and, with Starslayer, I had a primitive man in an ultra-futuristic world. He's a Celtic chieftain who gets transported basically into the middle of *Star Wars,* if you will. A shorthand description would be, '*Braveheart* meets *Star Wars*.' And it was actually on DC's schedule when the Implosion hit in the '70s and it got shelved. "[1]

FIRST IN LINE, SECOND ONE SERVED

Grell told Jon B. Cooke how he connected with the fledgling company. "I got the opportunity from Pacific Comics to create a project. I was approached by the Schanes brothers, Bill and Steve, who had this concept for a new company that would allow people to create and own their own characters, and thereby sharing a larger portion of the earnings on it. You'd keep the copyright, and things like that, and it was exactly what I was looking for… So Steve and Bill knew about *Starslayer*, and they said, 'I understand you have a project, and we'd be very interested in having you come over and do it.' I was actually the first person to sign with them; Jack Kirby signed a couple of weeks later." He added with a laugh, "But because Jack was Jack, he'd draw half a book while we were speaking! He delivered his first, and it was printed first, but I was actually the first person to sign."[2]

Was he nervous signing with the first truly independent publisher of color comics in the direct market? "I wasn't the least bit nervous about it," the artist replied. "This was another step. I was doing the *Tarzan* comic strip at the time, and *The Warlord* was continuing… in fact, that was sort of the point where I decided that my energy needed to be a bit more focused, and that was the reason I stepped back from doing the artwork and writing the scripts. I sort of phased myself back, and had a lot more time to devote to what I knew was the coming wave."[3] *Starslayer* #1 hit shops in late 1981 and sold 140,000 non-returnable copies.

STARSLAYER
the Log of the Jolly Roger

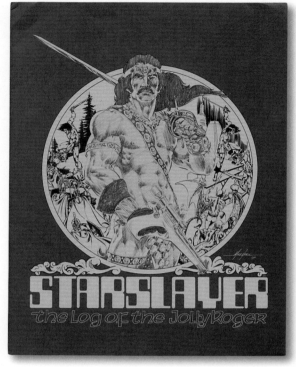

Before 1982 had ended, Grell had completed his first *Starslayer* story arc with six issues and then, wary of Pacific's solvency, jumped ship with his creation to join a brand-new independent publisher of color comics — First Comics — where the artist/writer had a run of 28 *Starslayer* issues, ending that series in 1985. (Bill Schanes bid Grell a friendly adieu in a publisher's note in *Starslayer* #6.)

Previous page: *Ms. Mystic* #1 [Oct. 1982]. **Above:** Pacific actually published a *Starslayer* portfolio first before debuting the comic book series. **Below:** Neal Adams [left] and Mike Grell, 1977 Chicago Comic-Con.

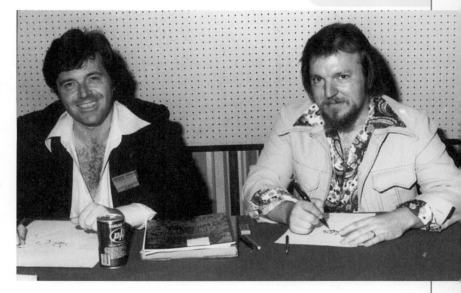

The Starslayer Portfolio Plates

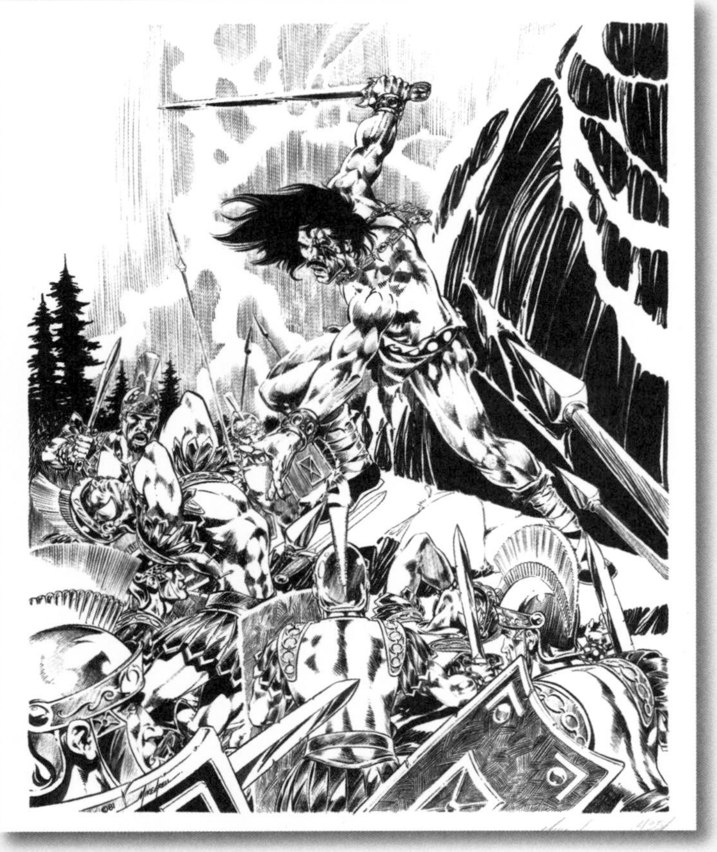

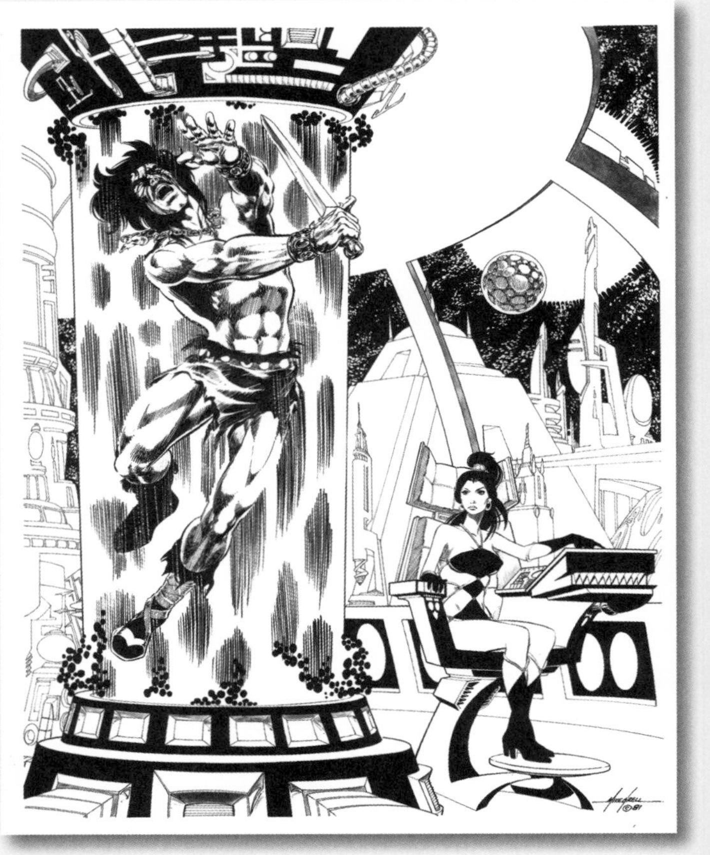

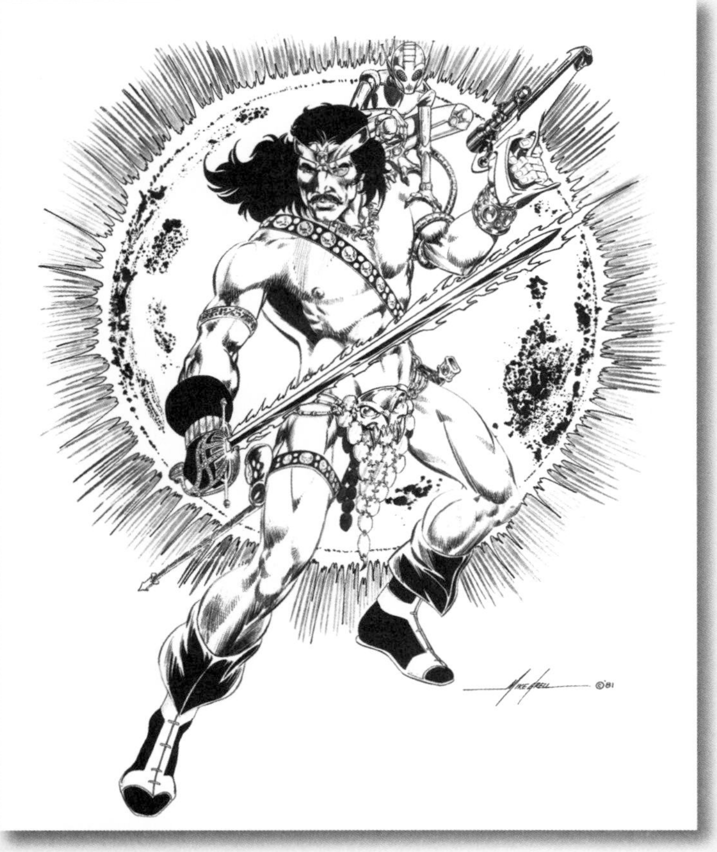

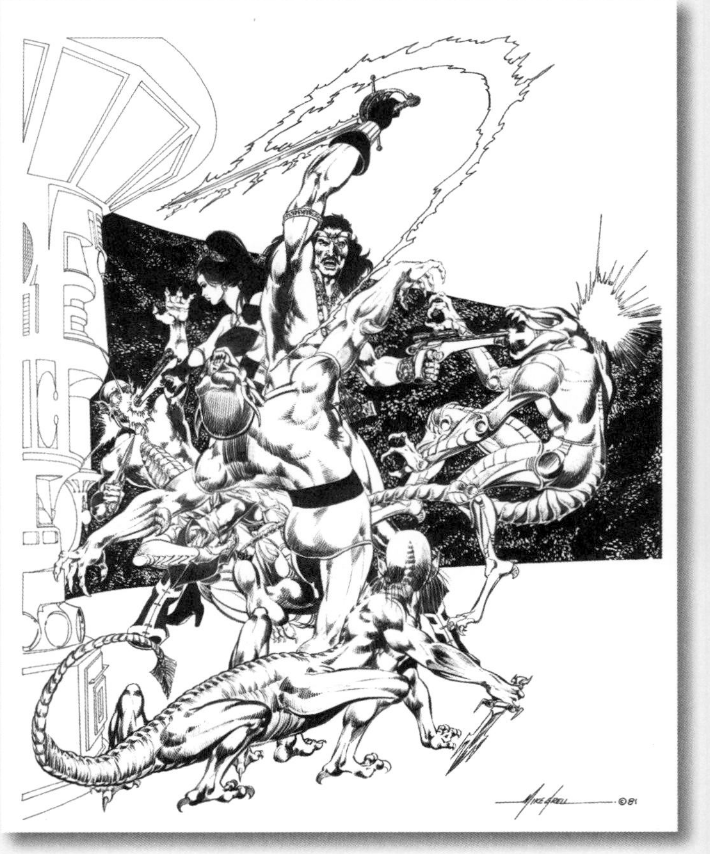

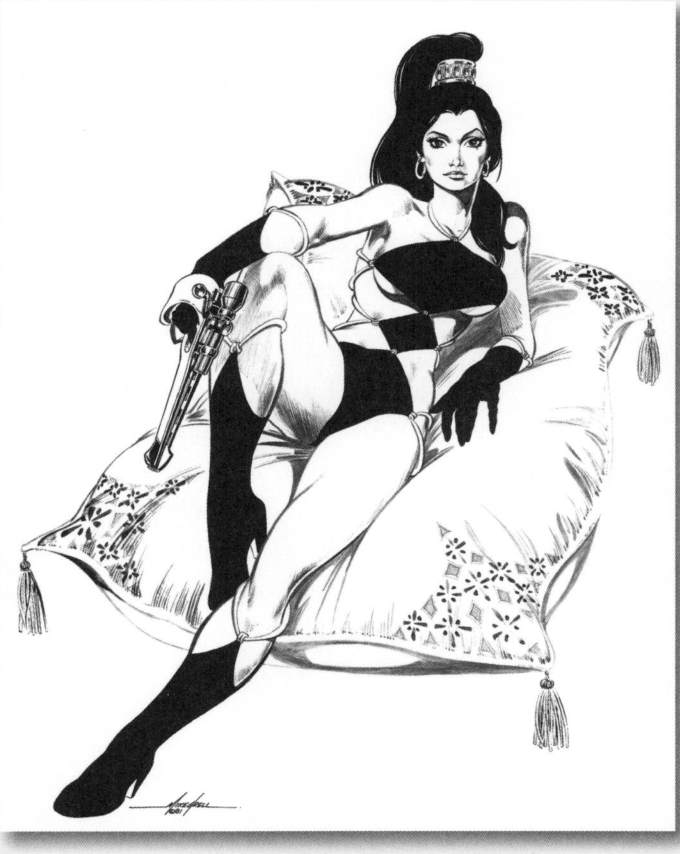

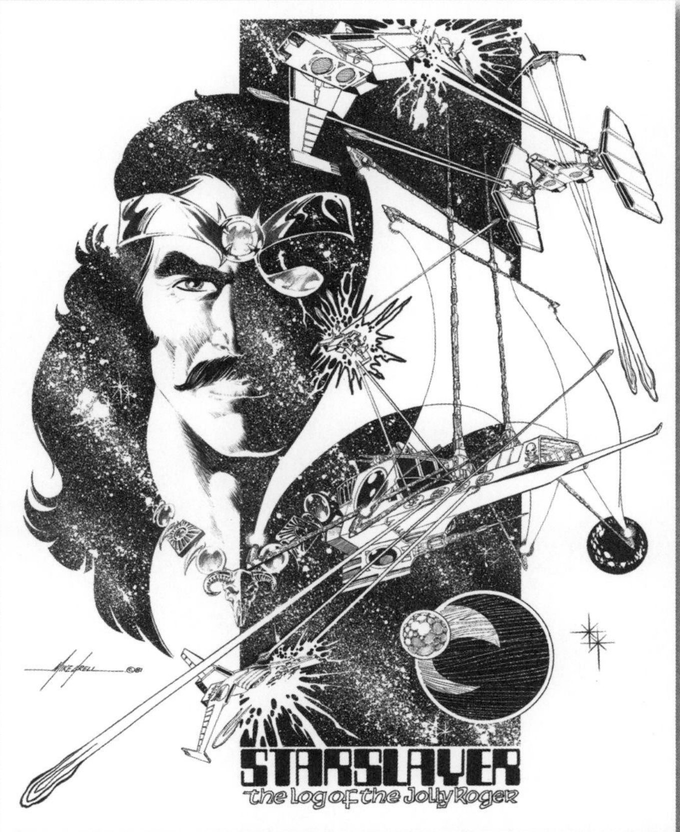
STARSLAYER
the log of the Jolly Roger

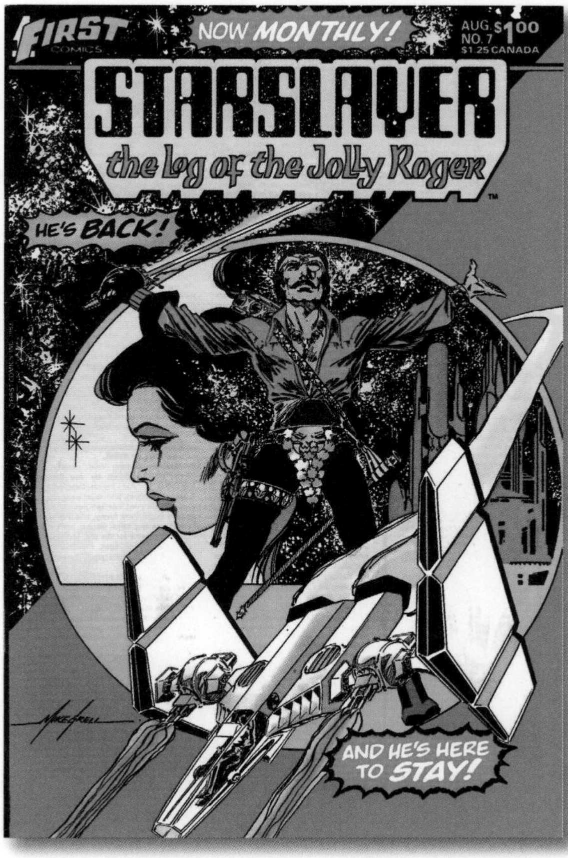
FIRST COMICS
NOW MONTHLY!
AUG NO. 7 $1.00 $1.25 CANADA
STARSLAYER
the log of the Jolly Roger
HE'S BACK!
AND HE'S HERE TO STAY!

STARSLAYER AFTERLIFE

Continuing *Starslayer* was only part of Mike Grell's agreement with upstart newcomer First Comics. "I signed on to do *Sable*, created the concept for *Sable*, and agreed that, after that," he told Jon B. Cooke, "I'd stay with *Starslayer* and do the launch with them, write the first few issues for them, and turn it over to the able hands of [writer] John Ostrander."[4]

Left: All six of the *Starslayer* b-&-w plates published by the Pacific Comics sub-division, Schanes & Schanes. Interestingly, this set was produced *before* the advent of Grell's science-fiction comic series that launched in 1982.

Pacific Profiles

Mike Grell

Born: *Sept. 1947*

Mike Grell's professional career actually started off in the realm of syndicated newspaper comic strips, assisting cartoonist Dale Messick on her feature, *Brenda Starr*. He would go on to greater fame as creator of *Jon Sable, Freelance,* which he originated at First Comics following his brief stint at Pacific Comics.

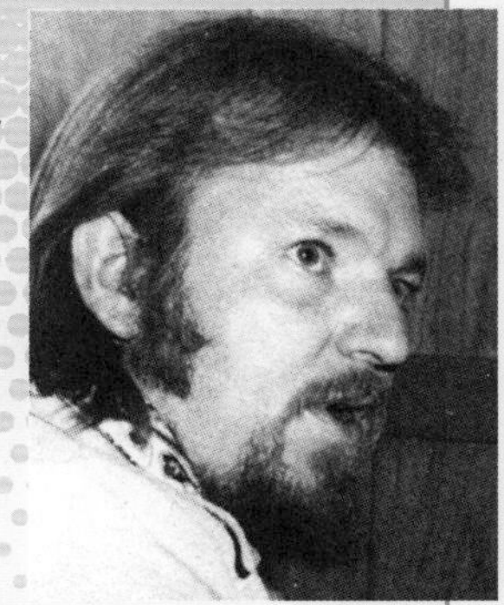

Above: Mike Grell in a photo that was included in the *Starslayer* portfiolio.

Top: First issue of First Comics' *Starslayer* series, #7, 1983.

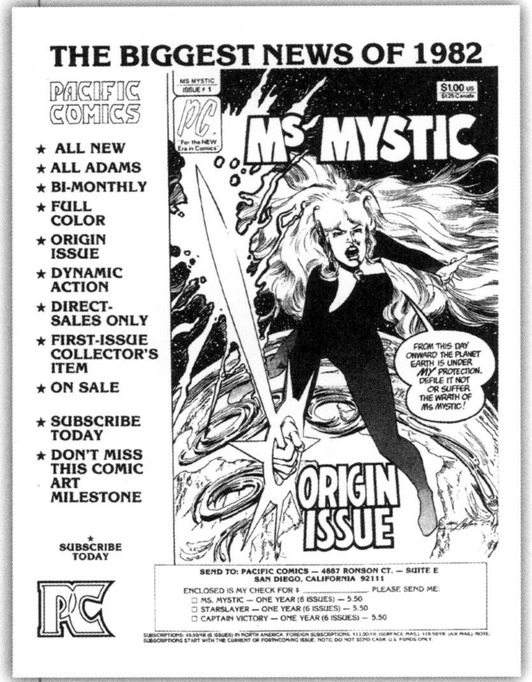
THE BIGGEST NEWS OF 1982
PACIFIC COMICS
★ ALL NEW
★ ALL ADAMS
★ BI-MONTHLY
★ FULL COLOR
★ ORIGIN ISSUE
★ DYNAMIC ACTION
★ DIRECT-SALES ONLY
★ FIRST-ISSUE COLLECTOR'S ITEM
★ ON SALE
★ SUBSCRIBE TODAY
★ DON'T MISS THIS COMIC ART MILESTONE
★ SUBSCRIBE TODAY
MS MYSTIC
$1.00 US
MS MYSTIC
FROM THIS DAY ONWARD THE PLANET EARTH IS UNDER MY PROTECTION. DEFILE IT NOT OR SUFFER THE WRATH OF Ms MYSTIC!
ORIGIN ISSUE
SEND TO: PACIFIC COMICS — 4887 RONSON CT. — SUITE E
SAN DIEGO, CALIFORNIA 92111
ENCLOSED IS MY CHECK FOR $ ______ PLEASE SEND ME:
☐ MS. MYSTIC — ONE YEAR (6 ISSUES) — 5.50
☐ STARSLAYER — ONE YEAR (6 ISSUES) — 5.50
☐ CAPTAIN VICTORY — ONE YEAR (6 ISSUES) — 5.50

THE COMING OF MS. MYSTIC

On Dec. 7, 1981, *Captain Victory and the Galactic Rangers* #3 [Mar. 1982] went on sale and it included a tantalizing four-pager that introduced the comics world to Ms. Mystic, a sensational new character produced by one of comics' greatest creators. At the time, Neal Adams shared with Gary Groth how the super-heroine went to Pacific, a description that included a young artist who had found work at Continuity Associates, Adams' art agency. "I'm doing a feature called *Ms. Mystic* for Pacific that I was originally going to do with Michael Nasser. Mike thought it would be a good idea to do a female character, and I came up with all the concepts behind Ms. Mystic. We decided to do it together, but Mike has since deserted various forms of civilization in favor of living a very, very different life from what most of us live. So, until and unless he comes back and wants to join in, I'm doing *Ms. Mystic* for Pacific Comics on my own. It'll be 12 bi-monthly issues. That's about it. It's a good character, an interesting character. It's one of the five characters I created for a portfolio for Sal Quartuccio.

Above: Before confirming with Neal Adams, who was backing away from committing himself to such an ambitious schedule given his advertising workload, Pacific promoted the new title as a bi-monthly series. Alas, over the next two years, only two issues would emerge at the imprint. **Below:** Adams introduced Ms. Mystic as one of his "New Heroes," in a portfolio published in 1979 by Sal Quartuccio.

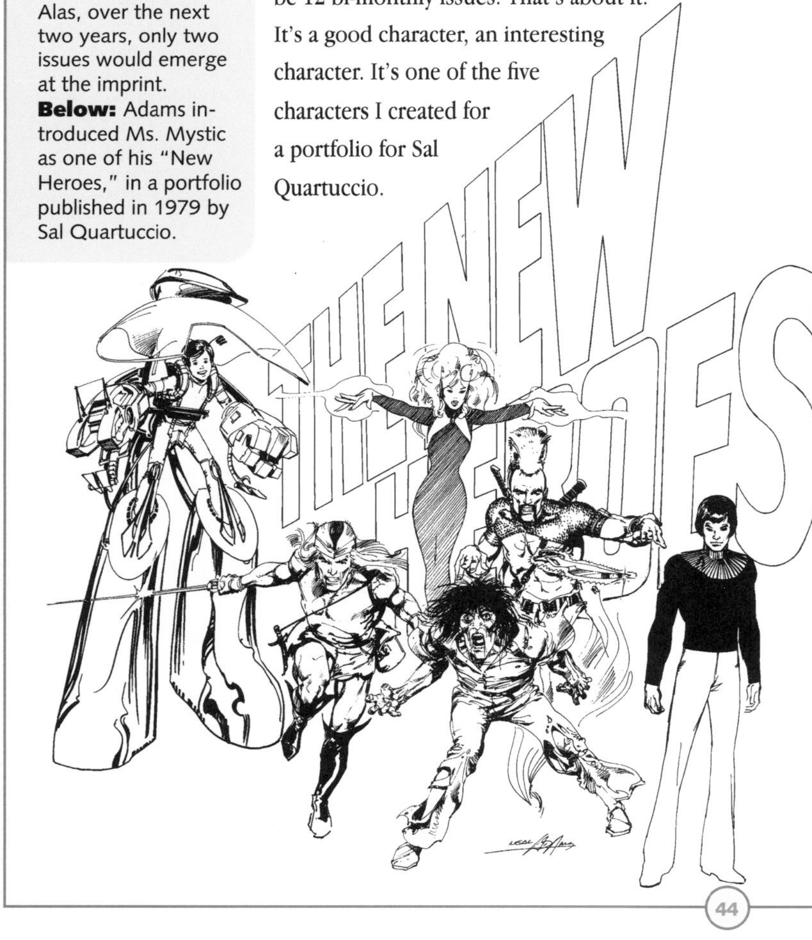
THE NEW HEROES

"I didn't go to Pacific. Pacific came to me. The reason I agreed to do it with Pacific is that, first of all, I don't intend to be a comic book publisher. I intend to be a comic *book* — with [*emphasis*] on *book* — publisher, in that Continuity will do the graphic novels. Pacific Comics is interested in doing comic books, a field I still wish to be involved in. The reason I went with Pacific is because Pacific was willing to allow me to keep my character, not interfere with any other rights that I would have in the character, not give me a work-for-hire agreement, and pay me a reasonable, though not exorbitant, amount of money for the right to publish it as a comic book. I felt it was a fair deal. In return, my job is to give them a comic book that will sell well and make money for them. It seemed incredibly fair compared to the deals that Marvel and DC offer."[5]

The *New Heroes* portfolio contained a striking plate featuring Ms. Mystic and it included an explicit credit: "Character © 1979 Neal Adams and Mike Nasser," but Adams would later describe the heroine's creation as one he came up with completely on his own. In 2015, Adams said, "Pacific was approaching me to do a comic book and I said, basically, 'Look, I really haven't got time to do this. Maybe I'll give it a shot.' But in the studio, there was a guy named Mike Netzer* who kind of drew like me. Well, he drew exactly like me, or as much as he could. I said, 'Look, y'know, I can have a guy in my studio work on this and maybe he can do it and I'll do layouts, blocking out and all the rest of it.' I was trying to really support Pacific Comics, because I sort of had convinced Jack Kirby to work for them. And also Sergio Aragonés to work for them. I had told them that they not only would pay them, but they would let them keep the rights to their character. They could hardly believe that. At that time, that was actually a phenomenon.

"So, partially the reason I turned the thing into a character was I wanted to promote a company that would do the right thing by the creators. Although that may not have been the first time it was being done, it certainly was the first where you had three well-known, official people out there — myself, Jack Kirby, and Sergio Aragonés — doing characters for more than normal rates, and also that they owned their characters. I was kind of killing about 80 birds with one stone there."[6]

The omission of Netzer from the story of Ms. Mystic's creation was the result of all that had transpired between the two artists over the decades.

* During Michael's initial extended stay in Israel, he changed his last name of "Nasser" to Hebrew-transliterated "Netzer."

THE NASSER/NETZER VERSION

In 2015, Michael Netzer shared with Shaun Clancy his recollections of the beginnings of Ms. Mystic and his being the catalyst for her creation. "It starts about the time Jenette Kahn became publisher of DC, around late 1976. Vinnie Colletta was the art director and was working with me on the *Wonder Woman* [#232, June 1977] story that he inked. On one of my visits, he told me that the new publisher would probably like some proposals for a new female super-hero and asked me to come up with a pitch. I was about 20 years old and lacking the type of experience to compete professionally on that level of creating a new character and storyline… but I must have had a lot of ambition because I took the challenge and told Vinnie I'd have an idea for him in a couple weeks."[7]

Netzer detailed his conceptualization: "I thought of a character that would be 'the spirit of the Earth' type. A girl who grew up with senses and abilities such as making plants grow quickly or making it stop raining if she tried hard enough. She'd later discover that she was a reincarnation of a witch that was burned at the stake in a previous life, because of having these abilities. She'd grow up to understand that her consciousness was one with the consciousness of the Earth and that her ultimate mission, this time around, was to stop civilization from destroying itself and the planet they lived on… I also thought she could be connected to Rama Kushna from 'Deadman,' or that she would actually be a physical embodiment of her, for DC continuity, but wasn't sure how that could work out yet. It was all happening quickly, within an hour or two, and I hadn't had enough time to think it through. I had just finished the *Starspawn* four-piece portfolio for Bob Keenan, one of Sal Quartuccio's friends, around then. That simple body figure with the body-length hair [*left*] seemed like a good place to start for a character design, and I began working out a costume that would preserve that look, that I thought had an ethereal feel that expressed the character well. It's one of the few things that was preserved from my early ideas on it, and still strongly resembles what Ms. Mystic's look later became through Neal's embellishment of that design… Neal looked at my sketches and then, to my surprise, suggested that we do it together because I wouldn't have the experience to

MS. MYSTIC
The New Heroes is Copyright © 1979 Sal Q. Productions
Art Copyright © 1979 Neal Adams
Character Copyright © 1979 Neal Adams and Mike Nasser

Above: *New Heroes'* Ms. Mystic plate by Adams. **Inset left:** *Starfawn* plate by Netzer.

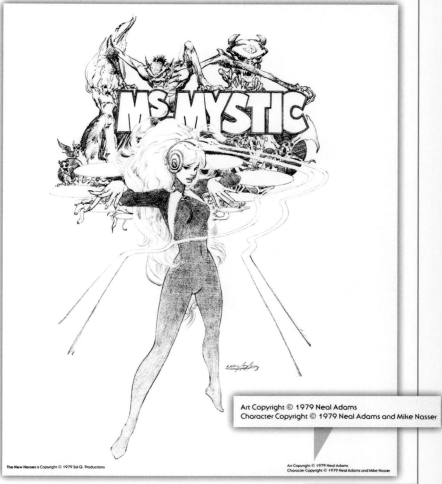

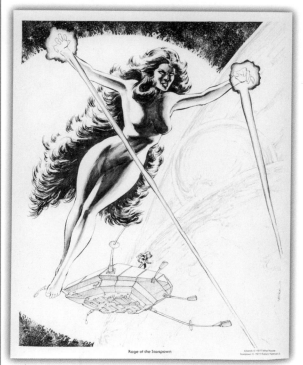

Rage of the Starspawn

Pacific Profiles
Neal Adams

Born: *June 1941*

Among the most celebrated comic book artists of all time, Adams started his professional career drawing Archie Comics gag pages. He soon earned his own syndicated newspaper strip, *Ben Casey,* which he drew 1962–66, and, before entering the industry, he worked for Johnstone Cushing, an ad agency specializing in comics.

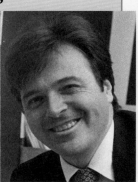

Above: Neal Adams, 1979, in pic taken after the promotion of his masterpiece, *Superman vs. Muhammad Ali* [*All-New Collectors' Edition* #C-56, Mar. 1978].

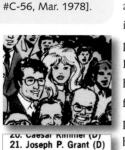

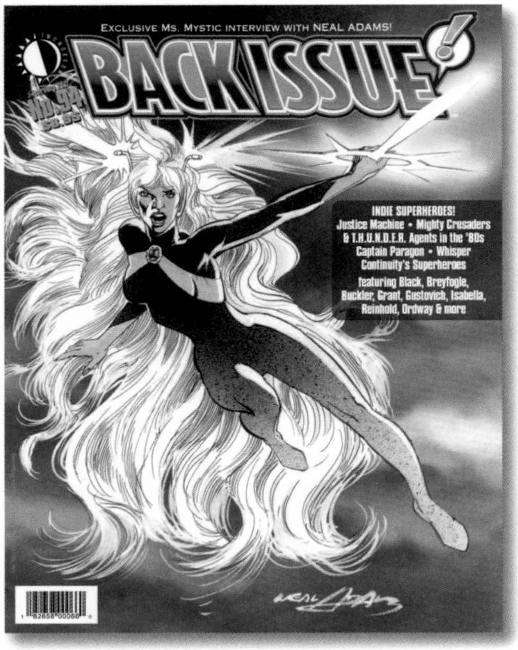
EXCLUSIVE MS. MYSTIC INTERVIEW WITH NEAL ADAMS!
BACK ISSUE!
INDIE SUPERHEROES!
Justice Machine • Mighty Crusaders & T.H.U.N.D.E.R. Agents in the '80s
Captain Paragon • Whisper
Continuity's Superheroes
featuring Black, Breyfogle, Buckler, Grant, Gustovich, Isabella, Reinhold, Ordway & more

go it alone. He said it would be a much better project if he wrote it and I drew it, and that he'd be able to negotiate a much better creator-owned deal with DC for it than I would. He then extended his hand out for a handshake and said, 'Fifty/fifty partners, what do you think?'"[8]

Netzer's regard for Neal Adams was considerable, "Not only as a mentor of the drawing and storytelling craft, but also as the moral/humanistic magnet and leader that he was to the community of creators," Netzer explained. "I extended my hand in return and we shook on it: 'Partners, fifty/fifty,' I said, and Neal went back to the front room. The next day he came in with a drawing of Ms. Mystic, with the Zip-A-Tone on the costume, preserving the direction I'd started with my first sketches. We'd spend the next few days developing the character's history and motives. Neal pushed for the less ethereal and more ambiguous alien-like persona, that I wasn't totally in favor of but conceded to him as the writer. We were now on our way to making this project come to life and Neal would handle the negotiations with DC for a creator-owned project."[9]

Above: *Back Issue* #94 [Feb. 2017] cover by Neal Adams of his and Mike Nasser/Netzer's creation. **Inset right:** Before the demise of Pacific Comics, Neal Adams established his own imprint (named for his studio), Continuity Comics, where he found a home for *Ms. Mystic.* This is the cover by Adams of #3 [Jan. 1989]. **Below:** The conceptualization of the character stretches back to the latter '70s, as evidenced by Ms. Mystic's appearance (albeit as a blond and not white-haired) in the back cover crowd scene on the fabled *Superman vs. Muhammad Ali* [*All-New Collectors' Edition* #C-56, Mar. 1978].

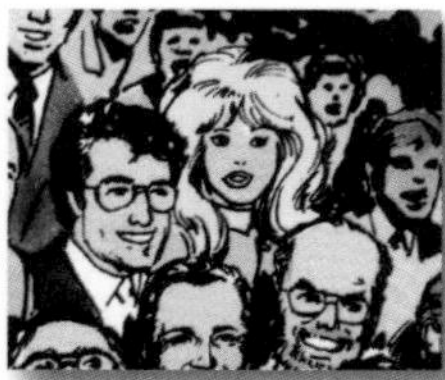

21. Joseph P. Grant (D)
22. Bert Wasserman (D)
23. Byron Preiss (G)
24. Ms. Mystic (H)
25. Frank Herrera (D)
26. Albert Sarnoff (D)
27. Dick Giordano (G)

During this era of Jenette Kahn's experimental Dollar Comics and the stellar Adams production of the *Superman/Muhammad Ali* book, "It was a big year all around for Continuity and the comics industry in general — and Ms. Mystic became an integral part of it, though had never been formally announced," Netzer said. "DC approved it as their very first creator-owned project, which is why she appears on the cover in the crowd, and is listed on the inside cover of the *Superman/Ali* book. Neal worked out a plot for the first issue and general thrust for the character. It veered away from the more mystical direction I initially had in mind… I spent the summer of '77 penciling the first 17-page story for DC. Probably some of the best pencils I'd done 'til then, which were mostly inked for the book just as they were. There was a splash page where she first appears in the story that Neal re-did. I liked mine a little more and was sorry to not see it used. I think Neal eventually reversed the angle on it to show Ms Mystic confronting the one-wheeled robot. My focus was more on showing her close up, front and center, to get to better know the character. It had the regal/mystical feel that I'd first intended for her and it was a very good drawing. Towards the end of summer, the job was done. DC paid me for the pencils and the job awaited production."[10]

Michael left to spend time in California and, "The upshot, relative to *Ms. Mystic*, was that when I came back a month later, Dick Giordano had left the studio, Neal and Jenette were no longer together, and *Ms. Mystic* was dropped by DC altogether… On one of my trips back to the studio, Neal showed me he'd produced the *New Heroes* portfolio with Ms. Mystic as one of the heroes, and properly crediting me with co-ownership of the character."[11]

Netzer was out of the country when the Pacific Comics *Ms. Mystic* edition was published and, he said, "A couple of years later, I saw Continuity's first *Ms. Mystic* [#1, Oct. 1987] comic book in a used bookstore in Beirut, where I'd stopped over for a family visit before continuing to Israel."[12] In the ensuing years, Netzer returned to work at Continuity, but suffered a dramatic falling-out with Adams and there were lawsuits regarding the character's creation and accusations of libel, which were all later dismissed.

In the final analysis, Michael concedes, "*Ms. Mystic* was, in most of its published totality, an almost exclusive Neal Adams production. The difference between layouts and pencil credits is a minor issue in the big picture, though I remain disappointed that Neal doesn't acknowledge

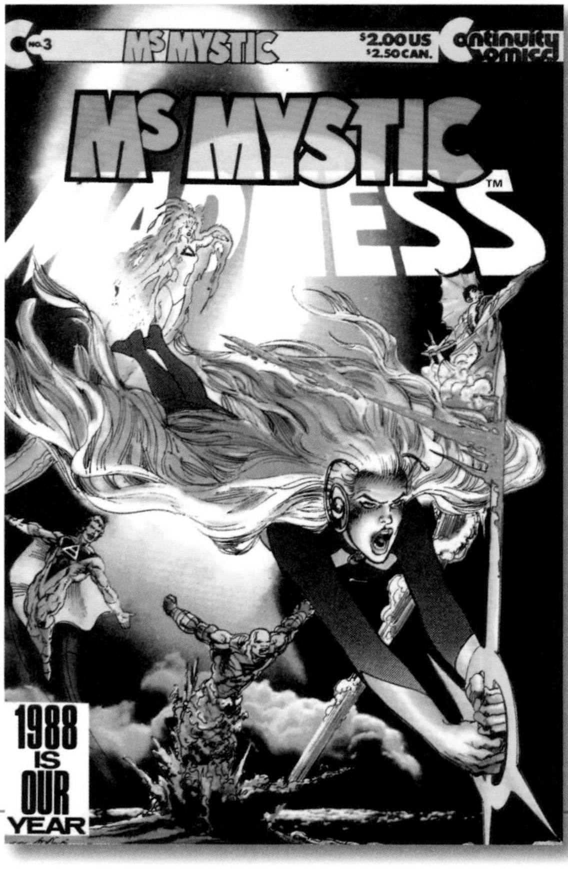
NO.3
MS MYSTIC
$2.00 US
$2.50 CAN.
Continuity Comics
MS MYSTIC
1988 IS OUR YEAR

the very well-done, tightly drawn full pencils I did for the original 17-page story for DC. In time, Neal eventually made the character what she has become, regardless of the initial input I had into her."[13]

Only two issues of *Ms. Mystic* were published by Pacific, 16 months apart, despite the publisher promoting the book as a bi-monthly (in a full-page ad trumpeting the first issue as "The Biggest News of 1982").

"While *Ms. Mystic* may not have been Neal Adams' apex creatively," David Scroggy admitted, "it was certainly Pacific Comics' biggest hit commercially. Appearing in the early days of the direct-sales comics specialty market, the first issue sold a whopping 250,000 copies.

"It was an interesting experience trying to cajole the subsequent issues out of Neal. He maintained, correctly I would say, that we jumped the gun soliciting the title before more issues were in the drawer. On the other hand, it was also true that Neal's commercial assignments played hob with his sincerely planned delivery schedule. As everyone knows, Neal believed strongly in creator rights, and he came to Pacific to support our endeavor to cement these rights across the industry. We only got the first two issues out before the company folded, but Neal started his own company and continued *Ms. Mystic* for six more issues."[14]

Above: Used as a basis for the cover of *Captain Victory* #9, this Jack Kirby-penciled page was inked by no less than his wife, Roz! **Below:** Pacific revamped its logo in mid-1982.

MEANWHILE… BACK ON PLANET KIRBY

With Jack Kirby burning the midnight oil to maintain a bi-monthly schedule (all the while maintaining his animation gig during daylight hours), "Bill and Steve were simultaneously floating their proposals to many top talents, notably Mike Grell, Neal Adams, Sergio Aragonés, and others," David Scroggy explained. "Steve and Bill were also engaging in a crash course in finding printers, color separation, and other aspects of comic book production. Initially, we approached the existing vendors, who were World Color Press, in Sparta, Illinois, for printing, and Chemical Color Corp., in New Jersey, for the color separation. Pacific Comics was off to the races!"[15]

On occasion, that race got bumpy, such as when the publisher sought a wee bit of control over its product. David continued, "In many cases, Pacific Comics really did not have a lot to do with the editorial content of the comics they published. That may seem strange to hear, but we took the concept of 'creator ownership' literally — sometimes to a fault. Early on, as Jack Kirby continued to send in issues of *Captain Victory*, and his follow-up, *Silver Star* [*to be introduced in November of 1982*], we made a few editorial suggestions. We were quickly informed that he was Jack Kirby, and we were a bunch of kids in San Diego, and he would come up with whatever he wanted, and we would publish it. Jack may have received some editorial input from others in his circle, but that was, I think, very little, if any at all. I did suggest that he come up with some back-up material [*in early issues*], such as a page of insignias of the Galactic Rangers. Jack liked that idea, so he did it. This creator control also included the letters pages, which I put together. In an early issue, I once ran a letter that was mildly critical. Jack called up and said it was a 'knock letter,' and he didn't want to see any more 'knock letters' in the letter's column of his comics. 'Nuff said."[16]

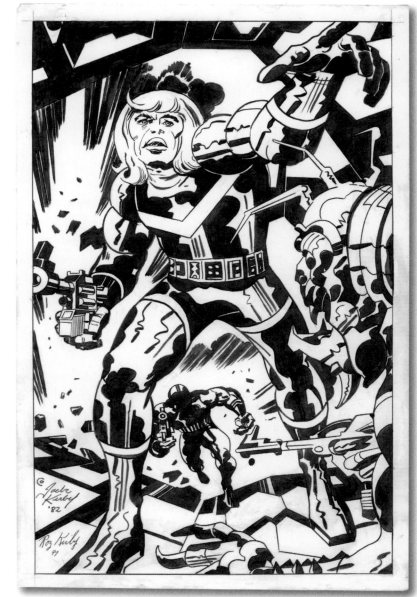

Inset right: *Pacific Presents* #1 cover [Oct. 1982], by Stevens and Ditko. Scan of the original art. **Below:** Dave Stevens illustration that graced the cover of IDW's *The Rocketeer: The Complete Adventures* collection [2009].

LAUNCHING THE ROCKETEER

Look in any comic book price guide under the listings for *Starslayer* and, as entertaining and collectible as is Mike Grell's intergalactic saga, you'll note that #2 [Apr. 1982] and #3 [June 1982] fetch higher prices than the typically coveted first issue. Why is that so? Two words answer the riddle: Dave Stevens.

If Neal Adams' *Ms. Mystic* #1 was Pacific Comics' best-seller, than artist Dave Stevens was the publisher's greatest creative discovery, and Stevens' creation of The Rocketeer was sheer serendipity. Kelvin Mao, the director of the full-length feature film documentary on the late artist, *Dave Stevens: Drawn to Perfection* [2022] — Stevens died at age 52, in 2008 — shared, "Dave... was an extraordinary artist and complicated person who lived life the way he drew: without compromise or yielding to adversity. Everything he produced shined with an unmistakable polish, a feeling of effortlessness that masked his obsessive struggle for perfection."[17]

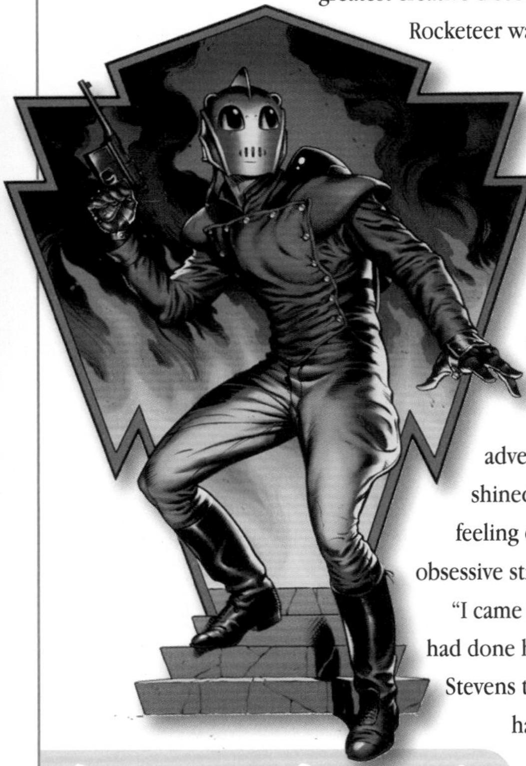

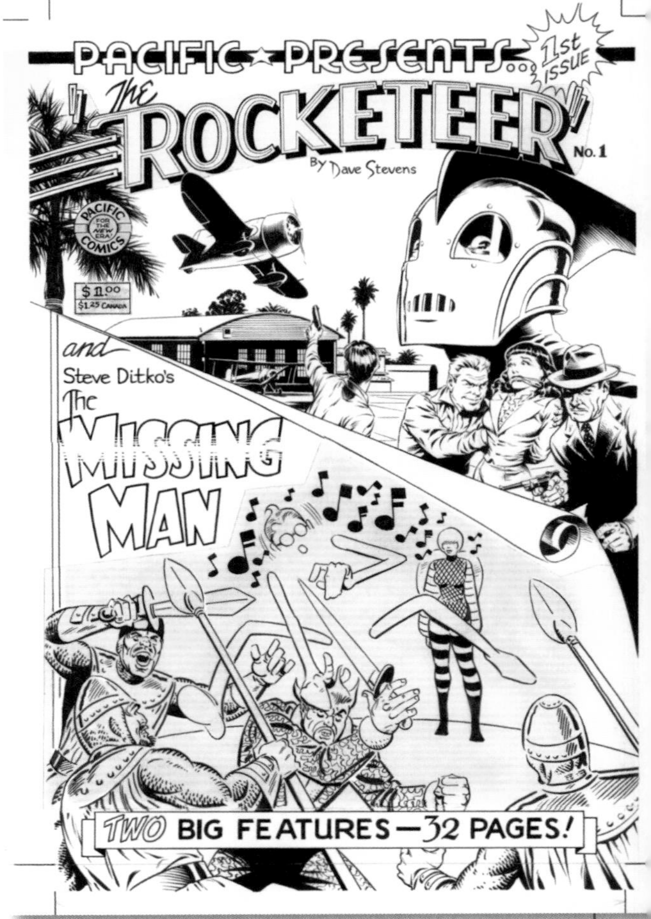
PACIFIC PRESENTS...
1st ISSUE
The ROCKETEER
By Dave Stevens
No. 1
PACIFIC COMICS
$1.00
$1.25 CANADA
and Steve Ditko's The MISSING MAN
TWO BIG FEATURES—32 PAGES!

"I came into Pacific Comics right after Jack had done his first issue of *Captain Victory*," Stevens told Jon B. Cooke, "and Mike Grell had done his first issue of *Starslayer*. The only reason I was even approached was because Grell's second issue was shy a few pages and they had to fill those pages with something, and they knew that I drew."[18] And, boy howdy, could that man *draw!*

Stevens explained he knew the Schanes brothers from their comics shop days. "I was a customer when I lived in San Diego, five years earlier," he said. "So, at the San Diego Comic-Con in 1981, they made the offer: 'Do whatever you want, but we need two installments of six pages.' So I said I'd see what I could come up with and went home and started kicking around some ideas."[19]

The conversation, he said, was casual. "I think they were trying to decide how best to fill that spot and I was around, so either Steve or Bill mentioned it to me. I really didn't regard it as anything important at the time; just 'filler' material… the Schaneses just told me to bring them something and left it entirely up to me. So, I came up with a promo drawing (which was also used as the first back cover), and wrote it around that image."[20]

Stevens added, "In the first issue of *Starslayer*, they ran a full-page ad: 'Coming next issue,' so, by the time the character appeared, it had already gotten some buzz and people really responded to it. By the time the second chapter came out, Pacific was getting a lot of calls and the immediate thought was that they had a potential cash cow."[21]

David Scroggy recalled the development of a book that could showcase the newcomer in a title he would share with a legendary creator. "We had succeeded in attracting Jack Kirby, Mike Grell, and Neal Adams to our upstart comics line-up," David said. "Why not Steve Ditko? I reached out to Steve Ditko, calling him and explaining our new approach to publishing, with its creator-ownership

Pacific Profiles

Dave Stevens

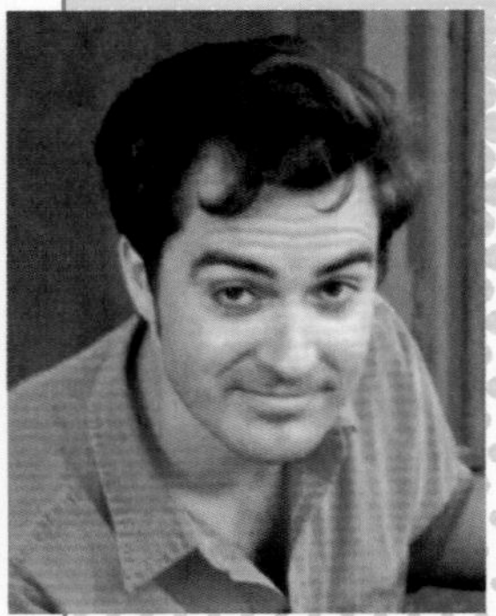

Above: Dave Stevens on set during the filming of *The Rocketeer*.

Born: *Apr. 1954*
Before becoming an industry sensation with The Rocketeer, Dave worked as an assistant to Russ Manning on the syndicated *Tarzan* strip and he worked in the Saturday morning cartoon animation industry. Stevens also had a career as movie storyboard artist before seeing *The Rocketeer* film released by Disney in 1991.

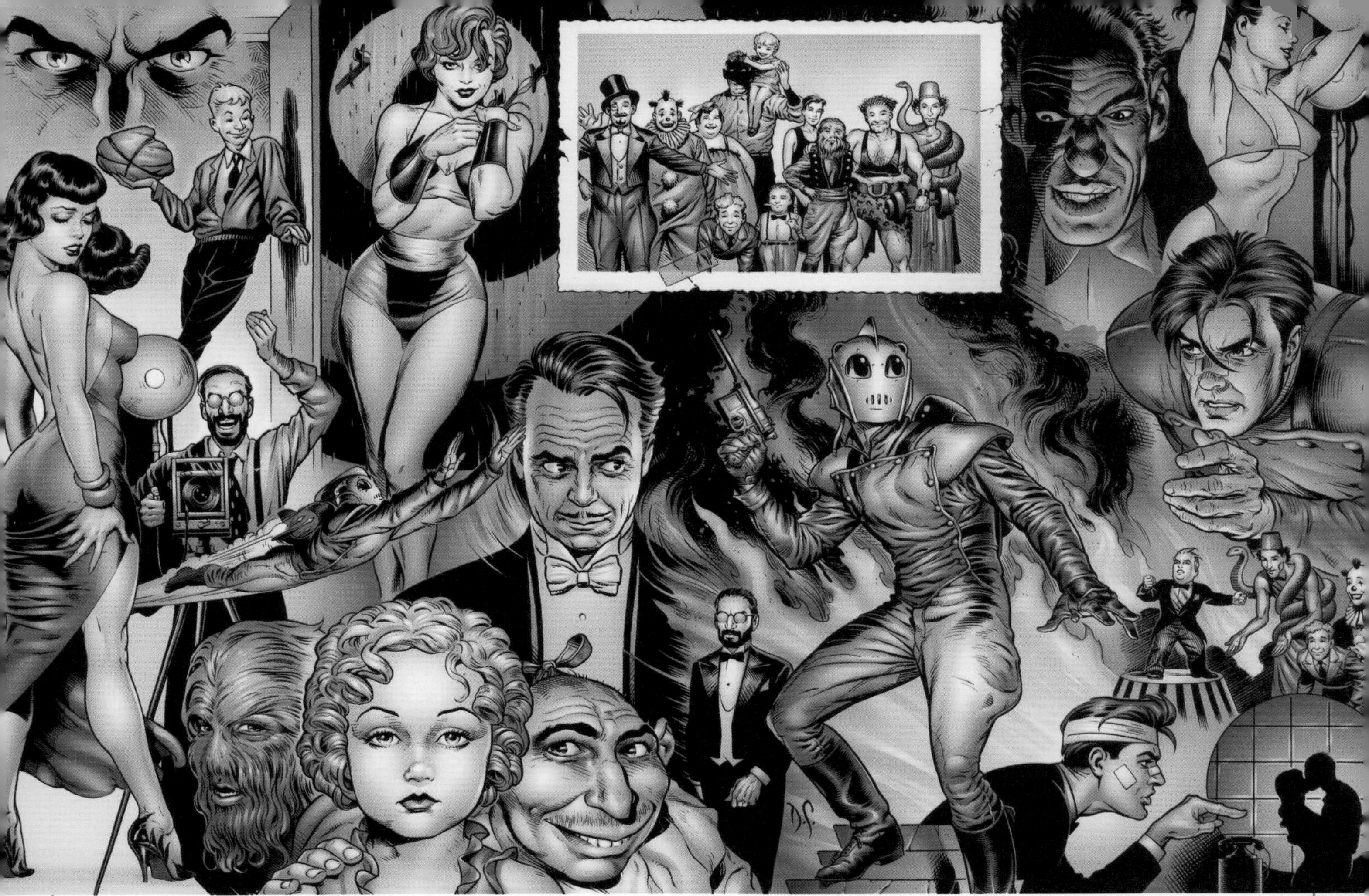

and the other benefits. To my elation, he was interested. We wasted no time in signing him up, and gave him a free hand to, as I put it, 'Do the character he had always wanted to.' We eagerly awaited his first submission."[22]

Scroggy continued, "At the same time, we had been looking for a way to get Dave Stevens involved in our books. Dave was a local and we all were familiar with him due to our time together working on Comic-Con. Everybody who ever saw Dave's work reckoned him to be a major talent — the guy just had it."

But Scroggy and the Schaneses understood the young artist was meticulous and painstakingly slow. "We didn't think Dave was able to generate an entire book, however. Dave didn't either. We realized Ditko's fame and following among comics fans would mean strong interest in his in-development comic and was certain to enjoy strong support from retailers and fans. It seemed a great idea to have Dave create a back-up strip for Ditko's lead feature."[23]

Scroggy then described the gestation of Stevens' trademark character. "Dave was a big fan of the old serials, such as Republic's *Commando Cody and His Lost Planet Airmen.* The various versions of these 1940s genre stories featured a character called Rocket Man. Dave was a big fan of this character and thought he could update it effectively. Originally, we considered simply coming forward with the underlying property clearly acknowledged, but were afraid of getting sued. None of us knew anything much about licensing or how to determine intellectual property ownership of this old material. Dave said he would re-work the concept and change it enough that it couldn't be mistaken for the original property or character. He came back with The Rocketeer. It didn't take a genius to realize that this was something really special. There was a unanimous green light given, and Dave began to work on it."[24]

Above: Anniversary Rocketeer print by Stevens. **Below:** Dave Stevens illo.

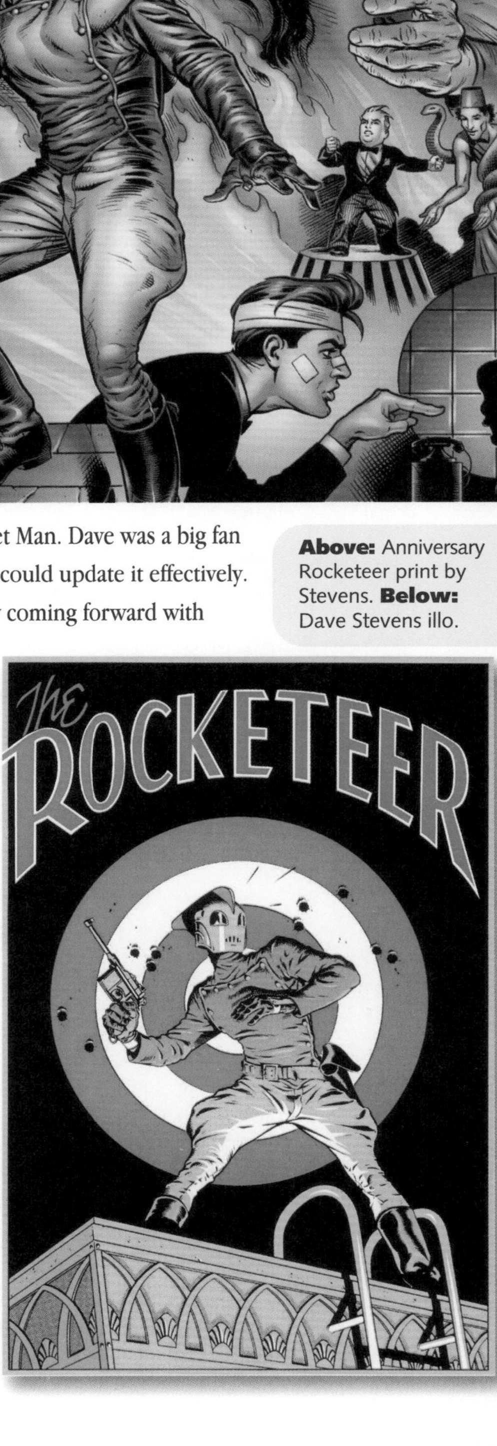
The
ROCKETEER

Pacific Profiles

Steve Ditko

Born: *Nov. 1927*
Co-creator of Spider-Man, the artist was, with the imminent closure of Charlton Comics, essentially reduced to being without a steady publisher by the time he contributed to Pacific. But, having established a creative partner in Robin Snyder, Ditko was on his way to self-publishing.

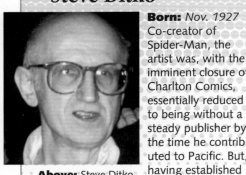

Above: Steve Ditko in the mid-1980s, taken at a family function.

REPRINTS PLUS
Steve Ditko's
80 PAGE
$9.00 US
PACKAGE
THE
MISSING
MAN
PLUS NEW PAGES of
1st HAND EXPERIENCE
2

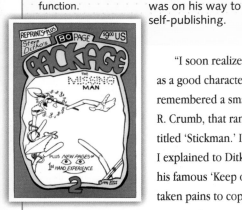

Above: Steve Ditko reprinted his "Missing Man" work in 1999. **Inset right:** Apparently this Ditko artwork featuring his "Missing Man" — modified to become an interior page — was intended as the cover of *Pacific Presents* #3 [Mar. 1984]. **Below:** Panel from *Pacific Presents* #1 [Oct. 1982].

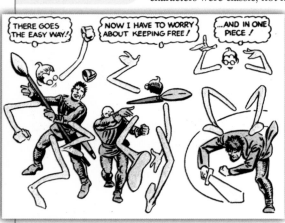

SOMETHING MISSING

Scroggy explained, "Meanwhile, the Ditko proposal arrived. It was titled 'Stick Man,' and was exactly that — a stick figure drawing who leapt about battling crooks with guns. There was no particular plot and any backstory was nonexistent. We were genuinely flummoxed. We didn't know how to respond. Was Ditko having a joke on us? Did he really mean it? Were we supposed to 'hang some clothes' onto the stick figure and flesh it out for him? I very tentatively phoned Mr. Ditko to find out.

"I soon realized that this was, indeed, what he viewed as a good character and viable proposal. Thinking fast, I remembered a small strip, by underground comix artist R. Crumb, that ran in the margins of one of his comics, titled 'Stickman.' It was a throwaway strip, but it did exist. I explained to Ditko that Crumb had been ripped off with his famous 'Keep on Truckin'' image and, ever since, had taken pains to copyright his stuff. Ditko accepted this and promised to rework the character. In short order, he sent us a draft of 'Missing Man.' There seemed no way to reject it again and still have Ditko do work for us, so we told him to proceed with it.

"When we launched *Pacific Presents*, we had the interesting situation of the back-up feature being the hit, and the lead feature not going over very well. It was truly a case of the tail wagging the dog. 'The Rocketeer' was immediately embraced by readers. It was the first wide exposure of Dave Stevens, and readers were stunned. His characters were classic, not least [*due to*] The Rocketeer's girlfriend, Betty, who, as we all know, was a thinly disguised Bettie Page. The marketplace wanted more. Dave Stevens realized it was his work selling the title, not Ditko's, and wanted to be featured more prominently. We tried juggling the story placement and splitting the front cover in order to showcase Dave's art. At the same time, Dave's legendary perfectionism made the pace of him finishing the pages slower and slower. I found myself as the first in what was to become a long line of editors trying to cajole, demand, or otherwise come up with an accelerated delivery schedule."[25]

THERE GOES THE EASY WAY!
NOW I HAVE TO WORRY ABOUT KEEPING FREE!
...AND IN ONE PIECE!

R. Fiore, in his "Funnybook Roulette" review column in *The Comics Journal,* noted the imbalance in *Pacific Presents.* "'The Rocketeer' works mostly because of artist/writer Dave Stevens' excellent feel for '30s pulp illustration; better than Michael Kaluta's, actually," he wrote. "While it suffers a bit from Marvelo-Schmarvelo characterization (main character who becomes a hero to impress his girlfriend, cantankerous employer), the air-show background is novel and the action is fast enough to preclude bothersome activities like thinking. And when's the last time you saw a new comics artist that reminded you more of Lou Fine than Neal Adams?

"On the other hand, you could miss 'The Missing Man' and not miss anything. Steve Ditko's eccentricities have been losing their charm for some time now, and here it's descended into self-indulgence. The title character is a page out of Ron Goulart's 'Second Banana Superheroes': Parts of him are, well, *missing*, so he can beat people up without being grabbed in return. Or something. Beneath the gimmicks is a lot of stale gangster nonsense."[26]

PACIFIC PRESENTS...
$1.50
$2.00 CANADA
No. 3
MISSING MAN by Steve Ditko
MA
AJAX
OLD TIMER
TODI

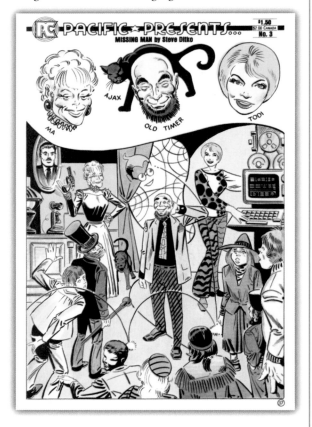

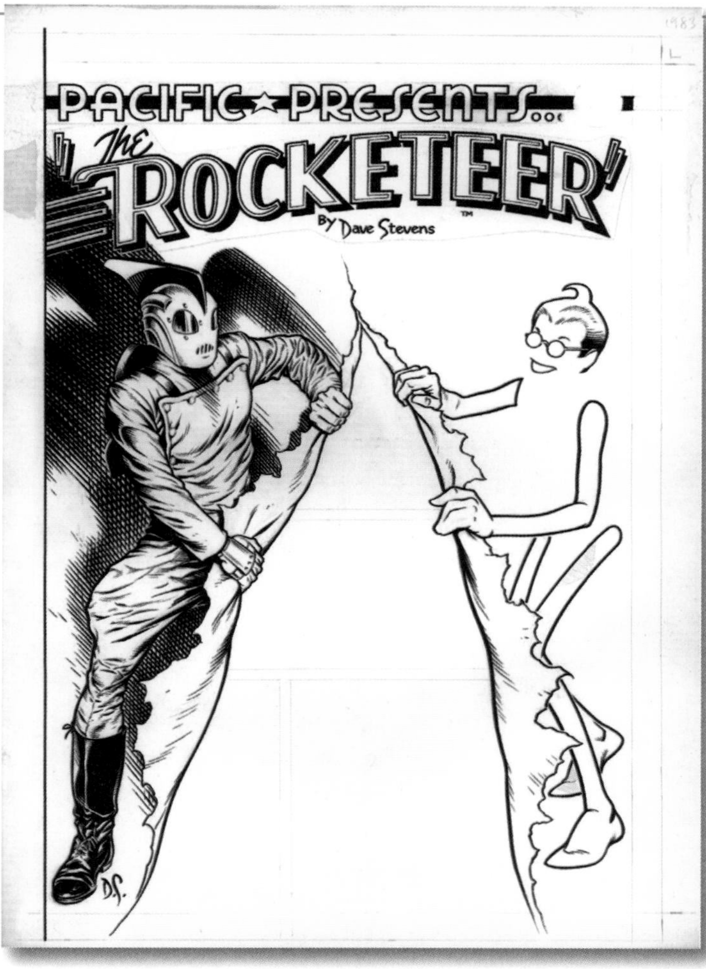
PACIFIC ★ PRESENTS...
The ROCKETEER
By Dave Stevens
TM

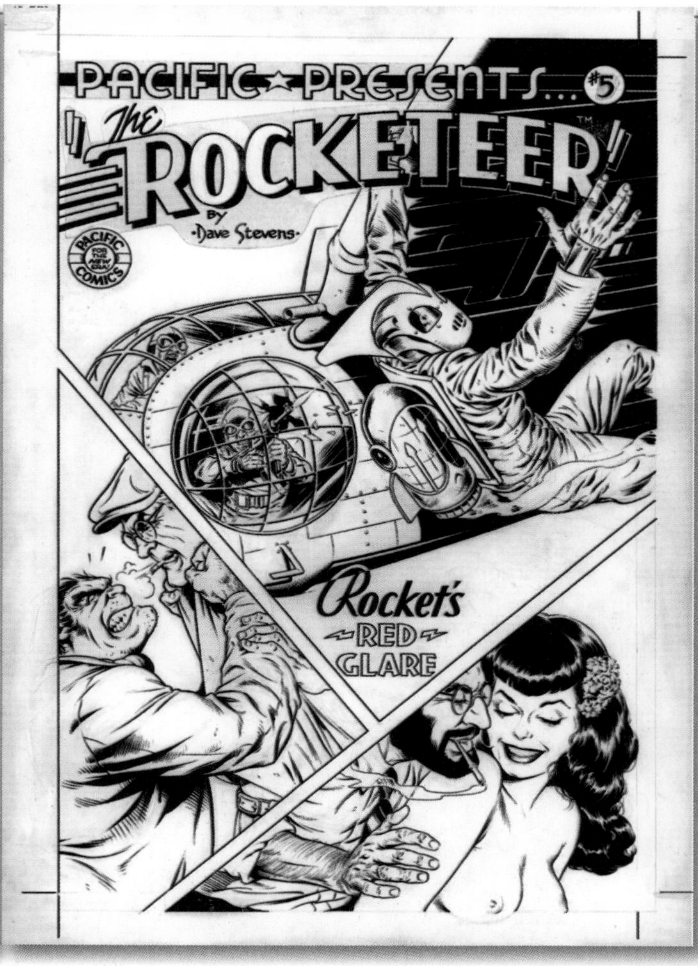
PACIFIC ★ PRESENTS... #5
The ROCKETEER
TM
By
Dave Stevens
PACIFIC COMICS
Rocket's
RED
GLARE

SELLING STEVENS

"In those days, at Pacific Comics, at least, there was no formal marketing department," David Scroggy shared. "I found myself doing the best I could at crafting Pacific's press releases, organizing creator signings and convention appearances, and anything else I could think of to promote the publications and increase their visibility. 'The Rocketeer' was a good example. We had some great art to show and a property we could pitch with pride.

"One time, Dave [*Stevens*] was going to be returning to Boise, Idaho for a visit with his parents. I rang up a local comic shop, whose owner I was acquainted with through Comic-Con, and asked him to host a signing for Dave, and do what he could to pitch it to the local press. I sent advance copies and backgrounds to the main newspaper. It was a big success — there was a full-page story in the paper, about Dave and lots of his art. The signing had good attendance.

"On another occasion, Dave and I traveled to Las Vegas, where a store appearance had been set up with local comics retailer Page After Page. It was a memorable excursion. Retailer Leonard Pederson was a superb host; his father, Pete, drove Dave and I to a brunch at a casino and ensconced us in a two-story hotel suite, spiral staircase and all. He had constructed oversize painted wooden panels depicting scenes from 'The Rocketeer' that filled the shop's large glass front display windows. For the actual appearance, Dave dressed as close to Cliff Secord as he could: wearing a vintage aviator helmet, jodhpur-style pants, high boots, and an old military-style tight coat. He was driven to the store perched on the running board of a 1930s automobile. Although the appearance didn't generate a lot in the way of press, and sales were modest, it is still one of the most noteworthy store signings of my experience, and I have been involved with quite a few."[27]

Scroggy continued, "*USA Today* ran a story about Pacific Comics, casting a light on us as a new kind of publisher with a new approach to comic books. It pictured some Dave Stevens art. We were excited, but something we had not realized was how many radio stations across the country used *USA Today* as a source for their radio news. The phones at Pacific Comics rang off the hook. Bill Schanes, Steve Schanes, me, and probably the janitor were all simultaneously engaged in doing live telephone on-the-air interviews with radio stations in markets like Iowa or Indiana. It was a zoo."[28]

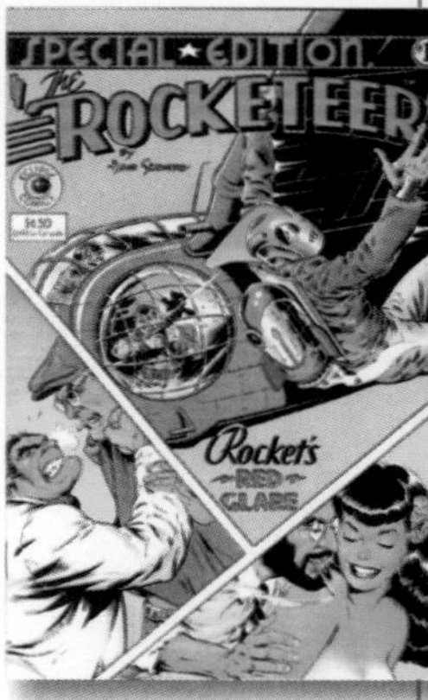
SPECIAL ★ EDITION 1
The ROCKETEER
Rocket's
RED
GLARE

This page: Original art of unused *Pacific Presents* covers by Dave Stevens, both courtesy of Scott Dunbier. On the left, the Rocketeer figure is used on this book's cover (originally shared with *Comic Book Artist* magazine back in 2001). On the right, this art was adapted by Eclipse for *The Rocketeer Special Edition* #1 [Nov. '84].

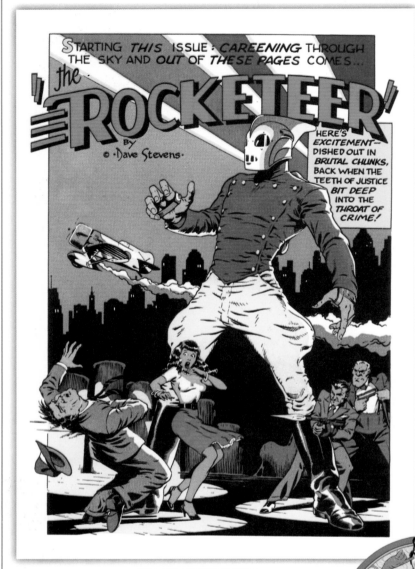

STARTING THIS ISSUE: CAREENING THROUGH THE SKY AND OUT OF THESE PAGES COMES...
the ROCKETEER
BY © Dave Stevens
HERE'S EXCITEMENT— DISHED OUT IN BRUTAL CHUNKS, BACK WHEN THE TEETH OF JUSTICE BIT DEEP INTO THE THROAT OF CRIME!

This page: Above is the back cover of *Starslayer* #2 [Apr. 1982]. Inset right is cover illo, *Movie Star News* [1990]. Below is *Pacific Presents* #2 [Apr. 1983] cover and call-out detail.

PACIFIC PRESENTS 2
The ROCKETEER
ON THE SPOT!
Girls! ENTER our "BETTY" LOOK-ALIKE CONTEST!

IT'S ALL ABOUT BETTY

Of course, from the very first appearance of The Rocketeer, on the back cover of *Starslayer* #2, one huge attraction in his adventures was Betty, Cliff Secord's sultry-yet-wholesome girlfriend, sensually rendered by Dave Stevens, soon to be renowned as a much-in-demand pin-up master.

About the full-pager [*above*] adorning the second issue of Mike Grell's title, Stevens told Diana Schutz, making up a filler story for *Starslayer*, "It sounded like an easy thing to do: just two issues and it didn't have to be a continuing feature — just one story in two parts. So I went home and thought about it over a month or so, and then the time came to *do* something, and I thought, 'Uh oh, I'd better get to it.' So I did a full-page drawing and just threw everything into it — I didn't know what I was going to write. And that was the back cover of that first one, with him standing there, very posed, with all the characters running around his legs. And I wrote it around that scene, using all those elements."[29]

Betty's likeness — in face and in figure — was based on 1940s/50s cheesecake model Bettie Page, and Page's likeness in "The Rocketeer," often scantily-clad and always curvaceous, rocketed her to hitherto unimagined fame before an entirely new generation of admirers. Stevens, who himself would become friends with the actual model late in her life, was undoubtedly the catalyst for an enduring appreciation for the pin-up queen, which even resulted in a feature-length motion picture, *The Notorious Bettie Page* [2005]. Page would outlive Stevens — who was tragically struck down at the age of 52 by leukemia — by almost nine months, passing away at 85 years old in 2008.

The cover of *Pacific Presents* #2 included a blurb announcing Pacific Comics' "Betty Look-Alike Contest." "Actually," Stevens told Diana Schutz at the time, "I had thought of doing something similar as a kind of a gimmick for personal appearances or something like that, just something fun. I think maybe I might have mentioned it to Scroggy, but it was *his* idea to do it in the book as a legitimate thing — only Pacific didn't come up with a prize to offer. I said, 'David, you can't just give these girls subscriptions. Girls don't read comic books — they don't want funnybooks! They want cash!'"[30]

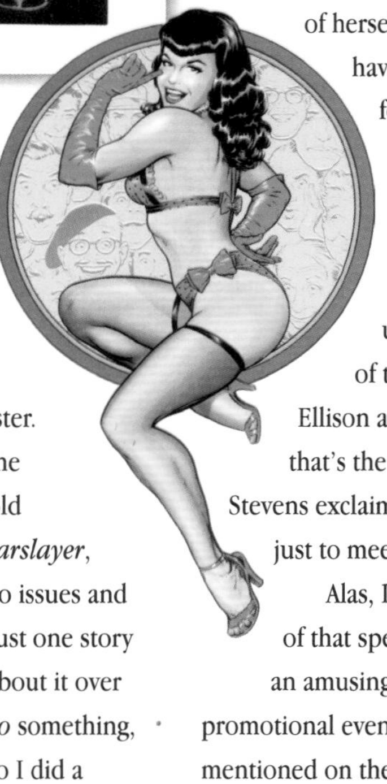

He continued, "If you want a girl to send in a photo of herself to some lookalike contest, you'd better have some kind of cash prize or something for the winner, and [*Pacific*] didn't come up with anything. I said, 'Well, at least give them a $50 gift certificate or something,' and they didn't want to do that either, so I had to come up with the ungodly commitment of doing a portrait of the winner!" Stevens added that Harlan Ellison admonished the young artist, "Stevens, that's the sleaziest thing I ever…!" About which Stevens exclaimed, "Because he assumed I was doing it just to meet some great-looking gals!"[31]

Alas, David Scroggy doesn't recall the results of that specific contest, though he did remember an amusing incident that occurred at the Las Vegas promotional event attended by Stevens and Scroggy mentioned on the previous page.

Referring to the *Pacific Presents* #2 contest, David said, "That idea sometimes gets confused with Dave's

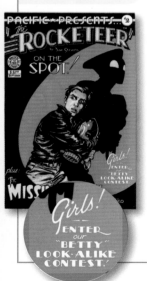

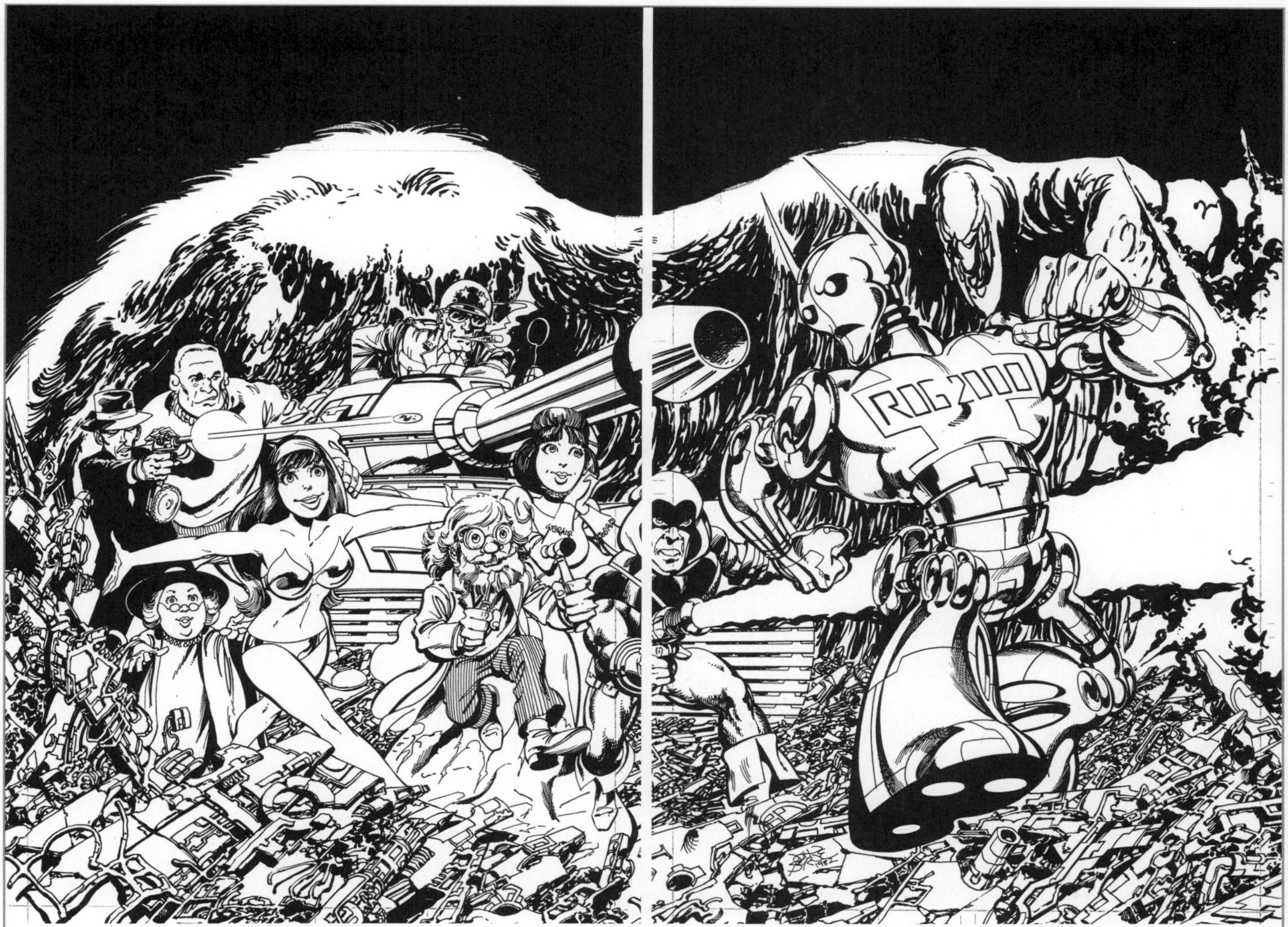
ROG 2000

notable store appearance at Leonard Pederson's Page After Page in Las Vegas, which I accompanied Dave to. They *did* hold a Bettie look-alike contest, unbeknownst to Dave and me. It was kind of a bust. There were only a couple of contestants, and they didn't really look at all like Bettie. Then some kid's mom showed up to collect her son, and we immediately proclaimed her the winner.* She had no idea who Bettie Page was, or Dave, or The Rocketeer. But she was a brunette cutie and close enough for us. She was a good sport about it, and kindly posed for a couple of snapshots."[32]

ROG 2000 REDUX

Out of the blue — and likely prompted by the artist's stellar success courtesy of his *Uncanny X-Men* work with Chris Claremont and Terry Austin over at Marvel Comics — Pacific obtained permission from artist John Byrne to reprint his charming "Rog 2000" material, which had originally appeared in Charlton Comics' *E-Man* between 1974–75. Printed magazine-size on higher-quality stock than usual, *The Complete Rog 2000*, weighed in at 40 black-&-white pages with the then rather high cover price of $2.95, though the spiffy new wraparound cover by Byrne and colorist Steve Oliff is quite splendid.

* *The Rocketeer Special Edition* #1 [Nov. 1984] announced that Ms. Diedre Mills of San Diego was the comic's contest winner.

This page: At top is John Byrne's original art for *The Complete Rog 2000* [July 1982]. Below is the printed edition with Steve Oliff's gorgeous coloring job.

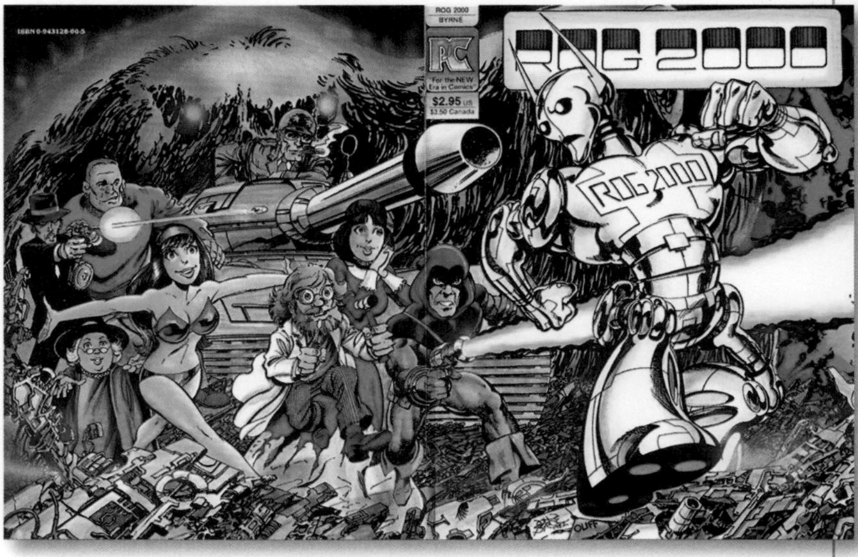
ROG 2000
ROG 2000

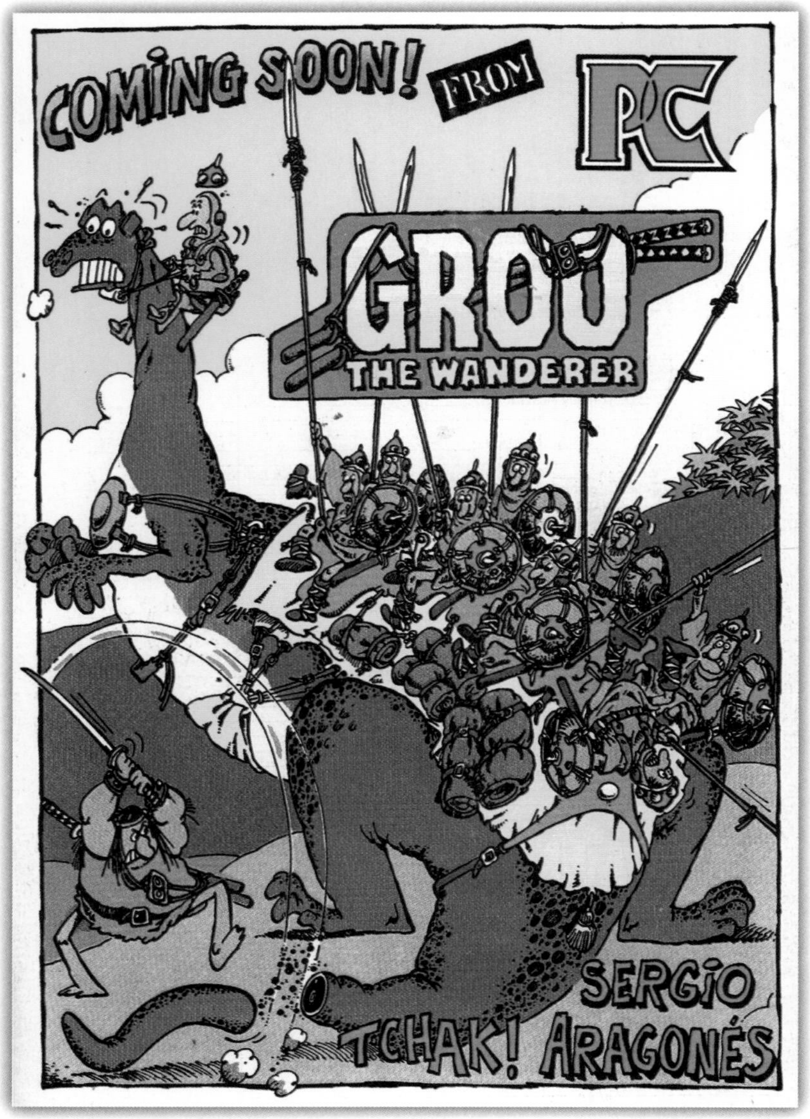
COMING SOON! FROM
PC
GROO THE WANDERER
SERGIO ARAGONÉS
TCHAK!

Pacific Profiles
Sergio Aragonés

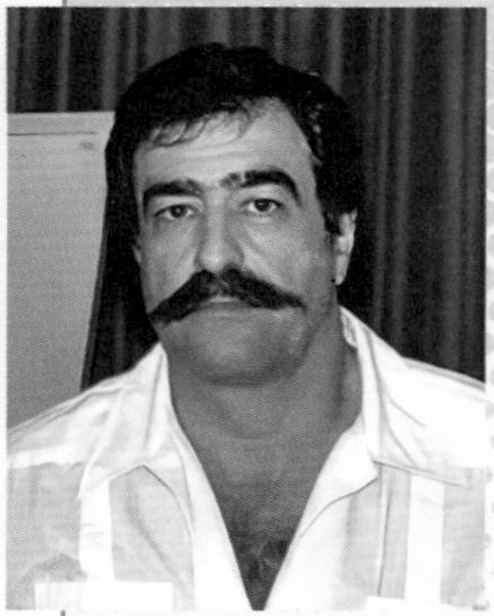

Born: *Sept. 1937* Besides his celebrated stint at *MAD* magazine, lasting over 50 years, the prolific cartoonist was also a writer for DC Comics from about 1967–77, scribing or plotting stories in numerous genres, including romance, Westerns, and humor. He left DC in a dispute over their work-for-hire policy.

Above: Sergio Aragonés at the 1982 San Diego Comic-Con. Photo by Alan Light. **Top:** Back cover, *Starslayer* #4 [Aug. 1982].

LOOK WHO WANDERED IN…

In the 1970s, despite U.S. comics publishers being utterly resistant to the idea of creators owning their own material, Sergio Aragonés, the great *MAD* magazine "marginal" cartoonist, pondered developing some of his own characters, creations of which he adamantly vowed to retain the rights. "I had already a few stories that I wanted to do, since the '60s," he told Jon B. Cooke. "But [*to have them published by DC or Marvel*] there was no way; in that market, no way. There was no way I was doing comics if I didn't own them, [*like it was*] in Europe. So I had different characters that I wanted to use, but there was no way. There was no publishing house that would share copyright, none. And, for many years, I just drew them with no way to have them published." The cartoonist had two concepts in particular he was pondering, one being "a Conan parody type of thing."[33]

The Spanish-born/Mexican-raised artist continued, "And I liked it a lot, because I thought it could be a very funny character — not Conan, but another barbarian [*done with*] humor. He was not a satire on Conan; he was just another barbarian, but an idiot. So I talk about doing a comic, but nobody wanted to publish it until 1980-something."[34]

Since butting heads with DC editorial in the latter '70s, Aragonés had paused his longtime association with the publisher, after having ended his humorous one-pagers for the mystery and war books. The reason for the kerfuffle was over creators owning the rights to their own creations. That disrespectful attitude — dismissing any notion of creator's rights — was the same over at Marvel. "They later changed their mind," Aragonés told Kim Thompson, "but at that time, there was no way."[35]

Aragonés' friend Mark Evanier told Dan Johnson about his introduction to a completely new character: "Sergio had this beautiful house up in the hills and we were up there one day, and he said, 'Let me show you something.' He pulled out these wonderful drawings… and they were all these barbarian characters, and this one in particular named Groo. I asked Sergio, 'Why Groo?' He said, 'I believe that name means nothing anywhere in any language.'"[36]

Evanier, who had been a one-time assistant to Jack Kirby, continued, "I somehow volunteered to assemble [*Destroyer Duck*] and Jack Kirby offered to draw the lead story. We needed a back-up series, and the first person I went to was Sergio. I told him about the project, and before I was halfway finished telling him about it, he went to his drawer of series that had not been published and told me, 'Take anything you want. If it's not right, I'll draw something special.' I said, 'This is the perfect place to put Groo in, as you'll own the copyright to it.' Sergio had one four-page 'Groo' story completed, and it was one of only two 'Groo' stories I was never involved with because it had no words. I said, 'Let's just publish this.'"[37]

Aragonés remembered to Cooke, "But the first thing we did is, I had done a pantomime story of Groo just to see how he'd work in comic books. And I had that [*to show*]. And Mark told me that they were doing a comic benefit for Steve Gerber, [*Destroyer Duck,* published by Eclipse]… the lawsuit issue. So he said, 'Well, why don't we use that thing?' 'Yeah, great, sure.' So they used it. That was the first appearance. And it looked good."[38]

Aragonés continued, "So I got to the point when I called Mark and we had a nice conversation, and I said, 'Mark, if I do a [*regular*] comic book, would you help me with the dialogue? Because I know I cannot [*dialogue*] it totally. But you can and you're my friend.' And he was very young then. So I said, 'Well, now I have a person who can *really* help me and who knows English and who knows humor, and I can work very comfortably with.' So I went to Pacific Comics, which was starting, and I asked them if they would distribute the comic."[39]

He said to Kim Thompson, "So I had a meeting with the Schanes brothers at Canter's [*a Los Angeles delicatessen*] and I showed them my project… I talked to the Schanes brothers and they said, 'Not only will we distribute it, but we'll publish it for you,' which was terrific. It saved me the trouble of having to spend time doing things other than drawing. And it came out and that was it."[40]

Aside from an ad promoting the barbarian's debut at the Schanes brothers' imprint, Groo's first Pacific appearance was a five-pager backing up *Starslayer* #5 [Nov. 1982] and, soon thereafter, *Groo the Wanderer* #1 [Dec. 1982] appeared, and the title lasted for eight issues at the San Diego company.

Aragonés admitted to Thompson that the Schaneses were not completely comfortable publishing a humorous title. "They weren't too happy with it, because it was humor. Every second issue they wanted to cancel it again, and I would tell them, 'Okay, I'll buy it, I'll publish it. I'll be the publisher. Let's make an arrangement. It'll be my company.' And immediately the publishers would say, 'Well, we'll do another issue.' But they never had too much faith in the humor comic."[41]

The cartoonist was not privy to the sales figures, as he told Thompson: "I have never been able to get out of anybody how many they printed, but in the beginning,

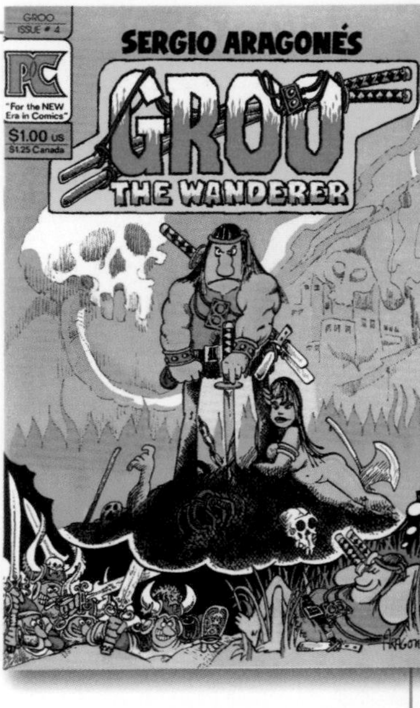
GROO
ISSUE # 4
PC
"For the NEW Era in Comics"
$1.00 US
$1.25 Canada
SERGIO ARAGONÉS
GROO
THE WANDERER

This page:
Above is Aragonés' Frazetta-esque *Groo the Wanderer* #4 cover [Sept. 1983]. Below, two-page promo, *Starslayer* #4 [Aug. 1982].

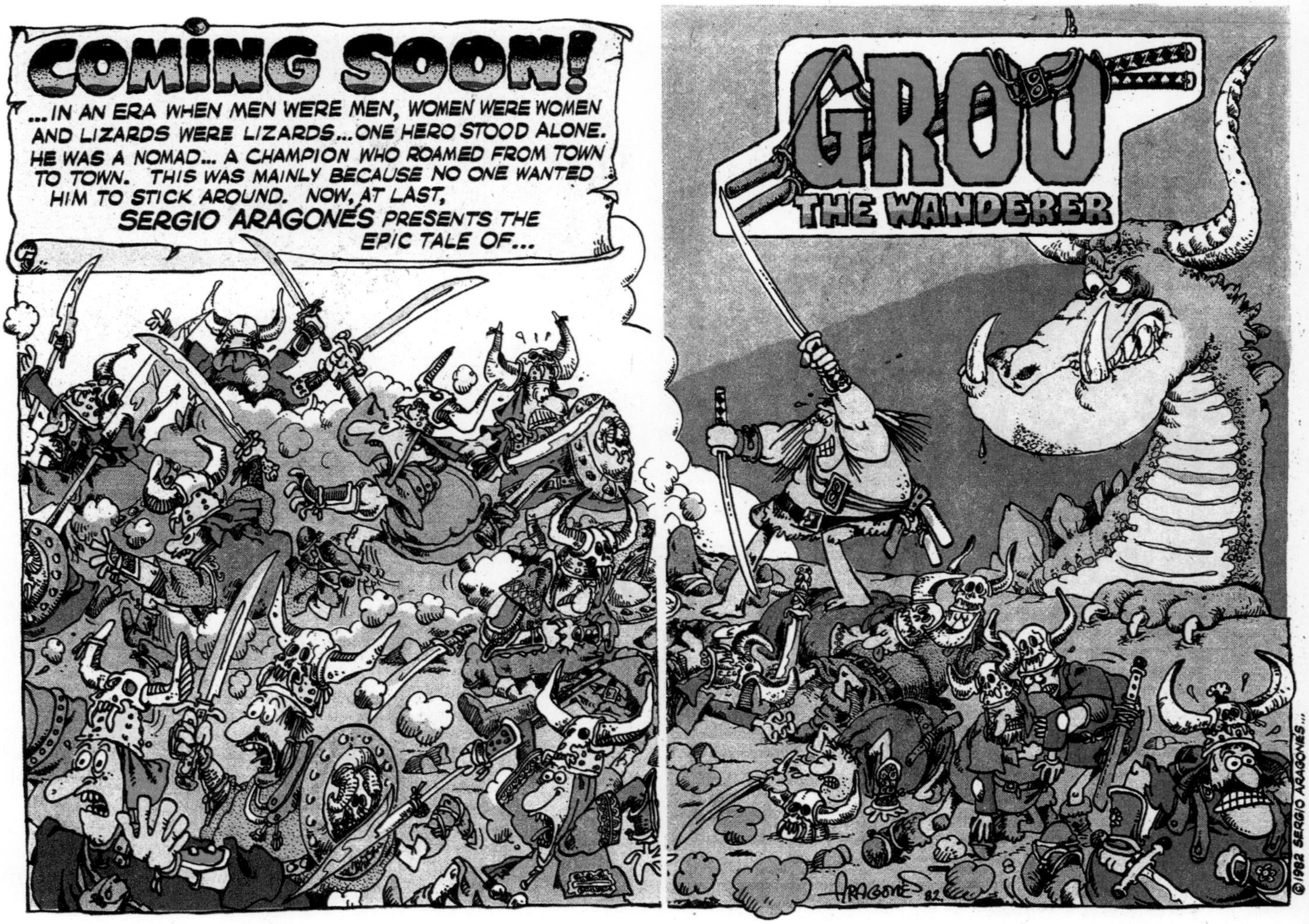
COMING SOON!
...IN AN ERA WHEN MEN WERE MEN, WOMEN WERE WOMEN AND LIZARDS WERE LIZARDS...ONE HERO STOOD ALONE. HE WAS A NOMAD... A CHAMPION WHO ROAMED FROM TOWN TO TOWN. THIS WAS MAINLY BECAUSE NO ONE WANTED HIM TO STICK AROUND. NOW, AT LAST, SERGIO ARAGONÉS PRESENTS THE EPIC TALE OF...
GROO
THE WANDERER
ARAGONÉS '82
© 1982 SERGIO ARAGONES...

at issue #1, it was probably about 50,000 copies. Later issues were lower, to the point that they were only printing 30,000 or less of the early *Groo*s. Sales were average — not too good because, again, it was humor. The only thing that probably saved me was that I had been working with *MAD* for so many years that I had a certain following that liked humor — or liked what I do."[42]

With the closing of Pacific's comics line looming on the horizon — "I don't think they were that interested in the publishing end of it; they were more into distributing and big business,"[43] the creator surmised to Thompson — Aragonés, with Evanier's help, pursued the idea of Marvel continuing the series, under their new Epic creator-friendly imprint, a move that would guarantee *Groo* would be distributed to newsstands.

Evanier told Johnson, "I called [*Marvel executive*] Carol [*Shaley*] at home one night and said, 'I think Pacific Comics is going the way of the passenger pigeon, and, even if they don't, they won't be publishing *Groo* much longer.' I asked her if Marvel would be interested, and she said, 'Absolutely.'"[44]

"So we started negotiating contracts," Aragonés told Thompson. "I told the people at Pacific, and everything was all right — they were going out of business and I said, 'Well, I'll continue with you until we start with Marvel,' and they said fine. It just happened that they were planning to do a special issue, and, by then, they'd gone out of business. I couldn't give it to Marvel because we were still negotiating, so it went to Eclipse."[45]

Thereafter, Groo the Wanderer has had a long life, certainly among the longest of any character to emerge from Pacific Comics. The cheese dip-loving swordsman lasted for 120 issues at Marvel, 12 issues at Image, and many mini-series at Dark Horse, which continue to the present day. (Evanier estimates a total of 200 or so issues to date.)

After the character's introduction in *Destroyer Duck,* Evanier quipped, "*Groo* then went to Pacific Comics and destroyed it. *Groo* then went to Eclipse Comics and destroyed it. *Groo* then went to Marvel, and I think when we left Marvel, it was in bankruptcy, if I'm not mistaken. One of the nice things about owning your own books is that you can survive. The fact that a publisher goes under doesn't mean your comic property is sold in a bankruptcy auction and it's passed around like a baseball card. They stay with the person who should own them, who in this case is Sergio Aragonés."[46]

David Scroggy recalled he had little to no editorial input on *Groo the Wanderer*. "Sergio and Mark Evanier sent in the pages essentially camera-ready. I got to open the envelopes and read them first, a genuine thrill, but that was about the extent of any editing I did. I did find a typo once, which Evanier could not believe when I phoned him. It was a red-letter day around Scroggy's desk. I might add that none of us were outstanding proofreaders. I often had to proof my own copy, which is, of course, a recipe for disaster. I wanted to have a cover blurb created that said, 'No Typos This Issue!,' but I don't know if I would have ever had a chance to use it."[47]

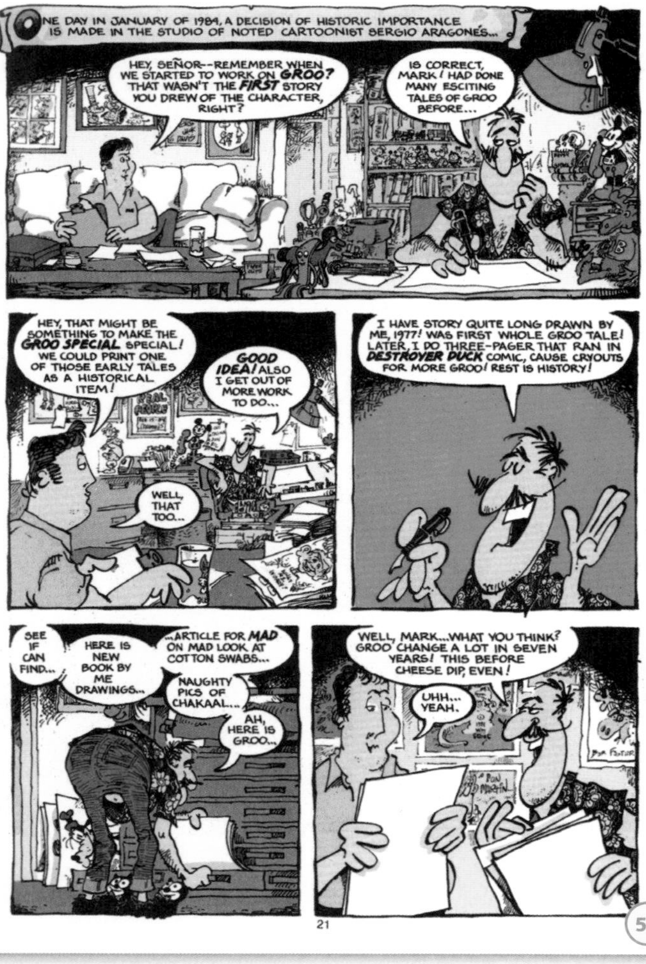
ONE DAY IN JANUARY OF 1984, A DECISION OF HISTORIC IMPORTANCE IS MADE IN THE STUDIO OF NOTED CARTOONIST SERGIO ARAGONÉS...
HEY, SEÑOR--REMEMBER WHEN WE STARTED TO WORK ON GROO? THAT WASN'T THE FIRST STORY YOU DREW OF THE CHARACTER, RIGHT?
IS CORRECT, MARK! HAD DONE MANY ESCITING TALES OF GROO BEFORE...
HEY, THAT MIGHT BE SOMETHING TO MAKE THE GROO SPECIAL SPECIAL! WE COULD PRINT ONE OF THOSE EARLY TALES AS A HISTORICAL ITEM!
GOOD IDEA! ALSO I GET OUT OF MORE WORK TO DO...
WELL, THAT TOO...
I HAVE STORY QUITE LONG DRAWN BY ME, 1977! WAS FIRST WHOLE GROO TALE! LATER, I DO THREE-PAGER THAT RAN IN DESTROYER DUCK COMIC, CAUSE CRYOUTS FOR MORE GROO! REST IS HISTORY!
SEE IF CAN FIND...
HERE IS NEW BOOK BY ME DRAWINGS...
...ARTICLE FOR MAD ON MAD LOOK AT COTTON SWABS...
NAUGHTY PICS OF CHAKAAL...
AH, HERE IS GROO...
WELL, MARK...WHAT YOU THINK? GROO CHANGE A LOT IN SEVEN YEARS! THIS BEFORE CHEESE DIP, EVEN!
UHH... YEAH.
21
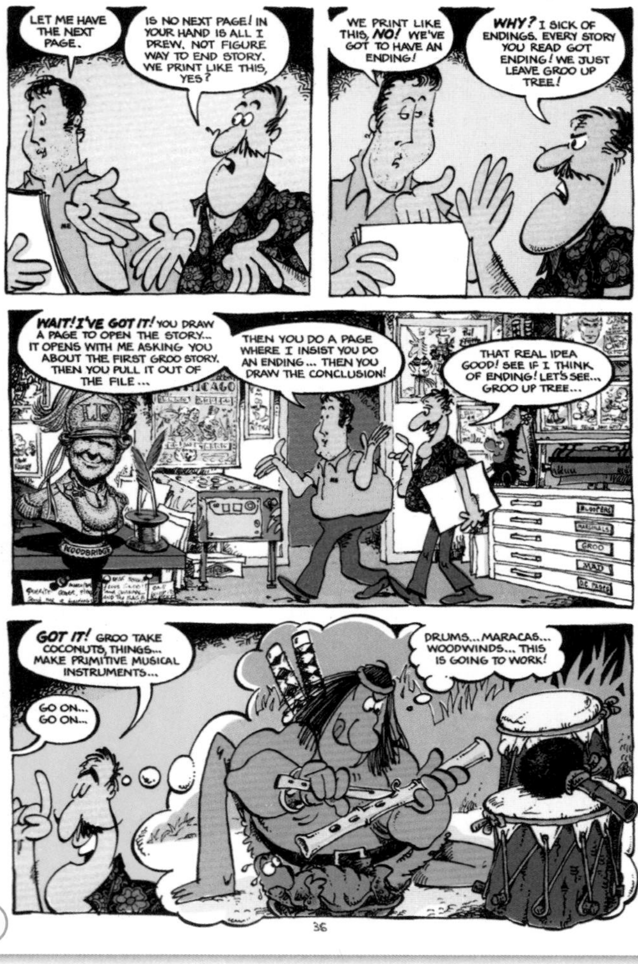
LET ME HAVE THE NEXT PAGE.
IS NO NEXT PAGE! IN YOUR HAND IS ALL I DREW. NOT FIGURE WAY TO END STORY. WE PRINT LIKE THIS, YES?
WE PRINT LIKE THIS, NO! WE'VE GOT TO HAVE AN ENDING!
WHY? I SICK OF ENDINGS. EVERY STORY YOU READ GOT ENDING! WE JUST LEAVE GROO UP TREE!
WAIT! I'VE GOT IT! YOU DRAW A PAGE TO OPEN THE STORY... IT OPENS WITH ME ASKING YOU ABOUT THE FIRST GROO STORY. THEN YOU PULL IT OUT OF THE FILE...
THEN YOU DO A PAGE WHERE I INSIST YOU DO AN ENDING... THEN YOU DRAW THE CONCLUSION!
THAT REAL IDEA GOOD! SEE IF I THINK OF ENDING! LET'S SEE... GROO UP TREE...
GROO
MAD
GOT IT! GROO TAKE COCONUTS, THINGS... MAKE PRIMITIVE MUSICAL INSTRUMENTS...
GO ON... GO ON...
DRUMS... MARACAS... WOODWINDS... THIS IS GOING TO WORK!
36

BJA brucejones associates

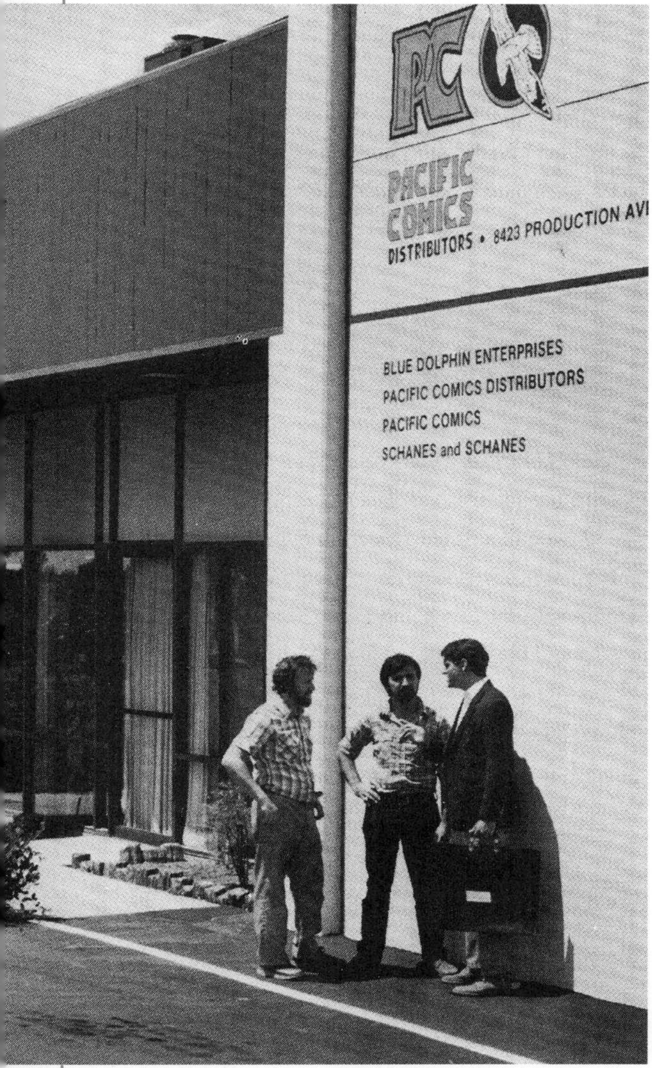

PACIFIC COMICS
DISTRIBUTORS • 8423 PRODUCTION AV
BLUE DOLPHIN ENTERPRISES
PACIFIC COMICS DISTRIBUTORS
PACIFIC COMICS
SCHANES and SCHANES

ALONG CAME JONES

"I came of age in the 1950s," editor/writer/artist Bruce Jones told Jon B. Cooke, "and, even though I sort of missed the EC heyday, I was still very influenced by the non-super-hero comic books (though comics were just one of the things I was reading). I was a voracious reader and most of the stuff I ended up doing for Warren [*Publications' horror comics*] — or anybody, really — was based on the short stories and novels I was reading, as well as comic books. The comic books were a factor because I was drawn to the short story-type of horror and science-fiction kind of comics rather than the super-hero or the funny animal stuff… It was always the more anthology-oriented short story stuff that I was drawn to. Super-heroes were on the way out and they didn't come back big until I was already in college, in the '60s."[48]

As an artist deeply influenced by Frank Frazetta and Al Williamson, Jones was among a new generation, one weaned on EC Comics and who came into the profession through comics and science-fiction fandom, a group that included Bernie Wrightson, Jeffrey Jones, and Michael W. Kaluta. Upon determining his strength was as a writer, Bruce scribed among the finest stories for Warren Publications during the '70s, under brilliant editor Louise Jones ("Weezie," then wife of Jeffrey Jones) and often teamed with the finest artists working for Weezie, among them Wrightson, Richard Corben, and Russ Heath. When Weezie switched to Marvel, so did Jones, and he worked on her titles, *Ka-Zar* and *Conan the Barbarian*.

"I got a call, when I was living in the Midwest, from Steve or Bill Schanes," Jones told Cooke, "and my intent was to move to California at that point, because I was really sick of the Midwestern winters. I was thinking of going to Los Angeles to investigate the film business and they were in San Diego, so they told me to come out and talk to them because they were interested in my work.

"When I got there, I just fell in love with San Diego — it's just the greatest town in the world. They made me a very good offer to be with their fledgling publishing company. So, for a time, I was doing work both for them and for Weezie at Marvel. Then Weezie got kicked upstairs and was replaced by an editor I really didn't get along with that well. So it became very hard to continue with the *Ka-Zar* and *Conan* stuff. Plus, the fact I was single-handedly writing

Above: BJA — Bruce Jones Associates — business logo that appeared at the conclusion of the *Somerset Holmes* [1987] graphic novel. **Previous page:** Two non-consecutive pages featuring the cartoonist and his writing collaborator, Mark Evanier, from Sergio Aragonés' *Groo Special* #1 [Oct. 1984], intended to be a Pacific release, but published by Eclipse. **Inset left:** Photo of Bruce Jones, with briefcase and all suited-up, and the casual Schanes bros outside the Pacific Comics HQ, from a photo feature in *Somerset Holmes* #1 [Sept. 1983].

Pacific Profiles

Bruce Jones

Born: *Oct. 1946*

The Missouri native actually first emerged from the fanzine world, where he was recognized as an artist, but it would be his writing for editor "Weezie" Jones in the Warren horror magazines where he gained renown as one of the best in the field. At Pacific he would also prove a great comics editor and anthologist.

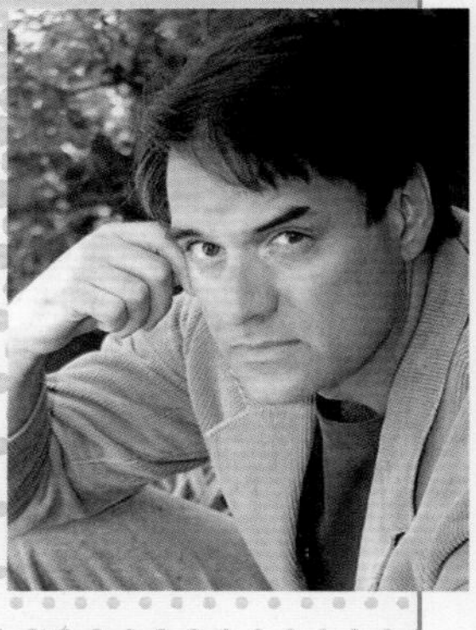

Above: Bruce Jones in a publicity shot, circa 1980s.

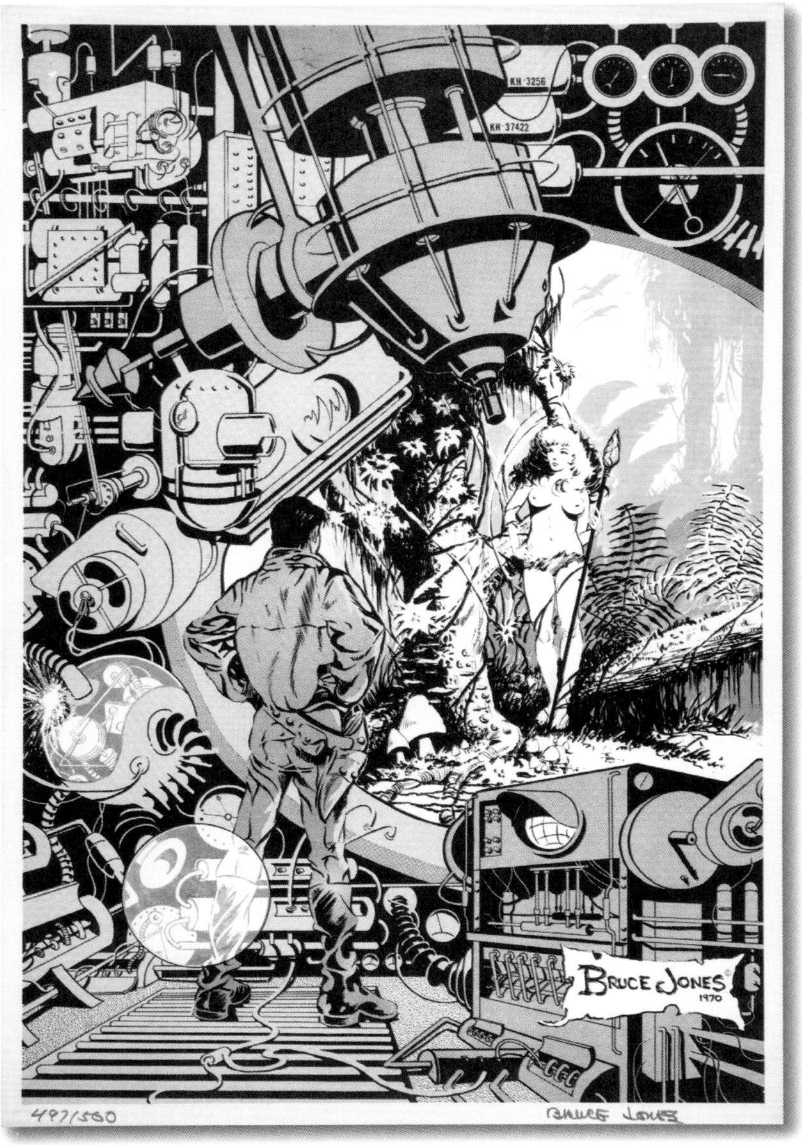
KH·3256
KH·37422
BRUCE JONES
1970
497/500

and drawing *Twisted Tales* and *Alien Worlds* was really too much work; something had to go. Security was with Marvel, but the fun was with Pacific, so (being the idiot that I was — and still am) I chose the fun."[49]

Not then recognized for editing comic books, Jones was asked whose suggestion was it for him to helm a set of titles at Pacific. "That wasn't their idea at all; it was all mine," he explained. "They wanted me as a writer and they didn't have a clue what they wanted to do. I came out and said, 'Look, guys: There's only one way I'm going to do this: I want to do an anthology book and I want control.'

"Essentially I wanted to become a packager. I said, 'I'll deliver the books completely finished. I'll hire the artists, and do all the writing, and all the design — virtually all the work.' This sounds like an ego trip, but it was a wonderful thing for them because I was a one-man machine and it took a lot of work from their hands. We did the first full-color covers and a lot of crazy stuff that people had never done. Steve and Bill were really responsible for handing out the first creator-owned contracts — and I don't think that they've been praised nearly enough for that. I was very proud of those books, for the most part; it was too much effort… I was writing too much, so some of the stories suffered, but that was a very good time. I was happy to do it and they were happy to go with that. I really got to form my own company, which sort of became an adjunct to their company; it was a great relationship until they ran into financial problems — then it all kind of fell apart."[50] (That decision to pay the contributors out of his own pocket would unfortunately come back to haunt Jones when he was left, as they say, holding the bag.)

A few years earlier, when Jones was in his native Missouri, he developed some fumetti book projects — basically comics stories told in staged photographs — and he met model/actress April Campbell. "We did some modeling work together for the *Kansas City Star*'s newspaper ads and got to know each other," Jones told Richard Arndt. "April was very bright, looked terrific, had a Playmate figure and — most importantly — had acting experience. I hired her and we began shooting *Dime Novel* and a second [*fumetti*] novel, *Vampira*, simultaneously with April in both lead roles… However, neither presentation interested New York publishers, which was the only game in town back then. So, broke and weary, I closed up shop and went back to comics."[51]

This page: While primarily revered as a writer, Bruce Jones is also an artist, as one can see in the plate above from the *Abyss Portfolio* [1970]. When Jones focused on scripting, his work at Warren Publications was among the best. Splash from *Creepy* #63 [July 1974] and "In Deep" cover of *Creepy* #101 [Sept. 1978].

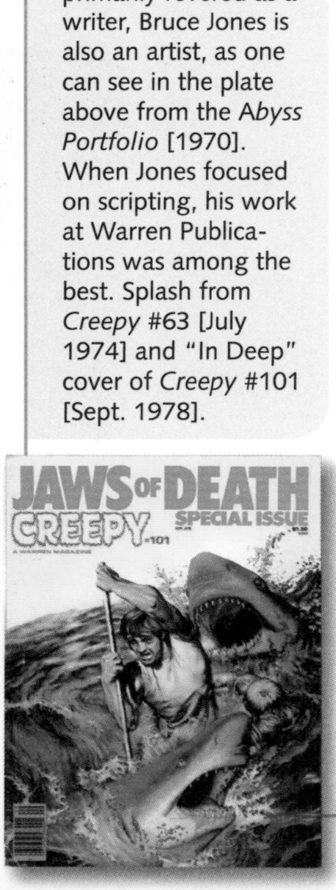
JAWS OF DEATH
CREEPY #101
SPECIAL ISSUE
A WARREN MAGAZINE

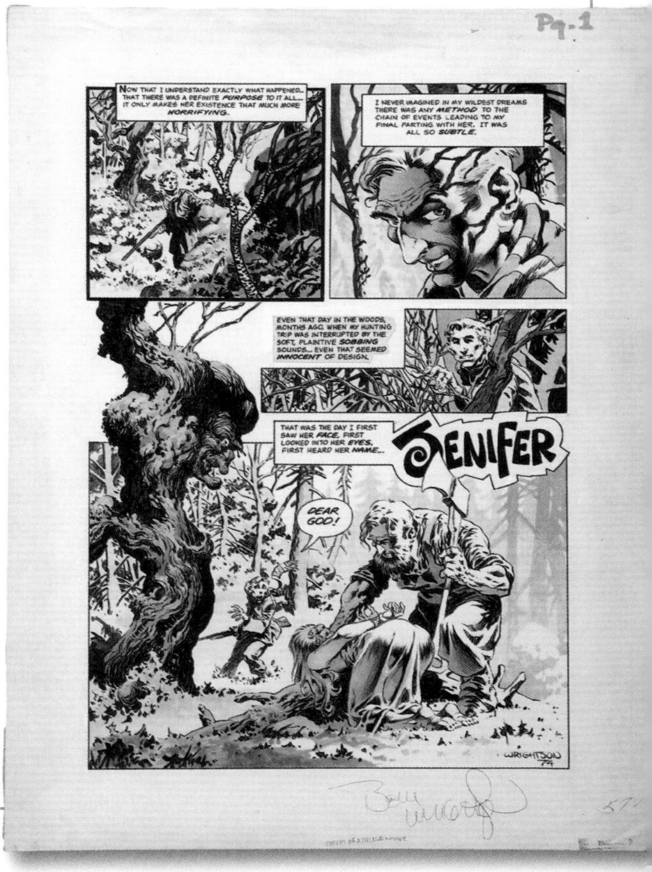
Pg.1
NOW THAT I UNDERSTAND EXACTLY WHAT HAPPENED... THAT THERE WAS A DEFINITE PURPOSE TO IT ALL... IT ONLY MAKES HER EXISTENCE THAT MUCH MORE HORRIFYING.
I NEVER IMAGINED IN MY WILDEST DREAMS THERE WAS ANY METHOD TO THE CHAIN OF EVENTS LEADING TO MY FINAL PARTING WITH HER. IT WAS ALL SO SUBTLE.
EVEN THAT DAY IN THE WOODS, MONTHS AGO, WHEN MY HUNTING TRIP WAS INTERRUPTED BY THE SOFT, PLAINTIVE SOBBING SOUNDS... EVEN THAT SEEMED INNOCENT OF DESIGN.
THAT WAS THE DAY I FIRST SAW HER FACE, FIRST LOOKED INTO HER EYES, FIRST HEARD HER NAME...
JENIFER
DEAR GOD!
WRIGHTSON 74

BJA

Jones and Campbell's association grew beyond the professional while working on the fumetti projects. "April and I had been together every day for months; meanwhile, working far into the wee hours and the close proximity eventually evolved into a romantic relationship, though a complicated one as both of us were married to others," he told Arndt. "When Neal Adams called and offered me the graphic novel that became *Freak Show,* with art by Bernie Wrightson, April and I moved in together and she helped me plot the graphic novel. After that, we began working together on things like *Ka-Zar* and *Conan* for Marvel, always with the idea of getting [*his company, Bruce Jones Associates*] up and running again.

"Soon after this, Steve Schanes at Pacific Comics called and offered me some writing work. I countered with my own offer to package a group of comics the way BJA had packaged *Amberstar** for Warner's — but only if I could retain editorial, writing and design control over the thing and pick out the artists."[52]

Jones continued, "April and I met with Steve and Bill in San Diego and cemented a deal. You could see right away, though, that having the control I insisted on was only going to work if we were in their proximity, so April and I moved to California and rented a house on Coronado Island across the bay and not far from the Pacific offices. The result was *Twisted Tales, Alien Worlds, Somerset Holmes, Pathway to Fantasy,* and *Silverheels*. April and I were very hands-on, right down to the fonts used on the covers and how to advertise the books. It would never have been possible if I didn't have so many talented artist friends in the business. I had the cream of the crop. Brent Anderson, Joe Chiodo, and other artists we worked with eventually followed us out there [*to Coronado*] and we had a little art colony there for awhile. It was probably the hardest I ever worked and the most fun I ever had. I'm still pretty proud of those books."[53]

TO DELIBERATELY DISTURB

Among the best comic books released by Pacific during its short reign, *Alien Worlds* and *Twisted Tales* might well have carried the torch for the extraordinary EC science-fiction and horror comics of the 1950s, considering the books' smart design, quality of writing, and art excellence, though Jones would repeatedly deny he was attempting to replicate their unparalleled achievements. "But I want to state emphatically," he told Kim Thompson, "that I did not, at any time, try to consciously copy that line. I don't think *Twisted Tales* was like EC. I will say that I did consciously try to shock. I was trying to elicit, with *Twisted Tales,* the kind of feeling that I experienced as a child, which was that the EC books — and not just the EC books — the horror comics in general, in those days, were like forbidden fruit. You know what I mean? And that was a very exciting feeling. You knew you weren't supposed to be looking at it. I tried to do in the '70s and the '80s what those books did in the '50s and, of course, we've come a long way and you can't just show a walking corpse coming down the road. We tried to do it, to some degree, with sex and, to some degree, with violence, but more than that, I think, with content. I deliberately tried to disturb. It may be true that I overstepped myself at times, but it was never for shock's sake alone. I tried to do it to establish an attitude. Sometimes I think I was very successful, with stories like 'Banjo Lessons.' Sometimes, whether it was my fault or whether it was the artist's fault, I just wasn't successful at all and some of the stories ended up looking exploitative, which I think was unfortunate. I *never* wanted that. We tended to do that less in *Alien Worlds* and so some people think *Alien Worlds* was a superior book. I think that, in terms of taking chances, and being radical, *Twisted Tales* was a better book."[54]

* Aided by Richard Corben or at least his studio colorists — who handled the colorizing of black-&-white photography — Bruce Jones produced a *Star Wars*-inspired trade paperback fumetti adventure tale called *Amberstar* [Warner Books, 1980].

Pacific Profiles

April Campbell Jones

Born: *Nov. 1955*

These days, April is still writing with husband Bruce Jones, currently novels under the pen-name Campbell Jones, and she's also an active screenwriter and editor. April has also been a singer, model, actress, and photographer, and among her book series is *Mitzi Magee: Vampire Poodle.*

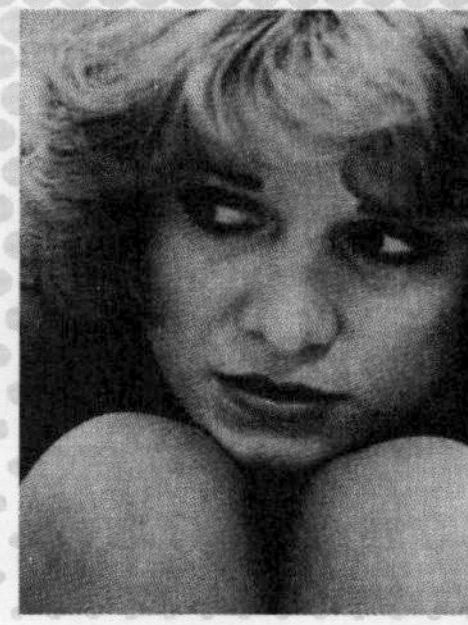

Above: April Campbell Jones posing as Somerset Holmes for artist Brent Anderson in 1983.

Below: Maybe the most controversial story to appear in the Bruce Jones-edited comics for Pacific was "Banjo Lessons," *Twisted Tales* #5 [Oct. 1983]. Story by Jones with art by underground regular Rand Holmes.

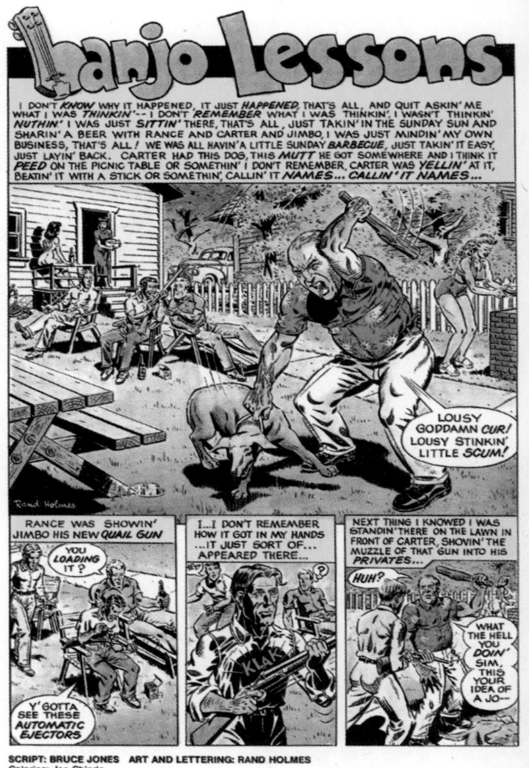
Banjo Lessons
I DON'T KNOW WHY IT HAPPENED, IT JUST HAPPENED, THAT'S ALL, AND QUIT ASKIN' ME WHAT I WAS THINKIN'-- I DON'T REMEMBER WHAT I WAS THINKIN', I WASN'T THINKIN' NUTHIN'! I WAS JUST SITTIN' THERE, THAT'S ALL, JUST TAKIN' IN THE SUNDAY SUN AND SHARIN' A BEER WITH RANCE AND CARTER AND JIMBO, I WAS JUST MINDIN' MY OWN BUSINESS, THAT'S ALL! WE WAS ALL HAVIN' A LITTLE SUNDAY BARBECUE, JUST TAKIN' IT EASY, JUST LAYIN' BACK. CARTER HAD THIS DOG, THIS MUTT HE GOT SOMEWHERE AND I THINK IT PEED ON THE PICNIC TABLE OR SOMETHIN' I DON'T REMEMBER, CARTER WAS YELLIN' AT IT, BEATIN' IT WITH A STICK OR SOMETHIN', CALLIN' IT NAMES... CALLIN' IT NAMES...
LOUSY GODDAMN CUR! LOUSY STINKIN' LITTLE SCUM!
Rand Holmes
RANCE WAS SHOWIN' JIMBO HIS NEW QUAIL GUN
YOU LOADING IT?
Y'GOTTA SEE THESE AUTOMATIC EJECTORS
I...I DON'T REMEMBER HOW IT GOT IN MY HANDS ...IT JUST SORT OF... APPEARED THERE...
?
KLAK
NEXT THING I KNOWED I WAS STANDIN' THERE ON THE LAWN IN FRONT OF CARTER, SHOVIN' THE MUZZLE OF THAT GUN INTO HIS PRIVATES...
HUH?
WHAT THE HELL YOU DOIN' SIM, THIS YOUR IDEA OF A JO--

SCRIPT: BRUCE JONES ART AND LETTERING: RAND HOLMES
Coloring: Joe Chiodo

Special Editorial

Because of the controversial nature of the last story in this issue, "Banjo Lessons," I've been asked to write an editorial stating our views on the subject of racism, just in case the completely anti-racist stance of the story is misinterpreted or the language in the story misunderstood as condoning the very behavior it condemns.

As an editor it is my job not only to choose what I believe are the very best stories in the way of script and art, but to set a policy with my co-editor as to the slant our book takes in regard to the type of material we print. Most magazines have this editorial slant; some barely discernible, others so politically or socially distinct that the reader can always guess as to the nature of the articles or stories certain editors will print. And as editor of *Twisted Tales*, *Alien Worlds*, and *Somerset Holmes*, I would be going totally against my own personal nature and the editorial policy of my publishers, Bill and Steve Schanes, to print *any* story promoting racism, sexism, or bigotry in *any form*.

However—and this is a big "however"—I reserve the right to print any worthwhile story *portraying* bigotry, *not* for the purpose of *promoting* it, but to remind our readers that it not only has existed in the past, but it exists in even more insidious forms today. Human beings have a history of becoming extremely touchy about issues when their own views on them are the most suspect. On the subject of censorship, George Bernard Shaw once said, 'A nation's morals are like its teeth; the more decayed they are, the more it hurts to touch them." I am of the opinion that no issue is sacred, and to "touch" an issue is only dangerous if your readers are afraid to examine their own consciences.

Bigotry in any form is abhorrent, but so is censorship. For an editor to tell a writer not to write on a topic because the readership of the magazine might misinterpret his *characters'* thoughts and actions as *approval* of those actions is for that editor to put a straitjacket on creative thought and to lie to the very public she or he wish to entertain and, perhaps, educate. What is more frustrating, perhaps, is that the comic book industry is the last to acknowledge that *most* people will understand what you're trying to say and will respect you for it. There seems to be no subject *television* won't deal with nowadays, from child molestation to abortion to venereal disease, but because comic books are thought to be a medium strictly for children, there seem to be some taboos about what you can reasonably deal with and what you can't.

Twisted Tales states on the cover, "Recommended for Mature Readers." I don't believe that there is a mature reader in the world who would misinterpret the strong *anti-racist* stance of "Banjo Lessons" as advocating bigotry simply because some of the characters in it are bigots. The first time I read this story, in script form, I felt it was one of the strongest and best written pieces I have ever read on the well-known ability of human beings to rationalize any action, especially when it involves the treatment of other human beings as *objects*. For when you come right down to it, that seems to be the very definition of bigotry: the ability to disregard the humanity of another human being and treat him or her as an object. Witness the Holocaust, or the incredible Klu Klux Klan lynchings, or any of the thousands of rapes that take place daily. As long as we are able to disregard the humanity of *any* human being, bigotry will flourish. If "Banjo Lessons" is a painful reminder of this, it has, for this editor, accomplished its purpose.

April Campbell
Editor

Above: Editorial inserted into the inside front cover of *Twisted Tales* #5 [Oct. 1983], regarding "Banjo Lessons." **Below:** Blackthorne Publishing released a collection of Jones prose tales in 1987.

BRUCE JONES
TWISTED
TALES

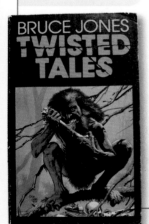

THE TROUBLE WITH 'BANJO LESSONS'

Years after Jones expressed his pride with the *Twisted Tales* #5 story, interviewer Arndt described "Banjo Lessons" to its author as an attempt at an EC *Shock SuspenStories*-style tale and asked whether it was a mistake to include an inside front cover editorial in that issue defending the story before anyone had a chance to read it. Jones responded, "Actually I did everything I could to avoid writing EC-type stories, as I knew the comparisons were likely inevitable. Every time someone mentioned how our stories were like the old EC material, I just rolled my eyes and walked away. I wasn't interested in nostalgia. I saw *Twisted* and *Alien* and our other books as a way to continue the kind of adult-oriented stories I'd been doing all along. Sounds crazy, but I really wanted adults to read comics, too. If it came off as pandering, it wasn't intentional."[55]

Then, about the controversial story itself, Jones said, "That was quite a little adventure — actually quite a headache. After I wrote 'Banjo Lessons' (in long hand in those days) I handed it to April and she said, 'This is one of the best things you've ever written.' I thought no more of it until Steve Schanes called. He said 'Uhh, we have to talk.' His parents helped fund the company and his mother, at least, was offended by some of the elements in 'Banjo Lessons.' To this day, I don't know how anyone could find the least racist thing about the story. But Steve wanted some kind of editorial to appear after the story assuring readers we weren't the KKK and to also eliminate the last panel showing the rednecks cooking the Black guy. I thought doing either would both ruin the plot and make us appear defensive.

"I finally elected to pull the story. I think it was April who insisted, 'Don't throw out the baby with the bathwater.' She suggested moving the editorial to the front of the book to look more like our regular letters page and less like a clumsy apology. I agreed. For all I knew, people weren't even reading the letters page. I think she also came up with the idea of putting a dark Zip-A-Tone dot pattern over the last panel to lessen (cloak) the visual impact. I agreed to that, too. Problem was, the heavy-handed dot pattern of Zip-A-Tone called attention to itself and made the art look even more salacious than everyone was worried about. I think I talked to Steve and tore the Zip-A-Tone off the art at the last minute. I don't recall. We weren't really obligated to answer to Pacific contractually, but they'd been good to us and kept their word up to then about a hands-off approach regarding our books, and I didn't want to create a climate of mistrust or hard feelings. Pacific and Warren (under Louise Jones) were the two most freely creative places I ever worked and I appreciated the freedom, believe me. Anyway, there was little gray area among readers when it came to their reaction to the published story. People either derided it out of hand or applauded our efforts at pushing the envelope. I never promised anyone *Twisted Tales* would be a pleasant read, just an entertaining and sometimes (hopefully) an insightful one. I mean, what the hell was I apologizing about? It was a horror comic. Personally, I'm just glad 'Banjo Lessons' saw the light of day. In some ways, it made up for all that hard work on *Dime Novel* and *Vampira* that never did come out except as promotional ads or brochures. Those two books were some of the best unfinished work I ever did. Kind of a shame."[56]

Besides Jones' often gripping and usually excellent scripts (sometimes illustrated with his own artwork), his anthology titles boasted some of the industry's finest delineators, including pros Corben, Williamson, Wrightson, Doug Wildey, Mike Ploog, and Frank Brunner, as well as the artist of "Banjo Lessons," Rand Holmes. Sometimes said artists' behavior could be less than professional, as David Scroggy recalled. "Bruce Jones and April Campbell Jones were the sole editors and packagers of their titles: *Twisted Tales, Alien Worlds, Somerset Holmes, Silverheels,* and the sadly short-lived *Pathways to Fantasy.* Steve Schanes worked with them on certain production issues and color separation, but other than that, the comics were edited 100% by Bruce and April without any editorial contribution from Pacific, other than occasionally suggesting creative talent when Bruce was stuck for an artist and the deadline loomed.

"I did help Bruce once on an editorial matter. Bruce had hired the great underground comix artist Rand Holmes as a contributor. I had worked with Holmes earlier on *The Portfolio of Underground Art*, so was able to help bring them together initially. After that, it was only Bruce and Rand creating his stories. I forget the specifics of the situation, but Bruce was, as usual, up against his deadline, and urgently needed to contact Rand Holmes, who did not have a telephone. Of course, this was in the pre-internet days, so what might normally be an inconvenience was a crisis. Holmes lived on Lasqueti Island, a tiny place situated off the eastern coast of Vancouver Island, in Canada's Georgia Strait. It was a very small place, with fewer than 500 inhabitants. Facing an apoplectic Bruce Jones, I came up with an idea. Using directory assistance, I located a general store on Lasqueti Island, and rang them up. I explained to the person who answered that I was calling from San Diego, and urgently needed to reach artist Rand Holmes. Might they possibly know him? 'Oh yeah… he stops in here,' was the reply. I said that Bruce Jones was desperately trying to reach him and gave them Bruce's number to pass along to Rand. They said they would. And they did! Bruce phoned me later that day; he had talked to Rand, and his problem was solved. I don't know if that qualifies as editorial input to most people, but it does in my book."[57]

Bruce Jones also enlisted the work of a number of young artists new to the field, including Dave Stevens, William Wray, Ken Steacy, Thomas Yeates, Scott and Bo Hampton, and one total newbie who, soon enough, would take the industry by storm. "I still recall being at the Pacific Comics table at an early San Diego Con," David Scroggy shared, "when this tall, skinny kid with long hair came up with his art portfolio, and showed it to us. After we picked ourselves up from the floor, we asked if we could maybe publish his stuff. Starting tomorrow would be fine. He said, in an 'aw, shucks' sort of way, that Marvel had just hired him to do a book called *Longshot*. Undaunted, Bruce Jones got him to squeeze in a five-pager for *Three Dimensional Alien Worlds*, which I think was the first widely-seen Art Adams work. The rest, of course, is history."[58]

PC
"For the NEW Era in Comics"
$1.50 US
$2.00 Canada
PLOOG
CONRAD
MAVERIK
HOLMES
Twisted
Tales
NO.2
BERNI WRIGHTSON 1982

Above: Bernie Wrightson contributed this cover for *Twisted Tales* #2 [Apr. 1983]. The artist had been, of course, a frequent collaborator with Bruce Jones in the 1970s, when they memorably worked together on Warren's horror mags.

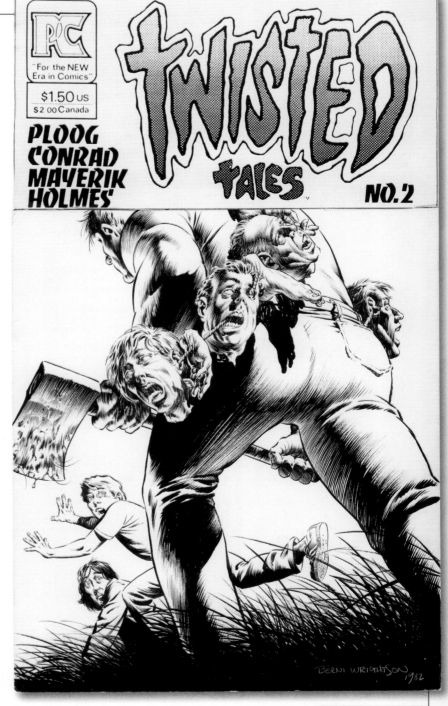

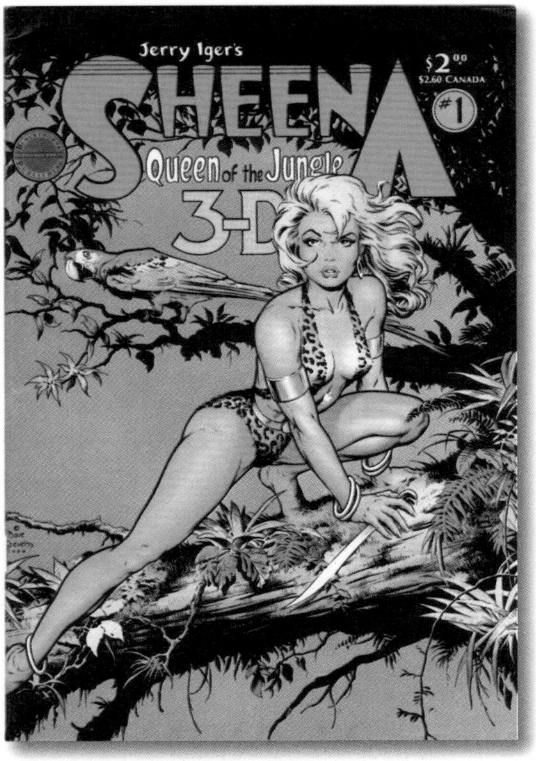
Jerry Iger's
SHEENA
Queen of the Jungle
3-D
$2.00
$2.60 CANADA
#1

COVER BOY

Dave Stevens explained to Jon B. Cooke about becoming the premiere cover artist in the independent comics scene. "That just followed a course already set in place before Pacific went under," the artist said. "I guess it started when [*editor*] Bruce Jones had come on board and was producing *Alien Worlds.* He was only two issues in and some artist had just flaked on him for 12 pages. He had seen 'Aurora' and asked if he could use it in a pinch. So, I let him doctor it and rescript it. And I created a new cover for [*Alien Worlds* #2, May 1983]."[59]

The story behind "Aurora," which was Stevens' first comic book effort, goes back to 1977, when Sanrio Films, a Japanese studio, was looking to get into publishing. Stevens told Diana Schutz, "At the time, they were trying to put together a magazine that would rival *Heavy Metal**… so they thought they wanted to do that, but only in Japan. They wanted to get together a bunch of West Coast artists or 'American' artists, and then put them together in one big book… a lot of the characters were female heroes rather than men, which I thought was real interesting. They seemed to be gearing it to a female audience."[60]

Stevens told Cooke, "The rights had reverted to me a couple of years earlier, but I had no plans to ever run it in the States. I thought it was pretty stiff, stilted." The artist grew to regret the Bruce Jones rewrite. "At this point, looking back at it, I probably should have just left it alone. Not that he did anything wrong; it was just a completely different tone. Anyway, when it came out, apparently the cover really sold the issue, so they asked me to do the next cover as well, and ink the feature story [*Alien Worlds* #4, Sept. 1983], 'Princess Pam.' After that, I sort of became the 'cover guy.' Whatever titles they had that really needed a good launch, I did the cover art for."[61]

This spread: Clockwise from above is published version of Dave Stevens' cover art that went missing, *Sheena 3-D Special* [1985]; William Stout's original color art, *Alien Worlds* #3 [July 1983]; Stevens' *Alien Worlds* #2 [May 1983] cover art; and Stevens portrait by Greg Preston.

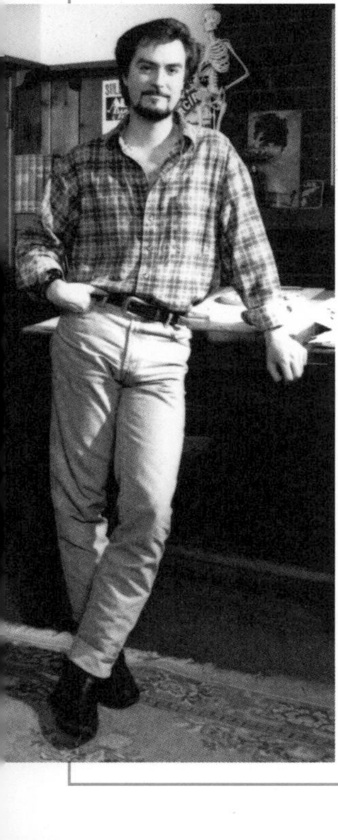

* Writer Mark Evanier, who worked on the project, recalled, "[*Sanrio*] might have been thinking more about competing with *Métal Hurlant* than its American version."[62]

The cover rate, Stevens estimated, was, "Somewhere between $300 and $500 for an inked drawing. So I kept doing covers, along with my own feature. By the summer of 1984, they wanted cover art for a *Sheena 3-D* book and, although nobody knew it at the time, the company would be bankrupt within a couple of months. I remember I had just finished the last issue of 'The Rocketeer,' handed it in, then did the *Sheena* cover. And I waited and never heard anything. So I called and reminded them I hadn't gotten the original art back yet. There was a hesitation on the other end of the line and it turned out that the original had 'disappeared' from the offices the day it was shot, and it's never been seen since. Someone there had decided to take home a bonus!

"Boy, that one hurt. I was crushed, because I felt it was my best work to date, and I didn't even have a negative of it. Anyway, they did a quick fade right after that; within a matter of weeks, they were basically gone as a publishing entity. So, even though I did a lot of covers for Eclipse, Pacific was really the starting point for all that. I had no idea that I'd be any good as a cover artist or that anyone would want to see me drawing girls before then. What a concept!"[63]

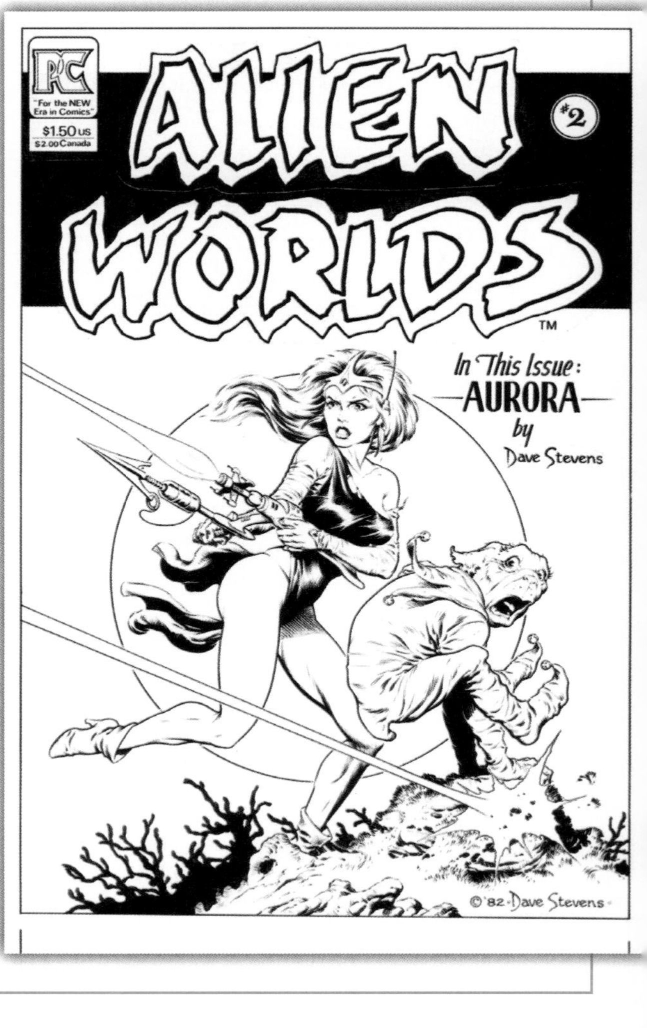
PC
"For the NEW Era in Comics"
$1.50 US
$2.00 Canada
ALIEN WORLDS
#2
TM
In This Issue:
AURORA
by
Dave Stevens
©'82 Dave Stevens

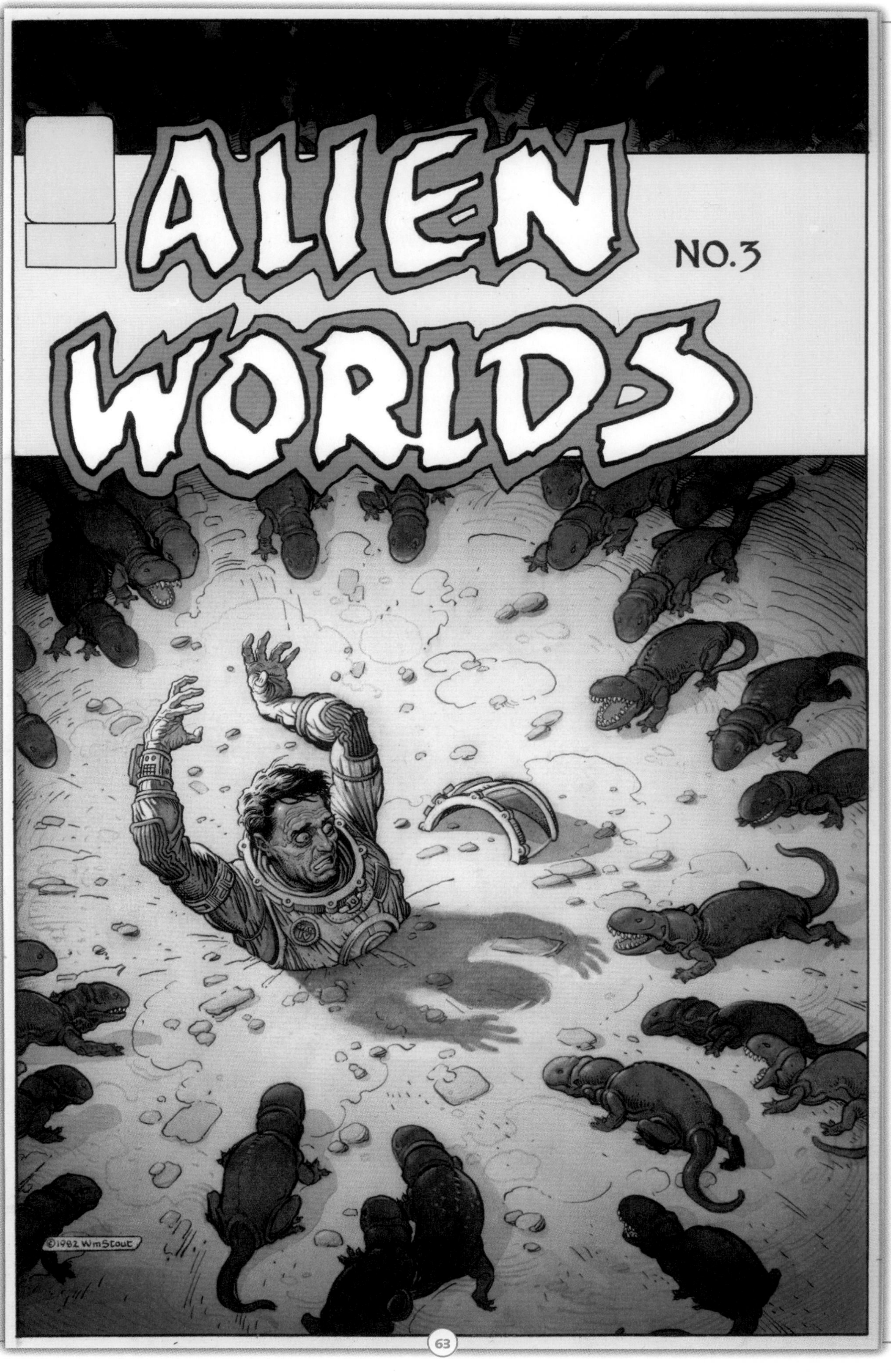
ALIEN WORLDS
NO.3
©1982 Wm Stout

Inset right: One of Arthur Adams' earliest pro jobs resulted from the Pacific crew meeting Adams at the San Diego Comic-Con, where he was recruited to contribute to *Three Dimensional Alien Worlds* #1 [1984]. This page was scanned omitting the 3-D effect. **Below:** The legendary Doug Wildey illustrated and colored "Off Key," for *Twisted Tales* #3 [June 1983]. **Next page:** Dave Stevens actually drew this story in 1977, years before it appeared in *Alien Worlds* #2 [May 1983].

BEHIND THE CURTAIN

Bruce Jones talked to Arndt about production realities of compiling the comics for Pacific. "It's just about impossible to think up these stories, then commit them to paper, then get the artwork back on them, then see them colored and published (pant-pant), and *still* retain any kind of distance from them. If readers went through in reading what we went through in creating and manufacturing the comics, it would kill all the fun. Happily, it doesn't work that way. They don't have to get exposed to all the frustrations and time limits and egos of production. But readers also don't see the disappointment when, for whatever reasons, something you've slaved over and nurtured and think is really exceptional just doesn't live up to expectations on the printed page, no matter what you do. This happens more often than we like to admit.

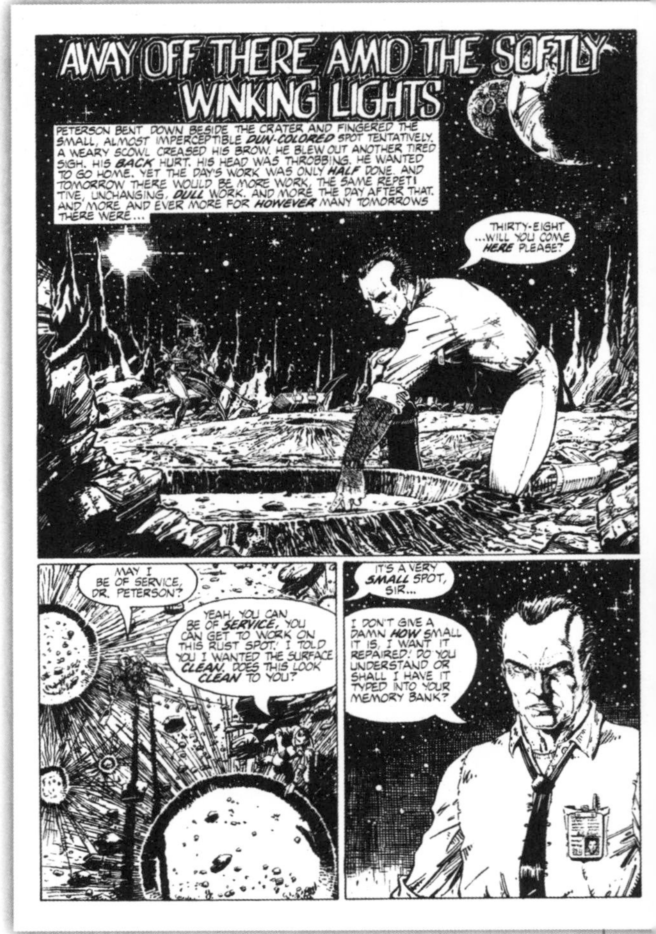
AWAY OFF THERE AMID THE SOFTLY WINKING LIGHTS
PETERSON BENT DOWN BESIDE THE CRATER AND FINGERED THE SMALL, ALMOST IMPERCEPTIBLE DUN-COLORED SPOT TENTATIVELY. A WEARY SCOWL CREASED HIS BROW. HE BLEW OUT ANOTHER TIRED SIGH. HIS BACK HURT. HIS HEAD WAS THROBBING. HE WANTED TO GO HOME. YET THE DAY'S WORK WAS ONLY HALF DONE. AND TOMORROW THERE WOULD BE MORE WORK, THE SAME REPETITIVE, UNCHANGING, DULL WORK. AND MORE THE DAY AFTER THAT. AND MORE AND EVER MORE FOR HOWEVER MANY TOMORROWS THERE WERE...
THIRTY-EIGHT ...WILL YOU COME HERE PLEASE?
MAY I BE OF SERVICE, DR. PETERSON?
YEAH, YOU CAN BE OF SERVICE. YOU CAN GET TO WORK ON THIS RUST SPOT. I TOLD YOU I WANTED THE SURFACE CLEAN. DOES THIS LOOK CLEAN TO YOU?
IT'S A VERY SMALL SPOT, SIR...
I DON'T GIVE A DAMN HOW SMALL IT IS. I WANT IT REPAIRED! DO YOU UNDERSTAND OR SHALL I HAVE IT TYPED INTO YOUR MEMORY BANK?

"It's collaborative like movies and TV — you can't be everywhere at once, oversee every line and nuance. You just have to live with it and move on to the next thing. Comics and movies and even novels are like trying to control your dreams. You can look like you are, to a point, but ultimately, like your children, they go *their* way. In reality, there is no control. I think knowing this and secretly loathing it is the reason most writers write — to keep trying to exercise a control they don't find in real life — but with something that just won't acquiesce. It's like nailing Jello to a tree. But we keep doing it anyway. We keep doing it. It really makes much more sense to sell insurance for a living."[64]

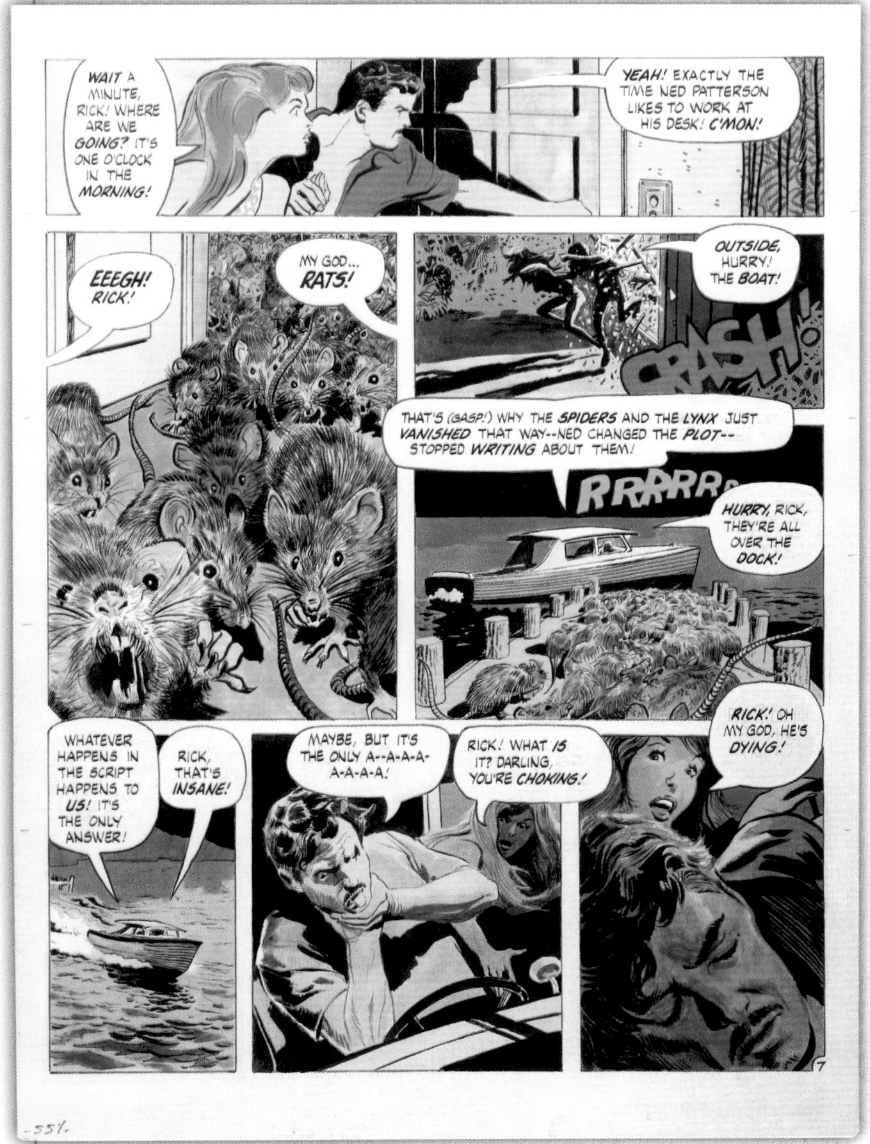
WAIT A MINUTE, RICK! WHERE ARE WE GOING? IT'S ONE O'CLOCK IN THE MORNING!
YEAH! EXACTLY THE TIME NED PATTERSON LIKES TO WORK AT HIS DESK! C'MON!
EEEGH! RICK!
MY GOD... RATS!
OUTSIDE, HURRY! THE BOAT!
CRASH!
THAT'S (GASP!) WHY THE SPIDERS AND THE LYNX JUST VANISHED THAT WAY--NED CHANGED THE PLOT--STOPPED WRITING ABOUT THEM!
RRRRR
HURRY, RICK, THEY'RE ALL OVER THE DOCK!
WHATEVER HAPPENS IN THE SCRIPT HAPPENS TO US! IT'S THE ONLY ANSWER!
RICK, THAT'S INSANE!
MAYBE, BUT IT'S THE ONLY A--A-A-A-A-A-A-A!
RICK! WHAT IS IT? DARLING, YOU'RE CHOKING!
RICK! OH MY GOD, HE'S DYING!
7

Jones shared about a gimmicky one-shot published at the end of his tenure, the same publication to which he enticed young Art Adams to contribute. "*Three Dimensional Alien Worlds* took longer to produce than the average issue, so we had to slot it in when it was finally done, hence the 'special.' But I think [*3-D process expert*] Ray Zone did an exceptional job with the 3-D conversion and some of the artists really took full advantage of the format. It's generally the most sought after Pacific title we did."[65]

AURORA
AND PLAY THEY DID, WHILE THE SHIMMERING APPARITION ABOVE THEM WHEELED AND DIPPED AND SPUN--
--AND UNLEASHED SUDDEN SHRIEKING DEATH!
A MOMENT OF STUNNED, SHOCKED SILENCE... THEN--
SEIZE HER! KILL HER, YOU IDIOTS! SHE'S SLAIN A HIGH PRIEST!
©1977 Dave Stevens
SCRIPT: BRUCE JONES STORY AND ART: DAVE STEVENS
Colors: Steve Oliff Letters: Carrie McCarthy
THE SHIP! WHERE DID UNK PUT THE SHIP?
FIND HER! KILL HER! I WANT HER HEAD, DO YOU HEAR ME? I WANT HER SKINNED ALIVE!
CALMLY, EFFICIENTLY, THE GOLDEN-HAIRED BEAUTY SLIPS INTO MORE PRACTICAL ATTIRE--ONE EYE GLUED TO THE HEAVING UNDERBRUSH...
...AND SILENT AS A SHADOW SLIPS IN BESIDE HER WAITING COMPANION...
HI! MISS ME?
SORRY, UNK! I KNOW YOU HATE WAITING IN THE DARK, BUT MY AUDIENCE JUST COULDN'T BEAR TO SEE ME GO!
SO LONG, FELLAS! IT WAS FUN! EVEN IF THAT FLUTE-PLAYER WAS OFF-KEY!

"WE'RE NOT LAST GASP COMICS HERE"

Jones told Kim Thompson in 1986 of his frustrations working with certain artists. "I'm proud of the books for the most part. But it is very hard to take chances and to do stories where you feel like you're stretching yourself, particularly when you're working with an artist who simply doesn't understand what you're going for… [M]ost of the time, it's simply the artist not having any idea — either having not any idea of what you're talking about or, more precisely, not caring. And I was *constantly* getting this with *Twisted Tales*. I would suggest the most tastefully polite bedroom scene or nude scene and *invariably* I would get stuff back that was unprintable! Because we were essentially R-rated comics, these artists would vent their spleens and I would get gigantic bazooms and penetration shots, stuff you wouldn't *believe*. In as many cases as I could, I would send that stuff back, and say, 'My god, give me a break, how in the world can we publish this stuff. You must be joking. We're not Last Gasp Comics here. We have a certain ethic to maintain.' I would get that stuff redrawn, but invariably the artist who would do that to me would be the wildest, the most spaced-out, and the latest.

"I used to live in constant fear because we had no backlog; none. We were going from moment to moment to moment, from minute to minute. Anything that was late was a disaster."

Threatening the company's survival, Jones said in 1986, "was that Pacific couldn't afford to miss a single issue. The comics-buying public — and, in fact, even people working for the bigger companies — don't realize and can't imagine that the smaller independent companies *must not* miss an issue. I mean, they *can* occasionally be late, they occasionally do it, but they can never do it without being hurt very badly… It was extremely true of Pacific. We just couldn't afford to be late and, toward the end, we were always late. Had we not been late toward the end — and when I say 'we' collectively, I'm being generous because I'd like to think it was not my fault; I was scrupulous about getting my issues in on time because I knew where my bread and butter was coming from.

"It was mostly the fault of the artists, several key artists who are friends of mine and so I don't want to talk about them. But had we not been late with those issues, Pacific unquestionably would have gone on longer than they went and might indeed have survived. They simply ran into a cash-flow problem that became so compounded they eventually went under. That is really sad. I know the same thing could be happening to Eclipse today, if Eclipse weren't in a situation where their overhead is so unbelievably low; that wasn't true of Pacific. You have to remember that Pacific was a distribution company and a

Geo. WASHINGTON
JOHN ADAMS
THOS. JEFFERSON
JAMES MADISON
JAMES MONROE
JOHN QUINCY ADAMS
ANDREW JACKSON
MARTIN VAN BUREN
WM. H. HARRISON
JOHN TYLER
JAMES K. POLK
ZACHARY TAYLOR
MILLARD FILLMORE
FRANKLIN PIERCE
JAMES BUCHANAN
ABRAHAM LINCOLN
ANDREW JOHNSON
ULYSSES S. GRANT
RUTHERFORD B. HAYES
JAMES A. GARFIELD
CHESTER A. ARTHUR
GROVER CLEVELAND
BENJ. HARRISON
WM. McKINLEY
THEO. ROOSEVELT
WM. H. TAFT
WOODROW WILSON
WARREN G. HARDING
CALVIN COOLIDGE
HERBERT C. HOOVER
FRANKLIN D. ROOSEVELT
HARRY S TRUMAN
DWIGHT D. EISENHOWER
JOHN F. KENNEDY
LYNDON B. JOHNSON
RICHARD M. NIXON
GERALD R. FORD
JAMES E. CARTER
RONALD W. REAGAN
THE PRESIDENTS OF THE UNITED STATES ©1982 RICK GEARY SAN DIEGO CALIFORNIA

Above: Rick Geary's brilliant, if nonsensical, back cover for *Wild Animals* #1 [Dec. 1982]. **Below:** Detail from *Wild Animals* #1's cover featuring Scott Shaw!'s ape naturalist.

FEATURING THE RETURN OF
YOU-ALL GIBBON
the JUNK-FOOD MONKEY!

publishing company second, so when they began to plow some of their distribution money into their publishing, the publishing company had, at all times, to remain solvent and there, towards the end, it just didn't. The only way it could remain solvent was if it produced its issues on time. That's *abso-lute-ly* imperative for a small house. You *have* to get the issues out and they have to sell a certain amount. They almost always will sell enough, but only if they get out there, and get out there with regularity; that's the key to running a small company. That was one of the main factors that killed Pacific Comics."[66]

Before the comic book imprint's demise, Jones and Campbell's peak at Pacific Comics lay ahead, with their greatest collaboration as a team — which included artist Brent Anderson — a crime thriller set for release in 1983 about an amnesia victim.

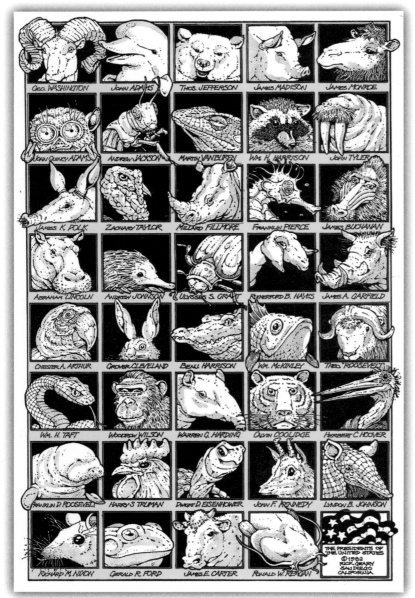

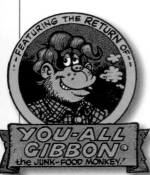

ANIMALS GONE WILD

As mentioned, cartoonist and San Diegan Scott Shaw! drew for the Pacific Comics ads and catalogues, so, when the Schanes brothers needed some help, they gave the chummy humorist a call. Shaw! told the author, "Sergio Aragonés and I were planning to publish *Wild Animals* together, but divorces soaked up all our funds. The material sat in a drawer for a few years — some of my pages still needed to be fully inked and I had yet to come up with a cover — until someone from Pacific Comics contacted me out of the blue. I think it was Steve Schanes, who told me that they printed their titles four at a time, and that, for some reason or another, one of the planned books had suddenly dropped out. Steve asked if I had anything laying around that PC could fill their slot with. I suggested *Wild Animals* and Steve immediately jumped on it."[67]

Interestingly, the lead story of the issue — *Wild Animals* did not last beyond #1 — was the conclusion of a You-All Gibbons two-parter, delayed since *Quack* #4 [June 1977]. (A terse editor's note in *Quack* #6 [Dec. '77] implied an acrimonious falling out between Shaw! and Star*Reach publisher Mike Friedrich, who added, "At last word, Scott is editing a funny animal magazine called *Wild Animals* for Krupp Comics [Kitchen Sink Press] in Wisconsin, so we'll see his animal creations elsewhere."[68]

"I designed the cover to look like an animation cel and background," Shaw! said, "and hired a guy named Richard Lester to finish inking my You-All Gibbon story, 'The Land That Time Ignored!' Mark Evanier suggested that *Groo the Wanderer* colorist Gordon Kent would be a good fit since he was between *Groo* issues. Pacific Comics — probably Dave Scroggy — got Los Angeles' Richard Hescox to paint the cover's background and someone else to transfer and paint my inked characters on a cel. I had no input on any of that, because the print-day was breathing down PC's collective breath."[69]

As for the other contributors, Shaw! explained, "I was already friends with Gordon Kent, who I met in 1976 when I was managing the American Comic Book Company, in Studio City, and later, in the animation industry; Jim Engel, a Chicago cartoonist who I met at the 1975 San Diego Comic-Con and became my instant pal; Sergio, of course, who I met at the 1972 San Diego Comic-Con, the first one held at the El Cortez; Brian Narelle, a San Diego cartoonist, actor — 1974's *Dark Star* — and puppeteer; and Rick Geary, who'd moved to San Diego a few years earlier, creating his first comic book story for my *Fear and*

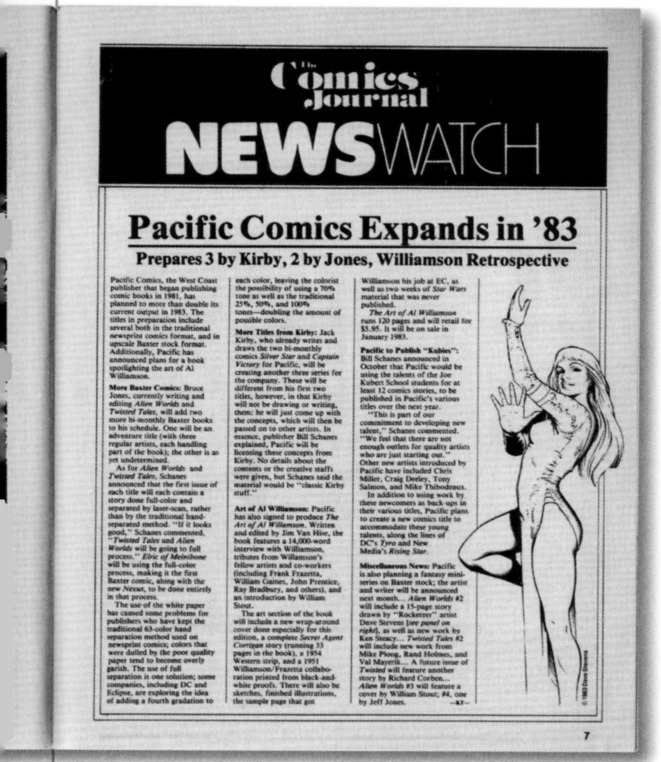

The Comics Journal

NEWSWATCH

Pacific Comics Expands in '83

Prepares 3 by Kirby, 2 by Jones, Williamson Retrospective

Pacific Comics, the West Coast publisher that began publishing comic books in 1981, has planned to more than double its current output in 1983. The titles in preparation include several both in the traditional newsprint comics format, and in upscale Baxter stock format. Additionally, Pacific has announced plans for a book spotlighting the art of Al Williamson.

More Baxter Comics: Bruce Jones, currently writing and editing *Alien Worlds* and *Twisted Tales*, will add two more bi-monthly Baxter books to his schedule. One will be an adventure title (with three regular artists, each handling part of the book); the other is as yet undetermined.

As for *Alien Worlds* and *Twisted Tales*, Schanes announced that the first issue of each title will each contain a story done full-color and separated by laser-scan, rather than by the traditional hand-separated method. "If it looks good," Schanes commented, "*Twisted Tales* and *Alien Worlds* will be going to full process." *Elric of Melnibone* will be using the full-color process, making it the first Baxter comic, along with the new *Nexus*, to be done entirely in that process.

The use of the white paper has caused some problems for publishers who have kept the traditional 63-color hand separation method used on newsprint comics; colors that were dulled by the poor quality paper tend to become overly garish. The use of full separation is one solution; some companies, including DC and Eclipse, are exploring the idea of adding a fourth gradation to each color, leaving the colorist the possibility of using a 70% tone as well as the traditional 25%, 50%, and 100% tones—doubling the amount of possible colors.

More Titles from Kirby: Jack Kirby, who already writes and draws the two bi-monthly comics *Silver Star* and *Captain Victory* for Pacific, will be creating another three series for the company. These will be different from his first two titles, however, in that Kirby will not be drawing or writing, them: he will just come up with the concepts, which will then be passed on to other artists. In essence, publisher Bill Schanes explained, Pacific will be licensing these concepts from Kirby. No details about the contents or the creative staffs were given, but Schanes said the material would be "classic Kirby stuff."

Art of Al Williamson: Pacific has also signed to produce *The Art of Al Willamson*. Written and edited by Jim Van Hise, the book features a 14,000-word interview with Williamson, tributes from Willamson's fellow artists and co-workers (including Frank Frazetta, William Gaines, John Prentice, Ray Bradbury, and others), and an introduction by William Stout.

The art section of the book will include a new wrap-around cover done especially for this edition, a complete *Secret Agent Corrigan* story (running 33 pages in the book), a 1954 Western strip, and a 1951 Williamson/Frazetta collaboration printed from black-and-white proofs. There will also be sketches, finished illustrations, the sample page that got Williamson his job at EC, as well as two weeks of *Star Wars* material that was never published.

The Art of Al Williamson runs 120 pages and will retail for $5.95. It will be on sale in January 1983.

Pacific to Publish "Kubies": Bill Schanes announced in October that Pacific would be using the talents of the Joe Kubert School students for at least 12 comics stories, to be published in Pacific's various titles over the next year.

"This is part of our commitment to developing new talent," Schanes commented. "We feel that there are not enough outlets for quality artists who are just starting out." Other new artists introduced by Pacific have included Chris Miller, Craig Deeley, Tony Salmon, and Mike Thibodeaux.

In addition to using work by these newcomers as back-ups in their various titles, Pacific plans to create a new comics title to accommodate these young talents, along the lines of DC's *Tyro* and New Media's *Rising Star*.

Miscellaneous News: Pacific is also planning a fantasy mini-series on Baxter stock; the artist and writer will be announced next month... *Alien Worlds* #2 will include a 15-page story drawn by "Rocketeer" artist Dave Stevens [*see panel on right*], as well as new work by Ken Steacy... *Twisted Tales* #2 will include new work from Mike Ploog, Rand Holmes, and Val Mayerik... A future issue of *Twisted* will feature another story by Richard Corben... *Alien Worlds* #3 will feature a cover by William Stout; #4, one by Jeff Jones. —KT—

7

Laughter underground comix, for Kitchen Sink, in 1977. I didn't know George Erling personally, but I liked his work in fanzines at the time — he's now a popular magazine gag cartoonist — and I already loved Larry Gonick's dinosaurs in his *The Cartoon History of the Universe* when he got wind of the project and contacted me. We've never interacted since, but I still love his work."

Shaw! continued, "I don't recall who I handed the pages over to, or sent to, but I think it's likely that I drove from Van Nuys to San Diego to deliver the work in person." The cartoonist then added, "I swiped the comic's logo from a Topps candy box that San Diego cartoonist John Pound and I found in a dime store near our high school in 1967, drawn and lettered by the great Wallace Wood. The little cardboard box, designed to resemble a zoo cage housing a maniacal gorilla, contained some stale taffy and a cheap gumball machine toy. It was called 'Wild Animals' and John and I loved it."[70]

THE DUCK MAN COMETH (NOT)

David Scroggy revealed that he asked the most celebrated of all funny animal comic book artists to join the team. "When I was editorial director of Pacific Comics," he shared, "I wrote Carl Barks, explained our then-new creator ownership deal, and asked him if he would like to contribute a comic or two to our line. What chutzpah. But hey, we had succeeded in enlisting Jack Kirby, Steve Ditko, and Neal Adams, so why not? Carl replied with a lovely letter, which I still have, gently-but-respectfully turning us down. He remarked that, given the then-current comics he was seeing, anything he would come up with would be 'as out of place as a fringed surrey in an automobile showroom.' I thanked him anyway and have come to realize that if anybody asked me to work on today's comic books, I might have to write them a similar letter myself."[71]

EXPANSION YEAR

In their Dec. 1982 issue, *The Comics Journal* led its "Newswatch" section with good news headlined, "Pacific Comics Expands in '83," reporting that the company "planned to more than double its current output in 1983," announcing an upgrading of paper stock, and plans for a book spotlighting artist Al Williamson.[72]

A particular intriguing item in the full-page article by Kim Thompson involved the King: "Jack Kirby, who already writes and draws the two bi-monthly comics, *Silver Star* and *Captain Victory* for Pacific, will be creating another three series for the company. These will be different from his first two titles, however, in that Kirby will not be drawing or writing them: he will just come up with the concepts, which will then be passed on to other artists. In essence, publisher Bill Schanes explained, Pacific will be licensing these concepts from Kirby. No details about the contents or the creative staffs were given, but Schanes said the material would be 'classic Kirby stuff.'"[73]

Competition was getting heavy into the new year, with First Comics making the scene with *Warp* #1 being released in November and *E-Man* #1 hitting shops in mid-December. Eclipse began its color line the previous spring, with *Sabre* #1. The fight for rack space by independent publishers in the direct market was just heating up!

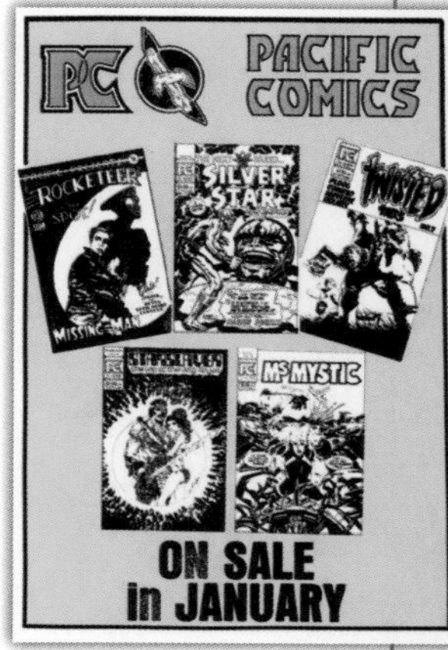
PC
PACIFIC COMICS
ROCKETEER
SILVER STAR
TWISTED
MS. MYSTIC
ON SALE
in JANUARY

Above: This promotional ad featuring the inaugural release for 1983 included *Ms. Mystic* #2, which actually wouldn't appear until a year later, in Jan. 1984. **Inset left:** Pacific's ambitious plans for 1983 headlined *The Comics Journal* #78 [Dec. 1982] "Newswatch" section. **Below:** Jack and Roz Kirby at a signing during the artist's Pacific years. Note the imprint's titles on the stands.

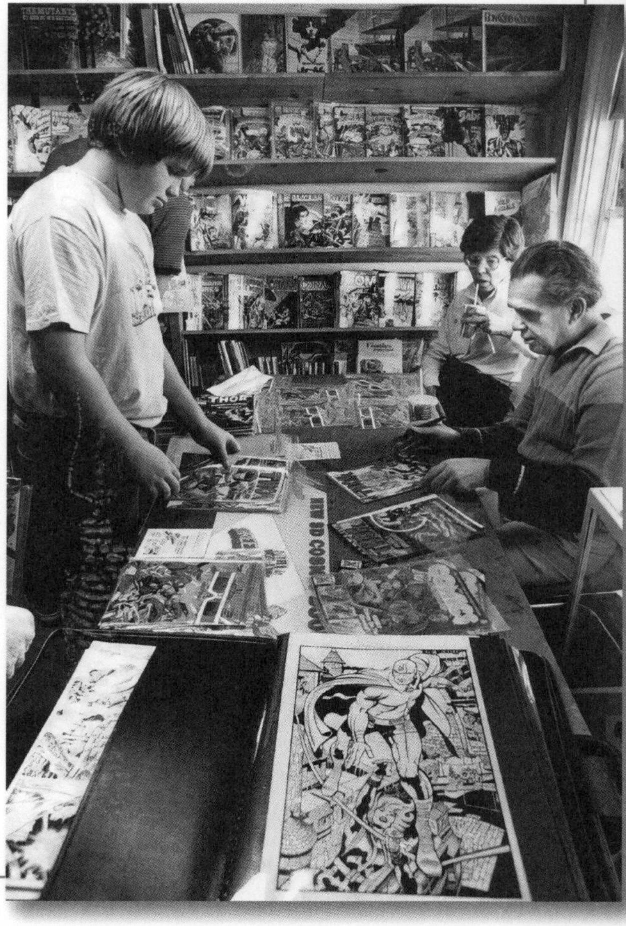

In the New Age of Comic Book Color

Next page: David Scroggy shares here the interesting fate of *Seven Samuroid*, Frank Brunner's graphic novel that ended up being used by Pacific to pay off a substantial debt owed to a vendor.

Christopher Lawrence, in his book *The Art of Painted Comics* [2016, Dynamite], put the achievements of the San Diego comic book publishing company in perspective regarding production advances made in the industry.

"It could be done," Lawrence wrote. "Painted sequential stories *could* be published in comic book format, they *could* be produced regularly, and they *could* be profitable.

"Credit for that discovery — the earliest evidence to support such claims — belongs neither to DC Comics nor to Marvel, but to an early 1980s upstart publishing house owned by brothers Bill and Steve Schanes: Pacific Comics. The Schaneses' decision to use a higher quality of paper stock than that typically utilized by the comic world's 'Big Two' enabled Pacific to reproduce the work of its artists at a much higher, magazine-quality level, an ability they put to good use on titles such as *Alien Worlds* and *A Corben Special*."[74]

Steve Oliff, who would become maybe the most prolific colorist at Pacific Comics, discussed that era at his website. "Every company was exploring color on their own. No one was really happy with the old 64-color hand-separated look. A variety of styles were tried. Everyone liked full color, but the costs were too high. Flat color was still the approach as they searched for new technologies. Blueline systems were kind of mysterious, and the double print system at Marvel had been pretty well abandoned due to registration problems.

"Pacific Comics launched two Bruce Jones anthology books in 1982. *Twisted Tales* and *Alien Worlds* were modeled after the EC horror stories — short, with a trick ending. I colored the first issues of each with the understanding that they were going to be hand-separated somewhere. The first issue of *Twisted Tales* gave me the opportunity to color a Richard Corben story, which was designed to be full-color. The rest of the issue was hand-separated…

"The first issue of *Alien Worlds* was going to be

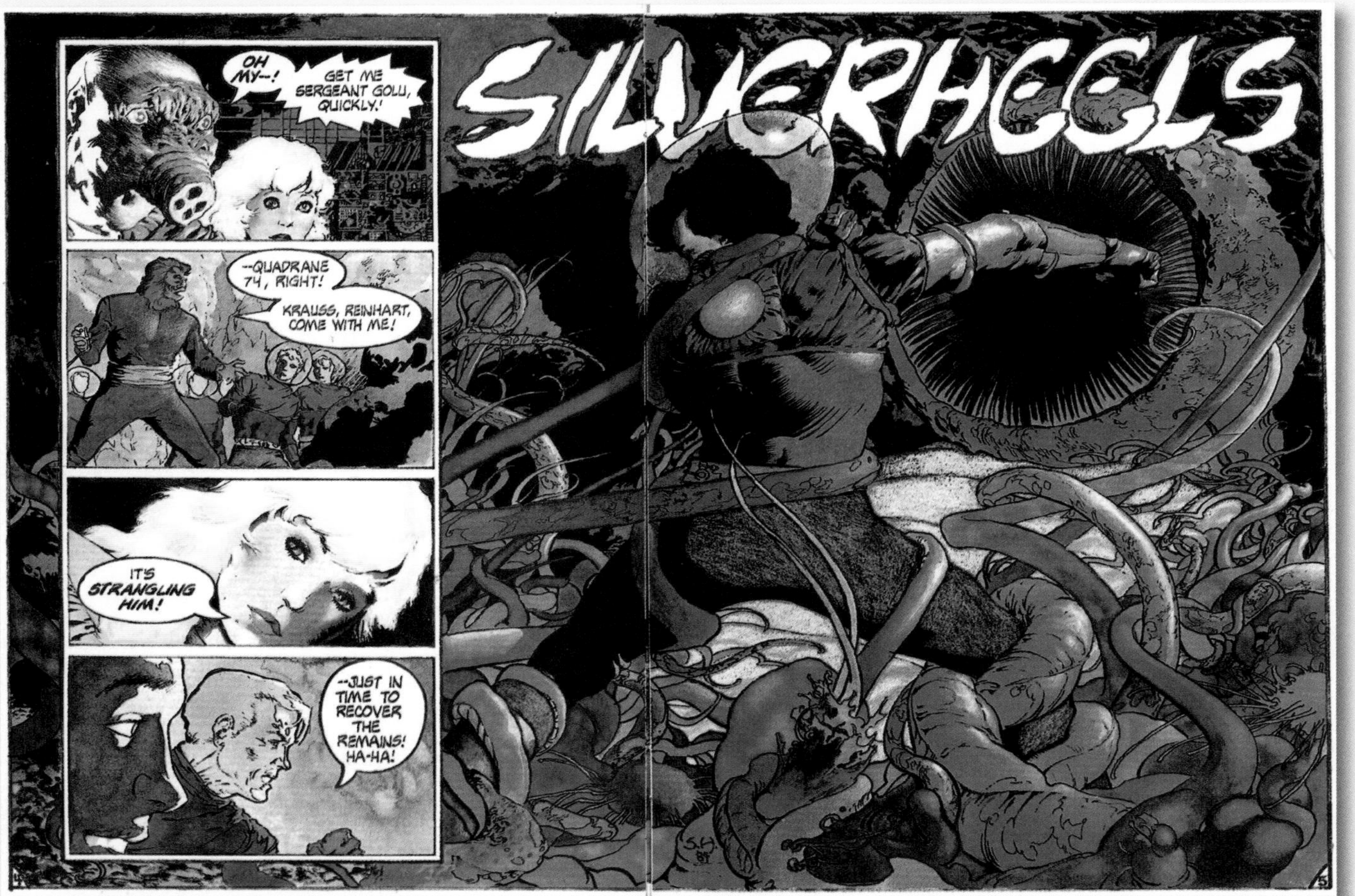
OH MY--!
GET ME SERGEANT GOLU, QUICKLY!
--QUADRANE 74, RIGHT!
KRAUSS, REINHART, COME WITH ME!
IT'S STRANGLING HIM!
--JUST IN TIME TO RECOVER THE REMAINS! HA-HA!
SILVERHEELS

Below: Striking double-page painted spread by Scott Hampton. From *Silverheels* #3 [May 1984].

all hand-separated but, at the last minute, on one Al Williamson science-fiction story, they decided to try something different. Apparently they liked my color guide so much that they took off the acetate with the [*color*] codes and shot my colors as full color. The results were great — so much so that Al sent me an original *Rip Kirby* daily strip to thank me for what he called, 'One of the best color jobs,' he'd ever gotten. It was right there that I realized how much it meant to an artist to have a colorist who enhanced his art rather than destroyed it. Too many times the color in comics has been truly wretched.

"There's an old saying in comics that: 'Bad color can ruin good art, but good color can't save bad art.'

"As a result of Al's story, both of Bruce's books began using full-color. For Pacific at that time, I was just doing full-color on Photostats. They shot the color and the black from the same art. I worked the same size as the comic, and had to make sure that I used transparent colors so I didn't mess up the line art. The separations were probably shot four pages at a time to save money. They were just developing the drumscanner technology at that time, so the pages needed to be flexible to wrap around the drum. Prior to then, I usually mounted my coloring onto illustration boards."[75]

Lawrence called the work in *Alien Worlds* "paintings easily comparable to those appearing on the pages of [*Heavy Metal* and *Epic Illustrated*]." And the author of *The Art of Painted Comics* continued, "Pacific again broke new ground in 1983, by releasing what many consider the first fully-painted comic series in the history of the American market: *Silverheels*. The three-issue story, reprinted by Eclipse as a 'color graphic album' [*with unpublished #4*] after Pacific's collapsed, featured the earliest professionally-rendered artwork by a young painter named Scott Hampton.

"The artist remembered the creation of *Silverheels* as a confluence of technology and 'the influence of *The Studio* guys on a bunch of young painters like me. I had been a big fan of Jeff Jones and Bernie Wrightson for a long time, and I had been doing a lot of paintings for my portfolio. I was tapped to do a story for *Alien Worlds* and, once I did that, they hit me up to do an ongoing series, *Silverheels*. Because I had those examples in my portfolio, it was natural enough for them to ask me to do it as a painted comic.'"[76]

Hampton also shared with Lawrence, "When Pacific, which was burning hot at the time, put out a comic book

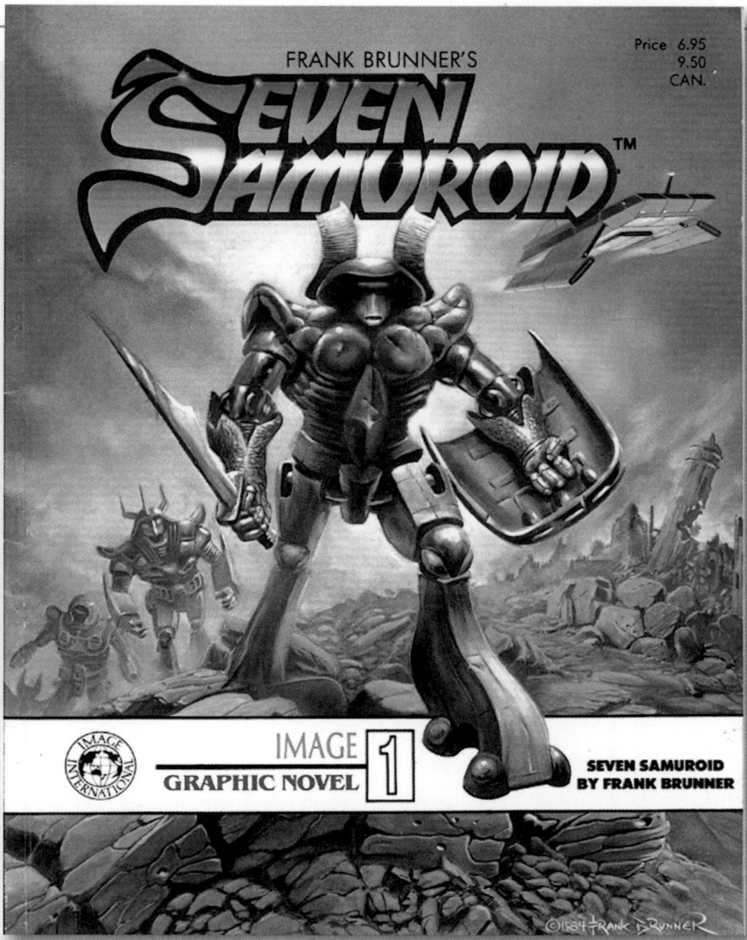
Price 6.95
9.50
CAN.
FRANK BRUNNER'S
SEVEN SAMUROID
TM
IMAGE
GRAPHIC NOVEL
1
SEVEN SAMUROID
BY FRANK BRUNNER

that was painted, it was like, people went, 'Ah-ha.' They saw this was something that could be used to put out a normal comic book, not just a special sort of album. It was eye-opening."

David Scroggy shared an anecdote about a vendor Pacific utilized. "When Pacific went down, they owed the [*New Zealand-based*] color separator company, Image International, a ton of dough. Their U.S. rep was a prince of a fellow and, against his home office's better judgment, he extended Pacific Comics' credit further than was prudent. And then extended it some more.

"When Pacific was finally throwing in the towel, they gave him an asset that had some value, since they didn't have any money. That asset was Frank Brunner's 'graphic novel,' *Seven Samuroid.* I think the finished book was 64 pages; maybe 60 pages of art and story. All by Frank Brunner with coloring by Jan Brunner. Painted color.

"They took it, grudgingly, and being a large printing concern as well as a color separator, published it under their Image International imprint. I don't think they were able to interface with the U.S. direct sales distribution network very efficiently and likely lost more money publishing it than if they had just eaten the bad debt, but it is indeed a Pacific Comic (at least sort of)."[77]

Note: Steve Oliff shared about working on *Captain Victory*: "In fall 1981, I got the job coloring Jack Kirby's *Captain Victory* and Mike Grell's *Starslayer*. It was the first time I'd tried flat, coded, hand-separated color. I had visions of doing flat color like it had never been done before by using some of the full-color tricks I'd learned… I even went so far as to add Zip-A-Tone to Jack's original art on *Captain Victory* #1 to get the added tonal values. My good intentions aside, the coloring came out dark and muddy rather than dramatic and moody… I'm afraid I really wasn't giving it the look he wanted, so he fired me. I've never really been comfortable with flat color."[78]

STRATOSPHERIC SCRIBBLINGS

Chapter Notes

[1] Mike Grell, interviewed by Dewey Cassell, *Mike Grell: Life is Drawing Without an Eraser* [TwoMorrows, 2018], pg. 71.

[2] Mike Grell, "Mike Grell, Freelance, interviewed by Jon B. Cooke, *Comic Book Artist* #8 [May 2000], pg. 104.

[3] Ibid.

[4] Mike Grell, *CBA* #8, pg. 105.

[5] Neal Adams, "Neal Adams," interviewed by Gary Groth, *The Comics Journal* #72 [May 1982], pg. 68–69.

[6] Neal Adams, "The Neal Adams Ms. Mystic Interview," interviewed (in 2015) by Shaun Clancy, *Back Issue* #94 [Feb. 2017], pgs. 2–3. This interview so incensed Michael Netzer, who felt his contributions were intentionally ignored by Adams, that Netzer waged a written counter-offensive via Facebook in 2017.

[7] Michael Netzer, "The Origin of Ms. Mystic," essay provided to Shaun Clancy [2015].

[8–13] Ibid.

[14] David Scroggy, interviewed by the author.

[15] Ibid.

[16] Ibid.

[17] Kelvin Mao, e-mail to Jon B. Cooke [Apr. 10, 2023].

[18] Dave Stevens, "Of Hollywood & Heroes," interviewed by Jon B. Cooke, *Comic Book Artist* #15 [Nov. 2001], page 22.

[19] Ibid.

[20] Stevens, *CBA* #15, pgs. 22–23.

[21] Stevens, *CBA* #15, pg. 23.

[22] David Scroggy, interviewed by the author.

[23] Ibid.

[24] Ibid.

[25] Ibid.

[26] R. Fiore, "Funnybook Roulette," reviews, *The Comics Journal* #78 [Dec. 1982], pgs 34–35.

[27] David Scroggy, interviewed by the author.

[28] Ibid.

[29] Stevens, *Telegraph Wire* #10, pg. 11.

[30] Stevens, *Telegraph Wire* #10, pg. 17.

[31] Ibid.

[32] David Scroggy, e-mail to Jon B. Cooke [Apr. 10, 2023].

[33] Sergio Aragonés, unpublished interview conducted by Jon B. Cooke [Jan. 2004].

[34] Ibid.

[35] Sergio Aragonés, "Sergio Aragonés," interviewed by Kim Thompson, *The Comics Journal* #128 [Apr. 1989], pg. 78.

[36] Mark Evanier, "Pro 2 Pro: Much Ado About Groo," interviewed by Dan Johnson, *Back Issue* #11 [Aug. 2005], pg. 2.

[37] Evanier, *Back Issue* #11, pgs. 3–4.

[38] Aragonés, unpublished interview.

[39] Ibid.

[40] Aragonés, *TCJ* #128, pg. 78.

[41] Aragonés, *TCJ* #128, pgs. 78–79.

[42] Aragonés, *TCJ* #128, pg. 79.

[43] Ibid.

[44] Aragonés, *Back Issue* #11, pg. 4.

[45] Aragonés, *TCJ* #128, pg. 79.

[46] Evanier, *Back Issue* #11, pg. 4.

[47] David Scroggy, interviewed by the author.

[48] Bruce Jones, "The Bruce Jones Touch," interviewed by Jon B. Cooke, *Comic Book Artist* V1 #4 [Spr. 1999], pg. 104.

[49] Bruce Jones, unpublished portion of *Comic Book Artist* V1 #4 interview conducted by Jon B. Cooke [Feb. 1999].

[50] Ibid.

[51] Bruce Jones, "A 2008 Interview with Bruce Jones," conducted by Richard Arndt [2008], *https://enjolrasworld. com/Richard%20Arndt/The%20 Warren%20Magazines%20Interviews. htm.*

[52] Ibid.

[53] Ibid.

[54] Bruce Jones, "Interview: Bruce Jones," interview conducted by Kim Thompson, *Amazing Heroes* #90 [Mar. 1, 1986], pg. 32.

[55] Jones, interviewed by Arndt.

[56] Ibid.

[57] David Scroggy, interviewed by the author.

[58] David Scroggy, Facebook post [Apr. 5, 2022].

[59] Stevens, *CBA* #15, pg. 26.

[60] Dave Stevens, "Rocketing to Fame: An Interview with Dave Stevens," interviewed by Diana Schutz, *The Telegraph Wire* #10 [July–Aug. 1983], pgs. 10–11.

[61] Stevens, *CBA* #15, pg. 26.

[62] Mark Evanier, e-mail to Jon B. Cooke [Apr. 9, 2023].

[63] Stevens, *CBA* #15, pgs. 26–27.

[64] Jones, interviewed by Arndt.

[65] Ibid.

[66] Jones, *AH* #90, pgs. 32–33.

[67] Scott Shaw!, interviewed by the author.

[68] Mike Friedrich, editor's note, *Quack* #6 [Dec. 1977], nn.

[69] Shaw! interview.

[70] Ibid.

[71] David Scroggy, Facebook post [Mar. 27, 2022].

[72] Kim Thompson, "Pacific Comics Expands in '83," news item, *The Comics Journal* #78 [Dec. 1982], pg. 7.

[73] Ibid.

[74] Christopher Lawrence, *The Art of Painted Comics* [2016, Dynamite], pg. 155.

[75] Steve Oliff, "History," Olyoptics website, *https://www.olyoptics.com/ history/#section2.*

[76] Lawrence, pgs. 155–156.

[77] David Scroggy, e-mail to Jon B. Cooke [Apr. 12, 2023].

[78] Oliff.

Top: Presumably drawn by Bruce Jones, on this page is the letters column header for *Alien Worlds* and, next page top, is William Stout's letter col header for *Twisted Tales*, reproduced from the original art.

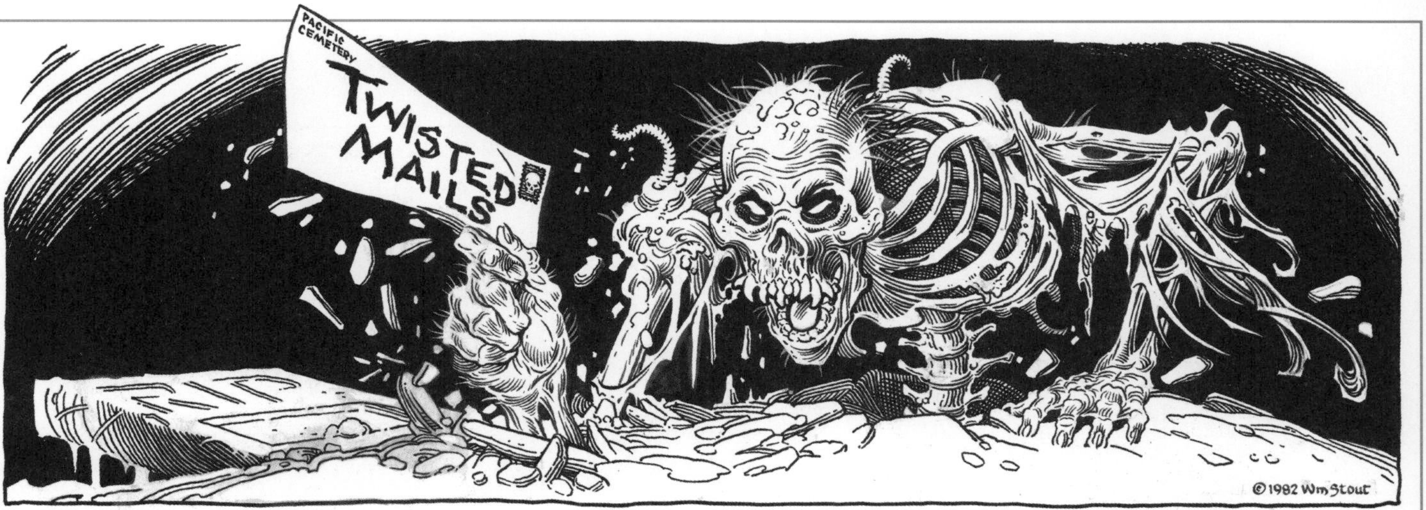
PACIFIC CEMETERY
TWISTED MAILS
©1982 Wm Stout

The Rocketeer Postcards by Dave Stevens

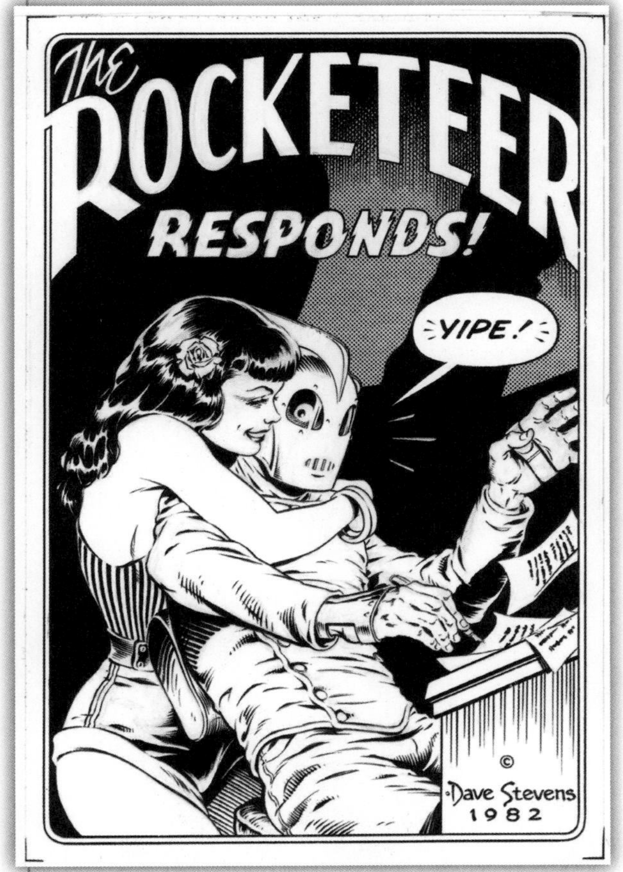
THE ROCKETEER
RESPONDS!
YIPE!
© Dave Stevens 1982

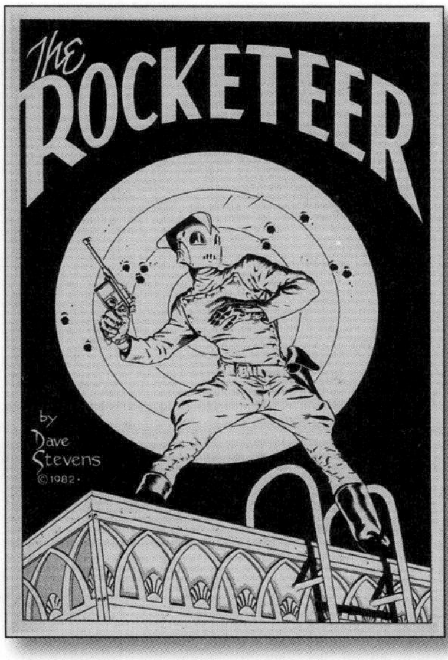
THE ROCKETEER
by Dave Stevens ©1982

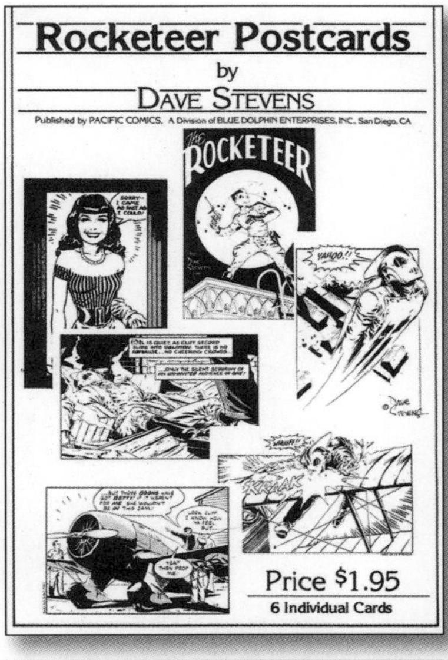
Rocketeer Postcards
by
DAVE STEVENS
Published by PACIFIC COMICS, A Division of BLUE DOLPHIN ENTERPRISES, INC., San Diego, CA
Price $1.95
6 Individual Cards

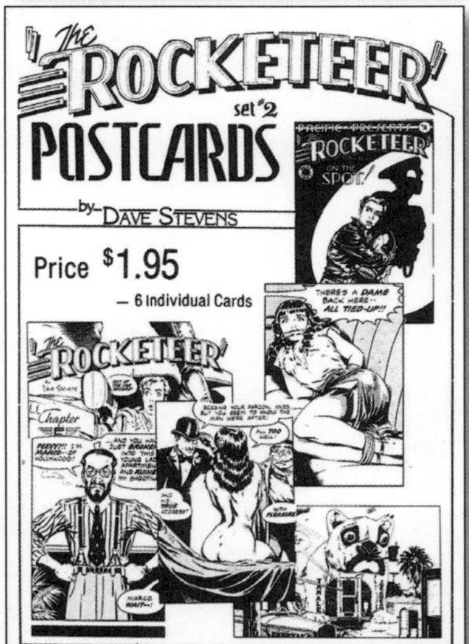
THE ROCKETEER
set #2
POSTCARDS
by DAVE STEVENS
Price $1.95
– 6 Individual Cards
Published by PACIFIC COMICS, a division of BLUE DOLPHIN ENTERPRISES, INC., San Diego, CA 92121

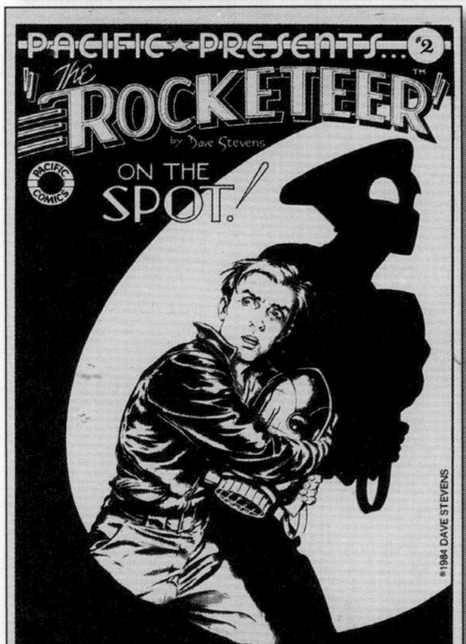
PACIFIC PRESENTS... 2
THE ROCKETEER
by Dave Stevens
ON THE SPOT!
PACIFIC COMICS
©1984 DAVE STEVENS

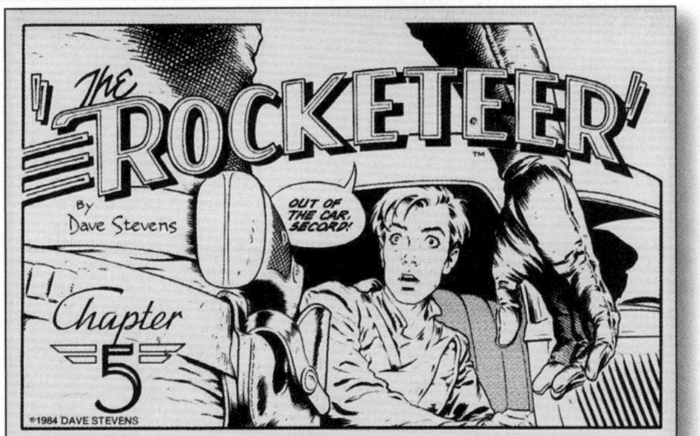
THE ROCKETEER
By Dave Stevens
OUT OF THE CAR, SECORD!
Chapter 5
©1984 DAVE STEVENS

To reply to the mountain of fan mail he received, Dave Stevens created the "Rocketeer Responds" postcard (scanned here from the original art, courtesy of Scott Dunbier). He also permitted Pacific Comics to produce two sets (of six per) of postcards, as well as a poster, which proved to be popular items.

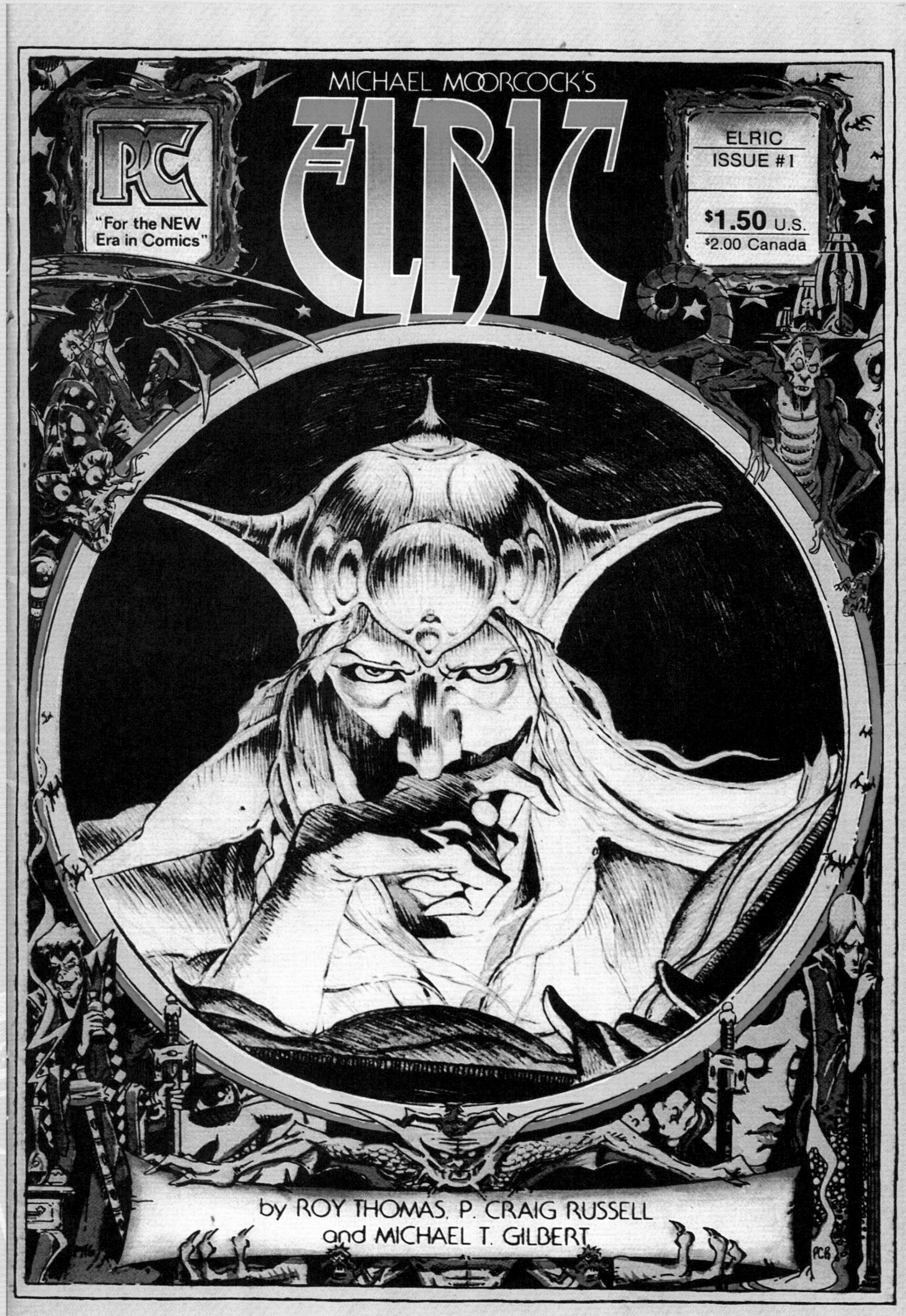
MICHAEL MOORCOCK'S
ELRIC
PC
"For the NEW Era in Comics"
ELRIC ISSUE #1
$1.50 U.S.
$2.00 Canada
by ROY THOMAS, P. CRAIG RUSSELL and MICHAEL T. GILBERT

The Age of Independents

Looking good on paper…

"When the folks at Pacific Comics realized there was room in the market for a company that gave creators ownership of their work* and paid them higher royalties," observed Steve Duin and Mike Richardson, "Bill Schanes came up with another idea to make Pacific's books unique: he asked Spartan Printing if they had a better quality of newsprint than DC and Marvel were using.

"In all the years Spartan had been around," said Pacific's former editor David Scroggy, "no one had ever asked them that question. They'd only been asked if Spartan had something cheaper."[1]

Spartan, of course, was also known as World Color Press, the largest printer of comic books in the industry,[2] predominately based in the town of Sparta, Illinois. As *The Comics Journal* reported, "Ever since the '60s, most newsstand comics have been printed on 20-lb. newsprint, the lowest grade of paper available from World Color Press. The Sparta-based printer has now, upon request from Pacific Comics, made available a heavier (37-lb.) brand of paper called Mando paper."

TCJ continued, "This, in fact, is the same stock of paper that was used for comics through the '60s until, bowing to publishers' demands for cheaper reproduction, World Color Press began offering the 30-lb. newsprint."[3]

Improving the quality of paper stock was to follow a trend, *TCJ* relayed. "Pacific's latest move reflects a general inclination of the alternative publishers to avoid the newsprint format. It is generally assumed that the direct-sales customer is more willing to spend extra money on comics that feature higher production values, and sales on specialty products have for the most part borne this out."[4]

"At that time," Steve Schanes told Jay Allen Sanford, "Marvel and DC were printing on the cheapest low-end newsprint paper with the most economical ink. We started experimenting, partly because we didn't know any better, with upgraded paper and ink. We went from standard newsprint to Mando book stock, coated covers, and then something called Baxter paper, perfectly white so that the inks don't bleed and the colors appear perfectly bright and almost three-dimensional. Our comics ended up looking far superior to what Marvel and DC were putting out."[5]

* Proof that creators had entered a new paradigm was in the fact that Mike Grell, in late 1982, decided to take his *Starslayer* over to a brand-new independent publisher emerging in the Midwest, First Comics. Pacific put up no fight to retain the title.

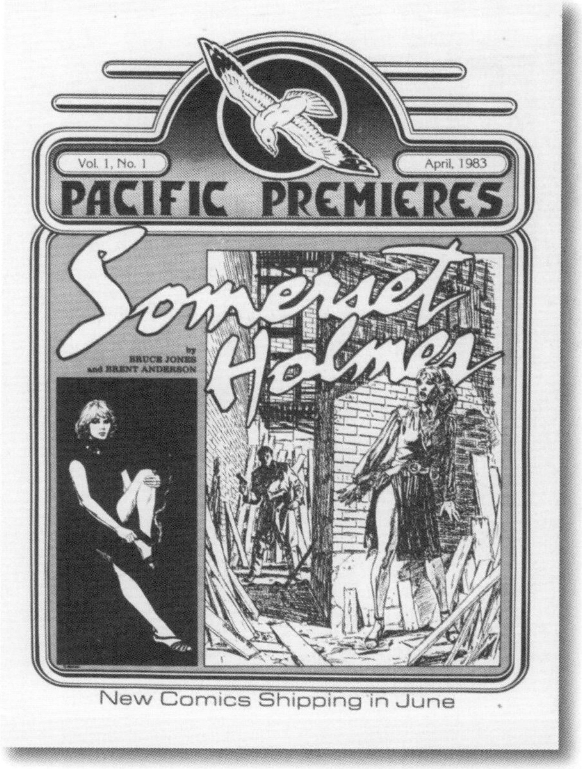
Vol. 1, No. 1
April, 1983
PACIFIC PREMIERES
Somerset Holmes
by BRUCE JONES and BRENT ANDERSON
New Comics Shipping in June

The move to print its entire line on Baxter paper wouldn't begin until the latter half of 1983 — when, as *TCJ* reported, "in order to sweeten the inevitable price leap"[6]— Pacific planned for six titles to switch to all-white ("quality paper" in the company's marketing parlance) for $1.00 rather than the industry standard of $1.50.

Pacific Comics came roaring into the new year. In September 1982, the local weekly alternative paper, the *San Diego Reader*, had featured a cover story devoted to the brothers entitled, "Two Boys and Their Comic Books," and, according to Sanford, Steve Schanes told the *Reader*, "Pacific had already grossed $3.5 million that year and expected to take in over $5 million in 1983."[7] Sanford also revealed, "The Schaneses were printing about 500,000 comic books in Sparta every month. They employed around 40 people at their San Diego operation alone."[8] Business at 8423 Production Avenue was booming.

Previous page: *Elric* #1 [April 1983]. **Above:** In April 1983, Pacific launched its newsletter for dealers, *Pacific Premieres*, which David Scroggy would produce from start to finish.

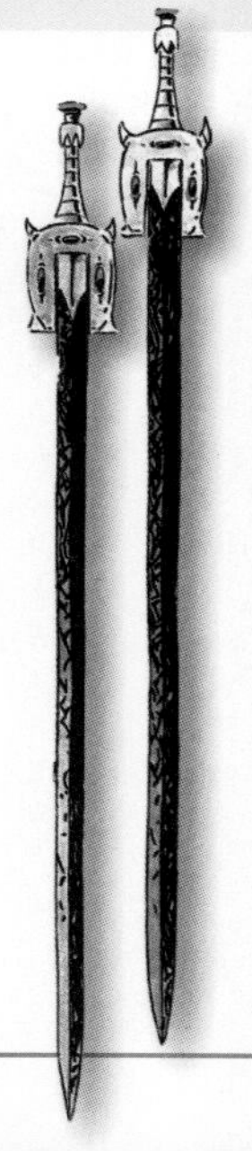

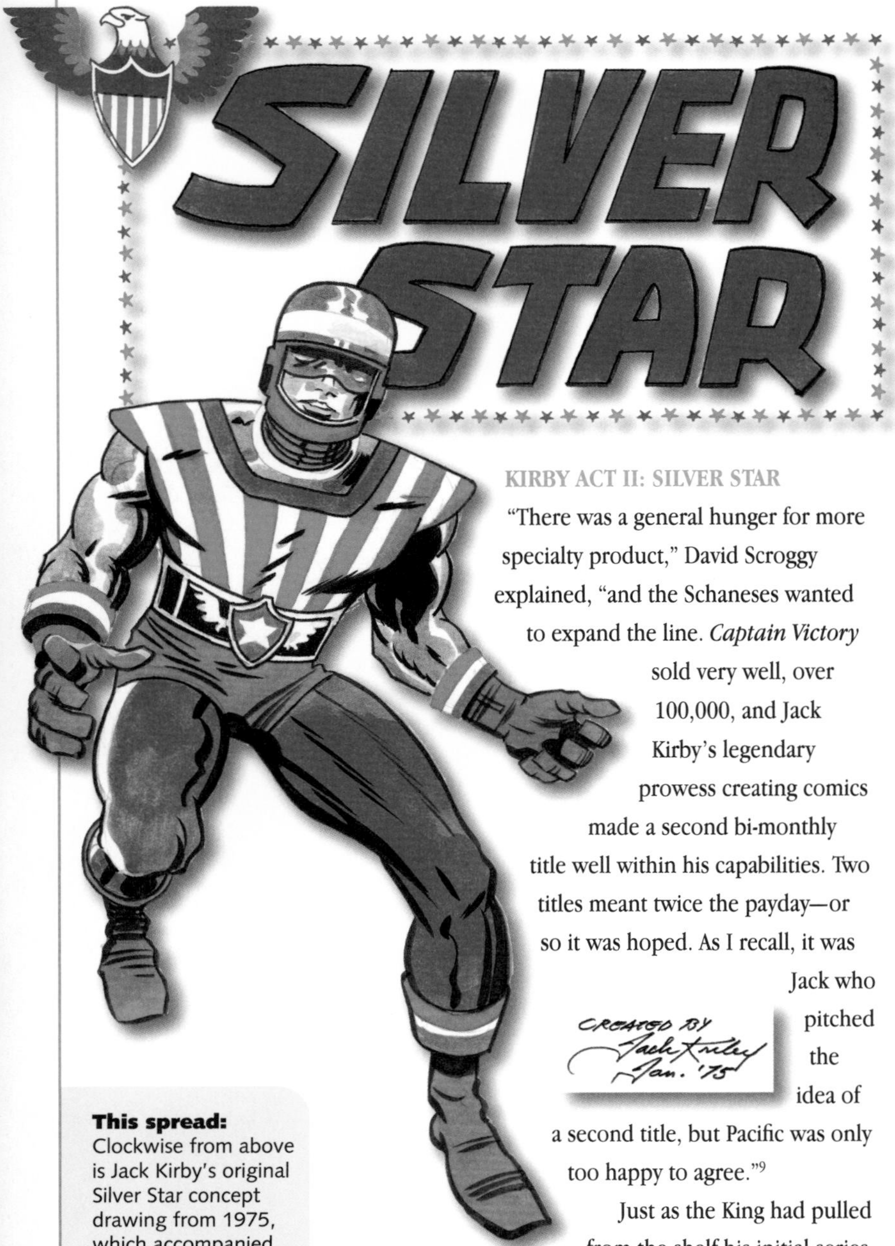
SILVER STAR
CREATED BY Jack Kirby Jan. '75

KIRBY ACT II: SILVER STAR

"There was a general hunger for more specialty product," David Scroggy explained, "and the Schaneses wanted to expand the line. *Captain Victory* sold very well, over 100,000, and Jack Kirby's legendary prowess creating comics made a second bi-monthly title well within his capabilities. Two titles meant twice the payday—or so it was hoped. As I recall, it was Jack who pitched the idea of a second title, but Pacific was only too happy to agree."[9]

Just as the King had pulled from the shelf his initial series for Pacific to publish, Kirby dusted off a screenplay he had written in 1975 with then assistant Steve Sherman for the Schanes brothers to consider as that second title.

"The concept had started with that single drawing in 1975," John Morrow explained, "and morphed into a movie screenplay… (complete with Kirby illustrations to help potential investors visualize the idea). Finding no takers for it as a film, the idea languished in the Kirby files until Pacific came a'calling. The original screenplay… provides some extra depth to the characterizations that isn't evident in the six-issue Pacific Comics series."[10]

Morrow continued, "It's unclear if Kirby intended *Silver Star* to be an ongoing, open-ended series or if it was meant to last just six issues from the start. He tended to view all his comics work as having unlimited potential; as long as the audience kept buying it, he'd keep creating new scenarios for the characters. As the series progressed, payments from Pacific Comics reportedly came slower and slower, and the company went into bankruptcy* not long after Kirby's final issue. But the finale to Kirby's tale doesn't seemed to be forced in the final issue, leading me to believe that, at the very least, Kirby intended to wrap-up the tale of Darius Drumm in a six-issue arc before continuing the adventures of Silver Star with another antagonist."

The *Jack Kirby Collector* editor explained a singular problem during the series' run: "Despite Kirby having a full-time job as an animation conceptual artist at the time, the book stuck to a strict bi-monthly schedule throughout its run, with the only glitch being an extra month between issues #4 and #5. This is more than likely attributed to the switch to D. Bruce Berry as inker with #5 (the Disney [*animators'*] strike ended in mid-series [*mid-Oct. 1982*], sending Mike Royer back to his day job), rather than Jack's ability to deliver."[11]

Though the relationship with Pacific and Kirby could be strained — *de facto* business manager Roz Kirby, Jack's wife, told Gary Groth amid laughter, "We had to call every minute [*and ask*] 'Where's the money? Where's the check?' 'It's in the mail'… But, they usually finally got it to us"[12] — there were plans for even more Kirby projects beyond *Captain Victory* and the *Silver Star* limited series.

* Technically, Pacific never declared bankruptcy, but went into receivership and had its assets liquidated (albeit the same end).

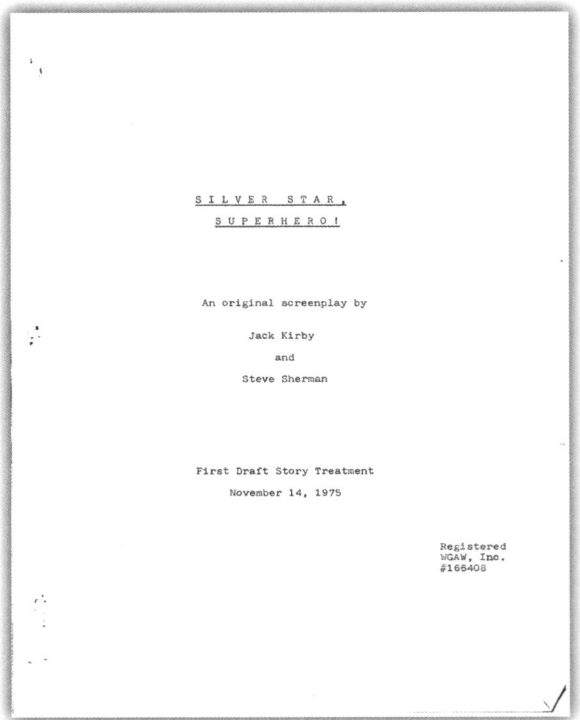
SILVER STAR,
SUPERHERO!

An original screenplay by

Jack Kirby
and
Steve Sherman

First Draft Story Treatment
November 14, 1975

Registered
WGAW, Inc.
#166408

This spread: Clockwise from above is Jack Kirby's original Silver Star concept drawing from 1975, which accompanied his and Steve Sherman's screenplay; nice full-page panel by Kirby from *Silver Star* #2 [Apr. 1983]; Pacific promo featuring Kirby's Silver Star; Steve Ditko's cover art adorns *Jack Kirby's Secret City Saga* #1 [May 1993]; the first page of Kirby's "The Secret City" proposal, which included character designs for the starring heroes; and cover page of Kirby and Steve Sherman's "Silver Star, Superhero" first draft screenplay, 1975.

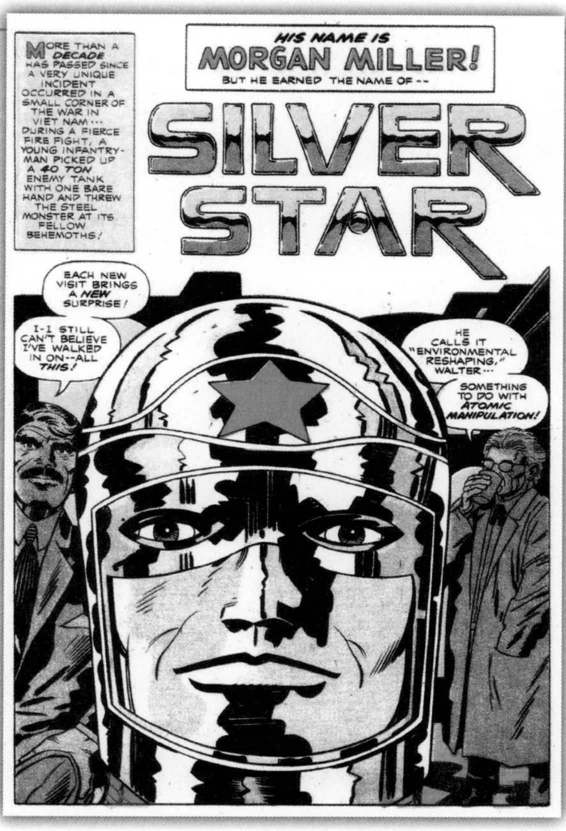

MORE THAN A DECADE HAS PASSED SINCE A VERY UNIQUE INCIDENT OCCURRED IN A SMALL CORNER OF THE WAR IN VIET NAM··· DURING A FIERCE FIRE FIGHT, A YOUNG INFANTRY-MAN PICKED UP A 40 TON ENEMY TANK WITH ONE BARE HAND AND THREW THE STEEL MONSTER AT ITS FELLOW BEHEMOTHS!
HIS NAME IS MORGAN MILLER! BUT HE EARNED THE NAME OF --
SILVER STAR
EACH NEW VISIT BRINGS A NEW SURPRISE!
I-I STILL CAN'T BELIEVE I'VE WALKED IN ON--ALL THIS!
HE CALLS IT "ENVIRONMENTAL RESHAPING," WALTER···
SOMETHING TO DO WITH ATOMIC MANIPULATION!

Somewhere along the way, plans for *The Midnight Men* hit a snag. "There were some Kirby-generated concepts that were intended to be worked up by others under Jack's approval," David explained recently. "We put together a proposal, but Jack rejected it.

"There was never an opportunity for us to rework anything. My memory of the exact timing is unreliable, but it was around then that various financial and other pressures were reaching a crescendo at Pacific, and the Kirby project fell by the wayside."[14] David subsequently added, "I went to Jack's house once and listened as he verbally explained some of the characters."[15]

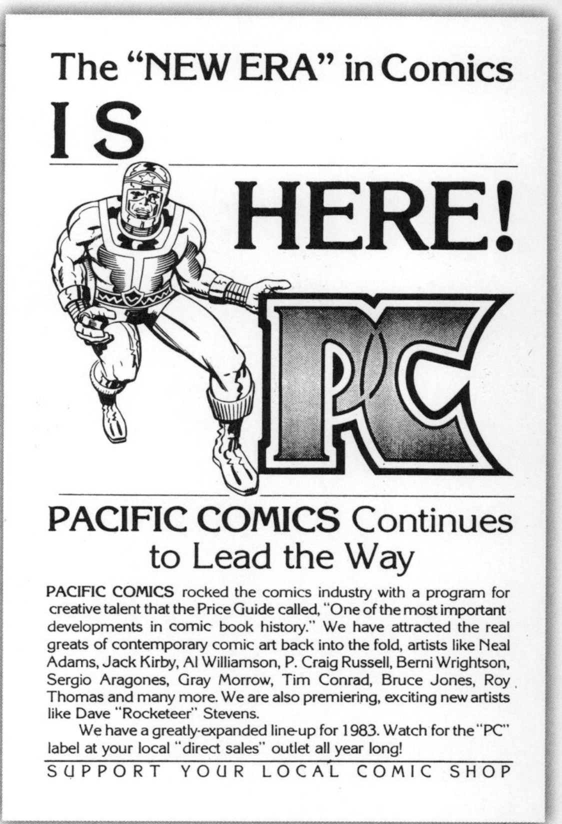

The "NEW ERA" in Comics
IS
HERE!
PC
PACIFIC COMICS Continues to Lead the Way
PACIFIC COMICS rocked the comics industry with a program for creative talent that the Price Guide called, "One of the most important developments in comic book history." We have attracted the real greats of contemporary comic art back into the fold, artists like Neal Adams, Jack Kirby, Al Williamson, P. Craig Russell, Berni Wrightson, Sergio Aragones, Gray Morrow, Tim Conrad, Bruce Jones, Roy Thomas and many more. We are also premiering, exciting new artists like Dave "Rocketeer" Stevens.
We have a greatly-expanded line-up for 1983. Watch for the "PC" label at your local "direct sales" outlet all year long!
SUPPORT YOUR LOCAL COMIC SHOP

JACK KIRBY: COMIC BOOK PACKAGER

In the wake of the San Diego Comic-Con, David Scroggy announced in August 1983 bombshell news via his "Happy Anniversary" editorial in *Captain Victory and the Galactic Rangers Special* #1 [Oct. 1983]: "There will be some intriguing new projects coming from Pacific Comics in the next year which involve Jack Kirby," he wrote. "Over the past several months, we have been developing a new series based on Jack's concepts — *The Midnight Men*. Top comics writer Roger McKenzie has been working on this series, developing his concepts in script form. While the series will ultimately be illustrated by another artist, Jack has generously agreed to handle the pencils on a 48-page introductory extravaganza slated for release at the end of the year."[13]

Rather than another unused Kirby concept withering since the '70s, *The Midnight Men* was derived from a new proposal, written in Feb. 1982 specifically for Pacific, called *The Secret City*. Truth to tell, illustrations attached to the proposal were, with one exception, drawn previously for other concepts, including animation pitches. (The one original character was "Night Glida," a flying super-heroine later renamed "Nightglider.") As widely known, in 1993, Topps Comics released *Jack Kirby's Secret City Saga* as part of its set of "Kirbyverse" titles, where writers Roy Thomas, Gary Friedrich, Gerry Conway, and Kurt Busiek made use of the King's 1982 proposal. During the all-too-brief run of the interconnected series, Captain Victory (here simply called "Victory") and Silver Star were revived by Topps.

Below: One of nine "Kirbyverse" titles published by Topps Comics in 1993–94.

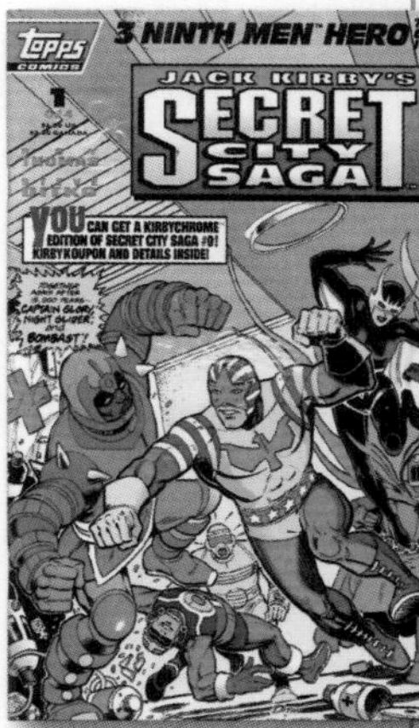

Topps COMICS
3 NINTH MEN HERO TRADING CARDS INSIDE!
JACK KIRBY'S
SECRET CITY SAGA
1
YOU CAN GET A KIRBYCHROME EDITION OF SECRET CITY SAGA #1! KIRBYCOUPON AND DETAILS INSIDE!

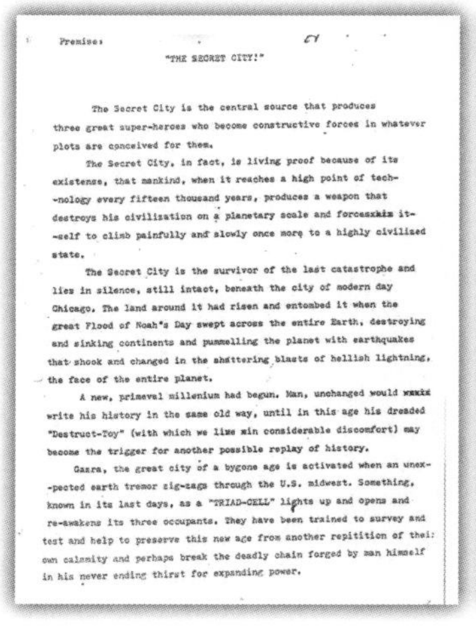

Premise:

"THE SECRET CITY!"

The Secret City is the central source that produces three great super-heroes who become constructive forces in whatever plots are conceived for them.

The Secret City, in fact, is living proof because of its existense, that mankind, when it reaches a high point of tech--nology every fifteen thousand years, produces a weapon that destroys his civilization on a planetary scale and forcesxhim it--self to climb painfully and slowly once more to a highly civilized state.

The Secret City is the survivor of the last catastrophe and lies in silence, still intact, beneath the city of modern day Chicago. The land around it had risen and entombed it when the great Flood of Noah's Day swept across the entire Earth, destroying and sinking continents and pummelling the planet with earthquakes that shook and changed in the shattering blasts of hellish lightning, the face of the entire planet.

A new, primeval millenium had begun. Man, unchanged would wxxix write his history in the same old way, until in this age his dreaded "Destruct-Toy" (with which we lime min considerable discomfort) may become the trigger for another possible replay of history.

Gazra, the great city of a bygone age is activated when an unex--pected earth tremor zig-zags through the U.S. midwest. Something, known in its last days, as a "TRIAD-CELL" lights up and opens and re-awakens its three occupants. They have been trained to survey and test and help to preserve this new age from another repitition of thei: own calamity and perhaps break the deadly chain forged by man himself in his never ending thirst for expanding power.

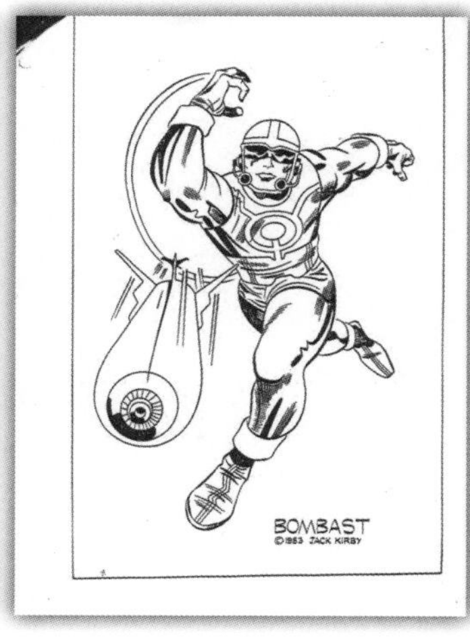

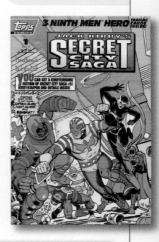

BOMBAST
©1983 JACK KIRBY

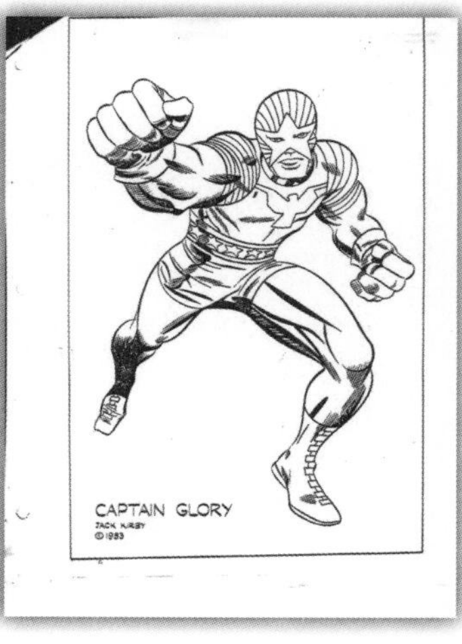

CAPTAIN GLORY
JACK KIRBY
©1983

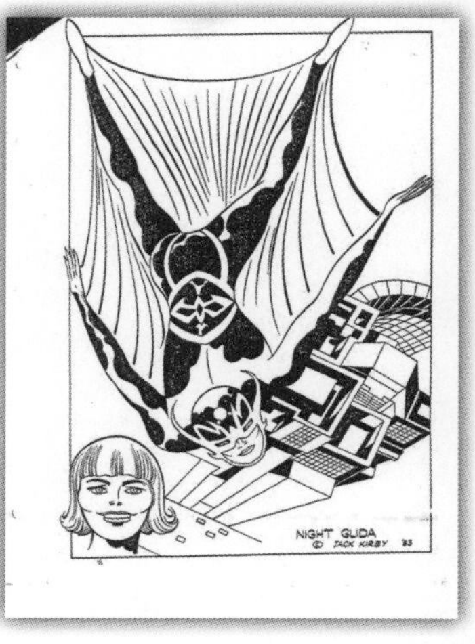

NIGHT GLIDA
© JACK KIRBY '83

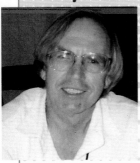

Pacific Profiles

Roy Thomas

Born: *Nov. 1940* One of the most highly regarded writers in comics, Roy is also a fan historian of the highest caliber as editor of *Alter Ego*, a magazine that numbers almost 200 issues as of this writing. Also, as Marvel's editor-in-chief in the 1970s, he helmed the bullpen during one of its most fertile creative periods.

Above: Roy Thomas.

ENTER MIKE FRIEDRICH

Maybe the earlier publishing model that most resembled Pacific Comics the most was Mike Friedrich's Star*Reach, a "ground-level" comics company that spawned the same-name black-&-white anthology title (which lasted for 18 issues between 1974–79). Historian Richard J. Arndt explained, Star*Reach — both publishing house and comic book — showed "the industry a new way to sell comics, particularly comics that were neither mainstream (at least, not at the time) nor underground. [*Friedrich*] demonstrated a method of sales and publication that also gave writers and artists a chunk of the financial action to boot."[16]

MARVEL GRAPHIC NOVEL
N°2
$5.95
MICHAEL MOORCOCK'S
ELRIC
the Dreaming City
By Roy Thomas and P. Craig Russell

Inset right: Doubtless, Steve Schanes got the notion to approach Mike Friedrich and suggest an *Elric* series for Pacific because of writer Roy Thomas and artist P. Craig Russell's 1982 graphic novel adapting Michael Moorcock's novella, *The Dreaming City*. Friedrich's Star*Reach Productions brokered the deal for RT/PCR.

The Schanes brothers, whose distribution arm had carried Friedrich's titles, took note of the publisher's breakthroughs in direct sales and enticements to top talent to contribute to his grand experiment, despite Star*Reach having gone belly-up in 1979. Soon enough, Friedrich would enter the orbit of Pacific Comics.

"I went bankrupt as a publisher," Friedrich shared with Jon B. Cooke, "and I worked at Marvel as a marketing and sales executive for a couple of years, setting up their direct sales department, and I used my salary to pay off my printer, which took me two years, and then I came home [*to Berkeley, Calif.*]. The first thing I did was enter into a three-month consulting agreement with Pacific Comics, with the option for me to agree to join the company in their publishing efforts."[17]

Friedrich and the Schaneses had previously interacted in his role as head of Marvel's direct sales department. "I had been working with Pacific on behalf of Marvel," he said. "They were one of my customers, as a distribution company that I dealt with and, while I was at Marvel, they started their publishing branch, immediately publishing Jack Kirby and then publishing Neal Adams, and it was, like, 'Okay, something's going on here.' So, once I left Marvel, the first phone call I made was to Pacific and they came back with this very generous offer. What I wound up doing was helping them draft a publishing deal in detail that they could use to appeal to the artist community. Pacific publicly released that document as a marketing tool, so a lot of small press people used it as a template for their own deals. So, as an agent five years later, I would get a contract in the mail on behalf of one of my clients and it had been the one I had drafted! So I didn't have an argument with the terms!"[18]

For whatever reason, at the end of his 90-day consulting gig, both parties agreed mutually that Friedrich wasn't a good fit at the company. But one of the Schanes brothers did make a parting suggestion that would retain a sustained connection between them, and it involved a certain stoic albino emperor with a soul-stealing blade.

THE MAN FROM MELNIBONÉ

Mike Friedrich's connection with the sword-&-sorcery character created by Michael Moorcock stretched back to his *Star*Reach* days. "I first encountered Elric as a reader while in college… but, in comics, I'm publishing *Star*Reach* and this incredibly detailed, 20-page, fully finished story by two guys I never heard of before shows up in my mailbox. It was an original Elric story… and I

Pacific Profiles

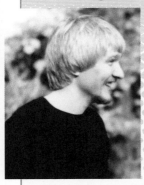

P. Craig Russell

Born: *Oct. 1951* First known for his "Killraven" collaboration with writer Don McGregor, besides his frequent work with superstar author Neil Gaiman, the artist is highly regarded for his magnificent series of opera adaptations rendered in comic-book form. Recent work includes *Norse Mythology*.

Above: Philip Craig Russell in the 1980s. Photo courtesy of Michael T. Gilbert.

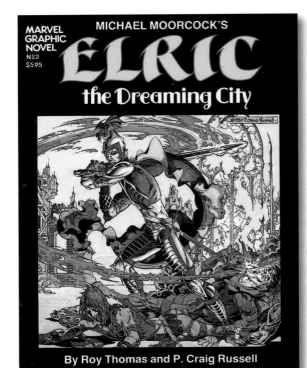

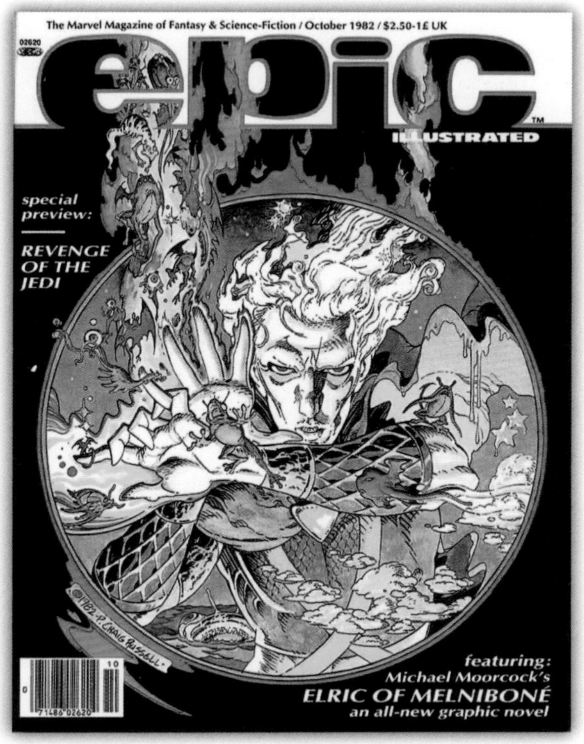

The Marvel Magazine of Fantasy & Science-Fiction / October 1982 / $2.50-1£ UK
epic
ILLUSTRATED
special preview:
REVENGE OF THE JEDI
featuring:
Michael Moorcock's
ELRIC OF MELNIBONÉ
an all-new graphic novel

immediately wanted to publish it and (though I don't know how I did it) I tracked down Michael Moorcock's agent in New York. I got permission — for something like $100 — to publish the story, and [*Star*Reach* #6, Oct. 1976] was the most successful comic I published."

Friedrich continued, "I followed that up by meeting Michael in London a year later and began a long association thereafter. We did [*Elric*] comics for Marvel. There was a Craig Russell story printed in *Epic Illustrated*, I believe, and then one of the Marvel graphic novels was an Elric story, and the next step was the Pacific Comics material."

While it "just didn't make any sense" to take on a permanent managerial position at Pacific, Friedrich explained, "Bill Schanes made the suggestion of why don't I package the Moorcock Elric material for Pacific Comics. So I quickly checked to see if Roy Thomas and Craig Russell were available, and Roy was available but, while Craig was somewhat available, he needed help, so I connected him to Michael Gilbert (though I don't remember how that came about) and they hit it off with each other and they had an art partnership for five, six, or seven years… maybe even longer." As packager, Friedrich also served as the bi-monthly's editor. *Elric* lasted for six issues at Pacific before switching to First Comics.

Renowned science-fiction/fantasy writer and editor Michael Moorcock was the first prose author Friedrich ever dealt with, and coming to an agreement was seamless. When they met, he said, "We subsequently agreed on an underlying license where [*Moorcock*] got a percentage of the page rate and the royalties. Another nice thing about him was he said he really didn't care about the money upfront; he just wanted the back-end. So I made an argument for what I thought was a fair percentage and that lasted for 25 years. It wasn't until the mid-2000s when I relinquished the license."

The longest tenure Friedrich would serve in the comic book industry was as an agent for comics creators, a career lasting about two decades. "I started the [*Star*Reach*] agency when I left Pacific, using the [*Elric*] packaging deal for the basis of the agency," he said. "I probably represented 50 or 60 different clients over the years."[19]

TEAM RUSSELL/GILBERT

The last person contacted when Friedrich was organizing an *Elric* series for Pacific had a prior connection to the nascent packager, as Michael T. Gilbert previously had his work published in Friedrich's *Star*Reach*, *Imagine*, and *Quack*. "They already hired Roy Thomas to do the writing," Gilbert told Jon B. Cooke, "and they had Craig Russell to do the artwork, but Craig didn't want to spend all his time just working on a bi-monthly comic. Mike

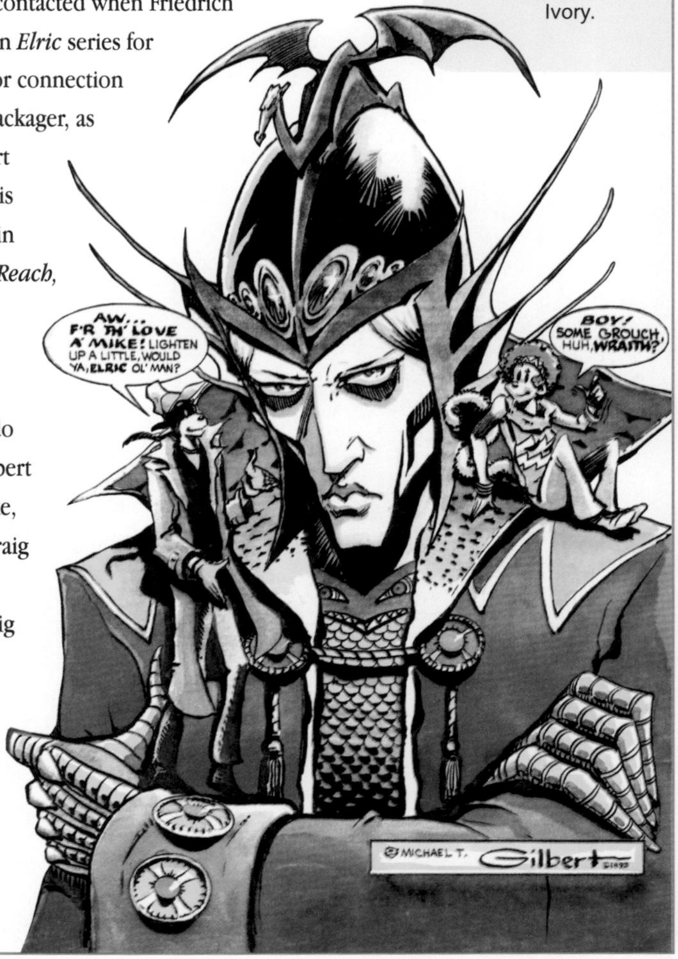

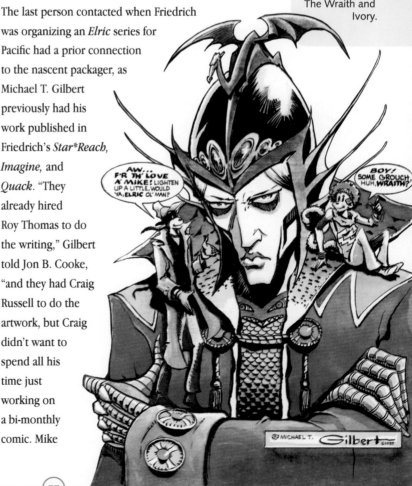

AW... F'R TH' LOVE A' MIKE! LIGHTEN UP A LITTLE, WOULD YA, ELRIC OL' MAN?
BOY! SOME GROUCH, HUH, WRAITH?
©MICHAEL T. Gilbert

Pacific Profiles

Michael T. Gilbert

Born: *May 1951*

As celebrated an artist/writer as MTG is, the creator will likely always be best remembered for his classic character, Doc Stern… Mr. Monster, a monster-killing doctor with his own cult following. Gilbert has served as the "Comic Crypt" for Roy Thomas' *Alter Ego* magazine for some 25 years.

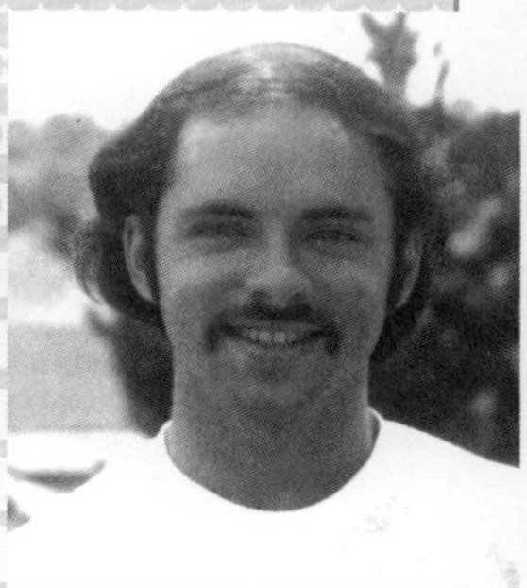

Above: Michael Terry Gilbert posing in his days living in Berkeley, California, in the 1980s.

Inset left: P. Craig Russell cover art for *Epic Illustrated* #14 [Oct. 1982]. **Below:** Vignette from MTG's cover for *The Comics Journal* #84 [Sept. 1983], which includes his characters, The Wraith and Ivory.

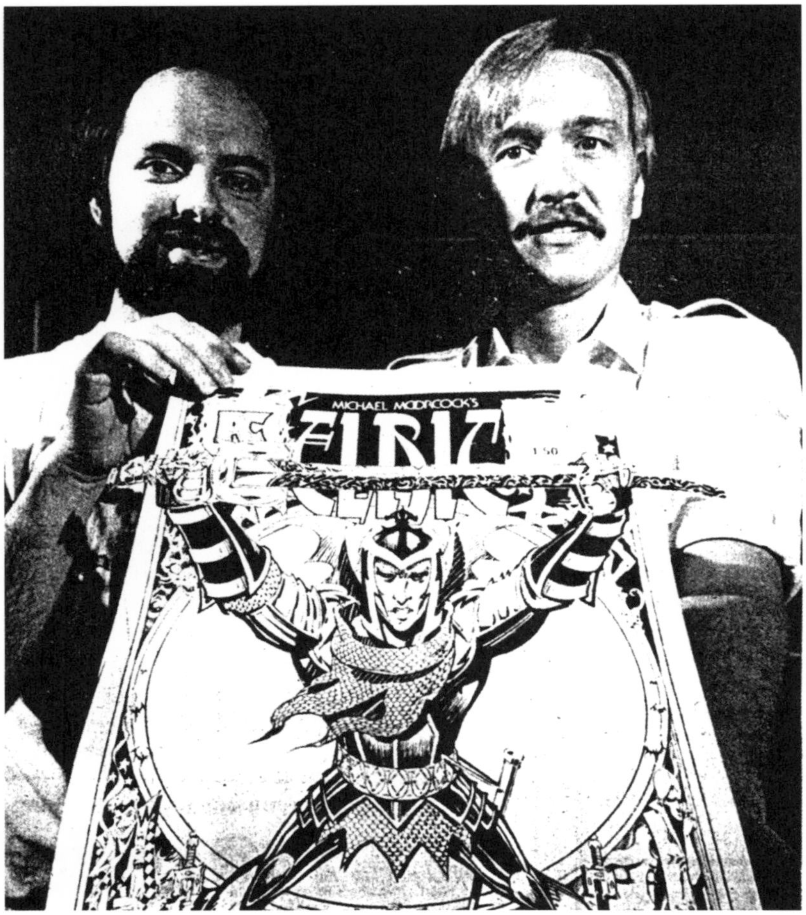
MICHAEL MOORCOCK'S
ELRIC

Above: *Kent-Rolvenna Record Courier,* Oct. 11, 1983 news photo with MTG (left) and PCR. **Inset right:** First took over the Elric title in 1986 with this mini-series. **Below:** PCR art from *Elric* promo ad.

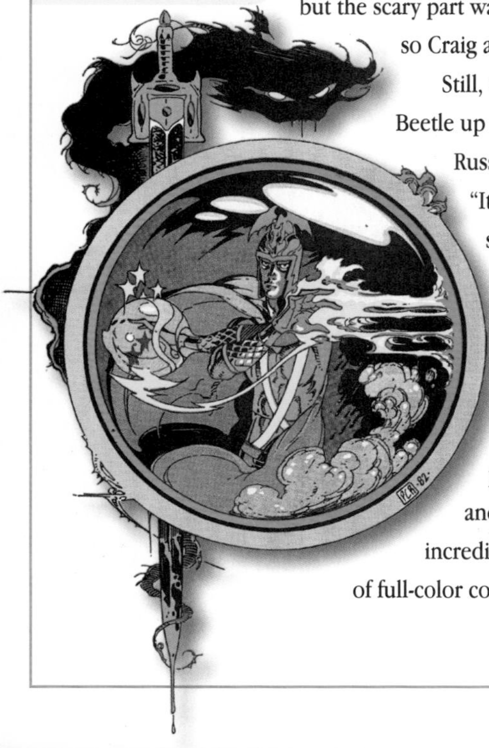

remembered me, and I had met Craig just briefly at some convention. We both liked each other's work, so they offered me the job. I did a couple of samples, which were mixed, but Mike finally said, 'Let's give it a try.' The tricky part was about this point (1982 or thereabouts), my [*first*] wife and I had split. It was just a terrible time for me, and then this offer came — which perked me up quite a bit — but the scary part was they wanted me to move to Ohio, so Craig and I could work together."[20]

Still, Gilbert drove his 1959 Volkswagen Beetle up to the Buckeye State and proved the Russell/Gilbert team was an effective one. "It worked," he said. "I've had people say they liked the blend because I brought a little more humor to the thing and, of course, Craig did most of the inking and such. He's got his elegant linework and everything, gave it this really beautiful look. I put together the letter pages and stuff, and we both did the coloring, which was incredibly difficult. This was the early days of full-color comics, so we were really just learning as we went along, trying to figure out how to make this coloring thing work."[21]

For his efforts, did P. Craig Russell find satisfaction in inking another artist's pencils? "I enjoy it. I really do," Russell told Steve Ringgenberg in 1983. "If I had to do it constantly, I don't know if I would, but since about '78, I've been inking people here and there. I've been able to play around with a real variety and range of artists. It's a nice break for me between drawing. Inking is almost like time off to me. It's a real skill, a real craft to develop, but it's not as mentally draining as starting out with a blank page, which is the real challenge."[22]

He continued, "And now I'm inking Michael Gilbert on the *Elric* book. He moved here to Kent, Ohio. He was living down in Austin, Texas, and now he's living right across town, five minutes away. He comes over here almost every night, and we work in the same studio, passing the pages back and forth. Mostly, I'm doing a combination of breakdown and layout, and he's doing all the penciling, and I'm inking that. He's a totally different artist from anyone else I've been inking. And there's a challenge there. Gilbert's is a much more morbid-looking Elric than what I do. He's also much looser than I am as a penciler, more like Will Eisner. With Gilbert's work, there's a 'creepier' feel to the whole story. If you want to compare studio styles, I play Lou Fine to his Will Eisner."

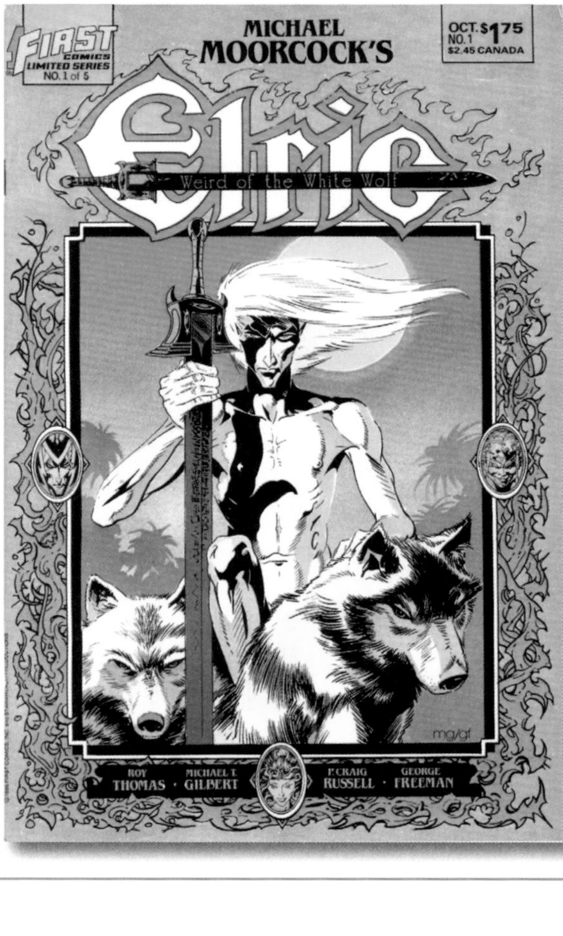
FIRST COMICS
LIMITED SERIES NO. 1 of 5
MICHAEL MOORCOCK'S
OCT. NO.1 $1.75
$2.45 CANADA
Elric
Weird of the White Wolf
ROY THOMAS · MICHAEL T. GILBERT
P. CRAIG RUSSELL · GEORGE FREEMAN

As penciler and inker, Russell already had to his credit chapters of an Elric adaptation published in *Epic Illustrated* [#3–4, Fall–Winter 1980], a story completed in *Marvel Graphic Novel #2 — Michael Moorcock's Elric The Dreaming City* [1982], as well as a standalone story in *Epic* #14 [Oct. 1982], and the artist hoped the new series would visually mesh with that earlier Elric work (which were all Star*Reach Productions). "Well, we're trying to keep it consistent with the Elric books I've already done," he told Ringgenberg, "but, by the second one, our styles are meshing a bit more — more of his is coming through."[23]

Elric's creator shared with the packager that he was pleased with the results. "What [*Moorcock*] said to me at the time was he wasn't wedded to any particular approach," Friedrich said to Cooke. "He appreciated what I had published, appreciated what Craig Russell did for the many years he was involved, and he liked what Michael Gilbert did when he was in partnership with Craig. He wasn't wedded to any particular interpretation."[24]

QUALITY CONTROL

Determined to maintain a superior level of consistency for their prestige release of 1983, when substandard samples of the first printing of *Elric* #1 arrived at Pacific, a dramatic decision was made by the Schanes siblings. The Recalled Comics website shared, "Error copies don't seem to have made it into the distribution chain, it seems the publisher received a batch of comics to check and they were not happy with the paper or the print quality, so [*they*] asked that all the comics were pulped and reprinted."[25] In the following issue, Friedrich discussed the matter:

"As this is being written, the first issue has not yet come from the printer. We understand there were some quality-control problems that necessitated a considerable, unforeseen delay. We're certainly glad here on the creative end that the publishers care enough about the quality of the comics they produce that they are willing to accept the criticism of distributors and retailers who want everything shipped on announced schedules. This isn't to say that dealers don't have a point; after all, it's you readers who want your favorite comics to come out on time. The all-important first issue, though, has to be 'just right'; otherwise, what's the point in releasing it? The writer and artists wouldn't have it any other way."[26]

Recalled Comics reported, "In recent times, one of the comic's editors (Bill Schanes) confirmed that the first printing was destroyed due to the quality and the print reoriented on better paper stock. He also confirmed

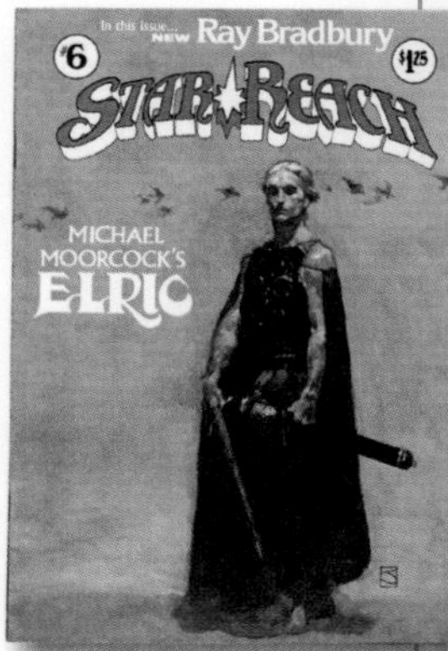
In this issue... NEW Ray Bradbury
#6
$1.25
STAR*REACH
MICHAEL MOORCOCK'S
ELRIC

Above: Packager Mike Friedrich's association with Elric stretches back to 1976, when he received a blind submission: a spectacular Elric story by Eric Kimball, Steven Grant, and Bob Gould, which he published in *Star*Reach* #6 [Oct. '76], behind this Jeff Jones cover. **Below:** Michael T. Gilbert/P. Craig Russell tryout which scored the *Elric* gig.

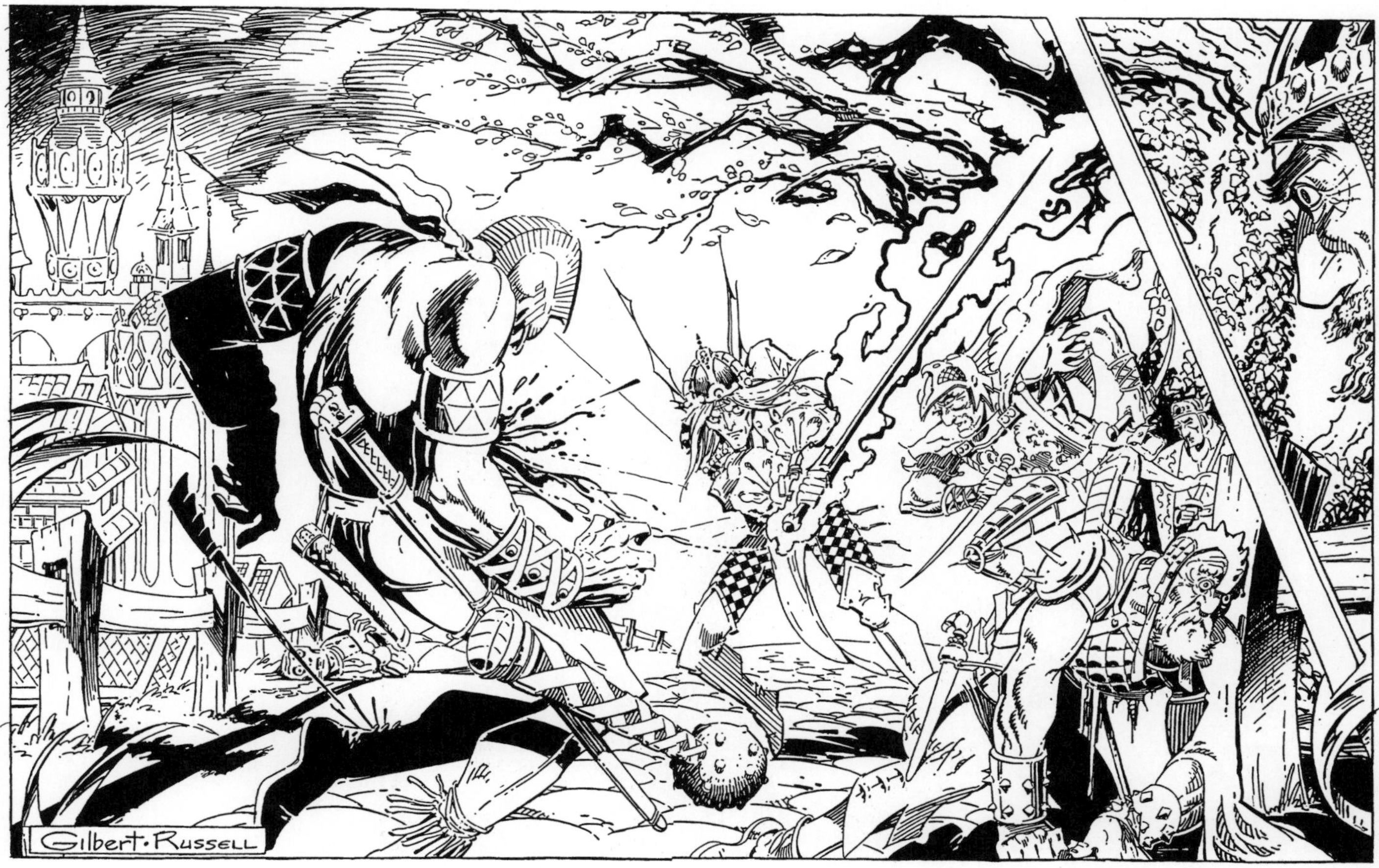
GILBERT·RUSSELL

Inset right: P. Craig Russell's favorite of his Elric drawings, this from *Elric: The Weird of the White Wolf* ['91]. **Below:** A gag drawing featuring Michael T. Gilbert's characters, The Wraith and Ivory, residing in the world of Elric, commenting on the Elric "tryout" drawing seen on the previous page. This MTG/P. Craig Russell piece appeared in the last Pacific Comics edition of the title, *Elric* #6 [Apr. 1984]. (The Wraith was a so-called "funny animal" strip created as homage to Will Eisner's The Spirit and it appeared first in Mike Friedrich's Star*Reach Comics title, *Quack* #1 [July 1976].)

around 200 copies were not destroyed (presumably those sent to the publisher when the quality issues were noticed)."[27]

KUDOS TO THE SCHANESES

In that same *Elric* #2 editorial, Friedrich gave a shout-out to the head honchos at Pacific. "All of us, readers and professionals alike, owe them a lot for blowing the entire comics field wide open. For years, comics have been locked into a two-company oligarchy, with only peripheral competition (I should know, I was one of those dinky publishers a few years back). Pacific was the first to recognize that the so-called specialty distribution system (the 'direct market') had grown to such a point that a publisher could publish 'regular' full-color comics at a price competitive to the major companies and pay the creative people comparable earnings."[28]

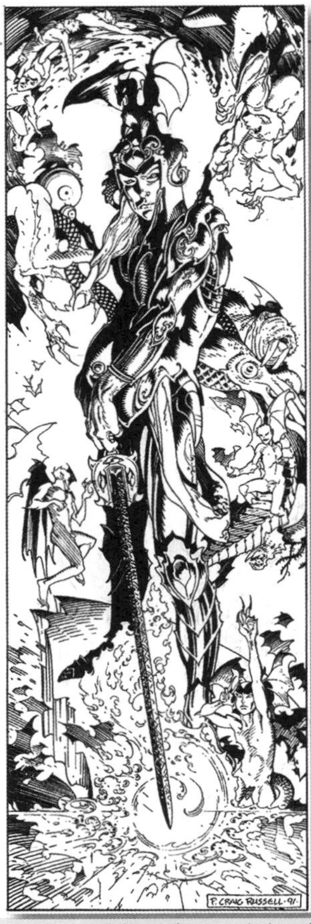
P. CRAIG RUSSELL-91

Friedrich continued, "Blessed with this insight and also with the naïve ignorance of all the potentially discouraging production, financial, and creative headaches that attend to publishing comics, the Schaneses forged ahead. *Captain Victory* #1 changed the landscape of comics. Within months, there were more new entrants into the field. The major publishers began directing even more attention than before on the desires of the comic store reader, and there has begun (and continues to this day) a mad scramble on the part of all publishers to sign up new artists and writers and develop new characters. The potential earnings of creators doubled and tripled in months. The creative explosion of new comics, new 'Baxter' comics (such as *Elric*) and the new 'graphic novels' are the result. All because two young men said, 'What the heck, let's do it!' Thanks, guys."

Today, Friedrich remains equally effusive as he was in the '80s about the accomplishments of the Schanes boys. "They were certainly instrumental in expanding the creator's rights business by publishing people like Jack Kirby and Neal Adams. What they did that no one else had done before was that they used the traditional comic-book format — the size and the paper stock, and all that — to publish their comics, where the smaller press before them (like what I had done) was working in black-&-white... in magazine-size formats. Pacific Comics were the first ones to use the traditional super-hero format to publish creator-owned material. That, of course, laid the groundwork for Image Comics to show up a few years later and just take over the universe."[30]

Some of you may be wondering about the rather strange illustration below. Well, to celebrate the completion of our series, we wanted to do something a little special. Now, in issue #1 we had a two page pin-up page that we claimed was our very first try-out to see how well our two very different styles would work together. Well, we lied. That page was actually our *second* attempt. Our first is below just before we worked the few remaining bugs out. I had just finished a story featuring my funny animal creations, The Wraith and Ivory (for Aardvark-Vanaheim's ''Strange Brew''), and still hadn't fully adjusted to this new art style. Our editor thought something looked a little . . . *off* . . . (though he couldn't quite put his finger on it) and suggested doing the second page mentioned above. Go figger' it! (And if you believe that. . .)

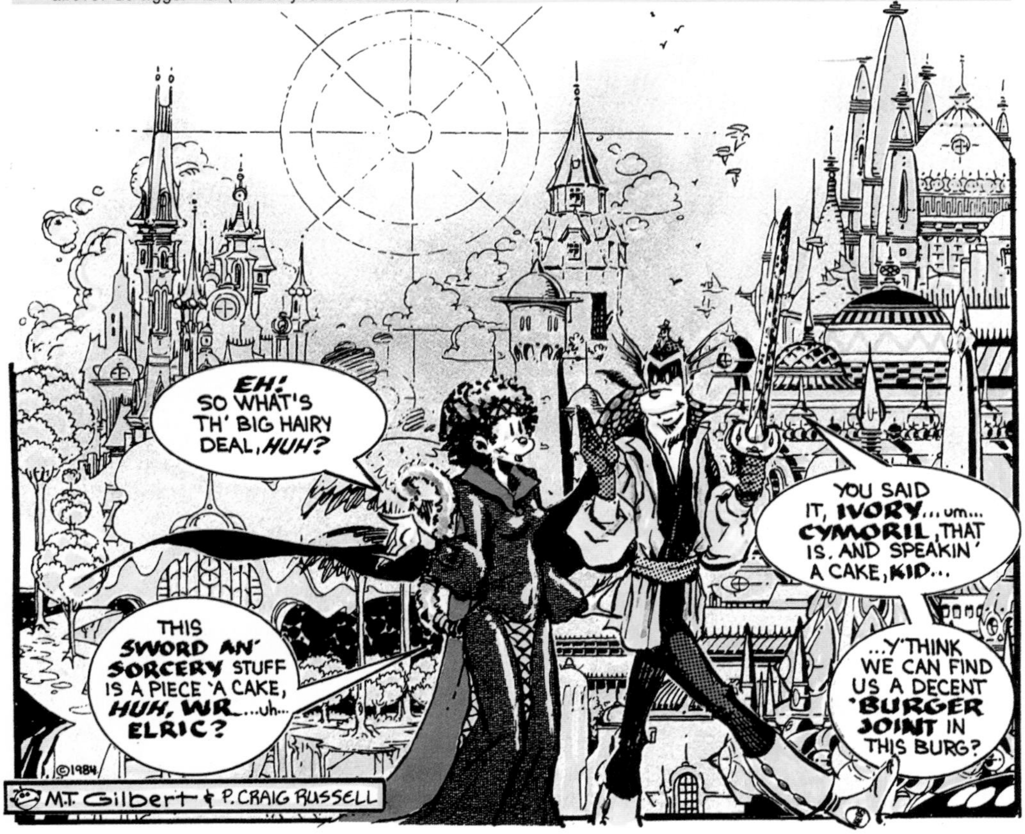
EH! SO WHAT'S TH' BIG HAIRY DEAL, HUH?
THIS SWORD AN' SORCERY STUFF IS A PIECE 'A CAKE, HUH, WR ...uh... ELRIC?
YOU SAID IT, IVORY... um... CYMORIL, THAT IS. AND SPEAKIN' A CAKE, KID...
...Y'THINK WE CAN FIND US A DECENT 'BURGER JOINT IN THIS BURG?
©1984
M.T. Gilbert & P. CRAIG RUSSELL

So was Pacific Comics a significant aspect in the history of comics? “Oh yes,” Friedrich replied. “Short-lived, but an important stepping stone to where the field is today.”

ELRIC AFTER PACIFIC

Roy Thomas, who wrote the Elric adaptations at Marvel and Pacific, has few distinct memories regarding the Schanes brothers’ operation, though he did share, “I can’t really remember much, except that Mike Friedrich, as my agent (and controller then of the Elric rights), set it up. I seem to recall having lunch with one with the owners, and they were very enthusiastic, but that’s about it.”[31] Along with his artist collaborators on *Elric*, all three would continue working on the character after the demise of Pacific.

By February 1985, First Comics relaunched the comic-book version of the character in an *Elric: Sailor on the Seas of Fate* limited series, with Thomas writing and Gilbert contributing layouts and rough pencils, and finishes by George Freeman. The same team produced *Elric: The Weird of the White Wolf* [First, 1986], and Russell would return 10 years later, only this time as writer and solo artist, for the Topps *Elric: Stormbringer* [1997] run.

BERNIE AT HIS BEST

Before Warren Publications would give up the ghost in 1983, Steve Schanes reached out to Jim Warren’s operation to reprint some of its finest horror material. “We had a relationship with them,” Steve recalled. “We dealt with them for several years as distributors. I contacted them about reprinting stories, made a deal, and we picked up the rights to reprint. But I had to make sure they had the right to give us permission. I wrote Bernie [*Wrightson*] and he wrote me a letter back saying, yes, his understanding was that, when he did work for Warren along with everybody else, that Warren retained all the rights. So that gave me an idea that I could publish these materials without having backlash. We didn’t want to be publishing stuff without creator rights, which was our basic philosophy. We contacted Bernie and we contacted writers. We made sure it’s all kosher.”[32]

Steve added, “Bernie was just such a nice guy. I got to have meetings several times. He was just delightful.”

Bruce Jones edited the *Berni Wrightson: Master of the Macabre* series (subsequently picked up by Eclipse), a title singularly devoted to Wrightson’s work, which featured Steve Oliff’s colorized versions of the artist’s *Creepy* and *Eerie* black-&-white stories, as well as some of Wrightson’s fanzine material. (The evocative comic book logo was rendered by Wrightson pal William Stout.)

BERNI WRIGHTSON MASTER OF THE MACABRE

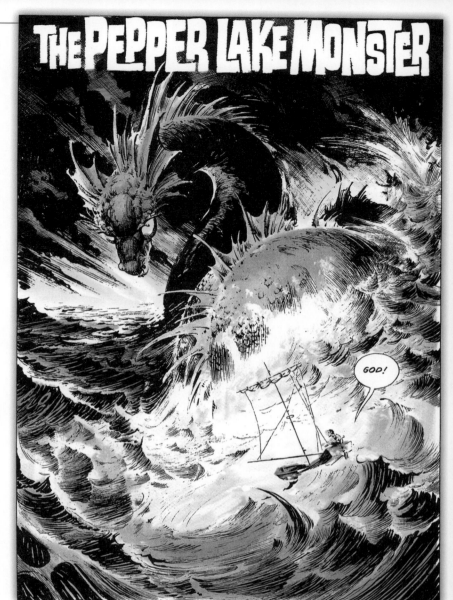

THE PEPPER LAKE MONSTER
GOD!

Above: Splash of the colorized version of Wrightson’s *Eerie* #58 [July ’74] tale. **Inset left:** William Stout was the logo creator. **Below:** July 4, 1975 pencil drawing of his “Jenifer” character from *Creepy* #63 [July 1974]

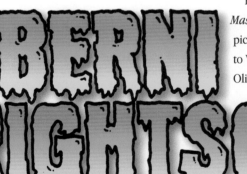

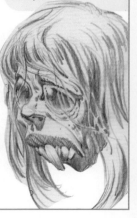

The Story of Blue Dolphin Books

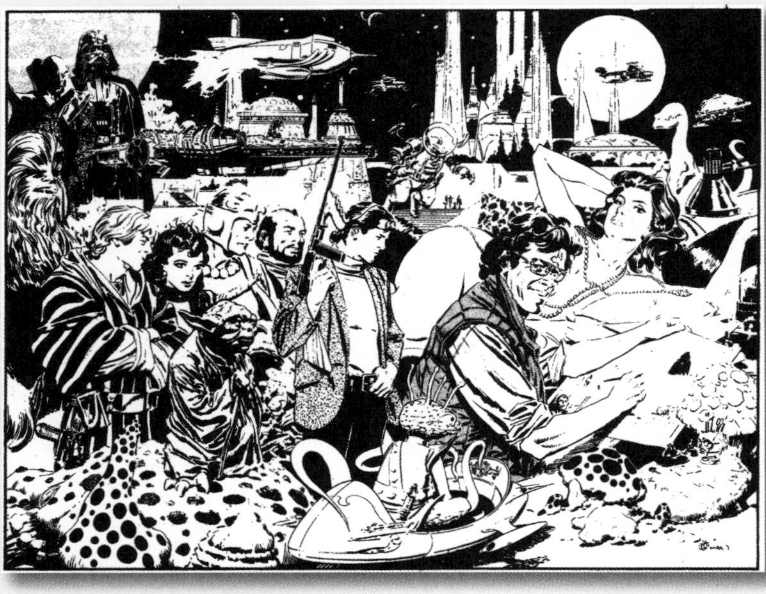

Above: Al Williamson's cover art for his *Art of...* book, published by Blue Dolphin in Apr. 1983. **Inset right:** Page from Scott Shaw!'s *Oddball Comics* book that was scheduled for Summer 1983 release by Blue Dolphin, but was never published. **Below:** Blue Dolphin's first release was a history of paperback books translated from Dutch [1982].

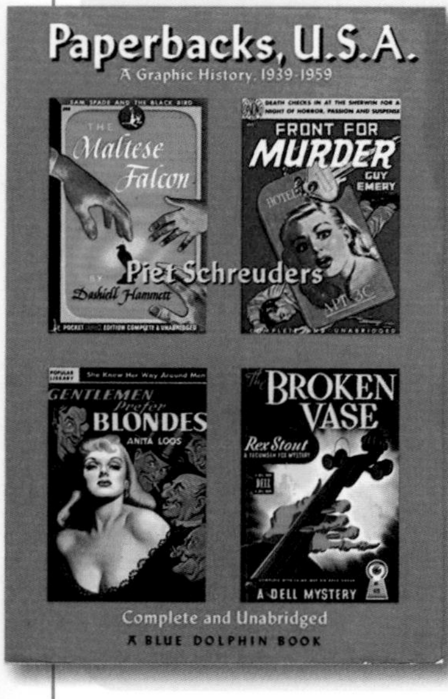

Paperbacks, U.S.A.
A Graphic History 1939-1959
The Maltese Falcon
Dashiell Hammett
FRONT FOR MURDER
GUY EMERY
Piet Schreuders
GENTLEMEN Prefer BLONDES
ANITA LOOS
BROKEN VASE
Rex Stout
A DELL MYSTERY
Complete and Unabridged
A BLUE DOLPHIN BOOK

Incorporated on Jan. 20, 1981, Blue Dolphin Enterprises was the umbrella corporation name as well as a book publisher imprint established by the Schanes brothers that was distinct from the comics. "I think the Schaneses' goal with Blue Dolphin," David Scroggy said, "was to separate the publishing entities in order to better penetrate the bookstore market. We were learning as we went.

"We were offered Piet Schreuders' *Paperbacks, U.S.A.* book. This was subtitled 'A Graphic History 1939–1959,' and was a compendium of cover art from mass-market paperback books. It was entirely packaged when we received it and is an excellent book. We were presented it by a colorful Dutch fellow named Hugo Van Baren... I don't think we ever figured out how to obtain an ISBN number, but were proud to have discovered how to get it assigned a Library of Congress catalogue number. The book got a review in *Library Journal* and we started to receive a ton of purchase order from libraries across the U.S. It was like a Tower of Babel, in that there was no standard system used by libraries to order; they all seemed to have their own diverse fulfillment procedures. We probably lost money filling these orders in a 'one-potato, two-potato' fashion, but were happy to do it, envisioning our title on the library shelves. What never did happen, unfortunately, were purchase orders from chain bookstore operations."[33]

Blue Dolphin also produced book tie-ins for a highly anticipated movie release coming in June 1982. "The *Blade Runner* titles were something I was very involved with and I still view them as one of my most satisfying accomplishments while at Pacific Comics... This was the early days of licensing — the Ladd Company practically thrust the license on us. I don't think they could find anyone else. Bill Schanes took their call, and we discussed the tantalizing opportunity. They wanted us to make comic books, but there wasn't time. We realized that, even if we crashed the boards and jammed out a comic adaptation as fast as we knew how, it would never see print until long after the film's release. So we wound up with a few projects we could turn around relatively quickly: *Blade Runner Sketchbook* (which I wrote and edited), *The Illustrated Blade Runner* (the script and whatever production art we could find), and *Blade Runner* portfolio (a set of color photos)."

David continued, "I drove up to the Ladd Company offices in my old VW and they opened a closet stacked high with art — mostly Syd Mead's design sketches for the film.

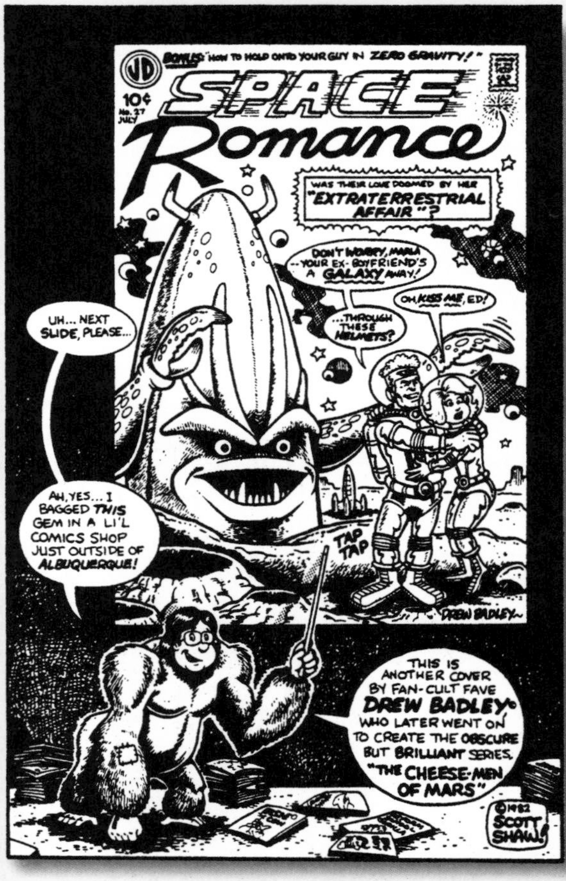

BONUS: HOW TO HOLD ONTO YOUR GUY IN ZERO GRAVITY!"
SPACE Romance
10¢
No. 27
JULY
WAS THEIR LOVE DOOMED BY HER "EXTRATERRESTRIAL AFFAIR"?
DON'T WORRY, MARLA --YOUR EX-BOYFRIEND'S A GALAXY AWAY!
OH, KISS ME, ED!
...THROUGH THESE HELMETS?
UH... NEXT SLIDE, PLEASE...
AH, YES... I BAGGED THIS GEM IN A LI'L COMICS SHOP JUST OUTSIDE OF ALBUQUERQUE!
TAP TAP
DREW BADLEY
THIS IS ANOTHER COVER BY FAN-CULT FAVE DREW BADLEY WHO LATER WENT ON TO CREATE THE OBSCURE BUT BRILLIANT SERIES, "THE CHEESE-MEN OF MARS"
©1982 SCOTT SHAW!

They let me take a huge pile of them to use for the books. This was truly the old days — no inventory or anything; it was the honor system.

"I was already acquainted with designer Syd Mead. I called him and asked if he could help me better understand what I had. He said, 'Sure,' and I drove over to the house, on Gardner Street, in Hollywood, that he used as a studio. We sat in the living room, a pile of my recently obtained sketches on the coffee table and my cassette tape recorder running. Syd said that, although he was happy to help us out, he could not be directly quoted, since there were legal issues around attribution and he wasn't getting paid. I agreed. He started going through the pile of designs, explaining what he was thinking of while conceiving them: the parking meter, the Voight-Kampff machine, the outdoor lunch counter (which wasn't used, by the way). To say this session was fascinating is an understatement.

"We engaged local graphic designer Jim Cornelius to help us put the books together. It was a very fun time for me; I got to work with Jim at his studio rather than at the office. I supervised the image selection and wrote text for each, based on my interview with Syd Mead. Jim created a logo for the book, chose the sepia-tone color treatment, and laid out the pages.

"When we got to *The Illustrated Blade Runner*, some challenges presented themselves. Our original idea was to use the film's storyboards to accompany the script. It seemed like there would be a coherent ongoing series of pictures related to the dialogue. This was not the case. Director Ridley Scott shot quite a bit of the picture without using storyboards. Where there were storyboards, they were mainly drawn by Scott himself. The production crew called these 'Ridleygrams,' and they were a visual aid in communicating what he wanted in a specific shot. We phoned the Ladd Company and begged for more artwork. We received as much as they had available, including several of Michael Kaplan and Charles Knode's costume designs and art by production illustrator Sherman Labby. In what we viewed as something of a coup, they also gave us an introduction by Ridley Scott. We did the best we could with this material, led by Jim Cornelius, and finished the book in time.

"The *Blade Runner* portfolio was a comparatively easy project. We were used to doing portfolios, so it was pretty straightforward to select a set of color still photos and package them in a folder. The American Booksellers Association trade show was upcoming and that year was being held in Anaheim, just up the freeway from San Diego. Pacific Comics was able to get an exhibit booth and we set up a stand featuring our *Blade Runner* books, the forthcoming Donald M. Grant hardcover of Stephen King's *The Gunslinger: Dark Tower,* and our various comic books. The Ladd Company provided us with posters, what today we would call a 'sizzle reel' of the film, and a few cases of promo buttons to give away. It was, in many ways, a frustrating exhibiting experience; although these hot book releases were physically sitting on the table and booksellers could hold them in their hands, it was as if the books weren't 'real.' We got few orders and fewer nibbles from the chain bookstores. Therefore, the distribution of these publications was once again confined, for the most part, to comics specialty market retailers."

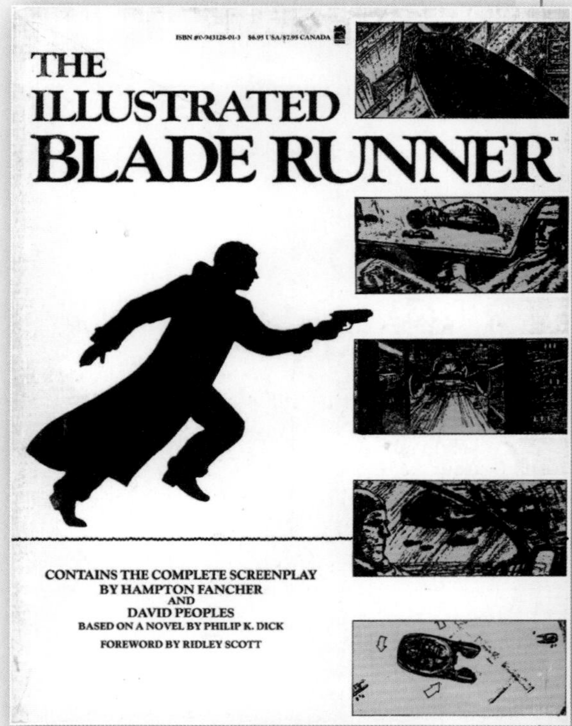
THE ILLUSTRATED BLADE RUNNER
CONTAINS THE COMPLETE SCREENPLAY BY HAMPTON FANCHER AND DAVID PEOPLES
BASED ON A NOVEL BY PHILIP K. DICK
FOREWORD BY RIDLEY SCOTT

Above: One of three *Blade Runner* tie-ins published by Blue Dolphin. **Below:** Pacific had planned for its first graphic album to be *Seven Samuroid* written and illustrated by Frank Brunner, and packaged by Bruce Jones Associates.

In late 1982, *Amazing Heroes* included this intriguing item: "Pacific will also be issuing Scott Shaw!'s collection of *The Craziest Comic Books of All Time*, under its 'Blue Dolphin Books' imprint. The book, which is scheduled for Summer 1983 release, is based on Shaw!'s 'Esoteric Comics' slide show which he has been presenting at conventions all over the country for the past several years. The book will reprint the covers and some interior pages from such comic books as *Negro Romance, Dagwood Splits the Atom, Space Western,* and *It's Fun to Stay Alive*." Alas, even after being rechristened *Oddball Comics,* the Shaw! tome was not to be.

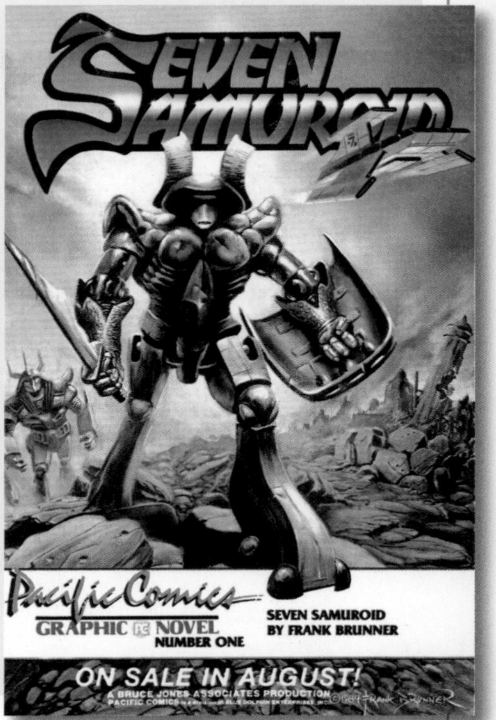
SEVEN SAMUROID
Pacific Comics
GRAPHIC NOVEL
NUMBER ONE
SEVEN SAMUROID BY FRANK BRUNNER
ON SALE IN AUGUST!
A BRUCE JONES ASSOCIATES PRODUCTION

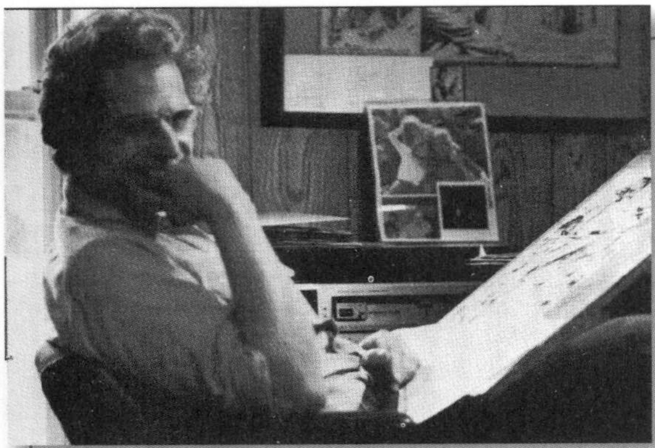

BONANZA OF BACK-UPS

With little to no outside advertising appearing in the Pacific Comics titles, there always seemed to be room for short back-up stories to fill out the comics. So, when freelancers would show up at Pacific HQ, they'd often walk out with an assignment to help get an issue on press.

This page: Clockwise from above is Al Williamson; his "Cliff Hanger" page from *Somerset Holmes* #1 [Sept. '83]; pin-up from *Skateman* #1 [Nov. '83]; and Sage trading card [1995].

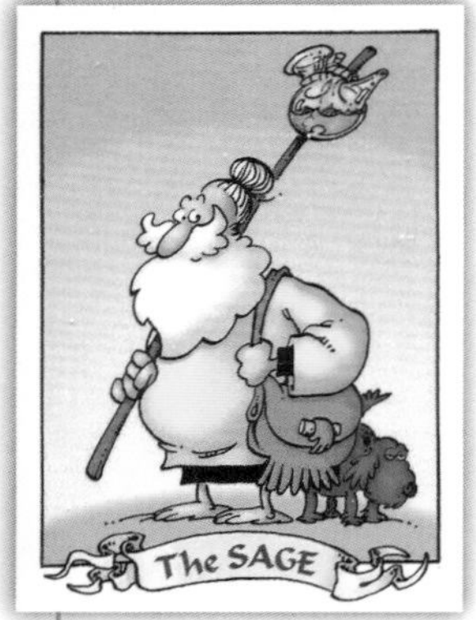
The SAGE

Paul S. Power, an Aussie cartoonist living in Southern California, shared about a tale (with pin-up) he did for the imprint. "In 1982, I visited Steve Schanes and David Scroggy, at Pacific Comics, in San Diego, to see if I could score a comic-book gig. They said they had eight or nine pages to fill and I could write and draw a story. That book turned out to be *Skateman* #1 [Nov. 1983]… So I went back to my place and thought about a story that involved my characters of Professor Om, Boxer, Ed Bidgee, and the Rock Warrior, about Ed's baby daughter who drives our heroes into a near nervous breakdown over the Moon."[35]

Power added, "I wanted to draw an adventure comedy. I created all these characters back in the early 1970s… Schanes and Scroggy were very easy to work for… I tried to get Alex Toth to submit to them, a story that he had about UFOs over the Hollywood Bowl. Toth lived almost next to the place."

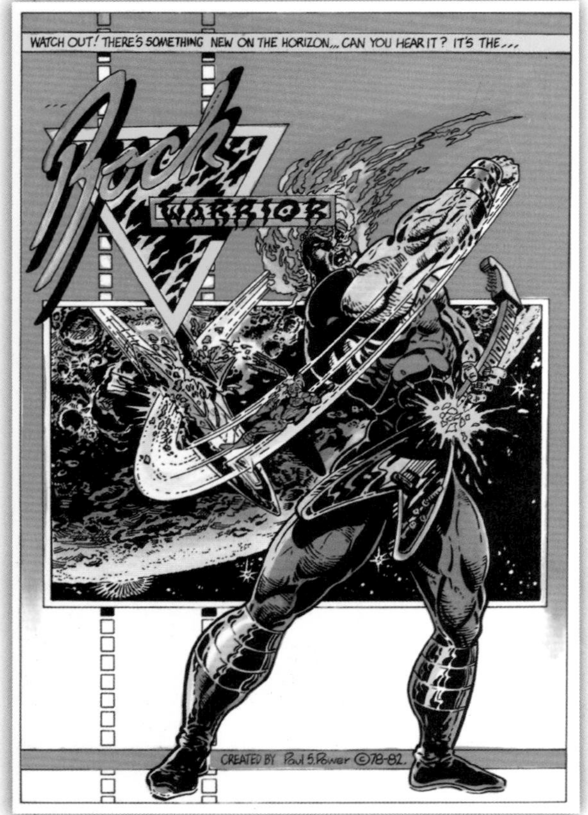
WATCH OUT! THERE'S SOMETHING NEW ON THE HORIZON… CAN YOU HEAR IT? IT'S THE…
Rock
WARRIOR
CREATED BY Paul S. Power ©78-82.

A comic book legend who did contribute a regular back-up feature was the great Al Williamson, who was recruited by packager Bruce Jones to draw the "Cliff Hanger" episodes in *Somerset Holmes.* The beautifully rendered six-episode series was written by Jones and was an "affectionate tribute to those thrill-a-minute Saturday morning adventure serials," said Paul Gravett. "Movie style opening and closing credits with blackout-style panel borders reinforce the cinematic effect."[36]

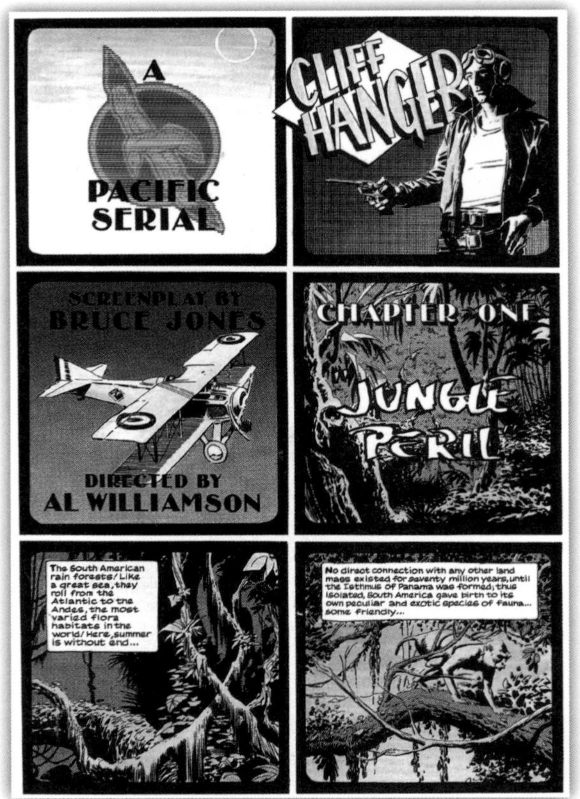
A
PACIFIC SERIAL
CLIFF HANGER
SCREENPLAY BY BRUCE JONES
DIRECTED BY AL WILLIAMSON
CHAPTER ONE
JUNGLE PERIL
The South American rain forests! Like a great sea, they roll from the Atlantic to the Andes, the most varied flora habitats in the world! Here, summer is without end…
No direct connection with any other land mass existed for seventy million years, until the Isthmus of Panama was formed; thus isolated, South America gave birth to its own peculiar and exotic species of fauna… some friendly…

Seasoned professionals Steve Ditko and Sergio Aragonés contributed back-ups, the former with "The Mocker," featuring a crime-fighting character in the mold of The Question and Mr. A, which appeared in *Silver Star* #2 [Apr. 1983]. The latter artist produced "The Sage," a back-up series in *Groo the Wanderer,* which directly related to the lead feature and it starred a wise old man, who advises the buffoonish Groo. The Sage also has a dog, Mulch.

Ditko wrote, "Unknown to me, the first Mocker episode was sold to Pacific Comics. And I was surprised to discover it published in Jack Kirby's *Silver Star* #2, April issue. 'The Mocker' was intended for magazine-size, so its page proportions didn't fit the comics-size page. There was a lot of wasted space. Worse, 'The Mocker' was never intended for color. I eventually got back the original art."[37]

The magazine originally set to feature "The Mocker" was New Media's *Adventure Illustrated*, edited by Richard Howell, who shared that Ditko and he had a falling out over production issues. Howell explained, "I think he had a 'Mocker' [*episode*] in his pocket all along, but I pushed my luck and encouraged him to produce it in black-&-white wash, like so many of his classic Warren stories."[38]

About the sale to Pacific, Howell surmised, "New Media was definitely experiencing some financial problems at the time, so (and this is a guess) they traded away some original comics material in order to pay back debts."[39]

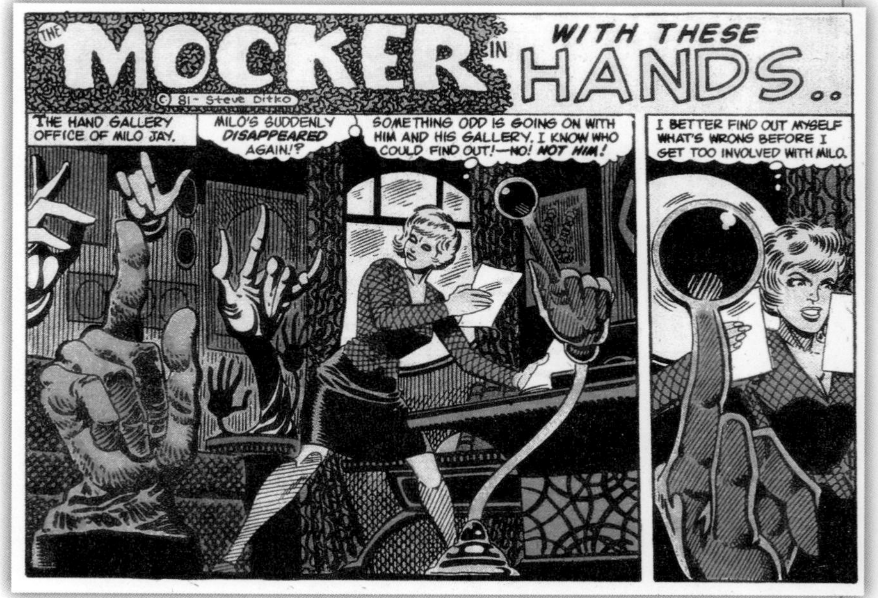
THE MOCKER IN WITH THESE HANDS..
© 81 - Steve Ditko
THE HAND GALLERY OFFICE OF MILO JAY.
MILO'S SUDDENLY DISAPPEARED AGAIN!?
SOMETHING ODD IS GOING ON WITH HIM AND HIS GALLERY. I KNOW WHO COULD FIND OUT!—NO! NOT HIM!
I BETTER FIND OUT MYSELF WHAT'S WRONG BEFORE I GET TOO INVOLVED WITH MILO.

An incongruous combination that Pacific published was Chris Miller's "Tales of Zed" backing up the two issues of *Ms. Mystic*. Miller's well-drawn pair of whimsical (if superfluous) fantasy vignettes featured a white-bearded, flute-playing old geezer, a co-feature as different from the super-heroic, environmentalist-themed lead series as can be imagined. (Miller would go on to produce a portfolio for Schanes and Schanes, and was represented by David Scroggy. Miller drew a story, "The Darkling Chronicles," for Blackthorne's one-shot, *Outposts* #1 [June 1987], and then evidently left the comics field.)

Newcomer to the scene Paul Smith, already something of a fan sensation during that period with his artwork for *Doctor Strange* and *Uncanny X-Men*, found time to produce a charming back-up series in the pages of *Sun Runners*. "His stories will have nothing to do with *Sun Runners*: they will be set in the 1940s," Kim Thompson explained. "Mike is a detective in the tradition of Sam Spade, and Mike Hammer — and, especially, Howdy Doody. Mike, you see, is a wooden dummy."[40] The humorous crime noir series lasted four episodes (the last with Eclipse Comics), all written by Roger McKenzie.

Michael Thibodeaux's "Last of the Viking Heroes," which started as a back-up in *Silver Star* #1 [Feb. 1983] had a much longer existence, into the 1990s. The artist had been Jack Kirby's inker on *Captain Victory* and was given the chance to do his own strip. "I was trying to come up with a concept of my own," Thibodeaux told John Morrow, "and [*Kirby*] kept saying, 'Do something you love. What do you love?' And I thought the Vikings were the coolest guys ever! They were the ultimate adventurers. Traveling all over the world, with their incredible, mythical gods. The visuals have such endless possibilities. Most importantly, it gave me the opportunity to draw scantily-clad women. He was more of a mentor in showing me the importance in pursuing things you are passionate about; don't try to follow formulas. Formulas can sometimes create barriers for the imagination. Along with this advice, he also drew three *Viking Heroes* covers for me."[41]

Between 1987–92, Thibodeaux's *Last of the Viking Heroes* ran for 12 issues as a standalone title, plus various specials, with some, as mentioned, sporting Kirby covers.

This page: Clockwise from above, "The Mocker" from *Silver Star* #2 [Apr. '83]; *Last of the Viking Heroes* #1 [Mar. '87]; spread from *Silverheels* #2 [Mar. '84]; and page from *Ms. Mystic* #1 [Oct. '82].

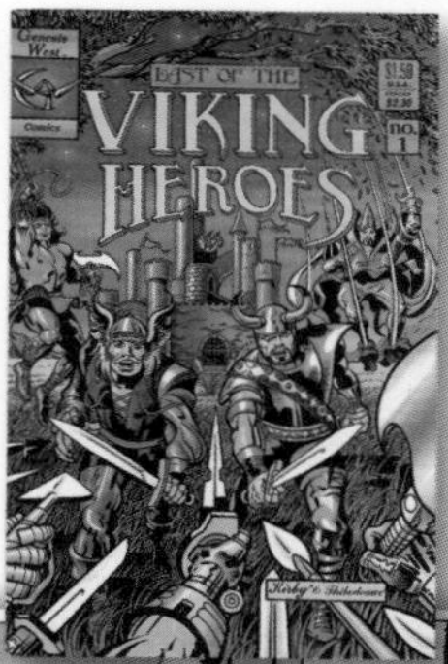
LAST OF THE VIKING HEROES

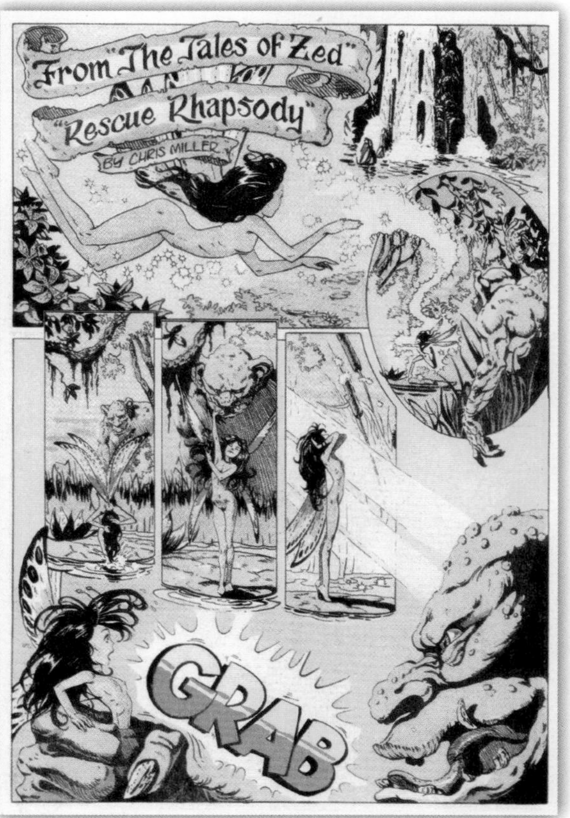
From "The Tales of Zed"
"Rescue Rhapsody"
BY CHRIS MILLER
GRAB

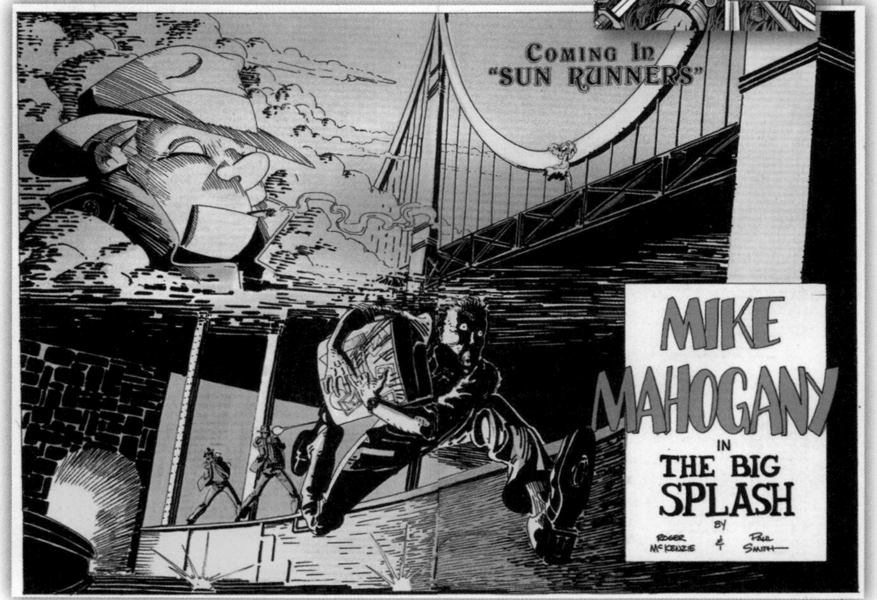
COMING IN "SUN RUNNERS"
MIKE MAHOGANY
IN
THE BIG SPLASH
BY
ROGER McKENZIE & PAUL SMITH

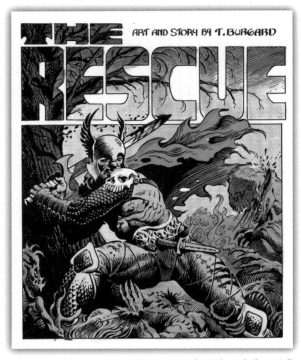

THE RESCUE
ART AND STORY BY T. BURGARD

Having attended a few San Diego Comic-Cons, Tim Burgard was familiar with the Schanes brothers and, after graduating art school, "I talked with Bill and Steve at the old Pacific Comics warehouse," he told Jon B. Cooke. "They liked the work I had. I had done (for junior college or whatever) a short story and basically just redid it. That was 'The Rescue,' for *Edge of Chaos* [#2, Nov. 1983] and then did 'Face to Face'[*Vanguard Illustrated* #5, May 1984]. And, not only did I do those two stories, I also did a portfolio of something like six plates [*Blood Sisters*, 1982]."[42]

Above: Tim Burgard's splash panel from "The Rescue," a back-up in *Edge of Chaos* #2 [Nov. 1983]. **Next page:** Poster art promoting Gray Morrow's series. **Below:** Double-page "Flynn" spread by D. Bruce Berry from the *Silver Star* #3 [June 1983] back-up.

During that time, Burgard became friendly with Dave Stevens. "I think he had already done 'The Rocketeer,' and he had the original art from 'Aurora,' about the girl on the rocketship and her little companion, and he was in the process of erasing all the faces of the woman. I was kind of horrified because he was erasing so much that the paper was looking ready to go, too! He said, 'This is my ex-wife's face. If this [*concept*] goes anywhere, I don't want it to be her likeness. So I saw a few pages that still had Brinke's face, so that was interesting."

One highlight working for Pacific was, after turning in his story, "Face to Face," it was chosen to be the basis for the cover art by Michael W. Kaluta. "He used my story for the cover," Burgard exclaimed. "That was awesome!"

The artist added, "About the same time I got the work at Pacific Comics, I started drawing the 'Huntress' back-up stories in *Wonder Woman,* and I also did an unpublished story about 'The War that Time Forgot,' for *Secret Origins*, written by James Robinson." The artist additionally did jobs for First Comics and Eclipse, but ended up working in animation and creating storyboards for Hollywood movies. Today, Burgard is also teaching storyboarding for the film department at Art Center College of Design, in Pasadena.

"Pacific was always great," Burgard summarized. "Finally, there wasn't anything left for me to do over there, because they had stopped doing the portfolios. I was midway in doing one, and I think I did get paid an upfront amount, so I did get partial payment for one that never went to print. I was always on good terms with them."[43]

Of course, there were numerous other back-up strips that helped fill out the Pacific titles, some notable and some less so. Among the former was a story illustrated by Jaime Hernandez, "All My Love, Aliso Road," in *Silver Heels* #3 [May 1984], as well as the curious "Detective Flynn" episodes by writer Richard Kyle and artist D. Bruce Berry, in *Silver Star* #3 and 4 [June–Aug. 1983], a story based in the New York City of 1884.

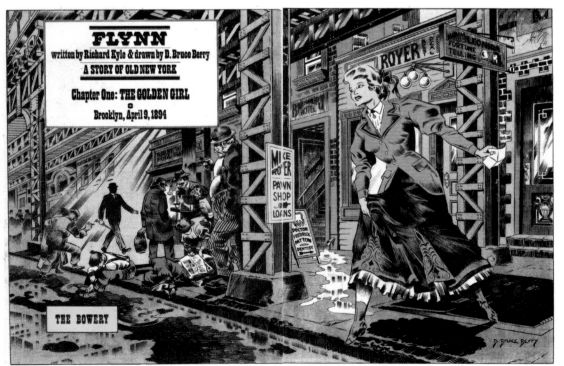

FLYNN
written by Richard Kyle & drawn by D. Bruce Berry
A STORY OF OLD NEW YORK
Chapter One: THE GOLDEN GIRL
Brooklyn, April 9, 1894
ROYER
FORTUNE TELLING
MIKE ROYER
PAWN SHOP
LOANS
DOCTOR FREDRICK PATTON DENTIST
THE BOWERY
D. BRUCE BERRY

In the last analysis, after back-ups had been first utilized to sample coming titles, they were later intended to help give exposure to fledgling artists and writers, as well as introduce any number of wild and wacky comic book concepts. As any number of contributors will agree, it was a fun ride… while it lasted!

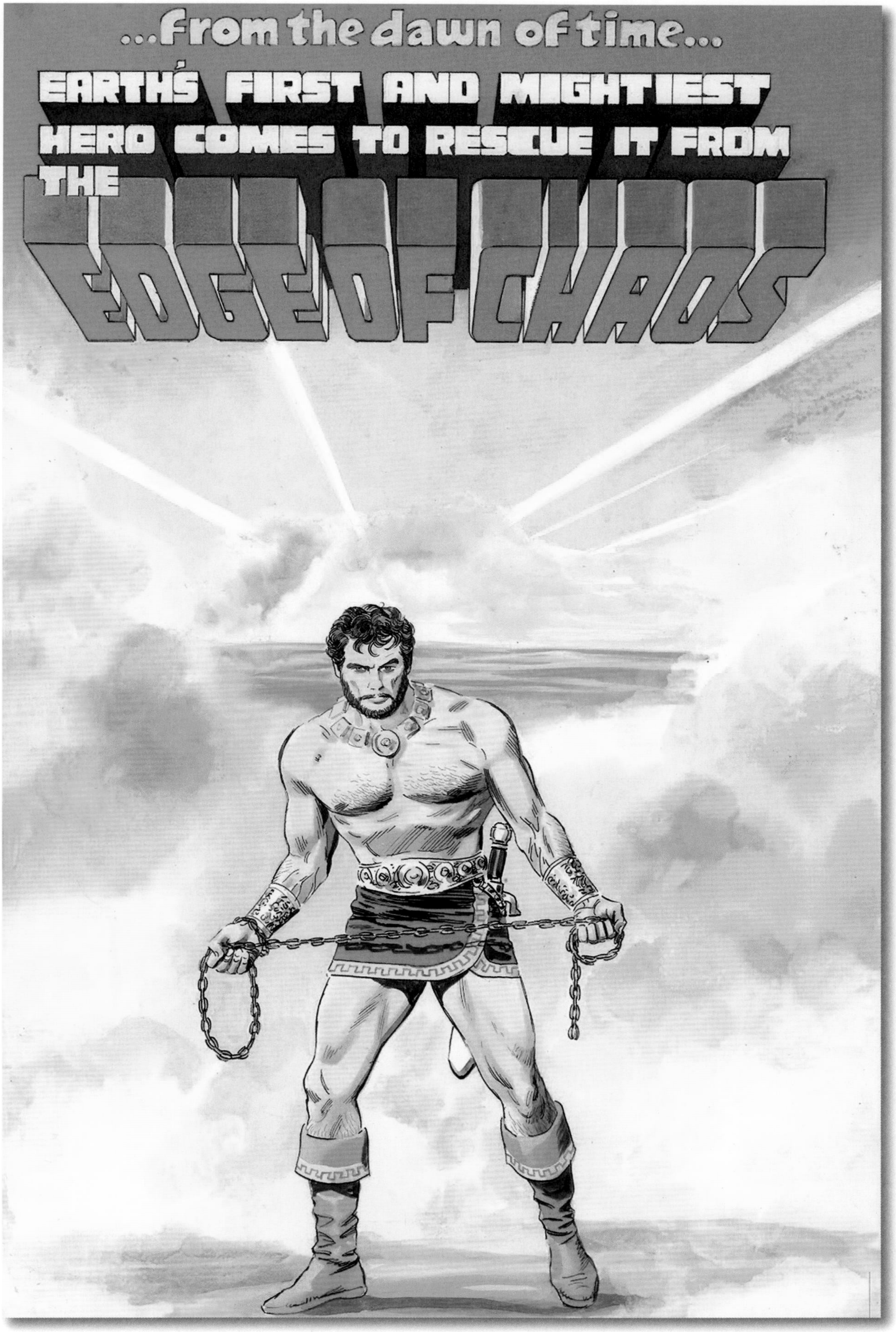
...From the dawn of time...
EARTH'S FIRST AND MIGHTIEST HERO COMES TO RESCUE IT FROM THE
EDGE OF CHAOS

EDGE OF CHAOS
PC
"For the NEW Era in Comics"
$1.00 US
$1.25 Canada
ORIGIN ISSUE!
GRAY MORROW

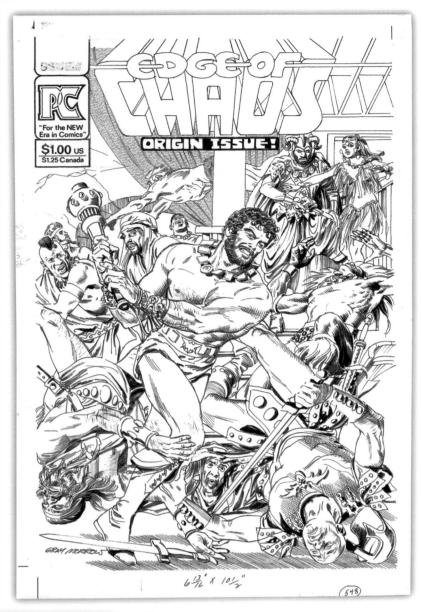

Above: Gray Morrow's *Edge of Chaos* #1 [July 1983] cover art. Courtesy of Ray Cuthbert. **Below:** *Edge of Chaos* was the cover feature in *Amazing Heroes* #26 [July '83].

AMAZING HEROES
Special Preview:
EDGE OF CHAOS!
PLUS:
The Nick Fury Hero History
Star Wars
Ron Goulart On Forgotten Heroes of The '40s
And More!

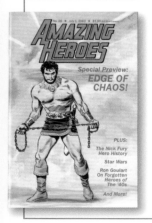

WITH AN EDGE OF GRAY

Veteran comic book master Gray Morrow, who had entered the comics field at the very end of the EC Comics era, bounced around the industry until he found his niche at Warren Publications in the mid-1960s. It was at that publisher where, for about three years or so, Morrow produced groundbreaking, magnificent artwork, from war stories to horror paintings to stunning single-pagers. While he subsequently found work outside the field, in comics, he would drift between companies, though significantly working as a quasi-packager for Archie Publications' Red Circle line in the early '70s, as well as for Charlton Comics' *Space: 1999* black-&-white magazine in the mid-'70s.

In a 1983 interview, the artist was asked why he had changed publishers in his career so often. "If you're referring to comic books," he replied, "there were always a lot of frustrations involved. There were a lot of things being discussed over the years that have finally come to pass concerning copyrights and residuals, and all that sort of thing. But they were just talk back then and, as a result, I was often busy working on what I thought was far more rewarding things. For example, for the last five years, I've been involved in syndication comic strips for the newspapers."[44]

With the advent of improved creators' rights and freedom afforded by the direct market, Morrow had just the thing for an adventurous publisher: an adult adventure title infused with mythological themes, which he had developed but was awaiting a receptive publisher.

Edge of Chaos was the name of Morrow's saga of Greek gods and lost Atlantis, a three-issue series he intended to write, pencil, ink, color, and even letter. As the first issue's editorial by David Scroggy gushed, "There are not many talents who even attempt to carry this load, and even fewer who are able to pull it off. Gray Morrow is one of those rare individuals who brings all the components together into a seamless package that is truly more than the sum of its parts — an adventure that reflects the vision of its creator crystal-clear."[45]

Many years later, Scroggy told the author that the comics creator and sometime packager wasn't solicited by Pacific but rather, "Gray brought it to us, initially through contact with Steve Schanes. The first issue [*was*] completely done. I didn't have much contact after that, other than maybe a phone call or two over deadlines with the following issues."[46]

From his perspective, the creator saw what transpired a bit differently. "Actually, they chose me," Morrow told interviewer Kevin McConnell in 1983. "They sent a bunch of material and a copy of their contract to me with a query as to whether or not I would be interested in working on some kind of project with them. I simply followed up on it. As it happened, I had a couple of projects of my own sitting on the shelf, which had been sitting there for a couple of years, and I sort of got them out and dusted them off. I reworked them a little bit and they took it."[47]

McConnell then asked Morrow to describe *Edge of Chaos*. "Oh, I guess the closest you could come is to call it fantasy. It involves pre-deluge Atlantis and events leading up to the cataclysm which wiped the continent out. It involves a man from our own time who is transported back into that time, and the story revolves around him. It also has a great deal of fantasy characters in it from mythology —

CREATION
EDGE OF CHAOS
by GRAY MORROW
CC
CREATION COMIX
Beginning in May — A three-issue mini-series by a master comics artist. Explore an ancient world of fantasy through the eyes of a modern-day hero. You've never seen adventure like this! Watch for it from PACIFIC COMICS

Allan Gross, in *Gray Morrow: Visionary* [2001, Insight], gave an overall assessment of the series: "This was a fast-moving tale of Eric Cleese,* a modern-day sailor who goes back in time to assume the role of Hercules. Gray's story ties together elements of ancient history, mythology, and even modern day theories of catastrophism as put forth in Immanuel Velikovsky's controversial book, *World in Collision.* Only Gray could combine such disparate ingredients into a story that was imbued with a solid sense of sexual play and heroic fun."

Unfortunately, there would be no interest from other publishers to resurrect *Edge of Chaos* and Morrow's comics work randomly appeared at various publishers over the remainder of his life. But the creator, even beyond his tragic passing in 2001, remained a much beloved "artist's artist," and *Edge of Chaos* is still fondly remembered.

* Say the name "Eric Cleese" three times fast and find out if it sounds like the moniker of a certain Greco-Roman demi-god!

Pacific Profiles

Gray Morrow

Born: *Mar. 1934*
The artist's first professional sale was a romance story for Toby Press, which went out of business in 1955 before the story could be published. Of course, Gray became a legendary illustrator, renowned for his Warren magazine work, science-fiction digest illos, and paperback covers.

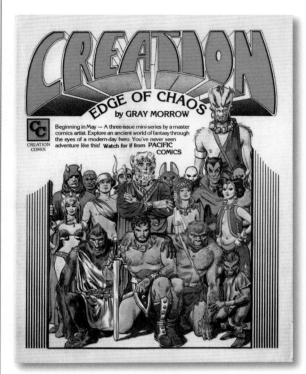

Above: Gray Morrow. Photo by Ray Cuthbert.

Inset left: Creation Con booklet with Gray Morrow's *Edge of Chaos* cover piece promoting the series in 1983. **Below:** Presentation artwork by Gray used to pitch his three-part *Edge of Chaos* series to potential publishers.

and not just Greek and Roman mythology, but other cultures, as well."[48]

The *Edge of Chaos* editor touched upon an aspect of the charm in the series in that first issue editorial, one that personalized it for the folks in the home office. "We knew we were dealing with a talent who had a sense of humor when we first received the cover for this issue," David explained. "After admiring the tumultuous action scene, we noticed a message penciled into the margin. It wasn't a coloring note or some other bit of technical direction, but the observation that, 'It looks like happy hour's over!' This humor is present throughout the script, giving *Edge of Chaos* a lack of pretension that is very refreshing in a genre that very often takes itself a mite too seriously. This in no way dampens the action and excitement of this saga, but adds one more dimension to an already well-rounded yarn."[49]

Out of curiosity, the *Amazing Heroes* interviewer asked about Morrow's relative speed as a creator. "It's funny," he answered, "you kind of get into a rhythm of doing a certain kind of thing in a certain way. Like, for the newspaper strips, I got very, very fast. I was able to do a week's worth in just a couple of days, which is not bad at all."[50]

Morrow continued, "I find that getting back into comics, I've lost a lot of speed that I used to have, and I've slowed down even more with *Edge of Chaos*, since I'm actually writing it as I draw it. Hopefully, that will pick up as time goes on."

THE SETTING IS PRE-DELUGE ATLANTIS- MU- AND LEMURIA WHERE IT ALL ACTUALLY HAPPENED -NOT THE DISTORTED VERSIONS PIECED TOGETHER AND MADE THEIR OWN BY THE GREEKS AND ROMANS CENTURIES LATER AFTER THE CATACLYSM...
ERIC UTILIZES VARIOUS MODES OF TRANSPORTATION- SUCH AS MANGA, THE MIGHTY WOOLY MAMMOTH....
...AND ON OTHER OCCASIONS THE VIHMANAS OR SKY CHARIOTS USUALLY USED BY ONLY THOSE FAVORED BY THE GODS OR THE GODS THEMSELVES.
THE GODS RESIDE IN THEIR CITY IN THE CLOUDS.
PREHISTORIC BEASTS ARE CONTEMPORARY WITH MAN HERE AND IN SOME CASES DOMESTICATED BY HIM...IN OTHERS, NOT!
THERE ARE GODDESSES TOO, OF THE CELESTIAL AND EARTHBOUND VARIETIES, MANY OF WHOM TAKE AN INTEREST IN OUR HERO.

This page: For decades, Frank Thorne was a journeyman comic book artist, knocking out assignments for an assortment of publishers, including Gold Key and DC, but in 1975 he drew *Red Sonja,* which changed his life. After 18 issues of his sexy version of the warrior, Thorne was kicked off the series, so he created his own Sonja, Ghita of Alizarr. Below is the collection title page and insert right, the volume Catalan published after Pacific's demise.

LOVELY GHITA

Comics veteran Frank Thorne, who had been relegated to war and Wild West stories on Joe Kubert's DC books and, before that, plenty of Gold Key adventure material, had come into his own when, in 1975, he was handed the *Red Sonja* assignment at Marvel. With 18 issues (including one *Marvel Feature* ish) to his credit starring the crimson-maned swordswoman, all drawn with unbridled enthusiasm and absolute panache, Thorne became permanently associated with the character. And, when the gig was taken from him, he created his own warrior women, including Ghita of Allizarr, a sexually-liberated character debuting in a Warren black-&-white magazine.

"Ghita" was the first series Thorne would write himself and, he told Gary Groth, "As I realized 'Ghita of Alizarr,' and before taking it to Warren, I was advised by Jim Lawrence to show it to Al Zuckerman, the owner of Writers House in Manhattan. Al represented Jim, who was an excellent writer and a good friend. Zuckerman took one look at 'Ghita' and signed me on. He loved my blonde, and loved my writing. To hear that from the head honcho of one of the most prestigious agents in New York was astounding. I mean, this guy reps the likes of Ken Follett and Stephen King! In truth, Maestro, I'd always wanted to write. It's easy for me, easier than drawing or painting… So, it was Zuckerman who contacted Jim Warren and set the deal; 'Ghita' would be serialized in *1984*, the hip new mag from Warren Publications. When I saw Warren for the first time in his office, he was impressed with my connecting with Writers House. I guess he hadn't dealt with a cartoonist's agent all that often."[52]

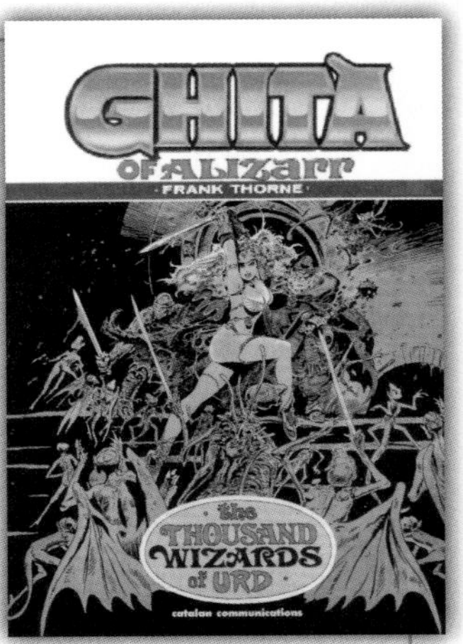
GHITA
OF ALIZARR
· FRANK THORNE ·
the THOUSAND WIZARDS of URD
catalan communications

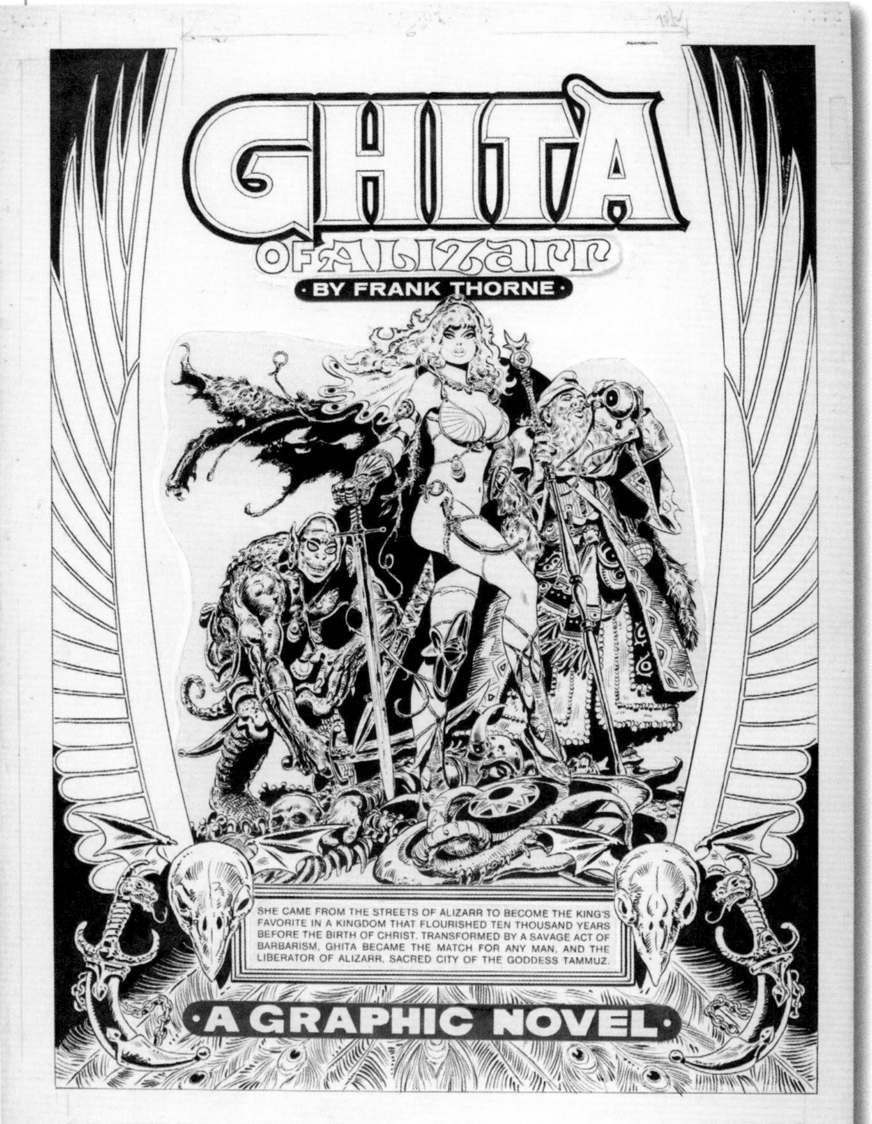
GHITA
OF ALIZARR
· BY FRANK THORNE ·
SHE CAME FROM THE STREETS OF ALIZARR TO BECOME THE KING'S FAVORITE IN A KINGDOM THAT FLOURISHED TEN THOUSAND YEARS BEFORE THE BIRTH OF CHRIST. TRANSFORMED BY A SAVAGE ACT OF BARBARISM, GHITA BECAME THE MATCH FOR ANY MAN, AND THE LIBERATOR OF ALIZARR, SACRED CITY OF THE GODDESS TAMMUZ.
· A GRAPHIC NOVEL ·

Thorne continued, "Jim and I got along really well. We're the same age, and he played the trumpet in swing bands around Philly, his hometown. I met Weezie Jones and Bill DuBay in my visits to the Warren offices. Weezie, now Louise Simonson, is a sweetheart. Bill just loved 'Ghita.' In 1981, I received the Warren Award for excellence — no money involved, but I had hoped I'd at least get one of the rubber Frankenstein masks that Jim sold in the magazines. I always keep my rubber chicken handy for a sight gag; it would've been nice to have the mask on while I took a shower! I wonder what ever happened to all that delightful kitsch that Warren pitched in his books?"[53]

With the fall of Warren Publications, Thorne's "Ghita" stories were eventually collected by the Schanes brothers, as they published the first volume of *Ghita of Alizarr* under the Blue Dolphin Enterprises book imprint before they, too, went under. Catalan Communications would release the second volume and reprint the first in 1985. *Ghita of Alizarr* was eventually translated into five languages and even optioned by a Hollywood producer.

Thorne told Groth, "When the book was published in Italy — in gravure, no less — [*a letter came*] from the great Italian film director Federico Fellini. In it, he describes how much he enjoyed the book and with it wishes me good luck. The letter and envelope hang, framed, on my studio wall."[54]

CORONADO DREAMIN'

In his introduction to the collected *Somerset Holmes* [1987, Eclipse], Bruce Jones sets the stage for the most memorable collaboration between creative/life partner April Campbell, artist Brent Anderson, and himself during the Bruce Jones Associates years at Pacific Comics:

"We moved to San Diego, and April and I not only wrote for the Schanes brothers, we started our own line of comics under my old [*Kansas City*] imprint, BJA. And I just may always think of the year-and-a-half that followed as the happiest time of my life. Think about it: I lived on this Pacific island called Coronado, across the bay from the most beautiful city in the world, San Diego; I was in love with this incredible, sexy, brilliantly intelligent woman; and I ran a comic book line over which I had complete and total creative and editorial control. I mean, for better or worse, the books were mine — nobody butted in with incongruous columns or insipid guidelines, nobody told me what to do. Some would no doubt call this too much power, but pal, it was heaven. I had never enjoyed that kind of artistic and creative freedom, I have never since. From cover to cover, our books had a *look*. I was and am very proud of them. Could I complain?

"Well… a little. I still wasn't making movies. Neither was April, and that was the whole idea in the first place, right? L.A. beckoned. What to do?

Left: Brent Anderson exhibiting at a local art show in California. Much of the work on display is from his *Somerset Holmes* assignment, including the cover painting for #2 [Sept. 1983]. **Below:** Campbell modeling for Anderson. **Inset bottom left:** Promo poster for the BJA Associates series by Bruce Jones, April Campbell, and Brent Anderson.

Somerset Holmes
ALONE
VULNERABLE
TERRIFIED
- She doesn't know
who she is . . .
Where she came from . . .
. . . or why they're
trying to kill her!
JONES & ANDERSON THIS SUMMER FROM

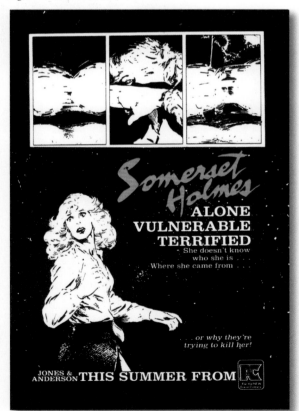

"'We should work with Brent Anderson on something,' suggested April one sunny California morning over breakfast. 'You two did such fun stuff on Marvel's *Ka-Zar* — imagine what we could turn out with a free rein.'

"'Like what?' I wanted to know. She shrugged. 'Let's call Brent, maybe he's got some ideas.'"[55]

Anderson shared with the author the origin of the series from his perspective. "As to the genesis of *Somerset Holmes*, Bruce Jones and I were big fans of Peter O'Donnell's Modesty Blaise character, of both his novels, and the Jim Holdaway-drawn comic strip. One day, I don't remember exactly where or when, I mentioned wanting to do some kind of take of our own on the character: a self-sufficient, independent, strong female hero who could hold her own in a patriarchal world, a super-spy like Blaise maybe. Bruce and I bandied the idea about, April Campbell was invited into the discussion, and a character began to develop. We talked about Hitchcock's film, *North by Northwest* [1959], starring Cary Grant and Eva Marie Saint, considered by many to be the first 'James Bond' film, made four years before *Dr. No* [1963], and played with the idea of

Pacific Profiles

Brent Anderson

Born: *June 1955*
Today, Brent is best known for his work with Kurt Busiek and Alex Ross on the celebrated *Astro City* comic series, which he co-created. Brent got his first regular pro assignment drawing *Ka-Zar the Savage* with writer Bruce Jones for Marvel, and he also drew *X-Men: God Loves, Man Kills*.

Above: Brent Anderson from *Somerset Holmes* #1.

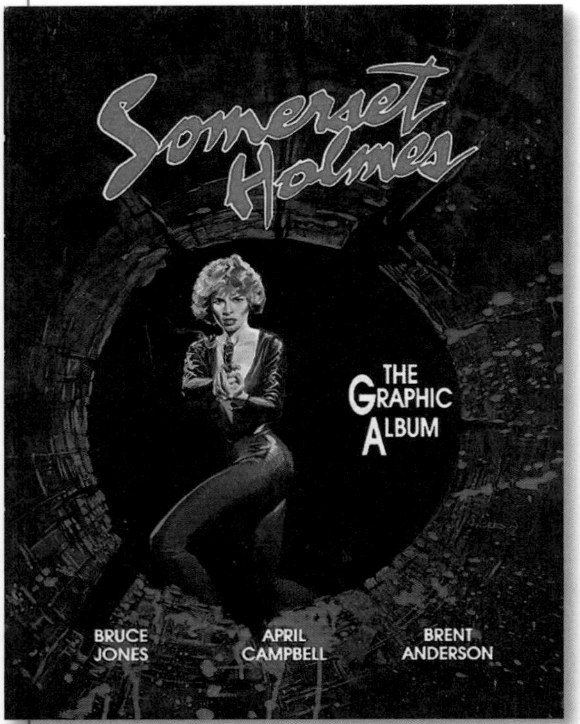
Somerset Holmes
THE GRAPHIC ALBUM
BRUCE JONES
APRIL CAMPBELL
BRENT ANDERSON

mixing in an international espionage-romance, à lá the relationship we had developed between Ka-Zar and Shanna in *Ka-Zar*, which our fan base found very appealing. I don't remember who put forward the mystery around the protagonist-having-amnesia trope, but Bruce and April wanted to call the book *Somerset*, in partial tribute to the works of W. Somerset Maugham, and because the nebulous title sounded romantic and mysterious. The *Holmes* came from Sherlock Holmes, the famous British detective, who brilliantly solved mysteries. As much as we liked the mysterious nature inherent in just calling the book *Somerset,* we decided that title alone was too vague and unspecific and soap-operatic by implication, so we added *Holmes* to the title to nail it down to one specific character, rather than implying an anthology series of unrelated romance mystery stories.

This page: Above is Brent Anderson's cover for the Eclipse graphic novel; inset is Jones during that era; and below is pencil preliminary, *Somerset Holmes* #1 cover art.

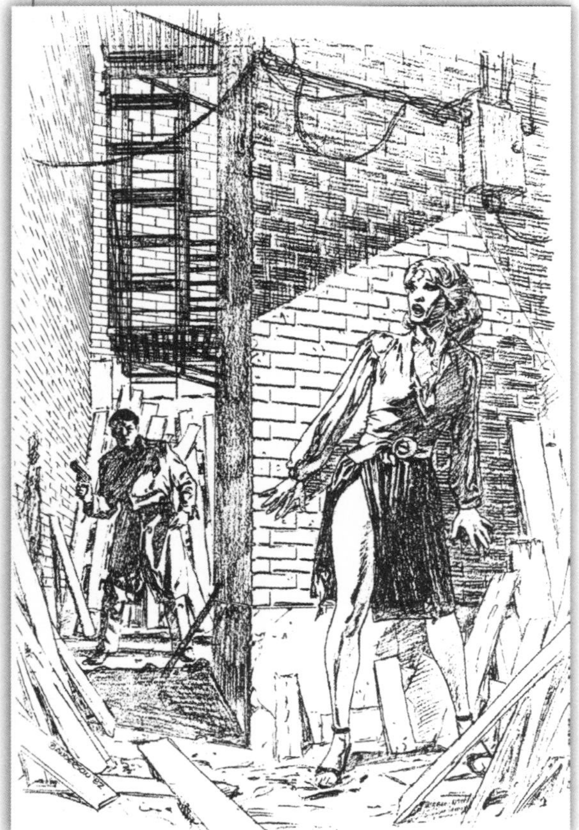

"I don't remember from where the inspiration came to have Somerset pull her auto fictive name from a billboard, but given the dark Hitchcockian nature of the story we were about to tell, Summerset Homes seemed like the perfect set-up, a dream of domestic normalcy giving birth to the nightmare story about as anomalous and exceptional and mysterious a character as Somerset Holmes."[56]

Jones did confess there was mercenary intent behind the series. "This is going to sound crassly commercial, but to tell it otherwise would be a lie. April and I put the *Somerset Holmes* idea together with artist Brent Anderson with the express notion of getting Hollywood interested. We felt, you know, if Spielberg and Lucas can make movies, so can we."[57]

Asked how long from initial concept of *Somerset Holmes* to printed first issue, Jones shared, "Not very long. I can't remember exact dates, but I know Pacific Comics was anxious to get product out in those days and get it out quickly, what with the boom in independent publishers, and the fact that Marvel was correspondingly flooding the market with product. But *Twisted Tales* and *Alien Worlds* had done well, so Pacific was willing to take a chance on this weird film noir piece with no horror and no super-heroes, which in those days, was taking a chance indeed. It all went pretty smoothly, as I recall. I was terribly manic about the production details, rushing around to printers and typesetters, and moving logos and color schemes all over the covers to get them just right — redesigning this, tinkering with that. If I'd been publishing a girlie mag like Hefner, I might have become rich through sheer force of will. I've learned since, to spread myself more evenly and conserve my energies a bit — save it for the close-up, you know?

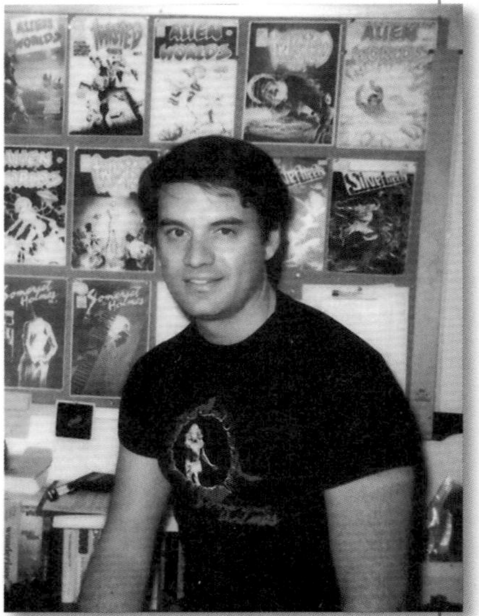

"As I mentioned, the cinema approach was both intentional and slaved over. I was very lucky to have someone like Brent who is not only an obviously gifted draftsman, but who was willing to put up with my Harvey Kurtzman-style rigidity during the course of the run. I actually did the storyboards on those first issues so Brent could see exactly what I had in mind. How the hell I did all that ridiculous amount of detail and wrote three other books at the same time, I'll never know. I doubt I could do it now. Inexhaustible youth, I suppose. But it was very rewarding creatively. We were breaking new ground at every turn back then with technical things — the coloring, the glossy stock, the painted covers, the whole darker, adult feel — it was a very kinetic, very experimental and fun time. And scary. We had no idea how this stuff was going to finally look or how it might be received. But it was exhilarating. I had total autonomy on my books — I was the packager, Pacific Comics was the publisher, and Steve and Bill Schanes just left me alone to run things my way. I doubt I'll ever see that kind of unbridled freedom again. I'm not sure anybody should have that much *carte blanche*; it's too easy to abuse it."[57]

Jones continued, "All the right circumstances just seemed to come into place to make those books happen; take any one of them away and I don't think it would have been the same. We were just very, very lucky. The strange thing is that none of us ever dreamed it would become this cult classic, we were just trying to do our best on the next job. It's only in retrospect I realize how serendipitous it all was."[58]

Though they would come close, the couple never would see their graphic novel — the final segments of which were published by Eclipse Comics after Pacific folded — translated into a major motion picture. Asked in 2012 if a movie was ever realized, Jones exclaimed, "Did it get close? It got made! A couple of times, I think. Just not by me — or with my consent! The first time I became aware of this was when Brent called and said, 'I think we just got ripped off,' referring to some picture with Geena Davis [*The Long Kiss Goodnight*, 1996], I think. Several months later, I remember watching TV one night with April and, about ten minutes into the film, we both looked at each other at exactly the same moment and said, 'Oh, sh*t....'

"Sometime later the phone rang, and Harlan Ellison was yelling: 'Some f*cker's filmed your comic!' He'd been recently ripped off by the first *Terminator* film and was very insistent that we go to court over the thing. But April and I were so exhausted with work at the time, we just let it go. It wasn't the first time."[59]

"Ultimately," Anderson said, "the series veered away from my original intention. We had talked about Somerset possibly being revealed as a globe-trotting super-spy, à lá James Bond or Modesty Blaise. The first three issues were devoted to developing the character and her mystery without actually revealing what that mystery was. With issue four, Bruce and April steered *Somerset* into the Hollywood entertainment arena, which was a complete surprise to me. I had visions of the character being pursued by a cadre of evil Bond villains or the like, much like the estranged amnesiac international assassin character Samantha Caine in *The Long Kiss Goodnight. Long Kiss* was obviously lifted from *Somerset Holmes,* long after a *Somerset* script had made the rounds of Hollywood."[60]

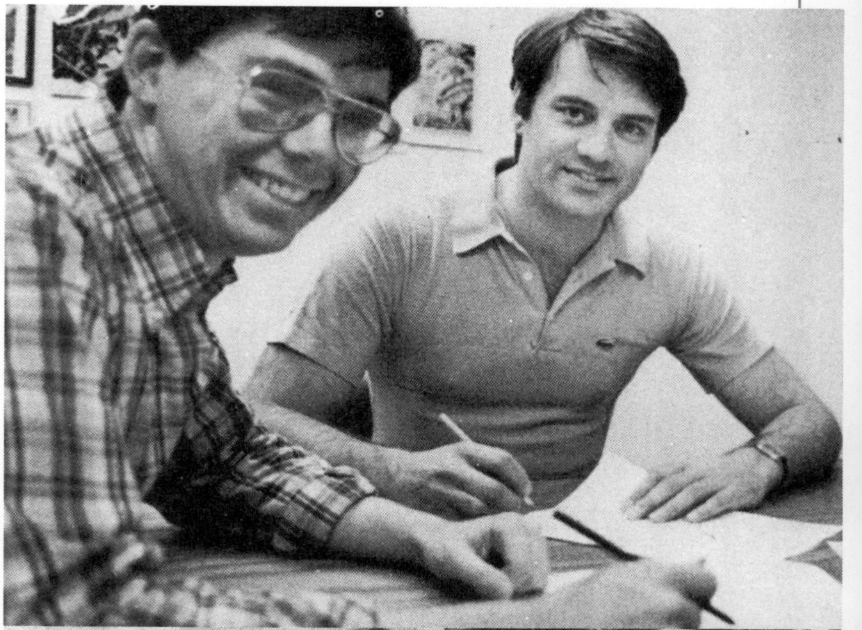
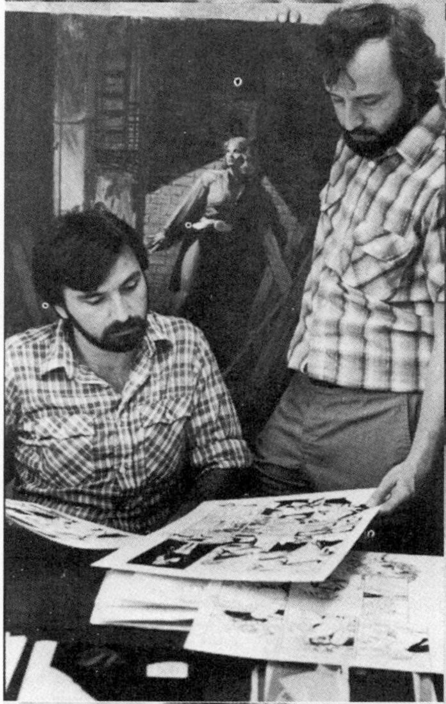
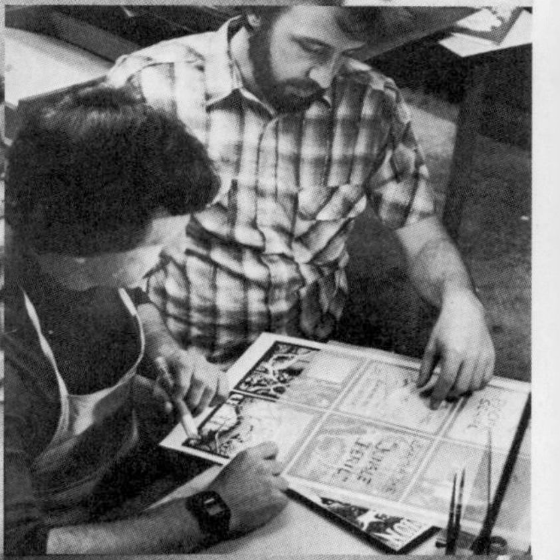
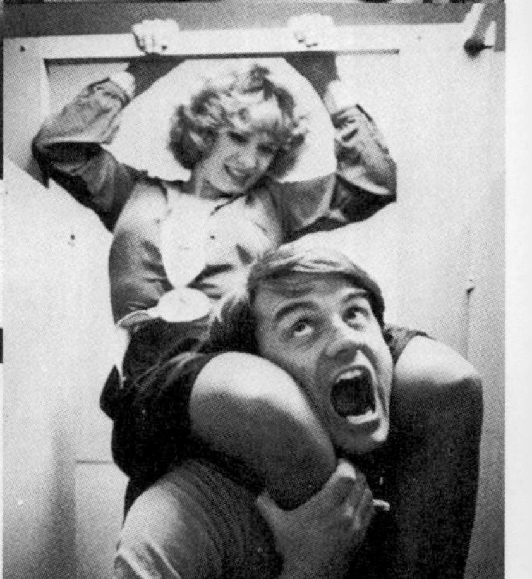
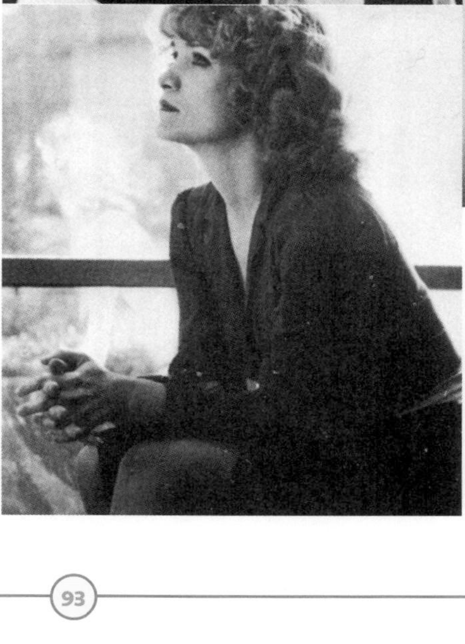

This: Select photos from the "Putting It All Together" behind-the-scenes feature in *Somerset Holmes* #1 [Sept. 1983]. Top is Bruce Jones and Brent Anderson; next row is the Schanes brothers and Steve Schanes with Paul Tallerday; above is April Campbell and Bruce.

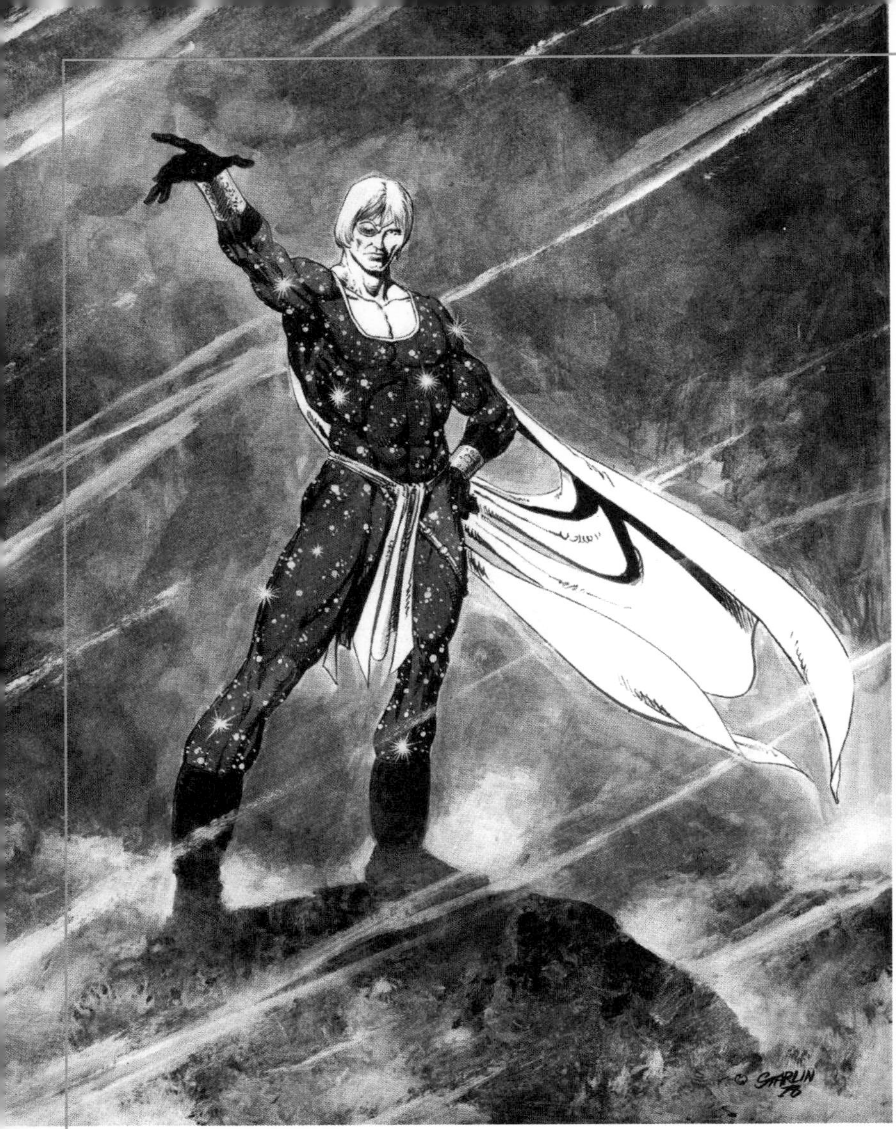
© STARLIN 78

Above: Jim Starlin Darklon pin-up from *Whizzard* #12 [1979]. **Inset right:** Scroggy poem from *Darklon* #1 [Nov. 1983]. **Below:** Starlin commission art.

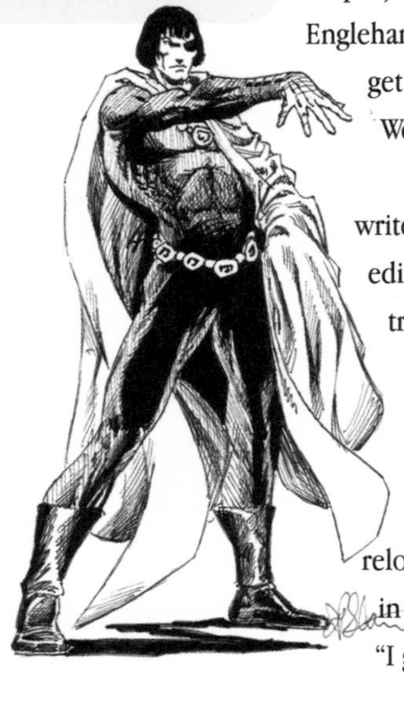

DARKLON IN LIVING COLOR

"In 1976, Starlin and Englehart finally rebelled against Marvel's work-for-hire policies," Steve Duin and Mike Richardson wrote in *Comics: Between the Panels*. "'We were both radical guys: we were both known to drop off projects if we didn't get what we thought was fair,' Englehart said. 'We were known as people who would get up and go. And we got up and went in 1976. We wanted reprint money. We wanted royalties.'"[61]

To be technical, writer Steve Englehart and artist/writer Jim Starlin quit the House of Ideas because of editorial interference in the bullpen. But it's just as true to say that creators' rights was an emerging issue in those days among young professionals, and Starlin, for one, was becoming intent on developing creator-owned properties.

Leaving Marvel behind, Starlin, who'd relocated to the West Coast, had to find a gig. "I was in California at the time," Starlin told Shaun Clancy. "I got some work with Warren [*Publications*] right away, doing 'Darklon'... They were always hiring, and they had this really good editor... Louise Jones [*Simonson*], who was the editor of *Creepy* and *Eerie* for the longest time. I knew her, but I just can't remember how it came about happening."[62]

Darklon was created, Starlin continued, "Just specifically for them. It sprang off some of that Moorcock's Elric stuff, somehow or another."[63] Replete with Ditko-like sorcery and Starlin's unique cosmic take on super-powered characters, the Mystic launched in *Eerie* #76 [Aug. 1976], as noted in a fanzine interview, with distinctly Alex Niño-like visuals. Starlin conceded the Filipino artist was indeed an influence: "Yes, I took a shot at Alex at that point," he told Jerry Durrwachter and Ed Mantels of *Whizzard*, in 1978. "I had only seen a little of his stuff, but thought, 'Wow, that's really nice.' I've had a tremendous respect for some of Niño's stuff and just had to try some of it."[64]

Starlin took full advantage of the black-&-white showcase *Eerie* offered and he decided to try new techniques. "I think I did a little charcoal work on 'Darklon the Mystic,'" he told Clancy. "There was a lot of experimentation on that... There was a lot of things in that. There was stuff like oil-painting marbley background. Most of it was done with a felt-point marker."[65]

The artist-writer stopped appearing in the Warren mags because another commitment arose. Starlin told Clancy, "I started working at Bakshi's animation studio and, in fact, the very last story I did after I worked at Bakshi's was the very last 'Darklon' story I ever did [*Eerie* #100, Apr. 1979].

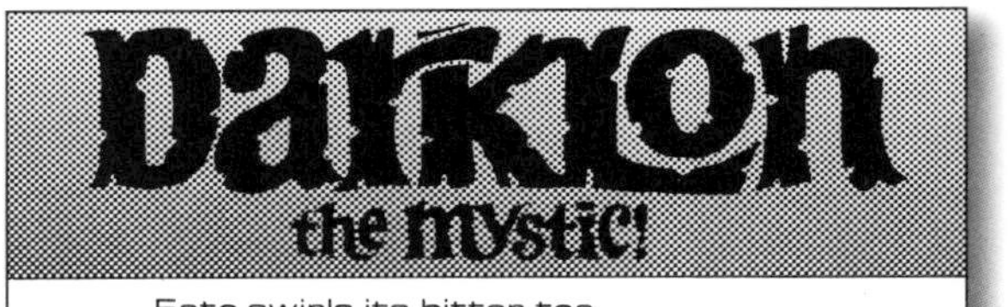
Darklon
the mystic!

Fate swirls its bitter tea
Into a cup called destiny,
Dredging up an evil bond
With a mystic prince, Darklon.

To aid his city, sire and kind
He ventures through the mortal veil
Into a nameless screaming skull
A lair of terror past the pale,
And with his last, lost tortured breath
He trades for power with his death

Becoming black and rolling dice
Of destiny, for that's the price
Of retribution, swift and fast,
A victory which cannot last.
A 'surge with power, cold as steel
His vengeance savage, bold and cruel
Until finally, his victory
but sets the stage for one last duel.

Fate laughs, and spews its bitter brew
Across a galaxy or two
Vitriolic conflict spans an age
No mercy tempers Darklon's rage.
These two must vie for their survival
Neither can tolerate a rival.
Their struggle, father 'gainst his son
The outcome favors only one.
Fate merely chuckles up its sleeve
The loser dies, the winner grieves.
— David Scroggy

It was just something I was doing. When I got one done, I'd send it to Warren. Then I'd get paid and then they'd print it. 'Darklon' would take awhile to do because it was in wash tone, markers, and all sorts of different things."[66]

With *Captain Marvel* and *Warlock*, Starlin had achieved superstar status as a top comics creator during the '70s, and, with his groundbreaking graphic novel, *The Death of Captain Marvel* [1982], he was once again on top. So, of course, the Schanes brothers had taken note and contemplated reprinting the five 'Darklon' episodes from *Eerie,* and a deal was made with Jim Warren's then-tottering imprint. 'This was another one from our deal with Warren magazines," Steve Schanes explained. "Jim Starlin was a prince. Just amazing."[67]

As with its *Berni Wrightson, Master of the Macabre* reprint series, Pacific decided to jazz up *Darklon the Mystic* for the direct market, thus it was decided the artwork — specifically designed to be presented in black-&-white — was to be colored. "Joe Chiodo colorized it," Starlin told Clancy. "I was rather surprised that he took on the job. Joe and I knew each other then and I think he was friends with the guys at Pacific Comics, and they asked him to do it."[68]

The results were decidedly mixed, with some observers preferring the original b-&-w appearances. "The Pacific reprint is in color, and is probably the easiest way to find a copy at this point," reviewer Mark Brett opined. "But I must admit, it's probably not the best way to read it. Starlin was working in black-&-white for Warren, playing with inks and textures and gray washes to good effect. And, while the colors do add to the book's psychedelic charm, they make the art muddy in a lot of places. Fine details get obscured and the grays all but vanish."[69]

(Interestingly, for a creator desiring to own his own material, Starlin apparently never had an explicit deal with Warren Publishing regarding the character. While, when asked if he owned 'Darklon,' Starlin said, "I would believe so. I let [*Pacific*] print it gratis and Warren never had any real work-for-hire contract."[70] Pacific was said to have negotiated with Warren to publish the reprint. And, it so happened, another writer, Rich Margopoulos, had revived the character twice for *Eerie* after Starlin's departure.)

THE DUBÉ'S BOLD ADVENTURE

With the demise of his editorship of the Warren magazines, Bill DuBay ventured over to Pacific to command *Bold Adventure*, an anthology title — projected to be four issues — with all stories written by the Dubé, featuring characters

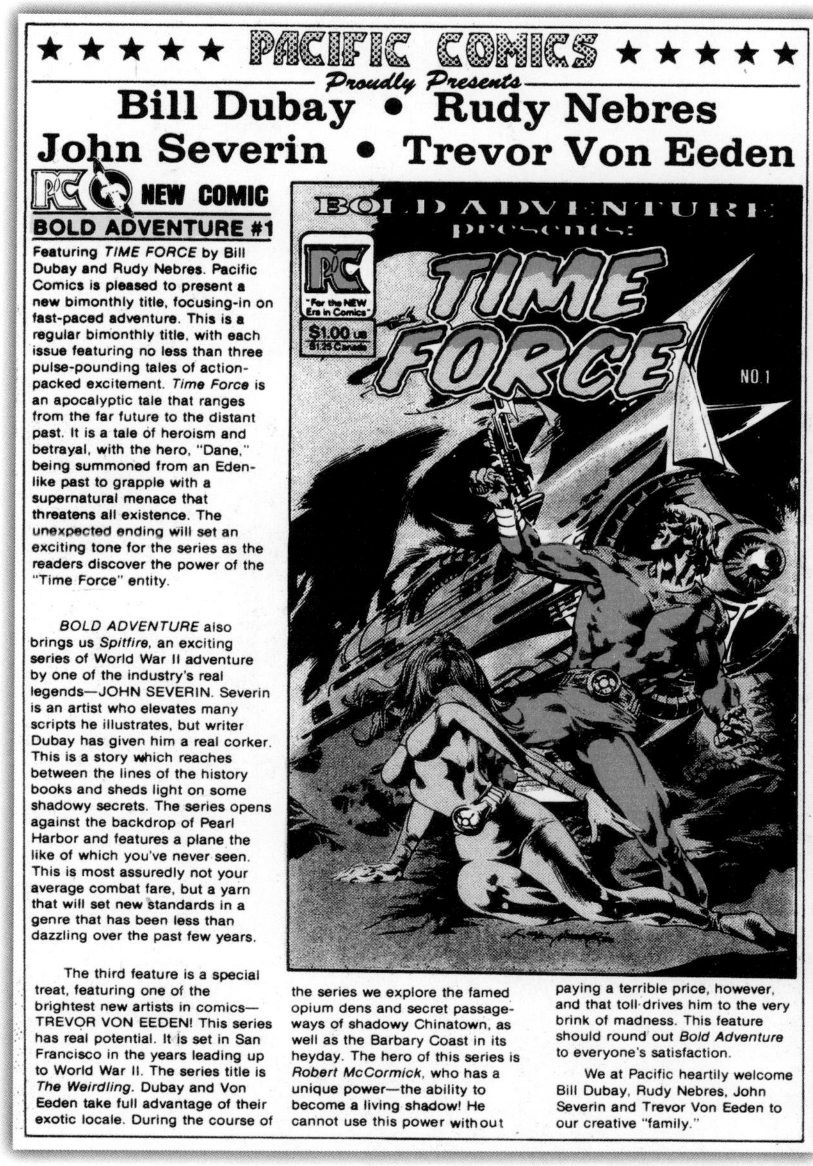

PACIFIC COMICS
Proudly Presents
Bill Dubay • Rudy Nebres
John Severin • Trevor Von Eeden
PC
NEW COMIC
BOLD ADVENTURE #1
Featuring TIME FORCE by Bill Dubay and Rudy Nebres. Pacific Comics is pleased to present a new bimonthly title, focusing-in on fast-paced adventure. This is a regular bimonthly title, with each issue featuring no less than three pulse-pounding tales of action-packed excitement. Time Force is an apocalyptic tale that ranges from the far future to the distant past. It is a tale of heroism and betrayal, with the hero, "Dane," being summoned from an Eden-like past to grapple with a supernatural menace that threatens all existence. The unexpected ending will set an exciting tone for the series as the readers discover the power of the "Time Force" entity.
BOLD ADVENTURE also brings us Spitfire, an exciting series of World War II adventure by one of the industry's real legends—JOHN SEVERIN. Severin is an artist who elevates many scripts he illustrates, but writer Dubay has given him a real corker. This is a story which reaches between the lines of the history books and sheds light on some shadowy secrets. The series opens against the backdrop of Pearl Harbor and features a plane the like of which you've never seen. This is most assuredly not your average combat fare, but a yarn that will set new standards in a genre that has been less than dazzling over the past few years.
BOLD ADVENTURE presents:
PC
"For the NEW Era in Comics"
$1.00 US
TIME FORCE
NO.1
The third feature is a special treat, featuring one of the brightest new artists in comics—TREVOR VON EEDEN! This series has real potential. It is set in San Francisco in the years leading up to World War II. The series title is The Weirdling. Dubay and Von Eeden take full advantage of their exotic locale. During the course of the series we explore the famed opium dens and secret passage-ways of shadowy Chinatown, as well as the Barbary Coast in its heyday. The hero of this series is Robert McCormick, who has a unique power—the ability to become a living shadow! He cannot use this power without paying a terrible price, however, and that toll drives him to the very brink of madness. This feature should round out Bold Adventure to everyone's satisfaction.
We at Pacific heartily welcome Bill Dubay, Rudy Nebres, John Severin and Trevor Von Eeden to our creative "family."

of his own creation. (In the editorial in #3, he wrote, "The stories within this comic book are, of course, simple fantasies. Still, while assembling this issue for the good people at Pacific, I came to realize that there's a great deal of myself within each of the heroic leads.")[71]

The science-fiction serial, "Time Force," with art by Rudy Nebres, headlined all three extant issues. "But forget 'Time Force,'" Marc Sobel implored. "The back-up features are the real draw. In both issues [#1–2], there's an outstanding tale called 'The Weirdling,' with art by Trevor Von Eeden and inked, on the second part only, by David Lloyd, an unlikely battery, but one that works exceptionally well. This was around the time that Lloyd was working on *V for Vendetta* and his style is similar here, but it's Von Eeden's pencils that really make this story shine."[72]

In 1984, David Lloyd discussed how he got the inking job through serendipity. "Sometimes commissions can

Above: *Bold Adventure* in-house ad featuring Rudy Nebres' "Time Force" cover art, which appeared in *Groo* #4 [Sept. 1983]. **Below:** A mad god by Rudy Nebres from *BA* #2 [Mar. 1984].

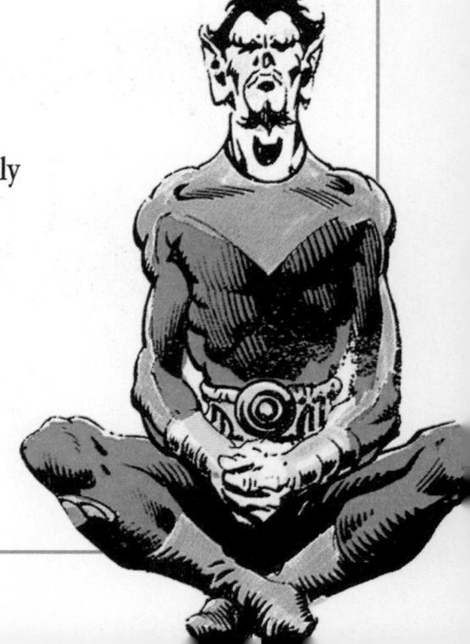

This page: Items from Bill DuBay's *Bold Adventure*, including Michael Wm. Kaluta's cover for #3 [June 1984], Alex Niño's splash panel from #2 [March 1984], and a poor repro of Niño's unpublished #4 cover. DuBay, best known as longtime editor at Warren Publications, also contributed two comedic strips to *Vanguard Illustrated* at Pacific Comics.

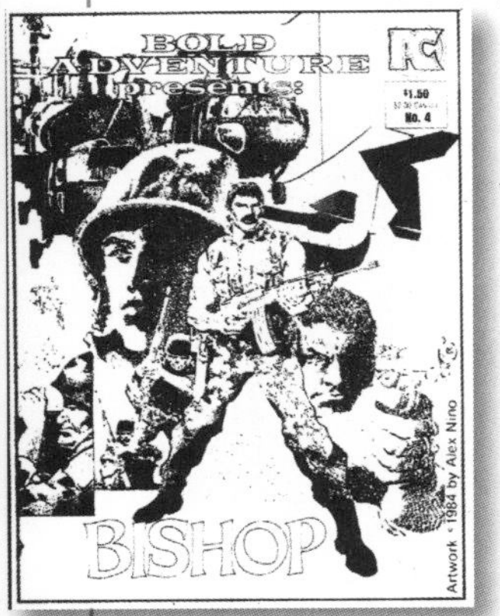
BOLD ADVENTURE presents
BISHOP
Artwork • 1984 by Alex Nino

come about by good luck," he said in *Warrior* magazine. "I was at [*artist*] Paul Neary's recently, when the American comic book editor Bill DuBay was visiting him, and Bill asked if I would re-ink some Trevor Von Eeden pencils for a strip called 'The Weirdling,' in Pacific Comics' *Bold Adventure*. I just happened to be there at the right time. It was only a one-off thing, and maybe we were a bit mismatched, but it was an interesting experience."[73]

Also in the series were fine stories rendered by Alex Niño — "Soldiers of Fortune" — and John Severin, though the second chapter of Severin's "Spitfire" would never appear, as Pacific folded before the finished #4 would see print.

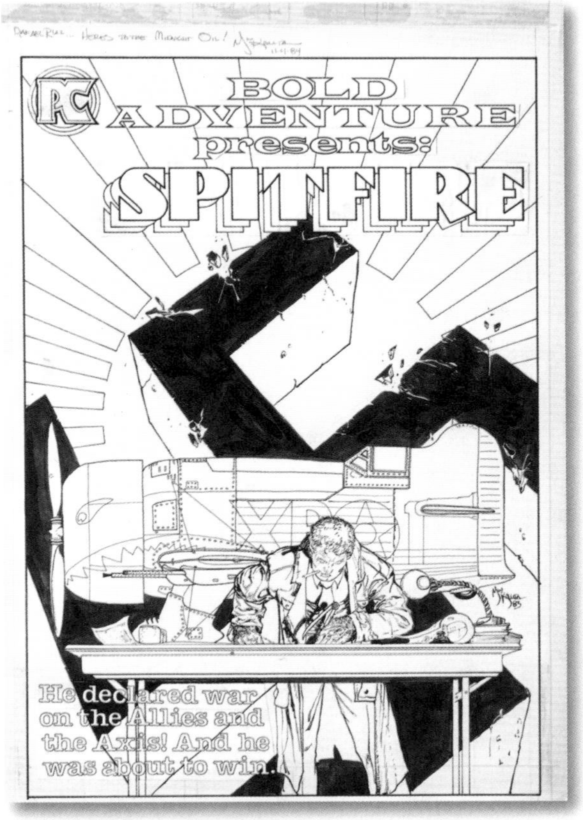
BOLD ADVENTURE presents:
SPITFIRE
He declared war on the Allies and the Axis! And he was about to win.

LO, THERE SHALL BE… SKATEMAN!

For a Neal Adams comic book, the one-shot *Skateman* [Nov. 1983] from Pacific might well be the most reviled of his considerable — and, overall, tremendously celebrated — body of work, but despite the credits therein, the comic book legend doesn't deserve all the blame!

In 1984, Neal Adams told Steve Ringgenberg, "We did *Skateman*, a reprehensible comic book… Because it wasn't intended to be for sale on this marketplace. It was intended to be a promotion for a potential movie that a producer named John Ballard wanted to do, and we sort of tailor-made it for that, for what he was trying to do. And he did that

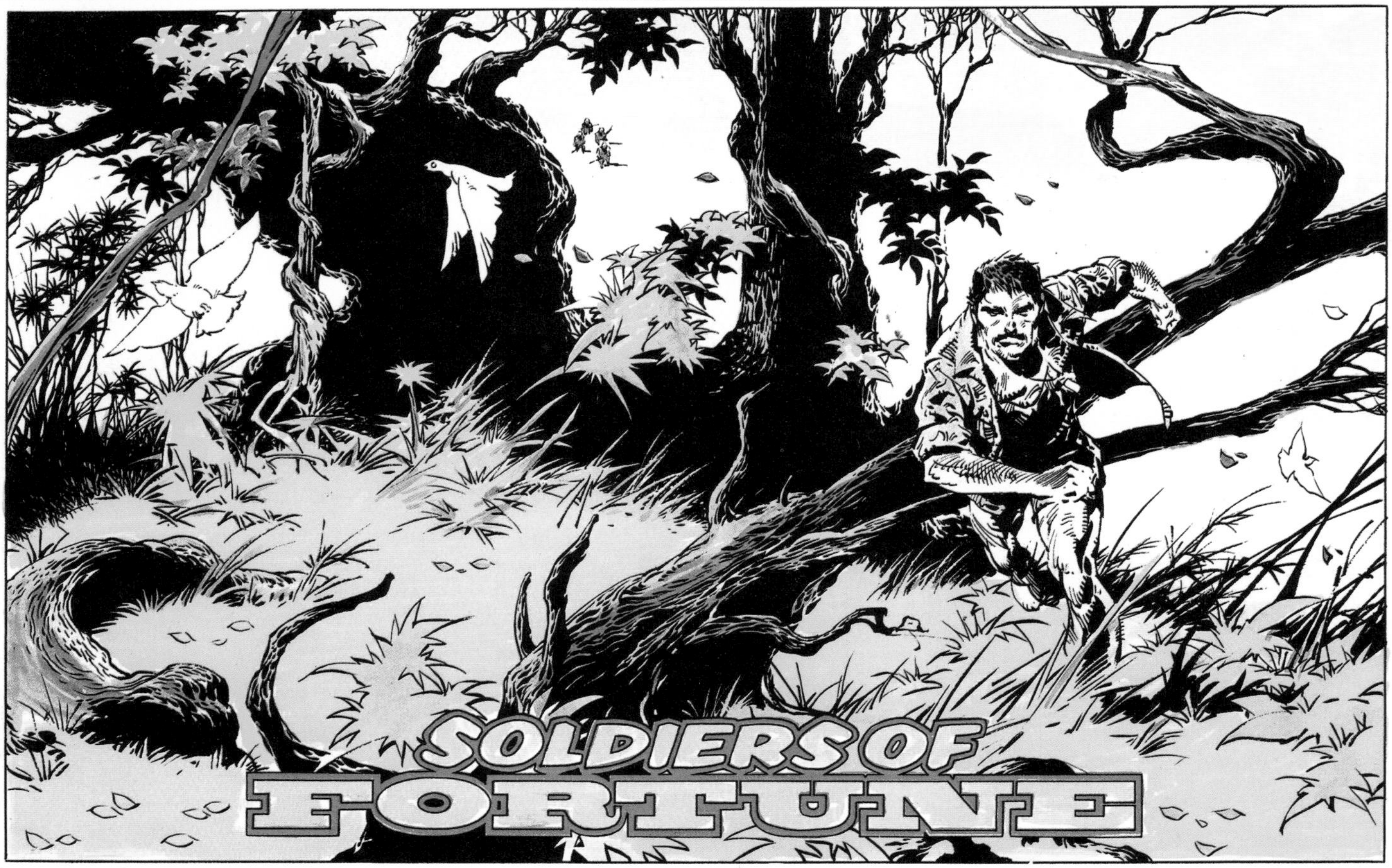
SOLDIERS OF FORTUNE

project when rollerskating was coming in [*as a fad*]. We finally got it to print — in other words, nothing happened with the movie for that period of time, and so when we were asked if we had anything lying around, *Skateman* was lying around. When we asked whether or not we could get permission to print the thing, well, that's when skating was not only out, but the door had shut.

"So I thought that we had done a fairly good job on the book and I thought that it held together very well, but it wasn't really intended to be the kind of book that we would think of ourselves as producing. But we did sell 70,000 copies of it and people sort of like it, and people are asking for a second issue... It's incredible. A lot of people like it. Actually, when you sit down with the book and read it, it holds together. You can take it into the bathroom and read it... *Ms. Mystic* sold 80,000 copies... In excess of 80,000 copies, through the direct sales market, it's not bad. For an imitator of Bill Sienkiewicz, I think it did pretty good."[74]

Indeed, *Skateman* was initially a screenplay by filmmaker Ballard, who had put together a promotional package in 1979 to attract investors, which included Neal Adams illustrations based on the movie script. A bookseller website offering the promo packet for sale shared, "While a feature film was never produced, a comic book with art by Adams was published by Pacific Comics in 1983. Originally intended as a tie-in for the film (as mentioned in the booklet), the comic was released as a standalone long after the rollerskating fad had ended, and is still widely considered one of the worst comics ever published. Ballard would continue to try to make *Skateman* happen, self-publishing three novels, changing the concept to skateboarding, and announcing a casting call for a film (though no film has been made) as recently as 2014."[75] (The website *www.skateman.com* promoting a new production is live as of this writing.)

When Adams was told maybe the best criticism received for the comic book was to call it "unfortunate," he told Peter Stone, "I don't think *Skateman* is unfortunate at all. In fact, I think it's one of the funnier things people criticize in comics. Most of that comic book was not drawn by me, oddly enough. It was drawn by Jim Sherman, a guy who worked in our studio at the time. A nice-looking guy and a decent artist whose style was a little bit like mine. And he did a great job. He got to do more than I did, so it was kind of a Neal Adams/Jim Sherman job."

SKATEMAN INDUSTRIES, INC.
CONFIDENTIAL 18AA
SKATE MAN
TM

Above: Presentation binder put together by filmmaker John Ballard to lure investors to support his *Skateman* movie. Neal Adams and his studio produced a comic book story for Ballard, which eventually was repurposed for a Pacific one-shot, *Skateman* #1 [Nov. 1983].

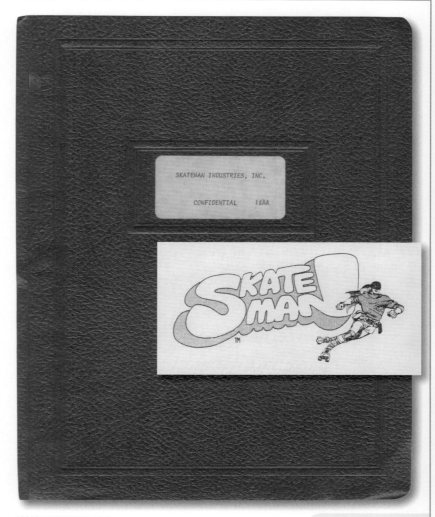

AT THE VANGUARD

On the cusp of Autumn 1983, Pacific Comics released yet another anthology, only this one was devoted to teaming fresh talent with seasoned vets. *Vanguard Illustrated* #1's editorial described the scenario: "There is a bumper crop of extremely talented newcomers with an interest in comics these days. As a result of the direct-sales marketing method, comics have become appealing to creative talents once again. The contracts have become fairer and more lucrative. The production values are getting better and better. All of this is acting as a powerful magnet — not only to old favorites who are returning to the fold in ever-increasing numbers, but

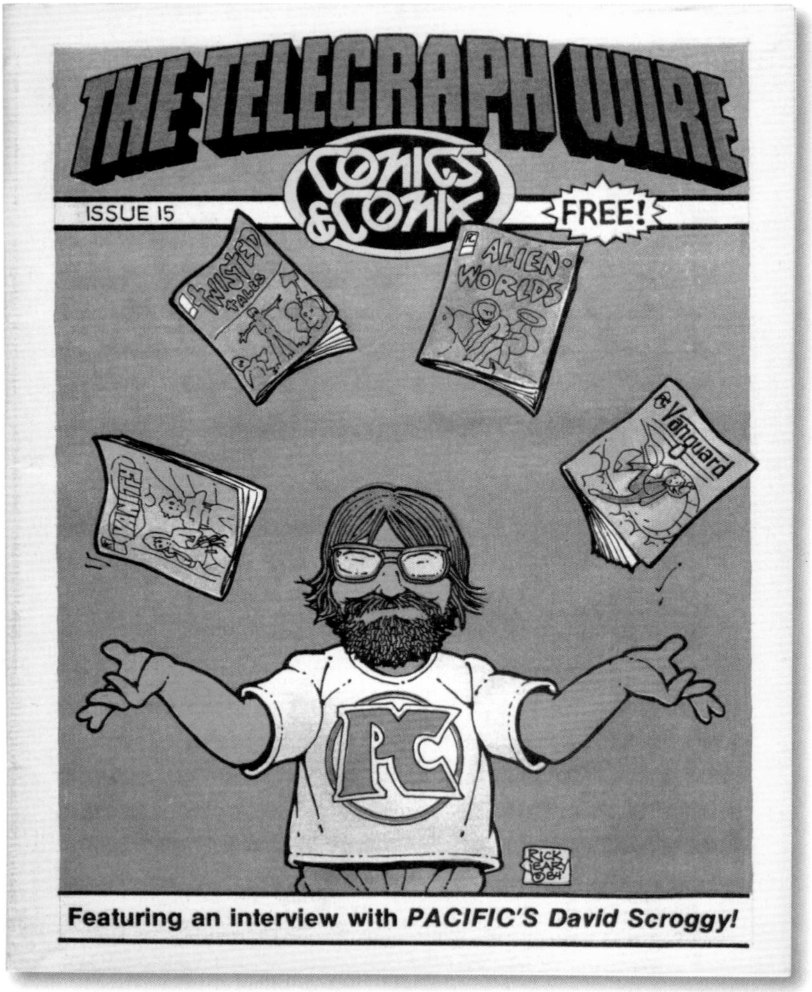
THE TELEGRAPH WIRE
COMICS & COMIX
ISSUE 15
FREE!
TWISTED TALES
ALIEN WORLDS
Vanguard
Featuring an interview with PACIFIC'S David Scroggy!

This page: Clockwise from top is the cover of *The Telegraph Wire* #15 [June/July 1984] featuring Rick Geary's caricature of Pacific editorial director David Scroggy; splash page from the Freakwave episode in *Vanguard Illustrated* #1 [Nov. 1983], Scroggy's pet title; and *Strange Days* #1 [Eclipse, Apr. 1984].

also to young artists and writers now pursuing careers in comic books, where not so long ago, they might well have been drawn to other fields."[77]

Those words were written by its editor, David Scroggy, who told the author, "The Pacific Comics title I am probably most associated with is *Vanguard Illustrated*. My idea was to pair a new talent with an established one. A new artist would illustrate a script from a veteran writer and vice-versa. We were getting a ton of submissions at Pacific, and some of them were pretty good. *Vanguard Illustrated* gave us a way to use some of them. We faced a problem that has continually plagued comics publishers: one can very quickly evaluate an art sample, but few have the time, resources, or frankly the interest to plow through a big stack of writing submissions. We were no different.

"Our friend, April Campbell Jones, was in my office one day and saw a large carton of scripts that had arrived over the transom. She was horrified. She volunteered to act as a 'reader.' She noted that most of them would be quick rejects, so the task wasn't as daunting as it appeared. She took the box home and began to plow through them.

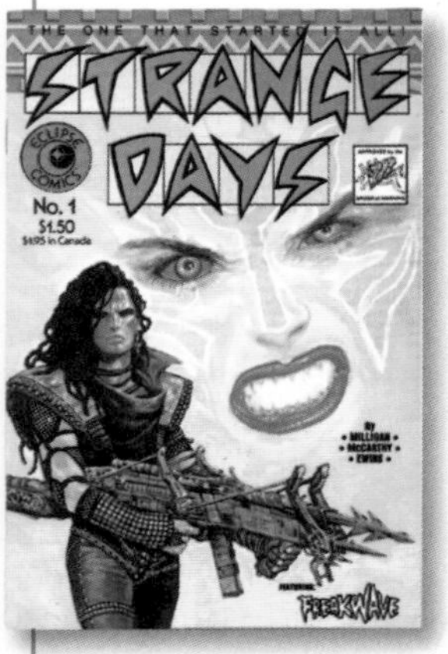
THE ONE THAT STARTED IT ALL!
STRANGE DAYS
No. 1
$1.50
FREAKWAVE

"When she returned, she had marked a few of special merit. She was enthusiastic about the samples from David Campiti, writing across one of his scripts 'We've got to give this kid something!' Reading the work, which was a draft of his Ray Bradbury-inspired story, 'Be What It Will, I'll Go to It Laughing,' we selected that one, and a second Campiti story, 'Libretto.' He was, of course, excited to be chosen, and we signed him up.

"I paired him [for *Vanguard* #1] with artist Tom Yeates, who was a Joe Kubert School graduate… I was truly thrilled by the results; the two stories were some of Yeates' most polished artwork to date, and the scripts were excellent."[78]

YEATES REMEMBERS

Thomas Yeates recalled, "My memory might be off after 40 years, but I think it was Bruce Jones who brought me on board with Pacific. I'd drawn a couple of his terrific short stories for DC mystery books before landing *Swamp Thing*. I guess Bruce liked working with me as he visited me at my place on Lake Hopatcong, in New Jersey, to talk about working with him at this new company, Pacific. We were both friends with Al Williamson and, to this day, I think the story Bruce did with Al in *Creepy* [#86, Dec. 1976, "Mother Knows Best"] is an all-time masterpiece. Drawing

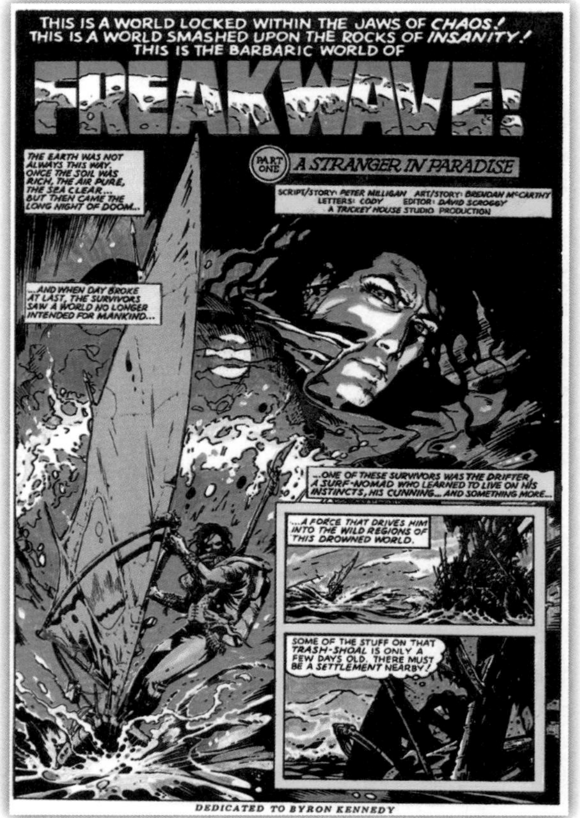
THIS IS A WORLD LOCKED WITHIN THE JAWS OF CHAOS!
THIS IS A WORLD SMASHED UPON THE ROCKS OF INSANITY!
THIS IS THE BARBARIC WORLD OF
FREAKWAVE!
THE EARTH WAS NOT ALWAYS THIS WAY. ONCE THE SOIL WAS RICH, THE AIR PURE, THE SEA CLEAR... BUT THEN CAME THE LONG NIGHT OF DOOM...
PART ONE A STRANGER IN PARADISE
SCRIPT/STORY: PETER MILLIGAN ART/STORY: BRENDAN McCARTHY LETTERS: CODY EDITOR: DAVID SCROGGY A TRICKEY HOUSE STUDIO PRODUCTION
...AND WHEN DAY BROKE AT LAST, THE SURVIVORS SAW A WORLD NO LONGER INTENDED FOR MANKIND...
...ONE OF THESE SURVIVORS WAS THE DRIFTER, A SURF-NOMAD WHO LEARNED TO LIVE ON HIS INSTINCTS, HIS CUNNING... AND SOMETHING MORE...
...A FORCE THAT DRIVES HIM INTO THE WILD REGIONS OF THIS DROWNED WORLD.
SOME OF THE STUFF ON THAT TRASH-SHOAL IS ONLY A FEW DAYS OLD. THERE MUST BE A SETTLEMENT NEARBY!
DEDICATED TO BYRON KENNEDY

a Bruce Jones script was sort of like working for EC Comics: about as good as it was going to get for me at that time. I think we only did two stories for Pacific though, both in *Alien Worlds*... During that period, 1983, David Scroggy contacted me about being Pacific's guest at the San Diego Comic-Con. This was my first time there and I had a wonderful time. My roommate at the hotel was Michael T. Gilbert — a great guy and great talent. Scroggy hosted some of us at his home for cocktails with his lovely wife, Rosemary. The Scroggys are a class act. Love that couple.

"Probably through David, I was asked to contribute to *Vanguard*, their new talent comic. David Campiti wrote two science-fiction stories for me to draw. Both seemed tailored for my tastes... Pacific, along with their competitor Eclipse, were spearheading better printing and coloring in comics. This appealed greatly to an illustrator like me and it was nice to be working with folks who were trying to take the industry up a notch."[79]

Above: Thomas Yeates' excellent *Vanguard Illustrated* #1 [Nov. 1983] cover art, illustrating his and writer David Campiti's opening story therein, "Liberetto." **Below:** Detail of Freakwave from house ad.

HAVING A FREAKWAVE

Maybe the highlight of the debut issue — or at least one that was quite startlingly original — was "Freakwave," featuring a dreadlocks-maned windsurfer sailing a post-apocalyptic globe now covered in water. Scroggy shared, "Around the time I was organizing *Vanguard Illustrated*, my desk phone rang one busy morning. I had been having a frustrating day and was in a bad mood. A British-accented voice said he was a comics artist visiting San Diego, and he wanted to call on me to pitch his portfolio. I asked him if he was published here, meaning the U.S.A., and he said no. I tersely said, 'Look — I'm busy and this is a bit inconvenient. We publish Dave Stevens here. Do you think you draw as good as Dave Stevens?' A pause. 'Well,' he replied, 'I have a little different style, but yes, I think I do draw as well.' 'Okay,' I retorted, 'if you really think you are able to do that, come on in, and I'll take a quick look at your stuff.'

"(I must hasten to add that I was rarely so curt with a new talent or in a portfolio review. I have, to this day, always tried to show respect for the person presenting their work, regardless of my opinion of its quality. You never go wrong by being polite, but can certainly go wrong by being rude.)

"Anyhow, not long thereafter, the fellow showed up, and that is how I met Brendan McCarthy and first saw his and writer Peter Milligan's 'Freakwave' strip. It was an impressive piece of work from an impressive talent, and I am happy to say that I hired him on the spot. 'Freakwave' ran in three parts in *Vanguard Illustrated* #1–3."[80]

McCarthy recalled that trip to Pacific: "I turned up in their offices in San Diego, with an introduction from the late and great Dave Stevens, whom I met in L.A. on my first visit there. They said yes to 'Freakwave' straight away."[81] The artist explained after the three-parter was finished, a movie treatment was put together before "Freakwave" reemerged in Eclipse's *Strange Days.*

Addressing his creative partner, writer Peter Milligan reminisced, "In any event, we did develop an amazing, large illustrated treatment. A work of art in itself, as I remember... How I remember it, Brendan, you came back from living and working in Australia with your head full of images of surfing"[82] (to which McCarthy added, "And the magnificent *Mad Max 2*,"[83] referring to George Miller's superb movie known stateside as *The Road Warrior*).*

* Brendan McCarthy would go on to co-write, with George Miller, the screenplay for *Mad Max: Fury Road* [2015].

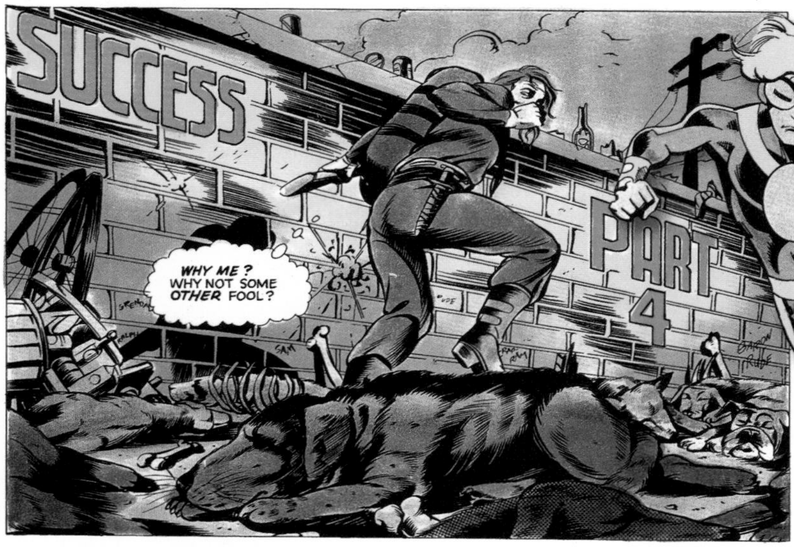
SUCCESS
PART 4
WHY ME ? WHY NOT SOME OTHER FOOL?

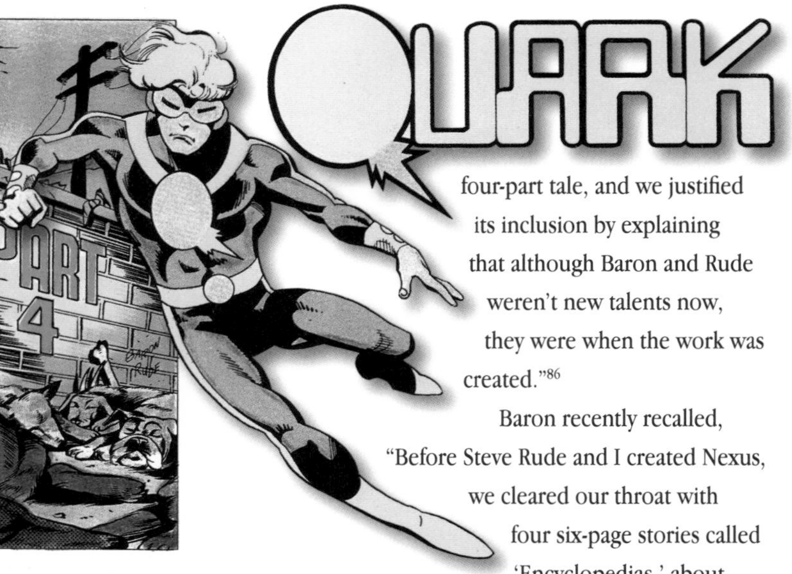
QUARK

This page: Clockwise from above is splash panel by Steve Rude to his and Mike Baron's "Encyclopedias" installment in *Vanguard Illustrated* #4 [Apr. 1984]; that same issue included another story by Baron, though "Quark" was drawn by then-newcomer Rick Burchett; and below is a panel detail from "The Guest," Darren Auck's tale in *Vanguard Illustrated* #2 [Jan. 1984].

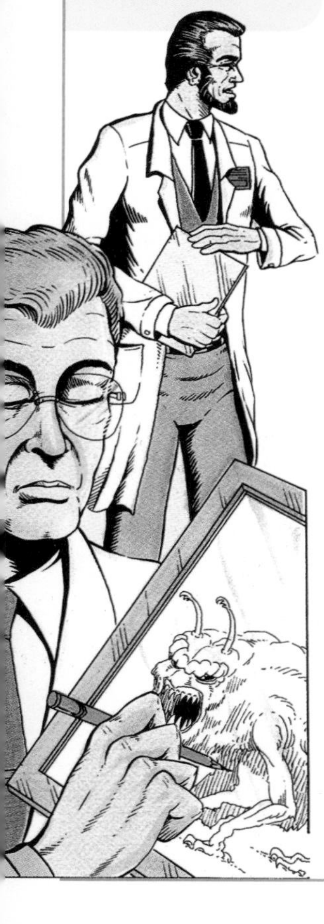

About the Drifter character becoming messianic, Milligan shared, "This is where 'Freakwave' really took off and came into its own. The freedom and allegorical nature of the comic and story has a lot to do with how we were producing it. It was a bit like a little cottage industry. There'd be a rough script and then the art would be produced, which, of course, didn't necessarily have a lot to do with the script. Then I would physically do the lettering. Often it was at this lettering stage that a lot of the writing was done, and this allowed me to riff off the art, and to allow the narrative to be as free and wild as Brendan's art was. I think I almost became addicted to tea, staying up late, and writing/lettering this thing."[84]

About their collaboration, McCarthy explained, "Because we were both fine arts painting graduates, we were aware of many different working methods we could use. So this wasn't a 'writer dictates story' set-up — which sometimes we would do if it suited us. The process of creating the comic had a lot of randomness thrown in. We were Brian Eno fans at the time, so anything accidental or left-field was treasured."[85]

BLOODY RED, THE DUDE, AND A GUY CALLED BURCHETT

Another serial that started in *Vanguard* #1 was by a creative team who had already been established as fan favorites over at a rival (though short-lived) publisher. David explained, "We were pitched an early collaboration by Mike Baron and Steve Rude, who were rocking the independent comics world with their character, Nexus, published by Capital City. Titled, 'Encyclopedias,' this student work was a story of a young slacker in a dystopian future, peddling encyclopedias. It was a four-part tale, and we justified its inclusion by explaining that although Baron and Rude weren't new talents now, they were when the work was created."[86]

Baron recently recalled, "Before Steve Rude and I created Nexus, we cleared our throat with four six-page stories called 'Encyclopedias,' about a door-to-door encyclopedia salesman in a dystopian future who's unable to make any sales. I was no seer or I would have foreseen the rise of the internet, obviating the need for encyclopedias. I'd have to reread those stories, which Pacific ran in four consecutive issues, to find out what I said. I have a nearly complete set of *Funk & Wagnalls,* which I consult all the time because it's more straightforward and honest than online sources, which often reflect the biases or lack of knowledge of whatever a cellar-dweller posted. Wikipedia, I'm looking at you."[87]

Steve Rude told Jon B. Cooke, "We were still in the very early days of Capital when *Nexus* had just come out and we got a call from Dave Scroggy from Pacific, and he wanted to know if we had any material that hadn't been published so he could capitalize (so to speak) what we were then doing with *Nexus* and the fact that we had just become 'an item' in the comic book world. We said, 'Well, we got this thing called, 'Encyclopedias,' which was the very first thing Baron and I had done together."[88]

The two first became acquainted in 1979, the artist related and, "'Encyclopedias' came about because, when I first met Baron, on the campus of the University of Wisconsin-Madison… I brought my portfolio and Baron always had a briefcase of some kind, and he hauled out this script about an encyclopedia salesman who went around after the world had blown up to try and sell people encyclopedias. Knowing nothing about discrimination, I said, 'Fine' — I said yes to anything back then — and it was a very good story. It made me laugh — anything Baron gave me back then made me laugh. It was 24 pages and it ended up taking me a year to do. Why? I don't know. But I lettered it and inked it, and a year later it

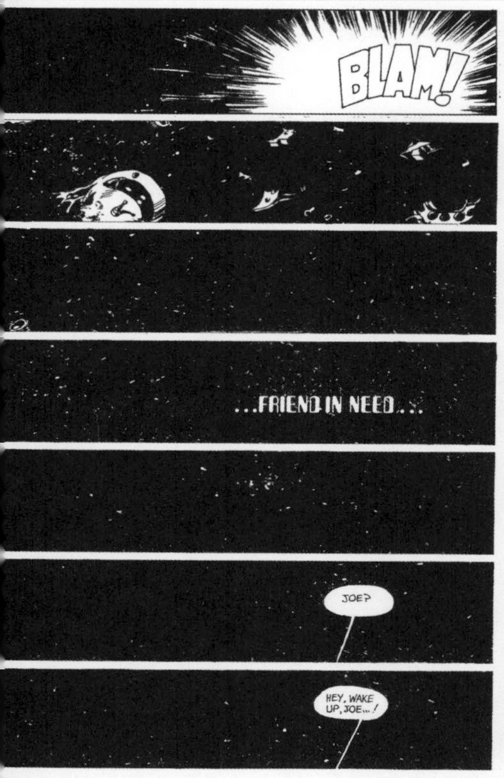
BLAM!
...FRIEND IN NEED...
JOE?
HEY, WAKE UP, JOE...!

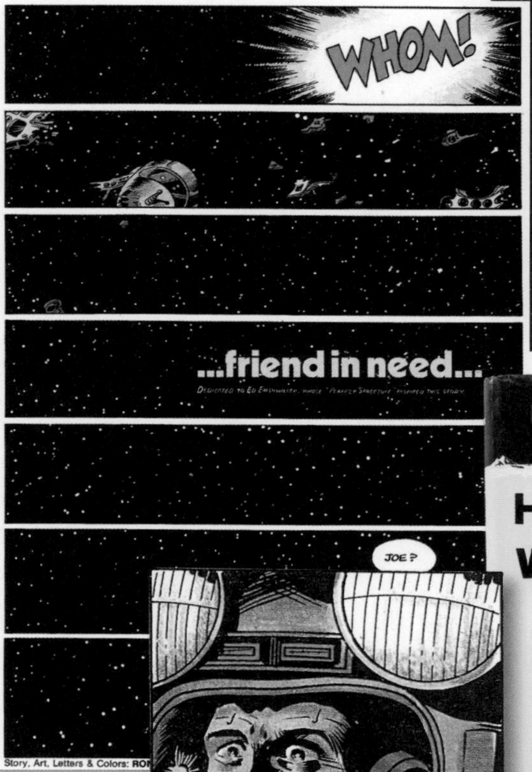
WHOM!
...friend in need...
JOE?
Story, Art, Letters & Colors: RON

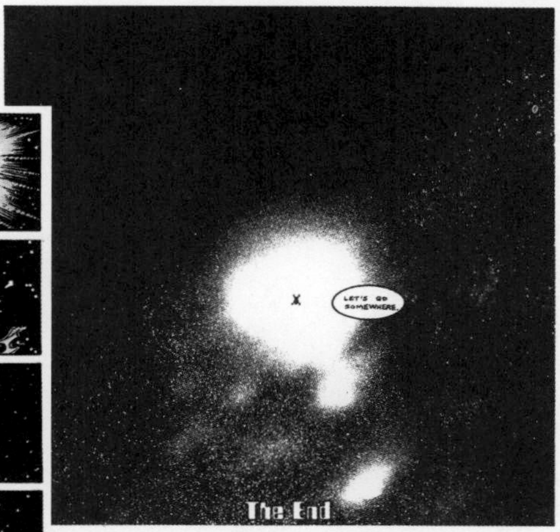
LET'S GO SOMEWHERE
The End

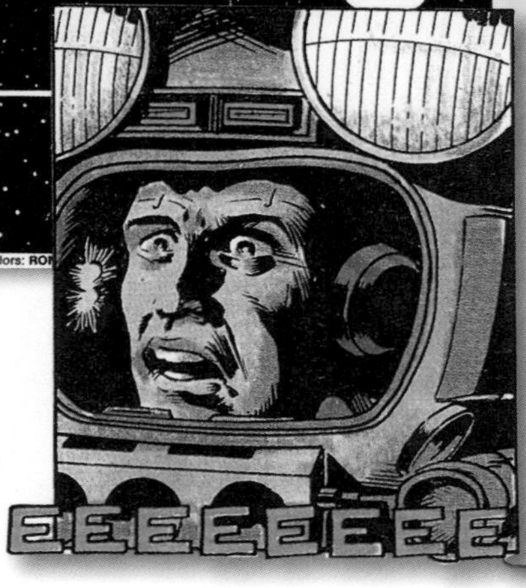
EEEEEEEEE

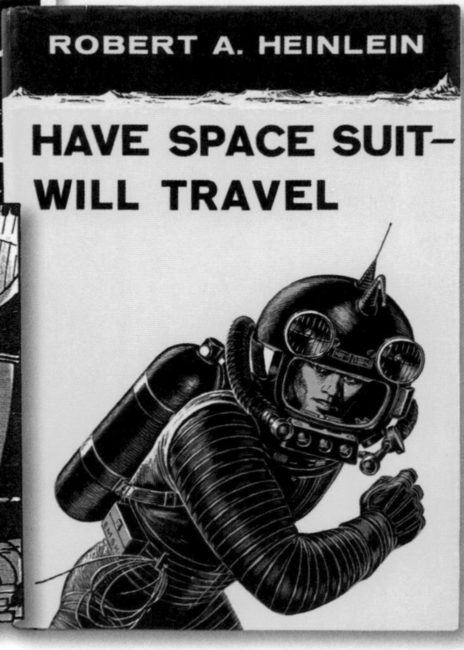
ROBERT A. HEINLEIN
HAVE SPACE SUIT—
WILL TRAVEL

was done, and that's what Dave Scroggy ended up buying from us. So, for us, it was just extra money, because we had already done this thing. They ended up publishing it and asked me for a new cover, and I said, 'Sure.' That's the only time I remember working for them."[89]

About his collaboration with Baron, Rick Burchett recently shared with Cooke, "I do indeed remember 'Quark.' During the big independent boom of the late '70s/ early '80s, I was sending out samples to every publisher in hopes of getting a foot in the door. One of the positive responses I received was from Pacific, who asked if I'd be interested in penciling a back-up strip written by Mike Baron. It was one of the first, if not *the* first professional job I was offered. The job was to design the characters and pencil the story. At the time, I was my own inker and I'm afraid my pencils were kinda loose. Fortunately, I think it was Steve Mitchell who inked the story, and he made the work look better than it had any right to.

"Working with Mike was fun. He would do small sketches of each page as a guide for the artist. This job led to my working with him again, penciling #2 and 3 of *The Badger* for Capital Comics.

"All in all, a great experience. I got some work in print which led to more work, had a good time working with Mike, and learned a few things. One of my first baby steps to a career in comics."[90]

THE KUBERT ASSIGNMENT

"'The Guest' in *Vanguard Illustrated* #2 was published when I was a third-year student at the Joe Kubert School, class of 1983," Darren Auck explained. "Joe had a deal with Pacific and this was one of his assignments. If I remember correctly, Joe set this up with David Scroggy, like the old comics studio deal with the publishers. This was my first published job (other than my self-published comics in high school) and I was thrilled to be in there with Mike Baron, Steve Rude, Dave Stevens, and the others!

"Along with back-up features in *Sgt. Rock* and DC's New Talent program under DC editor and instructor Sal Amendola, we had some great 'ins' for getting published.

"Joe was, of course, a masterful, firm editor. I hope I still have his pencil overlays and notes in my vault. His fixes were welcome and valuable lessons."

Auck would go on to serve as a letterer in the Marvel bullpen for a few years and, he said, "One of my highlights was working as John Romita's assistant art director, then becoming art director when he 'retired.'"[91]

Above: "Friend in Need," Ron Harris' submission in *Vanguard Illustrated* #5 [May 1984], was actually a remake of his same-named strip that appeared 10 years prior in an underground comic book, *Barbarian Comics* #3 [Apr. 1974]. As Harris explains here, the eight-pager was inspired by the very last panel in a Richard Corben story from *Fever Dreams* [July 1972]. The protagonist's space helmet was designed in homage to artist Ed Emshwiller's cover for Robert Heinlein's *Have Spacesuit— Will Travel* [1958].

When Vanguard Got Left Behind

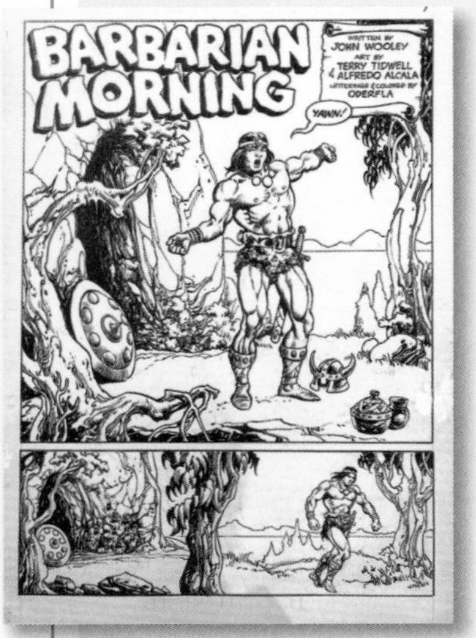
BARBARIAN MORNING
JOHN WOOLEY
TERRY TIDWELL & ALFREDO ALCALA
ODERFLA
YAWN!

Above: Splash page drawn by Terry Tidwell and inked by Alredo Alcala. Written by John Wooley and intended for *Vanguard* #10, it would, alas, go unpublished.

Writer John Wooley shared about the twilight days of Pacific, when he and artist Terry Tidwell sent in an unsolicited story, "Barbarian Morning," which eventually was inked by Alfredo Alcala and scheduled for *Vanguard Illustrated* #10, though Pacific would fold before it could see print. "The earliest correspondence I have about the story is a letter dated April 3, 1984, from Pacific editorial director David Scroggy," Wooley said. "I'd sent him a Xerox of the penciled 'Barbarian Morning,' which was then an eight-pager, and he responded by asking us to tighten it to six and for Terry to redraw the barbarian on the splash panel. He also sent along a sample contract.

"Quoting Scroggy's letter: 'We are currently dealing with a direct-sales marketplace which is flooded with new product. While our line is holding its own, sales are not what they should be. Consequently, *Vanguard*, one of our bottom-end books sales-wise, has not been generating royalties in excess of the advance. Furthermore, while two years ago we were able to budget an advance of $150 per page, excluding coloring, for a back-up, market conditions force us to offer only $130 per page for unsolicited short back-ups like 'Barbarian Morning.' I will need $55 for an inker like [Alcala] and $10 for letters. That leaves only $65 advance for you guys for script and pencils.'

"He went on to say he hoped the rate would be acceptable, and how appearing in *Vanguard* would provide us with 'valuable exposure.' 'You will also, of course, have copyrighted this story in your own names,' he added. 'In the happy event that *Vanguard*'s sales pick up enough, royalties beyond the advances will also be yours. Once again, I shouldn't count on that.'

"He closed by asking me to call him as soon as I could. Then, on April 10, another letter from Scroggy thanked me for the call and sent a voucher for payment. I have a copy, which was for $390, and, while I'm not 100% sure, I don't think we were ever paid.

"On May 5, he sent me Xeroxes of the Alcala-inked pages and, I think, a Xerox of Tim Truman's cover for #10, based on our story (which turned out not to be a 'back-up' after all)."[92]

Below: A miniature reproduction of Tim Truman's cover art intended for *Vanguard Illustrated* #10, appeared in *Pacific Premieres*, depicting John Wooley, Terry Tidwell, and Alfredo Alcala's "Barbarian Morning," which ultimately would never see print.

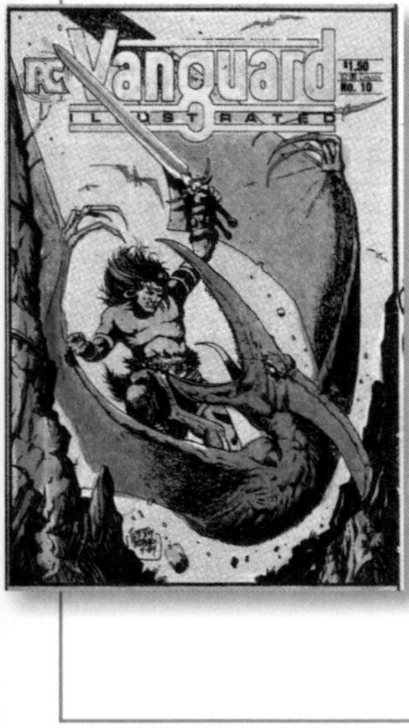
PC
Vanguard
ILLUSTRATED
$1.50
No. 10

IT CAME FROM *BARBARIAN COMICS*

Perhaps best known for his creation of *Crash Ryan*, a Marvel Epic Comics mini-series, and as artist on Roy Thomas' *Alter Ego* super-hero comic, Ron Harris recalled his *Vanguard Illustrated* #5 [May 1984] submission, "Friend in Need," which he explained to Cooke was actually a remake of a story he created in the early 1970s.

"I always liked 'Friend in Need.' To address the Pacific connection first, I was represented by Mike Friedrich (the first comic book artist agent!) and it was through Mike I made the sale. I never met Scroggy or anyone else nor did I get any feedback. I was rather cowed by the stature of the other *Vanguard* artists and figured my strip probably bombed.

"As I said, I liked the story [*a version of which was originally drawn for* Barbarian Comics *#3, Apr. 1974*]. I was generally happy with the breakdowns, but I could draw (a tiny bit) better by 1983 and wanted to update the artwork. I owned the strip, so there was no problem with my revising it, but I later learned that [Barbarian *editor/publisher*] Bob Sidebottom was disappointed that I didn't give him a shout-out. I regret that. I was working in Bob's Comic Collector Shop doing mail order when he decided to do *Barbarian Comics*. He invited me to contribute. The first thing I did was a barbarian/Japanese mash-up. I wanted to do a science-fiction strip and Bob okayed it, despite it not following the book's theme.

"When I was in elementary school, I won a contest from a reading show on local TV. The prize was a hardback of Robert Heinlein's *Have Spacesuit, Will Travel.* It was a juvenile novel set in the near future, about a teenager who wins a surplus spacesuit in a contest and stumbles into interplanetary intrigue. The moment I saw the gorgeous Emsh dust jacket, I fell in love with that suit and vowed to use it in a story some day.

"Strangely enough, 'Friend in Need' was sparked by the last panel of a Richard Corben s-f story ["To Meet the Faces That You Meet," *Fever Dreams,* July 1972]. As I recall, in it the dejected hero sails off into space with his robot assistant and the final panel was a starscape with the ship heading away from the camera. From the ship, the robot's balloon says, 'Let's go somewhere.' I don't know why it clicked, but I immediately thought of a guy adrift in space with an imaginary friend. Naturally, it would star the Emsh spacesuit.

"When I delivered the finished story to Bob, he suggested one change. In the original, when the hero reminisces about his girlfriend, I had him thinking of a sex scene. I figured, after all, this is an underground comic, so it should have a sex scene. Bob, who had no problem with sex scenes, pointed out that it didn't fit the tone of the rest of the story. Good call. I changed it so the hero remembers writing his girlfriend lousy poetry. It was a much better fit."[93]

"THE TRAINS BELONG TO US"

David Scroggy shared about *Vanguard* #6 and a super-star super-hero artist: "A memorable pairing was suggested by the great George Pérez. George, one of DC Comics' art superstars, was in a short window of availability between the expiration of one exclusive DC contract and the signing of another. He liked what Pacific Comics was up to and wanted to make his contribution to our line. He did a short story written by Bruce Jones for *Alien Worlds*, titled 'Ride the Blue Bus.' He also wanted to give a boost to a young writer, Joey Cavalieri. He had Joey, then unpublished, write a short script, 'The Trains Belong to Us,' which he illustrated for *Vanguard Illustrated*. Pérez also drew that issue's cover. When he sent in the original art, the image was of a gang of youths spraying graffiti onto subway cars in a moonlit rail yard. To my astonishment, he explained that he wanted our staff to provide the graffiti by scribbling whatever we liked onto the original art. Once we got up the nerve to deface a Pérez original, we gave it a shot. In hindsight, we were probably a tad tentative, but we did scrawl on the image. I couldn't resist the opportunity to scrawl my name on the side of the subway car."[94]

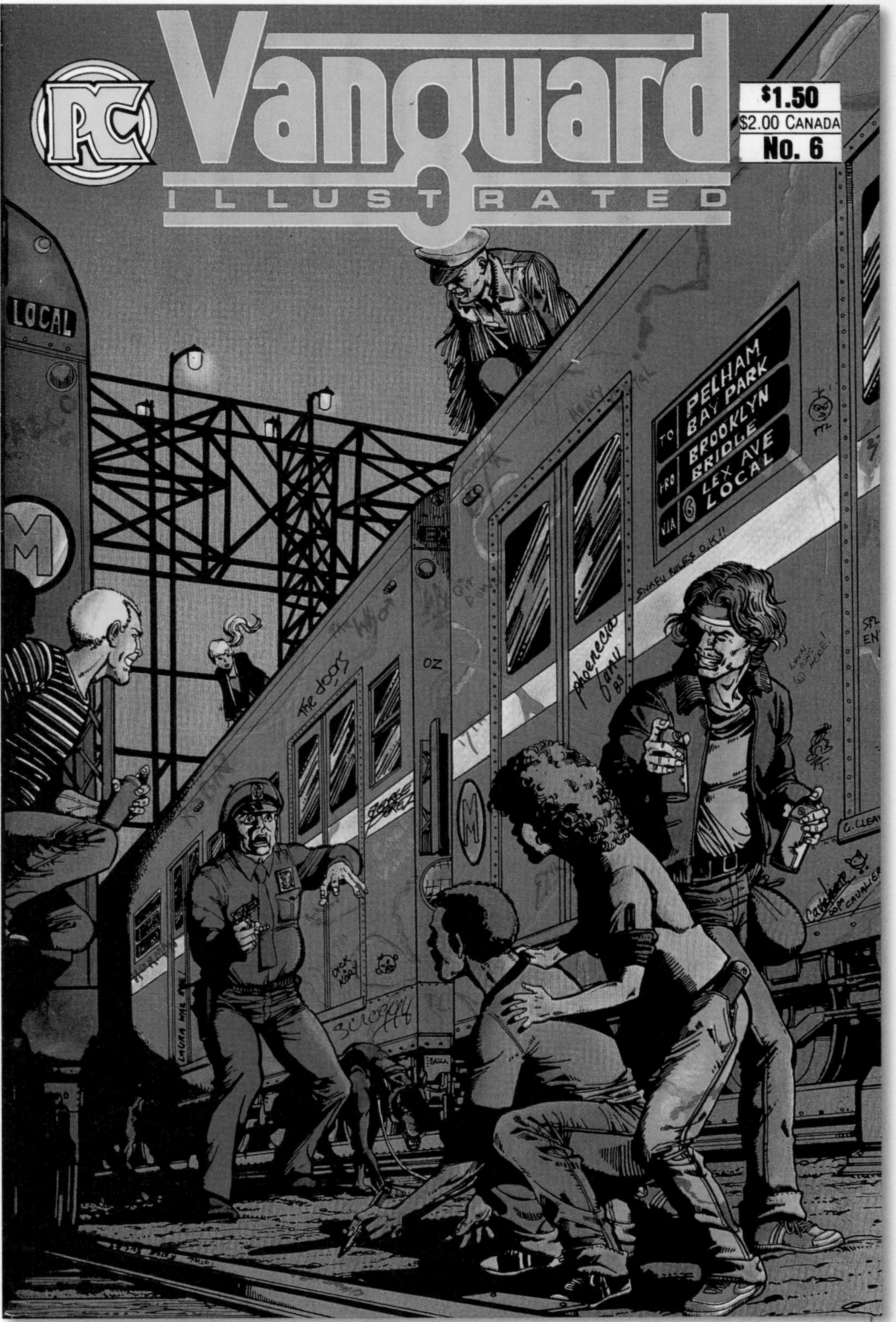
PC
Vanguard
ILLUSTRATED
$1.50
$2.00 CANADA
NO. 6
LOCAL
TO PELHAM BAY PARK
FRO BROOKLYN BRIDGE
VIA 6 LEX AVE LOCAL
M

Above: Reproduced big to read the Pacific staff's graffiti added per artist George Pérez's instructions, this is his *Vanguard Illustrated* #6 [June 1984] cover. Note "Scroggy" writ big by you-know-who!

THE GOLDYN AGE

Walter Stuart, who had a story in *Vanguard* #7, told Jon B. Cooke, "Steve [*Schanes*] and I went to high school together and then we took art classes together outside of school, and then we both ended up going to the Cleveland Institute of Art for a year together… We were just really, really good friends, in that I was his best man and he was mine. I pursued art and we took drawing classes, even

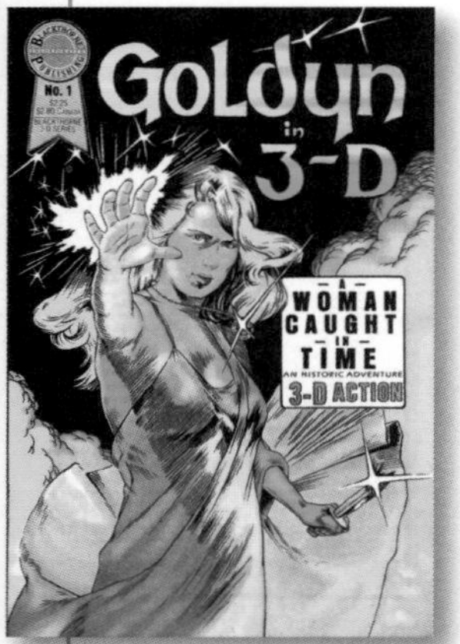
Goldyn in 3-D
No. 1
A WOMAN CAUGHT IN TIME
AN HISTORIC ADVENTURE
3-D ACTION

into adulthood and, at one point, he said, 'Walt, if you want to do a comic book, I'm sure I could publish it.' So I put together an idea and made a proposal."[95] Stuart's notion was about the time-traveling exploits of a linguistics expert named Goldyn, who gets stuck in 218 B.C. Stuart's character appeared in a 10-page story in *Vanguard*'s last issue and also starred in her own title, *Goldyn in 3-D*, published in 1986, by Steve's Blackthorne Publishing.

"I can't say that I studied comic book design more than any amateur might have," Stuart shared, "but I had some thoughts on what a story might and should look like, and I had a few ideas that were a little different than what people were doing. So I wrote up a treatment and Steve said, 'Okay, go ahead, do it,' and I penciled it." The plan, he explained, was for two back-up stories, but the demise of Pacific changed that. And, while Mike Gustovich did a "nice job" inking the *Vanguard* story, Stuart decided that he himself would ink *Goldyn in 3-D*. "And I thought it turned out kind of neat."

This page: Clockwise, top left, *Goldyn in 3-D* [June 1986] one-shot published by Blackthorne; splash page of Walter Stuart's *Vanguard Illustrated* #7 [July 1984] strip, which introduced his time-traveling scientist; splash page of the original Mr. Monster tale by creator Fred Kelly, appearing in *Super Duper Comics* #3 [May 1947], a Canadian publication which inspired Michael T. Gilbert to create his own version; and the splash panel by George Evans of his and writer Stephen Perry's contribution to *Vanguard* #7.

The premise of "Goldyn," Stuart explained, was unlike a typical time-travel story, where characters change history. "But I like the idea where you can't change the past… and if you try to change it, it's at your peril." The idea of doing a full-length *Goldyn* as a 3-D comic book came from Steve. "He said, 'I can sell it if you do the comic yourself and if I turn it into 3-D.' I said, 'Great! Let's do it.' Then I said, 'Will I make any money?' He said, 'Probably not.' In the end, I made a little bit of money and he made a little bit of money, but one of the wonderful things about Steve starting and running his own company is, he said, 'The only reason we can make a little money is because I'm only going to print as many as we can sell.'" Thus Blackthorne would not overprint, hence no need to warehouse any back-stock inventory.

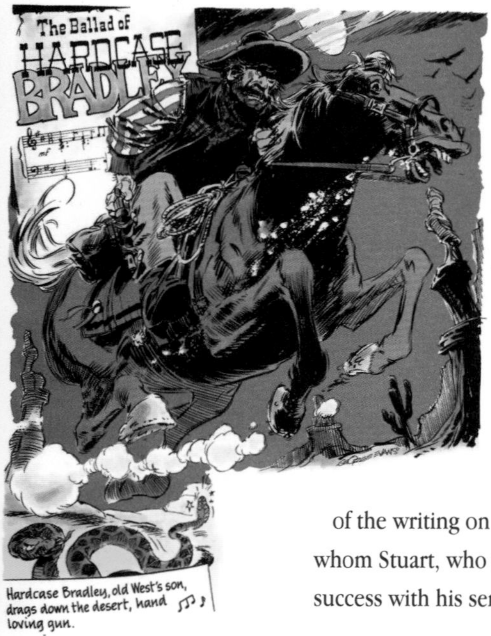
The Ballad of HARDCASE BRADLEY
Hardcase Bradley, old West's son, drags down the desert, hand loving gun.

After *Goldyn in 3-D*, Steve said to Stuart, "If you want to put together another issue, go ahead." So he did write a script and asked, "'Will we make any money?' And Steve said, 'Probably not,' so I didn't [*draw the story*]." Stuart went on to a successful career as a medical illustrator, and he and wife Pam (who helped with some of the writing on his comics) had a daughter together whom Stuart, who then daydreamed of achieving great success with his series, came close to naming 'Goldyn'!

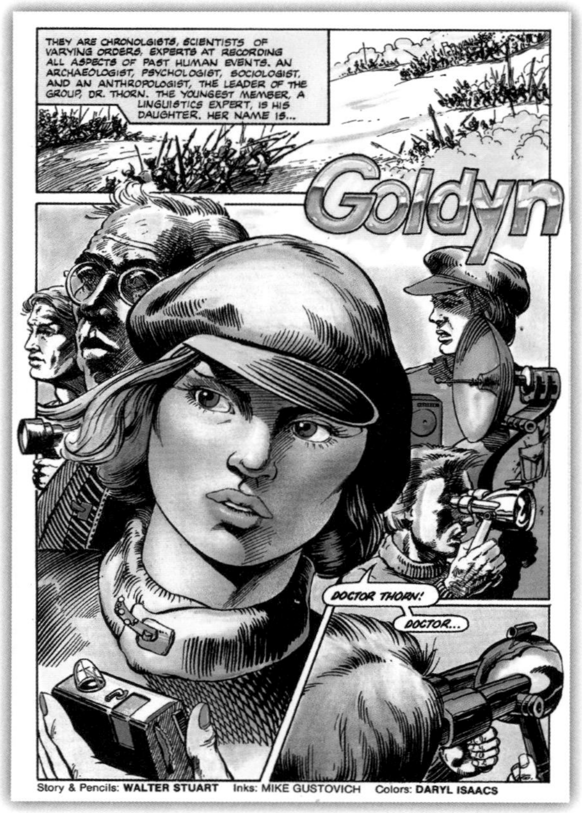
THEY ARE CHRONOLGISTS, SCIENTISTS OF VARYING ORDERS, EXPERTS AT RECORDING ALL ASPECTS OF PAST HUMAN EVENTS. AN ARCHAEOLOGIST, PSYCHOLOGIST, SOCIOLOGIST, AND AN ANTHROPOLOGIST, THE LEADER OF THE GROUP, DR. THORN. THE YOUNGEST MEMBER, A LINGUISTICS EXPERT, IS HIS DAUGHTER. HER NAME IS...
Goldyn
DOCTOR THORN!
DOCTOR...
Story & Pencils: WALTER STUART Inks: MIKE GUSTOVICH Colors: DARYL ISAACS

THEY CALL HIM… MR. MONSTER

"Doc Stearn… Mr. Monster" might be the most enduring creation to emerge from *Vanguard Illustrated*, and the character is certainly, along with The Rocketeer, one of the most endearing to debut at Pacific Comics. Creator Michael T. Gilbert shared with Jon B. Cooke about his experience: "Pacific Comics was one of the early independent publishers, and they'd gotten guys like Kirby and Ditko to do stuff for them. They had a comic called *Vanguard Illustrated*, and the premise of that was to match… it was sort of a 'new talent tryout' book, where they'd get a professional and team them up with an up-and-coming talent. Well, somewhere along the way, after we finished the first *Elric* series — Craig was leaving after that one, but I was going to continue with George Freeman. But there were a few months in-between, it would've been a dead time, so Mike Friedrich — who was my agent — worked out a deal where I would create a feature for *Vanguard Illustrated*. Dave Scroggy, the editor, said to come up with something, and we'd find a newcomer to

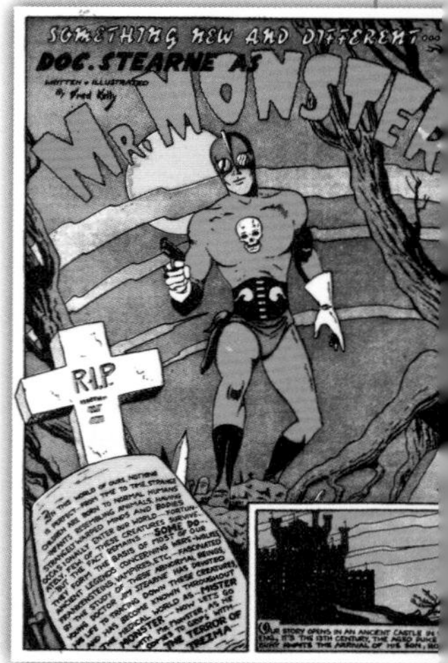
SOMETHING NEW AND DIFFERENT
DOC. STEARNE AS MR. MONSTER
R.I.P.

work with me. I thought this was great!

"It was a very exciting time for comics. Everyone was coming up with new ideas. Chaykin's *American Flagg!*, Dave Stevens' 'The Rocketeer,' and so on. There was a lot of really creative, fun stuff going on, and I wanted to be a part of it.

"After working on *Elric* a couple of years, I was delighted to create a character I'd own. I thought about doing 'The Wraith'* again, but I wanted to do something different. I started going through my old comic collection to see if there was any kind of neat idea I could use as the springboard for a new series. While digging through piles of comics, I found this old coverless comic book from 1947. It was an old anthology title with lots of different features… including a strange monster-fighting hero named Mr. Monster! I bought it at an old Seuling con for 50¢, back in the late '60s. Over the years, I'd look at this weird eight-page story and think, 'Someone should bring this guy back!' Turns out it was one of only two 'Mr. Monster' stories that had ever been done. So, anyway, I pitched Mr. Monster to Pacific. They were a little doubtful at first, but they approved it. And that's how he started."[96]

Plans were for a "Mr. Monster" three-parter. "Yeah, it was going to be three eight-page chapters of a single story," Gilbert told Cooke. "They came out with the first installment, I was working with Bill Loebs on the artwork — who was not exactly a newcomer, but I was able to make them think he was! I wanted to get someone with a real Eisner feel to the inks and whatnot; he was just perfect for it. So, I had done the scripts and the rough pencils, and then he did the finishes on the thing. Bill did a tremendous job, adding lots of Eisner-esque atmosphere."[97]

Gilbert was asked about the response to the first Mr. Monster chapter. He said, "Very positive. It's not like there were thousands of people writing in, but I got the feeling people did like it. Of course, it was kind of tricky, because the first issue of the three-part thing had come out in *Vanguard Illustrated,* and then the company went belly-up, it was like a continuation of the first time Mr. Monster had appeared 20 years earlier, but at Pacific Comics this time!… The first chapter had only appeared. So, the whole thing went under, and again, it was another one of these strange times because, at this point, I'd decided I had enough of Ohio. The first *Elric* series was over, and I didn't need to stay there any more. I wanted to move back to California to work on the next one, and take [*future spouse*] Janet with me. So, we packed up everything we owned into this huge, oversized U-Haul (much too dangerous for the size of our car — not that the U-Haul people cared!). The night before the big move, Mike Friedrich called to tell me Pacific Comics was dead.

"Suddenly, it's like, 'Oh, I don't have a job anymore! How grand!' What a good time to be moving! But it was too late to back out now, so a week later, we arrived in Berkeley and stayed at a friend's house. Luckily, while we were gone, Mike [*Friedrich*] had managed to sell *Elric* to First Comics and *Mr. Monster* to Eclipse. Eclipse was buying a lot of unused Pacific material, and they agreed to publish all three of the 'Mr. Monster' stories in a single one-shot comic. So suddenly, it was like, 'Oh, yes, I'm happy!'"

The monster-killing hero would go on to success for Gilbert at Eclipse and would even survive that company to bounce around companies over the years.

SO DON'T BELIEVE ME!!
I DON'T CARE. THEY EXIST!! (THEY DO!) AND THEY WAIT (OH YES..)
THEY WAIT, IN THE DARK. TO SUCK THE MARROW FROM YOUR BONES. TO SCOOP THE SOFT TASTY PARTS FROM YOUR SKULL! (FOR DESSERT!)
BUY IT...
OR ELSE!!
AND THEY'RE COMING, BROTHER! THEY'RE COMING... FOR YOU!!
AND ONLY ONE MAN CAN STOP THEM...
©MICHAEL T. Gilbert ©1984
DOC STEARN... MR. MONSTER
by Michael T. Gilbert & William F. Loebs
COMING SOON...TO VANGUARD!

Above: House ad for Mr. Monster. David Scroggy described Michael T. Gilbert's concept as "Dobie Gillis with werewolves." **Below:** Eclipse's *Doc Stearn… Mr. Monster* #1 [Jan. 1985].

MR. MONSTER

* The Wraith, a mash-up between a funny animal strip and The Spirit, was a Will Eisner homage about a canine private eye.

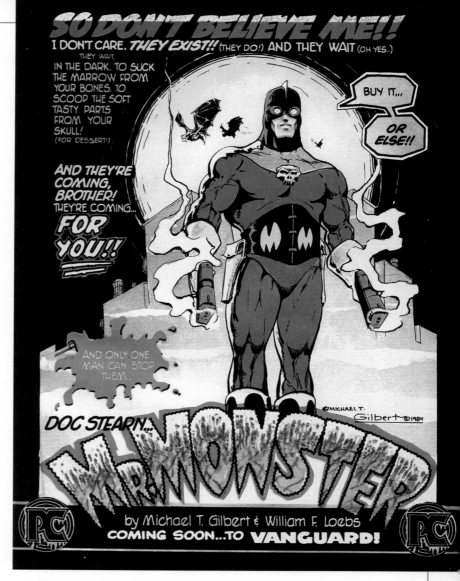

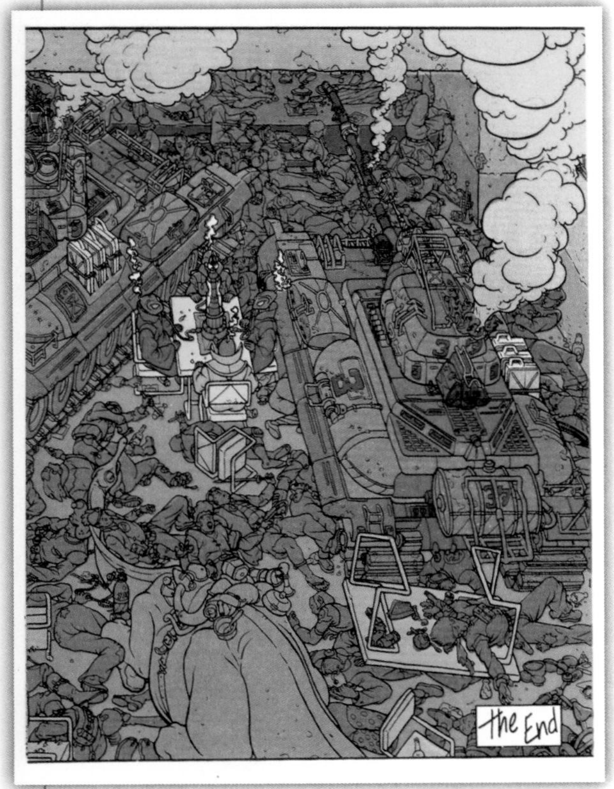

the End

SCROGGY'S STERN MEMORIES

David Scroggy shared about a cherished task. "The covers to *Vanguard Illustrated* were a high point of my time at Pacific Comics. I selected all the cover artists and worked with them on the assignments. I was able to get covers from Tom Yeates, Dave Stevens, Al Williamson, Steve Rude, George Pérez, and Michael Kaluta (twice!). Another noteworthy 'first' from *Vanguard Illustrated* was the debut of Michael T. Gilbert's 'Mr. Monster.' I had met Gilbert due to his collaborating with P. Craig Russell on the art for their adaptation of Michael Moorcock's *Elric of Melnibone*. Gilbert was living in Ohio, not far from Russell's home in Kent. One Christmas, Rosemary and I traveled to my hometown of Akron to spend the holiday with my family. Craig Russell invited us to his place for a dinner. Akron is only about 12 miles from Kent, so usually it isn't a very long drive. As the scheduled evening approached, the entire area was plunged into sub-zero temperatures, with a fresh blizzard dumping onto the already-accumulated snow. It was crazy to even attempt to drive, but we forged ahead into the night anyway. It took us many times longer than usual, inching our way towards Kent. We were an hour late for dinner, but we made it. We spent a long and convivial evening with Craig and Michael. This led to Gilbert sharing his creation, 'Doc Stearn… Mr. Monster,' based on an obscure 1940s Canadian comic character that only appeared twice. It was a wonderful fit for *Vanguard Illustrated*, and fortunately found its way into the final issue."

This spread: Counter-clockwise, below is opening to David Scroggy's interview in *The Telegraph Wire* #15 [June/July 1984], with Rick Geary's caricature; illo and ad with art by Jeffrey Jones; and a page of Geoff Darrow's "Bourbon Thret," originally intended for *Vanguard*.

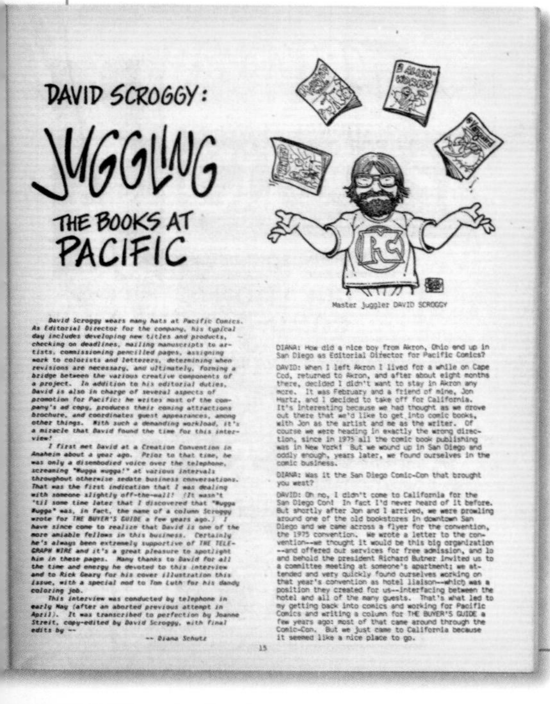

DAVID SCROGGY:
JUGGLING
THE BOOKS AT
PACIFIC

Master Juggler DAVID SCROGGY

David Scroggy wears many hats at Pacific Comics. As Editorial Director for the company, his typical day includes developing new titles and products, checking on deadlines, mailing manuscripts to artists, commissioning pencilled pages, assigning work to colorists and letterers, determining when revisions are necessary, and ultimately, forming a bridge between the various creative components of a project. In addition to his editorial duties, David is also in charge of several aspects of promotion for Pacific: he writes most of the company's ad copy, produces their coming attractions brochure, and coordinates guest appearances, among other things. With such a demanding workload, it's a miracle that David found the time for this interview!

I first met David at a Creation Convention in Anaheim about a year ago. Prior to that time, he was only a disembodied voice over the telephone, screaming "Wugga wugga!" at various intervals throughout otherwise sedate business conversations. That was the first indication that I was dealing with someone slightly off-the-wall! (It wasn't 'til some time later that I discovered that "Wugga Wugga" was, in fact, the name of a column Scroggy wrote for THE BUYER'S GUIDE a few years ago.) I have since come to realize that David is one of the more amiable fellows in this business. Certainly he's always been extremely supportive of THE TELEGRAPH WIRE and it's a great pleasure to spotlight him in these pages. Many thanks to David for all the time and energy he devoted to this interview and to Rick Geary for his cover illustration this issue, with a special nod to Tom Luth for his dandy coloring job.

This interview was conducted by telephone in early May (after an aborted previous attempt in April). It was transcribed to perfection by Joanne Streit, copy-edited by David Scroggy, with final edits by --

-- Diana Schutz

DIANA: How did a nice boy from Akron, Ohio end up in San Diego as Editorial Director for Pacific Comics?

DAVID: When I left Akron I lived for a while on Cape Cod, returned to Akron, and after about eight months there, decided I didn't want to stay in Akron any more. It was February and a friend of mine, Jon Hartz, and I decided to take off for California. It's interesting because we had thought as we drove out there that we'd like to get into comic books, with Jon as the artist and me as the writer. Of course we were heading in exactly the wrong direction, since in 1975 all the comic book publishing was in New York! But we wound up in San Diego and oddly enough, years later, we found ourselves in the comic business.

DIANA: Was it the San Diego Comic-Con that brought you west?

DAVID: Oh no, I didn't come to California for the San Diego Con! In fact I'd never heard of it before. But shortly after Jon and I arrived, we were prowling around one of the old bookstores in downtown San Diego and we came across a flyer for the convention, the 1975 convention. We wrote a letter to the convention--we thought it would be this big organization--and offered our services for free admission, and lo and behold the president Richard Butner invited us to a committee meeting at someone's apartment; we attended and very quickly found ourselves working on that year's convention as hotel liaison--which was a position they created for us--interfacing between the hotel and all of the many guests. That's what led to my getting back into comics and working for Pacific Comics and writing a column for THE BUYER'S GUIDE a few years ago: most of that came around through the Comic-Con. But we just came to California because it seemed like a nice place to go.

15

Scroggy also shared, "I have had the pleasure of knowing and occasionally working with Geof Darrow since assigning him his very first comic story, to be published in *Vanguard Illustrated.* [*Alas, it wasn't published.*] He is an astonishing talent. When Pacific folded, I was able to place the rest of the story in *Heavy Metal* [V8 #12, Mar. 1985]. Geof never looked back."[98]

About that tale "Bourbon Thret," Darrow told a radio interviewer, "Well, way back when, originally I'd done it — originally, it was actually David Scroggy. It used to be Pacific Comics, which had done 'The Rocketeer' originally. They were down in San Diego and I knew Dave Stevens. I'd met him. He was working at Filmation at the time. He said, 'Oh yeah, go down and talk to them.' I went down and I showed it to them. It was this thing I wanted to do and I showed them the drawings. They said, 'Oh yeah, we'd like to do that.' Of course, the company went under before it ever came out. But I always liked — I'm a big fan of Japanese films, especially Zatoichi. I wanted to do something kind of like Zatoichi. But I also liked spaghetti Westerns. He's got to have a six-gun and a sword! …it's all the way back to *Yojimbo* and *Seven Samurai*. For me, the archetype of all modern heroes is *Yojimbo*."[99]

THE EDITOR'S FUNCTION

For *The Telegraph Wire*, editor Diane Schutz interviewed David Scroggy, who discussed his level of involvement as editor. "It's in everyone's best interest to have the best possible package, so it's not really an adversarial relationship. Certainly some books that we publish are packages that people provide to us in total, and some of them are pages that we ourselves at Pacific Comics put together and commission, and that's the case with virtually all the books that I edit, so it really varies a lot depending on the package. On a book like *Groo*, my function will be minimal at best — basically just a coordinator. Certainly, when you're working with people like Sergio and Mark Evanier, there's very little for me to do input-wise — it's the best product we could possibly have.

"On a book like *Vanguard*, where you're dealing with new talent and people who are just getting into comics for the first time, and in many cases putting new talent with established talent, there's quite a lot of editing involved and quite a lot of working with writers on the script and the artists on the art and so forth. So my contribution will vary from book to book."[100]

ABANDONED QUEST

The financial woes over at Jim Warren's publishing firm finally caught up with Pacific after they had originally advertised a Jeffrey Jones comic collecting his work for the Warren magazines, but would never appear. David explained why in promotion copy for a subsequent one-shot compilation of Jones stories: "We are pleased to announce a second outstanding collection of graphic story material by Jeffrey Jones. There have been some unforeseen difficulties with our previously announced Jones anthology *Quest and Other Tales*. Scheduled for an October release, *Quest* consisted of material previously published in the Warren magazine line. Due to Warren's involuntary bankruptcy, our contracts for this material are tied up in court. Therefore, we are canceling *Quest* for now, and will resolicit for it when the material is released. We have collected a superb group of Mr. Jones' finest graphic story work from other sources, however, and it will ship in October as *Ravens and Rainbows*."[101]

It was one of the Schanes siblings who was the guy typically coordinating the reprint collections, but the Jones title was different, as David related. "Steve Schanes was very much involved with several of the reprint titles. One exception was the Jeff Jones reprint collection, which I titled *Ravens and Rainbows*. I was chagrined when I told Jones on the telephone that we had come up with the title, and his response was, 'I hate rainbows.' I offered to change it, but he really didn't seem to care.

"I think that attitude extended to the other reprint material creators — if they had a bone to pick regarding compensation, I think most of them realized that the conversation and complaint was one to have with Warren or whoever printed it originally, rather than Pacific Comics. So, while the other creators didn't support the reprints in any way, they didn't raise any public objections to them either. But they kept their distance from them and didn't want to, for example, create new cover art for these comics. I wrote a poem for the inside front cover of Jim Starlin's *Darklon the Mystic* reprint. [*See page 94.*] I never heard whether he liked it or not, but it was probably my most visible contribution to these titles. There was only enough of Jones' older material for a single one-shot comic, so it is not as if there was a second collection planned."[102]

Pacific Premieres #5 [Aug. 1983] mentioned that *Ravens and Rainbows* included the artist's fanzine work, material reprinted from *Swank* magazine, and plates from Jones' Middle Earth portfolio.

ISSUE #1
PC
"For the NEW Era in Comics"
$1.50 U.S.
$2.00 Canada
QUEST
and OTHER TALES
NEW JEFF JONES COVER!
June Release
QUEST . . .
And Other Tales
by JEFFERY JONES
Some of Jones' very finest graphic story work was originally presented in black-and-white in the Warren magazines. His output was small, but its quality glows like a cunningly cut, shiny jewel. The title story is a seven-page drama set in a prehistoric world. The collection also includes "Cold Cuts," a "chilling" narrative scripted by Jones' longtime colleague Berni Wrightson. This is one of their finest efforts. Also included is "Harry" where you'll discover just how disturbing a little girl and her teddy bear can be. This outstanding entertainment value is the first time ever this work has been presented in color. The coloring is being done by Steve Oliff, who is taking complete advantage of the full-process separation process. High quality "Baxter" stock. 32 pages.
—$1.50
4

The final nail was driven into the coffin of Jim Warren's storied company by August 29, 1983, when the G.E.M. Auction Corporation hosted a bankruptcy sale of the assets of the Warren Communication Corp., a.k.a. Captain Company. "The auctioneer's catalogue was 29 pages long and listed a total of 958,715 books."[103]

On January 4, 1984, over the objections of Bill DuBay and Frank Thorne — the artist there to plead for his ownership of *Ghita of Alizarr* — U.S. District Court Judge John Galgay approved the sale of what remained of Warren Publishing for $110,790 cash.[104] And, with that, one major source for Pacific Comics reprint titles was shuttered for good.

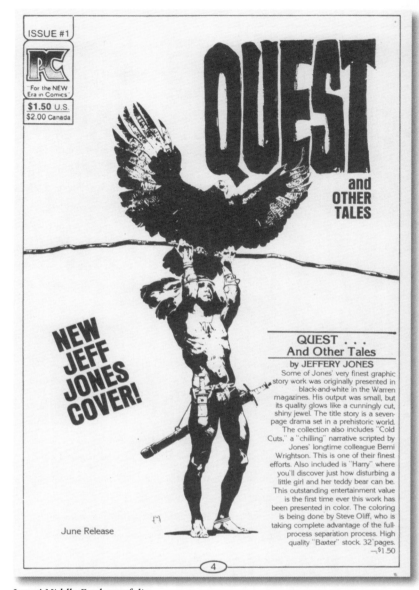

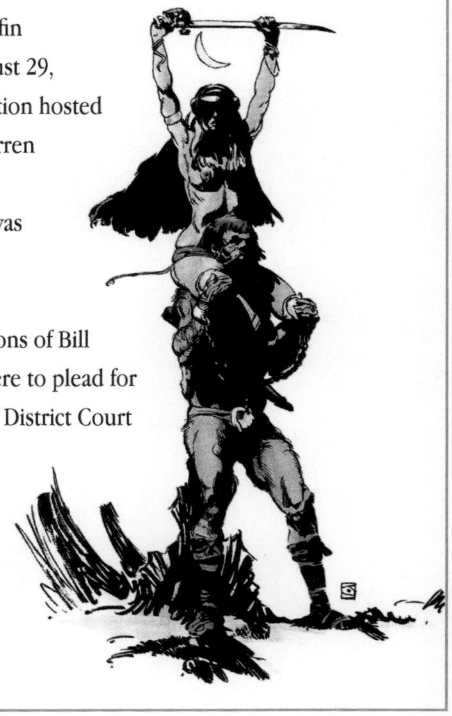

Inset right: Scott Hampton's evocative splash page in *Silverheels* #1 [Dec. 1983], the first fully-painted comic book in the United States.

An artist whose professed influences include Jeffrey Jones — as well as Jones' fellow Studio-mates Bernie Wrightson and Michael W. Kaluta — Scott Hampton produced extraordinarily fine work for Pacific Comics, and nowhere better than in the pages of *Silverheels,* a Bruce Jones Associates production. He shared with the author, "I had provided the art for a story Bruce wrote for *Alien Worlds* [#3, July 1983] called, 'The Inheritors.' Shortly after that, they asked me to work on *Silverheels*. They are great people. It was a blast working with them!... This was a Bruce Jones Associates production, and I'm pretty sure all my interactions were with April and sometimes Bruce."[105]

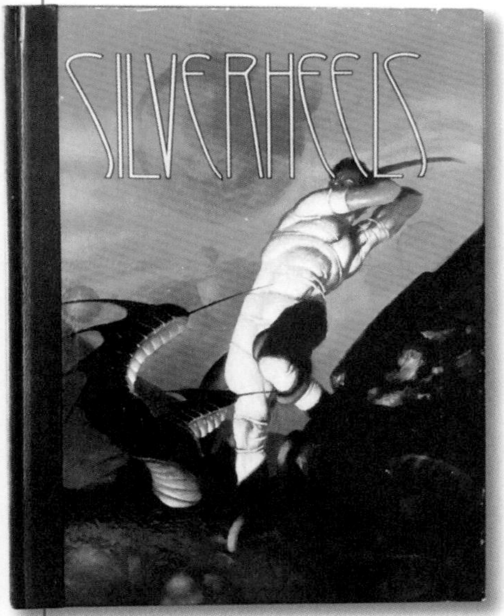
SILVERHEELS

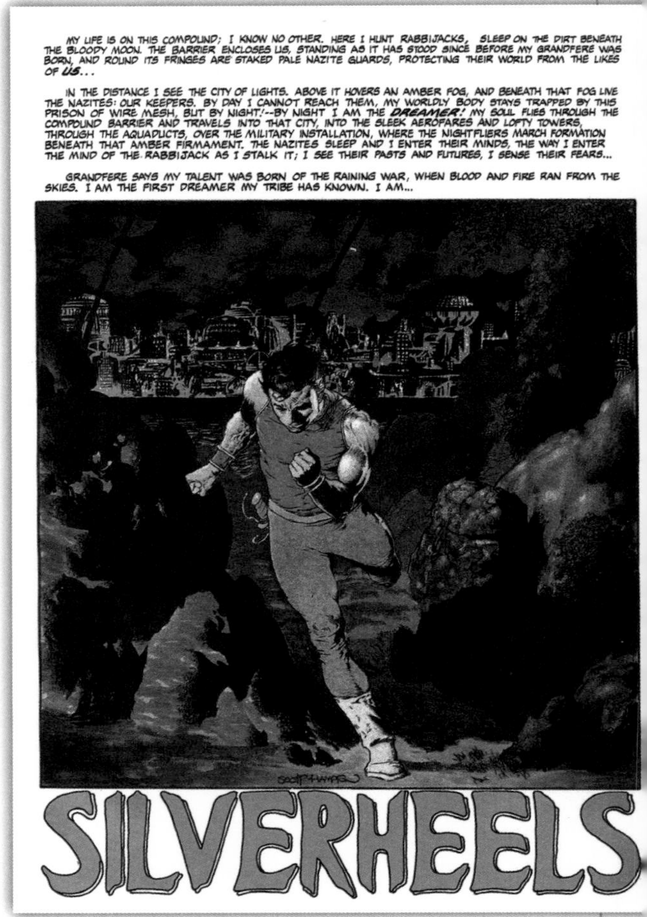
MY LIFE IS ON THIS COMPOUND; I KNOW NO OTHER. HERE I HUNT RABBIJACKS, SLEEP ON THE DIRT BENEATH THE BLOODY MOON. THE BARRIER ENCLOSES US, STANDING AS IT HAS STOOD SINCE BEFORE MY GRANDFERE WAS BORN, AND ROUND ITS FRINGES ARE STAKED PALE NAZITE GUARDS, PROTECTING THEIR WORLD FROM THE LIKES OF US...
IN THE DISTANCE I SEE THE CITY OF LIGHTS. ABOVE IT HOVERS AN AMBER FOG, AND BENEATH THAT FOG LIVE THE NAZITES: OUR KEEPERS. BY DAY I CANNOT REACH THEM, MY WORLDLY BODY STAYS TRAPPED BY THIS PRISON OF WIRE MESH, BUT BY NIGHT!--BY NIGHT I AM THE DREAMER! MY SOUL FLIES THROUGH THE COMPOUND BARRIER AND TRAVELS INTO THAT CITY, INTO THE SLEEK AEROFARES AND LOFTY TOWERS, THROUGH THE AQUADUCTS, OVER THE MILITARY INSTALLATION, WHERE THE NIGHTFLIERS MARCH FORMATION BENEATH THAT AMBER FIRMAMENT. THE NAZITES SLEEP AND I ENTER THEIR MINDS, THE WAY I ENTER THE MIND OF THE RABBIJACK AS I STALK IT; I SEE THEIR PASTS AND FUTURES, I SENSE THEIR FEARS...
GRANDFERE SAYS MY TALENT WAS BORN OF THE RAINING WAR, WHEN BLOOD AND FIRE RAN FROM THE SKIES. I AM THE FIRST DREAMER MY TRIBE HAS KNOWN. I AM...
SILVERHEELS

Asked about the process in which he participated, Hampton shared, "I got a full script, and I ran with that... [*This was*] the first ongoing comic book, as opposed to a graphic novel or anthology, to be fully-painted... I painted a lot of my early drawings and samples. Most of my assignments were to paint the stories since that was what I was comfortable with."

Above: The fourth issue was finally published, years after the first three chapters appeared, in the *Silverheels* collection, published by Eclipse in 1987.

Asked if filmmakers had influenced his storytelling, the artist replied, "Definitely! Stanley Kubrick, David Lean, animated Christmas specials, and Saturday morning cartoons were how I learned to tell stories visually."

Alas, when questioned if he recalled any interesting anecdotes working on this project, Hampton answered, "Not really. It was a long time ago, and I worked from home."[106]

However routine the assignment, *Silverheels,* chronicling a Native American living in a dystopian future, was a beautiful production and it spoke not only to Hampton's sublime talent, but also to the design sensibility of the book's co-writer and co-editor, Bruce Jones, who talked about visual consistency with Kim Thompson, in *Amazing Heroes*. "It was very hard to do given the proclivities of the average comic book artist and the average comic book reader, but I always tried to give the Pacific books a house look," Jones said. "Not just stand out of the racks so people would pick them up instead of something else. I got this from Hugh Hefner, who once said that a magazine should be like an old friend: it should be immediately recognizable and you should be very comfortable with it, but it should always be inspiring and there should always be a little nook or cranny of newness in there. That's what I strove for and it's not something I always succeeded at."[107]

When the interviewer mused that maybe Pacific failed because the comics had no consistent graphic identity, Jones replied, "I think you're absolutely right and the chief problem with that is a lack of art direction. That's always the case. Good art directors are hard to come by. I hate to say it this way, but most people who are good at it aren't going to waste their time in comic books, because the pay isn't good. They go on to the slick magazines."[108]

Silverheels, which, as Hampton said, has the distinction of being the first fully-painted American comic book series, was planned for a four-issue run, then cancelled after only three, and it would be years before Eclipse collected the series with the unpublished #4 in a graphic album.

Pacific Profiles

Scott Hampton

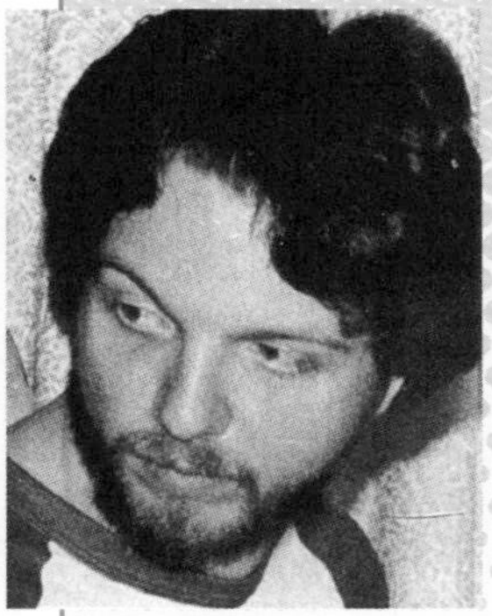

Born: *Apr. 1959*
The younger brother of fellow artist Bo Hampton, Scott studied under Will Eisner with his sibling in 1976 and had his first professional work published in *Vampirella* magazine. David Scroggy called his art "nuanced, ethereal, almost ghostly." Recent work includes *American Gods.*

Above: Scott Hampton, in a photo that appeared in a gallery section of his art in *Silverheels* #2 [Mar. 1984].

BRINGING UP THE REAR

Discussing *Silverheels* in his *Comics Journal* website piece, "Welcome to the Strip Mine," Marc Sobel recalled a fascinating back-up in that series, in the third issue: "*Silverheels* was a series published by Pacific in 1984," he wrote in the comments section. "Its main feature was a sci-fi adventure with really nice painted artwork by Scott Hampton (which was later collected by Eclipse). But the series had some great back-ups, including a six-page color story by Jaime [*Hernandez*] called 'All My Love, Aliso Road,' in the third issue. It was the first and only chapter and, when *Silverheels* was cancelled, Jaime abandoned the story. Years ago, I asked him about this story and he said, 'In the early days, when *Love and Rockets* started to get noticed, my brother and I started to get offers to work for other companies. Pacific Comics asked me to do a six-part back-up story in *Silverheels* about anything I wanted, and I took it thinking it would be fun. The comic was cancelled after my first chapter and that was that. Nobody ever offered me to finish it and that was okay. I might have felt bad about it if it was *Love and Rockets*.'"[109]

Canadian artist Ken Steacy was a frequent contributor on BJA Associate stories, notably the "Flan" back-ups in *Silverheels*. He recently shared, "My collaborations with Bruce Jones and his partner, April Campbell, for Pacific Comics were among the most satisfying (and downright fun!) of my 50-year career, as was my relationship with publishers Bill and Steve Schanes, and my old pal, Dave Scroggy, who was editorial director. I greatly admired their commitment to creators, offering substantially better deals on IP rights, royalties, and licensing than either Marvel or DC at the time.

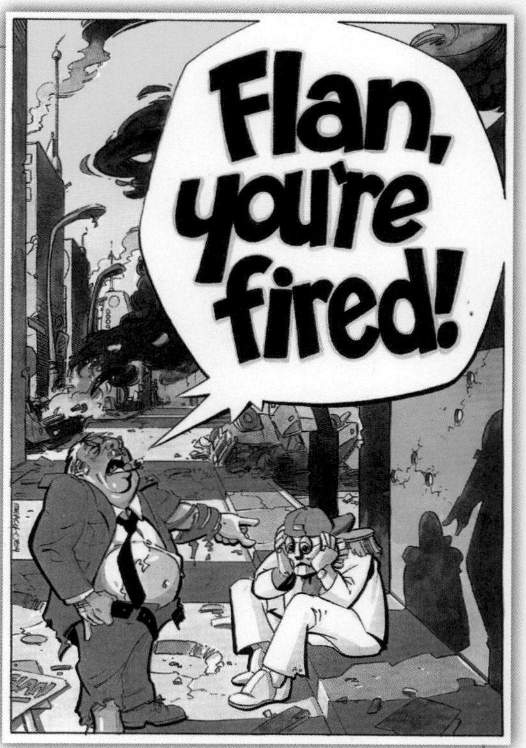
Flan, you're fired!

"I was already a fan of Bruce's work, as both writer and artist, and had long considered him kinda like the 'Fifth Beatle,' the other four being *The Studio* members: Jeff Jones, Michael Kaluta, Barry Windsor-Smith, and Bernie Wrightson. They were the first guys to work in the industry who didn't wear ties, paving the way for an entirely new generation of visual storyteller, and I was eager to join their ranks.

"I had always disliked the assembly-line approach of the mainstream industry, which insisted on specialization. With Bruce's support, Pacific Comics afforded me the opportunity to push the boundaries of what was possible at the time, enabling me to create fully-painted and airbrushed artwork, which their high-quality reproduction showcased admirably well."[110]

This page: Clockwise from above, Ken Steacy splash from *Silverheels* #3 [May 1984]; promotional drawing by Scott Hampton; and splash page of Jaime Hernandez's back-up strip in *Silverheels* #3.

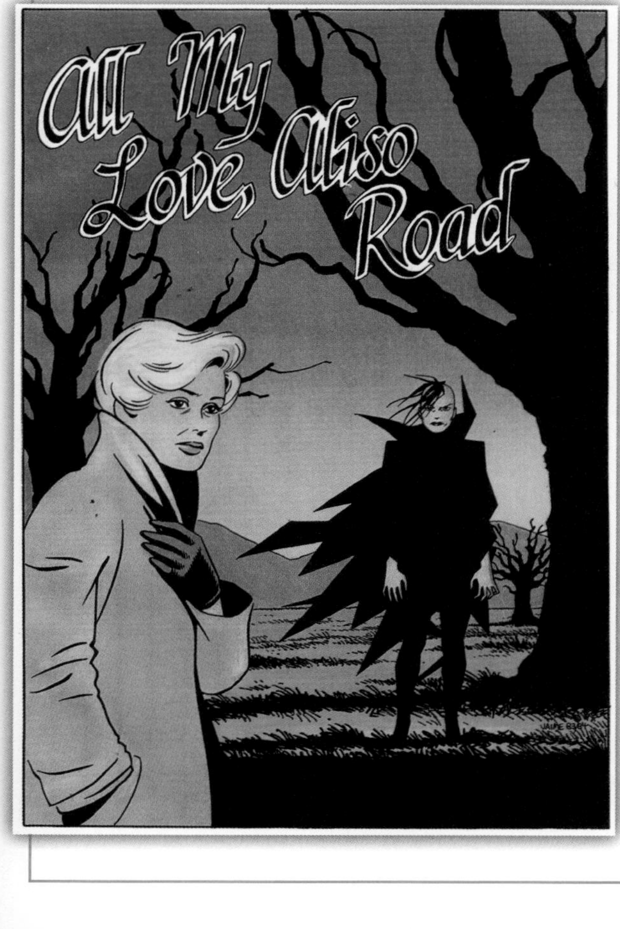
All My Love, Aliso Road

Steacy continued, "The only time we ever butted heads was once when I changed a caption, in "Pi in the Sky" [*Alien Worlds* #3, July 1983], from 'The Red Bear Sucks!' to 'The Red Bear Stinks!' Our boys were quite young at the time and I guess I felt the former phrase was kinda vulgar. April called and read me the riot act, after which I crossed my heart and promised never to do it again — at least not without asking first!

"Sadly, the Pacific Comics experiment was not to last, and market forces pushed me 'n' Bruce 'n' April in different directions. I'll always look back fondly on our time together, and greatly appreciate the opportunity to have collaborated with such boundlessly creative folks."[111]

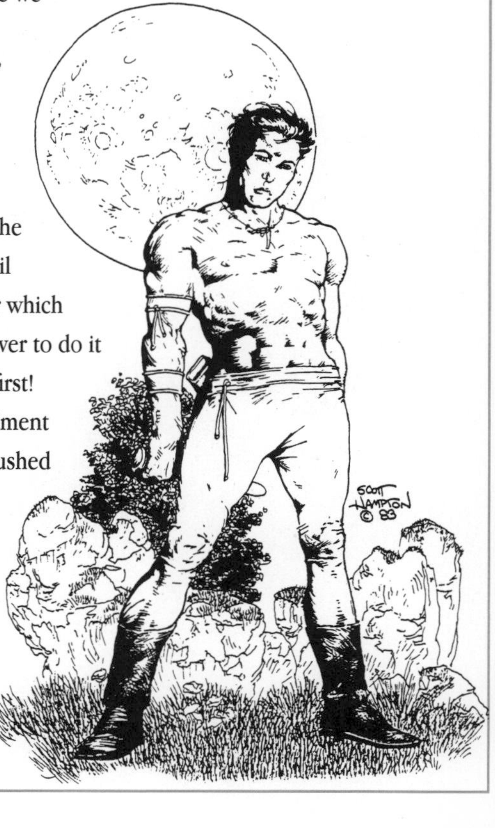
SCOTT HAMPTON © 83

The “Flan” Process Guide

At one point, we did a goofy photo-shoot of how I work, with me cosplaying as that idiosyncratic li’l robot, Flan, star of the back-up strip I drew in *Silverheels*.

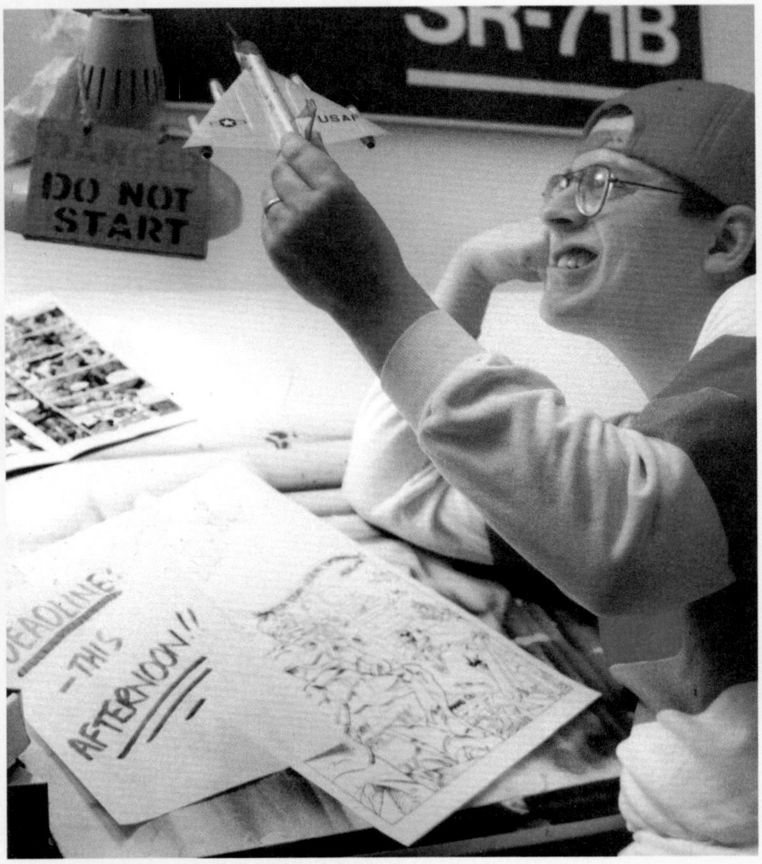
SR-71B
USAF
DO NOT
START
DEADLINE:
-THIS
AFTERNOON!!

Rule number one for making deadlines: don’t get distracted!

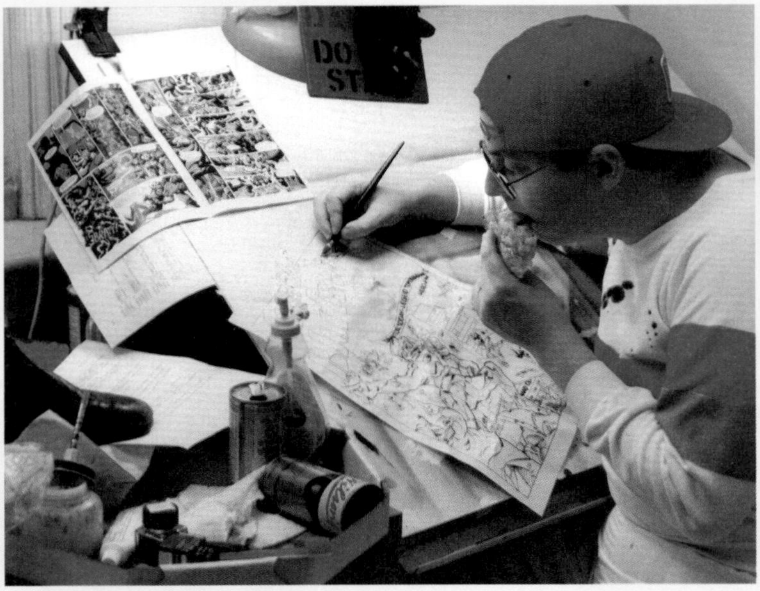

A clean, tidy workplace is a must to ensure positive productivity!

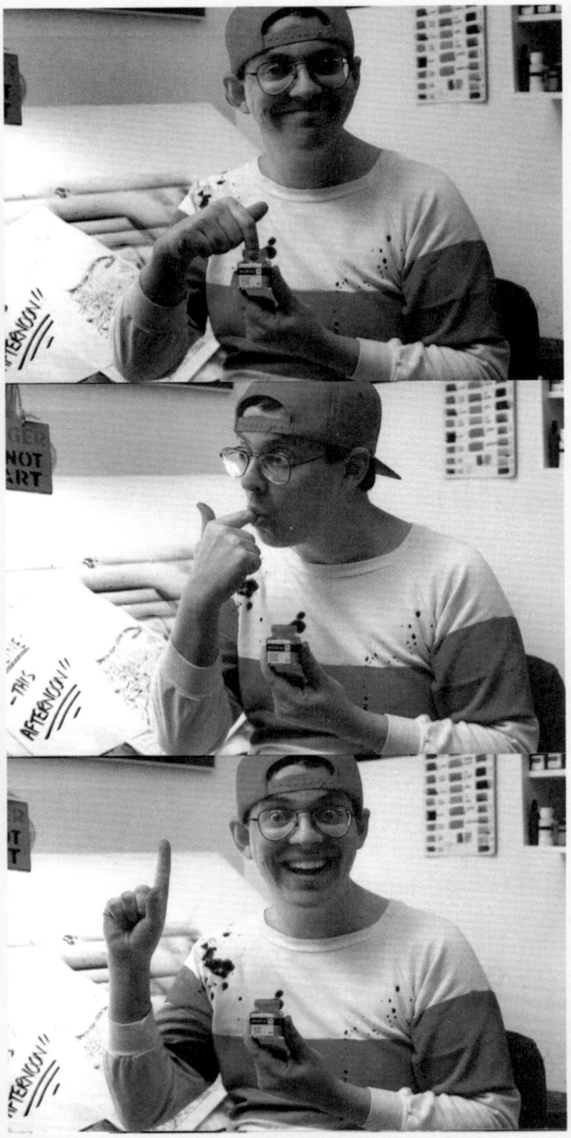

Choosing just the right red is largely a matter of good taste!

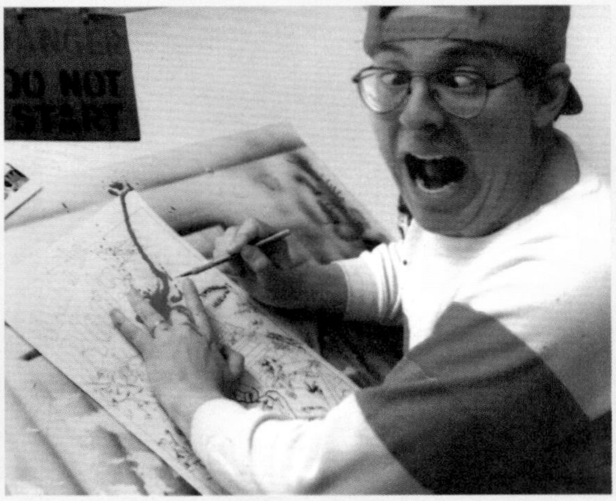

X-Acto blades are very sharp, so take care when cutting!

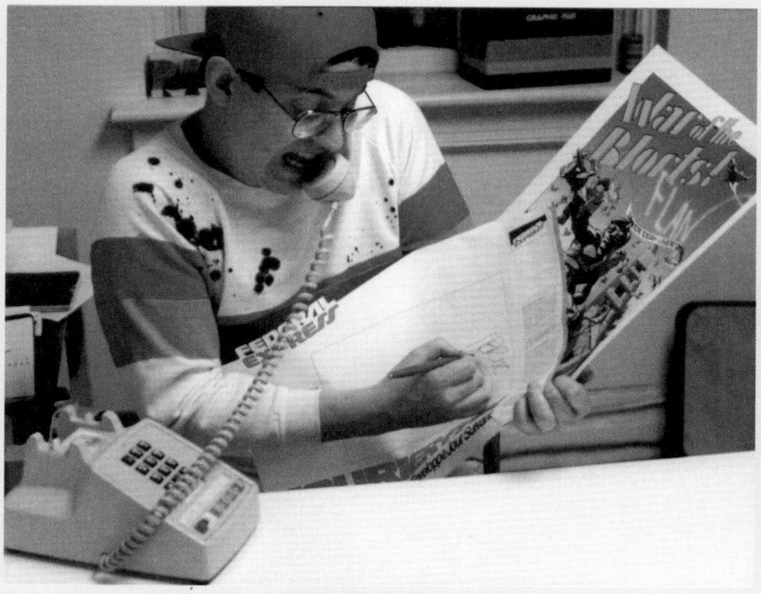
War of the Blasts!
Flan
FEDERAL EXPRESS

No worries, the fine folks at FedEx are just a phone call away!

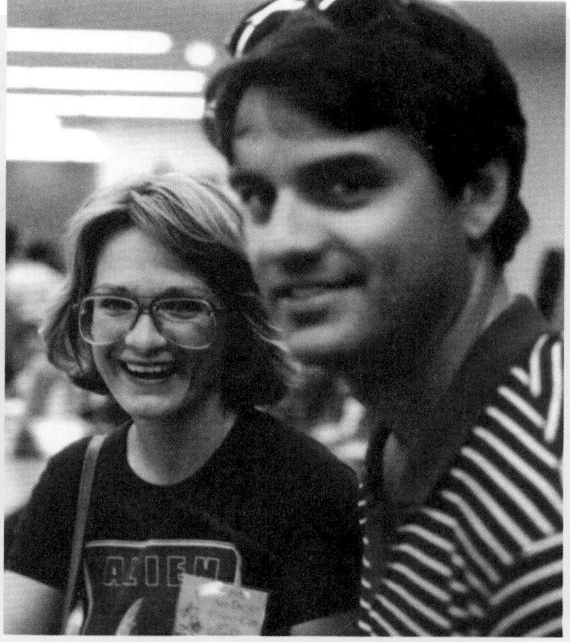

April and Bruce at the San Diego Comic-Con in 1982 — we were delighted to make one another's acquaintance!

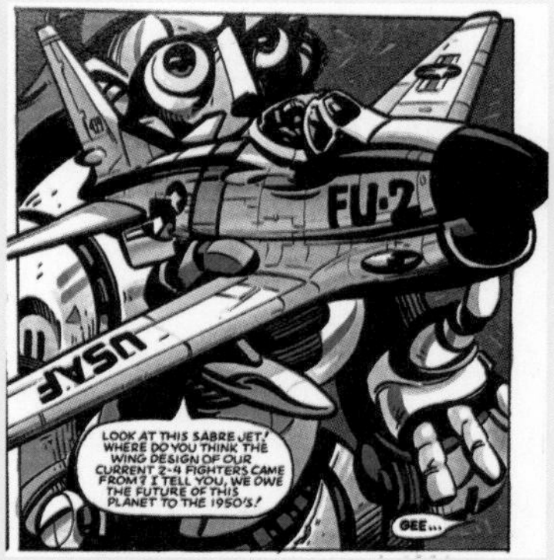
FU-2
USAF
LOOK AT THIS SABRE JET! WHERE DO YOU THINK THE WING DESIGN OF OUR CURRENT Z-4 FIGHTERS CAME FROM? I TELL YOU, WE OWE THE FUTURE OF THIS PLANET TO THE 1950'S!
GEE...

Robotus Ridiculous

Illustrating the goofy misadventure of Flan, an endlessly energetic little robot who's obsessed with the '50s and somehow gains the power to transform into anything that comes to mind, was a real treat. The three-part story ran as the back-up to Scott Hampton's beautifully painted feature, *Silverheels*. There were plans to give Flan his own book, but sales dictated otherwise.

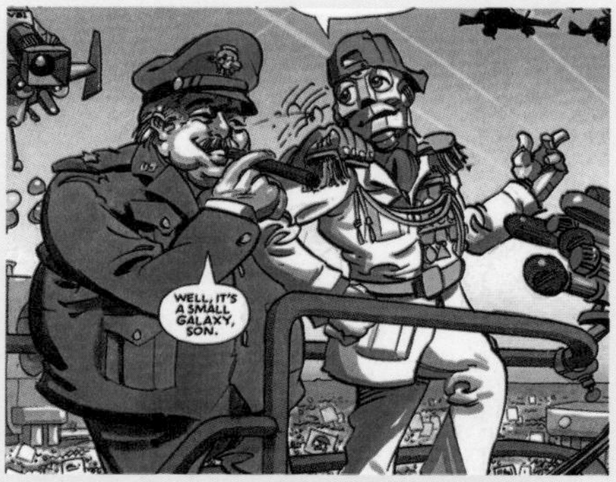
WELL, IT'S A SMALL GALAXY, SON.

The Blue/Gray Line

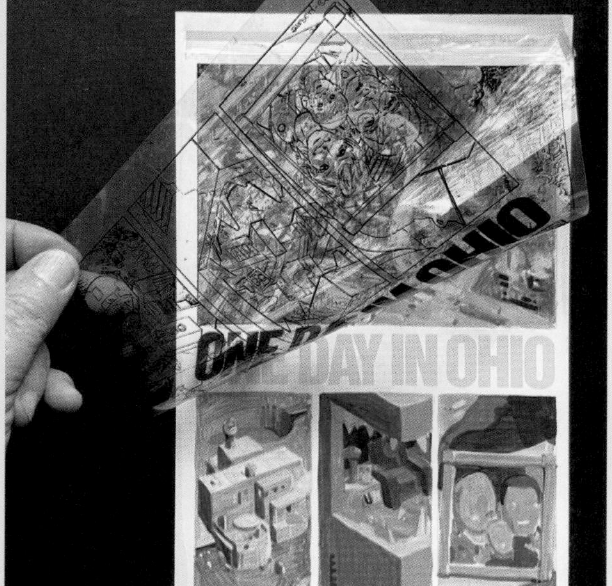
ONE DAY IN OHIO

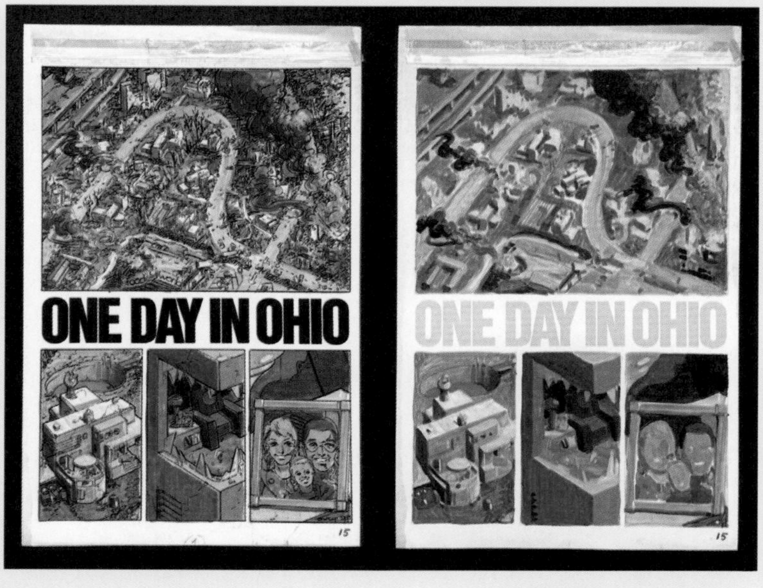
ONE DAY IN OHIO
ONE DAY IN OHIO

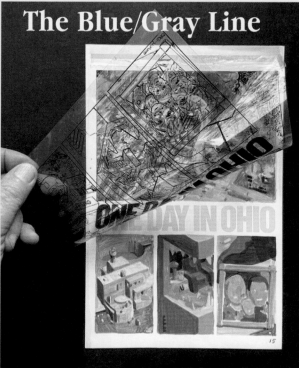

I really wanted to try the European 'blue line' method of full-process coloring, which involves painting over a copy of the line art printed in blue, or in this case, gray. The advantage is that the line art isn't color separated, so it prints as solid black. Bruce again demonstrates his mastery of creating stories that deliver a solid dramatic punch without losing his quirky sense of humor.

Pacific Comics and 'The Big Dump'

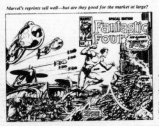

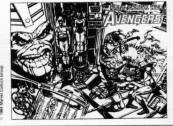

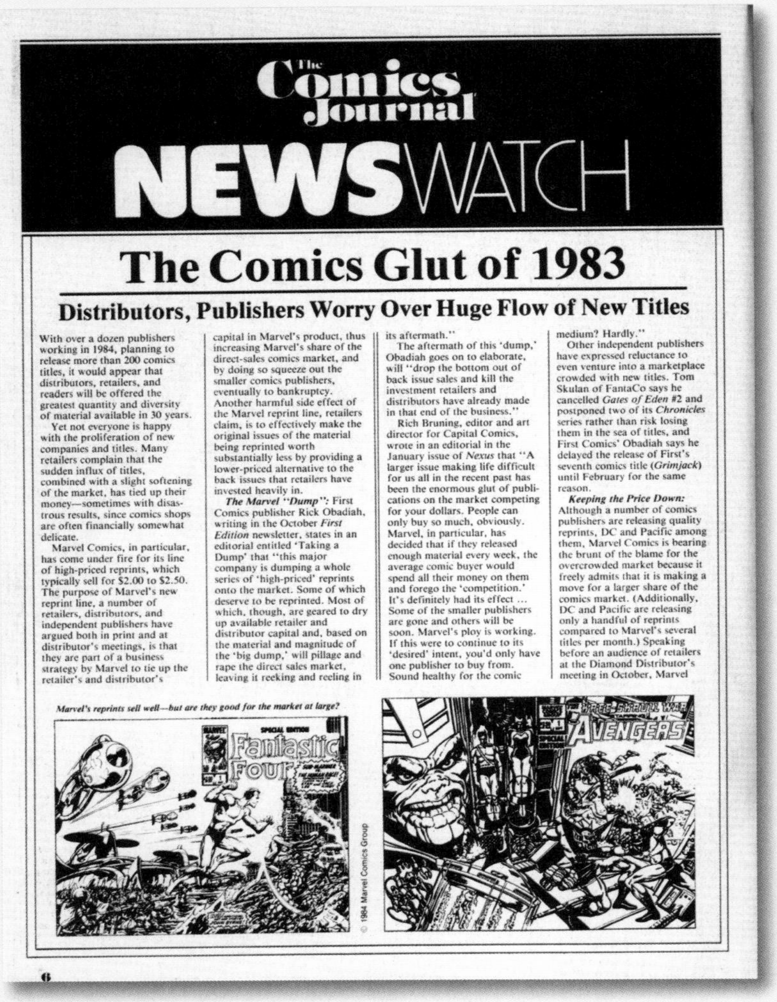

The Comics Journal

NEWSWATCH

The Comics Glut of 1983

Distributors, Publishers Worry Over Huge Flow of New Titles

With over a dozen publishers working in 1984, planning to release more than 200 comics titles, it would appear that distributors, retailers, and readers will be offered the greatest quantity and diversity of material available in 30 years.

Yet not everyone is happy with the proliferation of new companies and titles. Many retailers complain that the sudden influx of titles, combined with a slight softening of the market, has tied up their money—sometimes with disastrous results, since comics shops are often financially somewhat delicate.

Marvel Comics, in particular, has come under fire for its line of high-priced reprints, which typically sell for $2.00 to $2.50. The purpose of Marvel's new reprint line, a number of retailers, distributors, and independent publishers have argued both in print and at distributor's meetings, is that they are part of a business strategy by Marvel to tie up the retailer's and distributor's capital in Marvel's product, thus increasing Marvel's share of the direct-sales comics market, and by doing so squeeze out the smaller comics publishers, eventually to bankruptcy. Another harmful side effect of the Marvel reprint line, retailers claim, is to effectively make the original issues of the material being reprinted worth substantially less by providing a lower-priced alternative to the back issues that retailers have invested heavily in.

The Marvel "Dump": First Comics publisher Rick Obadiah, writing in the October *First Edition* newsletter, states in an editorial entitled 'Taking a Dump' that "this major company is dumping a whole series of 'high-priced' reprints onto the market. Some of which deserve to be reprinted. Most of which, though, are geared to dry up available retailer and distributor capital and, based on the material and magnitude of the 'big dump,' will pillage and rape the direct sales market, leaving it reeking and reeling in its aftermath."

The aftermath of this 'dump,' Obadiah goes on to elaborate, will "drop the bottom out of back issue sales and kill the investment retailers and distributors have already made in that end of the business."

Rich Bruning, editor and art director for Capital Comics, wrote in an editorial in the January issue of *Nexus* that "A larger issue making life difficult for us all in the recent past has been the enormous glut of publications on the market competing for your dollars. People can only buy so much, obviously. Marvel, in particular, has decided that if they released enough material every week, the average comic buyer would spend all their money on them and forego the 'competition.' It's definitely had its effect ... Some of the smaller publishers are gone and others will be soon. Marvel's ploy is working. If this were to continue to its 'desired' intent, you'd only have one publisher to buy from. Sound healthy for the comic medium? Hardly."

Other independent publishers have expressed reluctance to even venture into a marketplace crowded with new titles. Tom Skulan of FantaCo says he cancelled *Gates of Eden* #2 and postponed two of its *Chronicles* series rather than risk losing them in the sea of titles, and First Comics' Obadiah says he delayed the release of First's seventh comics title (*Grimjack*) until February for the same reason.

Keeping the Price Down: Although a number of comics publishers are releasing quality reprints, DC and Pacific among them, Marvel Comics is bearing the brunt of the blame for the overcrowded market because it freely admits that it is making a move for a larger share of the comics market. (Additionally, DC and Pacific are releasing only a handful of reprints compared to Marvel's several titles per month.) Speaking before an audience of retailers at the Diamond Distributor's meeting in October, Marvel

Marvel's reprints sell well—but are they good for the market at large?

Special Edition
Fantastic Four
Kree-Skrull War
Avengers
© 1984 Marvel Comics Group

6

Above: Opening page in the news section of *The Comics Journal* #86 [Nov. 1983] reports on Marvel's flooding the market with high-price reprint books, that forced retailers to buy less independent comics products, a debacle that was commonly termed "Black September."

Next page: Pacific advertised the *World of Wood* micro-series, though Eclipse would be the eventual publisher. Art by Dave Stevens.

With his imprint less than a year old, First Comics publisher Rick Obadiah took on the leading publisher in the industry with a scathing editorial in the October edition of his house newsletter, *First Edition*. Under the headline "Taking a Dump," he railed, "[T]his major company is dumping a whole series of 'high-priced' reprints onto the market. Some of which deserved to be reprinted. Most of which, though, are geared to dry up available retailer and distributor capital and, based on the material and magnitude of the 'big dump,' will pillage and rape the direct sales market, leaving it reeking and reeling in its aftermath."[113]

The 'major company' was, naturally, Marvel Comics, which had released nine limited series cover-dated 1982–83 featuring reprint material printed on high quality paper and carrying an expensive pricetag ($2–2.50), including (by one count) *Warlock* (six issues), *Doctor Strange/Silver Dagger* (one), *The Kree-Skrull War* (two), *Micronauts Special Edition* (five), *Moon Knight Special Edition* (three), *Nick Fury, Agent of Shield* (two), *Conan the Barbarian* (one), *Special Edition X-Men* (one), and—as apparently one *X-Men* series being simply not enough—*X-Men Classics Starring the X-Men* (three).

The head of the other Pacific Comics division saw an existential threat. Reported *The Comics Journal*, "Ken Kreuger, of Pacific Distribution, says that Marvel's flood of reprints, in addition to being extremely damaging to the small comic book dealer, is symptomatic of Marvel's desire to drive out its competition. States Kreuger, 'A lot of retailers don't know how to order any more. They haven't been cutting back on their orders to reflect the additional titles... Marvel really is trying to bleed the buying public out of their last buck, and trying to discourage the smaller publishers. They've just about destroyed the small comic book dealer.'"[114]

Over on the publishing side of Pacific, David Scroggy was asked for comment at the time by Diana Schutz regarding the "big dump." He replied, "Well, I think it's going to be touch and go. Currently, in the summer, we're seeing that some of the independents have to make some hard decisions. I feel that Pacific Comics is in perhaps the best position sales-wise of any independent, but we're all out there struggling very hard to increase our sales and increase our market share. It seems as though the generic name of a Marvel or DC is something that causes dealers to order the books in greater numbers. For example, when we talk to [*retailer*] Comics & Comix and ask John Barrett how our books are selling, he says that our books are selling great. And when we ask him how many *Alien Worlds* he ordered for his seven stores, he might say 800, and when we ask him how many [*Marvel Super-Heroes*] *Secret Wars* he ordered for his stores, he'll tell us 16,000, but our books 'are selling great'!

"A lot of the retailers tend to not stock the independent comics in depth. The reason for that is, in the early days, there came a time of the so-called 'big dump,' when dealers found themselves stuck with a lot of independents, because when collectors came in the store, along with their independents were a large number of very nice reprint packages from Marvel and DC at very high cover prices, and there's no question about it that many people bought the reprint before they bought the latest [First Comics'] *E-Man* or *Silverheels*. And, consequently, a lot of the retailers found themselves overstocked on independent comics, didn't feel comfortable speculating on them and, as a result, began to order to sell out.

"I think, in the case of at least a lot of our books, we have a huge audience for titles like *Alien Worlds* or *Groo* that is discovering them every day. And dealers who do stock them are reporting people coming in and buying complete sets. However, a lot of dealers feel as though they should order to sell out. And they might order 20 copies of *Groo,* sell out, and say to themselves, 'How nice, I'm not stuck with any *Groo*s.' And they're not really ordering ten more and ten more and ten more.

"Who knows. They might eventually sell 70, 80, or 100, but they'll never know! So, I think, to a degree, there's a conservatism on the part of the dealers that maybe is reducing the sale of a more potentially popular product. Hard to blame them, though, for being conservative. Ultimately, though, I think that the books are selling pretty well."[115]

Later in the interview with Schutz, David turned the conversation around to the quality of the Pacific Comics line. "Rather than talk about the 'big dump' though, we would like to take the profile that if we do good product, if we put out excellent comic books, we believe they will sell even if there are 100 comics around them on the stands. We go into publishing with that belief, and it seems that with our quality titles, the market bears us out."[116]

Distinguishing the Pacific reprints from Marvel's, David clarified, "Most of the reprints Pacific is doing are material that's never been in color before. And also it's material that hasn't been widely available before. Obviously, when you're doing a reprint, you don't have as much initial [*cash*] outlay, and when you're commissioning a [*new*] comic book, you're really putting out a lot of money that you don't see a return on for quite a long time."[117]

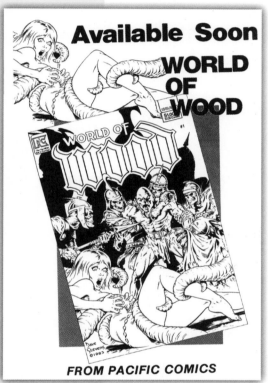

Available Soon
WORLD OF WOOD
FROM PACIFIC COMICS

THE MARK OF EXCELLENCE

Diana Schutz, as editor of *The Telegraph Wire,* wanted to know what distinguished Pacific Comics from the 20-plus publishers flooding the direct sales market. David Scroggy offered, "Well, I think we certainly lavish a lot of care on their production. When we entered comics publishing, our philosophy behind getting into the game was to motivate the creators to create their best work. By offering creators ownership and paying them on a royalty basis, we wanted to give them a free hand to create their best work. At the same time, we have tried to surround ourselves with the very best creators in comics, and I think, to a surprising degree, we've been successful. When people ask us what our house style is, we try to say 'excellence,' because we certainly have a diverse line. One of the interesting points our readers' surveys have borne out to us, and what a surprising percentage of people say to the question, 'What do you like best about Pacific Comics?' is 'diversity of art style' or 'different kinds of books'...

"So, one thing I hope that we're doing, to a degree anyway, is trying new things, and trying to do something a little different, a little better, and a little more considered. Sometimes it works and sometimes it doesn't, like anything else, but I think, to a large degree, we've not only been successful, but are improving now, noticeably. I suppose I should mention also that we're gearing a lot of our material for an older reader and, in some cases, this apparently is controversial."[118]

As 1983 closed, Pacific would face new — and devastating — realities in the coming new year as distributor wars flared up and the company's cash-flow problems threatened the very survival of the most successful arm of the Schanes brothers' operation. It would be, in more ways than one, a time of upheaval.

Collector's Edition #1
$1.00
"For the NEW Era in Comics"
"For the NEW Era in Comics"
$2.00 U.S.
GROO
ISSUE # 4
"For the NEW Era in Comics"

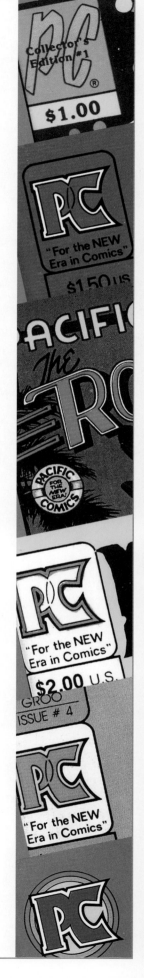

Chapter Notes

1 Steve Duin and Mike Richardson, "Pacific Comics" entry, *Comics: Between the Panels* [1998, Dark Horse Comics], pg. 345.

2 Bhob Stewart, "Comics a 'Penny Business,'" news item, *The Comics Journal* #84 [Sept. 1983], pg. 9. Stewart reports that World Color is "where 90–95% of all comic books are printed. Approximately 400 to 450 million comics a year are currently rolling off the World Color presses."

3 Kim Thompson "Two Publishers to Use Higher-Grade Newsprint," news item, *The Comics Journal* #76 [Oct. 1982], pg. 21.

4 Kim Thompson, "Pacific Upgrades All Titles to White Paper," news item, *The Comics Journal* #84 [Sept. 1983], pg. 10.

5 Jay Allen Sanford, "The Rise & Fall of Pacific Comics: The Inside Story of a Pioneering Publisher," *San Diego Reader* website [Aug. 19, 2004], https://www.sandiegoreader.com/news/2004/aug/19/two-men-and-their-comic-books/.

6 Thompson, *TCJ* #84.

7 Sanford.

8 Ibid.

9 David Scroggy, interviewed by the author.

10 John Morrow, introduction, *Silver Star: Graphite Edition* [2006, TwoMorrows], pg. 4.

11 Ibid.

12 Roz Kirby, "Jack Kirby," interviewed by Gary Groth, *The Comics Journal* #134 [Feb. 1990], pg. 99.

13 David Scroggy, "Happy Anniversary," editorial, *Captain Victory and the Galactic Rangers Special* #1 [Oct. 1983], inside front cover.

14 David Scroggy, e-mail to Jon B. Cooke [Apr. 24, 2023].

15 Ibid.

16 Richard Arndt, *Star∗Reach Companion* [2013, TwoMorrows], pg. 6.

17 Mike Friedrich, interviewed by Jon B. Cooke [Apr. 20, 2023].

18 Ibid.

19 Ibid.

20 Michael T. Gilbert, "Mr. Monster's Maker," interviewed by Jon B. Cooke, *Comic Book Artist* #8 [May 2000], pg. 38.

21 Ibid.

22 P. Craig Russell, "P. Craig Russell," interviewed by Steve Ringgenberg, *Comics Interview* #3 [May. 1983], pg. 11.

23 Ibid.

24 Friedrich, interview.

25 "Elric #1 Error Edition," entry, Recalled Comics website, https://recalledcomics.com/Elric1ErrorVariant.php.

26 Mike Friedrich, "Elric of Melniboné," editorial, *Elric* #2 [Aug. 1983], inside front cover.

27 Recalled Comics.

28 Friedrich, editorial.

29 Friedrich, interview.

30 Ibid.

31 Roy Thomas, e-mail to Jon B. Cooke [Apr. 10, 2023].

32 Steve Schanes, interviewed by the author.

33 David Scroggy, interviewed by the author.

34 "Funny Animals, Aliens, and Oddball Comics from Pacific," news item, *Amazing Heroes* #16 [Oct. 1982], pg. 24.

35 Paul S. Power, e-mail to Jon B. Cooke [Apr. 24, 2023].

36 Paul Gravett, "Al Williamson: Vistas of Other Worlds," review, Paul Gravett website [Nov. 12, 2006], http://www.paulgravett.com/articles/article/al_williamson.

37 Steve Ditko, "History of the Mocker," *The Mocker* [1990, Snyder and Ditko], nn.

38 Richard Howell, e-mail to Jon B. Cooke, [Apr. 26, 2023].

39 Ibid.

40 Kim Thompson, "Running for the Sun," *Amazing Heroes* #40 [Feb 1, 1984], pg. 39.

41 Mike Thibodeaux, "Interview with Mike Thibodeaux," interviewed by John Morrow, *The Jack Kirby Collector* #15 [Apr. 1997], pg. 43.

42 Tim Burgard, interviewed by Jon B. Cooke [April 25, 2023].

43 Ibid.

44 Gray Morrow, "The Long Road to Atlantis," interviewed by Kevin McConnell, *Amazing Heroes* #26 [July 1, 1983], pg. 32.

45 David Scroggy, "Words from the Edge," editorial, *Edge of Chaos* #1 [July 1983], inside front cover.

46 David Scroggy, interviewed by the author.

47 Morrow, *AH*, pgs. 32–33.

48 Morrow, *AH*, pgs. 33–34.

49 Scroggy, editorial.

50 Morrow, *AH*, pg. 36.

51 Allan Gross, "Visions of Life," biographical essay, *Gray Morrow: Visionary* [2001, Insight Studios Group], pg. 15.

52 Frank Thorne, "The Frank Thorne Interview," interviewed by Gary Groth, *The Comics Journal* #280 [June 2007], pgs. 64–65.

53 Thorne, *TCJ*, pg. 65.

54 Ibid.

55 Bruce Jones, "How I Got into the Movies," introduction, *Somerset Holmes* [Eclipse, 1987], nn.

56 Brent Anderson, interviewed by the author.

57 Bruce Jones, "The Main Event: Remembering Somerset Holmes," Scoop Diamond Galleries website [Nov. 8, 2013], https://tinyurl.com/ck6act7p.

58 Ibid.

59 Ibid.

60 Anderson.

61 Duin and Richardson, "Jim Starlin" entry, pg. 418.

62 Jim Starlin, "A Chat with Jim Starlin," interviewed by Shaun Clancy, *Back Issue* #48 [May 2011], pg. 31.

63 Ibid.

64 Jim Starlin, "Starlin Interviewed — At Last," interviewed by Jerry Durrwachter and Ed Mantels, *Whizzard* V2 #12 [Apr. 1979], pg. 6.

65 Starlin, *Back Issue*, pg. 22.

66 Starlin, *Back Issue*, pg. 31.

67 Steve Schanes, interviewed by the author.

68 Starlin, *Back Issue*, pg. 22.

69 Mark Brett, "Retro Review: Jim Starlin's Darklon the Mystic," Dork Forty website [Dec. 5, 2017], https://dorkforty.wordpress.com/2017/12/05/retro-review-jim-starlins-darklon-the-mystic/.

70 Starlin, *Back Issue*, pg. 22.

71 Bill DuBay, "This is a Bold Adventure?," editorial, *Bold Adventure* #3 [June 1984], inside front cover.

72 Marc Sobel, "Welcome to the Strip Mine," reviews, The Comics Journal website [Dec. 3, 2018], https://www.tcj.com/welcome-to-the-strip-mine/#_edn3.

73 David Lloyd, "Getting in on the Act: Hints and Tips on Starting Out," *Warrior* #20 [July 1984], pg. 17.

74 Neal Adams, "Adams: Echoes of Futurepast," interviewed by Steve Ringgenberg, *Comic Book Creator Bonus PDF Edition* #3 [Fall 2013], pg. 10, https://twomorrows.com/index.php?main_page=product_info&cPath=108&products_id=1140.

75 "Skateman," Royal Books website, https://www.royalbooks.com/pages/books/146598/neal-adams-john-ballard-comic-screenplay/skateman-original-screenplay-and-promotional-booklet-for-an-unproduced-superhero-film.

76 Neal Adams, "Neal Adams on Skateman," interviewed by Peter Stone, *Back Issue* #105 [July 2018], pg. 75.

77 David Scroggy, editorial, *Vanguard Illustrated* #1 [Nov. 1983], inside front cover.

[78] David Scroggy, interviewed by the author.
[79] Thomas Yeates, testimonial [May 14, '23].
[80] David Scroggy, interviewed by the author.
[81] Brendan McCarthy, "Pro 2 Pro: The Strange Worlds of Peter Milligan and Brendan McCarthy," interviewed by Roger Ash, *Back Issue* #63 [Apr. 2013], pgs. 55.
[82] Peter Milligan, "Pro 2 Pro: The Strange Worlds of Peter Milligan and Brendan McCarthy," interviewed by Roger Ash, *Back Issue* #63 [Apr. 2013], pgs. 55.
[83] McCarthy.
[84] Milligan.
[85] McCarthy.
[86] David Scroggy, interviewed by the author.
[87] Mike Baron, e-mail to Jon B. Cooke [April 29, 2023].
[88] Steve Rude, interviewed by Jon B. Cooke [May 2, 2023].
[89] Ibid.
[90] Rick Burchett, e-mail to Jon B. Cooke [May 1, 2023].
[91] Darren Auck, e-mail to Jon B. Cooke [May 1, 2023].
[92] John Wooley, testimonial [May 17, 2023].
[93] Ron Harris, e-mail to Jon B. Cooke [Apr. 21, 2023].
[94] David Scroggy, interviewed by author.
[95] Walter Stuart, interviewed by Jon B. Cooke [May 3, 2023].
[96] Michael T. Gilbert, "Mr. Monster's Maker," interviewed by Jon B. Cooke, *Comic Book Artist* #8 [May 2000], pg. 39.
[97] Ibid.
[98] David Scroggy, interviewed by author.
[99] Geof Darrow, "Running with Giants – Geof Darrow Interview in Full Text," radio interview transcript, Ink Studs Radio website [Dec 1, 2011], *http://www.inkstuds.org/running-with-giants-geof-darrow-interview-in-full-text/.*
[100] David Scroggy, "Juggling the Books at Pacific," interviewed by Diana Schutz, *The Telegraph Wire* #15 [June/July 1984], pg. 16.
[101] David Scroggy, "Rainbows and Ravens," listing, *Pacific Premieres* #5 [Aug. 1983], nn.
[102] David Scroggy, interviewed by author.
[103] Howard Wood, "Walking Off with Warren," *Comics Buyer's Guide* #516 [Oct. 3, 1983], pg. 1.
[104] Randy Palmer, "The Last Daze of Famous Monsters, Part 2, "*Ackermansion Memories* #2 [2016].
[105] Scott Hampton, interviewed by author.
[106] Ibid.
[107] Bruce Jones, "Interview: Bruce Jones," interview conducted by Kim Thompson, *Amazing Heroes* #90 [Mar. 1, 1986], pg. 29.
[108] Ibid.
[109] Sobel.
[110] Ken Steacy, testimonial [May 13 2023].
[111] Ibid.
[112] Ibid.
[113] Rick Obadiah, "The Comics Glut of 1983," *The Comics Journal* #86 [Nov. 1983], pg. 6.
[114] Steve Freitag, "The Comics Glut of 1983," *The Comics Journal* #86 [Nov. 1983], pg. 6.
[115] Scroggy, *Telegraph Wire*, pg. 19.
[116] Scroggy, *Telegraph Wire*, pg. 21.
[117] Scroggy, *Telegraph Wire*, pg. 20.
[118] Scroggy, *Telegraph Wire*, pg. 19.
[119] Jeff Gelb, "Pacific Comics," *Comics Scene* #9, May 1983], pg. 23.

Pacific Comics: A Good Life in the Comics Neighborhood

Jeff Gelb visited Pacific Comics and wrote a feature about meeting with the Pacific three — the brothers Schanes and David Scroggy — an admiring piece that was published in *Comics Scene* #9 [May 1983]. Here are the optimistic concluding paragraphs of Gelb's article:

"Ten years after the humble beginnings of Pacific Comics, the company seems to have just skimmed the surface of an iceberg of future activity. It's an exciting thought for both readers and the Pacific triumvirate, as well. Bill Schanes commented, 'The personal gratification comes from knowing that what we're doing is making people happy. And, of course, making us happy, as well — we're doing much better now than a few years ago. Of course, it helps when you're doing things you like to do, and that's where we're at. Sometimes this doesn't even seem like work.'

"David Scroggy offered, 'The reality of the jobs we do is probably quite different from people's fantasies. There's a lot of work, a lot of headaches. Creative people, after all, are usually temperamental people. But it's tremendously exciting to play a role in the birth of creative talents. And, since we all like comics ourselves, it's great to see the competition of all these companies producing better packages and better work. It's very gratifying to be a part of that process.'

"Steve Schanes has the final say: 'It's stressful and exhilarating at the same time. We're working for ourselves and with a very competent crew. We work with pros who are the cream of the crop — and that's a great neighborhood to be in.'"[119]

Pacific Comics

A look at one of the new-breed of comics publishers and what they offer readers

By JEFF GELB

The story of Pacific Comics is like a comic book fan's fairy tale: Ten years ago, Pacific Comics was a high school senior with a $50 collection of comics. Today, Pacific Comics is an organization that employs 25 people, works with about 50 professional freelancers, including Jack Kirby and Neal Adams, and publishers a full line of comic books, portfolios, and books. Along the way, Pacific Comics has become a force that has already caused ripples of significant change to spread throughout the comic book industry.

In 1972, Steve Schanes was a 17-year old high school senior in San Diego with a love for comic books and a few extra dollars in his pocket. He was at a swap meet and happened upon a collection of 900 comic books for sale for $50 (those were the good old days!), which he quickly paid. He took the collection home where he sold all the Marvel books to his 13-year old brother Bill for $30. And thus was born the nucleus of Pacific Comics. Bill and Steve began selling their books at the San Diego Comics Club (soon to become the San Diego Comic Convention), and, in early 1974, opened San Diego's first comic book store under the company title of Pacific Comics.

By 1978 there were four Pacific Comic shops throughout San Diego County, and the Schanes brothers had brought in fellow comics collector and fan David Scroggy to help run the operation. The three noticed two disturbing trends: first there was plenty of walk-in taffic in their stores, but no one distributor for the types of product those people wanted to buy. Second, the local comics distributor made comics a low priority item, which meant lateness problems, insubstantial discounts, and useless overstock. So Pacific called Marvel and became one of the first comic shops to get their books directly from the comics company. At this time, Pacific also began distributing Marvel's books to other Southern California comics shops, which was the start of a comics and related material distribution system now covering all 50 states and 20 countries. Distribution now contributes about 65 percent of Pacific Comics' income.

Pacific published its first professional artwork under the Schanes and Schanes logo, in 1977 in four portfolios of work by Howard Chaykin, Frank Thorne and Frank Cirocco. David Scroggy recalled, "We'd been distributing the portfolios and thought it was a field that would grow. They were marginal in sales for a long time, but we felt they had the potential of becoming accepted as a collectable." Some 30 portfolios later, with work published by such diverse talents as Wendy Pini, Alex Nino, Bil Stout, Chris Miller and Lela Dowling, Pacific has found its audience for portfolio art. Though portfolios account for only a single-digit percentage of the company's annual income, according to Bill Schanes, they can indeed be profitable as well as collectable. For example, Scroggy told this story: "For our latest *Elfquest* portfolio, there was much discussion about how many to do. We decided to press 3,000 and then got orders for about 8,000! So we're still trying to gauge the size of what is apparently a growing audience."

BUILDING THE BETTER COMIC BOOK

With professional comic artist contacts fostered through their portfolios, and having developed a strong network for distribution, it was only natural that the comics fans who ran Pacific decided in the late '70s to develop their own line of four-color comic books. The final impetus for getting started was the success of Marvel's *Dazzler* #1, a book that was marketed only through direct sales means at Steve Schanes's suggestion (at a 1980 San Diego Comic Convention meeting with Marvel), and which went on to sell a staggering 400,000 copies. David Scroggy commented, "This was the great awakening to everyone that the comics specialty shops had become a market of their own, fully capable of supporting a book's entire print run, often distributed through Pacific. We felt we were more in touch with the needs of these shops than anyone, including Marvel, and that we could probably do just as well or better at producing comics for that marketplace."

Of course, not every direct-sale comic book produced sells as dazzlingly as *Dazzler* #1. But, Bill Schanes pointed out, "It's more profitable to print 60,000 or 70,000 non-returnable comics for the comics shops than to print 125,000 and sell only 25 percent on the newsstands."

With those economic values in mind, Pacific contacted Jack Kirby, who soon presented Pacific with their first four-color comic book: *Captain Victory*, which sold 90,000 copies in the summer of 1981. Since then, the line has grown into nine titles, including *Victory*, *Starslayer* (soon to move to First Comics), *Twisted Tales*, *Alien Worlds*, *Groo the Wanderer*, *Pacific Presents*, *Elric*, and *Ms. Mystic* (the first copy of which sold a hefty 200,000 copies). Comics publishing now makes up 35 percent of Pacific's yearly income.

All of the Pacific triumvirate have editorial say over the comic book line, though their input varies depending on the book and its creator(s). Steve Schanes commented, "You don't really edit a Jack Kirby. You can give him an idea: do an origin story, create a superhero for us, but he's pretty well set in his ways so far as his book's direction is concerned. We do pass along all letters received from readers to each book's creator(s), which may help to determine editorial policy over a period of time."

David Scroggy recalled, "When Mike Grell presented us with his *Starslayer* concept, he had already plotted out all six issues in detail. So we had the chance to look at the entire package, discuss it in detail, and then give him the go-ahead to do the books based on those discussions. Similarly, there was a lot of give-and-take

Pacific Comic Number One

What was the first Pacific Comic book? If you said 1981's *Captain Victory*, you'd be wrong both in character and year. Actually, the first Pacific Comic is a 1977 title called (appropriately enough) *One*.

Beneath a cover by then-popular album cover artist Philip Carris, *One*'s lead feature was a photo-strip starring Pacific's Steve Schanes and a San Diego resident named Cliff Terry (now working for Embassy Pictures) in a quasi-underground looking superhero strip. The overall effect of the high-contrast photos is less than perfect, but it was an interesting experiment. Also on view in *One* number one are two shorter, traditionally-rendered superhero strips, one with inking by a young Brent Anderson. Interestingly, a full-page ad promises "One Unleashed" in the coming (never published) second issue, with an excellent graphic interpretation of a character by Alex Nino. And, on the inside back cover, and editorial says, in part, "Pacific Comics is the wave of the future. One is just the beginning. . ."

Is *One* destined to become the *Motion Picture Funnies* of Pacific Comics? Don't hold your breath—of the 10,000 copies printed, most still remain in Pacific's warehouse, unsold.

Suddenly, it's a whole new marketplace, a radically new ballgame. We're seeing a lot of new people attempting to enter the field because, for the first time, really, it can really be worth their while to draw comics for a living.

—Steve Schanes

A collection of titles Pacific has published in its first two years of existence. The Rocketeer has become their biggest fan favorite.

From left: Steve Schanes, David Scroggy and Bill Schanes pause for a moment in one of their spacious warehouses, filled with items they either publish and/or distribute.

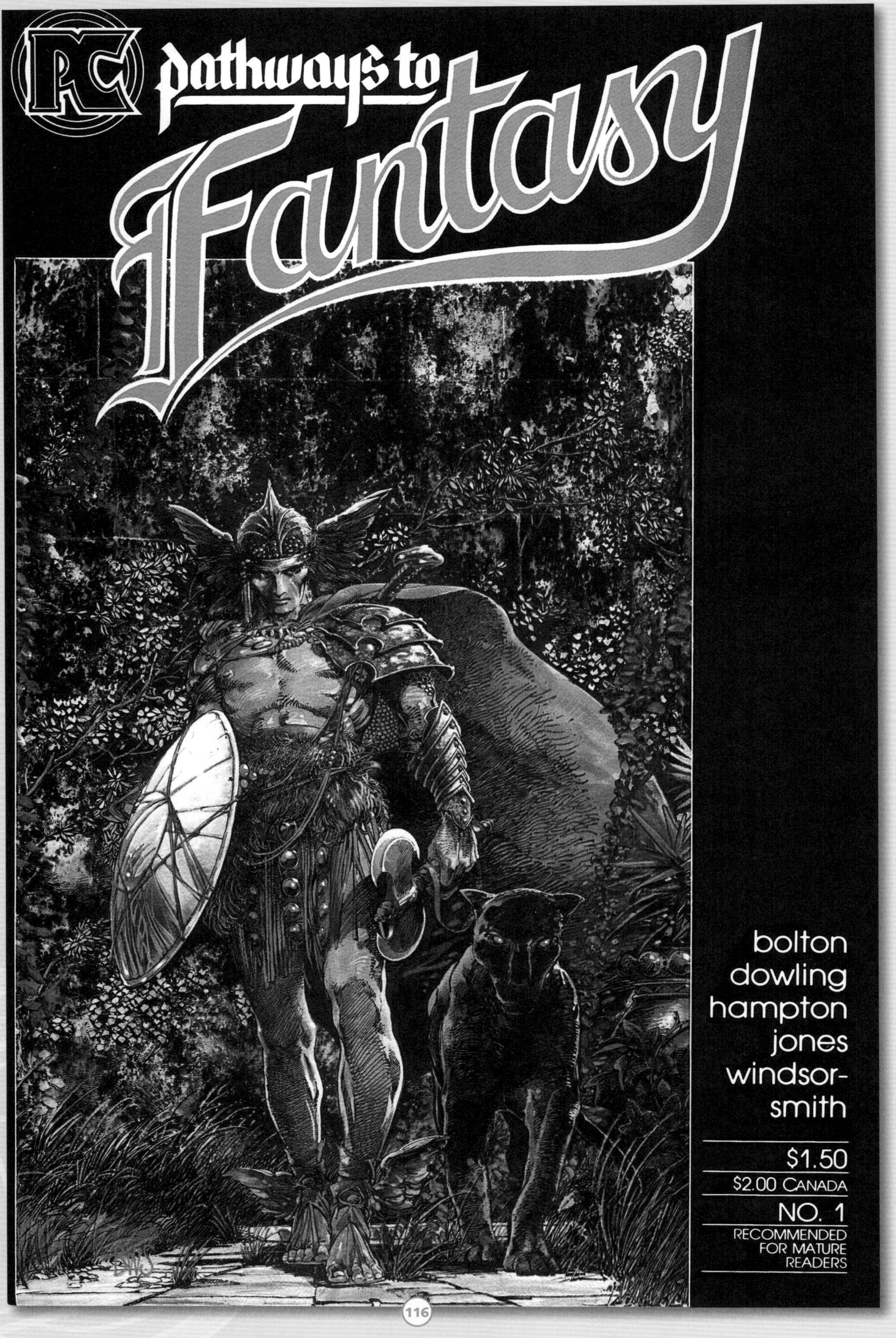
pathways to
Fantasy
bolton
dowling
hampton
jones
windsor-smith
$1.50
$2.00 CANADA
NO. 1
RECOMMENDED FOR MATURE READERS

Coming to the End of the Line

Inviting the British Invasion...

Alan Moore, the genius East Midlands scribe whose arrival in the U.S. would usher in a tsunami of U.K. writers and artists to the American comic book scene, had his utterly groundbreaking "Anatomy Lesson" story [*Saga of the Swamp Thing* #21, Feb. 1984] go on sale in mid-November 1983, which launched the cult of Moore on this side of the Atlantic. But, back on the British Isles, the writer had already made a notable reputation for excellence in the pages of *Warrior*, Dez Skinn's Quality Comics b-&-w monthly, with his "Marvelman" and "V for Vendetta" serials.

Over in Berkeley, California, the innovative proprietor of a burgeoning art agency took notice of Skinn's cutting-edge mag. "Star*Reach's Mike Friedrich said he loved *Warrior* and wanted to be our U.S. agent," Skinn explained to George Khoury. "I said, 'Sure.' Like with the *Doctor Who* strips that finally made it to Marvel U.S., we'd always planned on making four or five U.S. titles once we had enough material under our belts. The deal had been that, rather than all the creators having to phone the States and go over to sell their strips, Quality — as the originating publisher — would do it for them. We'd take 15% if we sold the stuff, 10% if they cut the deal. After all, if Quality hadn't forked out in the first place, there'd be nothing to syndicate, so I thought it was a good deal and they all signed up for it."[1]

Dummy copies of *Marvelman, Pressbutton, V for Vendetta,* and others were put together and sent to DC and then to Marvel, after DC blanched at the notion of printing a character called Marvelman. (Skinn said Moore wouldn't sanction a name change.) Marvel passed — again, because of Marvelman — and then Star*Reach arrived. "The deal that I was putting together," Skinn told Khoury, "was like the newspaper syndicate deal or films being sold to TV. If you want this one, you gotta take the rest. It's a package. It's not a pick and choose. It's not an à lá carte menu; it's a set meal. You take the lot or you get nothing. I knew strips like 'Spiral Past' — which I put into an anthology alongside 'Shandor' and 'Bojeffries Saga' — were not the stars of the show, but they deserved to get U.S. syndication. Everybody

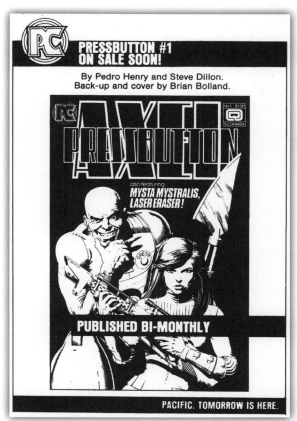

PC
PRESSBUTTON #1
ON SALE SOON!
By Pedro Henry and Steve Dillon.
Back-up and cover by Brian Bolland.
AXEL PRESSBUTTON
No.1 $1.50
$2 CANADA
also featuring
MYSTA MYSTRALIS, LASER ERASER!
PUBLISHED BI-MONTHLY
PACIFIC. TOMORROW IS HERE.

can't be the star; somebody has to be the warm-up, the back-up. Somebody has to have their name below the titles. So I figured it wouldn't be fair because, without these guys, we wouldn't have had an anthology, we would have just had a skinny little pamphlet. These guys deserved syndication, as well. So, the deal was all of them or none. Unfortunately, Marvel and DC couldn't do Marvelman. So enter Mike Friedrich.

"He said, 'Let's try Pacific Comics, they're expanding. They'll take them all with no problems.' But Pacific did the rudest thing of all; they had the audacity to go out of business just as they were about to publish them all. But this was far from instant. Pacific was understandably worried about the name Marvelman..."[2]

Friedrich recalled, "I have a very clear memory of meeting Dez Skinn in San Francisco. He came to California to meet with me to see whether I would represent the *Warrior* magazine talent. What he presented me was a document that gave me 'non-exclusive' rights to represent

Previous page: *Pathways to Fantasy* #1 [July 1984], with art by Barry Windsor-Smith. **Above:** Pacific house ad promoting *Axel Pressbutton* #1, which was eventually published by Eclipse (below) in Oct. 1984. Art by Brian Bolland

AXEL PRESSBUTTON
also featuring
MYSTA MYSTRALIS, LASER ERASER!

REBIRTH
by ALAN MOORE and GARRY LEACH

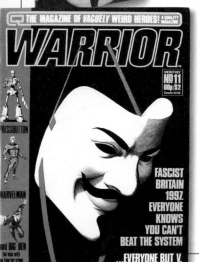

the strips because *he* did not have exclusive rights to represent them and I made the mistake — and I'll say this publicly — of agreeing to go forward, because I ended up with the biggest mess in my agency's history dealing with *Warrior* magazine properties. It was mixed. Some of it was very, very positive, and some of it was a mess."[3]

The year before Eclipse would publish — in the summer of 1985 — the first issue of *Miracleman,* David Scroggy explained to Diana Schutz the Pacific Comics plan to reprint the Quality material, starting with *Laser Eraser and Pressbutton* (which was retitled *Axel Pressbutton*): "Well, first of all, most of the reprints we're doing are material that's never been in color before, and also it's material that hasn't been widely available. Obviously, when you're doing a reprint, you don't have as much initial outlay, and when you commission a comic book, you're really putting out a lot of money that you don't see a return on for quite a long time. So, it's viable for us as a publisher faced with a kind of softening of sales… Certainly a reprint is less up-front money and can therefore be profitable while selling fewer copies. We have been very concerned about the *quality* of the material that we reprint, and I do think the things that we're reprinting are material that is well worth reprinting. Our main two reprint books now will be bi-monthly titles and they will alternate, very much like *Twisted Tales* and *Alien Worlds* do. And those will be British material, from Quality Communications, which has appeared in black-&-white in *Warrior* magazine, an import in some specialty shops. One of those titles will be [*Axel*] *Pressbutton*, and the other will be *Challenger*, an anthology title that will carry some regular features and some occasional stories. One of the regular features will be 'V for Vendetta,' by Alan Moore and David Lloyd, all newly colored… this is material that reached a very limited audience, and only in black-&-white, so we feel that, while it is a reprint, this one's almost like a first U.S. printing, you might say."[4]

Wholly original — and equally brilliant — material from British creators was to appear in Peter Milligan and Brendan McCarthy's *Strange Days,* a continuing title basically spun-off of the mind-blowing "Freakwave" appearances in *Vanguard Illustrated.*

This page: From top, *MIracleman* by Garry Leach and his cover for #1 [Aug. 1985]; cover for the hardbound collection of *V for Vendetta* [1990], and *Warrior* #11 [July 1983]. Art by David Lloyd.

V FOR VENDETTA
ALAN MOORE
DAVID LLOYD

THE MAGAZINE OF VAGUELY WEIRD HEROES!
WARRIOR
MONTHLY
No11
60p/$2
PRESSBUTTON
MARVELMAN
and BIG BEN
FASCIST BRITAIN 1997. EVERYONE KNOWS YOU CAN'T BEAT THE SYSTEM
...EVERYONE BUT V.

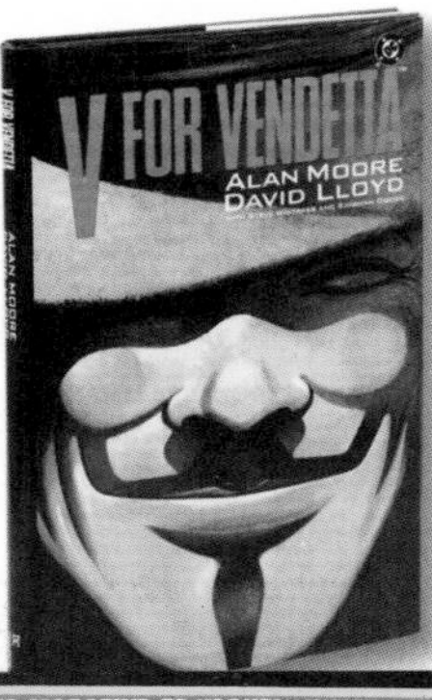

BLACK SEPTEMBER

Because Pacific Comics was a business encompassing distribution and publishing, pressures began to strain the company that were unique compared to the other independent imprints. "Distribution is a very marginal business," Steve Schanes explained in 1988 to Rod Underhill, "maybe working on five to eight percent gross margin. Extremely tough. You have to be very cautious, calculating, you have to really have good controls, and that is a problem all distributors have. Pacific didn't have good controls to make distribution work. There was a problem with buying too much — Pacific overbought with the assumption that it could sell the inventory. The critical overbuy was during a period [*in 1983*] called 'Black September.' It was when Marvel decided to release a tremendous amount of product, and the marketplace was impacted in a manner that caused the retailers to possibly order less 'independent' product."[5]

Steve continued, "The retailers and distributors underestimated the impact of the load. What happened was all the other stuff we bought, that we would have ordinarily sold over a period of time, three months to nine months, didn't turn. We built up massive quantities of inventory. We ended up with way too much inventory and it caused a real bottleneck on the cash-flow."

Pacific's main competitor of comparable size was Chicago-based First Comics, which took Marvel Comics to court regarding its over-saturating the marketplace. "Consumers have only a finite amount of money to spend, and retailers in the competitive marketplace must purchase their comic books on a no-return basis; with its monopolistic position, when Marvel is flooding the field, retailers cannot afford to give people a fair chance," First business manager Richard Felber stated publicly.[6]

"Marvel Comics historically has taken similar market-flooding actions when faced with the prospect of serious new competition… In November of 1982, when First Comics' initial publication was released, it would cost the consumer $42.05 to purchase one copy of each Marvel publication released in the competitive market during the month. In November 1983, one year later, it would cost the same consumer $109.35 to purchase one copy of each Marvel publication.

"Many of these additional Marvel publications were hastily put-together reprints and collections of inventory material, some of which was added retroactively. Retailers who were ordering items to be released in September

1983 would discover the addition of four last-minute reprint items during the preceding months… Additionally, after tying up retailer funds, Marvel Comics 'postponed' publication of a number of their announced releases, thereby tying up a substantial amount of retailer buying power and forcing its competitors to compete with 'phantom' titles."[7]

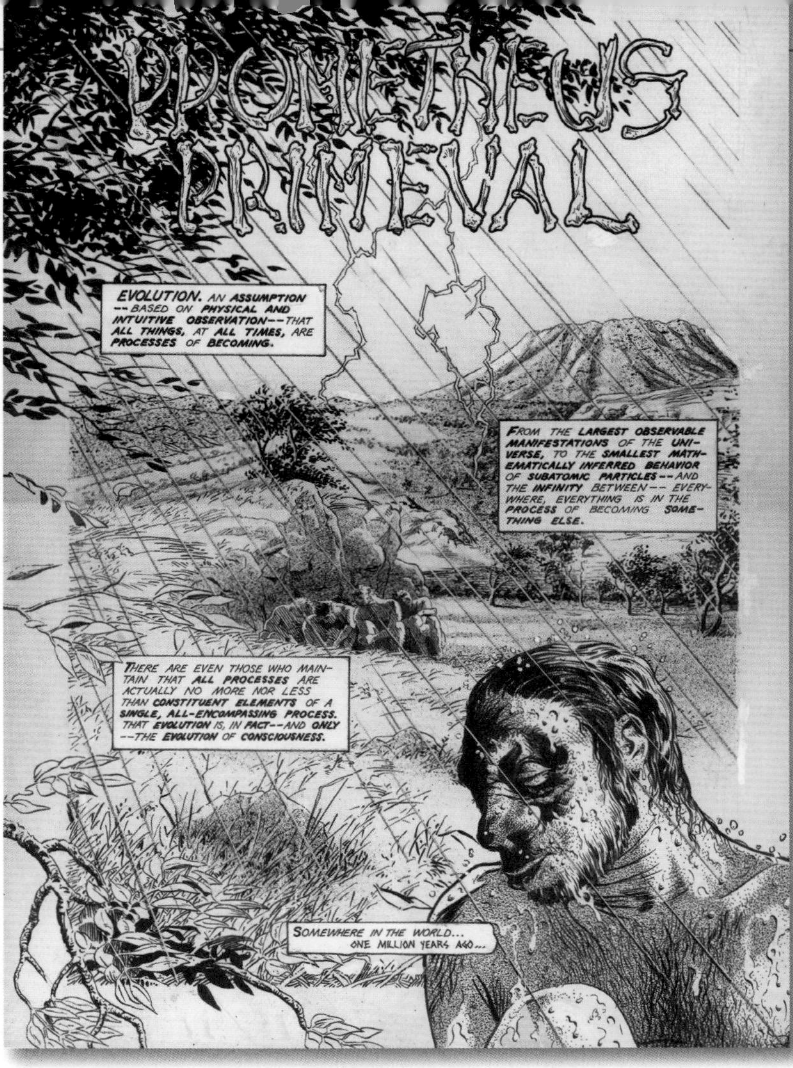
PROMETHEUS PRIMEVAL
EVOLUTION. AN ASSUMPTION --BASED ON PHYSICAL AND INTUITIVE OBSERVATION--THAT ALL THINGS, AT ALL TIMES, ARE PROCESSES OF BECOMING.
FROM THE LARGEST OBSERVABLE MANIFESTATIONS OF THE UNIVERSE, TO THE SMALLEST MATHEMATICALLY INFERRED BEHAVIOR OF SUBATOMIC PARTICLES--AND THE INFINITY BETWEEN-- EVERYWHERE, EVERYTHING IS IN THE PROCESS OF BECOMING SOMETHING ELSE.
THERE ARE EVEN THOSE WHO MAINTAIN THAT ALL PROCESSES ARE ACTUALLY NO MORE NOR LESS THAN CONSTITUENT ELEMENTS OF A SINGLE, ALL-ENCOMPASSING PROCESS. THAT EVOLUTION IS, IN FACT--AND ONLY --THE EVOLUTION OF CONSCIOUSNESS.
SOMEWHERE IN THE WORLD... ONE MILLION YEARS AGO...

THREE TIMES THE CHARM

David Scroggy enthused in *Pacific Premieres #4* [July 1983], "We have been featuring Tim Conrad's work in a number of our publications and response has been tremendous. Therefore, we have bowed to popular demand and created one that is all-new and all-Conrad. Titled *Thrillogy*, this comic is just that — a trio of thrillers!"[8]

The artist had, indeed, contributed work in several Pacific titles, including *Twisted Tales, Alien Worlds, Captain Victory,* and *Pacific Presents*, so naturally the author asked the artist how his involvement with Pacific came about: "As near as I can remember," Conrad replied, "I think they approached me and asked me to do a story for them. It was with Bruce Jones' *Twisted Tales,* and then "Talk to Tedi," in *Alien Worlds*. They then asked if I would do a single volume of my stuff and I did *Thrillogy*, which was a take-off on the word 'trilogy.'"[9]

The one-shot *Thrillogy* contained three stories written and drawn by Conrad, an artist who arose in the mid-1970s working on Marvel titles, including a notable adaptation of Robert E. Howard's "Bran Mak Morn," and a story for *Unknown Worlds of Science Fiction.* He later contributed to *Epic Illustrated* in the 1980s, painting the comics "Almuric" and "Toadswart," which were later collected respectively as graphic albums.

Conrad entered the field when, he said, "I had a couple of drawings I had done and went to a comic convention in New York City… one that was a drawing of my version of Barry Smith's Conan, and Roy Thomas purchased it and published it in the *Conan the Barbarian* comic book. Then Roy started giving me stories to do and it all went on from there. In the early '80s, I suddenly found myself with two babies, so I had to get out of the comic book business because I was unable to draw fast enough to raise my babies, so 'I had to get a real job.'"

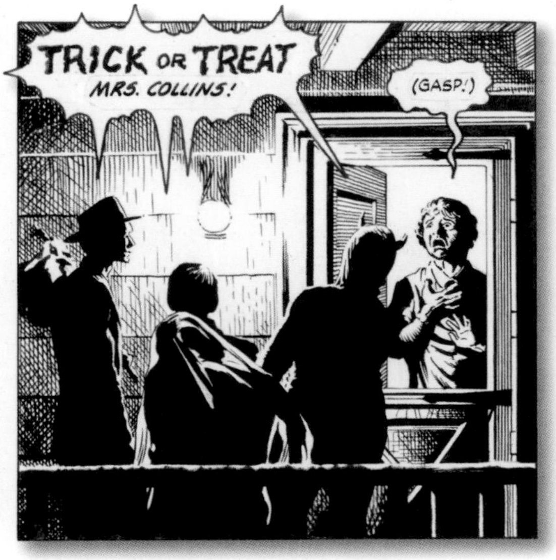
TRICK OR TREAT MRS. COLLINS!
(GASP!)

Conrad went into advertising and marketing for major production companies, and freelanced as painter of covers and posters. "Raising two sons during my comic life was the most wonderful thing I ever got to do," he shared.[10]

A tragedy put an end to Conrad's artistic career. "Thirty years ago," he revealed, "a 92-year-old driver ran me down on my motorcycle and put me in a coma for three months. Since I regained consciousness, I discovered I was no longer able to do the kind of artwork I was always used to doing. And then I heard John Lennon's line, 'Life is What Happens when You are Making Other Plans.'"[11] Today, Conrad lives in the Midwest with his wife, JoAnn.

Above: Original art splash for the first of Tim Conrad's trilogy in Pacific's *Thrillogy* #1 [Jan. 1984]. **Inset left:** Panel from the artist's "All Hallows" story, written and edited by Bruce Jones, in *Twisted Tales* #1 [Nov. 1982]. **Below:** Tim Conrad at a convention in 2019.

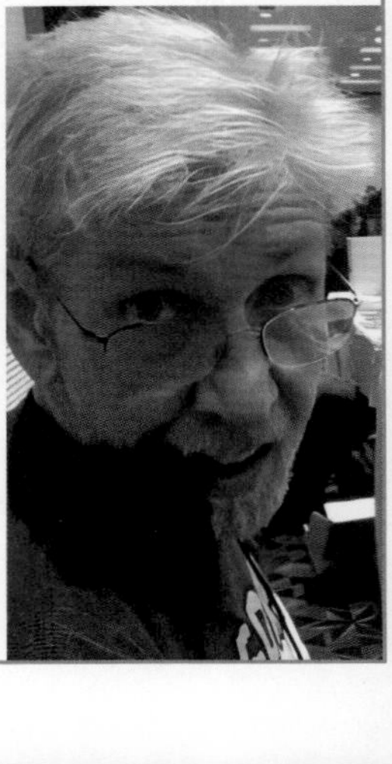

Pacific Profiles

Roger McKenzie

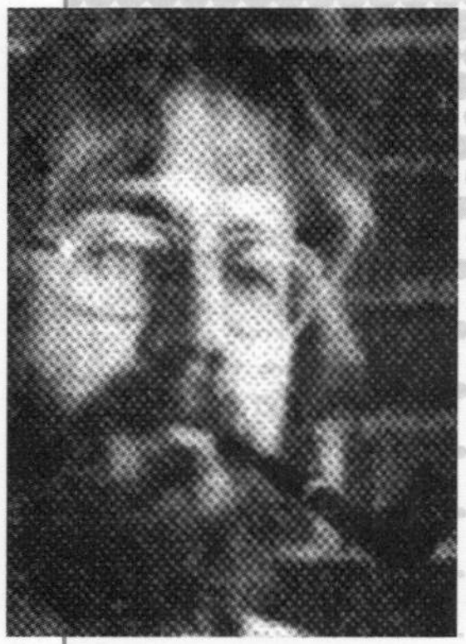

Born: *Nov. 1950*
The writer has had a wide-ranging career in the field, starting off at Warren Publications, and perhaps best known for work with artist Frank Miller on *Daredevil*. His *Sun Runners* series started at Pacific, moved to Eclipse [1984], then Sirius [1986], and finally landed at Amazing Comics [1987].

Above: Roger McKenzie in 1977.

Below: Spectacular double-page spread from the first issue of *Sun Runners* [Feb. 1984], rendered by Pat Broderick.

SUN RUNNERS RISE AND FALL

It is curious how Pacific Comics generally avoided creating its own super-hero universe, given the success of the "Big Two" competitors, who relied almost exclusively on their Spandex-clad characters, though *Captain Victory* and "The Rocketeer" certainly come close. *Sun Runners* by Roger McKenzie and Pat Broderick also came within spitting distance, and writer McKenzie was quite ambitious in the scope of his concept.

Bob Sodaro relayed in *Amazing Heroes*, "The Sun Runners are not just another group of super-heroes who go off to save the world (or, in this case, worlds); in fact, the Sun Runners are more than just the four characters who are the 'stars' of this book. There are several hundreds of Sun Runners. McKenzie's description of these people as being 'the electric company of the future' is more than just hyperbole."[12]

The cast includes an odd assortment, including Mark Dancer, the leader; Doc Gibralter; Delphi, a genetically altered dolphin; and a sexually rambunctious robot named Scooter. About Gibralter, artist Broderick shared with Sodaro, "Well, Roger told me that he was supposed to be as big as an elephant, so I thought, 'Why not make him a real elephant?'"[13] McKenzie's response? "I had no idea that Pat was going to turn Doc into an elephant. When I first saw Doc, I said, 'This isn't going to work.' But the more I looked him over, the more I liked him. Ultimately, it will have to be the fans who will decide if we made the right choice. I think we did."[14]

As observed by Sodaro, the road to Pacific Comics had some turns. "Eventually, our discussions with Roger and Pat turned to the question of their working for Pacific, rather than Marvel or DC," Sodaro wrote. "Broderick was quick to point out that he has not left DC and is working on several fill-ins for various titles… 'I decided to take on *Sun Runners* because I liked it a lot, and it was a science-fiction strip,' Broderick said… 'With *Sun Runners*, I really

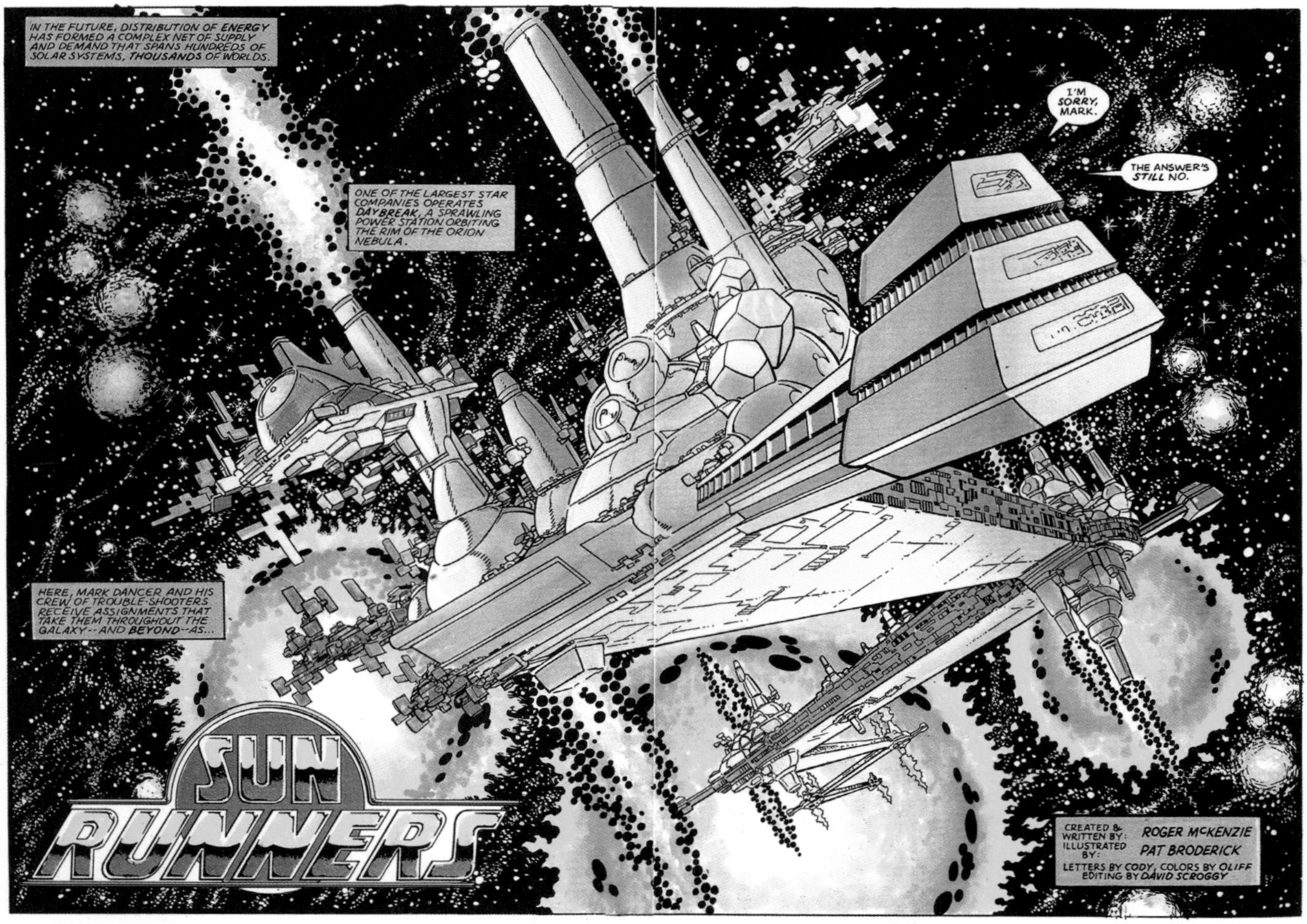
IN THE FUTURE, DISTRIBUTION OF ENERGY HAS FORMED A COMPLEX NET OF SUPPLY AND DEMAND THAT SPANS HUNDREDS OF SOLAR SYSTEMS, THOUSANDS OF WORLDS.
ONE OF THE LARGEST STAR COMPANIES OPERATES DAYBREAK, A SPRAWLING POWER STATION ORBITING THE RIM OF THE ORION NEBULA.
I'M SORRY, MARK.
THE ANSWER'S STILL NO.
HERE, MARK DANCER AND HIS CREW OF TROUBLE-SHOOTERS RECEIVE ASSIGNMENTS THAT TAKE THEM THROUGHOUT THE GALAXY-- AND BEYOND--AS...
SUN RUNNERS
CREATED & WRITTEN BY: ROGER McKENZIE
ILLUSTRATED BY: PAT BRODERICK
LETTERS BY CODY, COLORS BY OLIFF
EDITING BY DAVID SCROGGY

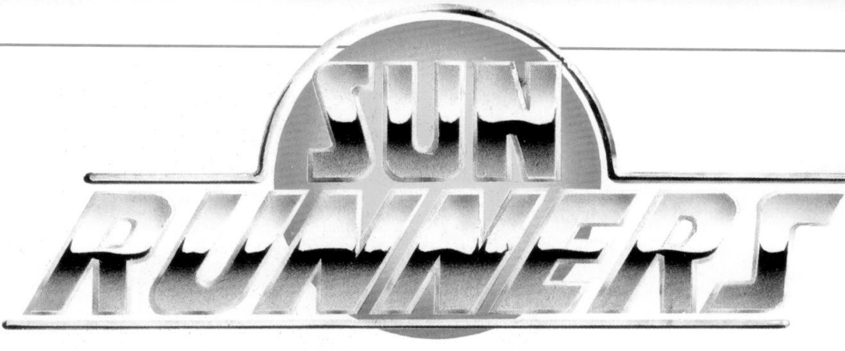
SUN
RUNNERS

get the chance to cut loose and do some wild stuff.'"[15]

Sodaro continued, "McKenzie's story is slightly different. 'I had this idea several years. It just sat around on the shelf, gathering dust.' With a story as exciting as *Sun Runners*, why let it sit around? 'Well, when you work for Marvel or DC, you have to give up the rights to your characters, because [*the companies*] want to own them,' says McKenzie.

"'Originally, I gave the strip to Jerry Bingham to come up with some character designs, and we took it around to the various companies. This was in January '83.' The first stop the two made was at Marvel, but 'we weren't treated real well.' Next up came DC, who wanted to turn *Sun Runners* into a mini-series. Unwilling to truncate the storyline, McKenzie kept looking.

"'First [*Comics*] liked it a real lot, but they just picked up *Starslayer*. Eclipse was also interested, but they too had just filled their schedule.' Then Pacific came up with the best offer but, by this time, Jerry had become busy with other projects. Casting around for a new penciler, McKenzie hit on Broderick, with whom he had previously worked. 'Pat and I never worked on a book that wasn't a hit,' he says. The first story the two of them worked on together was *Captain Marvel* #57, which co-starred Thor."[16]

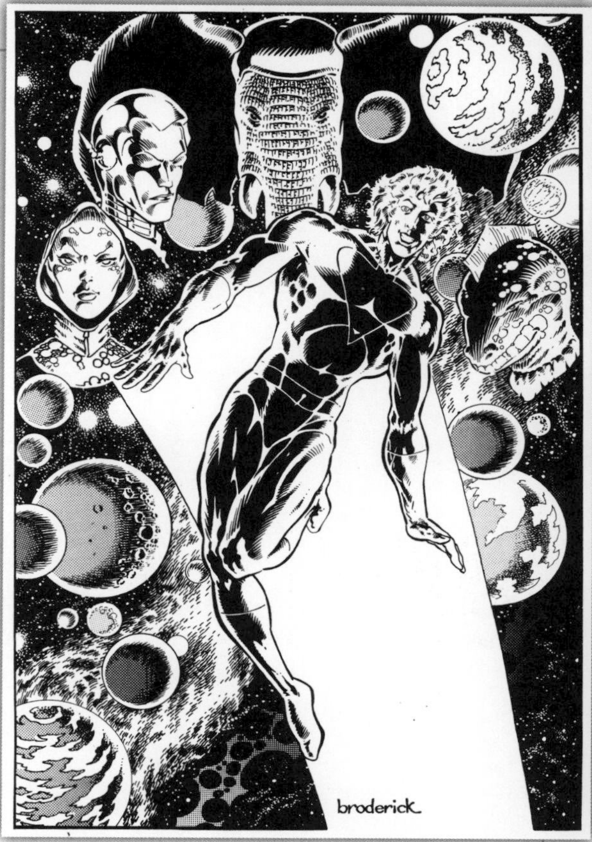
broderick

The *Amazing Heroes* cover feature also gave focus to the McKenzie/Broderick working relationship. "We asked Broderick how he enjoyed working with McKenzie," Sodaro shared. "'Roger is a good ol' Southern boy like myself,' he drawled reflectively. 'He and I work well together.' The affinity they have toward each other shows up in their work. 'Roger is great at characterization,' Broderick continues. 'He plots it all out and then phones me up, and we talk about it for a bit. Then I sit down and draw it out.' Although McKenzie is always open to suggestions on the stories, Broderick does not want to co-plot *Sun Runners*, because he feels it is really McKenzie's project and he wants to focus on the drawing."[17]

The series lasted three issues at Pacific, where there had been plans for a *Sun Runners* graphic novel, and the title moved over to Eclipse, with Glen Johnson taking on the art chores when Broderick left for steadier work.

In 1986, McKenzie wrote a scathing critique of his Pacific experience titled, "Me & Rod: Sun-Running in the Twilight

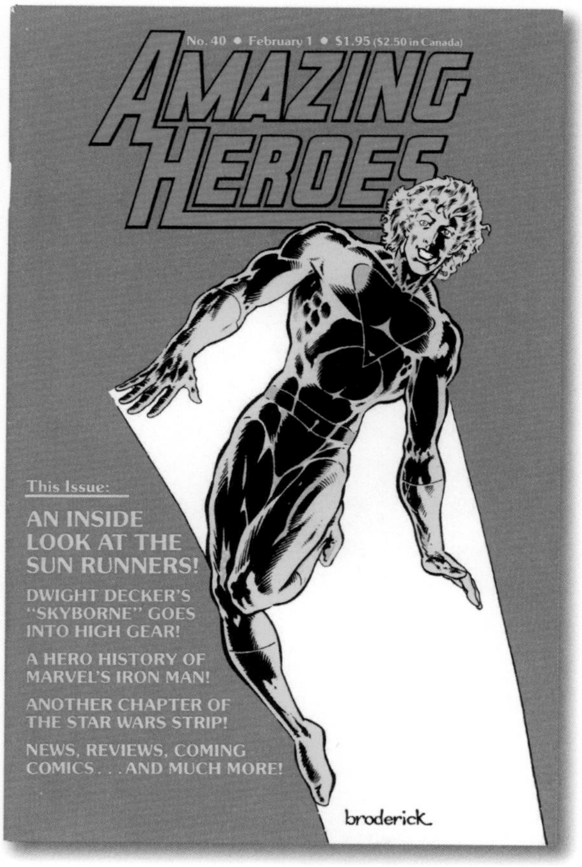
No. 40 • February 1 • $1.95 ($2.50 in Canada)
AMAZING HEROES
This Issue:
AN INSIDE LOOK AT THE SUN RUNNERS!
DWIGHT DECKER'S "SKYBORNE" GOES INTO HIGH GEAR!
A HERO HISTORY OF MARVEL'S IRON MAN!
ANOTHER CHAPTER OF THE STAR WARS STRIP!
NEWS, REVIEWS, COMING COMICS . . . AND MUCH MORE!
broderick

This page: Clockwise, from top left, is original art for the *Sun Runners* logo; pin-up page from the Pacific Comics series; and the cover art (using a detail of said pin-up) of *Amazing Heroes* #40 [Feb. 1, 1984].

Pacific Profiles

Pat Broderick

Born: *Nov. 1953*
The Florida native started a professional career at DC in the early '70s. After a brief stint at the short-lived Atlas/Seaboard (where his "Dark Avenger" is still fondly recalled), he joined up with Marvel and then back to DC again. He is currently drawing *Bronze Star*, a Western co-created with Mike Baron.

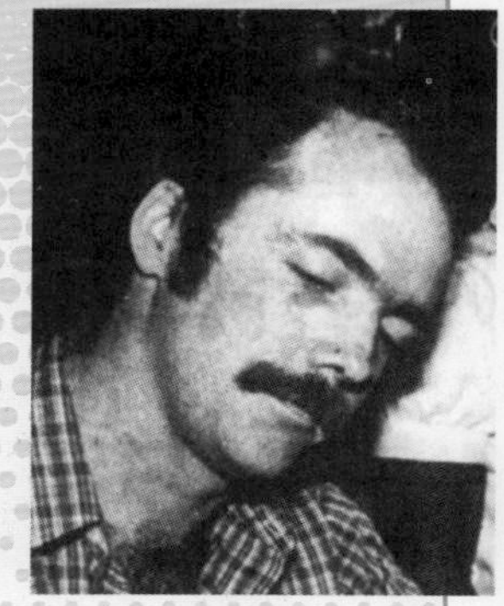

Above: Pat Broderick in a photo from the *Montgomery Advertiser* newspaper [Mar. 21, 1982], when he attended Alabama's Capital Comic Convention.

This page: Clockwise from above is Arthur Suydam's "Mudwog" detail; his Pacific title's logo; and a page from *Heavy Metal* Vol. 3 #4 [Aug. 1979] by Suydam, which was reprinted in *Demon Dreams* #2 May 1984], with the final panel repurposed as the cover art for that issue. Suydam's weirdo critters would be widely seen at that time as they also appeared in Continuity's *Echo of Futurepast.*

Zone," in *The Comics Journal* #106 [Mar. 1986]. He related, "I first sold the series concept to Pacific and was lucky enough to get Pat Broderick as artist/co-creator. We were given an initial four-issue contract. Pat and I completed all four issues either on or ahead of schedule. We signed to do a *Sun Runners* graphic novel and a limited edition portfolio. Things were looking great for a while. Then, almost overnight, they began to turn sour.

"Checks from Pacific kept getting later and later. Then they started bouncing. Then issue #4 was published late… Pacific just didn't print it because, they said, the printer was out of the right kind of paper(?). As it turned out, it was Pacific that was out of paper — the green kind routinely issued by the Federal Reserve."[18]

Still, Pacific wanted the team to sign a new six-issue contract, McKenzie said, "But we both knew that Pacific was in deep financial trouble. We hoped that they'd somehow recover… [*but*] things kept getting worse… It must have been frustrating for them seeing things going down the tubes and unable to prevent it."[19]

Arthur Suydam's DEMON DREAMS

DREAMING DEMONICALLY

After an intriguing debut in DC Comics' mystery books in the early '70s and then sudden disappearance, Arthur Suydam eventually came of age in *Heavy Metal* magazine by the end of that decade, when he received assignments from *HM*'s well-regarded art director. About the AD, Suydam told Steve Ringgenberg, "John Workman is the guy who got me the job at *Heavy Metal.* In just my dealings with him, he seems to have the greatest understanding of the medium — of artists, writers, and even the business end of the industry."[20]

In his two-issue Pacific Comics release, *Demon Dreams* [Feb.–May 1984], the artist included mostly work that had previously appeared in *HM*, a publication for which he expressed great fondness in 2005. "I used to go up to the offices and deliver my work by hand, then hang out with the editors," he told Dan Johnson in *Back Issue*. "It was a dad-and-daughter thing.* Now they're spread out and I don't get to meld with the *Heavy Metal* family like before. Still, I have a special place in my heart for *Heavy Metal. Heavy Metal* has always been the fertile ground for creativity in comics. Anthologies suffer terribly for not having ongoing properties. That's why they don't sell numbers like mainstream comics. Let's face it: Americans are obsessive about familiar characters for entertainment. It's no reflection on quality. It's a psychological thing. *Heavy Metal* is the one who revolutionized comics. The evolution from the more simplistic material from the 1960s and 1970s to what we see today. Nobody talks about it. Everyone's chasing numbers. They don't get the tie-in."[21]

Suydam, who also inked a story in *Alien Worlds* #6 [Feb. 1984] while at Pacific Comics, lavished special attention on some of the contents of *Demon Dreams*. "Bad Breath" in #1, for instance, originally in *HM* Vol. 3 #6 [Oct. 1979] as an eight-pager, was reconstructed and expanded with the artist adding new art and revising the coloring, inserting an additional 12 pages in the process.

* Actually, *Heavy Metal* editor Julie Simmons is the daughter of *HM* publisher Len Mogel's partner, Matty Simmons.

FIRST IN ITS CLASS

Anybody who knew Joe Kubert, the greatly beloved, veteran comics creator, recognized the artist-writer was a man who hustled and always strove to make the best use of his talents with tenacity. When the field demanded a new novelty, he co-created 3-D comic books, which became a sensation; when comics were in a tailspin in the mid-'50s, he found safe haven at DC as a stalwart, dependable artist; and, when comics were in flux by the mid-1970s, he decided to diversify and founded the Joe Kubert School of Cartoon and Graphic Arts, an institution that still thrives today, years after the man passed away, as it continues to instruct new generations on the art of creating comics.

By the early 1980s, graduates of the Kubert School, who dubbed themselves "Kubies," were making a major impact in the comics world, and Kubert, who remained a working comics professional through his years as top educator at the art school, was always on the lookout for opportunities where his students could benefit. One such possibility was located in San Diego, on Production Avenue. Steve Schanes recalled it was the Star*Reach Productions chief who connected Kubert with Pacific.

"Mike Friedrich was the point person on this project," Steve explained. "Mike knew Joe Kubert better than Bill or me. We wanted to offer Joe Kubert the opportunity to showcase his best students' work in a professional environment."[22]

COLOR HOLD / OVERLAM
THE JOE KUBERT SCHOOL PRESENTS:
1ST FOLIO
PC
ISSUE #1
$1.00 U.S.
$1.25 Canada
"For the NEW Era in Comics"
JOE KUBERT '83
YE
RED TS
BLACK TS
EDITOR: BLUE TS
6 13/16" x 10 1/2"

A MOMENT IN WAR!

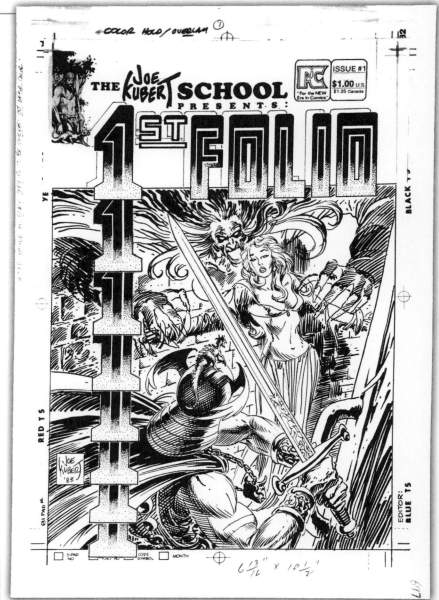

Friedrich's memory is fuzzy regarding the development of the Kubert/Pacific alliance, which resulted in a one-shot comic — though intended as an ongoing title — featuring work by Kubies (including father Joe's sons, Adam and Andy Kubert). "I remember Joe doing *1st Folio*, but I don't think I represented any of the artists, but I may have. Around this time, I was making presentations at the Kubert School, hoping to recruit graduating artists who had professional talent as clients. I know that Eric Shanower came out of that."[23] The retired art agent, whose friendship with Kubert went back to 1969, conceded he may well have been a part of that arrangement, but just couldn't recall.

Steve shared, "We handled all of the pre-publication production work once the pages were submitted. Joe was very pleased with the results."[24] (The satisfied patriarch, by the way, contributed the *1st Folio* cover art and a two-page war vignette that opened the issue.)

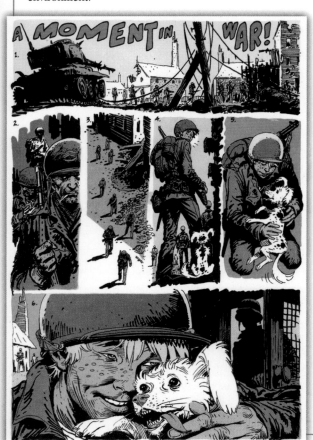

Above: Original art for *1st Folio* #1's cover, by Joe Kubert. David Scroggy's addendum to Joe Kubert's editorial gave a shout-out to the art agent: "We would also like to thank Mike Friedrich of Star*Reach Productions for his help in making this book possible." **Inset left:** Opening page of the issue, one of two by Joe Kubert. Spoiler alert: there's no happy ending for G.I., puppy, and the shadowy soldier.

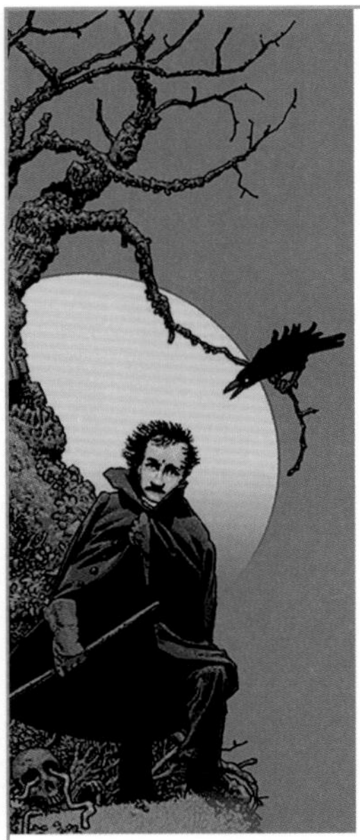

This page: Clockwise from above is Richard Corben cover art detail from *Spirits of the Dead*; the original cover design for *A Corben Special* #1 [May 1984]; and Corben never stopped adapting Poe, as evidenced by his 2013 Dark Horse *House of Usher*.

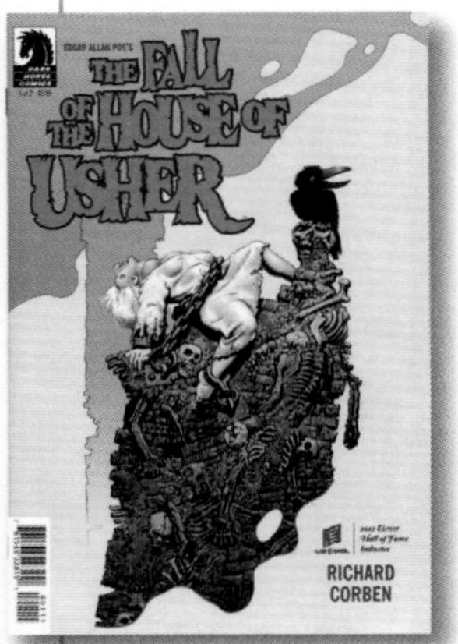
THE FALL OF THE HOUSE OF USHER
RICHARD CORBEN

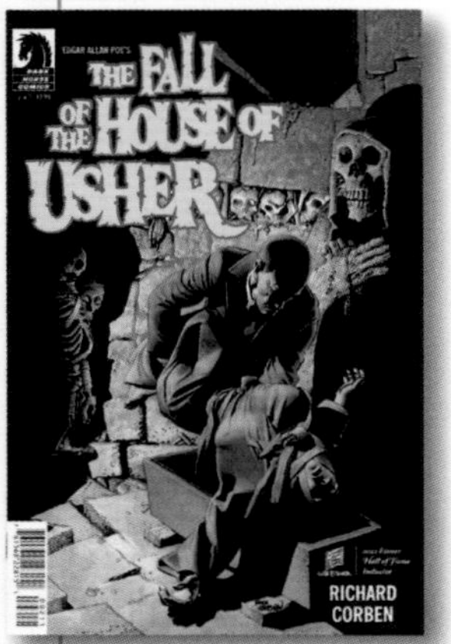
THE FALL OF THE HOUSE OF USHER
RICHARD CORBEN

POE MAN CORBEN

Simultaneous to the release of Pacific Comics' edition of *A Corben Special* [one-shot, May 1984], featuring Richard Corben's adaptation of Edgar Allan Poe's classic horror story, "The Fall of the House of Usher," the comics master's 28-page version was serialized in four issues of the Spanish version of *Creepy*, published by Toutain Editor. In 2013, Jon B. Cooke asked the artist-writer about his interest in the brilliant, tragic, world-renowned 19th century author.

"I think I was aware of Poe in a vague sort of way as an early teenager," Corben shared. "In college, we read some of his essays, as well as stories. Something clicked then and I was a fan. When Roger Corman did his Poe film adaptations, my interest was reinforced. I thought Corman/[*screenwriter Richard*] Matheson took some liberties with Poe's original themes, I didn't realize just how much. I looked for more renditions of the base material and found adaptations by other artists; these also were only remotely linked to the base material. So, at this point, it became my hobby to follow works inspired by Poe's stories."[25]

Starting in the mid-'70s, Corben produced his own versions of Poe classics, an author he returned to for inspiration again and again over the decades. "I'm afraid my own adaptations aren't any closer than the ones that went before," the artist confessed, "but then, my purpose was not merely to do a comic-book version of his literary work. For me, it was a matter of inspiration for a starting point. In fact, I feel it is virtually impossible to do a true visual rendition of a text story. Even if I could approach the same feeling of expression, other readers might feel I missed the point entirely."[25]

Asked for his assessment of Poe's fiction, Corben replied, "I'm afraid Poe generally had an unhappy life, with only a few high points. The themes in the stories and poems express much of the sadness and despair he must have felt, as well as his passions. Of course, his genius paraphrased his feelings and experiences into great art. I certainly don't think my life parallels his in any way except to the extent that he deals with universal feelings that we've all had to varied degrees. For instance, in 'The Cask of Amontillado,' I think he is expressing a little wish fulfillment for revenge that we all can relate to."

In response to Cooke's inquiry about the artist's Poe adaptation for Warren in 1974 (arguably Poe's best known work) of "The Raven" (a poem Corben adapted yet again for a Dark Horse version), the artist shared, "When Warren was running his Poe adaptations, I was very happy to

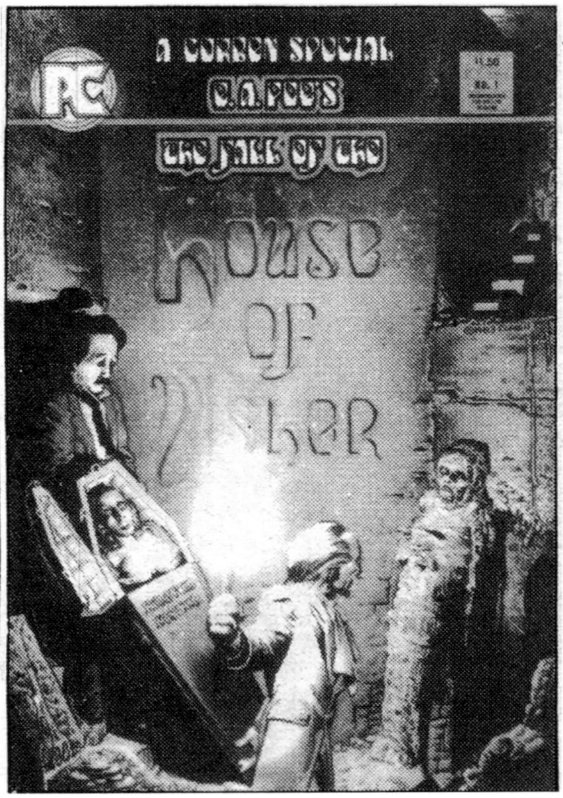
A CORBEN SPECIAL
E.A. POE'S
THE FALL OF THE
HOUSE OF USHER

work on some of them. In fact, I thought it was a perfect match for me. Richard Margopoulos' script, although very short, was true to the original theme. My good friend, Herb Arnold, and his wife modeled for the characters' poses. I also used it as an opportunity to stretch my efforts in the use of color. Years later, I also adapted the poem for an issue of Marvel's *Haunt of Horror*. Here, I was guilty of only loosely adapting the poem and inserted the character's guilt of a murder to the original symbolism of loss and despair. I have just finished a *third* adaptation of the poem and here I tried to return to the original idea of grief over the loss of Lenore, but told in a more visual and extreme fashion."[26]

About the relatively subtle horrors of Poe and H.P. Lovecraft compared to the explicit blood-splattered work of today, Corben said, "I think the appeal of gore or explicit cruelty and violence versus the appeal of more subtle qualities of mystery, mood, suspense, and character exposition has more to do with the maturity of the reader than any lacking of sophistication. Further, the appeal of shocking thrills generally fades as a person gets older, mainly because the explicit thrills are simpler and more elemental than subtle pleasures of atmosphere and mood.

"Personally, I'd like to express the full range of both explicit and subtle in my art. Actually, I have to curb some of the effects I might do for fear of alienating large groups of my audience. Not just for explicit gore, but for other effects that might be seen as lapses of good taste."

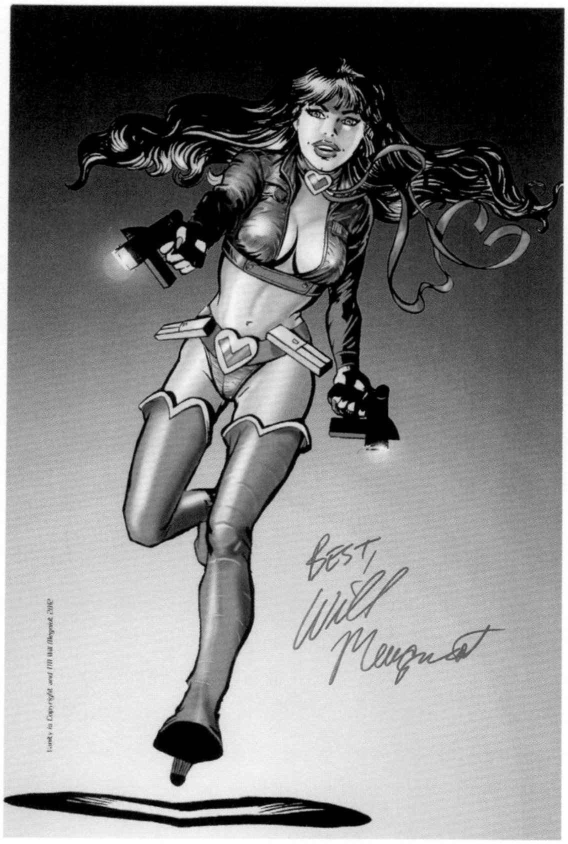
Best,
Will Meugniot

BLAME IT ON VANITY

"*Vanity* was the indie comic that I wanted to do," Will Meugniot recently shared, "but I knew I had to develop a track record before trying to sell that book, as I was relatively unknown in the comic book market. So I collaborated with my friend Mark Evanier and co-created *The DNAgents* to develop name recognition.

"I'd had *Vanity* on my mind from the early '70s and thought of her as a cross between [*Russian super-heroine*] Octobriana and [*Italian anti-hero thief*] Diabolik. She was an amoral adventurer who adventured out of boredom and the need to prove her superiority to normal humans. A very early and much more naked version of her made an appearance on the inside front cover of Bob Sidebottom's publication, Ira Harmon's *Superbitch* [July 1977].

"I first became aware of Pacific when my friend from our Hanna-Barbera days, Dave Stevens, dropped by Marvel Productions to make some 'free' Xeroxes of the first 'Rocketeer' story. I was excited by the notion that you could own your characters. And it was that exposure to the new indie market which inspired me to get in touch with Mark about creating our own book, with Pacific in mind as our probable publisher.

"When we took *DNAgents* out into the marketplace, five publishers were interested, but only Eclipse and Pacific would agree to publish the series without being attached to the media and merchandising, and, in the end, the numbers with Eclipse's $1.50 cover pricing seemed to work better. I often regretted the choice. So when I was ready to take *Vanity* out and Pacific made an offer, I jumped for it.

"I found that dealing with Pacific was much easier for me as our goals and intuition about the market were more in line. I was actually enjoying doing *Vanity* for them."[27]

Asked about drawing two books simultaneously, Meugniot replied, "At first, there was a bit of overlap and it was difficult. But I'd reached the realization that *DNAgents* was a dead-end for me, creatively and financially. Eclipse was starting to engage in editorial interference, and when I saw that some of the art for issue #11 had been altered without my knowledge or consent, that was the last straw. So I dropped the book and went back to Marvel Productions doing storyboards and development. My intention had been to do *Vanity* on weekends and evening time, but, when I was a few pages into issue #3, I got the call that Pacific was going out of business.

"I had a couple of offers to continue *Vanity*, and to do a new companion book. But Marvel was letting me produce, direct, and design more projects, and I felt that was where my future lay. When Pacific went under, I was busy enough that it was a relief to not have to worry about getting out even a bi-monthly comic. That said, of that era's indie publishers, Pacific was my favorite and I was glad to have had the chance to work with them."[28]

Pacific Profiles

Will Meugniot

Born: *July 1951*

While well-regarded for his "Tigra" and *DNAgents* work in comics, Will is far better known in the realm of cartoon animation, where he served as storyboard artist, director, and producer, among many other related jobs. He also ghost-drew 1970s European *Tarzan* and *Korak* comics.

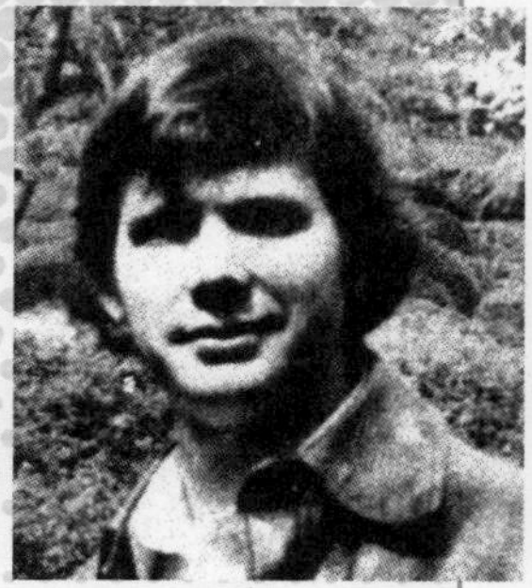

Above: Will Meugniot, circa 1980s, in a photo taken in Tokyo's Chinzanso Gardens.

Inset left: Signed specialty drawing of Vanity based on the character's first issue cover. Art and autograph by creator Will Meugniot. **Below:** The original art from a fun splash page published in *Vanity* #1 [June 1984].

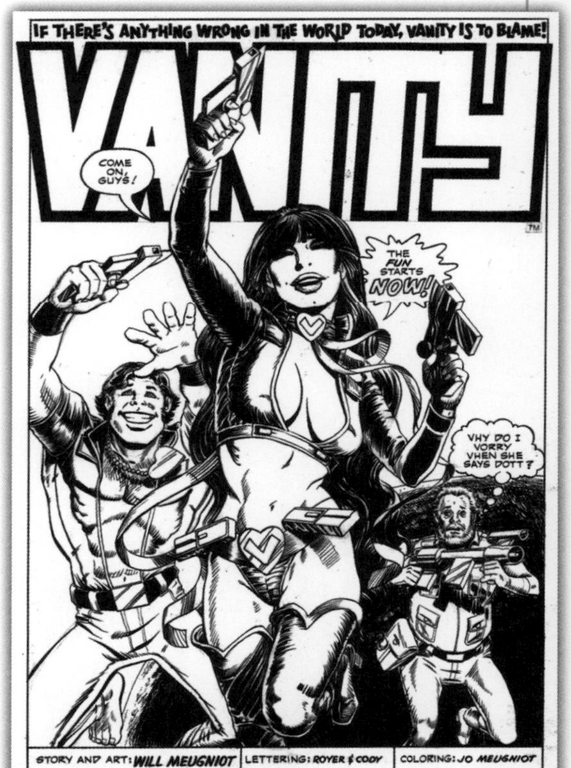
IF THERE'S ANYTHING WRONG IN THE WORLD TODAY, VANITY IS TO BLAME!
VANITY
COME ON, GUYS!
THE FUN STARTS NOW!
VHY DO I VORRY VHEN SHE SAYS DOTT?
STORY AND ART: WILL MEUGNIOT
LETTERING: ROYER & CODY
COLORING: JO MEUGNIOT

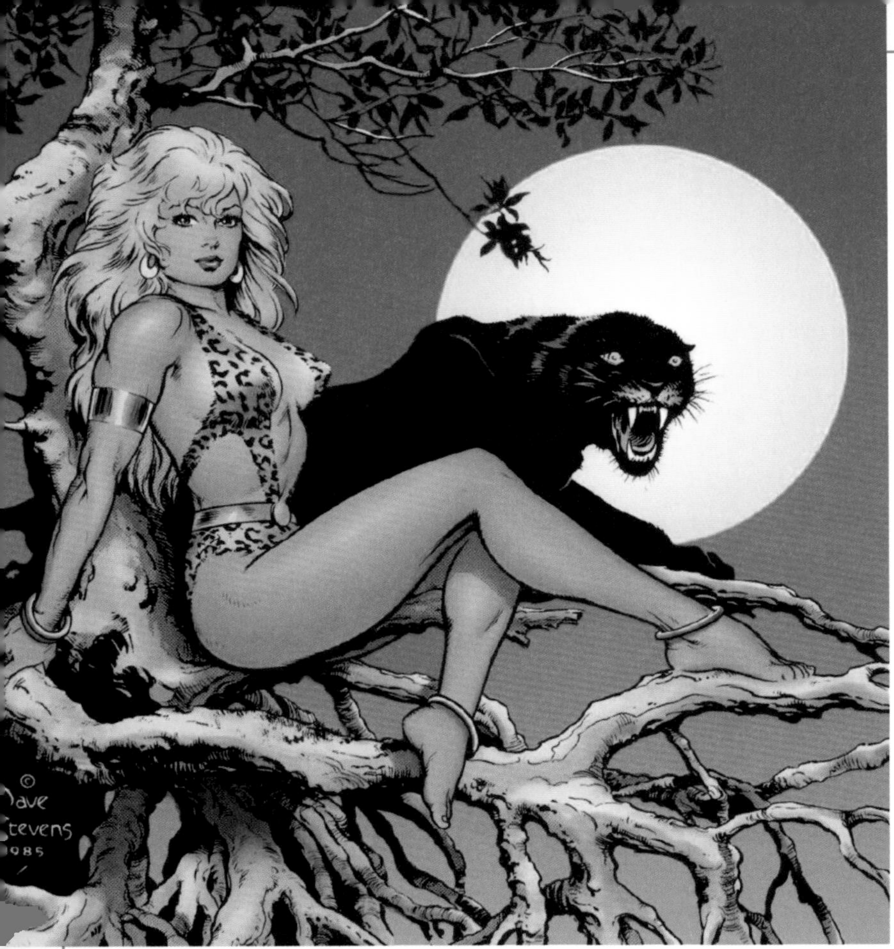

"I was unaware that Jerry Iger was still alive," Steve said, "but I did some research and found his partner at the time, Lee Caplin, and we talked on the phone. Lee was in Los Angeles and he connected me with Jerry, and I found out that Jerry still had a bunch of artwork on hand."

Because Iger lived in New York City, Steve enlisted the help of someone in the area whose name is now forgotten. "[*He*] was very surprised that the archive still existed and so was I. So that was very cool." Iger's artwork was borrowed and stats were made, Steve explained, "So we took hundreds of stats of Jerry's archives and it was very nice that Jerry let us borrow those, and I had some very nice conversations with Jerry Iger, a really nice, interesting fellow and one of the founders of the industry, so I was very honored to be able to talk with him. He answered all my questions about the creation of the industry and had some interesting Will Eisner stories."

One stunning discovery was an unpublished eight-page story drawn by the late "good girl" artist Matt Baker, starring the sultry Roma dancer, Flamingo, a character who had her own Iger-syndicated newspaper feature [1952–53]. Starring "the most beautiful girl ever drawn for a strip,"[30] Flamingo's tales of intrigue proved irresistible to Pacific, as Steve related: "So we hooked up with Jerry Iger and decided to do different things with his archives, and that's how it came about. We loved Matt Baker's 'Flamingo' work, a very unique comic book, and I just loved his artwork. I was unfamiliar with his work until I saw all the

Above: Dave Stevens' fabulous illustration of a vivacious Sheena, Queen of the Jungle, appeared on the cover of *The Iger Comics Kingdom* [1985] trade paperback history, by Jay Disbrow (published by Blackthorne). **Inset right:** *Pacific Premieres* #18 [Sept. 1984] page soliciting a square-bound reprinting of Quality's *Crack Comics* #1 [May 1940], which was never published. **Below:** A true curiosity is Pacific's pair of horizontal-formatted booklets dated July 1984.

EAGER FOR IGER

Steve Schanes recently explained, as a publisher, Pacific was always in need of material. "We were looking for more things to publish. We could do company-owned books, artist-owned books, or we could do reprints, which is basically a licensing thing, so we made a deal with Warren and then we were poking around, and we thought of Fiction House, and we said, 'That's interesting,'"[29]

Originally a pulp magazine imprint, Fiction House got into the comics game early, in 1938, and used the packaging firm of Eisner & Iger, run by comics greats Will Eisner and Samuel Maxwell "Jerry" Iger, and after Eisner's departure, the S.M. Iger Studio was established, supplying material for Fiction House's "Big Six" —*Jumbo, Jungle, Wings, Planet, Rangers,* and *Fight Comics.* Their most popular and successful creation was Sheena, Queen of the Jungle. But, by 1955, Fiction House had given up the ghost.

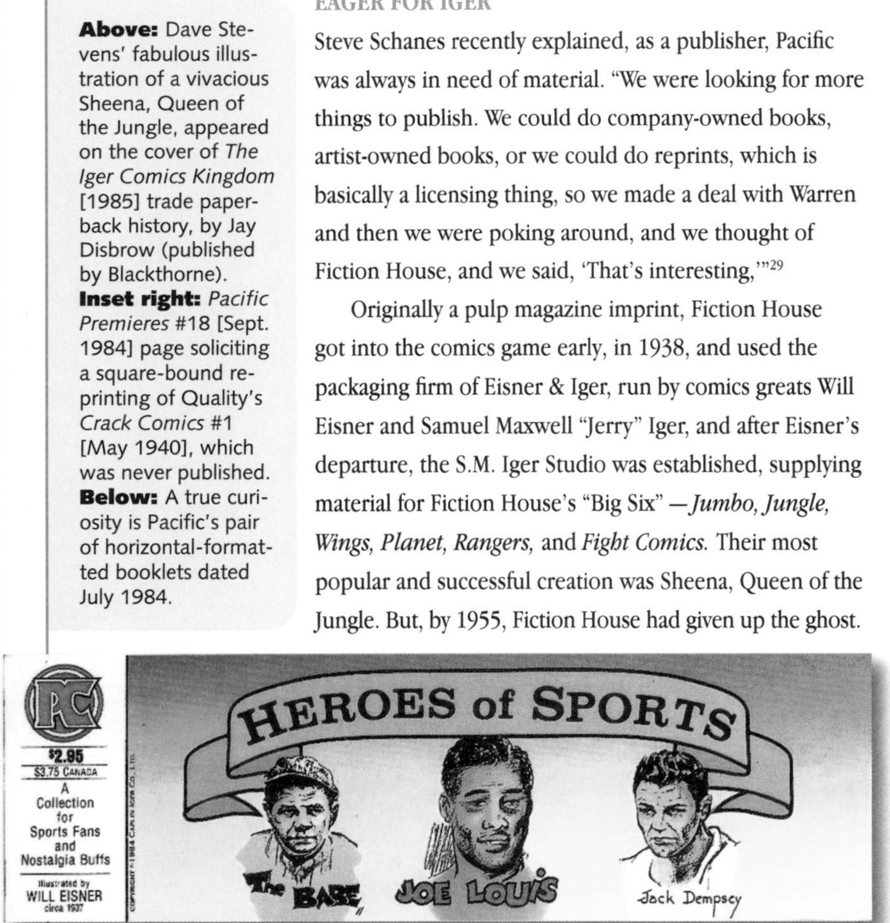

$2.95
$3.75 CANADA
A Collection for Sports Fans and Nostalgia Buffs
Illustrated by WILL EISNER circa 1937
HEROES of SPORTS
The BABE
JOE LOUIS
Jack Dempsey

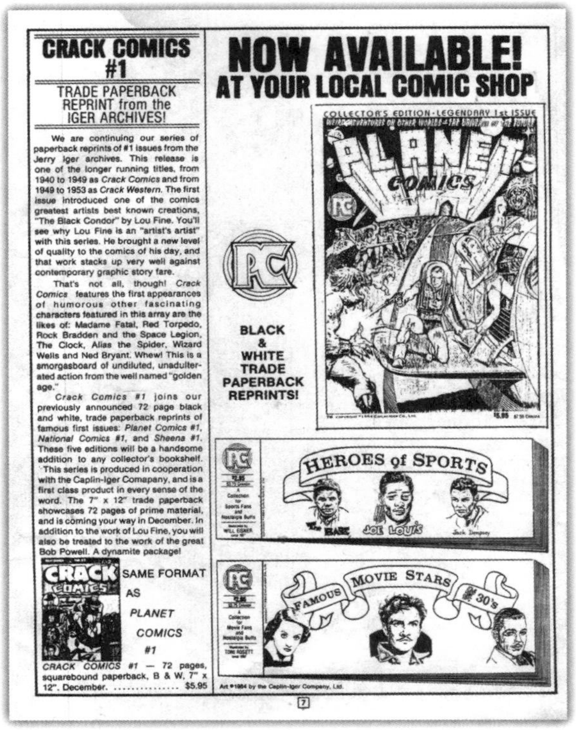

CRACK COMICS #1
TRADE PAPERBACK REPRINT from the IGER ARCHIVES!
We are continuing our series of paperback reprints of #1 issues from the Jerry Iger archives. This release is one of the longer running titles, from 1940 to 1949 as Crack Comics and from 1949 to 1953 as Crack Western. The first issue introduced one of the comics greatest artists best known creations, "The Black Condor" by Lou Fine. You'll see why Lou Fine is an "artist's artist" with this series. He brought a new level of quality to the comics of his day, and that work stacks up very well against contemporary graphic story fare.
That's not all, though! Crack Comics features the first appearances of humorous other fascinating characters featured in this array are the likes of: Madame Fatal, Red Torpedo, Rock Bradden and the Space Legion, The Clock, Alias the Spider, Wizard Wells and Ned Bryant. Whew! This is a smorgasboard of undiluted, unadulterated action from the well named "golden age."
Crack Comics #1 joins our previously announced 72 page black and white, trade paperback reprints of famous first issues: Planet Comics #1, National Comics #1, and Sheena #1. These five editions will be a handsome addition to any collector's bookshelf. This series is produced in cooperation with the Caplin-Iger Comapany, and is a first class product in every sense of the word. The 7" x 12" trade paperback showcases 72 pages of prime material, and is coming your way in December. In addition to the work of Lou Fine, you will also be treated to the work of the great Bob Powell. A dynamite package!
SAME FORMAT AS PLANET COMICS #1
CRACK COMICS #1 — 72 pages, squarebound paperback, B & W, 7" x 12". December. $5.95
NOW AVAILABLE!
AT YOUR LOCAL COMIC SHOP
PLANET COMICS
BLACK & WHITE TRADE PAPERBACK REPRINTS!
HEROES of SPORTS
FAMOUS MOVIE STARS of the 30's

artwork come through in stat form. It was just fantastic."[31] Flamingo's unpublished exploit, "The Face in the Golden Comb," an alternative version of which was later redrawn for the strip's debut continuity, was finally printed in *Jerry Iger's Famous Features* #1 [July 1984].

THE IGER METHOD

About his business partnership with Lee Caplin, Jerry Iger wrote in 1985, "Our new venture, the Caplin-Iger Company, Ltd., is dedicated to presenting features from the Iger shop in a historical context. It is my hope that relating my personal experience in connection with the evolution of 'Sheena, Queen of the Jungle,' as well as other features, will increase the understanding and enjoyment of these Golden Age creations for future generations of comic book collectors."[32]

As president of the partnership, Caplin shared in *The Iger Comics Kingdom*, "Historically, Jerry Iger never sold or transferred the copyright or trademark in any of his characters or titles. It was his practice only to negotiate a license to a publisher such as Farrell or T. T. Scott, etc., to publish a story or series of stories based on a given list of characters. Upon expiration of the license, all rights and title to those characters and stories reverted to Mr. Iger by the terms of the contract."[33]

Caplin had loved comics as a kid. "I got terrified by them when I saw the EC Comics," he recently shared. While he can't recall the exact circumstances how he met Iger, "Jerry and I became very close friends and eventually we formed a business and he transferred the rights to everything he created over to the company, including one of the first comics, *Jumbo Comics*."[34] The partnership started around 1982, when Caplin was 36 and Iger was 79, and when another party struck a deal with Columbia Pictures for a *Sheena* movie, "For the two of us, I saved the rights to do the classic comics and modern versions of those characters." Caplin recalled Sheena as part of the deal because, he said, "We were able to work with Dave Stevens on an iconic 3-D *Sheena, Queen of the Jungle* comic book, with the glasses, which I remember vividly… It was just breathtakingly beautiful."

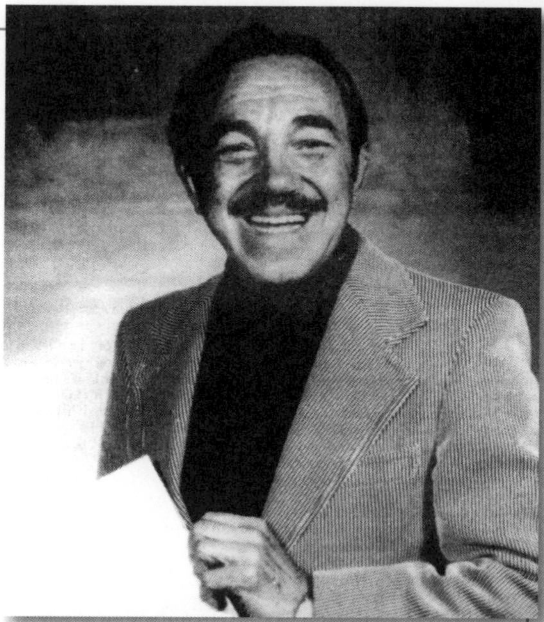

Caplin added, "Jerry was a bit of a pack-rat. He lived alone in a walk-up apartment, with one bedroom. He had stacks and stacks and stacks of material.

"We had a great time. He was so invigorated seeing all these old comics have new life and I think it made his life a lot more interesting, because he was solitary. He didn't get out and do very much. I bought him into Manhattan and introduce him to the intellectual property lawyers that we had. We did all of our deals in real partnership." Jerry Iger died in 1990, at the age of 87.

Though Pacific's plans called for a raft of titles, the only Iger-related productions to come from the outfit were the aforementioned *Jerry Iger's Famous Features* #1 (which reprinted that unseen "Flamingo" story in b-&-w) and an odd-sized pair of booklets featuring reprints of Iger-owned comic strip properties from the 1930s, *Heroes of Sports* and *Famous Movie Stars of the '30s*, each 48 pages printed 11" wide by 3.5" tall, as well as the 76-page square-bound *Planet Comics* #1, filled with reprints from the 1940s' Fiction House space opera title.

But, with his post-Pacific publishing enterprise, Steve would continue his association with Jerry Iger by producing six Blackthorne titles bearing Iger's name, along with other related comics. Unfortunately, though it was advertised as forthcoming in *Pacific Premieres*, the *Crack Comics* #1 trade paperback reprint, promoted as from the Iger archives and featuring reprints of Lou Fine material, never did appear.

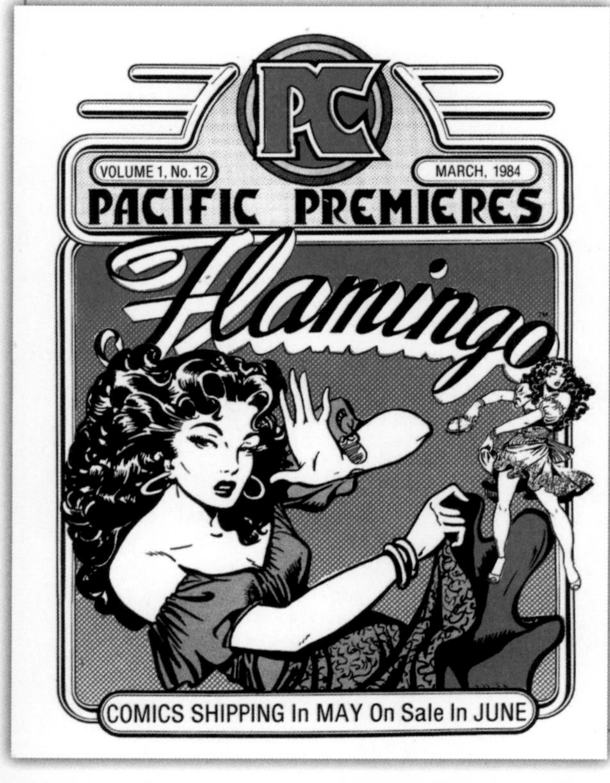
PC
VOLUME 1, No. 12
MARCH, 1984
PACIFIC PREMIERES
Flamingo
COMICS SHIPPING In MAY On Sale In JUNE

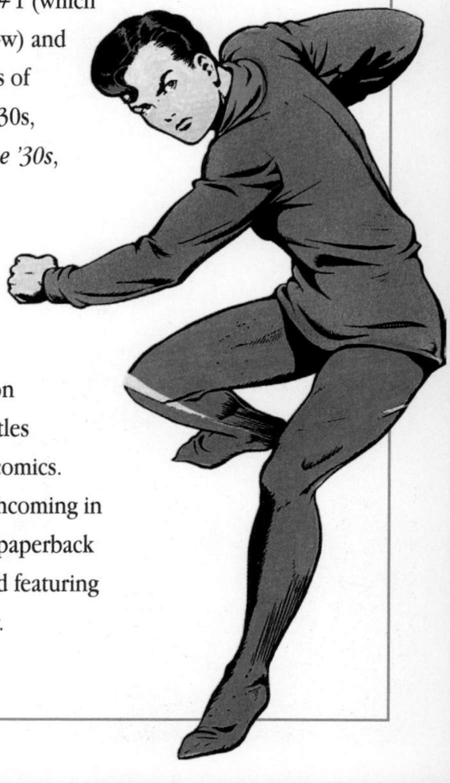

Above: Ebullient Jerry Iger in the 1970s. **Inset left:** Attractive two-color cover for *Pacific Premieres* #12 [Mar. 1984], graced with Matt Baker artwork. **Below:** Besides the eight-page "Flamingo" story in the same issue, another previously unpublished Matt Baker-drawn story was Wonder Boy's "The Amazing Plot of the Corpse Who Never Died," in *Jerry Iger's Famous Features* #1 [July 1984].

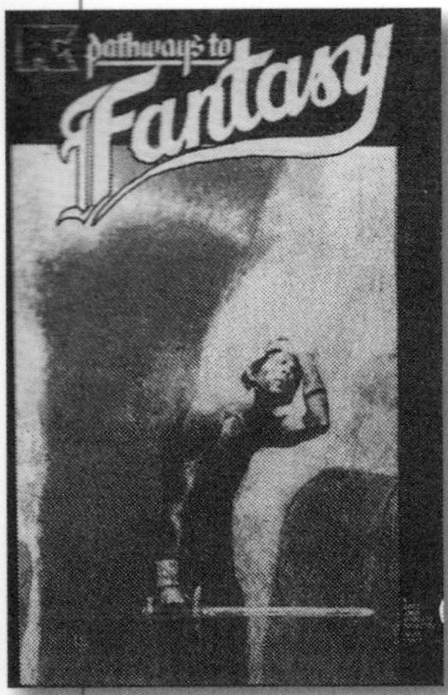
Pathways to Fantasy

This page: Clockwise, above is a fuzzy repro of the intended Jeffrey Jones cover for *Pathways to Fantasy* #2 (unpublished); Barry Windsor-Smith cover art to #1 [July 1984]; Danish edition of *Freak Show*; and *Pacific Premieres* #16 [July 1984] cover. *Pacific Premieres* #15 [June 1984] shared that *Pathways* #2 was to have stories by Frank Brunner, Bo Hampton, Jay Muth & Kent Williams, Scott Hampton, and the first chapter of a serial painted by Chris Miller.

OF FANTASY AND FREAKS

Ambitious to the end, Bruce Jones had long planned a third anthology title for Pacific Comics but, for one reason or another, *Pathways to Fantasy* #1 wouldn't be published until the twilight of the imprint's existence and, in fact, it was among the very last Pacific releases. The packager did have a number of projects in the works when the company collapsed, including the second issue of *Pathways*, which was to include a story, "The Reading," by Frank Brunner and a piece by Bo Hampton, who told *Back Issue*, "'The Maiden and the Dragon' was originally slated for an anthology titled *Pathways to Fantasy*. When that book was canned, Bruce used it for *Alien Worlds* [*at Eclipse*]. I colored that story on watercolor paper that had the black-&-white art printed on it, comic book-sized. As far as I know, that was the only time that technique was used in comics."[35]

As tragic as the demise of the company was for Jones' plans, *Pathways to Fantasy* #1 proved a cover-to-cover masterpiece from its exquisite Barry Windsor-Smith cover to all within. In 2020, commentator Geoff Rosengren enthused, "With five stories from some truly great creators, this book, which was released in 1984 from Pacific Comics for a couple of bucks or less, was worth every penny and can still be found today, if one is lucky, for the same amount, give or take. The only downside is that *Pathways to Fantasy* only lasted a single issue, a shame given the talent within its pages, but a gem that will surely enchant and delight those that are able to peruse its pages."[36]

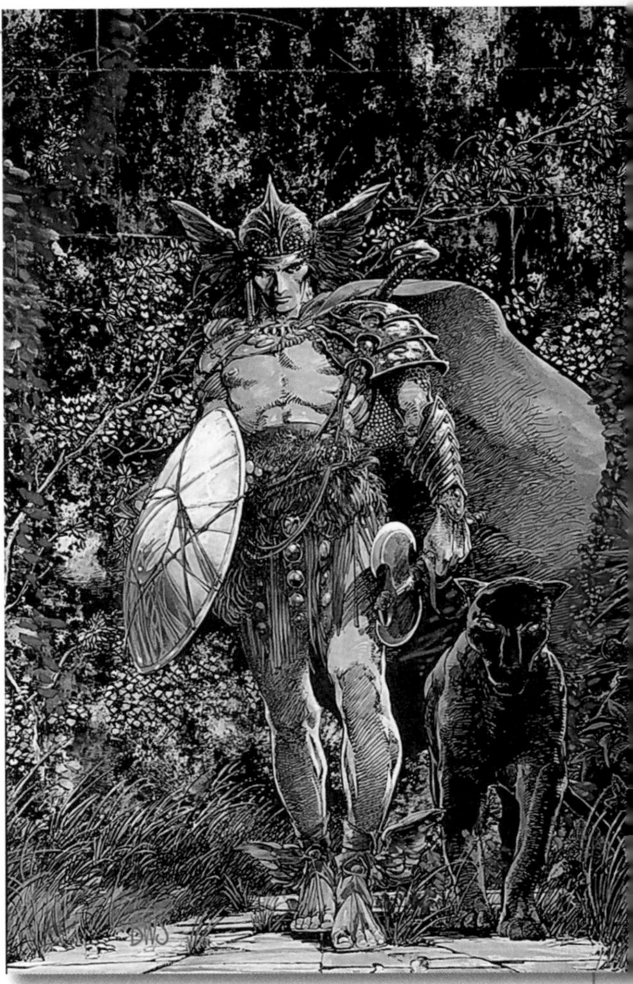

Said to have been originally intended as an annual, *Three Dimensional Alien Worlds* lasted but a single issue and the 36-pager (containing work by Dave Stevens, John Bolton, Bill Wray, and a very young Arthur Adams) wasn't just the last BJA production published by Pacific, it was also the final comic book printed under their banner. "The Schanes brothers ran into financial trouble right in the middle of our run on the books," Jones told *Back Issue*, "and one of the ways I tried to make sure every contributor got paid for their work was by continuing the books under the Eclipse colophon."[37]

Jones and Campbell had plenty of projects in the Pacific pipeline when all came to a screeching halt in the spring of 1984. There was the Pacific Comics graphic novel line to be edited by the couple, with the first being Frank Brunner's *Seven Samuroid*, a science-fiction saga of warring robots. The second was to collect Jones and Bernie Wrightson's "Freak Show" serial, featuring an artist at the peak of his exceptional abilities, which had run in *Heavy Metal* in 1982–83. (Curiously, post-Pacific, no other publisher in the U.S. picked up the property* — which was initiated at Continuity — though a European edition was produced in 1984 by Danish publisher Carlsen Comics.)

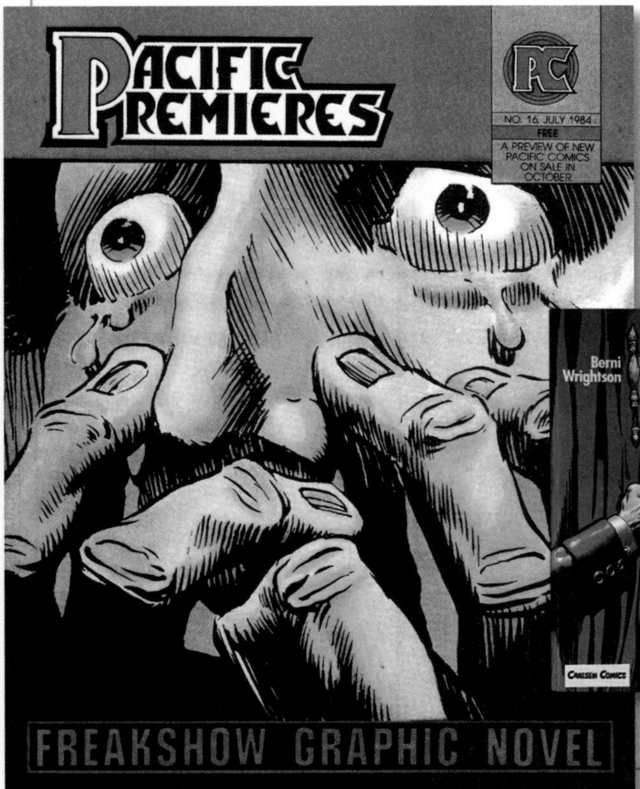
PACIFIC PREMIERES
PC
NO. 16 JULY 1984
FREE
A PREVIEW OF NEW PACIFIC COMICS ON SALE IN OCTOBER
FREAKSHOW GRAPHIC NOVEL

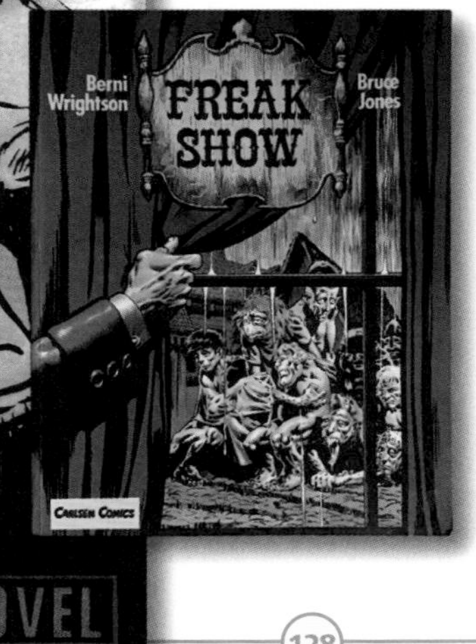
Berni Wrightson
FREAK SHOW
Bruce Jones
CARLSEN COMICS

* A *Freak Show* collection wouldn't see print this side of the Atlantic until an Image Comics edition was published in 2006. *Freak Show* was originally commissioned by Neal Adams, intended to be a graphic novel released by Continuity Graphics.

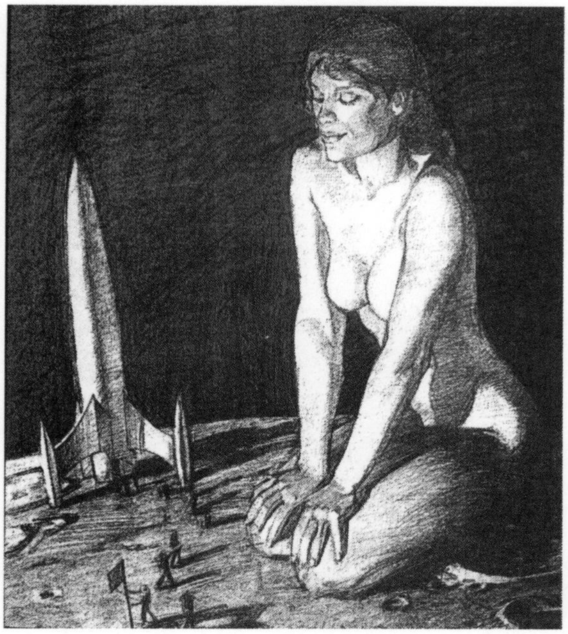

GROWN-UP FUNNY BOOKS

Bill Schanes told Ed Catto of his admiration for the BJA productions. "Personally, I really enjoyed almost all of the books that April Campbell and Bruce Jones packaged for Pacific Comics. April and Bruce put together a series of fantastic titles, with all-star talent involved. These included *Twisted Tales, Alien Worlds, Pathways to Fantasy, Somerset Holmes,* to name a few. Jeffrey Catherine Jones, Bernie Wrightson, Barry Winsor-Smith, Tim Conrad, Art Adams, John Bolton, Joe Chiodo, Bo and Scott Hampton, Brent Anderson, and a host of others, plus April and Bruce wrote the majority of the stories, which lent to wonderful continuity along the whole line."[38]

The pair were intent on fulfilling one promise of the direct market and cater to an adult audience who loved the comics form but had matured beyond super-men power fantasies. Anthony Dellaflora of the *Albuquerque Journal* reported in May 1984:

"Bruce Jones and April Campbell, creators of *Somerset Holmes,* are working on the premise that there is a market for classy comics; something with a dash of Alfred Hitchcock, an occasional erotic interlude, and some of the best artwork around.

"'We're aiming for a higher age market, 18 to 40 years old,' said Jones. 'Most of our readers are college-educated. It's a little more of an elitist group. We're dealing with the concept that, once you get past 15 or 16, super-heroes don't appeal to you.'

"The mature, socially pertinent themes in the latest wave of comic books have attracted a new audience.

"'Traditionally, the comic-book market has been for boys,' explained Ms. Campbell. 'Now women are reading them.'

"Perhaps more importantly, the new comics are attracting people who don't know Spider-Man from the Incredible Hulk — people like Ms. Campbell, who was not a fan of comic books as a child."[39]

The two would have much of BJA's remaining inventory published by Eclipse Comics in the months after Pacific's demise. And, despite their visionary approach to the comics field, it would be the allure of a more lucrative art form, based in a city 140 miles north of their Coronado Island abode, that drove Jones and Campbell from comics, as much as it was the collapse of their main client.

Inset left: This pencil preliminary drawing by Joe Chiodo appeared in *Pacific Premieres.* The finished painting graced the cover of *Three Dimensional Alien Worlds* #1 [July 1984]. **Below:** Article from New Mexico's *Albuquerque Journal* [May 13, 1984] about the creative forces behind BJA Associates, Bruce Jones and April Campbell.

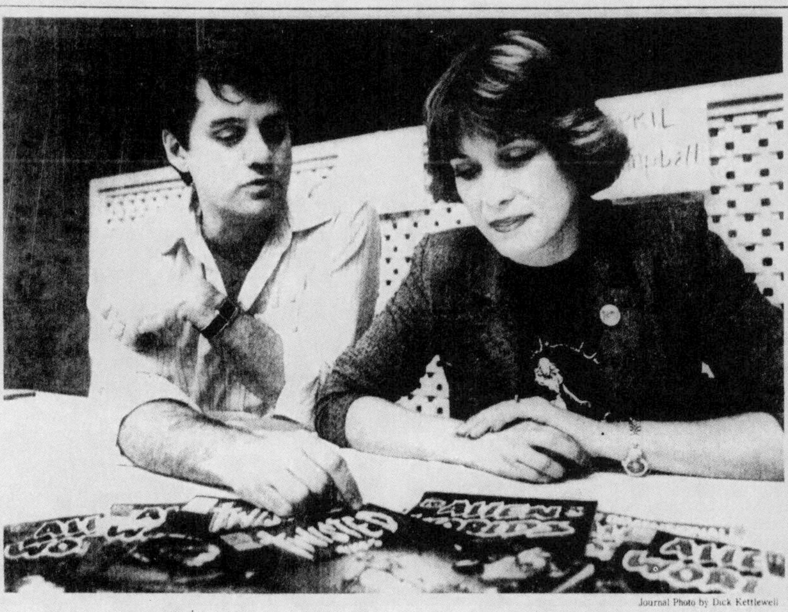

Journal Photo by Dick Kettlewell

Bruce Jones, Left, and April Campbell, Creators of New Wave 'Somerset Holmes'

New Comics Shun ZAP! BAM! POW!

By ANTHONY DELLAFLORA
Journal Staff Writer

It used to be people could tell something about a person, or thought they could, by the car he drove, the clothes he wore and the restaurants he frequented.

Well, they can now add comic books to the list of indicators of social status.

Do you go for the BIFF! BAM! BOOM! variety of superhero comic?

Or do prefer something a little more sophisticated like "Somerset Holmes?" — the saga of a woman who suffers total amnesia after being struck by a car, then must figure out her identity while eluding several people intent on murdering her.

Bruce Jones and April Campbell, creators of "Somerset Holmes," are working on the premise that there is a market for classy comics — something with dash of Alfred Hitchcock, an occasional erotic interlude and some of the best artwork around.

"We're aiming for a higher age market, 18 to 40 years old," said Jones. "Most of our readers are college educated. It's a little more of an elitist group.

"We're dealing with the concept that, once you get past 15 or 16, superheroes don't appeal to you."

The mature, socially pertinent themes in the latest wave of comic books have attracted a new audience.

"Traditionally, the comic-book market has been for boys," explained Ms. Campbell. "Now women are reading them."

Perhaps more importantly, the new comics are attracting people who don't know Spiderman from the Incredible Hulk — people like Ms. Campbell, who was not a fan of comic books as a child.

Along with Hitchcock, Jones and Ms. Campbell say, their inspirations include Edgar Allen Poe, Ray Bradbury and TV shows like "The Twilight Zone" and "Outer Limits."

"We do stories with a bite to them," Jones comments. "We don't like people in colored costumes hitting each other."

And unlike traditional comics, most of their stories don't have happy endings.

"Our protagonists often don't live," Jones points out.

"It's a real art form," continues Jones. "They're not throwaway products."

Independent companies like Pacific Comics, which distributes "Somerset Holmes" and other comics by Jones and Ms. Campbell, challenge the status quo by allowing writers and artists much more creative and financial control than the major companies.

Creators of comics now can package their efforts, much like producers put movies together, keep their copyrights and get paid royalties.

"The creators of Superman never got anything," laments Jones.

Jones and Ms. Campbell will be in town today for a comic-book convention at the Winrock Inn, from 10 a.m. to 6 p.m.

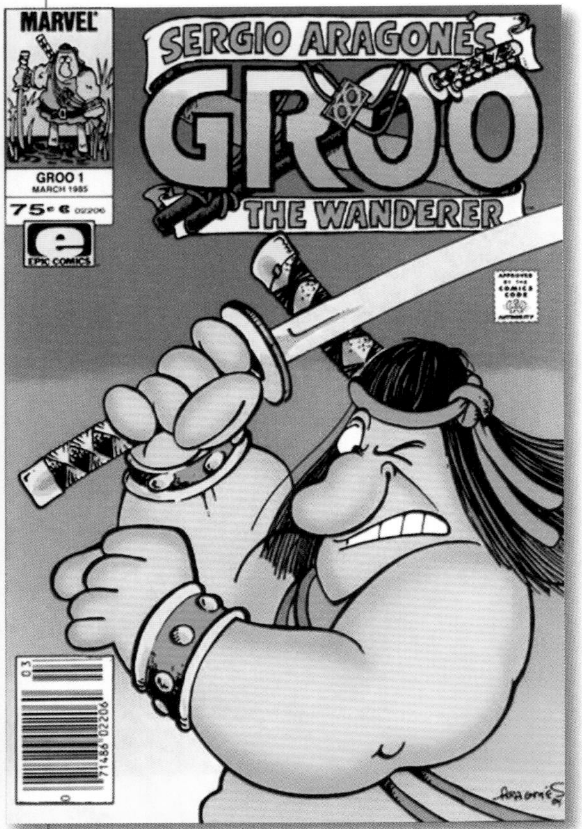
MARVEL
SERGIO ARAGONÉS
GROO
THE WANDERER
GROO 1
MARCH 1985
75¢
EPIC COMICS

GROO WANDERS OFF

Even before some of its freelancers took note of Pacific's difficulties in keeping afloat (like Mike Grell switching to First Comics), some marquee talents decided to jump ship before any proverbial iceberg was struck. Asked whether Pacific's creator rights gambit had resulted in more money for creators than they would have received with the mainstream "work-for-hire" outfits, Scroggy told Jeff Gelb, "Well, we still haven't seen results in such areas as major licensing. However, I believe that we are going to. Without saying more than I reasonably can, I know for a fact that there is definite interest, in both films and television, in some of the Pacific titles. Jack Kirby and Sergio Aragonés certainly enjoy greater revenues in the area of overseas licensing than they would have enjoyed through the old system. Certainly, Neal Adams made quite a lot more money on *Ms. Mystic* #1 — based on its high sale and therefore higher royalties — than he ever would have done under the old system. I think it's obvious that creator-owned comics have created a better deal for creators at every company, including the latest development we're seeing, the announcement of creator-owned newsstand comics through Marvel. One of those titles will be *Groo*."[40]

Above: Though suspicions regarding Pacific Comics' solvency were circulating at the time, Sergio Aragonés' decision to take *Groo the Wanderer* to Epic Comics, Marvel's new creator-friendly imprint, was predominately made because the *MAD* cartoonist wanted his title to have newsstand distribution, something the Schanes brothers could not offer. The title — officially, *Sergio Aragonés Groo the Wanderer* — lasted for 10 years and 120 issues at the House of Ideas. **Below:** Logo of Neal Adams' imprint.

Gelb then asked if Pacific's loss of *Groo* was frustrating. With a laugh, David replied, "Well, what do you think, Jeff? I'll be very sorry to see *Groo* go. But Sergio Aragonés will let you know, privately and publicly, that this is not the basis of us giving him a raw deal. It's an opportunity for him to reach a greater audience and wider marketplace and still retain the creator control and ownership that he feels is necessary to produce his work."

Mark Evanier offered an interesting observation about an advantage of his friend's creator-owned title. "Pacific published eight issues of *Groo the Wanderer,*" he said, "but the scent of their pending demise started to drift northward, from San Diego to our L.A.-based nostrils… they had comic-shop distribution, not access to regulation news outlets. Not only that, but the firm was in financial trouble… while the lawyers were playing ping-pong, Pacific Comics went belly-up. And right here is a splendid example of why creator-owned comics can better serve the creative community. Had *Groo* been owned by Pacific instead of Sergio, we couldn't have taken it elsewhere to keep it alive."[41] (Groo would prove to be a remarkably resilient comic book character, as he is periodically in print to present day, thus still wandering and still quite alive.)

MAKING THE (COMICS) WORLD A BETTER PLACE

The benefit of time suggests that, however short its existence, one aspect of Pacific's impact in the comics realm was to nudge publishers into a new direction, one favoring creators. Talking to Rod Underhill about the effect of his publishing company on competitors, Steve Schanes shared, "Well, we certainly allowed them to follow a beaten path. They have all continued to expand their market, and they have done a wonderful job. The main thing that it has done, is it took the creators from approximately $150 a page, maximum, to maybe upwards of $500 or $600 a page. In some cases, more; where the book is selling huge quantities, it put some writers on a royalty, and is, in fact, indirectly responsible for Marvel's Epic line, because that was a response to Pacific Comics… Marvel had to react. Pacific was pulling talent from the major companies, as an upstart company, because it could offer advantages that Marvel and DC couldn't. Pacific couldn't offer the marketing advantages, but it could offer ownership and royalties – which was, in the long term, worth more than the marketing. In order to compete with that, Marvel either had to match it on all its existing books or had to create a new label. I believe that they opted for a new division because, if they matched it on all their existing books, it would have cost them millions. So that is why I believe Epic came out."[42]

Citing that Pacific Comics had "made its mark," Steve Duin and Mike Richardson observed, "If Marvel and DC hastened Pacific's demise by flooding the market with upscale, high-priced reprints, they were forced to respond to the company's creator friendliness by offering higher compensation or venues such as the Epic line."[43] (Still, Jay Allen Sanford hinted that all was not always well

The Continuity Comics Connection

According to the Grand Comics Database, Continuity Comics lasted for almost 10 years and produced 142 issues, approximately 33 issues* more than Pacific's total. And it was quite possible the success of *Ms. Mystic* #1, the San Diego imprint's top-selling issue, prompted Neal Adams, owner of Continuity Associates — and the brilliant credited artist/writer of said *Ms. Mystic* — to branch out and launch his own line. But as a nascent imprint, New York City-based Continuity needed to enlist Pacific's help and expertise to get their publications to the direct market, with Pacific handling color separations, printing, soliciting, and distribution of the new titles.

At the time, David Scroggy shared about the first title to carry the Continuity logo, "Well, we have to distribute a book that costs $3 — Neal Adams' *Echo of Futurepast,* which I feel might have enjoyed a much larger sale at a lower price point. On the other hand, it really took an exceptional amount of work and involved exceptionally high production costs. We currently have no plans to sell any PC-imprint comic books for over $2. Neal Adams' Continuity Studios seems to feel $2.95 is an acceptable price for their 48-page package, and we have enough faith in *Echo of Futurepast* that we're certainly willing to distribute it... The logo on that comic book will be Continuity Graphic. Neal Adams is actually producing a line of comic books, of which *Echo* is the first title. By the time this interview is printed, you will probably have heard about *Zero Patrol,* also *Megalith*, and you will probably be hearing about other Neal Adams Continuity Comics. It's an ever-changing world, and who knows? Neal may decide, at some point, that he can support his own distribution and decide to break off, but for the foreseeable future, we are the exclusive distributor of Continuity Comics."[44]

* There are few greater challenges in comic book collecting than to figure out the precise order of the Continuity line, given the number of title reboots and imprint name variations, whether Continuity Graphic, Continuity Publishing, or Continuity Comics, so take any totals here with caution.

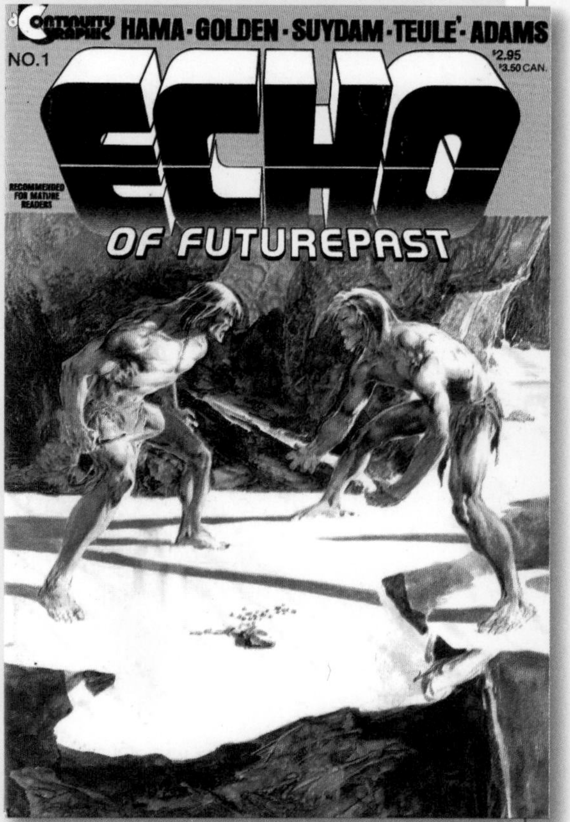
HAMA·GOLDEN·SUYDAM·TEULE'·ADAMS
NO.1
$2.95
$3.50 CAN.
ECHO
OF FUTUREPAST

Above: The first comic book to carry Neal Adams' Continuity branding, *Echo of Futurepast* #1 [Apr. 1984], with Neal Adams cover art, the debut of an anthology featuring the work of Continuity associates — including Larry Hama and Michael Golden's "Buck O'Hare" and Arthur Suydam's "Mudwogs" — and certain European artists who impressed publisher Adams.

The Comics Journal revealed that, in its coordinating with a more established publisher, Continuity had been previously able to "piggy-back" the printing of its comic books with Pacific's, as a larger print run decreases the per-copy cost, but the collapse of the Schanes brothers' company forced Continuity to scramble for a new solution. "Since this is no longer possible with Pacific, [*Continuity promotion manager Kristine*] Adams said that she has considered 'piggy-backing' with another publisher, but that no final decision has been made."[45]

Forced out of its proverbial nest, Continuity Comics quickly learned to fly independently and went about becoming completely self-sufficient. The *TCJ* article reporting on Continuity's dilemma with the California imprint concluded, "All in all, Continuity has completely severed its relationship with Pacific, and is redoubling its efforts to overcome the setback. 'We're out there on our own now,' [*Kris*] Adams said."[46]

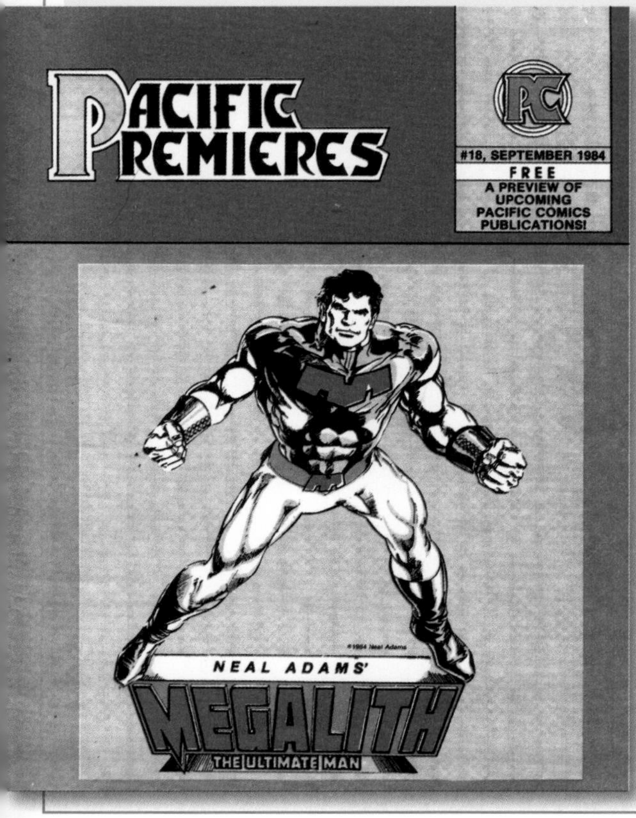
PACIFIC PREMIERES
#18, SEPTEMBER 1984
FREE
A PREVIEW OF UPCOMING PACIFIC COMICS PUBLICATIONS!
NEAL ADAMS'
MEGALITH
THE ULTIMATE MAN

Inset left: *Megalith*, a Continuity title poised to be distributed by the San Diego publisher, graced the cover of the Pacific Comics' solicitation newsletter for September 1984.

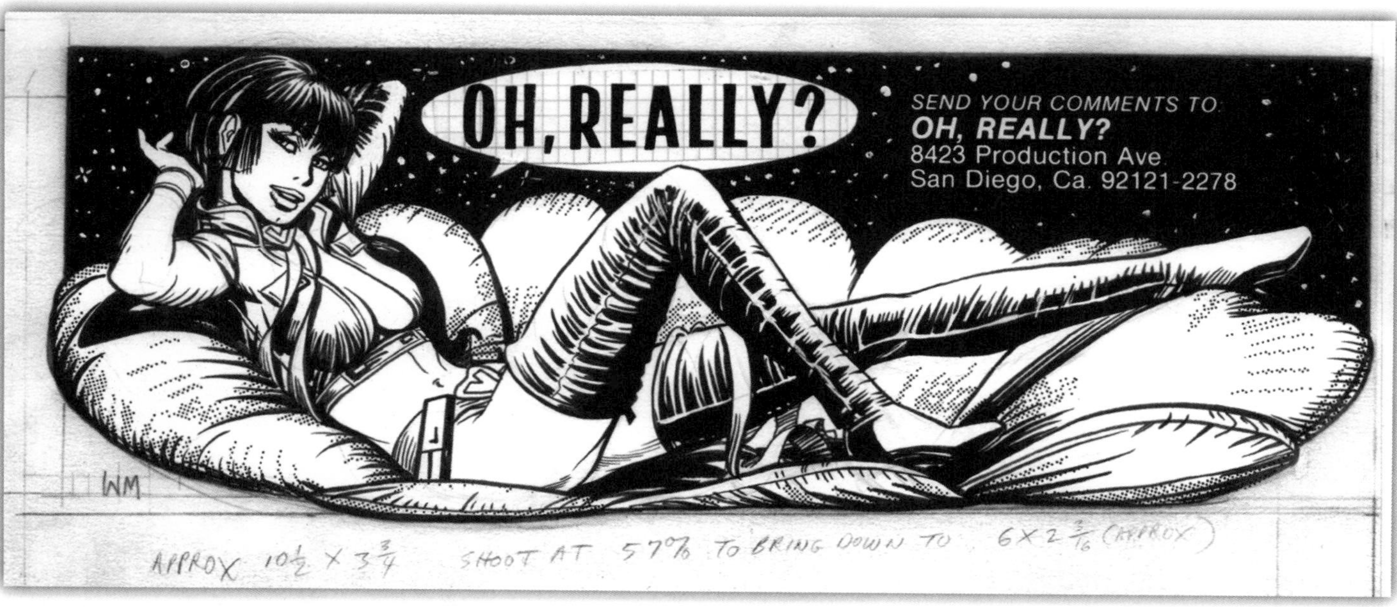
OH, REALLY?
SEND YOUR COMMENTS TO:
OH, REALLY?
8423 Production Ave
San Diego, Ca. 92121-2278
WM
APPROX 10½ X 3¾ SHOOT AT 57% TO BRING DOWN TO 6X2 3/16 (APPROX)

Above: Will Meugniot header art for the *Vanity* letters column page.

with Pacific/creator relations. Near the company's end, in his brief stint as foreign shipping manager, Sanford later revealed, "I fielded several terse phone calls from people claiming to represent comic creators like Sergio Aragonés and Neal Adams, attempting to confirm foreign circulation figures on titles for which their clients were owed royalties.")[47]

Next page: In 1984, Pacific published this 11" x 16" print by Dave Stevens depicting a memorable scene in the Rocketeer series.

BETTER LATE THAN NEVER?

One major complaint over much of Pacific's three-year existence as publisher was its difficulty keeping the periodicals on schedule. Asked by Jeff Gelb in 1983 why Pacific's books were sometimes late, David Scroggy answered, "Well, there's lots of different reasons. To be candid, part of the reason is that, when we began as publishers, we had to learn by doing and we made a lot of mistakes. Being in the public eye, we got to make our mistakes in public, in a lot of different areas. If you look at the Pacific comics coming out today, you'll see a definite improvement in all aspects. The key thing we're going for now is punctuality and a more considered product. I think the punctuality has gotten better, and I think the material, all in all, has gotten better — everything from our logo to the colors. As for why the books are late, part of it is that we are a smaller company. It's expensive to produce a comic, and artists and writers don't come cheap. It was difficult for under-capitalized publishers such as ourselves to get as far ahead as we really would like to be.

"But certainly no one is immune from deadline problems. We've seen it across the board, in other companies. I will tip my hat to First Comics as being the most punctual and I think that's helped their books a great deal."[48]

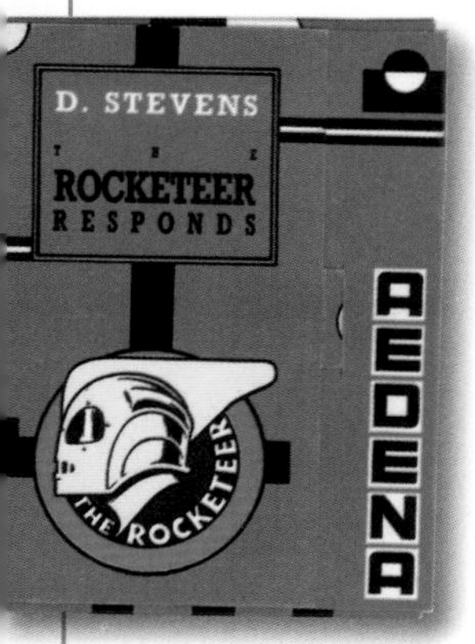
D. STEVENS
THE ROCKETEER RESPONDS
AEDENA
THE ROCKETEER

Below: A French mini-portfolio of Dave Stevens' Rocketeer artwork. Published by Aeden, the 16-card set was limited to 600 numbered copies, with one interior card signed in pencil by the artist.

During his years at Pacific, David had developed a side hustle as artist representative, repping John Pound, Chris Miller, Joe Chiodo, and Rick Geary by the time of his 1984 interview with Diana Schutz. When she asked if he sensed any conflict of interest being an agent and the editorial director at Pacific, he replied, "No, because I don't really represent comic book packages. If I was representing comic book packages in the sense that Mike Friedrich does, where I was offering these people's work to the highest bidder in the format of color comic book packages, I think there would be a definite conflict of interest, but most of the artists that I work with are primarily illustrators, painters who do covers for paperback books and comic books. And we have used them, but we would have used them anyway. I don't think there's a conflict of interest though; the only conflict of interest is if the agenting time begins to interfere with my time, with Pacific Comics' time or facilities. Bill and Steve are pretty understanding about it. I have been spending a lot of time wrestling with this time conflict, though. I am beginning to find that I'm somewhat restricted time-wise, and believe I should be putting more into the artist representation business. Since I obviously can't do *everything* at once, this will force some hard decisions."[49]

When the interviewer suggested he sounded as if he were contemplating quitting the comics company, David candidly replied, "Well, I guess it does. I have to go where my best interests lie and that would mean a career switch. I should have it all sorted out by the San Diego Comic-Con, so perhaps we'll do an update then."

If David didn't make his decision at the June 28–July 1 event, one would be made for him as, only a few months after the con, a reckoning was coming for Pacific Comics.

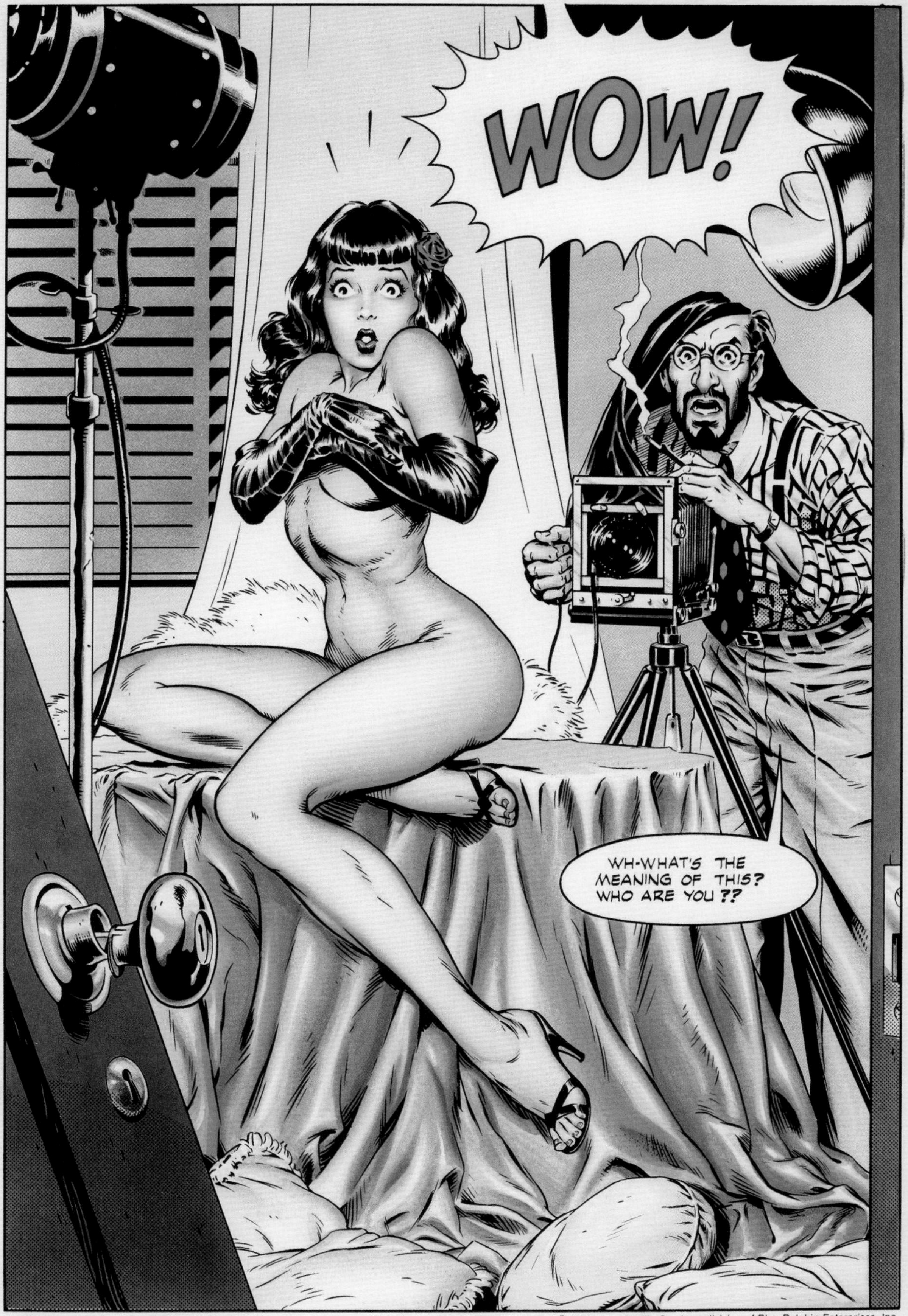
WOW!
WH-WHAT'S THE MEANING OF THIS? WHO ARE YOU??

Published by Pacific Comics a division of Blue Dolphin Enterprises, Inc.

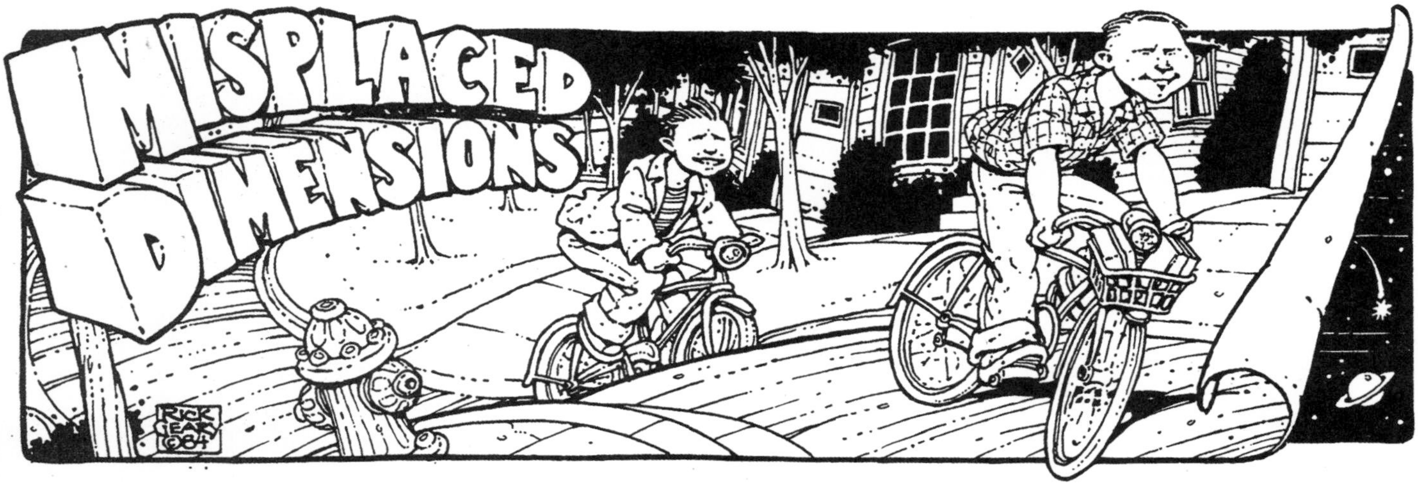
MISPLACED
DIMENSIONS
RICK GEARY ©84

Bill Schanes: The Great Diamond Distribution Boycott

In 1981, Pacific Comics started to publish full-color comic books, [when] DC Comics, Marvel Comics, Archie Comics, Harvey Comics, and Warren magazines, plus *Starlog* magazine [were being published]. There were also the underground comix publishers: Print Mint, Rip Off Press, Last Gasp, plus others, and a few new age publishers (ground-level publishers) like Star*Reach Productions and Eclipse Comics, as well.

We were so fortunate that our very first full-color comic book was by the biggest name in the business, Jack Kirby. *Captain Victory and the Galactic Rangers* was his first of two creator-owned titles for us (*Silver Star* came later). We decided to have a lead feature and then a much shorter back-up feature in each of our comic books. Most of the back-up features would focus on newer creators, who we wanted to give exposure to their works.

We had the "King" coming back to the industry (Jack had left comics to work in the animation field), so we knew this would be huge news.

We had gained tremendous support from comic book specialty retailers, distributors, and the media. As we continued to add titles, we started to branch out from the super-hero genre into science-fiction, fantasy, horror, and humor.

We had come to a special relationship with the incredibly talented team of April Campbell and Bruce Jones, who acted as editorial packagers on a wide range of new titles, some of which would stretch the boundaries of what might be considered politically correct at the time. Over the course of a couple of years, April and Bruce created *Alien Worlds, Twisted Tales, Pathways to Fantasy, Somerset Holmes,* and several others, as well.

One of our largest distributors at that time was Steve Geppi's Diamond Comic Distributors. We were aware that Steve was very conservative, and only distributed a few publishers prior to Pacific Comics (Archie, DC, Harvey, Marvel, as well as *Starlog*). That was Diamond's entire monthly product offerings. Other distributors offered much wider product ranges — Capital City and our own distribution company, to name just two.

As *Alien Worlds* and *Twisted Tales* started to be published, we had received a very strongly-worded letter from Geppi's Comic World (which was Steve Geppi's chain of comic book specialty retail stores on the East Coast). The letter went to great length as to how offended they were by the editorial direction some of our titles were heading in, and they wanted to let us know, under no circumstances, would any of the six stores support those controversial titles, and would also limit how deep the store chain would continue to support the more traditional titles. They also referenced potential concerns with some of their leases, as they didn't want the property management company who held the lease to say Geppi's Comic World was in violation due to unacceptable editorial matter. This letter was signed by each of the store managers; their general manager, Bob Cook; and Steve Geppi. This hit us hard and we were very worried other major distributors would follow suit. The other distributors didn't object or we would have been in real trouble.

A few years later, after Pacific Comics closed its doors in the summer of 1984, I took a few months off to contemplate what I wanted to do next. Ironically, I ended up moving to Baltimore to work for Steve Geppi, quickly getting promoted to vice president of purchasing, and being the person ultimately in charge of what types of products and publications Diamond would be offering to its comic book specialty retailers. The monthly product selection grew from 100–150 items on a two-page order form to well over 3,000 items in any given month, in a 600-page full-color illustrated catalogue.[50]

Chapter Notes

1 Dez Skinn, interviewed by George Khoury, *Kimota: The Miracleman Companion* [2001, TwoMorrows], pg. 44.

2 Skinn, pgs. 44–45.

3 Mike Friedrich, interviewed by Jon B. Cooke [May 3, 2023].

4 David Scroggy, "Juggling the Books at Pacific," interviewed by Diana Schutz, *The Telegraph Wire* #15 [June/July 1984], pgs. 20–21.

5 Steve Schanes, "Steve Schanes," interviewed by Rod Underhill, *Comics Interview* #55 [Summer 1988], pgs. 53–54.

6 Richard Felber, "First Comics Sues Marvel Comics for Anti-Competitive Activities," news item, *The Comics Journal* #89 [May 1984], pg. 8. (Attribution being unclear in the article, Felber is best guess, as the quote could also have been made by First publisher Rick Obadiah or text from court filing.)

7 Ibid.

8 David Scroggy, "Thrillogy" listing, *Pacific Premieres* #4 [July 1983], pg. 2.

9 Tim Conrad, interviewed by the author.

10 Ibid.

11 Ibid.

12 Bob Sodaro, "Running for the Sun," *Amazing Heroes* #40 [Feb. 1, 1984], pg. 31.

13 Pat Broderick, "Running for the Sun," *Amazing Heroes* #40 [Feb. 1, 1984], pg. 32.

14 Roger McKenzie, "Running for the Sun," *Amazing Heroes* #40 [Feb. 1, 1984], pg. 32.

15 Broderick, pg. 36.

16 Sodaro, pgs. 36–37.

17 Sodaro, pg. 33.

18 Roger McKenzie, "Me & Rod: Sun-Running in the Twilight Zone," commentary, *The Comics Journal* #106 [Mar. 1986], pg. 47.

19 Ibid.

20 Arthur Suydam, "Arthur Suydam," interviewed by Steve Ringgenberg, *Comics Interview* #18 [Dec. 1984], pg. 41.

21 Arthur Suydam, "Spotlighting the Fringe: Back Issue Talks With Arthur Suydam," interviewed by Dan Johnson, *Back Issue* #11 [Aug. 2005], pg. 80.

22 Steve Schanes, Facebook message to Jon B. Cooke [May 2, 2023].

23 Mike Friedrich, interviewed by Jon B. Cooke [May 3, 2023].

24 Steve Schanes, Facebook message.

25 Richard Corben, interviewed by Jon B. Cooke [Nov. 11, 2013].

26 Ibid.

27 Will Meugniot, testimonial [May 2, 2023].

28 Ibid.

29 Steve Schanes, interviewed by Jon B. Cooke [May 23, 2023].

30 Erwin Knoll, "Phoenix Features Offers New Comic Strips, Panel," "Syndicates" column item, *Editor & Publisher* Vol. 84 #51 [Dec. 15, 1951], pg. 48. (Knoll quotes syndicate promotional material.)

31 Schanes interview [May 23, 2023].

32 Jerry Iger, "Epilogue — Chapter 3: Historic Notes: Memories of Sheena," *The Iger Comics Kingdom* [1985, Blackthorne], pg. 83.

33 Lee Caplin, "Epilogue — Chapter 2: The Caplin-Iger Company, Limited," *The Iger Comics Kingdom* [1985, Blackthorne], pg. 79.

34 Lee Caplin, interviewed by Jon B. Cooke [May 24, 2023].

35 Bo Hampton, "The Gory Days of Pacific Comics: Bruce Jones and Company Recall *Alien Worlds* and *Twisted Tales*," interviewed by Dan Johnson, *Back Issue* #2 [Feb. 2004], pg. 69.

36 Geoff Rosengren, "One and Done — *Pathways to Fantasy* #1," review, The Tell Tale Mind website [July 18, 2020], *https://thetelltalemind. com/2020/07/18/one-and-done-pathways-to-fantasy-1/*.

37 Bruce Jones, "The Gory Days of Pacific Comics: Bruce Jones and Company Recall *Alien Worlds* and *Twisted Tales*," interviewed by Dan Johnson, *Back Issue* #2 [Feb. 2004], pg. 68.

38 Bill Schanes, "Ed Catto: The (Not Quite) Secret Origin of Pacific Comics," interviewed by Ed Catto, Comicmix website [Aug. 31, 2015], *https://www. comicmix.com/2015/08/31/ed-catto-the-not-quite-secret-origin-of-pacific-comics/*.

39 Anthony Dellaflora, "New Comics Shun ZAP! BAM! POW!," *Albuquerque Journal* [May 13, 1984], pg. 6.

40 David Scroggy, "David Scroggy," interviewed by Jeff Gelb, *Comics Interview* #11 [May 1984], pgs 68–69.

41 Mark Evanier, "The Rise & Fall of Pacific Comics: The Inside Story of a Pioneering Publisher," *San Diego Reader* website [Aug. 19, 2004], *https://www. sandiegoreader.com/news/2004/ aug/19/two-men-and-their-comic-books/*.

42 Steve Schanes, "Steve Schanes," interviewed by Rod Underhill, *Comics Interview* #55 [Summer 1988], pg. 52.

43 Steve Duin and Mike Richardson, "Pacific Comics" entry, *Comics: Between the Panels* [1998, Dark Horse Comics], pg. 345.

44 Scroggy, *Comics Interview* #11, pg. 68.

45 Tom Heintjes, "Pacific suspends operations," news item, *The Comics Journal* #93 [Sept. 1984], pgs. 9–10.

46 Heintjes, pg. 10.

47 Jay Allen Sanford, "The Rise & Fall of Pacific Comics: The Inside Story of a Pioneering Publisher," *San Diego Reader* website [Aug. 19, 2004], *https://www. sandiegoreader.com/news/2004/ aug/19/two-men-and-their-comic-books/*.

48 Scroggy, *Comics Intvw* #11, pgs. 59–60.

49 Scroggy, *Telegraph Wire*, pgs. 23–24.

50 Bill Schanes, Facebook post [Dec. 28, 2018].

This spread: On previous page is Rick Geary's header for the *Three Dimensional Alien Worlds* editorial page. At top is Al Williamson's header for *Pathways to Fantasy*.

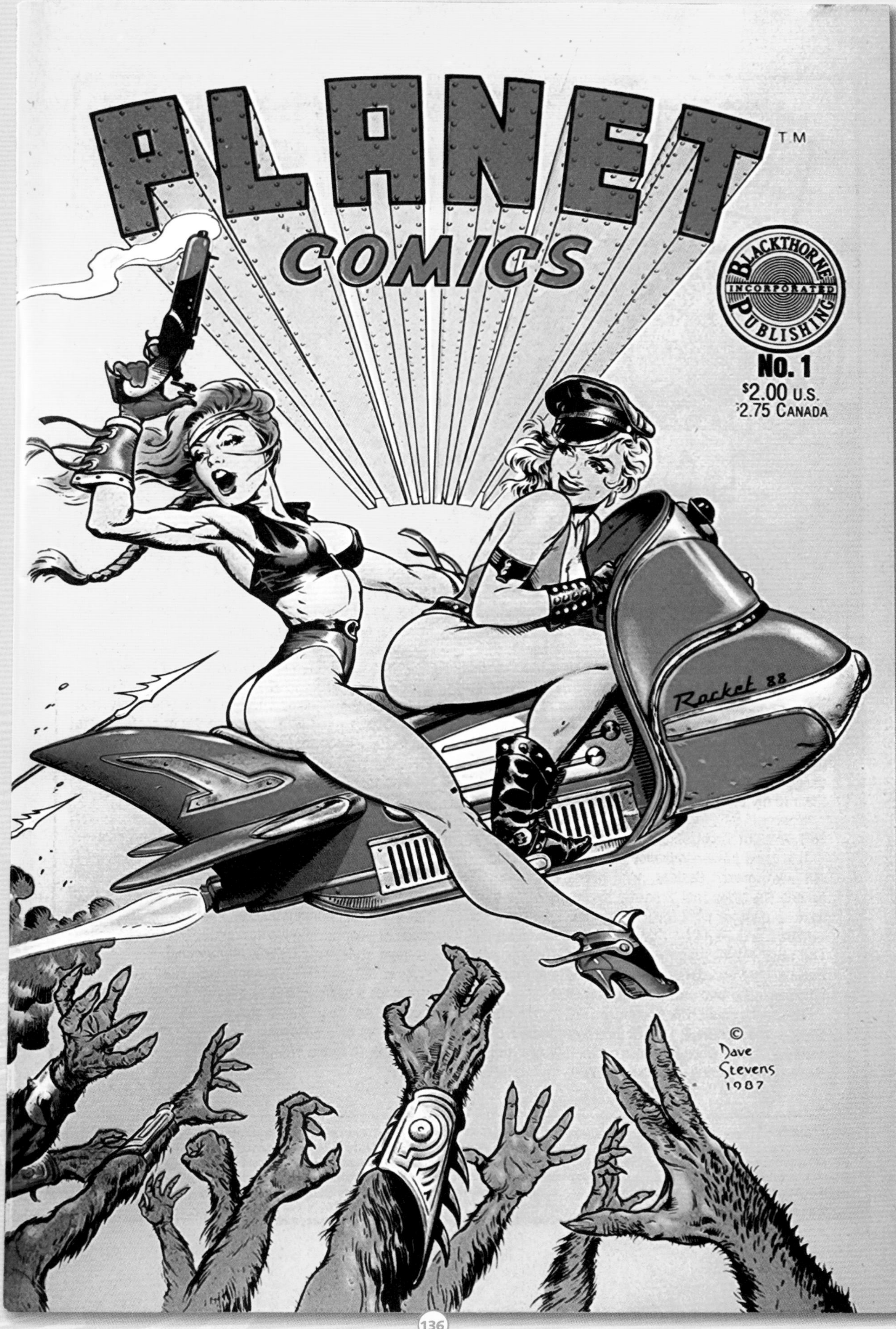
PLANET
COMICS
TM
BLACKTHORNE
INCORPORATED
PUBLISHING
NO. 1
$2.00 U.S.
$2.75 CANADA
Rocket 88
© Dave Stevens 1987

Pacific Comics Runs Aground

"It's like a bottomless pit…"

So said Steve Schanes regarding Pacific suspending operations in late summer 1984. "If you're losing money on distribution," he told *The Comics Journal*, "it doesn't matter if you're making money on publishing. You've got to correct distribution."[1] For six months, at least, the distribution division had been hemorrhaging cash. The aftershocks of 1983's "Black September" continued to decimate the company's finances. "There was a radical change in the marketplace last September," Steve said in 1984, "and we got adapting too slowly to it."[2]

The equal tragedy, of course, was the other half of the business also suffered as a result. "Perhaps most striking," *TCJ* reported, "is the fact that Schanes is suspending his publishing efforts, which are profitable, in order to tend to his ailing distributorship. While this does not completely cut off any income (the black-&-white trade books, as well as the portfolios, will come out as intended), it will interrupt the steady influx of money that the color comics provided. According to Schanes, this action was necessary in order to focus all manpower and attention on repairing distribution: 'Since the publishing is not making enough money to ward off the losses of distribution, I've got to put all my emphasis on distribution.'"[3]

Curiously, the inverse was expressed by the other Schanes sibling in Dan Gearino's 2019 book, *Comic Shop: The Retail Mavericks Who Gave Us a New Geek Culture*: "Pacific had gotten the attention of the industry when it became a comics publisher in 1981, in addition to being a distributor. 'We extended ourselves too far with too many publishing programs,' said Bill Schanes of Pacific. In some cases, the company gave advance payment to artists who did not complete the work or were late. Then the industry hit a mini-downturn, which led some shops to go out of business while owing Pacific money.

"'All of those things added up to us being in a negative cash-flow position, and we were unable to pull out,' Schanes said. He thinks the distribution side could have survived if not for the losses on the publishing side."[4]

Hey Retailer's! Here's this month's blockbusters from Pacific Comics

PACIFIC PRESENTS #6

George Perez cover and 6 page pencils. Dubay & Severin's "Spitfire", the first installment of a new character "Salimba", who will be the lead feature next issue. Written by Steve Perry, pencilled by Paul Chadwick, inked by Tom Palmer. Also an unpublished 4 pager by Neal Adams.

$1.50 x quantity ______ = ______

Pacific Presents #6 — 32 pages, quality stock, Perez cover, September.

FAMOUS FEATURES #4 (3-D)

Hot on the heels of *3-D Alien Worlds* comes this re-print of an obscure 50's 3-D book. All 3-D has been re-done by Ray Zone for this edition. A new Sheena cover by Dave Stevens is also reproduced in 3-D inside. 2 pairs of viewing glasses are bound in.

$2.00 x quantity ______ = ______

3-D Sheena (Jerry Iger's Famous Features #4) — 32 pages with 2 sets of glasses, Dave Stevens cover, September.

TWISTED TALES #11

Edited by Bruce Jones and April Campbell. An anthology of contemporary horror stories. A Joe Chiodo cover in the manner of the classic illustrators. Recommended for mature readers, who are responding with enthusiasm.

$1.50 x quantity ______ = ______

Twisted Tales #11 — 32 pages, quality stock, Chiodo cover, September.

ECHO of FUTUREPAST #4

Edited by Neal Adams, published by Continuity. All main features continue: Bucky O'Hare by Hama and Golden, Frankenstein / Dracula / Werewolf by Neal Adams, Mudwogs by Suydam, Hom by Giminez. Recommended for mature readers.

$2.95 x quantity ______ = ______

Echo of Futurepast #4 — 48 pages, quality stock, Suzuki cover, September.

PATHWAYS to FANTASY #2

Edited by Jones and Campbell. Frank Brunner provides one of his best recent stories, "The Reading". Also a Chris Miller/Roger McKenzie full-color fantasy, a Jay Muth/Kent Williams collaboration and Scott Hampton. A moody cover by Jeff Jones.

$1.50 x quantity ______ = ______

Pathways to Fantasy #2 — 32 pages, quality stock, Jones cover, September.

CHALLENGER #1

This new title will feature color material from *Warrior*, and will alternate bi-monthly with *Pressbutton*. V for Vendetta by Alan Moore and David Lloyd is featured, also lot of John Bolton. Great stuff, seen by many for the first time.

$1.50 x quantity ______ = ______

Challenger #1 — 32 pages, quality stock, Bolton cover, September.

FAMOUS STARS of the 1930's

Black and white trade paperback reproduces a very interesting newspaper strip from the Iger shop. Same impulse-priced 3½" x 11" format as *Heroes of Sport*, announced last month. Ships August.

$2.95 x quantity ______ = ______

Famous Stars of the 1930's — 48 pages, black and white on quality stock, 3½" x 11", August.

VANGUARD ILLUSTRATED #10

D. Scroggy, editor. Tim Truman barbarioan cover highlights "Barbarian Morning" by new talents Wooley & Tidwell, inked by Alcala. 2 pages of Dave Stevens from his new talent days. New appearance of a major character, "Bourbon Thret" by Geof Darrow. "Sentinel" by McKenzie & Van Hook.

$1.50 x quantity ______ = ______

Vanguard Illustrated #10 — 32 pages, quality stock, Truman cover, September.

Previous page: *Planet Comics* #1 [Apr. 1988] cover by Dave Stevens. **Inset left:** Solicitation page featuring items left unpublished by Pacific. **Below:** Steve Schanes and his wife, Ann E. Fera, founded Blackthorne Publishing immediately after Pacific's collapse.

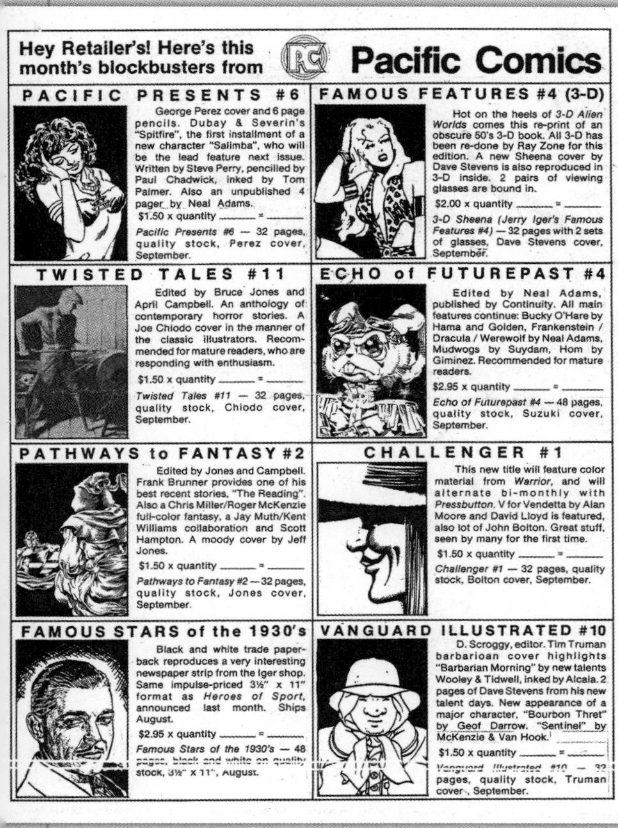

"BEYOND THE POINT OF TURNING BACK"

At least in theory, Steve offered that the company looked relatively solvent. "Pacific Comics, at the end, had, on paper, not a bad mix, or ratio, of receivables to payables," he told Rod Underhill. "Our receivables were around $500,000. Our payables were probably around $750,000. We had $500,000 of inventory paid for, on paper. It would have washed. The receivables were coming in too slow, the aging [*the amount of time a bill went unpaid*] couldn't bank the receivables because the receivables were over the aging limit, and the payables were due and the inventory was not selling. We did not see ourselves turning around no matter how many physical hours we were putting in — 80 or 100 hours a week — it wasn't going to turn around, so we decided to liquidate it… They were both under the same corporate umbrella: Blue Dolphin Enterprises. There was no way to salvage one without the other. So, therefore, we concentrated, at the end, to make profitable the unprofitable end, which was distribution. But it was beyond the point of turning back."[5]

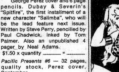

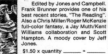

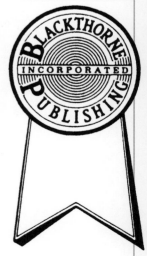

PUBLISHER'S STATEMENT

MARKET CONDITIONS: For a small publisher, like ourselves, the current market conditions are frustrating. The market place (comic stores) has switched emphasis, from back issues to new comics. Distributors have had to re-think their buying procedures. Publishers have had to come up with a better product mix. The two major publishers are in the best cash position to exploit these conditions.

Pacific is in a cash flow bind. We ask only for your understanding, while we work out our problems. Our releases will continue to be sporadic for the forseeable future. Comic book publishers are in the middle of a shake out. By the end of 1984 there will be significantly fewer publishers than there are now. Pacific will make it through this troubled time, and emerge as a strong company. We will be listing very few new titles until we catch up on the titles already solicited.

A revised schedule is listed below.

We thank you for your confidence.

STEVE SCHANES
Publisher

Above: Publisher statement appearing in the last issue of *Pacific Premieres*, #18 [Sept. 1984].

In spite of those fatal mistakes (which included Pacific taking out onerous loans of over $400,000, borrowed at interest rates in excess of 20%),[6] comics insider Mark Evanier opined, "Bill and Steve Schanes were able to succeed as long as they did as publishers because they had access to distribution through the direct sales market, including their stores. And, for a while, Pacific Comics as a publisher was a glorious experiment. It did not last, but that was not because the idea was flawed. It didn't last because this was a new field, a new kind of distribution, a new business, and people hadn't fully understood the business model. They hadn't figured out how to make it work yet. Pacific did not last very long, but it was very important, because a lot of other companies sprung up and a lot of them were successful, at least for a while. And DC and Marvel and the other established companies converted their business models accordingly. And now DC and Marvel sell through the direct sales market. And it's the reason that those companies are still in business, because newsstands are not a source of profit anymore."[7]

Inset right: *Amazing Heroes* #56 [Oct. 1, 1984] shares the sad announcement that, effective Aug. 31, Pacific Comics was suspending operations. Three weeks later, the Schanes brothers threw in the towel.

A PROUD LEGACY

Interviewed by Ed Catto, Bill Schanes assessed Pacific's short but unprecedented history: "Those early days were very innocent, as there really weren't any rules or boundaries at that time. Competition was limited in the 'super-hero' genre to DC and Marvel only, so we felt there was a fairly large gap into what we thought the market would respond to, which was to break out of the mold, and introduce new concepts that featured the creative teams as much, if not more than the character name, as any characters that Pacific Comics would be introducing would be brand new to both retailers and consumers.

"While we had a general idea as to what we wanted to publish, we didn't have a formal business plan at that time (silly looking back on it now).

"It's also important to remember that, in the late '70s

NEWSFLASHES

PACIFIC SUSPENSION: Effective immediately, Pacific Comics has suspended publication of its color comic book line for a period of "around two months," according to STEVE SCHANES, co-publisher of the company.

Schaner said that the company was experiencing "cash-flow problems" and that he was putting publishing on temporary hold so that he can reorganize his unprofitable distribution system. "It's like a bottomless pit," Schanes said, commenting on the distribution side of his business. "If you're making money publishing, it doesn't matter, if you're losing even more on distribution."

The sole exception to the suspension is ***Twisted Tales* #9**, which should ship sometime soon. The last books shipped by Pacific were: ***Echo of Futurepast* #2**, ed. by NEAL ADAMS; ***Pathways to Fantasy* #1**, ed. by BRUCE JONES; ***Vanguard Illustrated* #7**, ed. by DAVE SCROGGY; and ***Vanity* #2**, written and drawn by WILL MEUGNIOT.

Schanes listed 14 books that he has in film form, ready to be printed as soon as he rectifies his cash-flow problems. They are: ***Alien Worlds* #8**, ed. by BRUCE JONES; ***Berni Wrightson, Master of the Macabre* #5**; ***Challenger* #1**, by ALAN MOORE and DAVID LLOYD; ***Groo Special* #1**, by SERGIO ARAGONES and MARK EVANIER; ***Jerry Iger's Famous Features* #4**; ***Pacific Presents* #5**, by DAVE STEVENS; ***Pacific Presents* #6**; ***Pressbutton* #1**, by PEDRO HENRY and STEVE DILLON; ***Siegel & Shuster: Dateline 1930's***; ***Somerset Holmes* #5**, by BRUCE JONES, APRIL CAMPBELL, and BRENT ANDERSON; ***Strange Days* #1**, written by PETER MILLIGAN; ***Sun Runners* #4**, by ROGER McKENZIE and PAT BRODERICK; and ***Vanguard Illustrated* #8 and #9**.

The Continuity Publishing books (***Megalith, Echo of Futurepast, Zero Patrol***) will not be affected by the suspension, since Pacific only handled color separations and printing. They will continue independently.

Only the four-color comic books will be affected by the change. The upcoming portfolios, black-and-white reprint trade paperbacks, and other projects will continue to appear.

*Although titles like Pacific's **Berni Wrightson** reprints are on hold, Continuity projects should continue apace.*

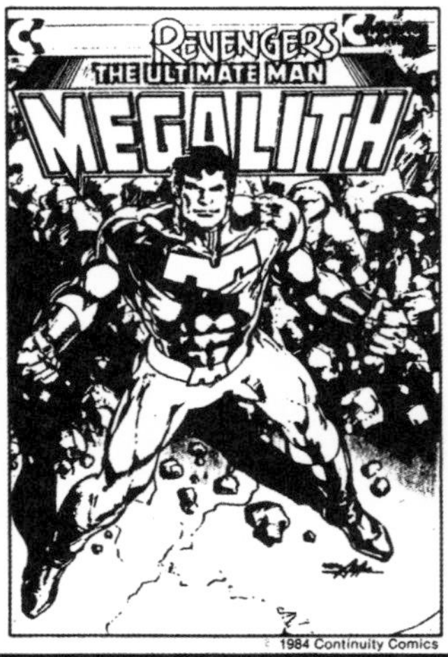
REVENGERS
THE ULTIMATE MAN
MEGALITH

© 1984 Continuity Comics

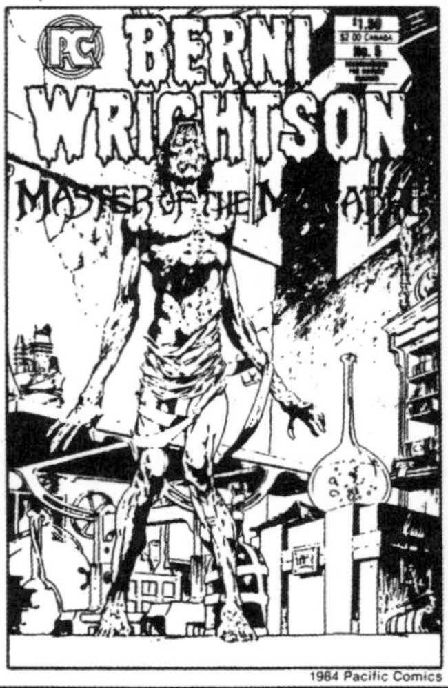
PC
BERNI WRIGHTSON
MASTER OF THE MACABRE
$1.50
$2.00 CANADA

© 1984 Pacific Comics

and early '80s, there weren't thousands upon thousands of comic book specialty retailers. Pacific Comics was also the largest wholesaler/distributor of comic books on the West Coast at the time, so we had a very good relationship with the vast majority of the comic book specialty retailers out West. We felt that they would treat us as one of their own, as DC and Marvel were those 'New York guys,' who really hadn't established any type of retailer programs yet.

"Pacific Comics was the first 'mainstream' comic book publisher who exclusively sold into comic book specialty market retailers (no newsstand), so the retailers really responded positively to this via very large initial order commitments. We combined key creators (Kirby, Ditko, Adams, Wrightson, Jones...) with what, at the time, was cutting-edge color separations (blue line/gray line), upscale paper stock, which allowed for higher quality reproduction, and heat-set printing. This basically means that once the ink was applied to the paper, the ink 'set' on top of the paper. This is opposed to the traditional cold press printing method of the previous 40-plus years, which the ink absorbed into the paper, and also transferred to the readers' hands fairly easily."[8]

Bill also shared a curious procedure he developed. "I had played with the idea of 'ranking' the talent/creators based on sales of the books they had worked on over the recent past few years (somewhat similar to sports stats). At that time (before [*spreadsheet software*] Excel), I put together a grid of sales stats (on a large oversized graph paper), broken down by writer, penciler, inker, letterer, colorist, editor, and any other individuals involved in the creative process. Each month, I'd update the data to include the most recent sales. I also put a 'point value' on each sales level for each category of creator, so, when we wanted to put together an editorial team, we wanted to make sure that each new book or story within a book would have a 'point value' which we felt would represent the best opportunity to achieve sales of previous books they had worked on. While it wasn't 100% scientific, it proved to be pretty helpful."[9]

CHANGING VIBES

San Diego resident Craig Deeley, who had a back-up story, "Donner Beck's Machine: A Cautionary Tale," in *Starslayer* #6 [Apr. 1983], recalled a changing atmosphere at Pacific over the course of its existence.

When he first arrived in its early days looking for work, "They were still just getting up a head of steam with publishing," he said. "I think they were open to ideas and didn't have an overload of scripts or material laying around to unload one on a budding artist."[10]

Deeley continued, "I interacted with Steve Schanes and mostly with David Scoggy. Dave was a super-mellow guy. Very open and totally into the business and seemed genuinely interested in boosting new talent. Everyone at the offices was very pleasant, totally into comics, and making their publishing business a hit... I recall coming into the offices later — probably to see the printed version of *Starslayer* #6. Things had got a lot more serious."

He explained, "The high page rates were a factor in Pacific's business. High production rates with no guarantee of sales seemed to be a major concern. I got the impression that everything was a fragile balance of expense to profit and with the publishing business and the newness of alternate supply chains being invented — that there was a lot of insecurity. Even then, on my last visits, some of the fun of being a new publisher seemed to be wearing off. My experience with the Pacific folks was good, but I could feel the change of vibe at the offices on my last visits."[11]

The writing was on the wall for the folks at Pacific.

PACIFIC COMICS DISTRIBUTORS 8423 PRODUCTION AVENUE SAN DIEGO, CALIFORNIA 92121-2278 (619) 566-3290

May 22, 1984

Dear Distributor:

For the first time in Pacific Comics history, we are now remaindering some of our overstock.

Prices from 80 to 90 percent off cover price. Here is a list of which books are being remaindered.

MIN. ORDER/TITLE		ORIGINAL RETAIL	SLASHED	NOW ONLY
50	ART OF AL WILLIAMSON	$ 7.95	80%	1.59 0
34	BLADE RUNNER SKETCHBOOK	6.95	80%	1.39 0
52	ILLUSTRATED BLADE RUNNER	6.95	80%	1.39 0
60	BLADE RUNNER PORTFOLIOS	9.95	80%	1.99 0
44	PAPERBACKS U.S.A.	10.95	82%	1.97 0
50	X-MEN INDEX	5.95	80%	1.19 0
50	DAREDEVIL INDEX	5.95	80%	1.19 0
36	ROBERT CRUMB CHECKLIST	10.95	82%	1.97 0
20	1983 OVERSTREET PRICE GUIDE	9.95	90%	.99 0
200	ROG 2000	2.95	80%	.59 0

TERMS: FIRST COME-FIRST SERVE
30 DAY CREDIT
FREIGHT: F.O.B.

We will accept phone orders, so call today.

Sincerely,

BILL D. SCHANES
President

Above: Intent on increasing cash-flow, even months before the end of the company, Pacific partner Bill Schanes sent out a notice to rival distributors offering massive discounts on its overstock, including the Blue Dolphin inventory. **Below:** Initially, Pacific declared a temporary two-month suspension, which was announced on Aug. 30, 1984. But, three weeks later, the company was liquidated as the corporation was turned over to a holding company. This headline appeared in *The Comics Journal* #95 [Feb. 1985].

character in 1938), Morrissey | asked Lee and Kirby to create a super-hero team because the | that he and Marvel have been in

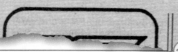

Pacific Comics liquidated

All assets being sold off; Pacific president Schanes starts new publishing company

Pacific Comics, which suspended its publishing efforts

on a per-share basis.
In determining who gets paid first, Sprink said that the banks ... Pacific get

paid, totalling $450,000.
The latter figure, according to Schanes, represents what ... retailers owe

Inset right: Promotional image for the HBO/USA Network cable TV horror anthology series, *The Hitchhiker,* initially broadcast in 1983–91. Bruce Jones and April Campbell wrote episodes for early seasons. **Below:** Eclipse Comics published the left-over *Alien Worlds* and *Twisted Tales* material after the collapse of Pacific Comics, and they also released *The Twisted Tales of Bruce Jones,* featuring reprints of his earlier comics work. **Inset bottom:** From left, Bill Schanes, Bruce Jones, David Scroggy, and April Campbell pose with *Twisted Tales* #2 [Apr. 1983].

The Hitchhiker

ALIEN WORLDS

THE TWISTED TALES OF
BRUCE JONES
Part 1 of 2

TWISTED TALES

HITCHHIKING TO HOLLYWOOD

While it would cost the couple to extract themselves from the comics realm,* Bruce Jones and April Campbell did land on their feet as writers on the HBO cable horror/thriller series, *The Hitchhiker.* Unfortunately, after Pacific's demise, the two were left holding the bag.

Asked in 2012 about his days at Pacific Comics, Jones offered, "Being an independent publisher is not unlike being an indy filmmaker. The upside is that you have total control; no one can interfere with your dream. The downside is that all those little things — and there are billions of them — from writing the checks to mollifying the next egomaniac artist falls squarely on your shoulders. So the danger is that you can become so caught up in business minutiae, you don't have as much time to concentrate on the creative.

"It helps to be young and naïve. We made some terrible business mistakes. I had a publishing concern in the Midwest before I came to San Diego to work with Pacific Comics. The tax laws in the Midwest provided for a much less expensive set-up than in California. It cost a lot just to get started in that state, just as it costs a lot to do anything in California. As a result, I kept Bruce Jones Associates a family run business so we could get off the ground, rather than protecting myself with high corporation costs. We never would have been able to do the books otherwise.

"Unfortunately, when Pacific went belly up and stopped with the paychecks — including mine — I was left holding the bag with the other creators to the tune of several thousand dollars. I wanted everyone I'd used on my books to get paid for what they did, even if it wasn't going to be published, so I did that by emptying my own bank account. It was very stupid of me, and no one but my close friends really understood the situation or what we went through. There's a price to pay for creative freedom, sometimes quite a high one. When you work for a studio or another publisher, there's little danger of this — but you also rarely get final cut and someone is always looking over your shoulder… usually someone who knows nothing about the creative process and whose chief interest is in the bottom line. It's a trade-off."[12]

Jones, who hasn't worked in comics since the early 2010s, was asked by Richard Arndt about the post-Pacific years. He replied, "That part of my life is a blur. There were so many things colliding simultaneously, I don't know how we wrapped our minds around it. *Somerset Holmes* had been [*optioned as a movie*] to Ed Pressman at Warner Bros., so April and I were working on the screenplay and on staff at HBO and trying to move our stuff from San Diego to Thousand Oaks — and then Pacific calls to say they're throwing in the towel. We took our line of books to Eclipse. They began meddling with the editorial pages and making life more difficult, just not getting the feel of the books at all. There were also some unscrupulous things going on in the background from various parties. April and I ended up paying some of the artists out of our own pockets, which was a hell of a drain, especially at the time. Even then, a few people apparently still never got reimbursed for their work, or so I'm told. Let's just say I learned pretty quickly who my friends were. I prefer to think that the good times and good people of San Diego made up for the bad, and leave it at that."[13]

* Bruce Jones did not leave comics completely. In fact, in addition to writing Richard Corben's *Rip in Time* in the mid-'80s, as well as the *Flash Gordon* comic strip in the early '90s, the writer scribed a sensational run of *The Incredible Hulk* between 2002–04, before signing an exclusive contract with DC in 2004.

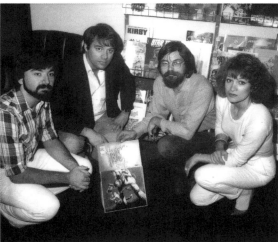

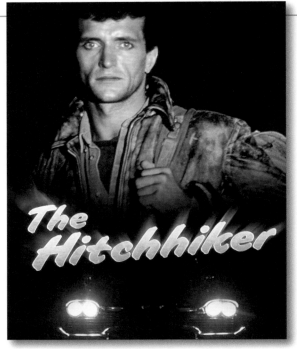

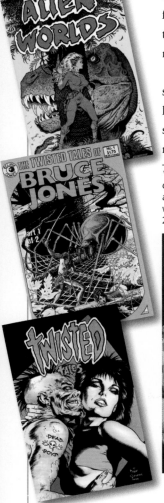

While the Joneses hitched a ride to Tinseltown, their San Diego-based brethren, now without tether after the disintegration of Pacific, had to each find a new job and, unsurprisingly, the top three guys would all secure refuge in the comic book industry they had helped to alter.

Even before the dissolution of Pacific, Steve Schanes maintained a determination to continue as a publisher, and he and wife Ann E. Fera founded Blackthorne Publishing, which existed between 1984–90, having produced (according to the Grand Comics Database) 156 separate titles and 538 individual issues. Their beginning was modest, Steve explained. "Blackthorne started with very little money. It started on *borrowed* money, $20,000 borrowed off of credit cards," he told Mark Borax.[14]

The publisher specialized in newspaper strip collections and, most prominently, in 3-D comics, with which they found great success with *California Raisins in 3-D*, as Blackthorne's novelty comics were being sold in non-traditional outlets, such as Spencer Gifts and Hallmark [greeting card] stores. One title that was a unexpected failure for the company was the heavily invested *Moonwalker in 3-D*, an adaptation of Michael Jackson's film.

(Curiously, one Blackthorne side gig was creating props for use in movies and television, such as a children's book produced to resemble one by Dr. Seuss for use in the *Amazing Stories* TV show.)

Bill Schanes would have a long career working as an executive for one-time business rival Steve Geppi. Bill would rise to the position of vice president for purchasing at Diamond Distribution and spend 28 years with Geppi's company until he retired in April 2018 to travel the world.

David Scroggy, drawing on his pre-Pacific experience with the San Diego Comic-Con, became an organizer for the annual San Diego Comic Book Expo and he also expanded his stable as artist rep for comics professionals. In 1989, he joined Dark Horse Comics, in Portland, Oregon, as an editor, and in 1993, he launched Dark Horse's product development department. David would also return as a columnist in the pages of the publication formerly known as *The Buyer's Guide*. In 2017, David retired from his position as DH vice president and is currently living in Scotland with wife Rosemary, a fellow Pacific Comics alumnus.

"We were a bunch of kids," David told Steve Duin and Mike Richardson, "who didn't know what we were doing, who latched onto something big and powerful and didn't know what to do when we evolved into a corporate structure and it all blew into a million pieces."[15]

While the business entity known as Pacific Comics was decisively liquidated into oblivion, the freelancer-friendly innovations it pioneered — epitomized by the contract the Schanes brothers enjoined Mike Friedrich to draft prior to publishing their first comic book — simply revolutionized the entire industry. The impact Steve, Bill, and Dave made through their Pacific Comics endeavors would forever change the course of comics history, whether in terms of the production of comics as in improving coloring techniques and using better grades of paper, forcing the major publishers to recognize the rights of creators to own their own work, or injecting an excitement into the direct sales marketplace that made the field as invigorating to be a part of as it had been in the Golden Age. For all this, and for many of its fine publications, Pacific Comics deserves to be remembered, studied, and celebrated.

Pacific Comics Knows You're Important.
Share Our New Era in Comics

Above: Certainly one of the most important developments in the history of creators' rights in U.S. comics was when Pacific Comics solicited artists and writers to join them with an entirely new type of contract, one composed by Mike Friedrich when he consulted for the company. The document was subsequently used as a template for contracts across the industry. Pacific actively sought creators with a pamphlet that listed the benefits. This is the booklet's cover, courtesy of Columbia University.

Remnant Sale: In the Wake of Pacific

Topps
VICTORY

SERGIO ARAGONÉS'
GROO
THE WANDERER

PRELUDE
DEATHWATCH 2000
Ms MYSTIC

NOW MONTHLY!
STARSLAYER
WANTED
DEAD or ALIVE

BERNI
WRIGHTSON
MASTER OF THE MACABRE

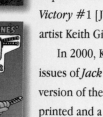

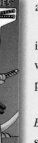

Perhaps the collapse of Pacific could have been foreseen, but it was a sudden and catastrophic end to the company all the same, as it had a number of planned releases in the pipeline, titles that suddenly were without a home... until other publishers came to their rescue, that is!

CAPTAIN VICTORY

Captain Victory would surface again in a Topps comic, *Victory* #1 [June 1994], with writer Kurt Busiek and artist Keith Giffen. Planned for five issues, it lasted one.

In 2000, Kirby grandson Jeremy Kirby published three issues of *Jack Kirby Comics*, a retelling and rearranged version of the *Captain Victory* story. Two issues were printed and a third was published online.

TwoMorrows produced *Captain Victory: Graphite Edition,* in 2003, featuring Kirby's pencil art in the supposed page order of the graphic novel as intended.

Marvel printed a six-issue mini-series, *Jack Kirby's Galactic Bounty Hunters,* under their Icon imprint in 2006. Based on discovered and originally rejected characters created for Kirby's "Wonder Warriors," youngest daughter Lisa co-wrote and is owner of the property. Captain Victory makes a guest appearance in the third issue.

In 2011–12, Dynamite Entertainment published a six-issue run of *Kirby: Genesis—Captain Victory* using the talents of a variety of creators and, again in 2014–15, with *Captain Victory and the Galactic Rangers* for six issues.

ALIEN WORLDS

Eclipse retained the Pacific numbering for the science-fiction anthology series, publishing #8–9 in 1984–85. Eclipse then launched *Alien Encounters,* their own science-fiction anthology series — unaffiliated with Bruce Jones Associates — using a logo quite similar to *Alien Worlds*. The knock-off series lasted 14 issues, from 1985–87, employing many of the same creators from *Alien Worlds*, including some scripts from Jones. In 1988, Eclipse convinced Jones to return with a new *Alien Worlds* series as a semi-annual "prestige format" special that only lasted one issue.

GROO THE WANDERER

Groo started in 1982 as a four-page wordless vignette in Eclipse's *Destroyer Duck* #1. After departing Pacific, Sergio Aragonés had Eclipse publish the *Groo Special* one-shot (originally intended to be a Pacific release) and he then went to Marvel, where *Sergio Aragonés Groo the Wanderer* endured for 120 issues as an Epic Comic release. The title was briefly published by Image Comics [1994–95] and, by 1998, he and his faithful dog, Rufferto, found a new home at Dark Horse Comics, where *Groo* has been irregularly published ever since, usually in four-issue standalone story arcs. One estimate is that 200 or so separate issues of *Groo* have been produced, all told.

MS. MYSTIC

After Pacific's end, Continuity Comics published *Ms. Mystic* and, between 1987–92, nine issues (including reprints of Pacific's #1 and #2) were produced. *Ms. Mystic: Deathwatch 2000* lasted three issues in 1993, and *Ms. Mystic* relaunched for four issues in 1993–94.

STARSLAYER

When his Pacific contract expired, Mike Grell elected to take *Starslayer* to First Comics, continuing Pacific's numbering, lasting for 28 issues [1983–85].

Grell later released an expanded version of the Pacific Comics issues at Acclaim Comics, that ran for eight issues in 1995, titled *Starslayer: The Director's Cut*.

TWISTED TALES

The Bruce Jones-edited horror anthology had three issues planned when Pacific tanked, and he took the *Twisted Tales* material over to Eclipse, which continued the Pacific numbering, publishing #9–10 in 1984. In 1986, Steve Schanes at Blackthorne produced *Twisted Tales 3-D* as a one-shot. That same year also saw a four-issue series from Eclipse, *Twisted Tales of Bruce Jones*.

Similar to its *Alien Encounters*, Eclipse produced its own horror anthology series, theirs titled *Tales of Terror,* for 13 issues between 1985–87. In 1986, they also wooed Bruce Jones back with a "prestige format" version of *Twisted Tales,* which only lasted but a single issue.

BERNIE WRIGHTSON: MASTER OF THE MACABRE

Eclipse published the fifth and final issue in 1984.

ELRIC

First Comics published multiple mini-series featuring Elric and the members of the creative team of the original series. *Elric: Sailor on the Seas of Fate* [seven issues, 1985–86], *Elric: The Weird of the White Wolf* [six, 1986–87], *Elric: The Vanishing Tower* [six, 1987–88], *Elric: The Bane of the Black Sword* [six, 1989], and others.

SILVER STAR

In 1993, Topps Comics announced the limited series, *Jack Kirby's Silver Star,* but only published one issue. In 2006, TwoMorrows Publishing put out *Silver Star: Graphite Edition*. Dynamite Entertainment published seven issues of *Kirby Genesis—Silver Star* [2011–12].

SOMERSET HOLMES

Eclipse Comics would conclude the *Somerset Holmes* series with #5–6 and collect the entire run in a graphic album in 1987.

JERRY IGER'S FAMOUS FEATURES

Pulling from the files of the man himself, Steve Schanes published *Jerry Iger's Famous Features* at Pacific in 1984. One issue was published, but five were solicited in *Pacific Premieres*. Blackthorne would take on the project and produce one issue each of *Jerry Iger's Classic Jumbo Comics, Jerry Iger's Classic Sheena,* and *Jerry Iger's National Comics,* in 1985. The following year would see one issue of *Jerry Iger's Classic Jungle Comics* and six issues of *Jerry Iger's Golden Features* [1986–87].

SUN RUNNERS

Eclipse picked up the title and published #4–8 [1984–85] and Sirius Comics later released two issues of a spin-off, *Tales of the Sun Runners* [1986]. Amazing Comics would then continue *Tales of the Sun Runners,* with #3, and release *Sun Runners Christmas Special*, both in 1987.

PACIFIC COMICS GRAPHIC NOVELS

Pacific advertised two graphic novels, *Seven Samuroid* by Frank Brunner and packaged by Bruce Jones Associates, which was intended to be the debut release. It was advertised in the pages of Pacific comics as early as 1983. It eventually was used to pay off debt to a New Zealand color separation outfit, Image International (no relation to the '90s comics imprint cited below), which published its edition in 1984. *Pacific Premieres* #16 solicited a second Pacific graphic novel, *Freak Show,* by Bruce Jones and Bernie Wrightson, collecting their serial from *Heavy Metal* magazine. Image Comics finally published an American edition in 2006.

The following were solicited but never published by Pacific, though the titles would find homes elsewhere:

AXEL PRESSBUTTON

In 1984, two issues of *Axel Pressbutton*, reprinting the *Warrior* magazine strip, were advertised with a Pacific logo in *Pacific Premieres*. Eclipse went on to publish six issues from 1984–85.

SIEGEL AND SHUSTER: DATELINE 1930'S

In 1984, Pacific advertised *Siegel and Shuster: Dateline 1930s,* but Eclipse published the two issues [1984–85].

STRANGE DAYS

In *Pacific Premieres*, two issues of Peter Milligan and Brendan McCarthy's *Strange Days* were scheduled by Pacific, but never appeared. Eclipse did publish three issues of that anthology title, in 1984–85.

CHALLENGER

In 1984, *Pacific Premieres* promoted *Challenger,* an anthology reprinting British comics from *Warrior* magazine. It was to rotate features that included Alan Moore and David Lloyd's "V for Vendetta"; Steve Parkhouse and John Bolton's "The Spiral Path"; as well as Steve Moore and Bolton's "Father Shandor"; and Alan Moore and Parkhouse's "The Bojeffries Saga." It never appeared, though *V for Vendetta* surfaced at DC Comics [1988–89], *The Spiral Path* had a two-issue Eclipse run [1988], one "Father Shandor" story was in Eclipse's *John Bolton's Halls of Horror* [#2, June 1985], and "Bojeffries" appeared in Fantagraphics' *Flesh and Bone* [1986].

SALIMBA

Paul Chadwick and Stephen Perry's *Salimba*, planned for Pacific release, appeared as a two-issue 3-D series [1986] and a "Deluxe Graphic Novel" [1989] from Blackthorne.

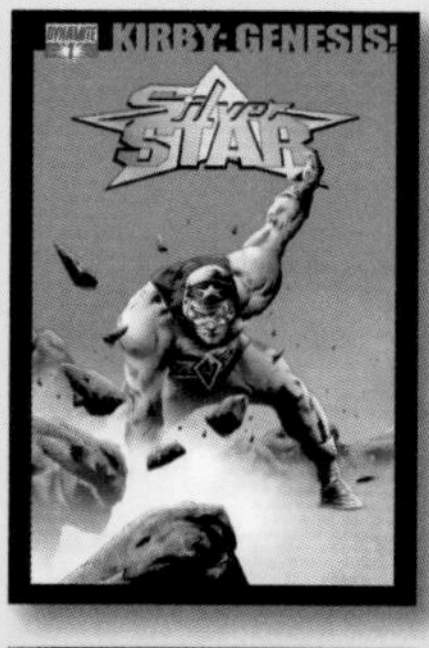
KIRBY: GENESIS!
Silver Star

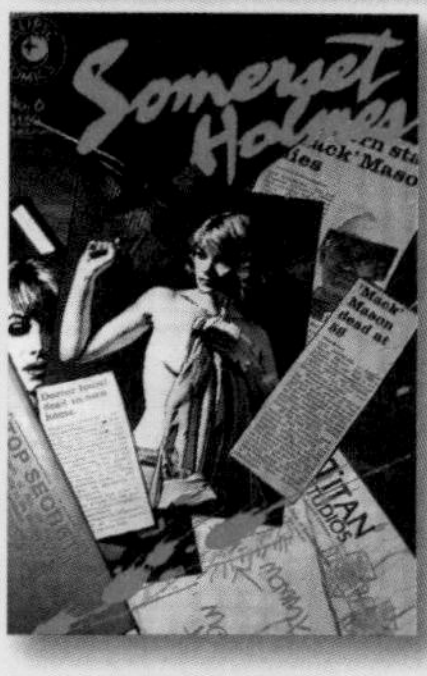
Somerset Holmes

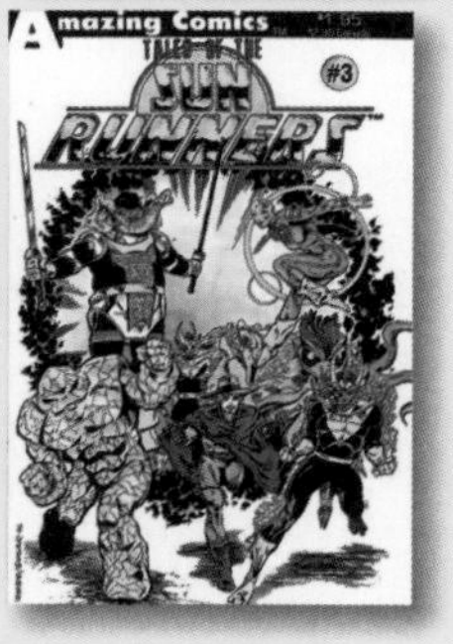
Amazing Comics
Tales of the
Sun Runners
#3

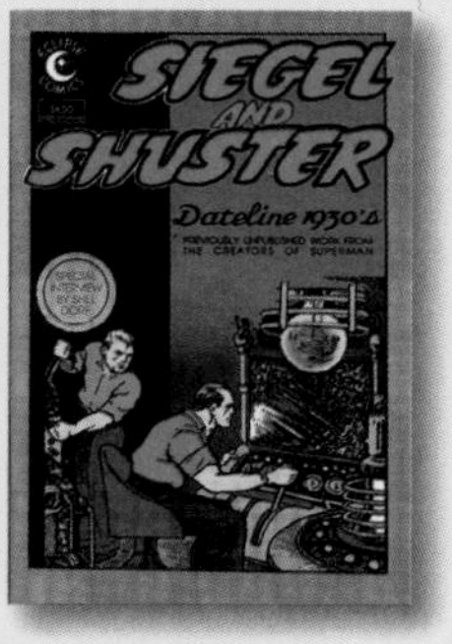
Siegel and Shuster
Dateline 1930's

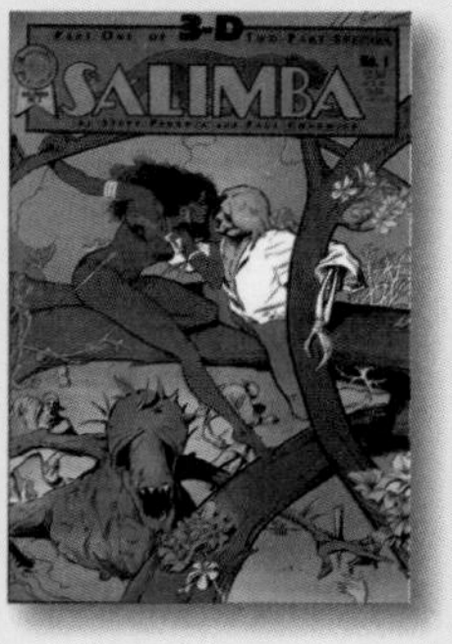
3-D
Salimba

Chapter Notes

[1] Steve Schanes, "Pacific suspends operations," interviewed by Tom Heintjes, news item, *The Comics Journal* #93 [Sept. 1984], pg. 8.
[2] Ibid.
[3] Tom Heintjes, "Pacific suspends operations," news item, *The Comics Journal* #93 [Sept. 1984], pg. 8.
[4] Dan Gearino, *Comic Shop: The Retail Mavericks Who Gave Us a New Geek Culture*, expanded edition [Swallow Press, 2019], pgs. 94–95.
[5] Steve Schanes, "Steve Schanes," interviewed by Rod Underhill, *Comics Interview* #55 [Summer 1988], pgs. 55.
[6] Rod Underhill, "Steve Schanes," *Comics Interview* #55 [Summer 1988], pgs. 55.
[7] Mark Evanier, testimonial, *See You in San Diego: An Oral History of Comic-Con, Fandom, and the Triumph of Geek Culture* [Fantagraphics, 2022], pg. 87–88.
[8] Bill Schanes, "Ed Catto: The (Not Quite) Secret Origin of Pacific Comics," interviewed by Ed Catto, Comicmix website [Aug. 31, 2015], *https://www.comicmix.com/2015/08/31/ed-catto-the-not-quite-secret-origin-of-pacific-comics/*.
[9] Ibid.
[10] Craig Deeley, interviewed by Jon B. Cooke [May 3, 2023].
[11] Ibid.
[12] Bruce Jones, "The Main Event: Remembering Somerset Holmes," Scoop Diamond Galleries website [Nov. 8, 2013], *https://tinyurl.com/ck6act7p*.
[13] Bruce Jones, "A 2008 Interview with Bruce Jones," conducted by Richard Arndt [2008], *https://enjolrasworld.com/Richard%20Arndt/The%20Warren%20Magazines%20Interviews.htm*.
[14] Steve Schanes, "Steve Schanes," interviewed by Mark Borax, *Comics Interview* #54 [Mar. 1988], pg. 34.
[15] David Scroggy, "Pacific Comics" entry, *Comics: Between the Panels* [1998, Dark Horse Comics], pg. 345.
[16] Bill Schanes, Facebook post [Dec. 8, 2016].
[17] Trina Robbins, e-mail to Jon B. Cooke [May 17, 2023].
[18] Steve Schanes, interviewed by author.
[19] Bill Schanes, Facebook post [Oct. 5, 2018].

Absolutely the Very Last Pacific Comics' Comic Book

The final comic book that would have the fingerprint of Pacific Comics — though with no obvious credit or company logo appearing within to indicate its origin — was *Getting the Olympics Story*, a 16-page, self-cover comic book printed on glossy stock. This rarity was produced in time for the Los Angeles-hosted 1984 Summer Olympic Games for client Pacific Bell, the California statewide phone company.

GETTING THE
OLYMPICS
STORY

Bill Schanes said, "The timeline to turn this around from when we won this contract to when the physical book being delivered was really tight, but the creative team took on the challenge and did a fantastic job!"[16] None other than fabled "herstorian" and feminist underground comix cartoonist legend Trina Robbins provided the art with her husband, Steve Leialoha. L. Lois Buhalis and Tom Orzechowski did the lettering.

"That was literally an in-house production!" Trina recently shared. "Tom and Lois lived downstairs, so we just took the finished art downstairs to them to letter. I guess Steve did most of the pencils and I inked. I can tell that the faces and clothes are mine, but that little cigar-chomping editor on page three is definitely by Steve, as are mechanical things like cars. I guess I did it because I needed the money."[17]

"We are always trying to figure out new markets," Steve Schanes explained. "We thought, 'Well, the Olympics would be a huge opportunity.'"[18]

Steve continued, "We made a deal with the Olympic Committee and they had this weird character [*named*] almost like 'f*ck you," or something like that. The weirdest name and it was almost inappropriate to put in a comic. We had to work it out and we did a lot of those comics!" He added, "I can't remember if it was a premium or we sold them, but there was a lot of the comics published. They were distributed all around the world, so that was great."

Bill Schanes on Getting Mind Blown by an EC Legend

I was working for Diamond Comic Distributors and, during the 1986 San Diego Comic Convention, I was walking the convention center floor between meetings when an older gentleman approached me. He was wearing a cowboy-type of hat, a country button-down shirt, bolo tie, jeans, and some boots. He looked at me, then the name on my badge a couple of times (I wasn't sure if he was having trouble reading my name in the small print).I introduced myself and offered to shake his hand, and he said his name was Al.

He told me he was a huge fan of our 1980s Pacific Comics line of comic books, and that many of the titles reminded him of the EC Comics which were published in the 1950s. I told him that was so nice of him; to reference and to compare our line to the incredible line that EC Comics published was more than flattering. It occurred to me that I didn't catch his full name, so I looked at his convention badge, and did a double-take, as it was none other than the great Al Feldstein, one of the all-time great comic book artists, and one of my personal favorites. I told him it was a great honor to meet him, what a huge admirer of his I was, and thanked him for producing so many memorable comics book stories. He told me that he always wanted to draw some new comic book series for Pacific Comics, but never reached out to us (nor did we to him). I told him that we would have been thrilled to be able to publish his works, and we both briefly laughed at the feeling of missed opportunities, and of the mutual respect we had for what each had accomplished. Al gave me his business card, and wrote on the back his home address and home phone number (his card showed a P.O. box), and told me if we ever started to publish comic books again, to please reach out to him.

Just incredible — *Al Feldstein!*[19]

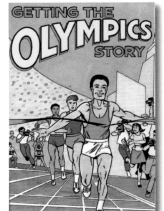

The Pacific Comics Index

the comics

It's remarkable how few comics titles and individual issues Pacific Comics produced in its short lifespan and, inversely, how many of those comic books were top-notch in content and production. And, to prove the point, below is an overview of the entire Pacific line — all 36 titles and 109 individual issues — including a couple of publications outside comics proper, but of interest to comics fans nonetheless.

Featured here are listings of all of the comics work in the titles themselves, though space restrictions forced us to omit pin-ups and editorial content details. Story titles are featured in boldface type accompanied by the number of pages therein. The creators are listed below story titles with the following bracketed designations:

[s] = Scripter
[p] = Penciler
[i] = Inker
[l] = Letterer
[c] = Colorist
[d] = Dialoguer
[p-a] = Plot assist or Co-plotter
[story] = Original author of work being adapted

We must acknowledge our sincere gratitude to the Grand Comics Database and its army of volunteers whose accomplishments make that website — *www.comics.org* — the invaluable reference resource it is for comics lovers and scholars everywhere. Referring to the GCD helped confirm and clarify the findings here.

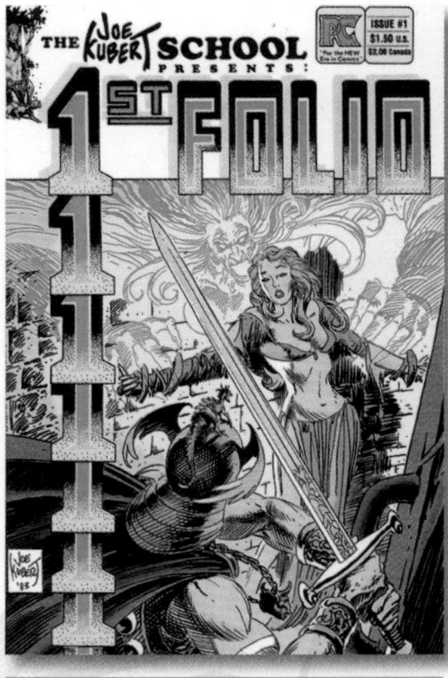
THE JOE KUBERT SCHOOL PRESENTS:
1ST FOLIO

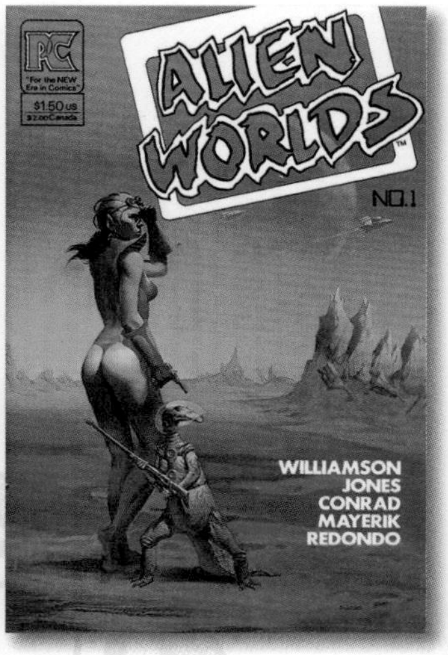
ALIEN WORLDS
NO.1
WILLIAMSON
JONES
CONRAD
MAYERIK
REDONDO

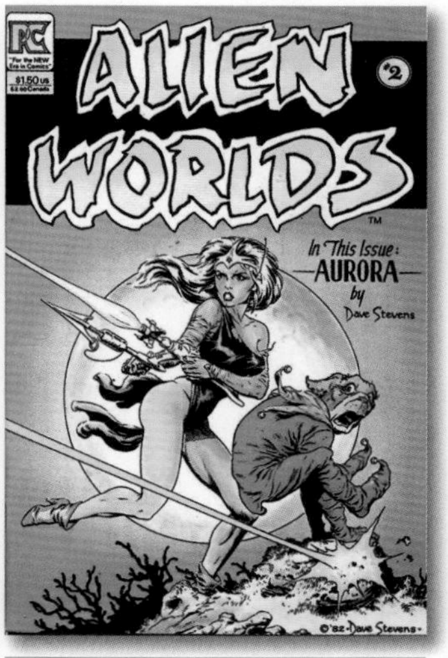
ALIEN WORLDS
#2
In This Issue:
AURORA
by
Dave Stevens

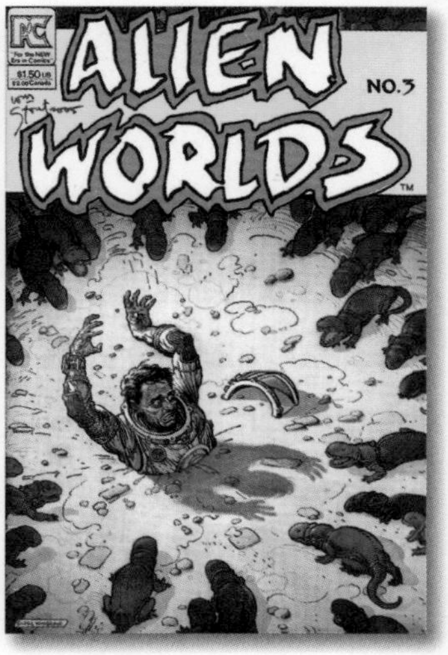
ALIEN WORLDS
NO.3

1st Folio

#1 Mar. 1984

Joe Kubert cover

"A Moment in War!" 2
Joe Kubert [s/p/i]

"Crown of Thorns" 5
Ron Randall [s/i]
Michael Chen [s/p]

"Physical Barriers" 2
Andy Kubert [s/p/i]

"The Trophy" 2
Andy Kubert [s/p/i]

"Dragon" 6
Andy Kubert [s/p/i]?

"Things That Go Bump in the Night" 3
Andy Kubert [s/p/i]

"Criminal Operations" 7
Rex Lindsey [s/p/i]
Andy Kubert [l]

"Tate's Hell" 3
Brad K. Joyce [s/p/i]

Additional editorial and in-house ad pages

Alien Worlds

#1 Dec. 1982

Joe Chiodo cover

"The Few and the Far" 6
Bruce Jones [s] Al Williamson [p/i]
Ed King [l] Steve Oliff [c]

"Domain" 7
Bruce Jones [s] Val Mayerik [p/i]
Carrie McCarthy [l] S. Oliff [c]

"Head of the Class" 7
Bruce Jones [s] Nestor Redondo [p/i] Redondo Studios [l]
Steve Oliff [c]

"Talk to Tedi" 10
Bruce Jones [s] Tim Conrad [p/i]
Ed King [l] Steve Oliff [c]

Additional editorial and in-house ad pages

#2 May 1983

Dave Stevens cover

"Aurora" 15
B. Jones [s] Dave Stevens [p/i]
Carrie McCarthy [l] S. Oliff [c]

"Vicious Circle" 8

Ken Steacy [s/p/i/c/l]
"A Mind of Her Own" 5
Bruce Jones [s/p/i]
C. McCarthy [l] Steve Oliff [c]
Additional editorial and in-house ad pages

#3 July 1983

William Stout cover
"The Inheritors" 10
B. Jones [s] Scott Hampton [p/i]
Carrie McCarthy [l]
"Pi in the Sky" 8
B. Jones [s] Ken Steacy [p/i/c]
Carrie McCarthy [l]
"Dark Passage" 15
Bruce Jones [s] Thomas Yeates [p/i] C. McCarthy [l]
Steve Oliff [c]
Additional editorial and in-house ad pages

ALIEN WORLDS
Dave Stevens ©1983

#4 Sept. 1983

Dave Stevens cover
"Princess Pam" 4
Bruce Jones [s/p] D. Stevens [i]
C. McCarthy [l] Joe Chiodo [c]
"Girl of My Schemes" 10
B. Jones [s] Bo Hampton [p/i]
C. McCarthy [l] Joe Chiodo [c]
"One Day in Ohio" 6
B. Jones [s]
Ken Steacy [p/i/c]
Carrie McCarthy [l]
"Deep Secrets" 2
Bruce Jones [s]
Jeffrey Jones [p/i/l/c]
"Land of Fire" 8
Bruce Jones [s]
Al Williamson, Angelo Torres, Roy Krenkel [p]
Al Williamson, Angelo Torres, Frank Frazetta [i]
C. McCarthy [l]
Joe Chiodo [c]
Note: Art reprinted from *witzend* #1 [1966], but Bruce Jones rewrote the story.
Additional editorial and in-house ad pages

ALIEN WORLDS
No.5

#5 Dec. 1983

John Bolton cover
"Lip Service" 10
Bruce Jones [s] John Bolton [p/i]
C. McCarthy [l] Joe Chiodo [c]
"Game Wars" 3
B. Jones [s] Ken Steacy [p/i/c]
"Plastic" 8
B. Jones [s]
Adolpho Buylla [p/i]
Ed King [l] Joe Chiodo [c]
"Wasteland" 8
Bruce Jones [s] Tom Yeates [p/i]
Tim Harkins [l] Joe Chiodo [c]
Additional editorial and in-house ad pages

ALIEN WORLDS
No. 6

#6 Feb. 1984

Frank Brunner cover
"Planet Prefect" 3
Bruce Jones [s]
Jim Sullivan [p]
Arthur Suydam [i]
Carrie McCarthy [l] Steve Oliff [c]
"The Test" 8
Bruce Jones [s] Val Mayerik, Roy Krenkel [p/i]
David Cody Weiss [l]
Joe Chiodo [c]
"Pride of the Fleet" 19
B. Jones [s]
Frank Brunner [p]
Mike Mignola [i]
Carrie McCarthy [l]
Joe Chiodo [c]
Additional editorial and in-house ad pages

ALIEN WORLDS
No. 7
william f. nolan
"THE SMALL WORLD OF LEWIS STILLMAN"
richard corben

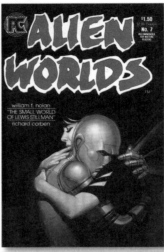

#7 Apr. 1984

Joe Chiodo cover
"The Small World of Lewis Stillman" 10
William F. Nolan [story]
Richard Corben [adaptation/p/i/c]
"Small Change" 2
Bruce Jones [s]
Brent Anderson [p/i]
"It All Fits" 10
Bruce Jones [s]
Gray Morrow [p/i]
"Ride the Blue Bus" 6
B. Jones [s] George Pérez [p/i]
Additional editorial and in-house ad pages

THE ART OF AL WILLIAMSON
BY JAMES VAN HISE · INTRODUCTION BY WILLIAM STOUT

The Art of Al Williamson

Apr. 1983

Al Williamson wraparound cover
Trade paperback about the artist includes introduction by William Stout, interviews with or testimonials by Williamson, Bill Gaines, Frank Frazetta, Al McWilliams, John Prentice, Ray Bradbury, Fred Fredericks, Roy Krenkel, Angelo Torres, Gray Morrow, George Lucas, and Archie Goodwin, and afterword by George Evans. Also includes the following reprints:
"The Hunter" 8
Reprint from *Two Gun Kid* #25 [Sept. 1955]
"The Little Earth" 10
Reprint from *Blast-Off* #1 [Oct. 1965]. (Pencils by Reed Crandall.)
"The Vicious Space Pirates" 12
Reprint from *Danger is Our Business* #1 [July 1953]. (Inks by Frank Frazetta.)
"The Lizard" 16
Reprint from *Mystery Tales* #51 [Mar. 1957]. (Inks by Ralph Mayo.)
"Robbie" 2
Reprint from *Fantasy Illustrated* #2 [Spr. 1964]. (Unsold comic strip.)
"Star Wars" 3
Unused *Star Wars* comic strips.
"Secret Agent Corrigan" 33
Reprints of newspaper strip.
"The Gunslinger" 4
Reprint from *Kid Slade, Gunfighter* #7 [May 1957].

ISSUE #1
BERNI WRIGHTSON
MASTER OF THE MACABRE

Bernie Wrightson: Master of the Macabre

#1 June 1983

Bernie Wrightson cover
"The Muck Monster" 7
Bernie Wrightson [s/p/i]
Steve Oliff [c] (Colorized reprint from *Eerie* #68 [Sept. 1975])
"The Pepper Lake Monster" 10
Bernie Wrightson [s/p/i]
Steve Oliff [c] (Colorized reprint from *Eerie* #58 [July 1974])
"Edgar Allan Poe's The Black Cat" 12
Edgar Allan Poe [story]

Bernie Wrightson [s/p/i]
Steve Oliff [c] (Colorized reprint from *Creepy* #62 [May 1974])
Additional editorial and in-house ad pages

ISSUE #2
BERNI WRIGHTSON
MASTER OF THE MACABRE

#2 August 1983

Bernie Wrightson cover
"Jenifer" 7
B. Jones [s] B. Wrightson [p/i] Steve Oliff [c] (Colorized reprint from *Creepy* #63 [July 1974])
"H. P. Lovecraft's Cool Air" 7
H.P. Lovecraft [story]
Bernie Wrightson [s/p/i]
Steve Oliff [c] (Colorized reprint from *Eerie* #62 [Jan. 1975])
"Four Classic Martians" 1
Bernie Wrightson [p/i] Steve Oliff [c]
"The Laughing Man" 6
B. Jones [s] B. Wrightson [p/i] Steve Oliff [c] (Colorized reprint from *Creepy* #95 [Feb. 1978]
"Clarice" 5
B. Jones [s] B. Wrightson [p/i] Steve Oliff [c] (Colorized reprint from *Creepy* #77 [Feb. 1976])
Additional editorial and in-house ad pages

ISSUE #3
BERNI WRIGHTSON
MASTER OF THE MACABRE

#3 [Oct.] 1983

Bernie Wrightson cover
"King of the Mountain, Man" 8
B. Wrightson [s/p/i] S. Oliff [c] (Colorized reprint from *Badtime Stories* [1972])
"A Martian Saga" 6
Nicola Cuti [s] Bernie Wrightson [p/i] Steve Oliff [c] (Colorized reprint from *Creepy* #87 [Mar. 1977])
"Nightfall" 8
Bill DuBay [s] B. Wrightson [p/i] Steve Oliff [c](Colorized reprint from *Eerie* #60 [Sept. 1974])
"The Last Hunters" 6
B. Wrightson [s/p/i] S. Oliff [c] (Colorized reprint from *Badtime Stories* [1972])
"Clarice" 5
B. Jones [s] B. Wrightson [p/i] Steve Oliff [c] (Colorized reprint from *Creepy* #77 [Feb. 1976])
Additional editorial and in-house ad pages

BERNI WRIGHTSON
MASTER OF THE MACABRE
No. 4

#4 Aug. 1984

Bernie Wrightson cover
"The Task..." 8
B. Wrightson [s/p/i] Marcus David [c] (Colorized reprint from *Badtime Stories* [1972])
(No title) 7
B. Wrightson [s/p/i] Marcus David [c] (Colorized reprint from *Badtime Stories* [1972]))
Werewolves illustration 1
B. Wrightson [p/i] Marcus David [c](Colorized reprint from *The Monsters Color the Creature Book* [1974])
"The Legend of Sleepy Hollow" 11
Washington Irving [story]
Mary Skrenes [s] Jeffrey Jones, Bernie Wrightson, Alan Weiss [p/i] Daryl Isaacs [c]
Additional editorial and in-house ad pages

Bold Adventure

#1 Nov. 1983

Rudy Nebres cover

BOLD ADVENTURE presents:
TIME FORCE
NO.1

"Time Force" 15
Bill DuBay [s] Rudy Nebres [p/i]
"Anaconda" 6
Bill DuBay [s] Bob McLeod [p/i] Bill Yoshida [l] Tom Ziuko [c]
"The Weirdling" 8
Bill DuBay [s] Trevor Von Eeden [p/i] Carrie McCarthy [l]
Additional editorial and in-house ad pages

BOLD ADVENTURE presents:
No. 2
TIME FORCE
GODS BATTLE!

#2 Mar. 1984

Rudy Nebres cover
"Time Force" 15
Bill DuBay [s] Rudy Nebres [p/i]
"Soldiers of Fortune" 7
Bill DuBay [s] Alex Niño [p/i] Daryl Isaacs [c]
"The Weirdling" 9
Bill DuBay [s] Trevor Von Eeden [p] David Lloyd [i]
Additional editorial and in-house ad pages

#3 June 1984

Michael W. Kaluta cover
"Spitfire" 6
Bill DuBay [s] John Severin [p/i] Tom Luth [c]
"Soldiers of Fortune: Apocalypse" 10
Bill DuBay [s] Alex Niño

BOLD ADVENTURE presents:
No. 3
SPITFIRE
He declared war on the Allies and the Axis! And he was about to win.

[p/i] Daryl Isaacs [c]
"Time Force: Creation" 11
Bill DuBay [s] Rudy Nebres [p/i]
"Cookie" 3
Bill DuBay [s/p/i]
Additional editorial and in-house ad pages

NEW - EXCITING - ORIGINAL!
IN DEFENSE OF OUR GALAXY
$1.00
CAPTAIN VICTORY AND THE GALACTIC RANGERS
FORCES FROM THE STAR WORLDS CLASH ON EARTH!

Captain Victory and the Galactic Rangers

#1 Nov . 1981

Jack Kirby & Mike Royer cover
"Captain Victory and His Galactic Rangers" 25
Jack Kirby [s/p] Mike Royer [i/l] Steve Oliff [c]
Additional editorial and in-house ad pages

#2 Jan. 1982

J. Kirby & Mike Thibodeaux cover
"Death Hive U.S.A." 25
Jack Kirby [s/p] Mike Royer [i/l] Steve Oliff [c]
Additional editorial and in-house ad pages

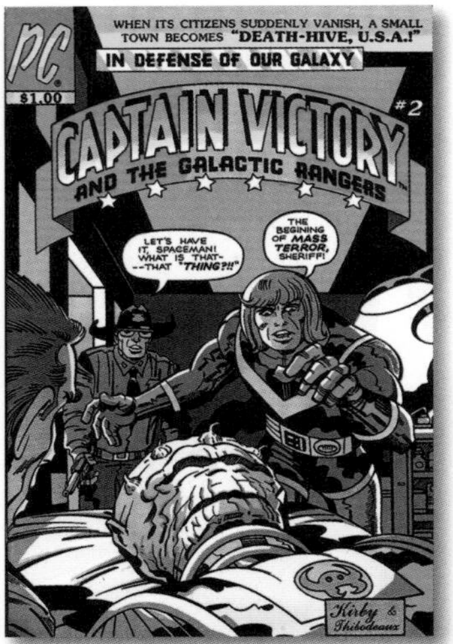
WHEN ITS CITIZENS SUDDENLY VANISH, A SMALL TOWN BECOMES "DEATH-HIVE, U.S.A.!"
IN DEFENSE OF OUR GALAXY
$1.00
CAPTAIN VICTORY AND THE GALACTIC RANGERS
#2
LET'S HAVE IT, SPACEMAN! WHAT IS THAT--THAT "THING?!!"
THE BEGINNING OF MASS TERROR, SHERIFF!
Kirby & Thibodeaux

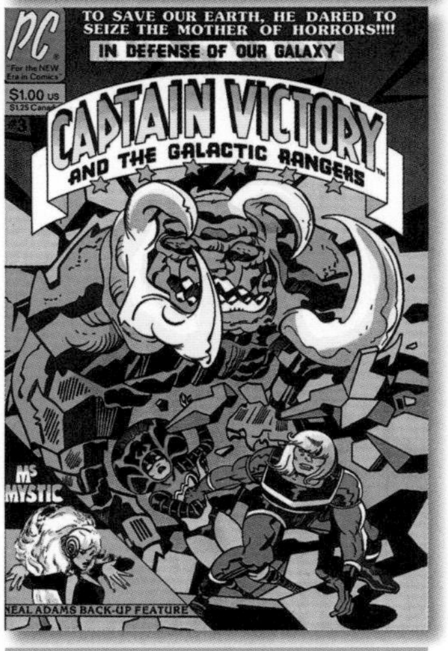
TO SAVE OUR EARTH, HE DARED TO SEIZE THE MOTHER OF HORRORS!!!!
IN DEFENSE OF OUR GALAXY
$1.00 US
CAPTAIN VICTORY AND THE GALACTIC RANGERS
MS MYSTIC
NEAL ADAMS BACK-UP FEATURE

#3 Mar. 1982

J. Kirby & Mike Thibodeaux cover (inset art by Neal Adams [p/i])

"Encounters of a Savage Kind" 25
Jack Kirby [s/p] Mike Thibodeaux [i/l] Steve Oliff [c]

"Ms. Mystic" 4
Neal Adams [s/p/i] S. Oliff? [c]

Additional editorial and in-house ad pages

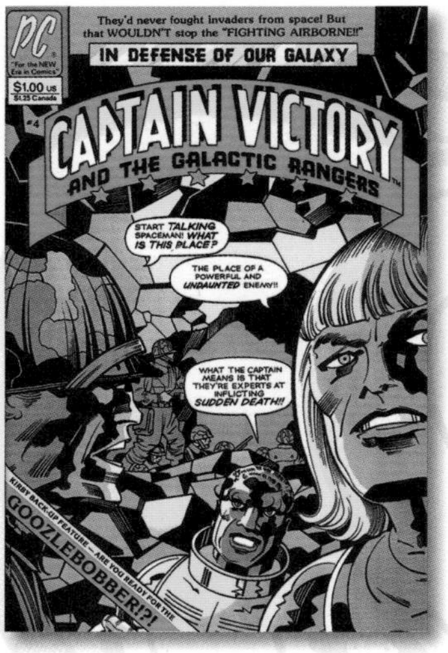
They'd never fought invaders from space! But that WOULDN'T stop the "FIGHTING AIRBORNE!"
IN DEFENSE OF OUR GALAXY
$1.00 US
CAPTAIN VICTORY AND THE GALACTIC RANGERS
START TALKING SPACEMAN! WHAT IS THIS PLACE?
THE PLACE OF A POWERFUL AND UNDAUNTED ENEMY!
WHAT THE CAPTAIN MEANS IS THAT THEY'RE EXPERTS AT INFLICTING SUDDEN DEATH!!
GOOZLEBOBBER?!?

#4 May 1982

J. Kirby & Mike Thibodeaux cover

"The Fighting Airborne" 25
J. Kirby [s/p] M. Thibodeaux [i/l] Steve Oliff [C]

"The Goozlebobber?" 4
J. Kirby [s/p] M. Thibodeaux [i/l] Steve Oliff [c]

Additional editorial and in-house ad pages

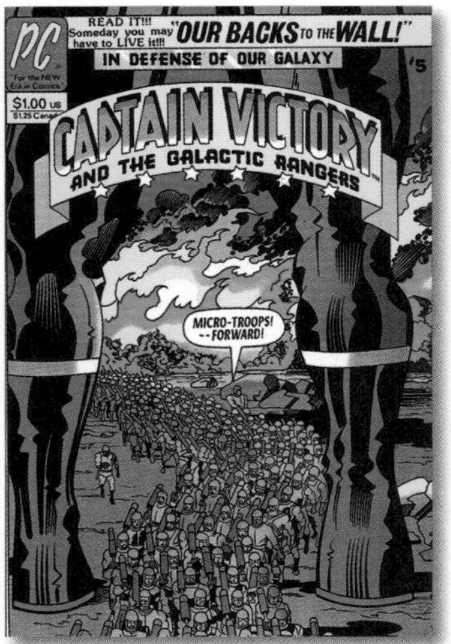
READ IT!!! Someday you may have to LIVE it!!!
"OUR BACKS TO THE WALL!"
IN DEFENSE OF OUR GALAXY
$1.00 US
CAPTAIN VICTORY AND THE GALACTIC RANGERS
MICRO-TROOPS! --FORWARD!

#5 July 1982

J. Kirby & Mike Thibodeaux cover

"Our Backs to the Wall" 25
J. Kirby [s/p] M. Thibodeaux [i] Palle Jensen [l] Steve Oliff [c]

"Goozlebobber, King of the Unwanted" 5
J. Kirby [s/p] M. Thibodeaux [i] Palle Jensen [l] Steve Oliff [c]

Additional editorial and in-house ad pages

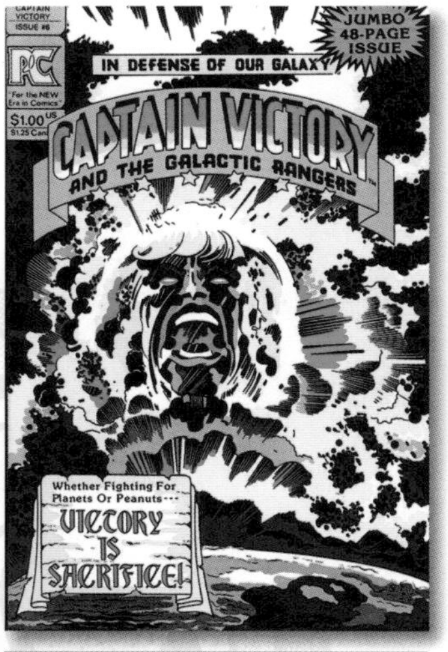
JUMBO 48-PAGE ISSUE
IN DEFENSE OF OUR GALAXY
$1.00
CAPTAIN VICTORY AND THE GALACTIC RANGERS
Whether Fighting For Planets Or Peanuts---
VICTORY IS SACRIFICE!

#6 Sept. 1982

J. Kirby & Mike Thibodeaux cover

"Victory Is Sacrifice" 25
J. Kirby [s/p] M. Thibodeaux [i] Palle Jensen [l] Steve Oliff [c]

"Goozlebobber" 5
J. Kirby [s/p] M. Thibodeaux [i/l] Steve Oliff [c]

"The Missing Man: The Khill Brothers" 5
Steve Ditko [s/p/i] Mark Evanier [d] S. Oliff [c]

Additional editorial and in-house ad pages

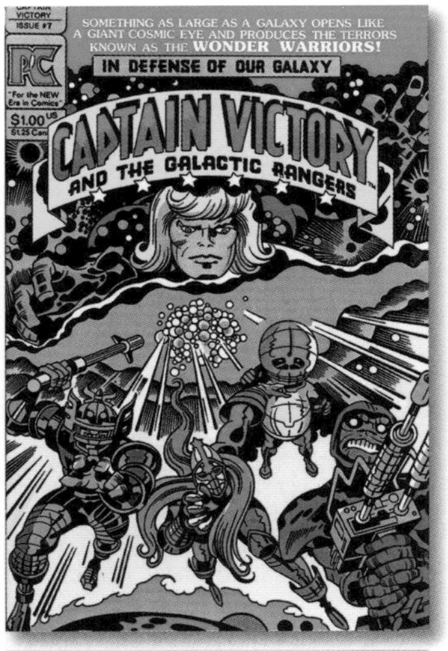
SOMETHING AS LARGE AS A GALAXY OPENS LIKE A GIANT COSMIC EYE AND PRODUCES THE TERRORS KNOWN AS THE WONDER WARRIORS!
IN DEFENSE OF OUR GALAXY
$1.00 US
CAPTAIN VICTORY AND THE GALACTIC RANGERS

#7 Oct. 1982

J. Kirby & Mike Thibodeaux cover

"Wonder Warriors!" 25
J. Kirby [s/p] M. Thibodeaux [i] Palle Jensen [l] Janice Cohen [c]

"Ranger Recruit— Martius Klavus!" 5
J. Kirby [s/p] M. Thibodeaux [i] Palle Jensen [l] Janice Cohen [c]

Additional editorial and in-house ad pages

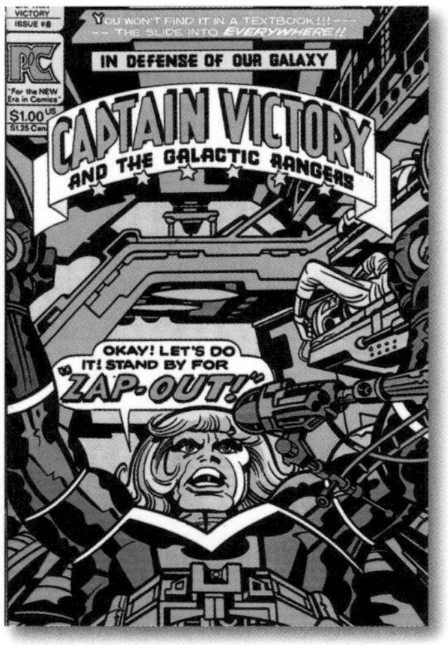
YOU WON'T FIND IT IN A TEXTBOOK!!! --- THE SLIDE INTO EVERYWHERE!!
IN DEFENSE OF OUR GALAXY
$1.00 US
CAPTAIN VICTORY AND THE GALACTIC RANGERS
OKAY! LET'S DO IT! STAND BY FOR ZAP-OUT!

#8 Dec. 1982

J. Kirby & Mike Thibodeaux cover

"Zap-Out" 25
J. Kirby [s/p] M. Thibodeaux [i] Palle Jensen [l] Janice Cohen [c]

"Martius Klavus: The Roman Syndrome" 5
J. Kirby [s/p] M. Thibodeaux [i] Palle Jensen [l] Janice Cohen [c]

Additional editorial and in-house ad pages

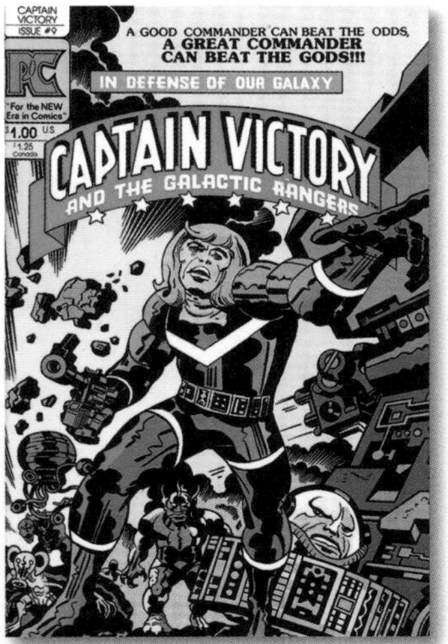
A GOOD COMMANDER CAN BEAT THE ODDS, A GREAT COMMANDER CAN BEAT THE GODS!!!
IN DEFENSE OF OUR GALAXY
$1.00
CAPTAIN VICTORY AND THE GALACTIC RANGERS

#9 Feb. 1983

J. Kirby & Mike Thibodeaux cover

"God's Many Mansions" 25
J. Kirby [s/p] M. Thibodeaux [i] Palle Jensen [l] Janice Cohen [c]

"Martius Klavus: The Unseen World" 5
J. Kirby [s/p] M. Thibodeaux [i] Palle Jensen [l] Janice Cohen [c]

Additional editorial and in-house ad pages

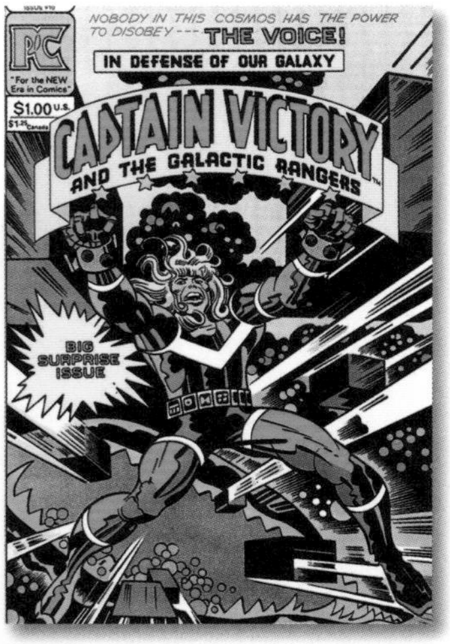
NOBODY IN THIS COSMOS HAS THE POWER TO DISOBEY---THE VOICE!
IN DEFENSE OF OUR GALAXY
$1.00 U.S.
CAPTAIN VICTORY AND THE GALACTIC RANGERS
BIG SURPRISE ISSUE

#10 Apr. 1983

J. Kirby & Mike Thibodeaux cover

"The Voice" 20
J. Kirby [s/p] M. Thibodeaux [i] Carrie McCarthy [l] J. Cohen [c]

"Rainmaker" 8
Tim Conrad [s/p/i]

Additional editorial and in-house ad pages

#11 June 1983

J. Kirby & Mike Thibodeaux cover

"Meet Big Ugly" 20
J. Kirby [s/p] M. Thibodeaux [i] Carrie McCarthy [l] J. Cohen [c]

"Off on a Comet" 8
Tim Conrad [s/p/i]

Additional editorial and in-house ad pages

A NEVER TO BE FORGOTTEN
ORIGIN ISSUE!
IN DEFENSE OF OUR GALAXY
$1.00 U.S.
CAPTAIN VICTORY
AND THE GALACTIC RANGERS
READ "BIG UGLY!!"

"ORIGIN TWO" -- END OF THE BOY ---BEGINNING OF THE MAN!!
IN DEFENSE OF OUR GALAXY
$1.00 U.S.
CAPTAIN VICTORY
AND THE GALACTIC RANGERS

#12 Oct. 1983

J. Kirby & Mike Thibodeaux cover
"Growing Up with the Lost Ranger" 20
J. Kirby [s/p] M. Thibodeaux [i] Carrie McCarthy [l] Tom Luth [c]
"An Eye for an Aye" 8
Bruce Jones [s] Kent Williams [p/i]
Additional editorial and in-house ad pages

"THE GANGS OF SPACE!!" IS THE FIRST OF ITS KIND!!! -- THE COMPLETION OF AN ORIGIN TRILOGY!!
IN DEFENSE OF OUR GALAXY
ISSUE #13 $1.50 U.S.
CAPTAIN VICTORY
AND THE GALACTIC RANGERS

#13 Jan. 1984

J. Kirby & Mike Thibodeaux cover
"Gangs of Space" 20
J. Kirby [s/p] M. Thibodeaux [i] Pallie Jensen [l] Tom Luth [c]
"Yesteryear" 8
Ed Foley [s/p/i] Marcus David [c]
Additional editorial and in-house ad pages

COMPLETE IN THIS ISSUE!!! A RIP-ROARING SPECIAL EDITION!! THE SPACE-MUSKETEERS!
IN DEFENSE OF OUR GALAXY
CAPTAIN VICTORY
AND THE GALACTIC RANGERS

Captain Victory and the Galactic Rangers Special

#1 Oct. 1983

J. Kirby & Mike Thibodeaux cover
"The Space Musketeers!" 25
J. Kirby [s/p] M. Thibodeaux [i] Pallie Jensen [l] Tom Luth [c]
Additional editorial and in-house ad pages

ROG 2000
$2.95 U.S.

The Complete Rog 2000

July 1982

John Byrne wraparound cover
"The Complete Rog" 1
John Byrne [s/p/i]
"Present at Conception" 1
Roger Stern [s] John Byrne [p/i]
"Who, How, and Where are They Now?" 1
Roger Stern [s] John Byrne [p/i]
"The Coming of the Gang" 6
Roger Stern [s] John Byrne [p/i] John Byrne & Roger Slifer [l] (Reprint from *Contemporary Picture Literature* #11 [1974])
"How to Draw Rogie 2000" 1
Nicola Cuti [s] John Byrne [p/i]
"What's a Nice Robot Like You..." 1
Nicola Cuti [s] John Byrne [p/i]
"That Was No Lady" 8
Nicola Cuti [s] John Byrne [p/i] (Reprint from *E-Man* #6 [Jan. 1975])
"Withering Heights" 7
Nicola Cuti [s] John Byrne [p/i] (Reprint from *E-Man* #7 [Mar. 1975])
"The Wish" 7
Nicola Cuti [s] John Byrne [p/i] Reprint from *E-Man* #9 [July 1975]
"Rog 2000 vs The Sog" 7
Nicola Cuti [s] John Byrne [p/i] Reprint from *E-Man* #10 [Sept 1975])

a CORBEN special
House of Usher
EDGAR ALLAN POE

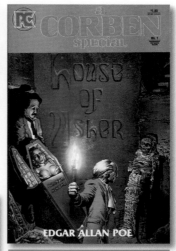

A Corben Special

#1 May 1984

Richard Corben cover
"The Fall of the House of Usher" 28
Edgar Allan Poe [story] Richard Corben [s/p/i] Herb and Diana Arnold [c]
Additional in-house ad pages

Darklon the Mystic

#1 Nov. 1983

Jim Starlin cover
"Beware Darklon the Mystic" 8
Jim Starlin [s/p/i] Gloria Cohen [c] (Colorized reprint from *Eerie*

Darklon
the mystic!
NO. 1
$2.00 U.S.

#76 [Aug. 1976])
"The Price!" 9
Jim Starlin [s/p/i] Basilio Amaro [c] (Colorized reprint from *Eerie* #79 [Nov. 1976])
"Retribution" 9
Jim Starlin [s/p/i] Basilio Amaro [c] (Colorized reprint from *Eerie* #80 [Jan. 1977])
"He Who Waits in the Shadows!" 6
Jim Starlin [s/p/i] Joe Chiodo [c] (Colorized reprint from *Eerie* #84 [June 1977])
"Duel" 13
Jim Starlin [s/p/i] Joe Chiodo [c] (Colorized reprint from *Eerie* #100 [Apr. 1979])
Additional editorial and in-house ad pages

Arthur Suydam's
DEMON DREAMS
$1.50
No. 1

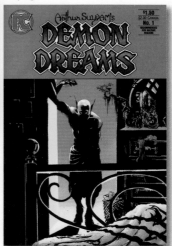

Demon Dreams

#1 Feb. 1984

Arthur Suydam cover
"Bad Breath" 20
Arthur Suydam [s/p/i/c] (Partial reprint from *Heavy Metal* vol. 3 #6 [Oct 1979])
"Christmas Carol" 9
Arthur Suydam [s/p/i/c] (Colorized reprint from *Heavy*

Metal vol. 3 #4 [Aug. 1979])
Additional editorial and in-house ad pages

Arthur Suydam's
DEMON DREAMS
No. 2

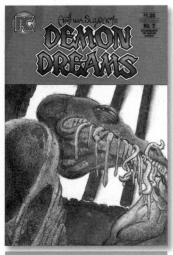

#2 May 1984

Arthur Suydam cover
"The Toll Bridge" 9
Arthur Suydam & Joe Koch [s]
Arthur Suydam [p/i/c] (Reprint from *Heavy Metal* vol. 5 #2 [May 1981])
"Mama's Place" 4
Arthur Suydam [s/p/i/c] (Reprint from *Heavy Metal* vol. 3 #4 [Aug. 1979])
"Food For the Children" 4
Arthur Suydam [s/p/i/c] (Reprint from *Heavy Metal* vol. 3 #9 [Jan. 1980])
"Mudwog" 3
Arthur Suydam [s/p/i/c] (Reprint from *Heavy Metal* vol. 6 #10 [Jan. 1983])
"Heads" 7
Arthur Suydam [s/p/i/c] (Reprint from *Epic Illustrated* #1 [Spr. 1980])
Additional editorial and in-house ad pages

ISSUE #1
EDGE OF CHAOS
ORIGIN ISSUE!
$1.00

Edge of Chaos

#1 July 1983

Gray Morrow cover
"Edge of Chaos" 22
Gray Morrow [s/p/i/l/c]
"The Redeeming Strain" 8
Don Lomax [s/p/i]
Additional editorial and in-house ad pages

ISSUE #2
EDGE OF CHAOS
$1.00

#2 Nov. 1983

Gray Morrow cover
"Edge of Chaos" 22
Gray Morrow [s/p/i/l/c]
"The Rescue" 5
Tim Burgard [s/p/i]
"Scaling the Heights" 2
Adam Kubert [s/p/i] Paul Tallerday & Barbara Marker [c]
Additional editorial and in-house ad pages

ISSUE #3
EDGE OF CHAOS
$1.50

#3 Jan. 1984

Gray Morrow cover
"Edge of Chaos" 22
Gray Morrow [s/p/i/l]
Daryl Isaacs [c]
"The World of Zand'or" 8
Rex Lindsay [s/p/i] D. Isaacs [c]
Additional editorial and in-house ad pages

MICHAEL MOORCOCK'S
ELRIC
ISSUE #1
$1.50
by ROY THOMAS, P. CRAIG RUSSELL and MICHAEL T. GILBERT

Elric

#1 Apr. 1983

M. T. Gilbert & P. C. Russell cover
"Book One: Out of the Dreaming City" 24
Michael Moorcock [story] Roy Thomas [s] P. Craig Russell & Michael T. Gilbert [p/i/c] Tom Orzechowski [l]
Additional editorial and in-house ad pages

MICHAEL MOORCOCK'S
ELRIC
ISSUE #2
$1.50
"KINDLY DR. JEST"
by P. CRAIG RUSSELL, MICHAEL T. GILBERT and ROY THOMAS

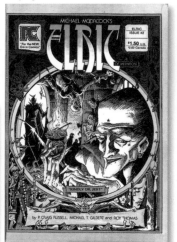

#2 Aug. 1983

M. T. Gilbert & P. C. Russell cover
"Welcome to the Domain of… Dr. Jest" 27
Michael Moorcock [story] Roy Thomas [s] P. Craig Russell & Michael T. Gilbert [p/i/c] Tom Orzechowski [l]
Additional editorial and in-house ad pages

#3 Oct. 1983

M. T. Gilbert & P. C. Russell cover
"Prologue: Aftermath of Battle" 29
Michael Moorcock [story] Roy Thomas [s] P. Craig Russell & Michael T. Gilbert [p/i/c] Tom Orzechowski [l]
Additional editorial and in-house ad pages

MICHAEL MOORCOCK'S
ELRIC
ISSUE #3
$1.50
by MICHAEL T. GILBERT, ROY THOMAS and P. CRAIG RUSSELL

MICHAEL MOORCOCK'S
ELRIC
$1.50
by ROY THOMAS P. CRAIG RUSSELL and MICHAEL T. GILBERT

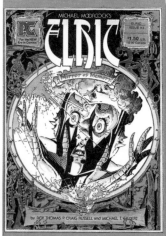

#4 Dec. 1983

M. T. Gilbert & P. C. Russell cover
"The Ship Which Sails Over Land and Sea" 28
Michael Moorcock [story] Roy Thomas [s] P. Craig Russell & Michael T. Gilbert [p/i/c] Tom Orzechowski [l]
Additional editorial and in-house ad pages

MICHAEL MOORCOCK'S
ELRIC
ISSUE #5
$1.50
by P. CRAIG RUSSELL, MICHAEL T. GILBERT and ROY THOMAS

#5 Feb. 1984

M. T. Gilbert & P. C. Russell cover

"Through the Shade Gate 28

Michael Moorcock [story] Roy Thomas [s] P. Craig Russell & Michael T. Gilbert [p/i/c] Tom Orzechowski [l]

Additional editorial and in-house ad pages

MICHAEL MOORCOCK'S
ELRIC
STORMBRINGER

#6 Apr. 1984

M. T. Gilbert & P. C. Russell cover

"At Last — Stormbringer" 28

Michael Moorcock [story] Roy Thomas [s] P. Craig Russell & Michael T. Gilbert [p/i/c] Tom Orzechowski [l]

Additional editorial and in-house ad pages

FAMOUS MOVIE STARS OF THE 30's

Famous Movie Stars of the '30s

July 1984

Toni Blum cover

No title 46

Toni Blum [s/p/i/l] (Reprints *Stars on Parade* newspaper strips from the 1930s)

GHITA
OF ALIZARR
BY FRANK THORNE
ADULT FANTASY

Ghita of Alizarr

Sept. 1983

Photo cover

"Ghita of Alizarr" 93

Modified versions of "Ghita" stories by Frank Thorne [s/p/i/l] that appeared in issues of *1984/1994* magazine [between #7, Aug. 1978–#14, Aug. 1980]

Additional editorial pages

SERGIO ARAGONÉS'
GROO
THE WANDERER

Groo the Wanderer

#1 Dec. 1982

Sergio Aragonés cover

"Friends and Enemies" 20

Sergio Aragones [s/p/i] Mark Evanier [p-a/d] Stan Sakai [l] Gordon Kent [c]

"Sage" 5

Sergio Aragones [s/p/i] Stan Sakai [l] Gordon Kent [c]

Additional editorial and in-house ad pages

SERGIO ARAGONÉS
GROO
THE WANDERER
DANGER QUICKSAND

#2 Feb. 1983

Sergio Aragonés cover

"The Missive" 20

Sergio Aragones [s/p/i] Mark Evanier [p-a/d] Stan Sakai [l] Gordon Kent [c]

"The Travels of the Wanderer" 2

Mark Evanier [s/l] Sergio Aragonés [p/i] Gordon Kent [c]

"Sage" 5

Sergio Aragones [s/p/i] Mark Evanier [p-a/d] Stan Sakai [l] Gordon Kent [c]

Additional editorial and in-house ad pages

SERGIO ARAGONÉS
GROO
THE WANDERER

#3 Apr. 1983

Sergio Aragonés cover

"The Caravan" 22

Sergio Aragones [s/p/i] Mark Evanier [p-a/d] Stan Sakai [l] Gordon Kent [c] Janice Cohen [color assist]

"Sage" 5

Sergio Aragones [s/p/i] Mark Evanier [p-a/d] Stan Sakai [l] Gordon Kent [c]

Additional editorial and in-house ad pages

SERGIO ARAGONÉS
GROO
THE WANDERER

#4 Sept. 1983

Sergio Aragonés cover

"The Turn of the Wheel" 22

Sergio Aragones [s/p/i] Mark Evanier [p-a/d] Stan Sakai [l] Gordon Kent [c]

"Sage" 5

Sergio Aragones [s/p/i] Mark Evanier [p-a/d] Stan Sakai [l] Tom Luth [c]

Additional editorial and in-house ad pages

SERGIO ARAGONÉS
GROO
THE WANDERER

#5 Oct. 1983

Sergio Aragonés cover

"Shanghaied" 20

Sergio Aragones [s/p/i] Mark Evanier [p-a/d] Stan Sakai [l] Tom Luth [c]

"The Voyages of the Wanderer" 2

Mark Evanier [s/l] Sergio Aragonés [p/i] Tom Luth [c]

"Sage" 5

Sergio Aragones [s/p/i] Mark Evanier [p-a/d] Stan Sakai [l] Tom Luth [c]

Additional editorial and in-house ad pages

SERGIO ARAGONÉS
GROO
THE WANDERER

#6 Dec. 1983

Sergio Aragonés cover

"The Wizard War" 23

Sergio Aragones [s/p/i] Mark Evanier [p-a/d] Stan Sakai [l] Tom Luth [c]

No title 4

Sergio Aragones [s/p/i] Mark Evanier [p-a/d] Stan Sakai

[l] Tom Luth [c]
Additional editorial and in-house ad pages

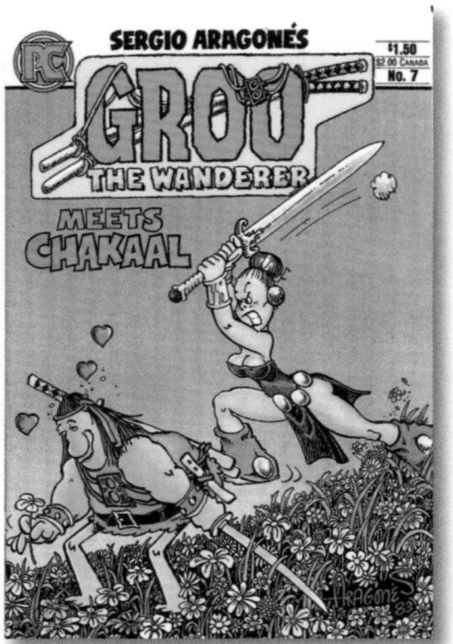
SERGIO ARAGONÉS
$1.50
$2.00 CANADA
No. 7
GROO
THE WANDERER
MEETS
CHAKAAL

#7 Feb. 1984

Sergio Aragonés cover
"Chakaal" 27
Sergio Aragones [s/p/i] Mark Evanier [p-a/d] Stan Sakai [l] Tom Luth [c]
Additional editorial and in-house ad pages

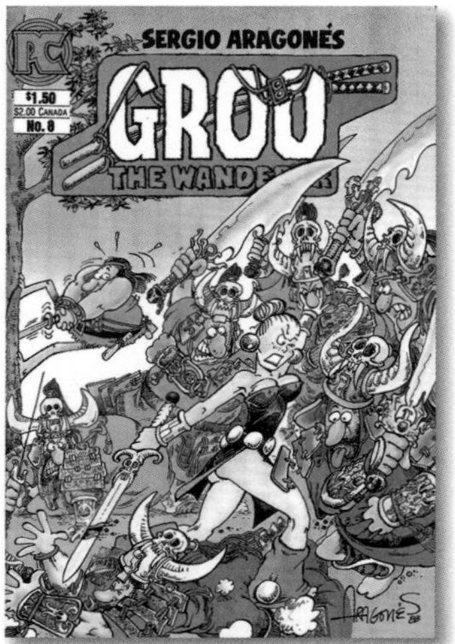
SERGIO ARAGONÉS
$1.50
$2.00 CANADA
No. 8
GROO

#8 Mar. 1984

Sergio Aragonés cover
"Warriors Two" 27
Sergio Aragones [s/p/i] Mark Evanier [p-a/d] Stan Sakai [l] Tom Luth [c]
Additional editorial and in-house ad pages

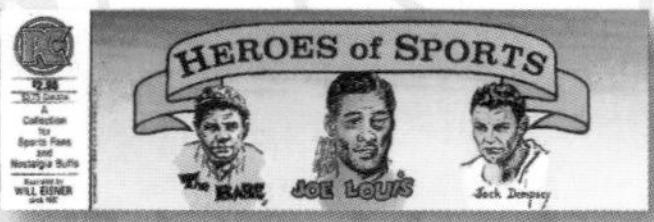
HEROES of SPORTS
JOE LOUIS

Heroes of Sports

July 1984

Will Eisner cover
No title 48
Will Eisner [s/p/i/l]? (Reprints *Heroes of Sports* newspaper strips from 1936)

Jerry Iger's Famous Features

#1 July 1984

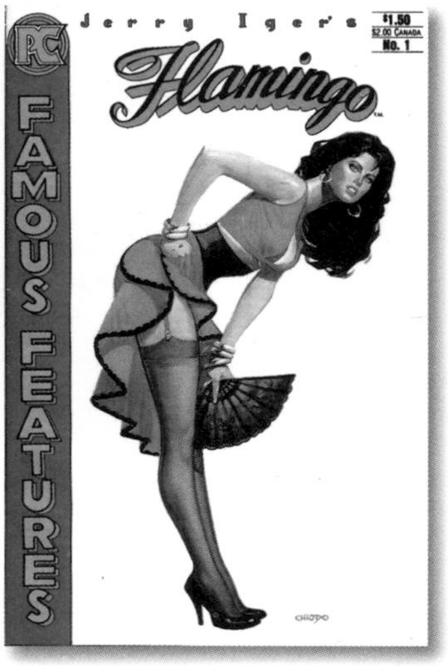
Jerry Iger's
$1.50
$2.00 CANADA
No. 1
Flamingo
FAMOUS FEATURES

Joe Chiodo cover
"Flamingo: The Face in the Golden Comb" 8
Ruth Roche [s] Matt Baker [p/i] Phil Phillipson [c]
"Ace of the Newsreels" 8
S. M. "Jerry" Iger [s] Matt Baker [p/i] Phil Phillipson [c] (Reprint from *Crown Comics* #6 [Sum 1946])
"Wonder Boy: The Amazing Plot of the Corpse Who Never Died" 10
S. M. "Jerry" Iger (as Jerry Maxwell) [s] Matt Baker [p/i] Jan Brunner [c]
Additional editorial and in-house ad pages

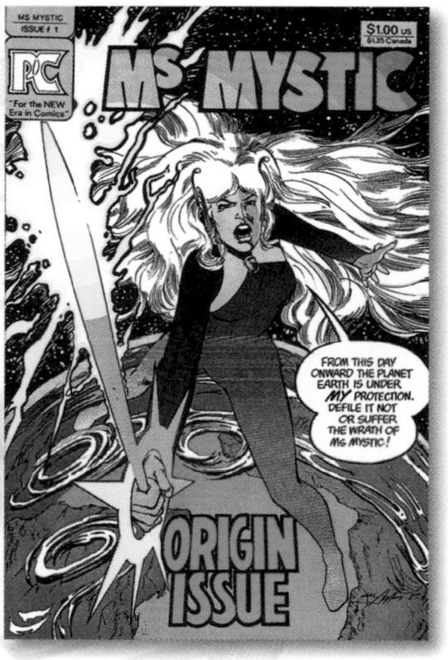
$1.00 US
MS MYSTIC
FROM THIS DAY ONWARD THE PLANET EARTH IS UNDER MY PROTECTION. DEFILE IT NOT OR SUFFER THE WRATH OF MS MYSTIC!
ORIGIN ISSUE

Ms. Mystic

#1 Oct. 1982

Neal Adams cover
"Ms. Mystic" 24
Neal Adams [s/p/i] Michael Netzer/Nasser [i] John Costanza [l] Cory Adams [c]
"Rescue Rhapsody" 5
Chris Miller [s/p/i] Carrie McCarthy [l] Daryl Isaacs [c]
Additional editorial and in-house ad pages

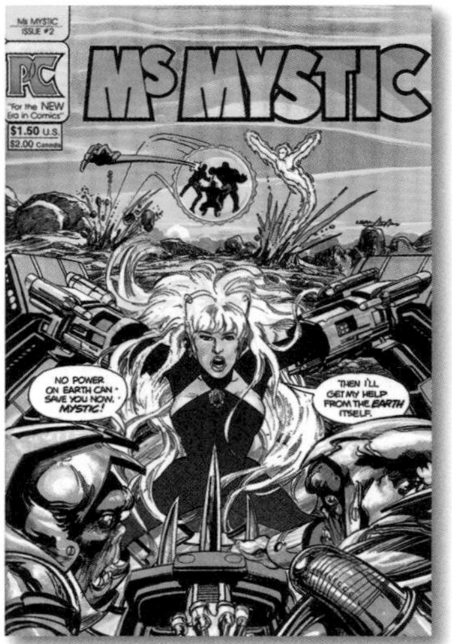
MS MYSTIC
$1.50 U.S.
NO POWER ON EARTH CAN SAVE YOU NOW, MYSTIC!
THEN I'LL GET MY HELP FROM THE EARTH ITSELF!

#2 Feb. 1984

Neal Adams cover
"Into the Womb" 24
Neal Adams [s/p/i] John Costanza [l] Cory Adams [c]
"Tales of Zad" 5
Chris Miller [s/p/i] Carrie McCarthy [l] Daryl Isaacs [c]
Additional editorial and in-house ad pages.

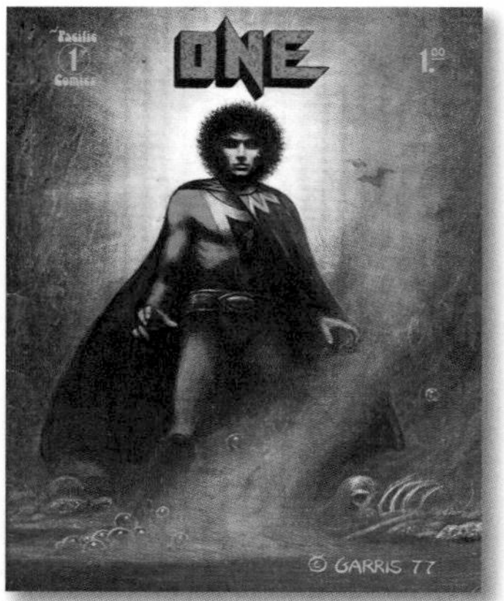
ONE
© GARRIS 77

One

#1 July 1977

Phillip Garris cover
"One" 19
Stephen Garris & Nathan Kingsbury [s/p/i]
"Hydro Celestial Battle" 4
Lana Evans [s] Lionel Sanders [p/i]
"Operation Changeling" 8
Wil Lund [s] David Cody Weiss [p] Brent Anderson, Frank Cirocco, and Gary Winnick [i] Shel Dorf [l]
Additional editorial and in-house ad pages

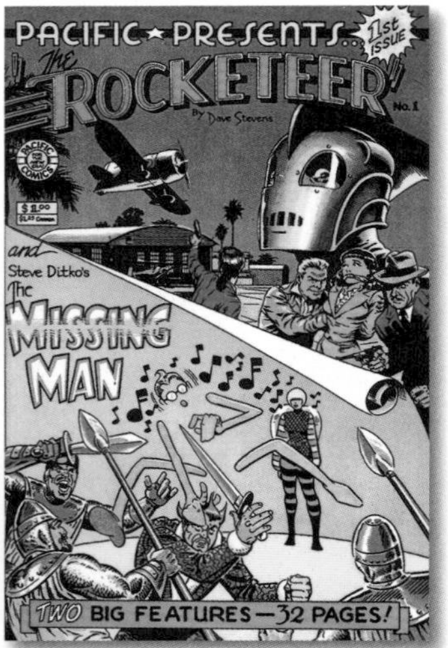
PACIFIC ★ PRESENTS...
1st ISSUE
the ROCKETEER
by Dave Stevens
and Steve Ditko's
The MISSING MAN
TWO BIG FEATURES—32 PAGES!

Pacific Presents

#1 Oct. 1982

Dave Stevens & Steve Ditko cover
"The Rocketeer: Chapter 3" 12
Dave Stevens [s/p/i/l]
"Missing Man Meets the Queen Bee" 18
Steve Ditko [s/p/i] David Cody Weiss [l] Steve Oliff [c]
Additional editorial and in-house ad pages

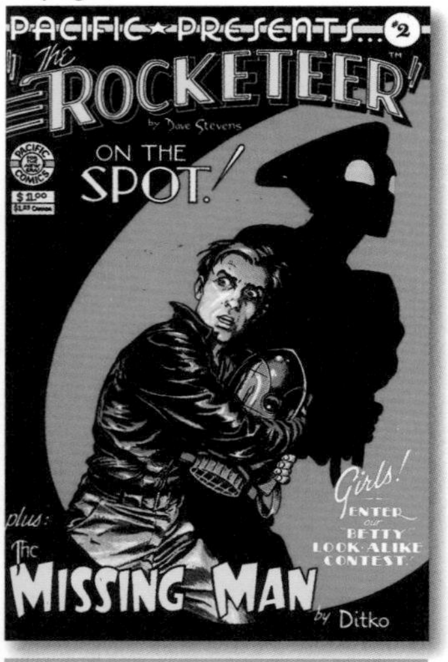
PACIFIC ★ PRESENTS... 2
the ROCKETEER
by Dave Stevens
ON THE SPOT!
Girls! ENTER BETTY LOOK-ALIKE CONTEST
plus: The MISSING MAN by Ditko

#2 Apr. 1983

Dave Stevens cover
"The Rocketeer: Chapter 4" 13
Dave Stevens [s/p/i/l]
"Missing Man Meets the Payne Family" 18
Steve Ditko [s/p/i] Robin Snyder [d] Andy Kubert [l] S. Oliff [c]
Additional editorial and in-house ad pages

PACIFIC PRESENTS
$1.50
No. 3
THE WILDLY PLAUSIBLE PLIGHT OF
EERIE SMITH and WALTER WEARY
WALTER! OUR SUBATOMIC ORGANIZATION HAS BEEN ALTERED!
WE'VE BECOME DWELLERS IN THE MULTIVERSE!
GREAT—
MISSING MAN AND Vanity BY WILL MEUGNIOT

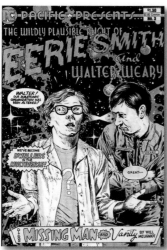

#3 Mar. 1984

Tim Conrad cover

"Eerie Smith and Walter Weary: When You Gotta Go — You Gotta Go…" 8
Tim Conrad [s/p/i] Robert Jessup [l] Jim Bertrand [c]

"Missing Man: Am I Maro, Roma, or Raem?" 18
Steve Ditko [s/p/i] Robin Snyder [d] Andy Kuber [l] D. Isaacs [c]

"Vanity: Scoop" 4
Will Meugniot [s/p/i] Jo Meugniot [c]

Additional editorial and in-house ad pages

PACIFIC PRESENTS
$1.50
No. 4
bruce jones • helmut eppich
"SHELL GAME"
ian akin • brian garvey

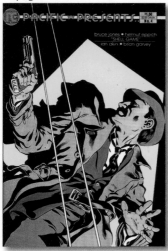

#4 June 1984

Ian Akin & Brian Garvey cover

"Doc .44: Take Two Slugs and Die" 10
Bob Haney [s] Mel Keefer [p] Ian Akin & Brian Garvey [i] Carrie McCarthy [l] Tom Luth [c]

"Mr. Brinks: The Shell Game" 8
Bruce Jones [s] Helmut Eppich [p] Ian Akin & Brian Garvey [i] David Cody Weiss [l] Marcus David [c]

"Eerie Smith and Walter Weary: Split Decision!" 8
Tim Conrad [s/p/i] Bob Jessup [l] Jim Bertrand & Daryl Isaacs [c]

Additional editorial and in-house ad pages

pathways to Fantasy
bolton
dowling
hampton
jones
windsor-smith
$1.50
NO. 1

Pathways to Fantasy

#1 July 1984

Barry Windsor-Smith cover

"Stalking" 7
Bruce Jones [s]
Barry Windsor-Smith [p/i]
Carrie McCarthy [l]
Tom Luth [c]

"Goblin Market" 10
Christina Rossetti [story]
John Bolton [s/p/i/c]
Carrie McCarthy [l]

"A Night to Remember" 4
Jeffrey Jones [s/p/i/c/l]

"Hunger" 5
April Campbell [s] Lela Dowling [p/i] Carrie McCarthy [l]
Tom Luth [c]

"Oh What a Lovely Estate We Have" 2
Bruce Jones [s]
Scott Hampton [p/i/c]
Carrie McCarthy [l]

Additional editorial and in-house ad pages

COLLECTOR'S EDITION • LEGENDARY 1st ISSUE
WEIRD ADVENTURES ON OTHER WORLDS—THE UNIVERSE OF THE FUTURE
PLANET COMICS
$5.95

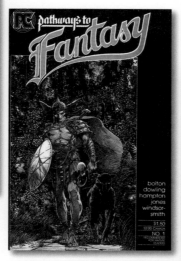

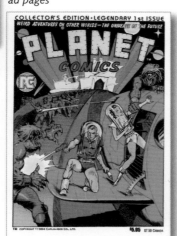

Planet Comics

#1 July 1984

Lou Fine cover

76-page book consists of reprints from *Planet Comics* #5 [May 1940] and #25 [July 1943], along with new editorial material

JEFFREY JONES
RAVENS & RAINBOWS
$1.50
NO. 1

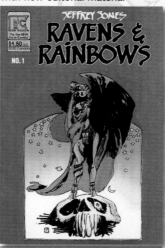

Ravens and Rainbows

#1 Dec. 1983

Jeffrey Jones cover

"Union" 8
Jeffrey Jones [s/p/i/l] Steve Oliff [c] (Colorized reprint from *Abyss* #1 [Nov. 1970])

"The Bridge" 3
Jeffrey Jones [s/p/i/l] Steve Oliff [c] (Colorized reprint from *Spasm* #1 [Apr. 1973])

"Toys" 1
Jeffrey Jones [s/p/i/l] Steve Oliff [c] (Colorized reprint from *Swank* vol. 19 #8 [Oct. 1972])

"Explored" 3
Jeffrey Jones [s/p/i/l] Steve Oliff [c] (Colorized reprint from Imagination #1 [1971])

"A Jeff Jones Portfolio" 5
Jeffrey Jones [s/p/i/l] Steve Oliff [c] (Colorized reprint from 1973 Jeff Jones-produced portfolio)

"Bias" 1
Jeffrey Jones [s/p/i/l] Steve Oliff [c] (Colorized reprint from *Swank* vol. 19 #5 [July 1972])

"Home" 4
Jeffrey Jones [s/p/i/l] Steve Oliff [c] (Colorized reprint from *Phase* #1 [1971])

"Spirit of '76" 4
Jeffrey Jones [s/p/i/l] Steve Oliff [c] (Colorized reprint from *Spasm* #1[Apr. 1973])

"Wholly Holy" 1
Jeffrey Jones [s/p/i/l] Steve Oliff [c] (Colorized reprint from *Swank* vol. 19 #6 [Aug. 1972]

"In Deep" 1
Jeffrey Jones [s/p/i/l] Steve Oliff [c] (Colorized reprint from *Swank* vol. 19 #9 [Nov. 1972])

Additional editorial and in-house ad pages

SILVER STAR ISSUE #1
THE NEXT BREED
SILVER STAR
$1.00 US
A VISUAL NOVEL
MEET MORGAN MILLER: HOMO GENETICUS!
Viking Heroes

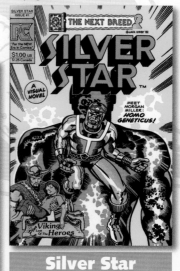

Silver Star

#1 Feb. 1983

Jack Kirby, Mike Thibodeaux, & Alfredo Alcala cover

"Silver Star: Homo-Geneticus" 20
Jack Kirby [s/p] Mike Royer [i/l] Janice Cohen [c]

"Last of the Viking Heroes" 10
Mike Thibodeaux [s/p] Alfredo Alcala [i] Carrie McCarthy [l] Shelly Leferman [c]

Additional editorial and in-house ad pages

SILVER STAR ISSUE #2
THE NEXT BREED...
SILVER STAR
$1.00 US
A VISUAL NOVEL
HOMO-GENETICUS
MAN MAY DESTROY TO GAIN POWER
HIS SUCCESSOR MAY DESTROY BECAUSE HE'S BORN WITH IT...
LOOK OUT FOR---
DARIUS DRUMM

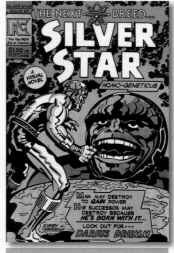

#2 Apr. 1983

Jack Kirby & M. Thibodeaux cover

"Darius Drumm" 20
Jack Kirby [s/p] Mike Royer [i/l] Janice Cohen [c]

"The Mocker: With These Hands…" 10
Steve Ditko [s/p/i] Janice Cohen [c]

Additional editorial and in-house ad pages

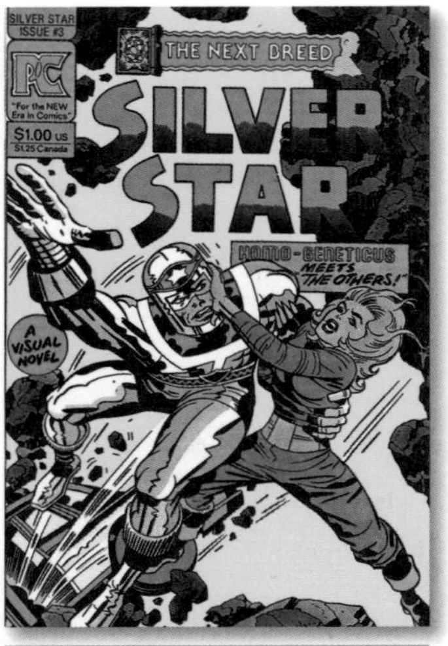
SILVER STAR ISSUE #3
THE NEXT BREED
PC
SILVER STAR
HOMO-GENETICUS MEETS THE OTHERS!
A VISUAL NOVEL

#3 June 1983

Jack Kirby & Mike Royer cover
"The Others" 20
Jack Kirby [s/p] Mike Royer [i/l] Janice Cohen [c]
"Detective Flynn: The Golden Girl" 10
Richard Kyle [s] D. Bruce Berry [p/i/l] Janice Cohen [c]
Additional editorial and in-house ad pages

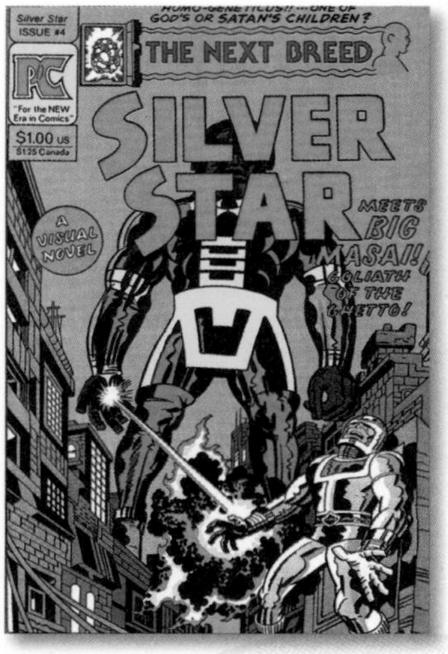
Silver Star ISSUE #4
THE NEXT BREED
PC
SILVER STAR
MEETS BIG MASAI!!
A VISUAL NOVEL

#4 Aug. 1983

Jack Kirby & Mike Royer cover
"The Super-Normals: Are They God's or Satan's Children?" 20
Jack Kirby [s/p] Mike Royer [i/l] Janice Cohen [c]
"Detective Flynn" 11
Richard Kyle [s] D. Bruce Berry [p/i/l] Shelly Leferman [c]
Additional editorial and in-house ad pages

#5 Nov. 1983

J. Kirby & D. Bruce Berry cover
"The World According to Drumm!" 20
Jack Kirby [s/p] D. Bruce Berry [i/l] Tom Luth [c]

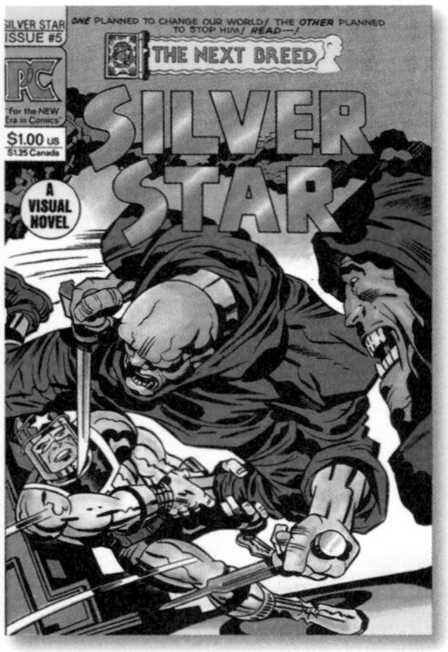
SILVER STAR ISSUE #5
THE NEXT BREED
PC
SILVER STAR
A VISUAL NOVEL

"Last of the Viking Heroes" 8
Mike Thibodeaux [s/p] Rudy Nebres [i] Palle Jensen [l] Tom Luth [c]
Additional editorial and in-house ad pages

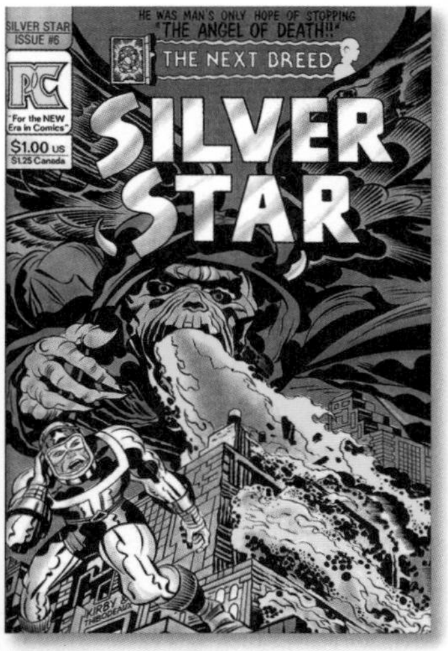
SILVER STAR ISSUE #6
"THE ANGEL OF DEATH!!"
THE NEXT BREED
PC
SILVER STAR

#6 Jan. 1984

J. Kirby & M. Thibodeaux cover
"The Angel of Death!" 20
Jack Kirby [s/p] D. Bruce Berry [i/l] Tom Luth [c]

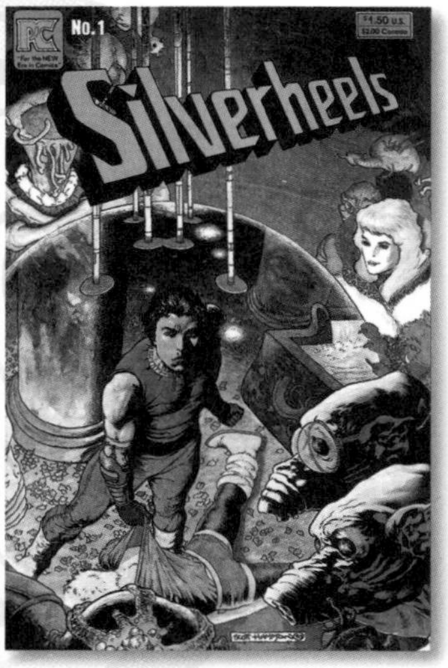
PC
No. 1
Silverheels

"Last of the Viking Heroes" 8
Mike Thibodeaux [s/p] Daerick Gross [i] Palle Jensen [l] Daryl Isaacs [c]
Additional editorial and in-house ad pages

Silverheels

#1 Dec. 1983

Scott Hampton cover
"Silverheels" 15
Bruce Jones & April Campbell [s] Scott Hampton [p/i/c] Carrie McCarthy [l]
"Robotus Ridiculous" 13
Bruce Jones & April Campbell [s] Ken Steacy [p/i/c] David Cody Weiss [c]
Additional editorial and in-house ad pages

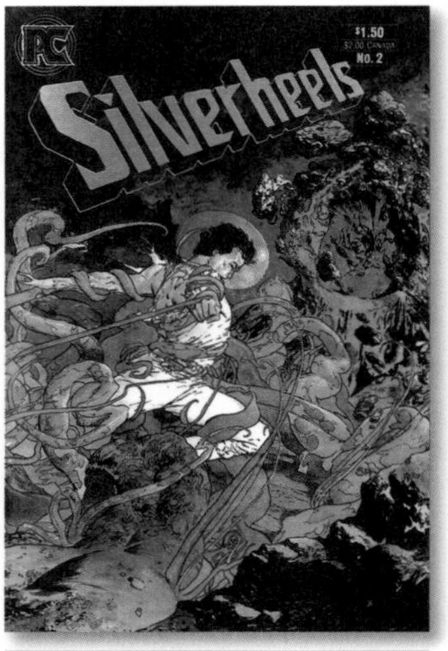
PC
$1.50
NO. 2
Silverheels

#2 Mar. 1984

Scott Hampton cover
"Silverheels" 8
April Campbell [s] Scott Hampton [p/i/c] Carrie McCarthy [l]
"War of the Blots!" 10
Bruce Jones [s] Ken Steacy [p/i/c] David Cody Weiss [l]

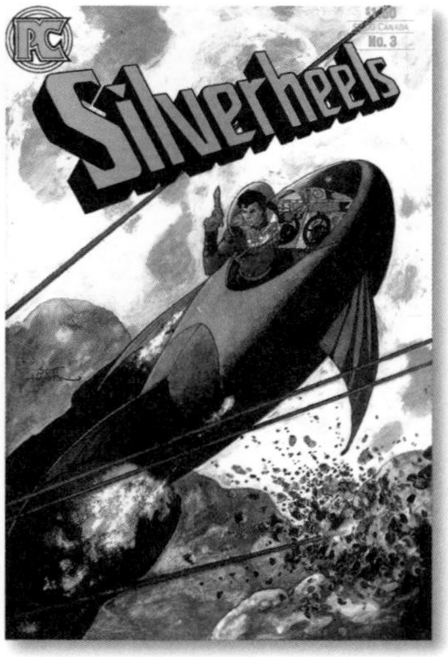
PC
No. 3
Silverheels

"A Steacy Gallery" 5
Ken Stacy [p/i/c]
Additional editorial and in-house ad pages

#3 May 1984

Scott Hampton cover
"Silverheels" 9
Bruce Jones & April Campbell [s] Scott Hampton [p/i/c] Carrie McCarthy [l]
"Flan, You're Fired" 13
Bruce Jones [s] K. Steacy [p/i/c]
"All My Love, Aliso Road" 6
Jaime Hernandez [s/p/i]
Additional editorial and in-house ad pages

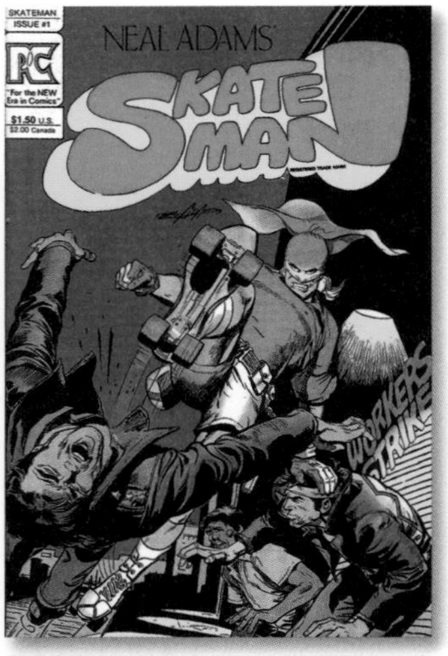
SKATEMAN ISSUE #1
NEAL ADAMS
PC
SKATEMAN

Skateman

#1 Nov. 1983

Neal Adams cover
"Skateman" 19
John Ballard [story] Neal Adams [s/p/i], James Sherman [p]
"Futureworld" 5
Jack Arata [s/p] Andy Kubert [i/l] Daryl Isaacs [c]
"The Rock Warrior" 5
Paul Powers [s/p/i/l] Daryl Isaacs [c]
Additional editorial and in-house ad pages

Somerset Holmes

#1 Sept, 1983

B. Anderson & A. Williamson cover
"Somerset Holmes" 21
Bruce Jones [s] April Campbell [p-a]; Brent Anderson [p-a/p/i/c] Ed King [l]
"Cliff Hanger: Chapter One: Jungle Peril" 8
Bruce Jones [s] Al Williamson [p/i] Ed King [l] Joe Chiodo [c]
Additional editorial and in-house ad pages

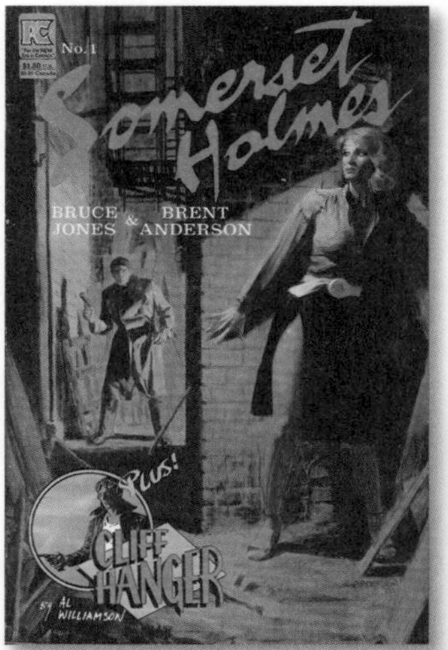
No. 1
Somerset Holmes
BRUCE JONES & BRENT ANDERSON
PLUS!
CLIFF HANGER
BY AL WILLIAMSON

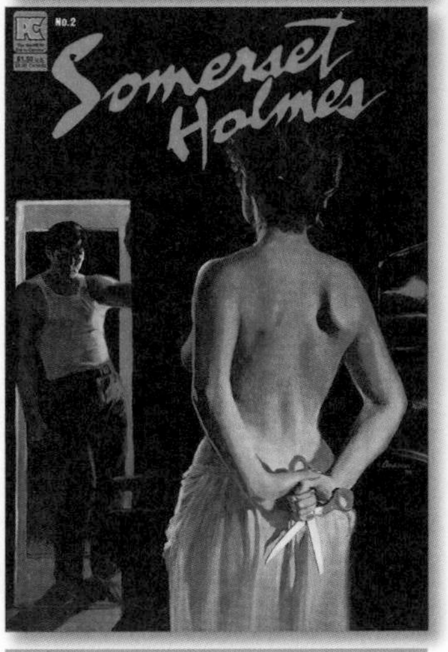
No. 2
Somerset Holmes

#2 Sept, 1983

Brent Anderson cover
"Strangers on a Train" 21
Bruce Jones [s] April Campbell [p-a] Brent Anderson [p-a/p/i/c] David Cody Weiss [l]
"Cliff Hanger: Chapter Two: Claws of Death" 8
Bruce Jones [s] Al Williamson [p/i] Ed King [l] Joe Chiodo [c]
Additional editorial and in-house ad pages

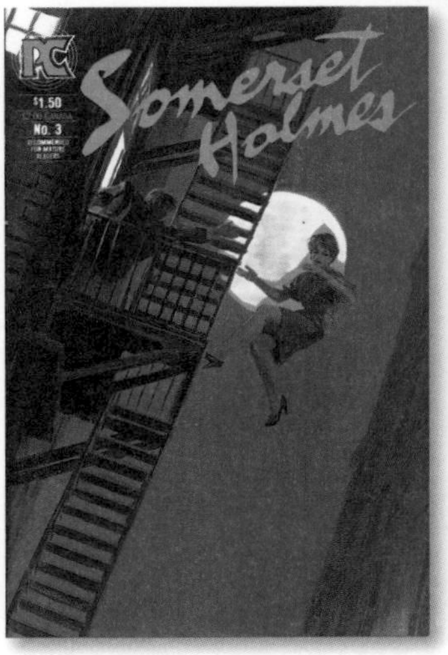
$1.50
No. 3
Somerset Holmes

#3 Feb. 1984

Brent Anderson cover
"Somerset Holmes" 20
Bruce Jones [s] April Campbell [p-a] Brent Anderson [p-a/p/i/c]
"Cliff Hanger: Chapter Three: Voice of Doom" 8
Bruce Jones [s] Al Williamson [p/i] Ed King [l] Joe Chiodo [c]
Additional editorial and in-house ad pages

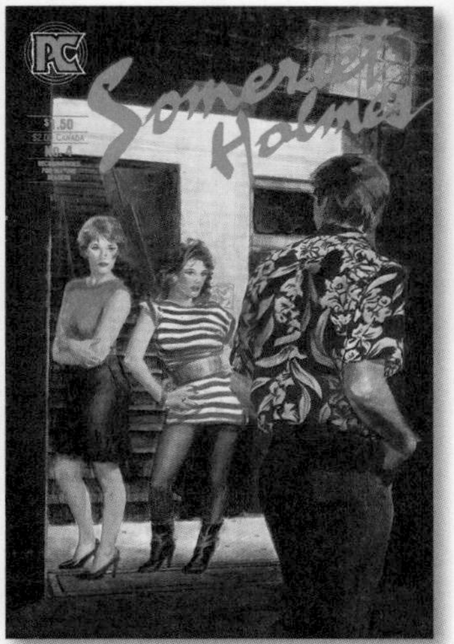
$1.50
Somerset Holmes

#4 Apr. 1984

Brent Anderson cover
"California Screamin'" 20
Bruce Jones [s] April Campbell [p-a] Brent Anderson [p-a/p/i/c] David Cody Weiss [l]
"Cliff Hanger: Chapter Three: Madman's Holiday" 8
Bruce Jones [s] Al Williamson [p/i] Ed King [l] Joe Chiodo [c]
Additional editorial and in-house ad pages

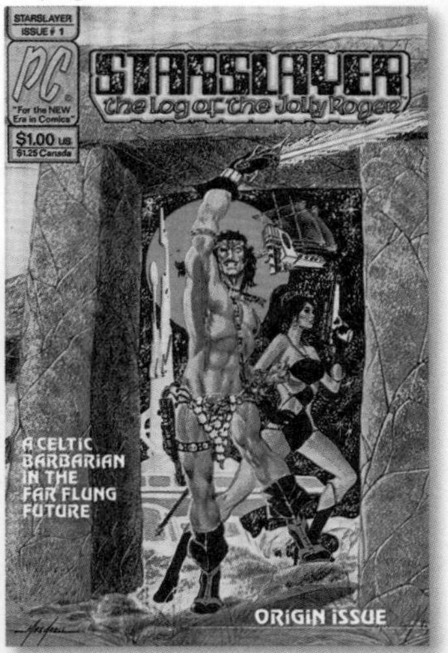
STARSLAYER ISSUE # 1
"For the NEW Era in Comics"
$1.00 US
$1.25 Canada
STARSLAYER
the log of the Jolly Roger
A CELTIC BARBARIAN IN THE FAR FLUNG FUTURE
ORIGIN ISSUE

Starslayer

#1 Feb. 1982

Mike Grell wraparound cover
"Starslayer" 25
Mike Grell [s/p/i/l] Steve Oliff [c]
Additional editorial and in-house ad pages

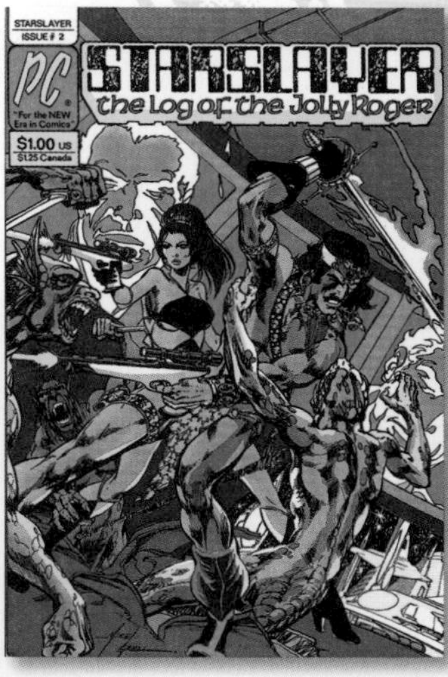
STARSLAYER ISSUE # 2
"For the NEW Era in Comics"
$1.00 US
$1.25 Canada
STARSLAYER
the log of the Jolly Roger

#2 Apr. 1982

Mike Grell cover
"Starslayer" 25
Mike Grell [s/p/i/l] Steve Oliff [c]
"The Rocketeer: Chapter 1" 6
Dave Stevens [s/p/i/l]
Additional editorial and in-house ad pages

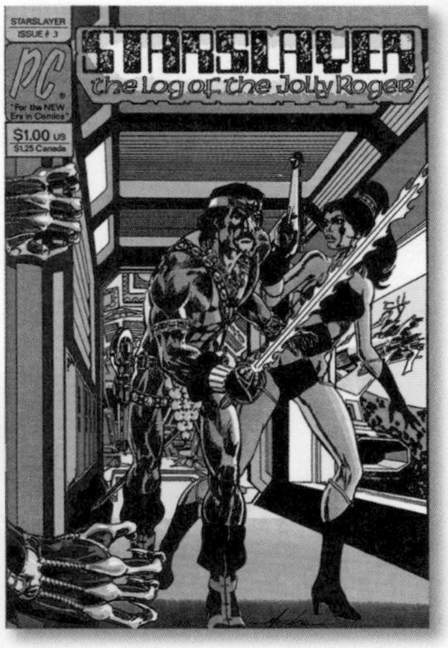
STARSLAYER ISSUE # 3
"For the NEW Era in Comics"
$1.00 US
$1.25 Canada
STARSLAYER
the log of the Jolly Roger

#3 June 1982

Mike Grell cover
"Starslayer" 25
Mike Grell [s/p/i/l] S. Oliff [c]
"The Rocketeer: Chapter 2" 5
Dave Stevens [s/p/i/l]
Additional editorial and in-house ad pages

#4 Aug. 1982

Mike Grell cover
"Starslayer" 25
Mike Grell [s/p/i/l] S. Oliff [c]
Additional editorial and in-house ad pages

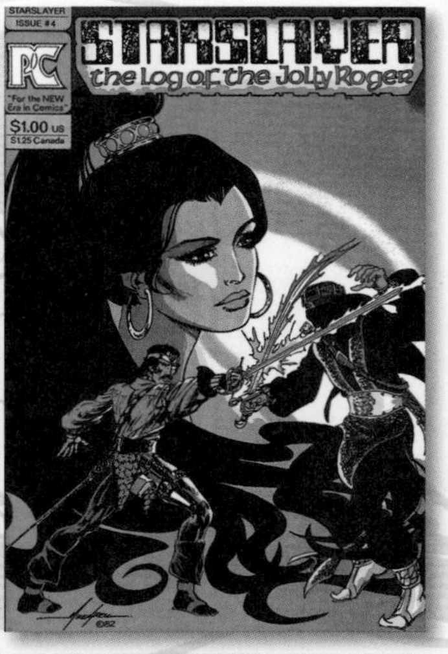
STARSLAYER ISSUE # 4
"For the NEW Era in Comics"
$1.00 US
$1.25 Canada
STARSLAYER
the log of the Jolly Roger

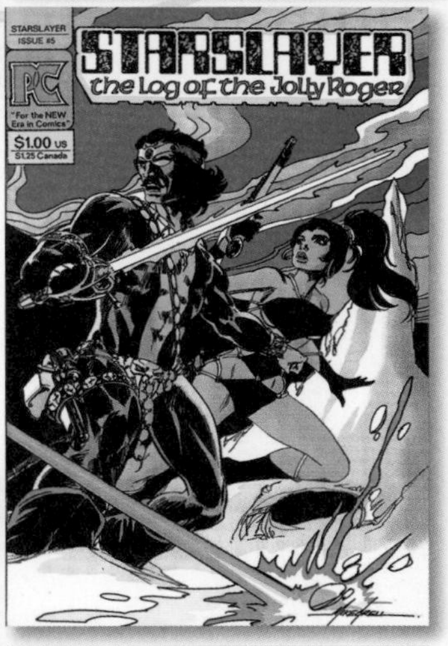
STARSLAYER ISSUE # 5
"For the NEW Era in Comics"
$1.00 US
$1.25 Canada
STARSLAYER
the log of the Jolly Roger

#5 Nov. 1982

Mike Grell cover
"Starslayer" 25
Mike Grell[s/p/i/l] S. Oliff [c]
"Groo the Wanderer" 5
Sergio Aragonés [s/p/i] Mark Evanier [d]
Additional editorial and in-house ad pages

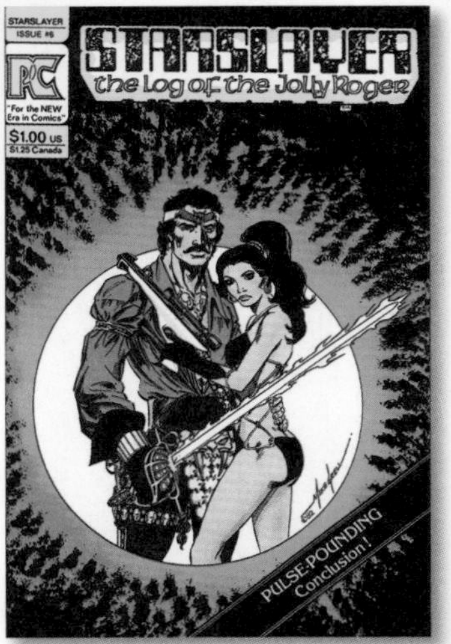
STARSLAYER ISSUE # 6
"For the NEW Era in Comics"
$1.00 US
$1.25 Canada
STARSLAYER
the log of the Jolly Roger
PULSE-POUNDING Conclusion!

#6 Apr. 1983

Mike Grell cover

"Starslayer" 25
Mike Grell [s/p/i/l] S. Oliff [c]
"Donner Beck's Machine: A Cautionary Tale" 5
Craig Deeley [story/p/i] Craig Ballad & D. C. Deeley [s]
Additional editorial and in-house ad pages

SUN RUNNERS
$1.50
$2.00 CANADA
NO. 1
broderick

Sun Runners

#1 Feb. 1984

Pat Broderick cover
"Sparky, I Want to Talk to You" 28
Roger McKenzie [s] Pat Broderick [p/i] David Cody Weiss [l] Steve Oliff [c]
Additional editorial and in-house ad pages

SUN RUNNERS
$1.50
$2.00 CANADA
NO. 3

#2 Mar. 1984

Cover by Pat Broderick
"Fort Dread" 22
Roger McKenzie [s] Pat Broderick [p/i] David Cody Weiss [l] Steve Oliff [c]
"Mike Mahogany: The Big Splash" 8
Roger McKenzie [s] Paul Smith [p/i] Daryl Isaacs [c]
Additional editorial and in-house ad pages

SUN RUNNERS
$1.50
$2.00 CANADA
NO. 2
broderick

#3 May 1984

Pat Broderick cover
"Masquerade" 22
Roger McKenzie [s] Pat Broderick [p/i] David Cody Weiss [l] Steve Oliff [c]
"Mike Mahogany: The Big Freeze" 8
Roger McKenzie [s] Paul Smith [p/i] Daryl Isaacs [c]
Additional editorial and in-house ad pages

THREE DIMENSIONAL!
ALIEN WORLDS
3D

Three Dimensional Alien Worlds

#1 July 1984

Joe Chiodo cover
"Misplaced Dimensions" 1
Bruce Jones [s] Rick Geary [p/i]
"Fair Play" 1
Bruce Jones [s] Jim Sullivan [p] Dave Stevens [i]
"Field Drill" 7
Bruce Jones [s] John Bolton [p/i/c]
"Gifts" 4
Bruce Jones [s] Bill Wray [p/i]
"Away Off There Amid the Softly Winking Lights" 5
Bruce Jones [s] Art Adams [p/i]
"Spaceman Go Home" 9
Bruce Jones [s]
Rand Holmes [p/i]
Additional editorial and in-house ad pages

Thrillogy

A CONRAD
THRILLOGY
$1.50 U.S.
$2.00 Canada

#1 Jan. 1984

Tim Conrad cover

"Prometheus Primeval" 8
Tim Conrad [s/p/i]
Bob Jessup [l] Jim Bertrand [c]
"All That Glitters" 13
Tim Conrad [s/p/i]
Bob Jessup [l] Jim Bertrand [c]
"Red Rover, Red Rover" 9
Tim Conrad [s/p/i]
Bob Jessup [l] Jim Bertrand [c]
Additional editorial and in-house ad pages

TWISTED TALES
NO. 1

Twisted Tales

#1 Nov. 1982

Richard Corben cover
"Infected" 8
Bruce Jones [s] Richard Corben [p/i/l] Steve Oliff [c]
"Out of His Depth" 8
Bruce Jones [s/c], Alfredo Alcala [p/i/l]
"A Walk in the Woods" 7
B. Jones [s/c] Bret Blevins [p/i/l]
"All Hallows" 7
Bruce Jones [s] Tim Conrad [p/i] Carrie McCarthy [l]
Additional editorial and in-house ad pages

TWISTED TALES
NO. 2

#2 Apr. 1983

Bernie Wrightson cover
"Over His Head" 8
Bruce Jones [s] Mike Ploog [p/i] Carrie McCarthy [l] Steve Oliff [c]
"Nightwatch" 6
Bruce Jones [s] Ken Steacy [p/i/c] Carrie McCarthy [l]
"Infant Terrible" 7
Bruce Jones [s] Val Mayerik [p/i] Carrie McCarthy [l] Steve Oliff [c]
"Speed Demons" 7
Bruce Jones [s] Rand Holmes [p/i] Carrie McCarthy [l] Steve Oliff [c]
Additional editorial and in-house ad pages

TWISTED TALES
NO. 3

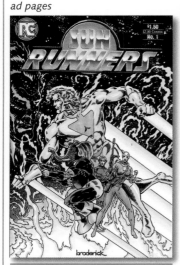

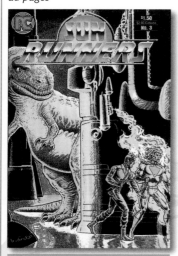

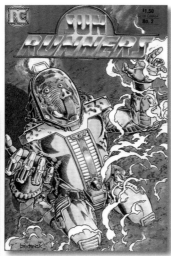

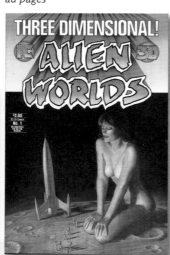

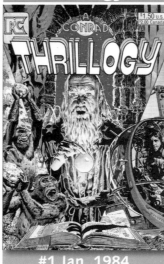

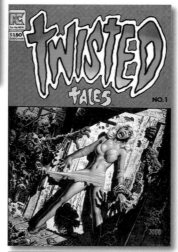

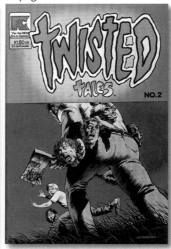

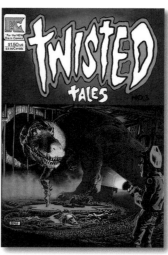

#3 June 1983

Richard Corben cover

"Me an' Ol' Rex" 8
Bruce Jones [s] Richard Corben [p/i/l] Steve Oliff [c]

"Offkey" 8
Bruce Jones [s] Doug Wildey [p/i/c] Carrie McCarthy [l]

"With Honor" 7
Bruce Jones [s] Bill Wray [p/i] Carrie McCarthy [l] S. Oliff [c]

"Sunken Chest" 7
Bruce Jones [s] Bret Blevins [p/i] Carrie McCarthy [l] S. Oliff [c]

Additional editorial and in-house ad pages

Twisted Tales
NO.4

#4 Aug. 1983

John Bolton cover

"The Well" 11
Bruce Jones [s] John Bolton [p/i] Ed King [l] Steve Oliff [c]

"Nick of Time" 10
Bruce Jones [s] Don Lomax [p/i] Carrie McCarthy [l] Phil Phillipson [c]

"Secret Place" 7
Bruce Jones [s/p/i] Carrie McCarthy [l] Joe Chiodo [c]

Additional editorial and in-house ad pages

#5 Oct. 1983

Richard Corben cover

"Terminated" 3
Bruce Jones [s] Richard Corben [p/i/l] Joe Chiodo [c]

"Scritch…Scritch…Scritch…" 8
Bruce Jones [s] Bill Wray [p/i] Carrie McCarthy [l]

"Majority of One" 8
Bruce Jones [s] Val Mayerik [p/i] Carrie McCarthy [l] Joe Chiodo [c]

"Banjo Lessons" 9
Bruce Jones [s] Rand Holmes [p/i/l] Joe Chiodo [c]

Additional editorial and in-house ad pages

Twisted Tales
NO.5

Twisted Tales
No. 6

#6 Jan. 1984

John Bolton cover

"You, Illusion" 8
Bruce Jones [s] John Bolton [p/i] Carrie McCarthy [l] J. Chiodo [c]

"Evening Walk" 2
Bruce Jones [s] John Totleben [p/i] Daryl Isaacs [c]

"Home Ties" 8
Bruce Jones [s] Mike Hoffman [p/i] Carrie McCarthy [l] Joe Chiodo [c]

"Roomers" 10
Bruce Jones [s] Attilio Micheluzzi [p/i] Carrie McCarthy [l] Joe Chiodo [c]

Additional editorial and in-house ad pages

#7 Mar. 1984

Cover by John Bolton

"Holly's Hobby" 4
Bruce Jones [s] John Bolton [p/i] C. McCarthy [l] Daryl Isaacs [c]

"Hooked" 7
Bruce Jones [s] Bill Wray [p/i] David Cody Weiss [l] J. Chiodo [c]

"Sasquatch" 10
Bruce Jones Ian Akin & Brian Garvey [p/i] David Cody Weiss [l] Joe Chiodo

Twisted Tales
No. 7

"Shut-In" 10
B. Jones [s] Tanino Liberatore [p/i] C. McCarthy [l] J. Chiodo [c]

Additional editorial and in-house ad pages

Twisted Tales
No. 8

#8 May 1984

John Pound cover

"Way Down There Below In the Dark" 11
Bruce Jones [s] Thom Enriquez [p/i] Carrie McCarthy [l] Joe Chiodo [c]

"First Impressions" 6
Bruce Jones [s] Butch Guice [p/i] D. Cody Weiss [l] Tom Luth [c]

"An Unsettling Incident" 1
Rick Geary [s/p/i/c]

"The Party" 10
William F. Nolan [s] Mike Hoffman [p/i] Carrie McCarthy [l] Joe Chiodo [c]

Additional editorial and in-house ad pages

Vanguard Illustrated

#1 Nov. 1983

Thomas Yeates cover

Vanguard Illustrated
No.1

"Libretto" 10
David Campiti [s] Thomas Yeates [p] Rick Bryant [i] Tom Harkins [l] Joe Chiodo [c]

"Encyclopedias (Part One)" 6
Mike Baron [s] Steve Rude [p/i] Phil Phillipson [l]

"Freakwave! Part One: A Stranger in Paradise" 10
Peter Milligan [s] Brendan McCarthy [s/p/i] David Cody Weiss [l]

Additional editorial and in-house ad pages

Vanguard Illustrated
#2

#2 Jan. 1984

Dave Stevens cover

"Legends of the Stargrazers" 10
David Campiti [s] Cynthia J. Wood & Bob McLeod [p/i] Daryl Isaacs [c]

"Sales Call (Encyclopedias Part Two)" 6
Mike Baron [s] Steve Rude [p/i] Phil Phillipson [c] David Cody Weiss [l]

"The Guest" 4
Darren Auck [s/p/i] David Cuccio [l] David Isaacs [c]

"Freakwave! Part Two: With Ceaseless Turmoil Seething" 10
Peter Milligan [s] Brendan

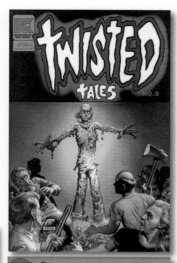

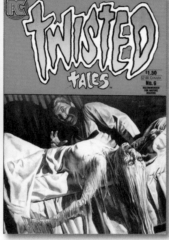

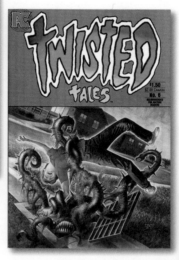

McCarthy [s/p/i] D. C. Weiss [l]
Additional editorial and in-house ad pages

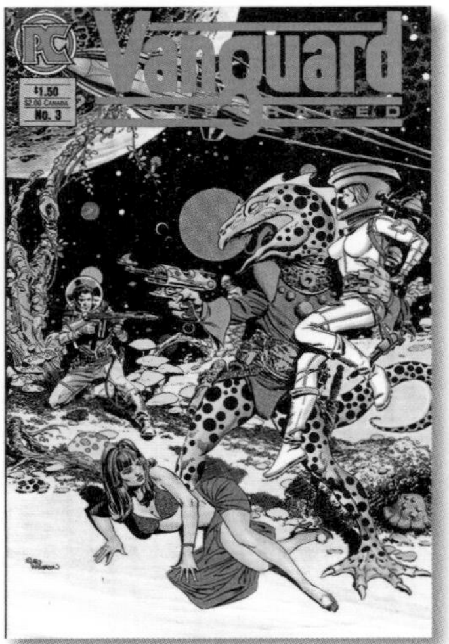
Vanguard
$1.50
$2.00 CANADA
No. 3

#3 Mar. 1984

Al Williamson cover
"Freakwave! (Part Three)" 8
Peter Milligan [s] Brendan McCarthy [s/p/i/c]
"Duel With Dorf Dishware (Encyclopedias Part Three)" 6
Mike Baron [s] Steve Rude [p/i] David Cody Weiss [l] Phil Phillipson [c]
"Killer in Orbit" 8
Rex Lindsay [s/p/i] D. Isaacs [c]
"Be It What It Will, I'll Go Laughing" 10
David Campiti [s] Thomas Yeates [p/i] Tim Harkins [l] Marcus David [c]
Additional editorial and in-house ad pages

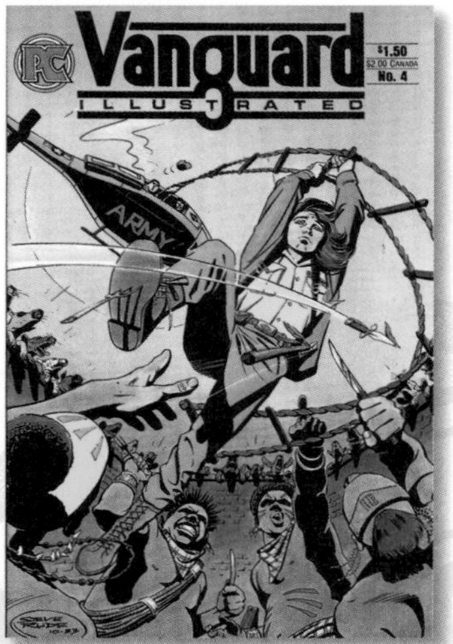
Vanguard
ILLUSTRATED
$1.50
$2.00 CANADA
No. 4
ARMY

#4 Apr. 1984

Steve Rude cover
"Quark" 10
Mike Baron [s] Rick Burchett [p/i] Carrie McCarthy [l] Marcus David [c]
"Success (Encyclopedias Part 4)" 6
Mike Baron [s] Steve Rude [p/i] Phil Phillipson [c]

"A Tangled Web" 3
Ruth Raymond [s/p/i] Barbara Marker [c]
"Low Level Diplomatic Immunity" 8
Paul Neary [s/i] Mick Austin [p] Marcus David [c]
"Student Filmmaker" 1
Rick Geary [s/p/i]
Additional editorial and in-house ad pages

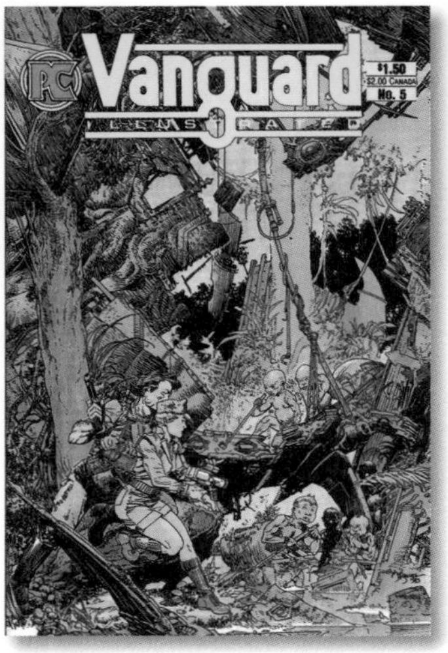
Vanguard
ILLUSTRATED
$1.50
$2.00 CANADA
No. 5

#5 May 1984

Michael Wm. Kaluta cover
"Quark" 10
Mike Baron [s] Rick Burchett [p] Steve Mitchell [i] Carrie McCarthy [l] Marcus David [c]
"...Friend in Need..." 8
Ron Harris [s/p/i/l/c]
"Adventures in Art" 2
Rick Geary [s/p/i/l] T. Luth [c]
"Face to Face" 8
Tim Burgard [s/p/i/c] David Cody Weiss [l]
Additional editorial and in-house ad pages

#6 June 1984

George Pérez cover [see pg. 103]
"The Trains Belong to Us" 4
Joey Cavalieri [s] George Pérez [p/i] Phil Phillipson [c]
"The Struggle's End" 8
Rex Lindsey [s/p/i] Adam Kubert [l] Daryl Isaacs [c]
"The God Run" 10
Peter Milligan [s] George Freeman [p/i] Ron Muns [l] Nick Burns & George Freeman [c]
"Hump Hammersmith" 6
Bill DuBay [s] Vince Argondezzi [p] Rick Bryant [i] David Cody Weis [l] Daryl Isaacs [c]
Additional editorial and in-house ad pages

#7 July 1984

Michael Wm. Kaluta cover
"Ballad of Hardcase Bradley" 6
Stephen Perry [s] George Evans

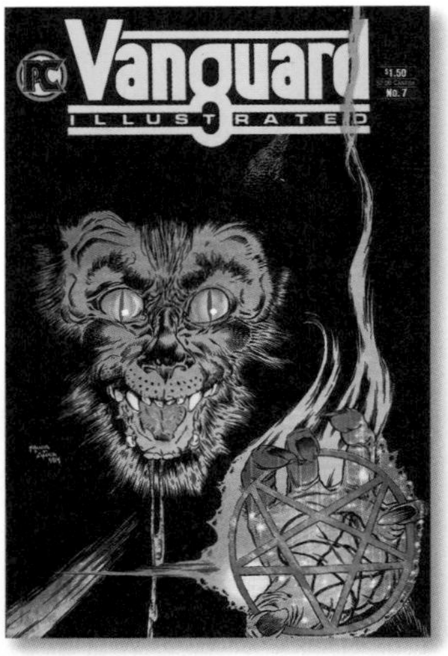
Vanguard
ILLUSTRATED
$1.50
No. 7

[p/i] Carol Petersen [l] T. Luth [c]
"Goldyn" 10
Walter Stuart [s/p] Mike Gustovich [i] Daryl Isaacs [c]
"Mr. Monster: The Case of the Reluctant Werewolf" 8
Michael T. Gilbert [s/p] William Messner-Loebs [p/i] Ken Bruzenak [l]
"Hump Hammersmith" 5
Bill DuBay [s] Vince Argondezzi [p] Rick Bryant [i] Mike Wade [l] Daryl Isaacs [c]
Additional editorial, in-house ad pages

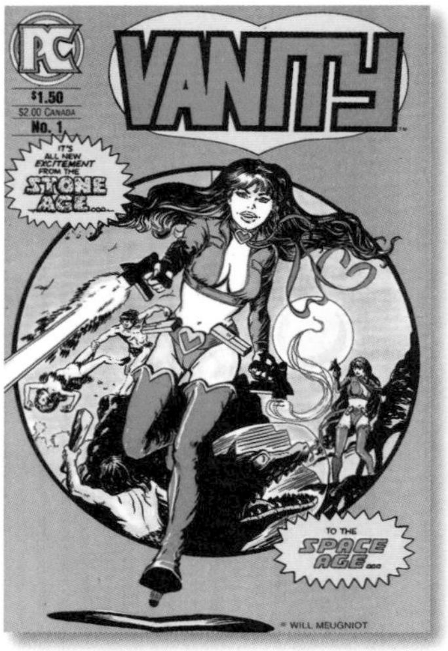
VANITY
$1.50
$2.00 CANADA
No. 1
STONE AGE
TO THE SPACE AGE
WILL MEUGNIOT

Vanity

#1 June 1984

Will Meugniot cover
"Vanity" 18
Will Meugniot [s/p/i] M. Royer & D.C. Weiss [l] Jo Meugniot [c]
"Escape from Fire" 7
Jim Rohn [s/p/i] M. David [c]
"Welcome Home" 5
Bjørn Ousland [s/p/i] D. Isaacs [c]
Additional editorial, in-house ad pages

#2 Aug. 1984

Will Meugniot cover
"A Scent of Lilac" 18
Will Meugniot [s/p/i] D. W.

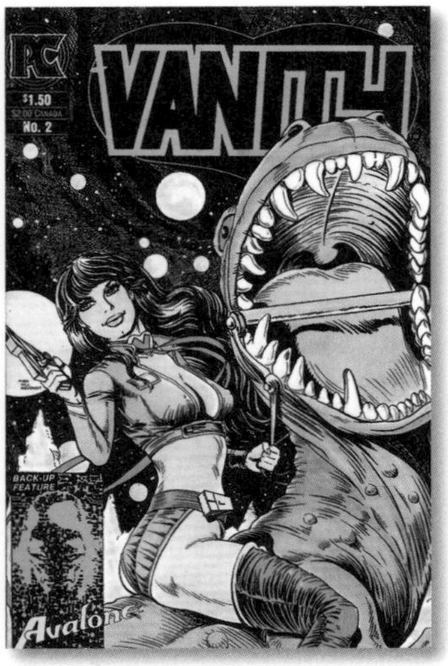
VANITY
$1.50
$2.00 CANADA
No. 2
Avalon

MacOda [l] Jo Meugniot [c]
"Avalon Episode One: Survival" 12
D. Campiti [s] David Ross [s/p] Dan Adkins [i] D. Cody Weiss [l]
Additional editorial, in-house ad pages

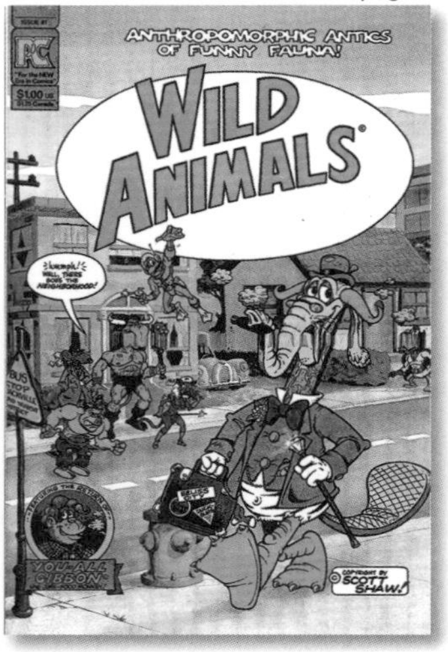
ANTHROPOMORPHIC ANTICS OF FUNNY FAUNA!
WILD ANIMALS

Wild Animals

#1 Dec. 1982

Scott Shaw! cover
"The Land That Time Ignored!" 12
Scott Shaw! [s/p/i] Richard Lester [i] Gordon Kent [c]
"The No-Luck Duck" 3
George Erling [s/p/i] G. Kent [c]
"Lackluster Lizard" 1
Jim Engel [s/p/i] G. Kent [c]
"Orange Sauce" 4
Larry Gonick [s/p/i] G. Kent [c]
"Toys Will Be Toys" 1
Jim Engel [s/p/i] Gordon Kent [c]
"Citizens Band Radio" 1
Jim Engel [s/p/i] Gordon Kent [c]
"A 'Short' Story" 2
Sergio Aragonés [s/p/i] G. Kent [c]
"The Rabbit Marauder" 1
Jim Engel [s/p/i] Gordon Kent [c]
Two strips 1
Brian Narelle [s/p/i] G. Kent [c]
"Presidents of the U.S." 1
Rick Geary [s/p/i/c]
Additional editorial, in-house ad pages

Editor's Afterword

Pacific and the New Paradigm

I was about done with comics

when somehow *Comics Scene* #2 crossed my path in the early months of 1982. Jack Kirby, by far my favorite comic book creator and someone to whom I felt deeply indebted for being such a supreme example of enormous creativity, had quit the industry, and mainstream comics seemed so stale and uninspired at that time. I attributed the doldrums to the great exodus of artists that culminated with the King leaving for the business of Saturday morning cartoons, but I had zero notion of "work-for-hire" and the "Big Two" refusing to return artwork. I was a terribly naïve outsider.

Reading the main feature in that issue of the nationally-distributed newsstand magazine simply blew my mind, and I confess it instantly radicalized me due to Jack giving a candid, angry, and astonishing behind-the-scenes look at his Marvel Comics experience. But almost as important was to learn that — *Great Glorious Godfrey!* — Jack was returning to the comics world, though not at DC or Marvel, but at some rinky-dink West Coast outfit called Pacific Comics! It was a thunderbolt to my sensibilities when I learned of *Captain Victory and the Galactic Rangers,* an entirely new, standalone Kirby series! Holy moley!

I can't precisely recall how quickly I got on the phone to my younger brother, Andy, who lived in New York City — and understood all too well my devotion to Kirby — but I do vividly remember begging him to go down to Forbidden Comics, buy the two available issues of *Captain Victory,* and mail 'em to me, a 23-year-old who lived in the boondocks, far from a comic book shop. And I will never forget opening the package and reveling in those two magnificent Mike Royer-inked issues. I was instantly transported into a fantastic new realm. (Thanks, bro!)

Soon enough, I was making monthly, then bi-weekly, then weekly visits to Starship Excalibur in Providence (and then Boston's Newbury Comics, New England Comics, and Million Year Picnic when I moved to Beantown), and I realized comics were exciting again, all due to the entry of new publishers with creator-friendly attitudes and willingness to share in the profits. Bruce Jones was reviving the EC spirit with *Alien Worlds* and *Twisted Tales,* bringing back the Warren crew, now printed on quality stock with full color. Then this youngster, Dave Stevens, just knocked me out in the back pages of *Starslayer* with his amazingly seductive and sensuous art style on "The Rocketeer"!

I honestly can't say whether I'd have remained a comics fan if not for Pacific. It's quite possible I would have missed out on the greatness that was to come in 1986, when comics truly came of age in the eyes of many (including mine!) during that wonderful year. But what I do know is that the Schanes brothers had a hell of a run, producing some kick-ass books to share with us, even if Pacific's lifespan was way too short — and I just had to be a part of Stephan Friedt's remarkable effort here, because Pacific Comics has meant so much to me. I'm grateful for Stephan being generous in allowing me to add so much to his manuscript and help mold his 40 years-in-the-making retrospective. I hope you've enjoyed our heartfelt tribute.

—**Jon B. Cooke**

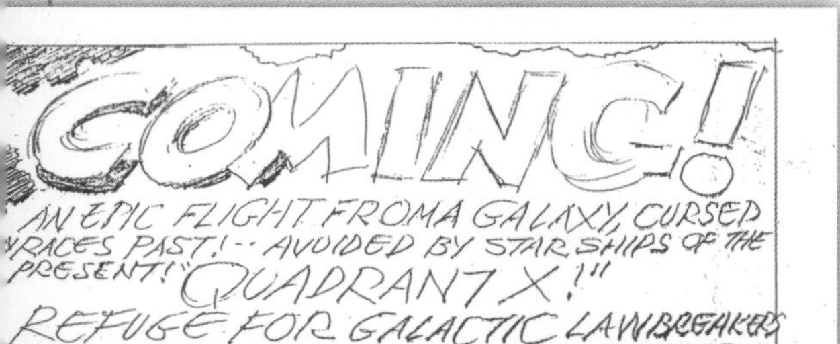
COMING!
AN EPIC FLIGHT FROM A GALAXY, CURSED BY RACES PAST!-- AVOIDED BY STAR SHIPS OF THE PRESENT! "QUADRANT X!"
REFUGE FOR GALACTIC LAWBREAKERS AND THE OPEN JAW OF HORROR FOR THEIR PURSUERS!!!
MEET THE FOUR WHO HID AMONG ITS MYSTERIES! THE DANGEROUS! THE DETERMINED! THE DARING-
WONDER-WARRIORS!
ALSO, ON ITS WAY--!
"BLOCK-BUSTER!" -- THE ONLY NAME ONE CAN GIVE TO AN ADDITIONAL NEW CONCEPT DESIGNED BY THE MASTER HIMSELF -- JACK KIRBY!!!
© JACK KIRBY 86

Inset left: Unused and uninked page by Kirby, likely intended for *Captain Victory,* publicizing his Wonder-Warriors concept and making mention of an tantalizing yet still unknown "Block-Buster" pitch by the King! Despite the copyright notation, were these two new Kirby comics proposals for Pacific in their final year?

TWO-FISTED COMIC BOOK ARTIST
JOHN
SEVERIN
by Greg Biga & Jon B. Cooke
Featuring Severin's
AMERICAN EAGLE

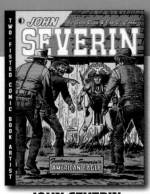

JOHN SEVERIN TWO-FISTED COMIC BOOK ARTIST

A spirited biography of EC Comics mainstay (with **HARVEY KURTZMAN** on Mad and Two-Fisted Tales) and co-creator of Western strip American Eagle. Covers his 40+ year association with Cracked magazine, his pivotal Marvel Comics work inking **HERB TRIMPE** on The Hulk & teaming with sister **MARIE SEVERIN** on King Kull, and more! By **GREG BIGA** and **JON B. COOKE**.

(160-page **COLOR HARDCOVER**) **$39.95**
(Digital Edition) **$14.99**
ISBN: 978-1-60549-106-6

Our ARTISTS at WAR
by Richard J. Arndt & Steven Fears
THE BEST OF THE BEST AMERICAN WAR COMICS

OUR ARTISTS AT WAR

Examines US War comics: **EC COMICS** (Two-Fisted Tales, Frontline Combat), **DC COMICS** (Enemy Ace, All American Men of War, G.I. Combat, Our Fighting Forces, Our Army at War, Star-Spangled War Stories), **WARREN PUBLISHING** (Blazing Combat), **CHARLTON** (Willy Schultz and the Iron Corporal) and more! Featuring **KURTZMAN, SEVERIN, DAVIS, WOOD, KUBERT, GLANZMAN, KIRBY**, and others! By **RICHARD ARNDT** and **STEVEN FEARS**, with an introduction by **ROY THOMAS**.

(160-page **COLOR SOFTCOVER**) **$27.95**
(Digital Edition) **$14.99**
ISBN: 978-1-60549-108-0

AMERICAN TV
COMIC BOOKS 1940s-1980s
by Peter Bosch
FROM THE SMALL SCREEN...
TO THE PRINTED PAGE

AMERICAN TV COMIC BOOKS

PETER BOSCH's history of over 300 TV shows and 2000+ comic book adaptations from the 1940s–1980s, from **STAR TREK & THE MUNSTERS** to **CAPTAIN GALLANT & PINKY LEE**. With artist profiles of **COLAN, TOTH, SPIEGLE, MANNING, BUSCEMA, HEATH**, and more!

(192-page **COLOR SOFTCOVER**) **$29.95**
(Digital Edition) **$15.99**
ISBN: 978-1-60549-107-3

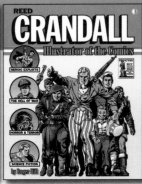

REED
CRANDALL
Illustrator of the Comics
HEROIC EXPLOITS
THE HELL OF WAR
HORROR & TERROR
SCIENCE FICTION
by Roger Hill

REED CRANDALL ILLUSTRATOR OF THE COMICS

ROGER HILL's history of Crandall's life and career, from Golden Age Quality Comics, to Warren war and horror, Flash Gordon, and beyond. With never-seen photos and unpublished artwork! **SECOND PRINTING—NOW IN SOFTCOVER!**

(256-page **COLOR SOFTCOVER**) **$39.95**
(256-page Digital Edition) **$13.99**
ISBN: 978-1-60549-102-8

MAC RABOY
MASTER OF THE COMICS
The Definitive Book on the Life and Art of the Legendary Golden Age Artist
by ROGER HILL

MAC RABOY MASTER OF THE COMICS

ROGER HILL documents the life and career of the artist of **BULLETMAN, SPY SMASHER, GREEN LAMA**, and his crowning achievement, **CAPTAIN MARVEL JR.**, with never-before-seen photos, a wealth of rare and unpublished artwork, and the first definitive biography of Raboy!

(160-page **COLOR HARDCOVER**) **$39.95**
(Digital Edition) **$14.99**
ISBN: 978-1-60549-090-8

AMERICAN COMIC BOOK CHRONICLES

The **AMERICAN COMIC BOOK CHRONICLES** is an ambitious series of **FULL-COLOR HARDCOVERS**, where TwoMorrows' top authors document every decade of comic book history from the 1940s to today! Don't miss all the other riveting, informative volumes, all edited by **KEITH DALLAS**.

Volumes: 1940-44 • 1950s • 1960-64 1965-69 • 1970s • 1980s • 1990s & 1945-49 (new volume, shipping Spring 2024)

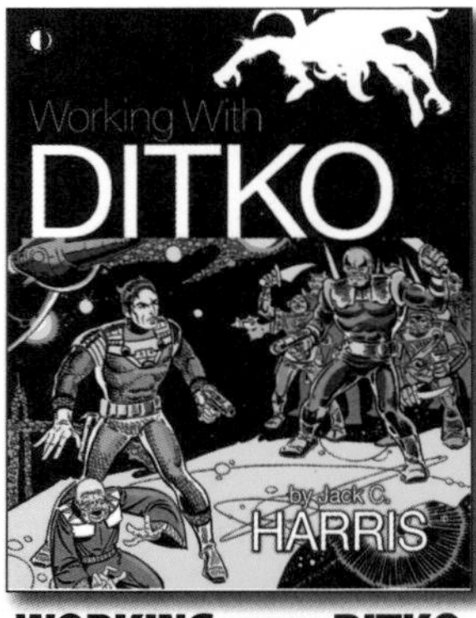

Working With
DITKO
by Jack C. HARRIS

WORKING WITH DITKO

JACK C. HARRIS recalls his collaborations with **STEVE DITKO!** Unseen art from The Creeper, Shade, Odd Man, Demon, Wonder Woman, Legion of Super-Heroes, The Fly, & Ditko's unused Batman design!

(128-page **COLOR SOFTCOVER**) **$24.95**
(Digital Edition) **$13.99**
ISBN: 978-1-60549-122-6

The Fascinating Story of the Action Heroes, Ghastly Ghosts, and Fun Comics of the Derby, Conn., Publisher
THE CHARLTON COMPANION
Derby CITY LIMIT

CHARLTON COMPANION

An all-new definitive history from the 1940s Golden Age to the Bronze Age of the '70s, with **CAPTAIN ATOM, BLUE BEETLE**, and more. By **JON B. COOKE**.

(272-page **COLOR SOFTCOVER**) **$43.95**
(Digital Edition) **$15.99**
ISBN: 978-1-60549-111-0

The Life & Art of
DAVE COCKRUM
BY GLEN CADIGAN

THE LIFE & ART OF DAVE COCKRUM

GLEN CADIGAN's bio of the artist who redesigned the Legion of Super-Heroes and introduced X-Men characters Storm, Nightcrawler, Colossus, and Logan!

(160-page **COLOR SOFTCOVER**) **$27.95**
HC: $36.95 • (Digital Edition) **$14.99**
ISBN: 978-1-60549-113-4

THE BEST OF SIMON & KIRBY'S
MAINLINE COMICS
BULLSEYE
FOXHOLE
POLICE TRAP
IN LOVE

BEST OF S&K's MAINLINE COMICS

Collects the best of **JOE SIMON** & **JACK KIRBY'S** 1954-1956 Mainline Comics titles: **BULLSEYE, FOXHOLE, POLICE TRAP**, and **IN LOVE**. With fully restored art, these are their final stories produced in the Western, War, Crime, and Romance genres, before the anti-comics backlash of the 1950s forced Mainline to shut down.

(262-page **FULL-COLOR HARDCOVER**)
$49.95 • (Digital Edition) **$15.99**
ISBN: 978-1-60549-118-9

KIRBY & LEE:
STUF' SAID!
EXPANDED SECOND EDITION
The complex genesis of the Marvel Universe, in its creators' own words

KIRBY & LEE: STUF' SAID (2nd Edition)

WITH 16 EXTRA PAGES OF "STUF' SAID"! Examines the complicated relationship of Marvel Universe creators **JACK KIRBY** and **STAN LEE** through their own words (and Ditko's, Wood's, Romita Sr.'s and others), in chronological order, from fanzine, magazine, radio, and TV interviews! By TwoMorrows publisher **JOHN MORROW**.

(176-page **COLOR SOFTCOVER**) **$26.95**
(Digital Edition) **$12.99**
ISBN: 978-1-60549-094-6

JACK KIRBY'S
DINGBAT Love
UNPUBLISHED '70s STORIES BY THE KING OF COMICS!
TRUE-LIFE DIVORCE!
DINGBATS OF DANGER STREET!
SOUL LOVE!

JACK KIRBY'S DINGBAT LOVE

The final complete, unpublished Jack Kirby stories in existence, presented here for the first time, in cooperation with DC Comics! Two unused 1970s **DINGBATS OF DANGER STREET** tales, plus **TRUE-LIFE DIVORCE**, and **SOUL LOVE** (the unseen black romance magazine)! With historical essays by **JOHN MORROW.**

(176-page **COLOR HARDCOVER**) **$43.95**
(Digital Edition) **$14.99**
ISBN: 978-1-60549-091-5

OLD
GODS
& NEW
A Companion to JACK KIRBY's FOURTH WORLD
by John Morrow

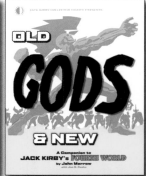

OLD GODS & NEW: A FOURTH WORLD COMPANION

Looks back at **JACK KIRBY**'s own words, as well as those of assistants **MARK EVANIER** and **STEVE SHERMAN**, inker **MIKE ROYER**, and publisher **CARMINE INFANTINO**, to show how Kirby's epic came about, where it was going, and how he would've ended it before it was cancelled by DC Comics! By **JOHN MORROW** with **JON B. COOKE**.

(160-page **COLOR SOFTCOVER**) **$26.95**
(Digital Edition) **$14.99**
ISBN: 978-1-60549-098-4

THE ULTIMATE GUIDE TO SILVER & BRONZE AGE TEAM-UP COMICS
The TEAM-UP COMPANION
By Michael Eury
TEAM-UP INDEXES
TEAM-UP CREATORS
TEAM-UP TRIVIA

THE TEAM-UP COMPANION

Examines team-up comic books of the Silver and Bronze Ages of Comics: Brave and the Bold, DC Comics Presents, Marvel Team-Up and Two-in-One, plus other team-up titles, treasuries, and treats—in a lushly illustrated selection of informative essays, special features, and trivia-loaded issue-by-issue indexes! By MICHAEL EURY.

(256-page **COLOR SOFTCOVER**) **$39.95**
(Digital Edition) **$15.99**
ISBN: 978-1-60549-112-7

TwoMorrows Publishing • www.twomorrows.com • 919-449-0344
Download our Free Catalog: https://www.twomorrows.com/media/TwoMorrowsCatalog.pdf